www.wadsworth.com

wadsworth.com is the World Wide Web site for Wadsworth and is your direct source to dozens of online resources.

At *wadsworth.com* you can find out about supplements, demonstration software, and student resources. You can also send e-mail to many of our authors and preview new publications and exciting new technologies.

wadsworth.com
Changing the way the world learns®

THE WADSWORTH CONTEMPORARY ISSUES IN CRIME AND JUSTICE SERIES
Todd Clear, Series Editor

1995
Close/Meier: *Morality in Criminal Justice: An Introduction to Ethics*
Klofas/Stojkovic: *Crime and Justice in the Year 2010*
Silberman: *A World of Violence: Corrections in America*
Wooden: *Renegade Kids, Suburban Outlaws: From Youth Culture to Delinquency*

1996
Belknap: *The Invisible Woman: Gender, Crime, and Justice*
Friedrichs: *Trusted Criminals: White Collar Crime in Contemporary Society*
Johnson: *Hard Time: Understanding and Reforming the Prison,* Second Edition
Karmen: *Crime Victims: An Introduction to Victimology,* Third Edition
Walker/Spohn/DeLone: *The Color of Justice: Race, Ethnicity, and Crime in America*

1997
Golden: *Disposable Youth: America's Child Welfare System*
Hickey: *Serial Murderers and Their Victims,* Second Edition
Irwin/Austin: *It's About Time: America's Imprisonment Binge,* Second Edition
Messner/Rosenfeld: *Crime and the American Dream,* Second Edition
Shelden/Tracy/Brown: *Youth Gangs in American Society*

1998
Bailey/Hale: *Popular Culture, Crime, and Justice*
Chesney-Lind/Shelden: *Girls, Delinquency, and Juvenile Justice,* Second Edition
Johnson: *Death Work: A Study of the Modern Execution Process,* Second Edition
Pollock: *Ethics, Crime, and Justice: Dilemmas and Decisions,* Third Edition
Rosenbaum/Lurigio/Davis: *The Prevention of Crime: Social and Situational Strategies*
Surette: *Media, Crime, and Criminal Justice: Images and Realities,* Second Edition
Walker: *Sense and Nonsense About Crime and Drugs: A Policy Guide,* Fourth Edition
White: *Terrorism: An Introduction,* Second Edition

1999
Arrigo: *Social Justice/Criminal Justice: The Maturation of Critical Theory in Law, Crime, and Deviance*

2000
Walker/Spohn/DeLone: *The Color of Justice: Race, Ethnicity, and Crime in America,* Second Edition

2001
Austin/Irwin: *It's About Time: America's Imprisonment Binge,* Third Edition
Karmen: *Crime Victims: An Introduction to Victimology,* Fourth Edition
Shelden/Tracy/Brown: *Youth Gangs in American Society,* Second Edition
Pope/Lovell/Brandl: *Voices from the Field: Readings in Criminal Justice Research*
Walker: *Sense and Nonsense About Crime and Drugs: A Policy Guide,* Fifth Edition
Wooden/Blazak: *Renegade Kids, Suburban Outlaws: From Youth Culture to Delinquency,* Second Edition

Crime Victims

An Introduction to Victimology

Fourth Edition

ANDREW KARMEN
John Jay College of Criminal Justice

WADSWORTH
THOMSON LEARNING
Australia • Canada • Mexico • Singapore • Spain
United Kingdom • United States

WADSWORTH

THOMSON LEARNING

Executive Editor, Criminal Justice: *Sabra Horne*
Editor: *Dan Alpert*
Development Editor: *Terri Edwards*
Assistant Editor: *Ann Tsai*
Editorial Assistant: *Cortney Bruggink*
Marketing Manager: *Jennifer Somerville*
Project Editor: *Susan Walters*
Print Buyer: *Karen Hunt*
Permissions Editor: *Joohee Lee*
Production Service: *Proof Positive/Farrowlyne Associates, Inc.*
Copy Editor: *Andrew Parker*
Cover Designer: *Laurie Anderson*
Cover Image: *PhotoDisc*
Compositor: *Black Dot Group*
Text and Cover Printer: *Von Hoffmann Press/Custom*

Printed in the United States of America
1 2 3 4 5 6 7 04 03 02 01 00

Library of Congress Cataloging-in-Publication Data
Karmen, Andrew.
Crime victims : an introduction to victimology / Andrew Karmen. — 4th ed.
p. cm. — (Wadsworth contemporary issues in crime and justice series)
Includes bibliographical references (p.) and index.
ISBN 0-534-51544-4 (alk. paper)
1. Victims of crimes—United States. I. Title. II. Contemporary issues in crime and justice series.
HV6250.3.U5 K37 2000
362.88 '0973—dc21 00-033363

Wadsworth/Thomson Learning
10 Davis Drive
Belmont, CA 94002-3098
USA

For more information about our products, contact us:
Thomson Learning Academic Resource Center
1-800-423-0563
http://www.wadsworth.com

International Headquarters
Thomson Learning
International Division
290 Harbor Drive, 2nd Floor
Stamford, CT 06902-7477
USA

UK/Europe/Middle East/South Africa
Thomson Learning
Berkshire House
168-173 High Holborn
London WC1V 7AA
United Kingdom

Asia
Thomson Learning
60 Albert Street #15-01
Albert Complex
Singapore 189969

Canada
Nelson Thomson Learning
1120 Birchmount Road
Toronto, Ontario M1K 5G4
Canada

About the Author

Andrew Karmen earned a Ph.D. in sociology from Columbia University in 1977. Since 1978 he has been a professor in the Sociology Department at John Jay College of Criminal Justice of the City University of New York. Since 1970 he has taught courses on victimology, criminal justice, criminology, drug abuse, delinquency, social problems, race relations, research methods, statistics, and general sociology. At John Jay College, he has served as a coordinator of the master's program in criminal justice, the advisor for the undergraduate majors in criminal justice and in criminology, and a member of the doctoral faculty.

Dr. Karmen has co-edited a reader (with Donal MacNamara) called *Deviants: Victims or Victimizers?* (Sage, 1983). He has authored chapters in books and journal articles on a number of subjects, including drug abuse, auto theft, police use of deadly force, vigilantism, research taboos, the Rosenberg atom spy case, news media ethics, providing lawyers for indigents, providing victim advocates, victims' rights, the victimization of women, and the likely situation of crime victims in the future. His latest book is entitled *New York Murder Mystery: The True Story Behind the Crime Crash of the 1990s* (NYU Press, 2000).

To everyone whose suffering is needlessly intensified or prolonged because of ignorance about crime victims or a lack of commitment to them.

—Andrew Karmen

Contents

Foreword

"What about the victim?"

This may seem like a mundane question, but when we hear it, most of the time we are hearing a rhetorical way to advocate a philosophy of justice, one which takes account of the problems and costs suffered by victims of crime. While the plight of victims of crime is an old one, the philosophy that embraces the plight as a justice priority is not. For most of the history of our nation, victims of crime were largely invisible in the criminal justice process. The very way we referred to criminal cases—*Wilson v. State*—made clear an overriding idea that criminal justice was concerned with a controversy between a defendant and the state. Victims, if they were considered at all, were only important as potential witnesses in that controversy.

Beginning in the last third of the 20th century, however, this isolation of victims from the justice process began to change. With concern about rising crime in the 1960s and 1970s came an increasing interest in the impact of the criminal justice process on victims. Perhaps this concern was inevitable, since rising rates of crime meant there were increasing numbers of crime victims, families with victims, and friends of victims, many of whom could recount all-too-frequent negative experiences with the way their cases were handled. The concern about victims was also a backlash against an era when the rights of criminal suspects were such a prominent issue in Supreme Court cases and public-policy debates. And it is also likely that as U.S. citizens came to demand more services in general, one of the constituencies calling for help would be crime victims.

Whatever the causes—and there are probably several—victims of crime became an important constituency in the last third of the 20th century. They were a significant political block, of course, since almost every politician in the country made "tough-on-crime" a cornerstone campaign promise. Even people who were never victims of serious crime and knew nobody in that category came to believe that a "tough" stance on crime was a victim-friendly stance on crime. For over 30 years, penalties for crime have become ever more severe—often with the justification that a concern for victims required tougher measures against offenders. But this was not the only expression of pro-victim sentiment in the political arena. Numerous local victims' advocacy organizations were formed, the most notable of which may be the Mothers Against Drunk Driving. The federal government established a national office on victims of crime in the U.S. Department of Justice, and many states passed new legislation that enumerated the rights of victims of crime. In many ways the last generation of criminal justice has been one dominated by the "voice" of the victim, at least as a symbol of alarm and a call for change. No set of ideas has had a more profound impact on the criminal justice system in the last 30 years than has the institutionalized, public concern about the victim of crime.

As public sentiment about the predicament of the victim grew, social scientists also developed a greater interest in the victim. A new field called "victimology" was established that investigated all aspects of victims of crime, from prevalence and demographics to needs and perspectives. The lessons that victimology gleaned about the social significance of crime have reshaped our understanding of crime and justice. From the time when it became popular to ask, "What about the victim?" to the contemporary ease with which we embrace concern about the victim in the justice system, much has changed and much has been learned. Today, anyone who wishes to be considered informed about crime and justice issues must understand what we know about victims of crime.

That is why I am delighted to announce the fourth edition of Andrew Karmen's superb, seminal text on the topic: *Crime Victims*. This book has been one of the most important contributions to the Wadsworth Contemporary Issues in Crime and Justice Series. The series gives detailed attention to important topics and controversies in crime and justice that are not usually covered in detail in traditional textbooks. As editor of the series, I am pleased to welcome this new edition as an excellent illustration of the role of the series in giving students of crime and justice in-depth analyses of important topics.

This new edition retains the reliable data, evenhanded analysis, and thought-provoking presentation of the previous editions. It adds completely updated statistics, new discussions of recent developments in victimology, and fresh perspectives on the future of the field. No book currently available provides a more balanced, comprehensive, or reliable discussion of the important controversies and dilemmas in criminal justice policy and practice regarding victims. This book supports its positions with data, provides statistics that question some of the typical myths about victims, and provokes the reader to think carefully about the importance of the victims' movement for justice policy.

Professor Karmen's earlier editions of this book were received with praise. This new edition continues and strengthens his contribution to our knowledge. I commend the book to you. To read it is to have your thoughts and opinions about crime victims become more informed and more effective. You will be changed by this book.

Todd R. Clear
Series Editor

Preface

In revising this book once again, I have retained the basic structure of the previous three editions and added a great deal of new material to expand and update the coverage of many subjects. When I wrote the first edition during the early 1980s, it was difficult to locate either reliable social science data or well-informed speculation about a number of crucial aspects of criminal victimization. When I prepared the second edition in the late 1980s, I encountered the opposite problem. Instead of a scarcity of material, there was too much: massive amounts of data and lengthy analyses, especially about rape, spouse abuse, child abuse, and elder abuse. By the mid-1990s, when I prepared the third revision, this "knowledge explosion" problem had become even more serious. Entire issues of scholarly journals had been devoted to, and whole books had been written about, the plight of these victims. When I began this fourth revision, the most striking change that I encountered was how the Internet could provide readily available and continuously updated information about a wide variety of victims. As a result, I have added an appendix of Internet Web sites that faculty and students can periodically check to find out the latest statistics and the most recent developments concerning laws and victim services.

As in the first, second, and third editions, I have tried to be as objective as possible when examining the controversies surrounding victims and their strained relations with offenders, the news media, social movements, profit-oriented enterprises selling security products and services, and criminal justice officials and agencies. I succinctly summarize both sides of emotionally gripping, passionately debated, and politically divisive issues. I do not necessarily endorse the points of view that I present or their implications for social policy. But I believe it is my obligation to call attention to sharp differences of opinion and interpretation whenever it is relevant. By the late 1990s, the passions inflamed by the burning issues of the 1980s and early 1990s had died down considerably, especially concerning the whereabouts of missing children, allegations about human sacrifices by Satanic cults, claims about repressed memories of childhood sexual abuse, and estimates about the frequency of husband beating, marital rape, and date rape on college campuses. However, new controversies have emerged, especially between the advocates of restorative justice (which seeks to bring about reconciliation between victims and their offenders) and the adherents of retributive justice (which emphasizes punishment). Besides focusing on controversies, I have also highlighted an unanticipated positive development that became evident as the century drew to a close: the impressive nationwide drop in the crime rate. Across the country, with each passing year, fewer people were being murdered, robbed, raped, and assaulted, or suffered burglaries and car thefts during the second half of the 1990s.

One negative trend continued: some prominent people who should have known better continued to use "victimology" as an epithet spit out through clenched teeth. I first detected this unfortunate development during the early 1990s. As I noted in the preface to the third edition, the name of an area of specialization within criminology—one that most people never heard of unless they took a college course about crime or criminal justice—had become incorporated into everyday language. However, as soon as it entered mainstream culture, *victimology* (undeservedly!) became a "dirty word."

Consider the following examples of how the term was misused during the 1990s:

- During a nationally televised interview, a critic of contemporary feminism (Paglia, 1993) declared "I hate *victimology*. I despise a victim-centered view of the universe. Do not teach young women that their heritage is nothing but victimization." (emphasis added)
- In a best seller that condemned the fragmentation of American society, allegedly brought about by multiculturalism, the author (Hughes, 1993, p. 9) argued "Meanwhile, the new orthodoxy of feminism is abandoning the image of the independent, existentially responsible woman in favor of woman as helpless victim of male oppression—treat her as equal before the law, and you are compounding her victimization. Conservatives have been delighted to cast their arguments in the same terms of *victimology*, with the difference that, for them, what produces victims is feminism itself . . . (emphasis added)
- In a newspaper opinion piece about the controversy over lifting the ban on homosexuals serving in the military, the author (Sullivan, 1993, p. A21) observed ". . . the effect that ending the ban could have on the gay community is to embolden the forces of responsibility and integration and weaken the impulses of *victimology* and despair. . . . A defeat would send a signal to a gay community at a crossroads between hopeful integration and a new relapse into the *victimology* of the ghetto." (emphasis added)

- In his syndicated column, a leading conservative partisan (Buckley, 1994, p. 30A) condemned the thinking of the 1960s Woodstock generation. "The countercultural music is the perfect accompaniment for the culture of sexual self-indulgence, of exhibitionism, of crime and illegitimacy and ethnic rancor and *victimology*." (emphasis added)
- In an angry denunciation of several different jury verdicts that found defendants "not guilty," a newsmagazine commentator (Leo, 1994) complained "We are deep into the era of the abuse excuse. The doctrine of *victimology*—claiming victim status means you are not responsible for your actions—is beginning to warp the legal system. . . .The irony of this seems to escape victimologists. A movement that began with the slogan, 'Don't blame the victim' now strives to blame murder victims for their own deaths." (emphasis added)

Attacks on victimology continued as the decade wound down. A collection of letters written to the editors of the *New York Times* (1996, p. E8) was published under the headline "What women want is a lot less victimology." A Pulitzer-Prize-winning conservative commentator (Will, 1998, p. 42) entitled his syndicated column opposing the Clinton administration's antismoking campaign as, "President feeds the culture of victimology." Another columnist (Seebach, 1999, p. 2B) berated liberal professors for producing college grads whom employers would reject because these students were "experts only in victimology or oppression studies." One journalist (Parker, 1999, p. B10) even insisted that, "Americans are fed up with 20th century victimology . . ."

Why is victimology being singled out for such harsh criticisms? Victimology is just one of many "ologies" (including such narrowly focused fields as penology, suicidology, and sociobiology). The suffix *ology* merely means "the study of." If the phrase "the scientific study of victims" is substituted for "victimology" in the excerpts quoted above, the usage makes no sense. Evidently those who denounce victimology are railing at something other than research into the plight of people harmed by criminals.

It appears that what they are deriding is a victim-oriented outlook on life, which can be categorized as the ideology of "victimism" (see Sykes, 1992). An ideology is a coherent, integrated set of beliefs that shapes interpretations and leads to political action. Whether or not victimism is understandable, justifiable, and politically effective, it is a popular outlook that is widely held by people who share a sense of common victimhood. Individuals who adopt this ideology believe that they and their fellow group members have been seriously harmed by some other group or by an unfair social system built upon oppressive and exploitive roles and relationships. Because they criticize the foundations of contemporary society, these victimist groups are condemned by conservative defenders of the status quo, as part of an ongoing battle for the hearts and minds of the American people that is often dubbed the "culture wars." But victimology, as an "ology" and not an "ism," is a neutral, evenhanded, nonpartisan, ongoing scientific endeavor that does not take sides, play favorites, or speak with just one voice. So there is no reason to condemn the whole scholarly enterprise of victimology and dismiss it as flawed, distorted, or biased, as the authors quoted above did.

The current spate of polemics directed against victimology for being too "pro-victim" is particularly ironic, since the academic discipline is still recovering from a series of attacks launched during the 1970s from the opposite political direction. In those days, victimology was (unfairly) branded by liberal critics as being inherently antivictim. There was a kernel of truth in these charges because the first few victimologists to gain recognition in academic circles were intrigued by the possibility that some crimes could be the "fault" of victims. Their research into the issue of shared responsibility provoked some detractors to charge that the entire discipline of victimology provided scientific trappings to cloak a mean-spirited impulse to blame the victim for his or her own plight. But as the field evolved, matured, and diversified, accusations about alleged antivictim biases faded away.

In sum, victimology has received a "bum rap" in common, everyday political rhetoric by those who mistakenly mock it. Read on, and this confusion will be dispelled. Victimology will emerge as a challenging, meaningful, balanced, and relevant field of study focusing on a deep-seated social problem.

In the prefaces of the previous editions, I listed my credentials not only as a victimologist but also as a crime victim. I know from firsthand encounters what it is like to be a victim of a wide range of street crimes (thankfully, none of them really serious). Before the first edition was written

- I was held up twice (in one month!) by pairs of knife-wielding robbers.
- I lost a car to thieves. (The police discovered it completely stripped, burned, and abandoned.)
- I experienced a series of thefts of car radios, hubcaps, and batteries.
- I suffered a break-in that left my apartment in shambles.

  By the time the second edition of this textbook came out, my already impressive résumé as a street crime victim had grown considerably.
- A thief stole the bicycle that I used to ride to the train station by cutting the fence to which it was chained.
- Someone ran off with a fishing rod I had left unattended on a pier for a few minutes while I was buying more bait.
- A teenager singled out my car in a crowded parking lot and smashed the rear window with a rock. An eyewitness pointed out the young man to the police, and his foster parents volunteered to pay my bills for the damage. I minimized their expenses by going to a salvage yard to find a replacement window.
- A thief broke into the trunk of my car and stole my wallet and my wife's pocketbook while we spent an afternoon at the beach. Our wallets were later recovered from a nearby mailbox, emptied of our cash and credit cards.
- One hot summer night, an intruder entered our kitchen through an unlocked screen door. He ran off with a purse while we talked to guests in the living room.

- A car I was riding in was sideswiped by a vehicle driven by a fugitive who was being hotly pursued by a patrol car. No one was hurt, but the offender escaped.
- A thief smashed the side window of my car, which was parked a block away from the college where I teach. Sitting in the passenger seat, he began to pry out the radio. When the alarm went off, he fled, leaving his screwdriver behind.

  By the third edition, I had a few more misfortunes to add to the list.
- My car was broken into two more times (on busy streets during the daytime). In each incident, the alarm sounded and apparently scared off the thief, cutting short his depredations and minimizing my losses.

  Shortly before this fourth edition was completed, my family was the victim of a "white collar" con game or scam.
- We picked a moving company out of the Yellow Pages because it advertised low rates and accepted credit cards. I should have been suspicious when they arrived in a rented truck, but I foolishly signed some papers authorizing them to charge me for packing materials. While we loaded computer components, valuables, and pets into our cars and shuttled them to our new house, they quickly used an enormous amount of shrink-wrap and cardboard boxes on our old furniture, cheap picture frames, and clothing. Before they would unload our stuff that night, they presented me with a bill that was inflated by about $1,000 worth of unnecessary packaging. Then they demanded payment in cash or else they would drive away with all our possessions and charge us for unloading and storage. I called the police but they insisted it was a business dispute and that they could not intervene. After visiting several ATMs and handing over the cash, I contacted some colleagues at John Jay College of Criminal Justice who have connections with law enforcement agencies. They made inquiries and warned me that this company was known to have mob ties. Since these gangsters literally "knew where we lived," a fear of reprisals intimidated me from pursuing my claims about fraud in civil court or through state regulatory agencies or consumer affairs bureaus.

Although others have suffered much more severely than I, these many brushes with an assortment of offenders have sensitized me to the kinds of financial losses, emotional stresses, and physical injuries that taken together constitute the "victim's plight." I suspect that many victimologists and victim advocates have been drawn to this humanistic discipline because their own painful experiences inspired them to try to alleviate the suffering of others.

ACKNOWLEDGMENTS

Before writing the fourth edition, I received useful feedback from these reviewers: Frankie Bailey, State University of New York, Albany; Scott Hedlund, Pierce College; Janice Joseph, Richard Stockton College of New Jersey; and

Thomas McDonald, North Dakota State University. Once again, I am grateful for the support this project received from the staff at Wadsworth. In particular, the revision process was efficiently supervised by executive criminal justice editor Sabra Horne, and by editor Dan Alpert, associate project editor Susan Walters, and editorial assistant Cortney Bruggink. Editorial and production services were professionally handled at Proof Positive/Farrowlyne Associates Inc. by Gail Savage, Andrew Parker, Kathleen Ermitage, and Ann Lindstrom, and at Black Dot Group by Sue Katkus and Sandy Reinhard.

Andrew Karmen
May 2000

Crime Victims

An Introduction to Victimology

1

The Rediscovery of Crime Victims and the Rise of Victimology

The Discovery, Decline, and Rediscovery of Crime Victims

The Discovery of Crime Victims

The Decline of Crime Victims

The Rediscovery of Crime Victims

The Rise of Victimology

The Emergence of a New Focus

The Need for Objectivity

Victimology Compared to Criminology

What Victimologists Do

Step 1: Identify, Define, and Describe the Problem

Step 2: Measure the True Dimensions of the Problem

Step 3: Investigate How Victims are Handled

Step 4: Gather Evidence to Test Hypotheses

Victimology Contributes to the Process of Rediscovering Victims

Stage 1: Calling Attention to an Overlooked Problem

Stage 2: Winning Victories, Implementing Reforms

Stage 3: Emergence of an Opposition and Development of Resistance to Further Changes

Stage 4: Research and Temporary Resolution of the Dispute

The Continuing Process of Rediscovery

Chapter Summary

Discussion Questions

Box 1.1 Highlights in the Brief History of Victimology and Victim Assistance

Box 1.2 The Kinds of Studies Victimologists Undertake

Box 1.3 Groups of Victims That Have Been Recently Rediscovered

THE DISCOVERY, DECLINE, AND REDISCOVERY OF CRIME VICTIMS

The Discovery Of Crime Victims

The word **victim** was connected to the notion of sacrifice in ancient cultures. In the original meaning of the term, a victim was a person or an animal put to death during a ceremony in order to appease some supernatural power or deity. Over the centuries the word has picked up additional meanings. Now the term commonly refers to individuals who experience injury, loss, or hardship for any reason. People can be victims of accidents, diseases, natural disasters, or social problems like warfare, discrimination, or other injustices. Crime victims are harmed because of illegal acts. **Victimization** is an asymmetrical relationship that is abusive, destructive, parasitical, unfair, and, in many cases, in violation of a law. While the crime is in progress, criminals temporarily force their victims to play roles (almost as if following a script) that mimic the dynamics between predator and prey, winner and loser, and even master and slave. **Direct** or **primary** victims experience the criminal act and its consequences firsthand. **Indirect** or **secondary** victims (such as family members) also suffer emotionally or financially but are not immediately involved or injured. **Survivors** are the relatives of people killed by murderers.

Laws that prohibit certain harmful actions define wrongdoers as criminals subject to punishment and at the same time specify that the injured parties are victims. The penal codes forbidding what are now called street crimes—murder, rape, robbery, assault, burglary, and theft—can be traced back to biblical times. Hence, victims of these "common-law offenses" were formally identified, officially recognized, and consequently **discovered** ages ago.

The Decline of Crime Victims

Scholars who study the history of the legal system report that in past centuries victims played a leading role in the resolution of criminal matters. To discourage retaliation by victims and their families—acts that could lead to endless feuding if offenders and their kin counterattacked—societies in simpler times established direct repayment schemes. Legal codes around the world enabled victims to receive money or valuables from wrongdoers to compensate for the pain, suffering, and losses they endured. This process of victim-oriented justice prevailed mostly in small villages engaged in farming where social relations were based on personal obligations, clear-cut family ties, strong religious beliefs, and traditions considered to be sacred. But the victim's role diminished as industrialization and urbanization brought about business relations that were voluntary, secular, impersonal, rationalized, and contractual. Victims lost control over the process of determining the fate of the offenders who harmed them. Instead, the local governmental structure dominated judicial proceedings and extracted fines from convicts, physically punished them, or even executed them. The seriousness of the wounds and losses inflicted upon victims were of importance only for determining the charges and penalties upon conviction. Restoring victims to the condition they were in before the crimes occurred was no longer the main concern. In fact, the recovery of damages became a separate matter that was handled in another arena (civil court) according to a different set of rules (tort law) after criminal proceedings were concluded (Schafer, 1968).

The situation of victims followed the same evolutionary pattern from the center of the legal process to its sidelines in U.S. history. In colonial America, police forces and public prosecutors had not yet been established. Victims were the key decision makers within the rudimentary criminal justice system and its direct beneficiaries. Victims conducted their own investigations, paid for warrants to have sheriffs make arrests, and hired private attorneys to indict and prosecute their alleged attackers. Convicts were forced to repay victims up to three times as much as they damaged or stole.

But after the American Revolution and the adoption of the Constitution and the Bill of Rights, crimes were reconceptualized as hostile acts directed against the authority of the state, which was defined as the representative of the people. Addressing the victims' suffering was deemed to be less important than dealing with the symbolic threat to the social order posed by lawbreakers. Public prosecutors, acting on behalf of the government and in the name of the entire society, took over the powers and responsibilities formerly exercised by victims. Federal, state, and district attorneys were granted the authority to decide whether or not to press charges against defendants and what sanctions to ask judges to impose upon convicts. The goals of deterring crime through punishment, protecting society by incapacitating dangerous persons in prisons or through executions, and rehabilitating lesser transgressors through treatment came to overshadow victims' demands to be restored to financial, emotional, and physical health.

Over the last two centuries, the government increasingly has assumed the obligation of providing jail detainees and prison inmates with food, clothing, housing, supervision, medical care, recreational opportunities, schooling, job training, psychological counseling, and legal representation—while leaving victims to fend for themselves. As victims lost control over "their" cases, their role dwindled to just two contributions: filing a complaint with the police that initiated an investigation and, if necessary, testifying for the prosecution as another piece of evidence in the state's presentation of damning facts against the accused. When plea negotiations replaced trials as the means of resolving most cases, victims lost their last opportunity to actively participate in the process by presenting their firsthand experiences on the witness stand to a jury. Victims rarely were included and consulted when the police and prosecution "team" decided upon its strategies and goals. To add insult to injury, often they were not even informed of the outcomes of "their" cases. Thoroughly marginalized, victims often sensed that they had been taken advantage of twice, the second time by a system that was ostensibly set up to help them but in reality seemed more intent on satisfying the needs of its core agencies and key officials (see McDonald, 1977; and Davis, Kunreuther, and Connick, 1984).

The Rediscovery of Crime Victims

After decades, even centuries, of neglect, crime victims were given renewed attention and in effect were **rediscovered** during the late 1950s and early 1960s. A small number of self-help advocates, social scientists, crusading journalists, enlightened criminal justice officials, and responsive lawmakers helped to direct public concern toward what they defined as a serious problem: the total disregard of victim issues. Through writings, meetings, and events such as rallies and petition drives, these activists got across their message that victims were forgotten people whose needs and wants had been systematically overlooked but deserved attention and action. Discussion and debate emerged in the late 1960s and intensified throughout the 1970s, 1980s, and 1990s over why the situation existed and what could be done about it. Various groups with their own distinct agendas formed coalitions and mobilized to campaign for reforms. As a result, new laws favorable to victims are being passed, and criminal justice policies are being changed.

Social Movements: Taking Up the Victims' Cause Aside from suffering harm at the hands of criminals, victims as a group may have very little in common. They may differ in age, sex, race, social class, political orientation, and in many other important ways. Therefore, it has been difficult to organize them into self-help groups and to harness the energies of these groups into a larger social movement. Despite these obstacles, a crime victims' movement emerged during the 1970s. It has developed into a broad alliance of activists, support groups, and advocacy organizations that lobbies for increased rights and expanded services, demonstrates at trials, educates the public, trains criminal justice professionals and caregivers, sets up research institutes and information clearinghouses, designs and evaluates experiments, and holds conferences to share experiences and develop innovative programs. The guiding principle holding this diverse coalition together is that victims who otherwise would feel powerless and enraged can regain a sense of control over their lives through practical assistance, mutual support, and involvement in the criminal justice process (see Friedman, 1985; Smith, 1985; Smith, Sloan, and Ward, 1990; Weed, 1995).

Several earlier social movements have greatly influenced the growth and orientation of the victims' movement. The most important contributions have been made by the law-and-order movement, the women's movement, and the civil rights movement.

The law-and-order movement was the first to proclaim in the 1960s that the plight of street crime victims merited more attention. Alarmed by surging crime rates, law-and-order advocates adopted a hard-line, conservative stance that the criminal justice system ought to crack down on deviants who disobeyed society's rules. To win over people who might have been reluctant to grant more power to the police, prosecutors, and prison authorities, they argued that the average American should be more worried about becoming a victim than about being falsely accused, mistakenly convicted, and unjustly punished (Hook, 1972). The scales of justice were said to be unfairly tilted in favor of the bad guys and against innocent, law-abiding citizens and their allies on the police force and in the prosecutor's office. In the victim-oriented justice system that law-and-order advocates envisioned, punishment would be swift and sure. Defense attorneys would no longer be able to take advantage of loopholes and technicalities that undermined the government's efforts to arrest, detain, convict, incapacitate, and punish wrongdoers. Permissiveness (unwarranted leniency) and the coddling of criminals would be ended: more offenders would be locked up for longer periods of time, and fewer would be granted bail, probation, or parole. People who opposed these get-tough policies were branded as "pro-criminal" and "antivictim" (see Carrington, 1975).

Activists in the women's movement understandably have focused their energies towards supporting women who were victimized by men and then failed to receive the help they needed from the male-dominated criminal justice system. Feminists launched both the antirape and the antibattering movements. The antirape movement originated in 1972 when the first rape crisis centers were set up in Berkeley, California, and Washington, D.C. These centers were not only places of aid and comfort in a time of pain and confusion. They were also rallying sites for outreach efforts to those who were suffering in isolation, meeting places for consciousness-raising groups exploring the patriarchal cultural traditions that encouraged males to subjugate females, and hubs for political organizing to change laws and policies (see Rose, 1977; Largen, 1981; and Schechter, 1982). Some antirape activists went on to protest street harassment, uniting behind the slogan "Take back the night" (see Lederer, 1980). Other activists helped to organize the battered women's movement and set up the first "safe house" in St. Paul, Minnesota, in 1974. Antibattering efforts paralleled antirape activities in a number of ways. Both were initiated for the most part by former victims who viewed their plight as an outgrowth of societal and institutional problems rather than personal troubles and individual shortcomings. Both sought to empower women by confronting established male authority, challenging existing procedures, providing peer support and advocacy, and devising alternative places to turn to for help in a time of need. The overall analysis that originally guided these pro-victim projects was that male-versus-female offenses (such as rape, wife beating, sexual harassment in the streets and at work, and incest at home) pose a threat to all women, and this kind of group intimidation slows down progress toward equality. The gravest dangers are faced by women who are socially disadvantaged because of racial discrimination and economic insecurity. Girls and women victimized by boys and men cannot count on the men at the helm of the criminal justice system to appreciate the seriousness of the problem and to effectively protect or assist them.

Composed of organizations representing the interests of a wide range of racial and ethnic minority groups, the civil rights movement opposes entrenched discriminatory practices that encourage members of the white majority to victimize people of color. Over the decades the movement has directed attention to the special threats posed by racist violence, from lynch mobs to Ku Klux Klan bombings and assassinations. In recent years one of the movement's major concerns has been protection for victims of hate-motivated

bias crimes, which range from vandalism and harassment to beatings and arson. Civil rights groups have been instrumental in getting legislatures to impose stiffer penalties for committing hate crimes and in establishing specialized police squads to deter or solve these divisive and inflammatory crimes that would otherwise polarize communities along racial and ethnic lines (see Levin and McDevitt, 1993). Civil rights organizations try to mobilize public support to demand evenhandedness in the administration of justice. A double standard, although more obvious in the past, may still infect the operations of the criminal justice system. Crimes by black perpetrators against white victims were always taken very seriously (thoroughly investigated, solved, vigorously prosecuted, and severely punished), whereas crimes by white offenders against black victims and lawbreaking by blacks against blacks (see *Ebony,* 1979) rarely evoked the same governmental response and public outrage. Activists also point out that members of minority groups still face greater risks of becoming victims of official misconduct in the form of police brutality (or even worse, the unjustified use of deadly force), false accusations, frame-ups, wrongful convictions, and other miscarriages of justice.

Social movements that champion the causes of civil liberties, children's rights, senior citizens' rights, homosexual rights, and self-help have also made significant contributions to bettering the situation of victims. The civil liberties movement's main focus is to preserve constitutional safeguards and due process guarantees that protect suspects, defendants, and prisoners from abuses of governmental power by criminal justice officials. However, civil liberties organizations have won court victories that have benefited victims of street crime in two ways: by furthering police professionalism and by extending the doctrine of "equal protection under the law." In professionalized police departments, officers must meet higher educational and training requirements and must abide by more demanding standards. As a result, victims are more likely to receive prompt responses, effective service, and sensitive treatment. If they don't, channels exist through which they can redress their grievances. Equal protection guarantees improve the chances that people whose calls for help were given short shrift in the past (due to their race, sex, age, social class, disability, or other disadvantage) will gain access to the police and prosecutorial assistance to which they are entitled (Walker, 1982; Stark and Goldstein, 1985).

Children's rights groups campaign against physical abuse, sexual abuse, gross neglect, and other forms of maltreatment of youngsters. Their successes include more effective parenting instruction programs; stricter abuse reporting requirements; improved procedures for arrest, prosecution, and conviction of offenders; greater sensitivity to the needs of victimized children as complaining witnesses; and enhanced protection and prevention services. Activists in senior citizens' groups have pressured some police departments to establish special squads to protect older persons from younger persons, convinced legislatures to pass stiffer penalties that apply when victims are over 60, and brought about greater awareness of the problem of elder abuse—financial, emotional, and physical mistreatment by family members or caretakers (see Smith and Freinkel, 1988). The gay rights movement originally called attention to the vulnerability of homosexuals and lesbians to blackmail, to exploitation by organized crime syndicates that ran some of the bars and clubs, and to police harassment of those who needed police protection (see Maghan and Sagarin, 1983). The movement now focuses on preventing gay-bashing street assaults against suspected homosexuals and lesbians, attacks that are motivated by the offenders' hatred for the victim's presumed sexual orientation.

Groups that are part of the self-help movement have set up dependable support systems for victims by combining the participatory spirit of the grass roots protest movements of the 1960s with the self-improvement ideals of the human potential movement of the 1970s. The ideology of self-help derives from the simple organizing principle that former victims who have directly experienced the pain and suffering of being harmed, and are still struggling to overcome these hardships, can provide mutual assistance that is more comforting and effective than the services offered by large, distant bureaucracies and detached professional caregivers (Gartner and Riessman, 1980).

The News Media: Portraying the Victim's Plight The news media—newspapers, magazines, and radio and television stations—deserve a great deal of credit for rediscovering victims. In the past the lion's share of coverage was devoted to offenders: their backgrounds, their motives, and what should be done with them (usually how much they should be punished). Scant attention was paid to the real flesh-and-blood individuals who suffered because of offenders. But now details about the injured parties are routinely included to inject some human interest into crime stories. Balanced accounts can vividly describe the victims' plight: how they were harmed, what losses they incurred, what emotions they felt, how they were handled by the legal system, and what helped or hindered their recovery. By remaining faithful to the facts, journalists can enable their audiences to transcend their own limited experiences with criminals and to see emergencies, tragedies, and triumphs through the eyes of victims. Skillful reporting and insightful observations allow nonvictims to better understand and empathize with the actions and reactions of victims.

Businesses: Selling Products and Services to Victims Commercial enterprises have rediscovered victims as an underserved market for crime prevention goods and services. After suffering through an unpleasant experience, many victims become willing, even eager, consumers, searching for services and devices that will protect them from any further harm. Potential victims—essentially everyone else—constitute a far larger market, if they can be convinced that their personal security purchases can reduce their odds of winding up as another statistic. Products that are promoted as reducing the chances of harm include firearms, pepper sprays, burglar alarms with monitoring systems, automobile antitheft hardware, cell phones, and assorted other specialty items such as bulletproof clothing, high-tech tracking devices, and surveillance cameras. Potentially useful personal services range from bodyguards to background checks of employees to insurance coverage.

THE RISE OF VICTIMOLOGY

The Emergence of a New Focus

The origins of the academic discipline of victimology can be traced back to several articles, books, and research projects initiated by criminologists during the 1940s and 1950s. At that time, attention was focused squarely on those who violated the law: who they were, why they engaged in illegal activities, how they were handled by the criminal justice system, whether they should be incarcerated, and how they might be rehabilitated. Eventually, perhaps through the process of elimination, several criminologists searching for solutions to the crime problem were drawn to—or stumbled upon—the importance of victims. Victims were considered to be worthy of serious study primarily because they were the completely overlooked half of the dyad (pair). The first scholars to consider themselves victimologists examined the resistance put up by rape victims (Mendelsohn, 1940); the presumed vulnerabilities of certain kinds of people, such as the very young, the very old, recent immigrants, and the mentally disturbed (Von Hentig, 1948); and the kinds of people, in terms of factors like age, sex, and race, whose actions contributed to their own violent deaths (Wolfgang, 1958). The first use in English of the term *victimology* to refer to the study of people harmed by criminals appeared in a book about murderers written by a psychiatrist (Wertham, 1949).

During the 1960s, as the problem of street crime intensified, the President's Commission on Law Enforcement and the Administration of Justice urged criminologists to pay more attention to victims (and for some to become victimologists).

> One of the most neglected subjects in the study of crime is its victims: the persons, households, and businesses that bear the brunt of crime in the United States. Both the part the victim can play in the criminal act and the part he could have played in preventing it are often overlooked. If it could be determined with sufficient specificity that people or businesses with certain characteristics are more likely than others to be crime victims, and that crime is more likely to occur in some places rather than in others, efforts to control and prevent crime would be more productive. Then the public could be told where and when the risks of crime are greatest. Measures such as preventive police patrol and installation of burglar alarms and special locks could then be pursued more efficiently and effectively. Individuals could then substitute objective estimation of risk for the general apprehensiveness that today restricts—perhaps unnecessarily and at best haphazardly—their enjoyment of parks and their freedom of movement on the streets after dark. (Task Force on Assessment, 1967, p. 80)

In this call for action, the commission's Task Force on Assessment stressed the potential practical benefits of a science of victimology: More crimes could be prevented and more criminals caught, unrealistic fears could be calmed and unwarranted complacency dispelled, and needless expenditures could be eliminated or reduced. These ambitious goals have not yet been attained. Other goals not cited by the commission that have been added over the years include reducing suffering, making the criminal justice system more responsive, and restoring victims to the financial condition they were in before the crime occurred.

During the 1960s and 1970s, criminologists, reformers, and political activists argued persuasively that offenders themselves were in some sense victims—of poverty, inferior schooling, run-down housing, job shortages, discrimination, disrupted family relations, and other social injustices. In reaction, many people asked, "But what about the real flesh-and-blood victims they preyed upon who were innocent, law-abiding, and vulnerable? What can be done to ease their suffering?" In trying to answer that question, people of goodwill came to recognize that such individuals were being systematically abandoned to their fates. Many acknowledged that institutionalized neglect had prevailed for too long. A consensus that certain categories of people harmed by illegal acts deserved better treatment began to emerge. Plans for financial assistance were the focus of early discussions; campaigns for enhanced political rights soon followed.

By the 1970s, victimology had become a recognized area of specialization within criminology, with its own national and international professional organizations, conferences, and journals. During the 1990s, victimology was studied at over 240 colleges and universities (see Box 1.1 for a compilation of the major events in victimology's short history).

Victimology is now recognized as the scientific study of the physical, emotional, and financial harm people suffer because of criminal activities. Victimologists not only investigate the impact of the injuries and losses inflicted by offenders but also the handling of victims by the criminal justice system—the interactions with agencies and officials, especially police officers, prosecutors, defense attorneys, judges, probation officers, and members of parole boards. In addition, researchers explore the public's reaction to the plight of victims, as indicated by relations with other societal groups and institutions (such as the news media, the medical and legal professions, and businesses selling anticrime hardware and protective services). Victimologists want to know if victims have been physically injured, economically hurt, robbed of self-respect, emotionally traumatized, socially stigmatized, politically oppressed, collectively exploited, personally alienated, manipulated, co-opted, neglected, ignored, blamed, defamed, demeaned, or vilified. Victimologists are equally curious to find out if victims are being empowered, assisted, served, accommodated, placated, rehabilitated, educated, celebrated, memorialized, honored, and even idolized. Note that victimologists are researchers, not practitioners or advocates who help injured parties to recover from their ordeals. Psychiatrists, psychologists, therapists, counselors, social workers, doctors, nurses, and lawyers provide the actual services to their clients. Victimologists evaluate the effectiveness of these kinds of assistance.

The suffering of victims and survivors always has been a popular theme for artists and writers to interpret and for political and religious leaders to address. But this long and rich tradition embodies what might be categorized as the *subjective* approach to the plight of victims, since issues are approached from the standpoint of morality, ethics, philosophy, and emotion. Victimologists endeavor

BOX 1.1 Highlights in the Brief History of Victimology and Victim Assistance

1941 Hans Von Hentig publishes an article focusing on the interaction between victims and criminals.

1947 Benjamin Mendelsohn coins the term *victimology* in an article in French.

1957 In Great Britain Margery Fry proposes legislation that would reimburse victims for their losses.

1958 Marvin Wolfgang studies the circumstances surrounding the deaths of murder victims.

1964 The U.S. Congress holds hearings on the plight of crime victims but rejects legislative proposals to cover their losses.

1965 California becomes the first U.S. state to set up a special fund to repay victims for crime-inflicted expenses.

1966 A research team carries out a nationwide survey to find out about crimes that were not reported to the police.

1967 A presidential commission recommends that criminologists study victims.

1968 Stephen Schafer writes the first textbook about victims.

1972 The federal government initiates a yearly *National Crime Victimization Survey* of the general public to uncover firsthand information about street crimes.

1973 The first international conference of victimologists is convened in Jerusalem.

1976 The first scholarly journal devoted to victimology begins publication.

1979 The World Society of Victimology is founded.

1981 President Reagan proclaims Victims' Rights Week in April.

1982 Congress passes a Victim and Witness Protection Act that suggests standards for fair treatment of victims within the federal court system.

1983 The President's Task Force on Victims of Crime recommends changes in the Constitution and in federal and state laws to guarantee victims' rights.

1984 Congress passes the Victims of Crime Act, which provides federal subsidies to state victim compensation and assistance programs.

1985 The United Nations General Assembly unanimously adopts a resolution that urges all members to respect and extend the rights of victims of crimes and of abuses of power.

1986 Victims' rights activists seek the passage of constitutional amendments on the federal and state levels guaranteeing victims' rights.

1987 The U.S. Department of Justice opens a National Victims Resource Center in Rockville, Maryland, to serve as a clearinghouse for information.

1990 Congress passes the Victims' Rights and Restitution Act.

1991 Congress enacts the International Parental Child Kidnapping Act.

1994 Congress passes the Violence Against Women Act.

1990s Victimology is mistakenly characterized as an ideology that encourages people to see themselves as victims rather than a scientific discipline that studies victims.

SOURCES: *Galaway and Hudson, 1981; Schneider, 1982; Lamborn, 1985; National Organization for Victim Assistance (NOVA), 1989, 1995.*

to examine the same topics from a fresh, new, **objective** social scientific perspective. Scientific objectivity requires that the observer try to be fair, open-minded, evenhanded, dispassionate, neutral, and unbiased. Objectivity means not taking sides, showing favoritism, allowing personal prejudices to sidetrack analyses, permitting emotion to cloud reasoning, or letting the dominant views of the times dictate conclusions and recommendations.

Prescriptions to remain neutral are easier to abide by when the incidents under scrutiny happened long ago and far away. It's much harder to maintain social distance when investigating the plight of real people right here and right now. These scientific tenets are extremely difficult to live up to when the subject matter—the suffering inflicted by offenders—draws upon widely held beliefs about what is good and evil, right and wrong, and just and unfair. Most offenders show such callous disregard and depraved indifference toward the human beings they cold-bloodedly targeted and mistreated as depersonalized objects that it is difficult to avoid being swept away by powerful emotions. Consider how natural it is to feel sorry for innocent victims and to feel hostility toward aggressors in the following real-life examples:

- An intruder walks into an evening biology class on a college campus and forces the instructor and the seven students to lie flat on the floor and hand over their valuables. The victims lose a total of $655 in cash, plus jewelry. "Being held up in class is unprecedented. It's a surrealistic situation. It was like a movie, watching it go on before your eyes," says the laboratory assistant. (Purdum, 1986)
- Two freshmen returning to their Jeep in a shopping center parking lot are confronted by a junior pre-med student from another college who is home for Christmas break. He draws a gun and forces his two hostages to drive to a deserted area. There he orders his captives out, reassuring them, "Don't be nervous. I'm not going to hurt you." As they lie face down in the snow, he shoots each of them in the back of the head, killing one young man and injuring the other. Then he drives off with his prize—the Jeep. (Hanley, 1994b)
- Two armed men accost a graduate student working a summer job as an ice cream vendor. Without saying a word they shoot him twice, take his money, and flee. He collapses in a pool of blood near his truck on the edge of a housing project. A crowd of over one hundred children and teenagers gather. But instead of helping him, they help themselves to his ice cream. He lies bleeding on the pavement for over an hour until the police arrive. "Some of them were happy that such a thing would happen, that an opportunity would come up, that they'd be getting something free," the victim says from his hospital bed. (Associated Press, 1984b)
- An author of a book that urges its readers to commit "random acts of kindness" toward strangers is mugged and beaten by three teenagers. True to his principle of accentuating the positive, he praises the police officers and hospital staff who attended to his wounds and notes optimistically that one of the teens did not assault him and that the trio did not get away with the bicycle he was riding. (Associated Press, 1994b)

Doesn't basic human decency demand that observers side with the downtrodden and underdogs and denounce the behavior of predators and aggressors like those shown in these examples? Why would victimologists consider maintaining objectivity to be a desirable prerequisite of any scientific analysis?

The Need for Objectivity

At first the importance of reserving judgments, refraining from jumping to conclusions, and resisting the urge to take sides might not be self-evident. The angry gut reaction might be to ask "What decent person could possibly side with criminals against their law-abiding, totally innocent victims? What is wrong with championing the interests of people who have been hurt by unjust and illegal actions? Why is neutrality a worthwhile starting point in an analysis?"

The simple and direct answer to the question "Why shouldn't victimologists be openly and squarely pro-victim?" is that on many occasions this formula provides no real guidance. Victimologists are not merely presented with clear-cut cases of guilt and innocence. Not all victims were weak, defenseless, unsuspecting, innocent "lambs" who, through tragic or ironic circumstances or just plain bad luck, were pounced upon by cunning, vicious "wolves." In some instances observers may have honest and legitimate disagreements over which party in a conflict should be labeled the victim and who should be stigmatized as the offender. These real-life situations dramatize the necessity for impartiality when untangling convoluted relationships in order to make a rational argument and a reasonable legal determination that one person should be arrested, prosecuted, and punished, and the other defended, supported, and assisted. Unlike the black-and-white examples presented above, many dramatic incidents can embody clashes between two people who to varying degrees are both victims, both offenders, or both victims and offenders simultaneously. Consider the following news accounts that though admittedly atypical, illustrate just how difficult it can be to try to establish exactly who misbehaved badly and who acted appropriately:

- A man riding a subway train is approached by two teenagers who ask him for $5 while two of their friends look on. Fearing that he is about to be robbed and injured, as in a previous incident, the man rises from his seat, draws an unlicensed revolver, and empties it of the bullets he has hollowed out for greater impact. He shoots two of the teens in the chest, one in the side, and the fourth twice, once in the back at close range. Dubbed the "Subway Vigilante" by reporters, he is widely hailed as a hero who stood up and fought back, striking a symbolic blow on behalf of all victims against all street criminals. Others, however (including some high officials), depict him as a trigger-happy gunman who overreacted to stereotypes and mowed down four unarmed teenagers—two of them fleeing—before they made their intentions clear.

  Amidst a growing controversy, a grand jury does not indict him, but the case is brought before a second grand jury which agrees to put him on trial for attempted murder, assault, and reckless endangerment. His lawyer pursues a prosecutorial defense, arguing that the four wounded youths are really injured robbers and that the accused is actually their intended prey who justifiably resorted to deadly force to protect himself. The jury convicts him only of possessing an unlicensed handgun. The judge sentences him to a jail term followed by probation, community service, psychiatric observation, and a fine (Fletcher, 1988b). The young man who was shot twice ends up in a wheelchair, paralyzed from the waist down. More than 10 years later he wins a multi-million dollar lawsuit against the man who crippled him when a civil jury decides that the fourth shot in the back was not fired in self-defense. (Nossiter, 1996)

- An ex-marine who works as a bouncer in a bar wakes up and discovers to his horror that his wife has sliced off his penis with a kitchen knife. Arrested for "malicious wounding," she tells the police that she mutilated him because earlier that evening he awakened in a drunken stupor and forced himself upon her. He is put on trial for marital sexual abuse but is acquitted by a jury that does not believe her testimony about a history of beatings, involuntary rough sex, and other humiliations. When she is put on trial (ironically, by the same prosecutor) for the bloody bedroom assault, many people rally to her side. To her supporters she has undercut the debilitating stereotype of female passivity; she literally disarmed him with a single stroke and threw the symbol of male sexual dominance out the window. To her detractors she is a master at manipulation, publicly playing the role of sobbing, sympathetic victim to divert attention from her act of rage against a sleeping husband who had lost sexual interest in her.

  Facing up to 20 years in prison, she declines to negotiate a guilty plea and demands her day in court. The jury accepts her defense that she was a traumatized battered wife, deeply depressed, beset by flashbacks, and susceptible to "irresistible impulses" because of years of cruelty and abuse, finding her not guilty by reason of temporary insanity. After 45 days of observation in a mental hospital, she is released, the couple divorces, and then they both cash in on all the international media coverage, sensationalism, titillation, voyeurism, and sexual politics. (Margolick, 1994; Sachs, 1994)

- Two brothers, 18 and 21, barge in upon their wealthy parents as they are watching television and eating ice cream in their mansion. The sons slay their father and mother with a salvo of 15 shotgun blasts. For 6 months the police search for the murderers; then the brothers concede they did it. On trial for first-degree murder and facing possible execution, the sons give emotionally compelling (but uncorroborated) testimony describing how their father sexually molested and emotionally abused them when they were little boys. The brothers contend they acted in self-defense, believing that their parents were about to murder them to keep the alleged incestuous acts a family secret. The prosecution argues that these college students killed their parents in order to get their hands on their $14 million inheritance (they quickly spent $700,000 on luxury cars, condos, and fashionable clothing before they were arrested). The jurors become deadlocked over whether to find them guilty of murder or only of the lesser charge of voluntary manslaughter, and the judge declares a mistrial. In the second trial the prosecution ridicules their abuse defense. They are convicted of premeditated murder and are sentenced to life in prison without parole. (Berns, 1994; Mydans, 1994; Associated Press, 1996a)

In each of the above cases, the people officially designated as the victims by the police and prosecutors—the wounded teenagers, the slashed husband, the dead parents—could be considered as wrongdoers who got what was coming to them, and, indeed, they were viewed just that way by substantial segments of the public and by some jurors. The defendants who got in trouble with the law—the subway passenger, the wife, the brothers—denied that they were criminals. They insisted that they were victims: an innocent commuter about to be robbed, a battered woman who was subjected to marital rape, two sexually molested children. When opinions differ sharply over who is genuinely the victim and who is actually the victimizer, any knee-jerk anticriminal, pro-victim allegiance loses its meaning. The confusion inherent in the unrealistically simplistic labels of "offender" and "victim" underscores the need for objectivity when trying to sort out who is responsible for what happened.

To further complicate matters, impartiality is called for when injured parties turn out to be offenders themselves. To put it bluntly, predators prey upon each other as well as upon innocent members of the general public. Researchers (see Singer, 1981; and Fattah, 1990) have noted that people who are routinely engaged in lawbreaking are more likely to be harmed than their law-abiding counterparts. Some individuals who get robbed, assaulted, or killed were engaged in illegal activities at the time. Hustlers, con men, high-stakes gamblers, pimps, prostitutes, fences, swindlers, smugglers, and others living life in the fast lane of the underworld often get hurt because they frequently find themselves in the company of persons known to be armed and dangerous and place themselves in volatile situations. When rival factions of organized crime families engage in a "mob war" and a gangster is "rubbed out," the dead man was not an upstanding citizen struck down by an act of randomly directed violence. Similarly, when a turf battle erupts between drug dealers and one vanquishes the other, it must be remembered that the loser aspired to be the victor. When youth gangs feud with each other by carrying out "drive-by" shootings, the young members who get gunned down are casualties of their own brand of retaliatory street justice. What could it possibly mean to be pro-victim in those rather common cases in which criminals victimize other criminals?

Next, consider the possibility of a cycle of violence over time that transforms a victim into a victimizer (see Fagan, Piper, and Cheng, 1987). For example, a group of picked-upon students may band together to ambush their tormentors, a battered wife may launch a vengeful surprise attack against her brutal husband, or a physically abused child may grow up to parent his sons in the same excessively punitive way he was raised. A study that tracked the fortunes of about 900 abused children over a follow-up period that ranged from 15 to 20 years concluded that being victimized substantially increased the odds of future delinquency and criminality (Widom, 1992). Similarly, the results of a survey of convicts revealed that they were much more likely to have been abused physically or sexually as children than their law-abiding counterparts (Harlow, 1999). Therefore, yesterday's victims might be tomorrow's offenders. Even more confusing are the situations of certain groups of people who continuously switch roles as they lead their twisted daily lives. For instance, desperate heroin addicts are repeatedly victims of consumer fraud (dealers constantly cheat them by selling heavily adulterated packets of this forbidden substance), but after being defrauded the addicts routinely go out and commit property crimes to raise the cash that pays for their habits (see Kelly, 1983).

Of course, it is possible for lawbreakers to be genuine victims deserving of protection and redress through the courts. For example, prostitutes who illicitly trade sexual favors for money are frequently beaten by sadistic "johns," robbed of their earnings by exploitive pimps (see Boyer and James, 1983), and targeted by serial killers. The victimizations they suffer are more serious than the offenses they commit. Convicts become victims entitled to press charges when they are assaulted, gang raped, or robbed by other, more vicious inmates in the same institution. Clearly, the dynamics between victims and victimizers need to be sorted out in an objective manner.

Striving for objectivity is very important for another reason. Victimologists do not limit their studies to the clashes between victims and offenders. They are very interested in the social reaction to victimization. Victims may also become embroiled in conflicts with other persons and groups besides the perpetrators who directly inflicted injuries and losses: journalists reporting about their cases; police officers and detectives investigating their complaints; prosecutors representing them; defense attorneys working on behalf of the individuals that victims accuse of harming them; lawyers handling their lawsuits in civil court; juries and judges deciding how to resolve their cases; probation, parole, and corrections officers supervising convicts who injured them; governmental agencies and legislative bodies shaping their legal rights; social movements ostensibly rallying to their side or openly opposing their wishes; and businesses seeking to sell them security products and services. Impartiality helps social scientists to understand why friction can develop and to find solutions to these antagonistic relations.

For example, consider the importance of remaining neutral when examining two alternative policies that both claim to be pro-victim. One proposes that a battered woman should decide if she wants to press charges against her husband/boyfriend who was arrested for beating her. The other mandates that the prosecution of the arrestee should proceed on the basis of the available evidence, even if the injured woman wants to drop the charges (presumably because she fears reprisals). Only an objective analysis can determine which approach best serves the long-term interests of domestic violence victims.

Victimologists need to start out as impartial when they check to see whether the new legislation bearing the names of victims turns out to be effective or ill-conceived and counterproductive. Elected officials discovered during the 1990s that naming a proposed law after a well-known victim insures its passage, since few officeholders will dare to argue against the bill, lest they be branded as "antivictim." Were vote-seeking politicians exploiting highly emotional but complex situations for their own personal advantage, or were these tragedies the final straw that dramatized festering problems, mobilized public opinion, and triggered much-needed and long overdue action by lawmakers? For example, the wave of new laws in most states mandating community notification about the release from incarceration of sex offenders was based on New Jersey's

"Megan's Law," named after a little girl slain by her new neighbor. The New York's state legislature passed a slew of statutes named after victims: a measure requiring lengthier sentences before parole eligibility, referred to as "Jenna's Law," in honor of a 22-year-old college student murdered by a man out on parole; a law mandating background checks of employees, dubbed "Kathy's Law," in recognition of the woman who was raped and impregnated by a health care worker, and died after childbirth—while remaining in a coma in a nursing home the entire time; and a regulation that children do not have to visit their imprisoned father if he killed their mother, called "Lee-Anne's Law," after the deceased woman (Henican, 1998). Also signed into law was a controversial measure called "Kendra's Law," named after a young woman murdered by a disturbed man who pushed her in front of a speeding subway train. This law empowered courts to detain and impose compulsory treatment on mentally ill patients who refused to take their medication (Cox, 1998).

Victims of highly publicized crimes often nurse grievances against the news media. Rather than side with angry victims or defend the way journalists cover stories, shouldn't a victimologist adopt the stance of a detached and disinterested observer who investigates these charges with an open mind?

For example, victims and their advocates often complain about sensationalism, a kind of coverage that can be branded as "scandal-mongering," "pandering," "yellow journalism," and "tabloidism." Newspapers, magazines, radio stations, and television networks may engage in sensationalism because they are profit-oriented businesses. Shocking stories attract readers, listeners, and viewers. Blaring headlines, gripping accounts, colorful phrasing, memorable quotes, and other forms of media "hype" build the huge audiences that enable media enterprises to charge advertisers high rates. Producers, editors, and reporters who seek to play up the human interest angle may exploit the victims' plight, having found that crime stories attract a lot of notice if they are spiced up with a heavy dose of sex, gore, and raw emotions. Victimologists might be able to objectively assess the seriousness of the problem by studying press coverage. It has been hypothesized that cases receive exaggerated importance only if some aspect of the victim-offender relationship stands out as an attention grabber: The act, the perpetrator, or the target must be unusual, unexpected, strange, or perverse. Victimization that is typical, commonplace, or predictable is just not newsworthy. Editors and journalists sift through an overwhelming number of real-life tragedies that come to their attention (largely through contacts within the local police department) and select the cases that are most likely to shock people out of their complacency or arouse the public's social conscience. The stories that are featured strike a responsive chord in audiences because the incidents symbolize some significant theme—for example, that anyone can be chosen at random to be brutally attacked (simply for being at the wrong place at the wrong time); that bystanders may not come to a victim's aid, especially in anonymous, big-city settings; or that complete strangers cannot be trusted (Roberts, 1989). Historically, the heinous crimes that have received the most coverage have one or more of these elements in common: a child or woman as the victim or the defendant; a high-class or well-known victim or defendant; intimations of promiscuous behavior by the victim or defendant; and some doubts about the guilt of the accused (Stephens, 1988). Predictably, the unsolved Christmas Eve murder of a 6-year-old beauty contest winner and daughter of locally prominent parents was the subject of incessant tabloid sensationalism during the late 1990s.

If reporters turn a personal tragedy into a media circus and a public spectacle, victims and their families may complain about an invasion of privacy. Overzealous journalists are frequently criticized for showing corpses lying in a pool of blood, maintaining vigils outside of victims' homes, or shoving microphones in the faces of bereaved, dazed, or hysterical persons at funerals. The injured party receives unwanted and intrusive publicity and experiences a loss of control as others comment upon, draw lessons from, and impose judgments on what the victim allegedly did or did not do. And yet, it can be argued that media coverage is a necessary evil. Reporters and news editors have a constitutional right arising from the First Amendment's guarantee of a free press to present information about crimes to the public without interference from the government. Illegal activities not only harm particular victims but also threaten society as a whole. The public has a right and a need to know about the emergence of dangerous conditions and ominous developments.

The problem is that the public's right to know about crime and the media's right to report about incidents clash with the victim's right to privacy. Journalists, editors, and victims' advocates are addressing questions of fairness and ethics in a wide variety of forums, ranging from the letters to the editor columns to professional conferences to lawsuits in civil court. Several remedies have been proposed to curb the abusive treatment of victims. One approach would be to enact new laws to protect victims from needless public exposure, such as the unnecessary disclosure of their names and addresses. An alternative approach would be to rely on the self-restraint of reporters and their editors. The fact that most news accounts of sexual molestations of children and of rapes no longer reveal the victims' names is an example of this self-policing approach in action. A third remedy would be for the media to adopt a code of professional ethics. Journalists who abide by the code would "read victims their rights" at the outset of interviews, just as police officers read suspects their Miranda rights when taking them into custody (see Thomason and Babbilli, 1987; and Karmen, 1989). Victimologists could play an important role in monitoring progress by studying how frequently and how seriously news reporters offend the subjects of their stories and how successfully the different reform strategies prevent exploitation, or at least minimize abusive invasions of privacy.

Just as the rediscovery of victims by the news media has its pros and cons, so too does the attention paid to the victim's plight by businesses. Along with the development of this new market for protective services and antitheft devices arises the possibility of commercial exploitation. Profiteers can engage in fear mongering and false advertising in order to cash in on the legitimate concerns and needs of customers who feel particularly vulnerable and even panicky. In situations where entrepreneurs issue bold claims about their products' effectiveness, objectivity takes the form of scientific skepticism. Victimologists must demand, "Prove it! Where is the evidence?" Consider the question of whether automobile antitheft devices actually work as well as their manufacturers say they do. For instance, do car alarms really provide the protection against victimization that their purchasers want and sales pitches claim? Rather than agreeing with those motorists whose cars have been stolen that the wailing sirens did no good or trying to defend the alarm industry's reputation (and profits), nonpartisan victimologists can independently evaluate the effectiveness of these antitheft devices in deterring break-ins, in minimizing losses of accessories like car stereo systems or air bags, and in aiding the police to catch thieves red-handed.

Even the impact of the victims' movement must be subjected to objective assessment (see Weed, 1995). Under the banner of advancing victims' rights, pressure groups might advocate policies that undermine whatever progress has been made toward securing humane treatment for offenders and inadvertently widen the net of formal social control exercised by the police and prosecution over dissenters and deviants. Victim activism can unnecessarily heighten fear and anxiety levels about the dangers of violence and theft, divert funds away from social programs designed to tackle the root causes of street crime, distract attention away from other socially harmful activities like polluting the environment or marketing unsafe products, and raise expectations about full recovery that cannot be reasonably met (Fattah, 1986). It is even possible that the victims' movement has metamorphosed into a "victim industry" that engages in the "mass production" or on-going identification of new groups of victims by promoting an ideology of victimization that covers suffering from such diverse problems as emotional abuse, sexual harassment, sexual addiction, and credit card dependency (Best, 1997).

In sum, when choosing projects to research and when gathering and interpreting data, victimologists must put aside their allegiances to causes (like preserving freedom of the press or advancing women's rights), their personal political orientations (such as conservatism or liberalism), and any positive or negative feelings toward entire groups (such as being pro-business or antipolice). Advocacy, whether for or against some policy or practice, should be kept separate from any assessment of the facts or conclusions based on evidence. Scientific skepticism—not self-interest—must prevail when evaluating whether criminal justice reforms, prevention strategies, antitheft equipment, and rehabilitative programs actually work on behalf of victims as intended, or are ineffective or counterproductive in reaching their stated goals.

Three types of biases undermine the ability of any social scientists (not just victimologists) to achieve objectivity (see Myrdal, 1944). The first may arise from personal experiences, taking the form of individual preferences and prejudices. For example, victimologists who have been personally harmed in some way (by a burglary, robbery, or rape, for example) might become so sensitized to the plight of their fellow victims that they can see issues only from the victim's point of view. Conversely, those who have never been through such an ordeal might be unable to truly grasp what the victim must endure. In either case, the victimologist may develop a bias, whether it be over-sensitivity and over-identification or insensitivity and lack of identification.

A second type of bias derives from the discipline itself. The language, concepts, theories, and research priorities can reflect the collective biases of its founders and their followers. For instance, it is widely acknowledged that the pioneers in the field injected a victim-blaming bias into the new discipline, but over the decades the tide has decisively turned, and the vast majority of victimologists today make no secret of their pro-victim commitment to devise means of aid and support.

Though subtle, a third type of bias can be traced back to the mood of the times. Victimologists, like all other members of a society, are influenced by their surroundings and social environment. The events that shape public opinion during different periods in history can also affect scientific thought. During the 1960s and early 1970s, for example, many people asked how the government could help victims recover financially and emotionally. These questions were rarely asked before these decades and were voiced less often during the 1980s and 1990s, when the themes of "less social spending by government" and "lower taxes" prevailed. Also, the argument that a closer look will reveal that many offenders were themselves seriously victimized earlier in their lives and therefore deserve help rather than punishment has fallen out of favor in an age that exalts the notion of individual responsibility for behavior.

Clearly, the study of how victims suffer at the hands of criminals and other groups is unavoidably a value-laden pursuit that arouses intense passions and biased views. As a result, some researchers believe that objectivity is an impossible and unrealistic goal that should be abandoned in favor of a forthright affirmation of values and allegiances. They say that victimologists (and other social scientists) should acknowledge their biases at the outset to alert their audiences to the slant that their analyses and policy recommendations will take. Others argue that objectivity is worth striving for because subjectivity thwarts attempts to accurately describe, understand, and explain what is happening, why it came about, and how conditions can be improved.

For the author of a textbook, the best course of action is to present all sides of controversial issues. Nevertheless, space limitations impose hard choices. This book focuses almost entirely on victims of street crimes (murder, rape, robbery, assault, burglary, larceny, and motor vehicle theft). There are many other categories of lawbreaking: crimes in the "suites" by high government officials against their "enemies" or the general public, and by corporate executives against their company's competitors, workers, or customers; white-collar crimes by employees against their employers or by citizens against government programs; organized rackets run by mobsters; crimes without complainants ("victimless crimes" to some, "vice" to others); political crimes, including acts of terrorism; and status offenses committed by juveniles. These other types of crime are serious and merit attention from scholars, law enforcement agencies, and concerned citizens. But they are not the lawless deeds that come to mind when people talk about "the crime problem" or express fears about being victimized. Street crime scares the public, preoccupies the police, and captures the notice of politicians. These conventional, ordinary, depressingly familiar, and all-too-common predatory acts have tangible, visible, readily identifiable victims who are directly affected and immediately aware of their injuries and losses. In contrast, in the other categories of crime harm might befall abstractions (like a competitive economy or national security), impersonal entities (like the U.S. Treasury or insurance companies), or vaguely defined collectivities (like taxpayers or consumers). It's harder to grasp who has suffered in these cases, and it's also more difficult to describe or measure their characteristics or reactions. But victims of street crimes can be easily observed, contacted, interviewed, and studied, so a wealth of statistical data has accumulated about their injuries, losses, and responses. For these reasons, victims of interpersonal violence and theft will be the primary focus of attention and concern throughout this text. But note that this decision immediately introduces a bias into this introduction to victimology, one that reflects the textbook author's experiences, the collective priorities of the discipline's founders and most prolific researchers, and the mood of the times!

Victimology Compared to Criminology

Victimology is an interdisciplinary field that benefits from the contributions of sociologists, psychologists, social workers, political scientists, doctors, nurses, lawyers, police officials, judges, and other professionals, advocates, and activists. Academically and organizationally, victimology is best conceived of as an area of specialization within criminology, on par with other fields of intensive study, such as delinquency, drug abuse, and terrorism, which merit elective courses and textbooks of their own in colleges and graduate programs.

Even though it is a recent offshoot, victimology parallels its parent, criminology, in many ways. Criminologists ask why certain individuals become involved in lawbreaking while others do not. Investigators concentrate upon the offenders' backgrounds and motives in order to uncover the root causes of crime. Victimologists ask why some individuals, households, and entities are targeted while others are not. Research focuses upon discovering the sources of vulnerability to criminal attack and the reasons some victims might have for acting carelessly, behaving recklessly, or even instigating trouble. Criminologists recognize that most people occasionally break certain laws (especially during adolescence) but are otherwise law abiding; only some who engage in delinquent acts graduate to become hard-core offenders and career criminals. Victimologists realize that anyone can suffer the misfortune of being at the wrong place at the wrong time but wonder why certain individuals are victimized over and over again. Although the law holds offenders personally accountable for their illegal conduct, criminologists explore how social, economic, and political conditions generate criminal activity. Similarly, although certain victims might be accused of sharing some degree of responsibility with offenders for specific crimes, victimologists examine personality traits, social factors, and cultural imperatives that compel some people to take risks and put their lives in danger. Just as aggressive criminal behavior can be learned, victims may have been taught to play (and accept) their subordinate roles.

As social scientists, both criminologists and victimologists place a great emphasis on following the proper methods of gathering and interpreting data. Criminologists collect and analyze information about individuals engaging in illegal behaviors, such as their ages and social backgrounds. Victimologists look over statistics about the ages and social backgrounds of the people who are harmed by unlawful activities. Criminologists apply their findings to devise crime-prevention strategies; victimologists use the patterns and trends they detect to develop and test out risk-reduction tactics.

Both criminologists and victimologists study how the criminal justice system *really* works, in contrast to the way the system is *supposed* to work according to agency regulations, official roles, federal and state legislation, and court decisions. Just as criminologists scrutinize how suspects, defendants, and convicts are actually handled, victimologists examine the way victims are really treated by police officers, prosecutors, defense attorneys, judges, and parole boards. Criminologists assess the needs of offenders for counseling, psychotherapy, additional education, job training, and drug treatment. In addition, criminologists evaluate the effectiveness of various rehabilitation programs available behind bars or offered to probationers or parolees that are intended to reduce recidivism rates. Similarly, victimologists want to diagnose the emotional problems that beset people after they have been harmed by offenders, and test out the usefulness of programs designed to facilitate their recovery (see Roberts, 1990; and Lurigio, 1990). Criminologists try to calculate the social and economic costs of criminal activity to a community or to society as a whole. Victimologists estimate the personal losses and expenses that individuals incur due to acts of violence, theft, or fraud.

Criminology and victimology differ in several important ways. Criminology is several hundred years old whereas victimology is only several decades old. Criminologists agree among themselves that they should limit their studies to illegal activities (and not forms of social deviance which do not violate any laws). Victimologists cannot reach a consensus about the appropriate boundaries of their field. Some victimologists argue that criminal victimization should not be the only form of suffering worthy of systematic study. They advocate adopting a broader scope that integrates studies about victims of oppressive political regimes, human-made disasters (like wars and famines), natural disasters (such as floods and earthquakes), and sheer accidents. The common goals would be to develop effective strategies for crisis intervention, short-run relief, and long-term solutions in order to alleviate human suffering from all kinds of calamities. (For the pros and cons of these alternative visions of what the scope of victimology ought to be, see Schafer, 1968; Galaway and Hudson, 1981; Scherer, 1982; Schneider, 1982; Friedrichs, 1983; and Viano, 1976, 1983, and 1990.) The line dividing harmful behaviors that are illegal and those that are perfectly legal (but lead to starvation, ill health, impoverishment, and other social problems) is artificial and politically determined (see Elias, 1986).

However, the majority of victimologists believe that the focus of the discipline should remain on criminal victimization so that there are precise, readily identifiable limits and clear directions for research and theorizing. Even though criminal victimization may not be more serious (financially), more injurious (medically), or more traumatic and longer lasting (psychologically) than other types of victimization, it is necessary to reign in the boundaries of the field in order to make it manageable for the practical purposes of holding conferences, publishing journals, writing textbooks, and teaching college courses (see Flynn, 1982; and Fattah, 1991).

Victimology does not have the distinct schools of thought that divide criminologists into opposing camps, probably because victimology lacks its own well-developed theories of human behavior. However, in both criminology and victimology, political ideologies—conservative, liberal, or radical-critical—can play a significant role in influencing the choice of research topics and in shaping policy recommendations. The conservative tendency within victimology focuses primarily upon street crimes. A basic tenet of conservative thought is that everyone—both victims and offenders—must be held strictly accountable for their decisions and actions. This translates into an emphasis on self-reliance rather than governmental assistance. Individuals should strive to take personal responsibility for preventing, avoiding, resisting, and recovering from criminal acts and for defending themselves, their families, and their homes from outside attack. Lawbreakers must be strictly punished on behalf of their victims (retribution or "just deserts"); such punishment should also act as further general deterrence (to make a negative example of them, to serve as a warning to other would-be offenders that they should think twice and decide not to break the law), and specific deterrence (to teach them a lesson not to commit any new crimes).

The liberal tendency sees the scope of the field as stretching beyond street crime to include criminal harm inflicted on persons by reckless corporate executives and corrupt government officials. A basic theme within liberal thought is to endorse governmental intervention to try to ensure fair treatment and to alleviate needless suffering. This position leads to efforts to extend the "safety net" mechanisms of the welfare state to cushion shocks and losses due to all kinds of misfortunes, including crime. To "make the victim whole again," aid must be available from such programs as state compensation funds, subsidized crime insurance plans, rape crisis centers, and shelters for battered women. Some liberals are enthusiastic about experiments that, instead of punishing offenders by imprisoning them, attempt to make wrongdoers repay their victims so that reconciliation between the two estranged parties might become possible.

The radical-critical tendency seeks to demonstrate that the problem of victimization arises from the exploitive and oppressive relations that are embedded within the entire social system. Therefore, the scope of the field should not be limited simply to the casualties of criminal activity in the streets. Inquiry must be extended to cover the harm inflicted by industrial polluters, owners and managers of hazardous workplaces, fraudulent advertisers, repressive law enforcement agencies, and discriminatory institutions. Victims might not be particular individuals but whole groups of people, such as factory workers, minority groups, consumers, or neighborhood residents. From the radical-critical perspective, victimology can be faulted for preferring to study the more obvious, less controversial kinds of harmful behaviors, mostly acts of violence and crude theft, instead of the more fundamental injustices that mar everyday life: the inequitable distribution of wealth and power that results in poverty, malnutrition, homelessness, chronic structural unemployment, and other social problems. The legal system and the criminal justice apparatus are considered part of the problem because they primarily safeguard the interests of influential groups and privileged classes (see Birkbeck, 1983; Friedrichs, 1983; Viano, 1983; Elias, 1986, 1993; Fattah, 1986, 1990, 1992a, 1992b; Miers, 1989; Reiman, 1990; Walklate, 1991; and Mawby and Walklate, 1993).

One last parallel between criminology and victimology needs to be highlighted. Criminology and victimology are not well-paying fields ripe with opportunities for employment and advancement. Becoming a criminologist or a victimologist rarely leads to fame and fortune and certainly doesn't make a person invincible to physical attacks, thefts, or swindles. Yet for several reasons a growing number of people are investing time, energy, and money to study victimology. First of all, victimologists benefit intellectually, as do all social scientists, by gaining insights, solving puzzles, appreciating life's subtleties, seeing phenomena more clearly, and understanding complex situations more profoundly. Second, individuals profit from pursuits that expand their horizons, transcend the limits of their own experiences, free them from irrational fears and unfounded concerns, and enable them to overcome gut reactions of fatalism, emotionalism, and deep-seated prejudice. Third, the findings generated from theorizing and research have humanistic applications that simultaneously ease the suffering of others and give the victimologist a sense of purpose, worth, and satisfaction.

Victimology is not the cold or dismal discipline it might appear to be at first glance. Victimologists are not morbidly curious about or preoccupied with misfortune, loss, death, tragedy, pain, and grief. Of course, because of its negative subject matter, the discipline is problem oriented by nature. Furthermore, victimologists and criminologists can be guilty of impersonal detachment when, for example, they study murder victims by counting corpses and noting the circumstances of death. But the dilemma of treating tragedies as mere "cases" or "statistics" is largely unavoidable and arises just as sharply in other fields, such as medicine, military history, police science, and suicidology. The redeeming value of victimology lies in its potential for human betterment. Victimology's allegiance to the principle of striving for objectivity doesn't detract from the discipline's overall commitment to alleviate needless suffering.

WHAT VICTIMOLOGISTS DO

The current parameters of the field are evident in the kinds of questions victimologists try to answer. In general, these questions transcend the basic who, how, where, and when. Victimologists explore the interactions between victims and offenders, victims and the criminal justice system, and victims and society. In the process, victimologists, like all social scientists, gather data to test hypotheses and refine theories. In the face of bold claims, they display a critical spirit and adopt a skeptical stance, declaring, "Prove it!" and "Where's the evidence?" In the search for truth, myth must be separated from reality by rejecting unfounded claims, dismissing public relations propaganda, and challenging commonsense notions. The following guidelines outline the step-by-step process that victimologists follow when carrying out their research (see Parsonage, 1979; Birkbeck, 1983; and Burt, 1983).

Step 1: Identify, Define, and Describe the Problem

The most basic task for victimologists is to determine all the different ways that an offense can cause harm: the extent of any physical injuries, psychological damage, and economic costs, plus any social consequences (such as loss of status). For example, severely abused children might suffer from posttraumatic stress disorder, dysfunctional interpersonal relationships, personality disorders, and self-destructive impulses (see Briere, 1992). Sometimes, a group is hard to study because there isn't an adequate expression to capture the nature of their plight. Now that terms like **date rape, stalking, carjacking, battering, elder abuse,** and **bias crime** have entered everyday speech, government agencies and researchers are exploring how the victims of these offenses are harmed. On occasion, victimologists help to break the silence about situations that long have been considered taboo topics by studying activities such as incestuous sexual impositions, sibling abuse, and marital rape.

Victimologists trace the short-term and long-run consequences of being harmed and also analyze how membership in the category "victims" is socially defined and constructed. They explore why only some people who suffer physical, emotional, or economic harm are designated and treated as full-fledged, bona fide, and officially recognized victims and as such, are eligible for aid, while other injured parties are left to fend for themselves. One key question is "Is the social standing of the two parties taken into account when government officials and members of the general public evaluate whether or not a person should get into legal trouble for what happened?" Another important query is "Who decides what is unacceptable and illegal?" For example, what action should be taken when consumers claim they were defrauded by exaggerated claims in advertisements? In what situations should elementary school students who are subjected to corporal punishment by headmasters, deans, and teachers (with parental permission) be considered victims of a physical assault?

Step 2: Measure the True Dimensions of the Problem

Because policymakers and the general public want to know how serious various kinds of illegal activities are, victimologists must devise ways to keep track of their frequency and consequences. Statistics kept by government officials and private agencies must be critically examined to ferret out any biases that might inflate or deflate the estimates to the advantage of those who, for some self-serving reason, wish to either exaggerate or downplay the real extent of the problem.

In order to make measurements, victimologists have to develop working definitions that specify essential characteristics and also mark boundaries, clarifying which cases should be included and which should be excluded. For example, when trying to determine how many students have been victims of school violence, should youngsters who were threatened with a beating but were not actually physically attacked be counted? Once victimologists measure frequency per year, they can begin to search for changes over time to see if a particular type of criminal activity is claiming greater or fewer victims with each passing year. To grasp the importance of making accurate measurements, consider the problem of child abuse. Statistics gathered by child protection agencies indicate a huge increase in the number of reported instances of suspected abuse. How can this upsurge be explained? One possibility is that parents are neglecting, beating, and molesting their children these days like never before. But another explanation is that new compulsory reporting requirements recently imposed on physicians, school nurses, and teachers are bringing many more cases to the attention of the authorities. Thus, the sharp rise in reports might not reflect a crime wave directed at children by their caretakers but just improvements in detecting and keeping records of mal-treatment. Victimologists can make a real contribution toward resolving this controversy by estimating the actual dimensions of the child abuse problem.

Other pressing questions that can be answered by careful measurements and accurate statistics include the following: Are huge numbers of children being snatched up by kidnappers? Or are abductions by strangers very rare? Are husbands assaulted by their wives about as often as wives are battered by their husbands? Or is female aggression of minor importance when compared to male violence? Is forced sex a common outcome at the end of an evening, or is date rape less of a danger than some people believe?

After determining **incidence rates** (how often a type of victimization takes place during a given time period, usually one year), victimologists can also estimate **prevalence rates** (the fraction of the population that has ever experienced this type of misfortune) and can even project **lifetime likelihoods** (the proportion of the population that will someday suffer in this way if current rates prevail). Additionally, researchers can establish which categories of people are preyed upon the most and the least. Then they can draw a **profile,** or statistical portrait, of the characteristics of typical victims (people who fall into high-risk groupings).

Step 3: Investigate How Victims Are Handled

Victimologists scrutinize how victims are actually treated by the criminal justice and social service systems that are ostensibly geared to help them. Researchers carry out needs assessments to identify just what the injured parties want, require, and get. Studies pinpoint the sources of tension, conflict, mistreatment, and dissatisfaction that alienate victims from the criminal justice and social welfare agencies that are supposed to serve them. Program evaluations determine whether stated goals are being met. For instance, victimologists want to know how well or how poorly the police, prosecutors, judges, mediators, and family therapists are responding to the plight of battered wives (see Hilton, 1993). Similarly, victimologists explore whether promises are being kept, and if reforms granting new rights are having any impact on business as usual. Are most victims wasting their time if they appear before parole boards to argue that the prisoners who harmed them should not receive early release, or are victims' arguments taken seriously?

Additionally, victimologists monitor the way the public, the news media, elected officials, and businesses react to the plight of people whose possessions are stolen or who are robbed, raped, beaten, or murdered.

Step 4: Gather Evidence to Test Hypotheses

Victimologists investigate claims, suspicions, hunches, and predictions. They collect data to see if there is any basis for widely held hypotheses, such as that wives beaten mercilessly by their husbands often don't flee their unhappy homes because they are too frightened of being hunted down and killed. Similarly, researchers want to find out whether most survivors are angry or relieved if the murders of their loved ones are resolved through plea negotiations (in which the assailants admit their guilt in return for some concession) rather than by highly publicized trials in open court. Testing hypotheses yields interesting findings, especially discoveries that cast doubt on commonsense notions (challenging what everyone "knows" to be true). All research findings serve to build victimology's knowledge base, and some have obvious practical applications. For example, how often do people who were just robbed fail to recognize the suspect and pick out an innocent person at a station house lineup? After elderly persons are robbed and injured, are they more likely than victims of other ages to take precautions, such as staying home at night? If police departments hire more female detectives, will the departments themselves be perceived as more user friendly and therefore will more women be willing to come forward and lodge date rape charges?

A sampling of the wide range of intriguing and imaginative studies carried out by victimologists appears in Box 1.2.

VICTIMOLOGY CONTRIBUTES TO THE PROCESS OF REDISCOVERING VICTIMS

The rise of victimology has furthered the rediscovery process. This process—through which formerly recognized and then neglectfully overlooked groups of victims become much more prominent—usually unfolds in predictable stages.

The rediscovery process is more than just a well-intentioned, humanitarian undertaking, media campaign, or special pleading; instead, rediscovery has far-reaching consequences for everyday life. The stakes are high. Groups of victims who gain the mantle of legitimacy and win public backing are in a position to make compelling claims on government resources (asking for compensation payments to cover the expenses they incurred from physical wounds, for example). Such groups also can advance persuasive arguments for reforming criminal justice policies concerning arrest, prosecution, trial procedures, sentencing standards, and custodial control over prisoners. Finally, rediscovered victims can assert that preventing others from suffering the same fate requires a change in prevailing cultural values. Victims even can make recommendations that are taken seriously about the ways people should and should not behave (for instance, how husbands should treat their wives and how closely parents should supervise their children) and about the proper role of government (such as how readily the state should intervene in "private" matters within violent families and whether certain offenses should be penalized more severely).

BOX 1.2 The Kinds of Studies Victimologists Undertake

Identifying the Cues That Trigger a Mugger Into Action

Pedestrians, through their body language, may signal to prowling robbers that they are "easy marks."

Men and women walking down a New York City street were secretly videotaped for several seconds, about the time it takes a criminally inclined person to size up a potential victim. The tapes were then shown to a panel of "experts"—prisoners convicted of assaulting strangers—who sorted out those who looked as if they would be easy to corner from those who might give them a hard time. Individuals who received high "muggability" ratings tended to move along awkwardly, unaware that their nonverbal communication might cause them trouble (Grayson and Stein, 1981).

Explaining the Indifference Toward Victims of Fraud and Con Games

People who have lost money to swindlers and con artists often are portrayed as undeserving of sympathy in the media, and they may encounter callousness, suspicion, or contempt when they turn to the police or consumer fraud bureaus for help. This second-class treatment seems to be due to negative stereotypes and ambivalent attitudes that are widely held by the public as well as criminal justice officials. A number of aphorisms place blame on the victims themselves: fraud only befalls those of questionable character, an honest man can't be cheated, and people must have larceny in their heart to fall for a con game. The stereotype of defrauded parties is that they disregarded the basic rules of sensible conduct regarding financial matters. They don't read contracts before signing and don't demand that guarantees be put in writing before making purchases. Their perceived stupidity, carelessness, or complicity undermines their credibility and makes others reluctant to activate the machinery of the criminal justice system on their behalf, to formally condemn and punish those who harmed them, and to validate their claims to be treated as authentic victims worthy of support rather than as mere suckers who were outsmarted (Walsh and Schram, 1980; Moore and Mills, 1990).

And yet a nationwide survey using a broad definition of fraudulent schemes (including dishonest home, auto, and appliance repairs and inspections; useless warranties; fake subscription, insurance, credit, and investment scams; phony charities, contests, and prizes; and expensive 900 number telephone tricks, among other rip-offs) found the problem to be widespread: more than half the respondents had been caught up in some deception or an attempt at least once in their lives, costing an average loss of more than $200. Contrary to the prevailing negative stereotype, the elderly were not any more trusting and compliant; actually they were duped less often than targets of other ages (Titus, Heinzelmann, and Boyle, 1995).

Examining How Victims Are Viewed by Pickpockets

According to twenty *class cannons* (professional pickpockets) working the streets of Miami, Florida, their preferred *marks* (victims) are tourists who are relaxed, off guard, loaded with money, and lacking in clout with criminal justice officials. Some pickpockets choose *paps* (elderly men), because their reaction time is slower, but others favor *bates* (middle-aged men) because they tend to carry fatter wallets. A *moll buzzer,* or *hanger binger* (sneak thief who preys on women) is looked down upon in the underworld fraternity as a bottom feeder who acts without skill or courage.

Interaction with victims is kept to a minimum. Although pickpockets may *trace a mark* (follow a potential target) for some time, they need just a few seconds to *beat him of his poke* (steal his wallet). This is done quietly and deftly, without a commotion or any jostling. They rarely *make a score* (steal a lot in a single incident). The class cannon *passes* (hands over) the *loot* (wallet, wad of bills) to a member of his *mob* (an accomplice) and swiftly leaves the scene of the crime. Only about one time in a hundred do they get caught by the mark. When the theft is detected, they can usually persuade their victims not to call the police. They give back what they took (maybe more than they stole) and point out that pressing charges can ruin a vacation because of the need to surrender the wallet as evidence plus the time wasted in court appearances. Cannons show no hatred or contempt for their marks. In general,

Continued

BOX 1.2 *continued*

they rationalize their crimes as impersonal acts directed at targets who can easily afford the losses or who would otherwise be fleeced or swindled by businessmen and other exploitive *legal types* (Inciardi, 1976).

Exploring the Bonds Between Captives and Their Captors

Hostages (of terrorists, skyjackers, kidnappers, bank robbers, rebelling prisoners, and gunmen who go berserk) are used by their captors to exert leverage on a third party—perhaps a family, the police, or a government agency. These victims frequently react in a surprising way to being trapped. Instead of showing anger and seeking revenge, these pawns in a larger drama may emerge from a lengthy siege with positive feelings for, and attachments to, their keepers. Their outrage is likely to be directed at the authorities who rescued them for acting with apparent indifference to their well-being during the protracted negotiations. This surprising emotional realignment has been termed the *Stockholm Syndrome,* because it was first noted after a 1973 bank holdup in Sweden.

Several psychological explanations for this *pathological transference* are plausible: the hostages may be identifying with the aggressor; they may be sympathetic to acts of defiance aimed at the Establishment; as survivors, they may harbor intense feelings of gratitude toward their keepers for sparing their lives; or as helpless dependents, they may cling to the powerful figures who controlled their every action because of a primitive emotional response called *traumatical infantilism.* After the ordeal, these terrorized victims need to be welcomed back and reassured that they did nothing wrong during—and right after—their captivity. People holding jobs that may place them at risk of being taken hostage—ranging from convenience store clerks and bank tellers to airline personnel and diplomats—need to be trained about how to act, what to say, and what not to do if they are captured and used as a bargaining chip during a stand-off. Police departments need to set up and train hostage negotiation units as an alternative to using heavily armed SWAT teams that might endanger the lives of the captives they are trying to save (see Fattah, 1979; Ochberg, 1978; Symonds, 1980a; Turner, 1990; Wolff, 1993; and Louden, 1998).

The sequential model that is proposed below incorporates observations drawn from several other models. The notion of *developmental stages* arises from the self-definition of the victimization process (Viano, 1989). The **natural history, career,** or **life-cycle** approach comes from models for examining ongoing social problems (see Fuller and Myers, 1941; Ross and Staines, 1972; and Spector and Kitsuse, 1987). The focus on how concerns about victimization are first raised, framed, and publicized arise from the **constructionist** approach (see Best, 1989b) and the idea of inevitable clashes of opposing interest groups battling over governmental resources and legislation comes from sociology's **conflict** approach. The realization that there is an ongoing struggle by victimized groups for respect and support in the court of public opinion comes from the concept of **stigma contests** (Schur, 1984).

Stage 1: Calling Attention to an Overlooked Problem

The rediscovery process is set into motion whenever activists begin to raise the public's consciousness about some type of illegal situation that "everybody knows" happens but few have cared enough about to investigate or try to correct. These **moral entrepreneurs,** who lead campaigns to win people over to their point of view, usually have firsthand experience with the problem and direct, personal knowledge of the pain and suffering it causes. Individuals deserving credit for arousing an indifferent public include the victims of hate-filled bias crimes, adults haunted by the way they were molested by their parents when they were young, women brutally raped by men they trusted, and wives viciously beaten by their husbands. These spokespersons called attention to a state of affairs that people took for granted as harmful but shrugged off with a "What can anyone do?" attitude. These victims responded, "Things don't have to be this way!" Exploitive and hurtful relationships don't have to be tolerated—they can be prevented, avoided, and outlawed; governmental policies can be altered; and the criminal justice system can be made more accountable and responsive to its "clients."

As Stage 1 moves along, activists function as the inspiration and nucleus for the formation of self-help groups that provide mutual aid and solace and also undertake campaigns for reform. Members of support networks believe that only people who have suffered through the same ordeal can really be trusted to understand and appreciate what victims are going through (a basic tenet borrowed from therapeutic communities that assist substance abusers to recover from drug addiction). Activists also state that victims' troubles stem from larger social problems that are beyond any individual's control (and so he or she is not to be blamed for the misfortunes). Finally, activists argue that recovery requires empowerment within the criminal justice process so that victims can pursue what they define as their own best interests (whether to see that the offender receives the maximum punishment permitted by law, is compelled to undergo treatment, and/or is ordered to pay their bills). Particularly effective self-help groups have been set up by mothers whose children were killed in collisions caused by drunk drivers, survivors of officers slain in the line of duty, and parents who endured the agony of searching for their missing children, among others.

To build wider support for their causes, moral entrepreneurs and self-help groups organize themselves into loosely structured social movements (like the antirape and antibattering movements). Usually, one or two well-publicized cases are pointed to as symbolic of the problem. Soon, many other victims come forward to tell of their personal experiences. Then, experts like social workers, detectives, and lawyers testify about the routine injustices these kinds of victims endure and to plead that legal remedies are urgently needed. Extensive media coverage is a prerequisite for success. The group's plight becomes the subject of exposés by investigative reports on television, talk radio discussions, magazine cover stories, and newspaper editorials. Meanwhile, press conferences, demonstrations, marches, candlelight vigils, petition drives, ballot initiatives, lawsuits, and lobbying campaigns keep the pressure on and the issue alive.

Sociologically speaking, what happens during the first stage can be termed the **social construction of a social problem** along with **claims making** and **typification** (see Spector and Kitsuse, 1987; and Best, 1989). A consensus about a pattern of behavior that is harmful and should be subjected to criminal penalties is "constructed." This crystallization of public opinion is a product of the activities of the moral entrepreneurs, the support groups, and their allies. Spokespersons for the victims' cause engage in a claims-making process to air grievances, estimate how many people are hurt in this manner, suggest appropriate remedies to facilitate recovery, and recommend measures that should prevent this kind of physical, emotional, and/or financial suffering from happening to others. Through the process of typification, advocates point out classic cases and textbook examples that illustrate the menace to society against which they are campaigning.

Stage 2: Winning Victories, Implementing Reforms

The rediscovery process enters its second stage whenever activists and advocacy groups begin to make progress toward their goals.

At first, it might be necessary to set up independent demonstration projects to prove the need for special services. Then government grants can be secured, or federal, state, and local agencies can copy successful models or take over some responsibility for providing information, assistance, and protection. For instance, the battered women's movement set up shelters, and the antirape movement established crisis centers. Eventually local governments funded safe houses, where women and their young children could seek refuge, and hospitals (and even some universities) organized their own 24-hour rape hotlines and crisis-intervention services. Originally, private organizations monitored incidents of hate-motivated violence and vandalism directed against racial and religious minorities, as well as homosexuals; in 1990, Congress passed the Hate Crime Statistics Act, which authorized the FBI to undertake the task of collecting reports from local police departments about bias crimes (see Levin and McDevitt, 1993).

Achievements that mark this second stage in the rediscovery process include legislative hearings that lead to new laws (for instance, to punish hate-motivated bias crimes more severely because they polarize communities and undermine the mutual respect and goodwill needed to make multiculturalism viable). Special law enforcement and prosecution units may be set up, such as those that investigate, solve, and pursue bias crimes). Training programs for professionals may be updated (for example, to recognize whether an assault was motivated by the offender's hatred of the "kind" of person the victim symbolizes).

The best example of a campaign that has won victories and secured reforms is the one waged since the early 1980s by an organization of parents, mostly mothers, who are outraged because their sons and daughters were injured or killed by drunk drivers. These anguished survivors argued that for too long the "killer drunk" was able to get away with a socially acceptable and judicially excusable form of homicide because more people identified with the intoxicated driver than with the innocent person who died from injuries sustained in the collision. Viewing themselves as the relatives of bona fide "crime victims," not merely "accident victims," these crusaders were able to move the issue from the obituary page to the front page by using a wide range of tactics to mobilize public support, including candlelight vigils, pledges of responsible behavior by children and family cooperation by their parents, and demonstrations outside courthouses. Local chapters of their national self-help organizations offered concrete services: Pamphlets were distributed through hospital emergency rooms and funeral parlors, bereavement support groups assisted grieving relatives, and volunteers accompanied victims and their families to police stations, prosecutors' offices, trials, and sentencing hearings. With the help of unprecedented favorable media coverage, their lobbying campaigns brought about a crackdown on DUI and DWI offenders (roadblocks, license suspensions and revocations, more severe criminal charges, on-the-spot confiscations of vehicles) and reforms of drinking laws (raising the legal drinking age to 21; lowering the blood-alcohol concentration levels that officially define impairment and intoxication) (Thompson, 1984). Along with the 55-mph speed limit, mandatory seat belt laws, improved vehicle safety engineering, better roads, and breakthroughs in emergency medical services, the efforts of Mothers Against Drunk Driving (MADD) have saved countless lives (Ayres, 1994).

Stage 3: Emergence of an Opposition and Development of Resistance to Further Changes

The third stage in the rediscovery process is marked by the emergence of groups that oppose the goals of the rediscovered victims' campaigns. Whereas these victims had to overcome public apathy during Stage 1 and bureaucratic inertia during Stage 2, during Stage 3 they encounter resistance from other quarters. A backlash arises against perceived excesses in their demands. The general argument of opponents is that the pendulum is swinging too far in the other direction, that people are uncritically embracing a point of view that is too extreme, imbalanced, and one sided and that special interests are trying to advance an agenda that does not benefit the law-abiding majority.

Spokespersons for the victims' cause might come under fire for a number of reasons. They may be criticized for overestimating the numbers of people harmed, when the actual threat to the public, according to the opposition, is much smaller. Advocates may be condemned for portraying all victims as totally innocent of any blame—and therefore deserving of unqualified support—when in reality some are partly at fault and shouldn't get all the help that they demand. Activists may be castigated for making unreasonable demands that will cost the government (and taxpayers) too much money. Advocates may also be denounced for insisting upon new policies that would undermine cherished constitutional rights, such as the presumption of innocence (which can be disregarded when charges about child abuse or elder abuse lead to investigations) (see Crystal, 1988).

When the antirape movement claimed to have discovered an outbreak of date rapes among students, opponents asked why federally mandated statistics about incidents reported to campus security forces showed no such upsurge. They contended that hard-to-classify liaisons were being redefined as full-fledged "sexual assaults," thereby maligning some admittedly sexually aggressive and exploitive college men as hard-core criminals (see Gilbert, 1991; and Hellman, 1993). When the battered women's movement organized a clemency drive to free certain imprisoned wives who had slain their abusive husbands (allegedly in self-defense), opponents charged that these killers would be getting away with revenge murders. When "incest survivors" insisted that new memory retrieval techniques had helped them recall repressed visions of sexual molestations by parents and stepparents, some accused family members banded together and insisted they were being mistakenly slandered because of a therapist-induced "false memory syndrome." Claims by some child-search organizations that each year tens of thousands of children were being kidnapped by complete strangers created near hysteria among parents until some journalists challenged their estimates as gross exaggerations (see chapter 5 for an in-depth analysis of these controversies).

Stage 4: Research and Temporary Resolution of the Dispute

It is in the fourth and final stage of the rediscovery process that victimologists can make their most valuable contributions. By getting to the bottom of the mystery, victimologists can become a source of accurate assessments, helping to evaluate the competing claims issued by those who, assuming the worst, generate high estimates and by those at the opposite end of the spectrum, who come up with very low estimates. By maintaining objectivity victimologists can serve as arbiters in these heated disputes. For instance, a blue-ribbon panel of experts convened by the U.S. Department of Justice in the late 1980s to make sense out of competing claims ascertained just how many children really are kidnapped by strangers each year. The researchers concluded that killings and long-term abductions by complete strangers were, thankfully, very rare and did not pose a dire threat to the well-being of the next generation.

During Stage 4, a standoff, deadlock, or truce might develop between victims' advocates, who want more changes, and their opponents, who resist any further demands. But the fourth phase is not necessarily the final phase. The findings and policy recommendations of neutral parties like victimologists and criminologists do not settle questions once and for all. Concern about some type of victimization can recede from public consciousness for years only to reappear when social conditions are ripe for a new rediscovery cycle of claims-making, opposition, and temporary resolution.

The Continuing Process of Rediscovery

There is no end in sight to the process of rediscovering victims. A steady stream of fresh revelations serves as a reminder that neglected groups out there still have compelling stories to tell, unmet needs, and legitimate demands for assistance and support. Some groups of victims whose plight is being examined scientifically include:

- People whose attackers cannot be arrested and prosecuted because they are members of foreign delegations granted diplomatic immunity. (Ferrigno, 1987; Trescott, 1987)
- Recipients of crank phone calls, laced with threats or obscenities, made by individuals that range from "heavy breathers" to bored teenagers. (Savitz, 1986)

- Unsuspecting consumers who lose money, time, and their reputations because of credit card scams in which thieves steal their identities, and purchase goods that are then billed to consumers' charge accounts. (Berreby, 1988; Hinds, 1988; Hansell, 1996; and O'Brien, 2000)
- Illegal aliens who feel they cannot come forward and ask the police for help without revealing that they lack the proper documents and are subject to deportation. (Davis and Murray, 1995)
- Children who are sexually molested by religious ministers whom they respected and their parents trusted. (Berry, 1992; Woodward et al., 1993)
- Students assaulted, robbed, even fatally shot by fellow students or by intruders in school buildings and yards. (Bastian and Taylor, 1991; Toby, 1983;. Dillon, 1994; and NCES, 1998)
- Homeless persons robbed, assaulted, and murdered on the streets and in shelters. (Holloway, 1995; Nieves, 1999)
- Hotel guests who suffer thefts and assaults because of lax security measures. (Prestia, 1993)
- Tourists who blunder into dangerous situations avoided by streetwise locals (Rohter, 1993a) and are easy prey because they let their guard down. (Boyle, 1994)
- Delivery truck drivers who feel compelled to wear bulletproof vests and illegally carry weapons to protect themselves against robbers and hijackers. (Sexton, 1994)
- Good Samaritans who try to break up crimes in progress and rescue the intended victims but wind up injured or killed themselves. (McFadden, 1993b)
- Innocent bystanders who are wounded or killed by stray bullets intended for others, often when caught in the cross fire between rival street gangs or drug dealers fighting over turf. (Sherman, Steele, Laufersweiler, Hoffer, and Julian, 1989; Onishi, 1994)
- People deceived and held up by robbers impersonating plainclothes detectives. (Sanchez, 1994; Holloway, 1994)
- Motorists and pedestrians slammed into by fugitives seeking to avoid arrest or by squad cars in hot pursuit during high-speed chases. (Gray, 1993)
- Unrelated individuals whose lives are snuffed out by vicious and demented serial killers. (Holmes and DeBurger, 1988; Hickey, 1991)
- Newborns abandoned or killed by their distraught mothers. (Yardley, 1999)
- Frantic relatives of missing persons who have vanished and are presumed dead but, since they they were adults with the right to privacy, can't be the objects of intense police manhunts unless there is evidence of foul play. (McPhee, 1999)
- Prisoners assaulted, gang raped, and stabbed by other inmates. (Lockwood, 1980; Silberman, 1995; O'Connell and Straub, 1999)

- Suspects brutally beaten by police officers and corrections guards. (AIUSA, 1999)

Several groups of victims have begun to receive the attention they deserve (as the process of rediscovery reaches Stage 2): law enforcement officers murdered in the line of duty, drivers robbed of their vehicles by carjackers, individuals hounded by stalkers, young lovers subjected to violence during courtship, and college students harmed right on their campuses. Their situations are examined in Box 1.3.

BOX 1.3 Groups of Victims That Have Been Recently Rediscovered

Law Enforcement Officers Wounded and Killed in the Line of Duty

Killing a police officer has always been considered one of the most heinous crimes. In many states it carries the death penalty. A patrolmen's benevolent association to take care of the widows and orphans of fallen officers was set up as early as 1894 in New York City. But, in recent decades, much greater efforts have been directed toward preventing victimization and assisting the survivors of officers who sacrificed their lives to protect the public.

Officers who work for law enforcement, probation, parole, or corrections agencies on the local, state, and federal level face unusual challenges and threats. Their jobs require them to come into daily contact with persons known to be armed and dangerous and not to back down from confrontations. These officers are called upon to deal with convicts, patrol high-crime locations, break up crimes in progress, search suspicious persons, and track down fugitives. Additional risks arise because uniforms are viewed as symbols of governmental authority. The police, in particular, as the first line of defense for the "system," serve as a lightning rod, absorbing the bolts of discontent emanating from hostile groups within the general public.

The Federal Bureau of Investigation (FBI) monitors line-of-duty deaths to determine the most dangerous situations officers face during their daily routines, so that improved training and tactics can reduce injuries in the future. During 1998, of the 61 officers slain on the job (not counting the additional 77 who died from accidents), 26% were murdered while answering calls about disturbances, 16% were ambushed, 15% were enforcing traffic laws, 11% were investigating drug situations, 10% were serving arrest warrants, another 10% were looking into suspicious circumstances, 7% were handling prisoners, and just 5% were confronting armed robbers. About 95% died from gunfire, mostly from handguns, even though 56% were wearing body armor; 10% were murdered with their own weapons. Only five cop-killers remained at large by the end of the year (*Uniform Crime Reports,* 1999).

In a study of slayings committed from 1983 to 1992, FBI analysts discovered that a deadly mix was a common element: An easy going, good-natured officer who was less inclined to use force than his colleagues entered into a fatal encounter with a suspect afflicted with a personality disorder and armed with a handgun. The homicides were often facilitated by some kind of procedural miscue (such as improperly approaching a vehicle pulled over for a traffic infraction). The typical law enforcement casualty was a white southern male, 36 years old, married, with a high school education and an average of nine years on the force. The typical assailant was a twenty-nine year-old white man, with a record of a previous arrest (*UCR* Section, 1993).

Although the average officer goes through a 20-year career without ever firing a shot (except for target practice), undercover officers face much greater chances than their uniformed colleagues of shooting their revolvers or getting shot. African-American officers in undercover and plainclothes assignments run an additional risk of being hit by "friendly fire" from the guns of officers who mistake them for armed criminals (Geller, 1992).

Probation and parole officers making field visits are getting firearms, bulletproof vests, body alarms, portable phones, armed escorts, and

BOX 1.3 *continued*

training in self-defense tactics and crisis management techniques to lessen their vulnerability to assault, robbery, and car theft when carrying out spot checks and home visits (Lindner and Koehler, 1992; Del Castillo and Lindner, 1994).

The families of law enforcement agents mistakenly were assumed to be stronger emotionally and better prepared than civilians to cope with losses and grief because they are part of a tightly knit community which "takes care of its own." But the inadequate responses of many police departments has brought about the establishment of counseling units, death-notification training, and peer support groups for injured and disabled officers (see Sawyer, 1987; Stillman, 1987; Martin, 1989; and "Does Your Agency Measure Up," 1999), as well as a national self-help and support group, Concerns of Police Survivors (COPS). The National Law Enforcement Officers Memorial Fund keeps track of changes in the death toll, as does the FBI.

Fortunately, and contrary to widespread impressions, law enforcement is not the most dangerous job (taxi driving is), and deadly assaults on police officers are subsiding, not rising. Reasons for the decline include regulations requiring officers to wear bulletproof vests, better training, improved weaponry, restrictions on the private ownership of assault weapons, and a diminishing violent crime rate nationwide (Butterfield, 1999). The number of officers feloniously (not accidentally) killed in the line of duty peaked in 1979 and since then has been dropping, even though there are now more people engaged in law enforcement (see Figure 1.1).

Carjacked Drivers

In the movies as well as in real life, motorists have been yanked out of their cars by highwaymen who hop in behind the wheel and make their getaway. In the early 1990s the catchy term *carjacking* was coined to describe this kind of robbery of a motor vehicle directly from a driver

Continued

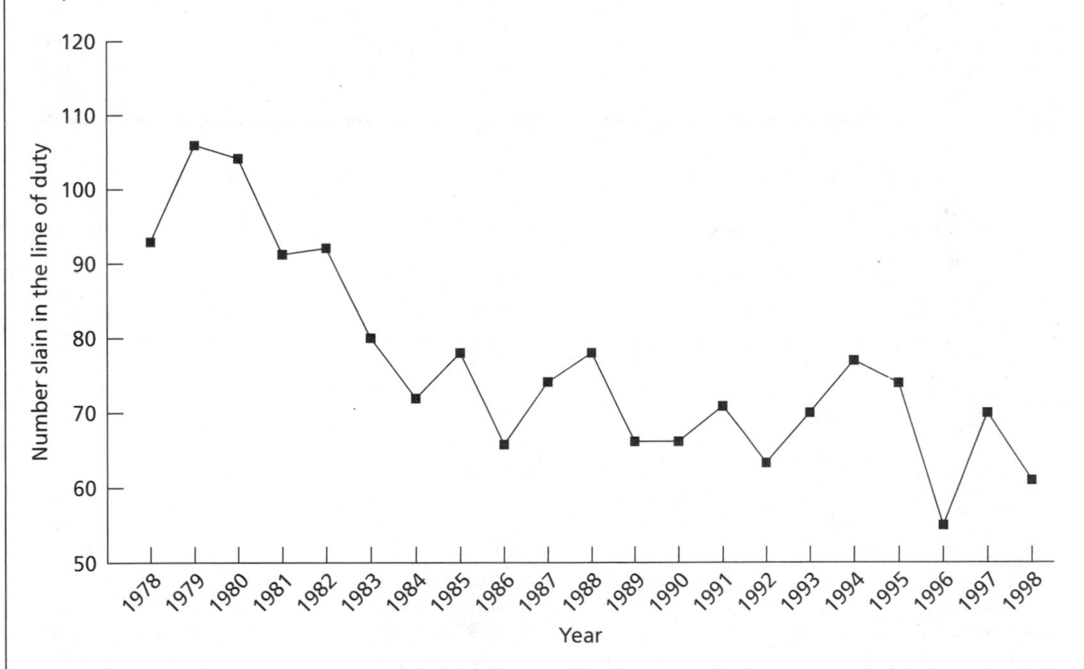

FIGURE 1.1 Trends in Murders of Law Enforcement Officers, 1978–1998

NOTE: Includes federal, state, and local officers feloniously killed.
SOURCE: FBI's annual *Uniform Crime Reports*, 1978–1998.

BOX 1.3 *continued*

(as distinct from a theft of a parked car). Once the crime had a name, some police departments began to keep track of it (broken out of the general category of "robberies of all types"), the news media started to report the most outrageous cases (such as the death of a woman who was dragged over a mile because she became tangled in her seat belt while trying to rescue her toddler from the back seat of her commandeered BMW), and legislators began to impose stiffer penalties for the crime. In 1992, Congress made carjackings ("robbery auto theft") carried out with a firearm a federal offense, since vehicles and guns are involved in interstate commerce (see Gibbs, 1993a).

A federally sponsored annual survey estimated that about 35,000 carjackings were carried out against motorists throughout the United States each year between 1987 and 1992 (Rand, 1994a). That number grew to almost 50,000 attempted or completed carjackings a year from 1992 to 1996, yielding a rate of about 25 victims for every 100,000 people in a year. As for the chances of being accosted, the groups facing the highest risks were men, drivers between the ages of 25 and 49, African Americans and Hispanic Americans, people who were not married, and city residents. In the vast majority of the incidents, the driver was alone, and in about half of all confrontations, the robber acted alone. Only about half of all these robberies were completed, and nearly all motorists reported the crime to the police if the carjackers drove off with the vehicle. About half of all victims were accosted by assailants armed with a gun, but most were not physically hurt. Only 4% suffered serious injuries, such as gunshot and knife wounds, broken bones, or internal injuries that required medical attention. More than one third of the drivers offered no resistance, but about one third tried nonconfrontational tactics like running out of the car and/or screaming for help; the rest fought back in one way or another. Only about one quarter of all victims never recovered their vehicles after the attack took place, but about half suffered some financial losses (Klaus, 1999).

This kind of robbery is very difficult for victims to anticipate and defend against, since there are no foolproof precautions and drivers must be on the alert for so many different scenarios when starting or stopping and while parking. Carjacking is an especially frightening type of confrontational crime because of its potential for escalation from a robbery into aggravated assault, abduction, rape, and even murder. Roughly 25 victims were killed each year by carjackers during the first half of the 1990s (Klaus, 1999).

Individuals Menaced by Stalkers

The term *stalking* was coined in the late 1980s and entered into everyday language after an actress was shot and killed by a mentally disturbed, obsessed fan. In 1990, California's legislature was the first to make this series of connected behaviors a crime, and soon afterward the Los Angeles Police Department set up a Threat Management Unit specifically to investigate complaints about being shadowed and hounded.

Two types of victim-offender relationships account for most complaints. In the first type, a well-known person (i.e., celebrity, star performer, media personality, professional athlete, or political figure) receives continuing unwanted contacts and intrusions from some unknown "admirer" or enemy. In the second type, which is much more common, the victim knows the offender and is shadowed in a frightening way after a dispute. Frequently, the terrorized party is a woman pursued by her jealous, possessive, violence-prone ex-boyfriend or ex-husband who refuses to accept her decision that their romantic relationship has ended. However, many variations on a "fatal attraction" or "murderous obsession" theme are possible: A man might be stalked by a woman who was formerly his lover, a man's new girlfriend can be trailed and threatened by his old girlfriend, a therapist can be besieged by a former patient who feels betrayed, or a boss might be chased after by a disgruntled worker who was fired.

Stalking begins with perfectly legal acts, such as a series of notes, phone calls, faxes, gifts, and visits, but soon the attention becomes a distressing reminder of someone's unwelcome, obsessive intrusions. Spurred on by victims' rights groups, by 1994 all 50 states had outlawed the act of willfully, maliciously, and repeatedly following and harassing a person. Antistalking laws fill a void in the patchwork of statutes forbidding menacing, trespassing, and threatening, and allow the

BOX 1.3 *continued*

authorities to take action before the object of the unwanted attention is seriously hurt. To have the stalker arrested before an attack is actually carried out, many state laws require that the targeted individual have a "reasonable fear of death or grave bodily injury" that arises from a credible threat of violence made by the perpetrator. In some jurisdictions stalking is a misdemeanor; in others it is a felony. Most states provide for both: First offenses are misdemeanors; repeated convictions, violations of orders of protection and injunctions to stay away, stalkings of children, and threats backed up with weapons are felonies. Stiffer punishments can be imposed if the offender actually inflicts bodily harm or confines or restrains the person being pursued. If unchallenged by legal intervention, stalking can escalate into kidnapping, sexual assault, and even murder. About 1 in every 12 women and 1 in every 45 men report that they have been stalked at some point in their lives. An FBI study discovered that 30% of all slain women had been stalked by their former boyfriends or husbands before these distraught intimates killed them (Beck et al., 1992; Hunzeker, 1992; Kolarik, 1992; Wright, et al., 1996; Office of Justice Programs, 1998; Tjaden and Thoennes, 1998).

Civil libertarians have challenged antistalking laws as unconstitutionally vague and overly broad on the grounds that alleged offenders won't realize that their persistent behavior is prohibited, and that the hastily crafted statutes grant too much discretion to the police, opening the door to arbitrary enforcement. Others criticize the legislation for being ineffective, especially if officers are not trained to recognize the recently outlawed pattern of behavior or if the targets are unable to provide documentary proof that the actions are threatening. Antivictim accusations abound: Female targets in particular are told they are imagining that they are in trouble, that they should be flattered by all the attention, or that they are somehow encouraging the stalking and should examine their own behavior and change it (see Meloy, 1998; and Endo, 1999).

Young Women Battered During Courtship

Today the plight of battered women is well known, as is the problem of date rape. Now a growing number of researchers are exploring the phenomenon of physical violence during courtship (especially, for the sake of convenience, among college students).

Courtship is the training ground for marriage, so controlling behaviors (like slapping, grabbing, shaking, kicking, choking, threatening with a weapon, and throwing things) that begin during dating may persist, and perhaps escalate, after the couple ties the knot. But in several crucial ways, violence during courtship differs from violence within marriage. First of all, less force is used over shorter periods of time. Second, young women are more likely to initiate violence against their dates/boyfriends/fiancés than wives are against their husbands (or unmarried women against their live-in lovers). Perhaps these young women feel they can assert themselves more freely because they are not trapped in a day-after-day cohabitation situation and can break off the relationship if the spiral of violence gets out of hand. Of course, much of the physical force exerted by females can, in all fairness, be classified as examples of "fighting back"—either acts of immediate self-defense, or of retaliation for earlier male aggression, or even as preemptive strikes to forestall impending assaults. However, when women are severely victimized, the question "Why does she stay?" inevitably arises. Clearly, some of the reasons married women cite as most important do not apply to dating situations: remaining together for the sake of the children, depending upon the husband financially, or believing that a failed marriage is shameful and divorce is wrong. So other explanations need to be tested. Perhaps some young women tolerate abuse because rules and behavioral limits in romantic relationships are currently in a state of confusion as traditional norms are challenged and rejected. Other women battered during courtship may interpret beatings as demonstrations of "deep feelings" and fits of jealous rage as signs of "really caring." Still others may consider violence within intimate relationships as normal because they were mistreated as children or their parents behaved abusively toward each other. A few might even feel comfortable being dominated by a "virile" man.

Even when the female is the aggressor and the male is the victim, or when mutual combat

Continued

BOX 1.3 ***continued***

breaks out, the adversaries are not evenly matched and it is not a fair fight. Young men usually have several advantages—larger size, greater strength, and better hand-to-hand combat skills—which protect them from serious harm and endanger their girlfriends' well-being. Male-initiated violence remains the more frequent and more serious problem (see Makepeace, 1981; Laner and Thompson, 1982; Allbritten and Allbritten, 1985; Stets and Pirog-Good, 1987; Demaris, 1992; and Follingstad et al., 1992).

College Students Harmed on Campus

College and university campuses used to be viewed as sanctuaries from the problems of the "mean streets" and "real world." But a number of highly publicized crimes and a spate of negligence lawsuits filed by distraught parents have forced administrators, faculties, and student governments to address questions of personal safety within the ivory towers. Despite opposition by college administrators, Congress passed a Student Right-to-Know and Campus Security Act in 1990 (amended by the Higher Education Act of 1992) that required all institutions receiving federal aid to issue annual crime reports.

Students can be victimized by other students or by outsiders. Interpersonal offenses usually take the form of assaults (including brutality against pledges during hazing and drunken brawls after sports events), gang rapes (at parties), date rapes, and hate crimes (gay bashings, racial attacks). As for property crimes, an abundance of bicycles, stereos, and personal computers in an open, unguarded environment attracts robbers, burglars, and thieves. In the late 1990s, larcenies (thefts of all kinds) topped the list, followed by burglaries; aggravated assaults outnumbered robberies; and, of course, murders were rare, according to the campus-by-campus compilation appearing in the Uniform Crime Report issued annually by the FBI.

But, for a number of reasons, official figures may not reveal the full extent of the growing problem. Many students do not report incidents to either the local police or the campus security force. Crimes that occur in the area immediately beyond the campus gates are not counted. Image-conscious administrators devise ways to downplay the risks their students actually face for fear that such revelations will damage their schools' reputations, scare away potential candidates from applying for admission, and hurt fund-raising campaigns. For example, cases involving allegations of date rape, assault, or threats with a weapon don't have to be publicly reported if they are handled by the campus judicial system and don't lead to an arrest.

Comparisons among campuses, although tempting to make, can be misleading, since their populations differ greatly in size. Furthermore, some institutions are situated in idyllic rural settings while others are located in dense urban neighborhoods or have several satellite centers, branches, or affiliated teaching hospitals. At some institutions, most students live in residence halls, while at others all are commuters. Finally, a growing number of colleges, especially public ones, have professionalized security forces that check out visitors and seek out incidents to investigate, while the remainder rely mostly on a few guards and on student/faculty judicial committees. To prevent incidents, many campuses now have gates and checkpoints, ID systems, better lighting, more patrols, outdoor emergency phones, evening shuttle buses, student escort services, crisis counseling centers, crime-on-campus columns in student newspapers, and workshops on date rape and crime prevention as part of first-year orientation (Purdum, 1988; Smith, 1988; Graham, 1993; Mathews, 1993; Lederman, 1994; Whitaker and Pollard, 1994; Molotsky, 1997).

CHAPTER SUMMARY

Victimization is an asymmetrical relationship that is abusive, parasitical, destructive, unfair, and illegal. Offenders harm their victims physically, financially, and emotionally. Laws that recognized that injured parties deserved governmental support and economic aid were passed centuries ago, but until the middle of the

20th century the plight of crime victims was largely overlooked, even by most criminologists. When some researchers began to study victims, their initial interest betrayed an antivictim bias: They sought evidence that the victims' behavior before and during the incidents contributed to their own downfall. Since the 1960s the majority of the social scientists attracted to this new discipline have labored to find ways to ease the suffering of victims and to prevent future incidents. But a commitment to strive for objectivity is the best stance to adopt when undertaking a research project that looks into the conflicts between victims and offenders, criminal justice officials, members of social movements concerned about the crime problem, journalists covering their situations, and businesses selling anticrime devices and services.

Victimology is best viewed as an area of specialization within criminology. Both criminologists and victimologists seek to be impartial in their roles as social scientists investigating both lawbreaking and the consequent response by the justice system and treatment programs. But criminology is much older than victimology and has more clearly defined schools of thought, which leads to sharply different analyses and recommendations.

Victimologists carry out studies that seek to identify, define, and describe all the ways that illegal activities harm targeted individuals; measure the seriousness of the problem; discover how victims' cases are actually handled by the legal system; and test research hypotheses to see if they are supported by the available evidence. Victimology's findings contribute to an ongoing rediscovery process, which constantly brings the plight of additional overlooked groups to the public's attention. But the rediscovery process goes through several stages. After a group's plight becomes known and reforms are implemented, an opposition frequently arises that resists further changes that might be to the group's advantage. Victimologists can help resolve disputes by studying how newly rediscovered groups suffer and whether efforts to assist them are really working as intended.

DISCUSSION QUESTIONS

1. Why should victimologists strive for objectivity rather than adopt a pro-victim bias?
2. Give several examples of the kinds of research questions that victimologists find interesting and the kinds of studies they carry out.
3. In what ways are victimology and criminology similar, and in what ways do they differ?
4. Discuss what can happen at each stage in the rediscovery process.
5. What are some of the important milestones in the history of victimology and victim assistance?
6. Choose a group whose plight is being rediscovered and pose some interesting questions that researchers ought to examine.

2

Digging Up the Facts About Crime Victims

CRIME IN THE STREETS: THE BIG PICTURE

Victimologists gather and interpret data in order to answer certain fundamental questions. For example, they want to find out how many people are harmed by street crimes each year, how rapidly their ranks are growing as time goes by, and which groups are targeted the most and the least. Victimologists want to find out where and when most crimes occur, whether offenders typically carry weapons and, if so, what kinds. Victimologists also want to determine whether attackers tend to be complete strangers, how people act when confronted by assailants, what proportion try to fight back or escape, how many individuals are injured, how many need to be hospitalized, and how much money they lose.

The answers to key questions like these, when taken together, constitute what can be termed the "big picture"—an overview of what is really happening across the United States at the close of the century. The big picture serves as an antidote to limited personal experiences, false impressions, misleading media images, baseless stereotypes, self-serving reports circulated by organizations with vested interests, and widely held myths. But putting together the big picture is not easy. Careful planning, formulation of the right questions, proper data collection techniques, and insightful analyses are required. Until the 1970s few efforts were made to routinely and systematically measure various indicators of the victims' plight. By the 1980s a great many social scientists and agencies were conducting the research needed to bring the big picture into focus. By the 1990s all sorts of special-interest groups began keeping count and disseminating estimates about a wide variety of victims, including innocent persons hit by stray bullets, police officers killed in the line of duty, children reported missing by their parents, and people attacked by assailants who hate their "kind."

Most of the statistics and analyses presented in this chapter concern the dreaded crimes of murder and robbery. Statistics about murders are more complete, consistent (over time and from place to place), accurate, and detailed than those for any other crime. Robbery statistics are far less precise and reliable but are still extremely important because robberies fuel the public's fears about crime in the streets.

The Use and Abuse of Statistics

Statistics are meaningful numbers that reveal important information. Victimologists need accurate statistics about crimes and victims in order to calculate the odds individuals face of being harmed, to estimate their personal financial losses and societal costs, to anticipate how many people might need help, to test theories that purport to explain why some groups experience higher rates of predation than others, and to evaluate the effectiveness of prevention strategies and recovery efforts. By collecting, computing, and analyzing statistics, victimologists can discover what kinds of people are robbed the most, the ways in which individuals protect themselves when robbers attack, the chances of being slain during a robbery, and whether robberies are becoming more or less of a threat.

Victimologists look at **raw numbers**, computed **rates**, detectable **patterns**, demonstrable **trends**, and statistically derived **profiles**. **Raw numbers** indicate the actual *incidence* of victimization. For example, 16,914 people were murdered in the United States during 1998. **Rates** are expressed as fractions or ratios that project the odds, chances, or risks of victimization. The numerator of the fraction counts the number of individuals harmed while the denominator is a standardized base (e.g., 1,000 households, 100,000 people, or 100,000 vehicles). Rates are the appropriate measurements to use when comparing the incidence of crime in populations of unequal size, such as murders in different cities or countries. During 1998 about 6 out of every 100,000 Americans were slain throughout the country. In Los Angeles 426 residents were killed by criminals, and in Detroit the body count was almost the same size, 429. But many more people live in Los Angeles than in Detroit. So when population is taken into account in the denominators, Los Angeles's 1998 murder rate (12 deaths for every 100,000 inhabitants) was much lower than Detroit's (43 killings per 100,000 inhabitants).

Patterns reflect relationships or connections that emerge from an analysis of data. For instance, murders generally occur at a higher rate in urban neighborhoods than in rural areas, with suburban communities somewhere in between these extremes. **Trends** reveal how conditions change as the years roll by. Are the dangers of being murdered increasing or decreasing with each passing year? An inspection of annual rates reveals that the nation's murder rate rose dramatically from the early 1960s until the early 1990s. But a pronounced downward trend in homicides took place during the remainder of the 1990s. **Profiles** are statistical portraits that yield an impression of what is usual or typical in a given situation. The profile of the typical murder victim is a poor young man from a city neighborhood.

After carefully examining data, victimologists can answer some interesting questions: What are the chances of becoming a victim during a single year? Victimization rates indicate the odds. Does crime burden all kinds of people equally? No. Victimization patterns indicate the persistence of **differential rates**: Certain groups are targeted much more often than others. Which unwanted event is a person more likely to personally experience—an accident, an illness, or a crime? **Comparative rates** enable people to assess the relative threat posed by each kind of misfortune. Is the crime problem as severe in other societies as it is in the United States? **International comparisons** enable researchers to rank countries according to their victimization rates. What are the chances that a person will become a victim by the end of a lifetime (not just during a single year)? **Cumulative risks** estimate these odds.

Statistics are of crucial importance to social scientists, policy analysts, and decision makers because they replace vague adjectives like "many," "most," and "few" with more precise numbers. Criminologists and victimologists either collect their own data or they scrutinize official statistics (gathered and published by government agencies). Yet, as useful and necessary as statistics are, they should always be viewed with a healthy dose of scientific skepticism. These numbers can be used by interest groups just like a lamppost is used by a drunkard—for support rather than for illumination. Though some mistakes are honest and unavoidable, it is easy to "lie" with statistics by using impressive and scientific-sounding numbers to manipulate or mislead. Whenever statistics are presented to underscore or clinch some point in an argument, their accuracy and interpretation must be questioned. What was the source of the data? How were key concepts defined? How valid and precise were the measurements? What kinds of biases and inaccuracies could have crept into the data? If the observed difference between samples that are being compared was small, was it within the margin of error? Are different estimates available from other sources?

For several reasons officials, agencies, and groups with vested interests and narrow agendas release statistics to influence decision makers or the public. Often these groups employ statistics to demonstrate that those in charge are doing their jobs well (for example, convicting murderers or preventing robberies). Their critics or opponents will try to make the contrary point that the incumbents are incompetent and need to be replaced. Statistics might also be cited to prove that existing laws and policies are having the intended effects (such as reducing the number of carjackings) or, conversely, to persuade people that new approaches are necessary. Data can be assembled to support the argument that more personnel, equipment, and money are needed to successfully combat crime and serve victims; different figures can be marshaled to convince people that current budgets are adequate or even bloated. Numbers can be used to calm the public (for example, by reassuring people that almost all robbery victims survive their confrontations without any physical injuries) or to arouse alarm (by emphasizing that some robbers kill even those victims who surrender their valuables and offer no resistance).

Statistics never "speak for themselves." The numbers must be placed within some context or put into perspective. Sometimes, the same numbers can be interpreted quite differently, depending on what spin commentators give them—what is stressed and what is downplayed.

For example, consider a set of statistics summarizing the big picture. These statistics are compiled and published comes each year from the Federal Bureau of Investigation's authoritative **Uniform Crime Report *(UCR)***; the picture they present illustrated under the heading of the "Crime Clock." The Crime Clock dramatizes the fact that with the passing of each and every second, minute, hour, and day, the victim toll keeps mounting (see Figure 2.1). The Crime Clock's statistics are computed in a straightforward manner. The number of incidents of each kind (reported to police departments across the country during the year) is divided into the total number of seconds ($60 \times 60 \times 24 \times 365 = 31{,}536{,}000$) or minutes ($60 \times 24 \times 365 = 525{,}600$) in an entire year. For instance, during 1998, 16,914 people were murdered across the country; the calculation $(525{,}600)/(16{,}914) = 31$ indicates that every 31 minutes another American is murdered. (Note that when working with impersonal statistics it is easy to forget that each case represents a terrible tragedy and devastating loss for the real people involved.)

Just a glance at this chart alerts even the casual reader to its chilling message. The big picture it portrays is that serious crimes of violence and theft are all too common. As the Crime Clock ticks away, a steady stream of casualties flows into morgues, hospital emergency rooms, and police stations. Practically every moment another person is joining the growing ranks of crime victims somewhere in the United States. These grim reminders give the impression that being victimized is

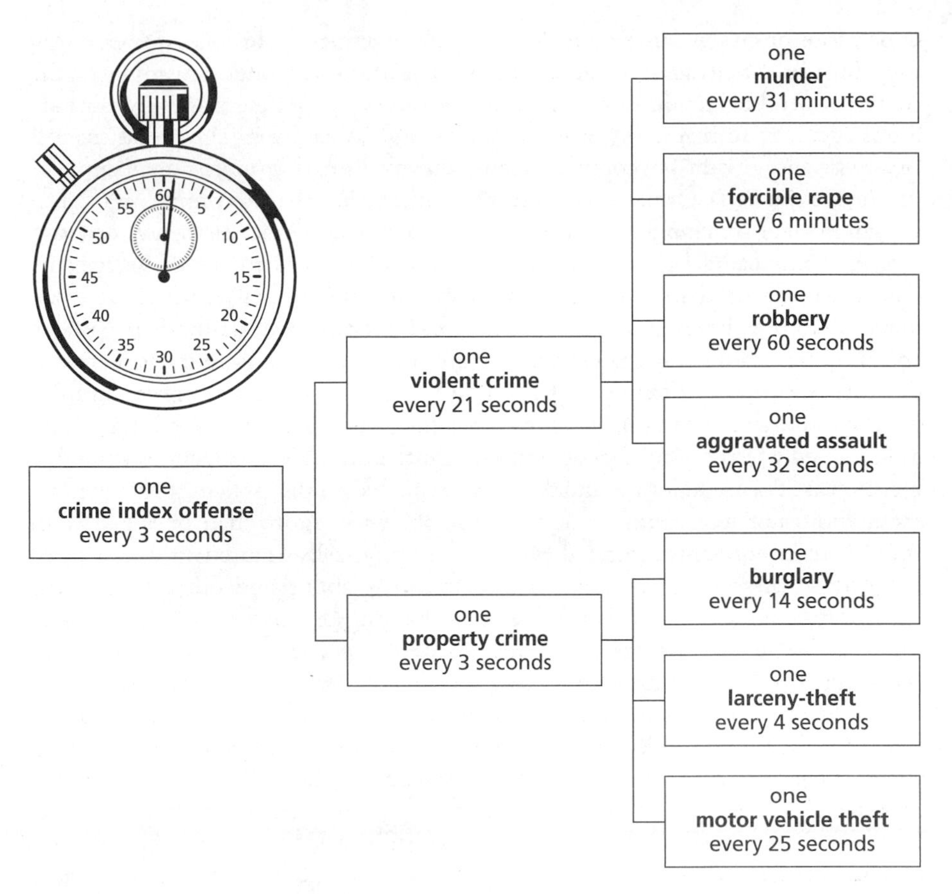

FIGURE 2.1 The FBI's Crime Clock, 1998

SOURCE: Reprinted from the FBI's *Uniform Crime Report* for 1998.
The FBI adds this note: "The crime clock should be viewed with care. Being the most aggregate represention of *UCR* data, it is designed to convey the annual reported crime experience by showing the relative frequency of occurrence of the index offenses. This mode of display should not be taken to imply a regularity in the commission of the Part I offenses; rather, it represents the annual ratio of crime to fixed time intervals."

inevitable. It is just a matter of time before disaster strikes. Sooner or later, everyone will be harmed in every one of these different ways—or so it appears (although an FBI disclaimer points out that crimes are not committed with such rigid regularity; these relative frequencies represent averages). Not surprisingly, this Crime Clock mode of presentation is frequently used in sales pitches for insurance policies, burglar alarms, or automobile antitheft devices because the immediate future seems so ominous. (Worse yet, these figures are based solely upon crimes reported to the authorities. The police do not find out about every instance in which someone is harmed, so the actual victimization rates must be even higher. See the discussions below and in chapter 4 about victim reporting rates.)

However, this "spin" is overly dramatic and unduly pessimistic, and consequently misleading. The social context is missing—the recognition that there are millions of potential targets across the country. The ticking away of the Crime

Clock is an unnecessarily frightening way of depicting the big picture because it uses a formula that ignores population size. Instead of seconds and minutes, the other part of the fraction should be some measure of people or possessions at risk. Since there are so many millions of residents, homes, and cars, the actual chances of any given individual becoming a victim during a single year are rather slim.

While the FBI's Crime Clock gives the impression that becoming an offender's target is a shockingly common occurrence, a different set of authoritative figures is circulated by another branch of the U.S. Department of Justice: the Bureau of Justice Statistics (BJS). The BJS circulates annual estimates that are derived from a different source—a **National Crime Victimization Survey *(NCVS)*** and the message is almost opposite. In fact, its yearly findings seem relatively reassuring. For example, the Crime Clock warned that a robbery unfolded every minute during 1998. However, the survey's findings indicated only about 4 out of every 1,000 people in the United States were robbed during that entire year (this includes the incidents not reported to the police). Furthermore, victims did not lose anything of value to robbers in more than one quarter of these hostile encounters, and they were not physically injured in about three quarters of these confrontations. Therefore, only about one out of every one thousand Americans was injured during a mugging or holdup in 1998. Despite their fears, 996 out of every 1,000 persons were not accosted by robbers during that year, 997 did not suffer any financial losses, and 999 were not wounded.

Both sets of data from sources in the federal government are reasonably accurate and trustworthy. What differs is the way the data is presented. Each format suggests a particular interpretation. The FBI's Crime Clock calculations accentuate the negative, highlighting the number of people harmed per hour, minute, or even second, while ignoring the fact that the overwhelming majority went about their daily lives throughout the year without interference from criminals. The BJS victimization figures juxtapose the small numbers who were preyed upon against the huge numbers who got away unscathed in a certain year. Clearly, crime statistics are analogous to the classic example of a partially filled glass of water that may be seen as either half empty or half full, depending upon the emphasis or "spin."

A CLOSER LOOK AT THE TWO OFFICIAL SOURCES OF VICTIMIZATION DATA

During the 1800s public officials began keeping records about crimes to gauge the "moral health" of society. Then, as now, high crime rates were taken as signs of social pathology—indications that something was desperately wrong. As they do now, the criminologists of the time used crime statistics to build and test theories about the kinds of people breaking the law and the reasons for their lawless deeds. Victimologists use the same data sets to discover who criminals are preying upon, and whether the crime problem is intensifying or subsiding.

Two different government reports containing statistical data are published yearly. The FBI's *Uniform Crime Report,* entitled *Crime in the United States,* is much older and better known than the BJS's *National Crime Victimization Survey,* entitled *Criminal Victimization in the United States.* Each of these official sources of facts and figures about crime and its victims is disseminated yearly by the U.S. Department of Justice. Each source has strengths and weaknesses in terms of the kinds of information victimologists find useful.

At first the establishment of a second, independent reporting system to measure the amount of street crime in contemporary society appeared to be a positive development in terms of bringing the big picture into focus. In theory, the federal government's two monitoring systems should support and confirm each other's findings, lending greater credence to all official statistics. But in practice, the *UCR* and *NCVS* estimates have diverged significantly for certain years or stretches of time. On occasion during the 1970s and 1980s, victimization rates appeared to be going up according to the *UCR,* but seemed to be going down according the *NCVS,* or vice versa, as a number of graphs presented later in this book will show. This lack of correspondence (technically speaking, this low correlation) caused confusion and touched off debates among victimologists, the general public, and the law enfoercement community. The divergence enabled some interested parties to contend that America's street crime problem was getting worse, while their opponents could marshal evidence from the other reporting system to argue that the problem was subsiding. However, during the second half of the 1990s, trend lines derived from the data from both of the government agencies were in synch, indicating that an across-the-board decline in criminal activity was taking place throughout the country.

The *Uniform Crime Report* The *UCR* was established in 1927 by a committee set up by the International Association of Chiefs of Police. The committee's goal was to develop a uniform set of definitions and reporting sheets for gathering crime statistics. Since 1930 the FBI has published crime data forwarded voluntarily by police departments. Since 1958 the annual reports have drawn upon reports from nearly 17,000 village, municipal, county, and state police, and sheriff's departments that serve about 96% of the nearly 260 million inhabitants of the United States.

Unfortunately, the *UCR* has been of limited value to those interested in studying victims as opposed to alleged perpetrators or incidents. In part I of the *UCR,* eight **index crimes** are the focus of attention. These are the illegal acts most people think about when they hear the term "street crime." Four index crimes concern violent attacks directed against persons: murder, forcible rape, robbery, and aggravated assault. The other four constitute crimes against property: burglary, larceny (thefts of all kinds), motor vehicle theft, and arson (added in 1979 at the request of Congress but still unreliably measured). The FBI compiles information about the number of incidents of each of these eight crimes that were reported to the police, the proportion of cases that were solved, and the characteristics of the persons arrested for these offenses. The number of acts of violence and theft known to the authorities is presented for big and small cities, counties, states, and even many college campuses (since the mid-1990s). In part II, the *UCR* furnishes data about the number of people arrested (but no estimates of the number of illegal acts committed) for an assortment of 21 offenses, including some crimes that could have directly harmed individuals, like fraud and vandalism. The *UCR* also contains a section about bias crimes motivated by the offenders' hatred of people of the victims' race, nationality, religion, sexual orientation, or type of disability. Another part of the report furnishes data about how many law enforcement officers were feloniously assaulted and killed in the line of duty, the weapons used against them, and the assignments they were carrying out when they were slain.

From a victimologist's point of view, the *UCR*'s method of data collection suffers from several shortcomings that undermine its accuracy and usefulness (see Savitz, 1982; and O'Brien, 1985). First of all, underreporting is a major problem. Since many victims do not inform their local authorities about the illegal acts committed against them and their property (see chapter 4), the FBI's compilation of "crimes known to the police" is unavoidably lower than the actual (but unknown) number of crimes that really took place in a jurisdiction. Second, the *UCR* focuses on accused offenders (keeping track of the age, sex, and race of arrestees) but does not provide any information at all about the victims who filed complaints with the police. (However, information about murder victims is collected routinely—see below.) Third, the *UCR* mixes together reports of attempted crimes (usually not as serious for victims) with completed crimes (in which offenders were successful in achieving their goals). Finally, when computing crime rates for cities, counties, and states, the FBI counts incidents directed against all kinds of targets, adding together crimes against impersonal entities and commercial establishments on the one hand, and individuals and households on the other. For example, figures for robberies include bank holdups as well as muggings, statistics about burglaries combine attempted warehouse break-ins with ransackings of homes, and figures for larcenies include shoplifting plus an assortment of other kinds of thefts (such as stealing packages from a parked truck in addition to pocket-pickings and car break-ins).

But the *UCR* is being overhauled and is becoming a more useful source of statistics for victimologists as the FBI converts its data collection format to a National Incident-Based Reporting System (NIBRS). Instead of just eight index offenses, FBI computers are prepared to keep track of 46 Group A offenses derived from 22 categories of crimes. In addition to the four crimes against persons and the four against property that part I included, the new Group A embraces a number of offenses with individual victims that formerly were listed in part II or were not previously collected. These crimes for which victim-oriented data are becoming available include simple assault, vandalism (property damage and destruction), blackmail (extortion), fraud (swindles and con games), nonforcible sex offenses (statutory rape and incest), and kidnapping (abduction). Details are now being collected about intimidation (categorized as a type of assault), justifiable homicide and negligent manslaughter (classified as types of homicides), and sexual attacks other than rape (forcible sodomy, sexual assault with an object, and forcible fondling). FBI computers are also storing a number of additional data elements about each incident, including the time and location of the occurrence; the weapons used; any injuries sustained; the kind of property stolen, its value, and whether it was recovered; the age, sex, race/ethnicity, and resident status of each victim and every arrestee (if any); and the nature of the relationship between them. Previously, only in cases of homicide were some of these details extracted from police files. Another major change is the abolition of the hierarchy rule in scoring incidents, which instructed police officials to report only the worst offense that happened during a sequence of events. Preserving these details will make it possible to determine how often one crime evolves into another, such as a carjacking escalating into a rape, or a robbery intensifying into a murder. However, keeping track of information about all victims and perpetrators (in addition to simply counting offenses and incidents) leads to many complications. Entering all the data from police files into the proper computer fields becomes very complicated when a single incident involves several different offenses, more than one victim, many offenders, and multiple arrests. The analysis of data from the NIBRS will appear in an annual supplement called *Victims and Offenders: Incident-Based Uniform Crime Reports* (Reaves, 1993; Office of Justice Programs, 1997; Chilton, Major, and Propheter, 1998; FBI, 1999). Austin, Texas, was the first to switch over to the comprehensive data collection and reporting system, but other big-city police departments that deal with a huge volume of crime reports have had trouble meeting NIBRS goals and timetables, so the complete implementation of the new recording system has been postponed repeatedly. As more local law enforcement agencies and state data collection clearinghouses phase in the NIBRS, the wealth of data in the FBI's *Uniform Crime Report* will increasingly resemble and then surpass the information derived from the *National Crime Victimization Survey* report. But one major difference will persist: *UCR* figures will continue to be based solely on crimes known to local police forces and sheriff departments.

The *National Crime Victimization Survey* Criminologists and victimologists have reservations about the accuracy of the official records kept by the police. The tallies are known to be incomplete and are suspected of being periodically either inflated or deflated by powerful groups manipulating the numbers churned out for public consumption in order to prove some point. Dissatisfaction with official record-keeping led criminologists to collect their own data. The first method used was the "self-report survey." Small samples of people were promised anonymity and confidentiality if they would "confess" on questionnaires about the crimes they had committed. This type of study consistently revealed greater volumes of illegal acts than were indicated by official statistics in government reports. Self-report surveys confirmed the hypothesis that a lot of people who broke the law were never investigated, arrested, or convicted, especially if they were members of the middle and upper classes.

After exploring the usefulness of self-report surveys about offenses, the next logical step for criminologists was to survey people from all walks of life about any street crimes that may have been committed *against* them rather than by them. These studies originally were called "victim surveys." But that label was somewhat misleading because most respondents answered that they had not been harmed in those specific ways during the time period in question.

Criminologists conducted the first national survey about victimization (based on a random sample of 10,000 households) in 1966 for the President's Commission on Law Enforcement and the Administration of Justice. It immediately confirmed one suspicion: A sizable percentage of the individuals in the sample who told interviewers that they had been victimized acknowledged that they had not reported the incident to the police. This additional proof of the existence of a "dark figure" of unreported crimes further undercut confidence in the accuracy of the FBI's *UCR* statistics for all offenses except murder and underscored the importance of continuing this alternative way of measuring victimization rates. In 1972 the federal government initiated a yearly survey of residents and businesses in 26 large cities, but this project was discontinued in 1976. In 1973 the Census Bureau began interviewing members of a huge randomly selected, nationwide, stratified, multistage sample of households (clustered by geographic counties). Until 1992 the undertaking was known as the *National Crime Survey* (*NCS*); after some revisions it was re-titled the *National Crime Victimization Survey* (*NCVS*).

NCVS respondents answer questions from a survey that runs for over 20 pages. They are interviewed every 6 months for 3 years. The questioning begins with a series of "screen" items such as "During the last 6 months did anyone break into your home?" If the respondent answers yes, follow-up questions are asked to collect details about the incident. When completed, the survey provides a great deal of data about the number of violent and property crimes committed against the respondents; the location and time of the incidents; the extent of any physical injuries or financial losses; their descriptions of the perpetrators and their weapons; any prior relationship between the victim and the offender; the reasons why the crime was or was not reported to the police; and the age, sex, race/ethnicity, marital status, income level, educational attainment, and place of residence of the victims disclosing their misfortunes to survey interviewers.

The survey focuses on four crimes of violence (forcible rape, robbery, simple assault and aggravated assault), two kinds of theft against persons (personal larceny with and without contact), and three types of stealing directed at the common property of households (burglary, larceny, and motor vehicle theft). The list of crimes analyzed in the *NCVS* is shorter than in the *UCR* and is far from exhaustive. For example, instances of kidnapping, swindling, blackmail, extortion, and property damage due to vandalism or arson are not probed. The survey is person-centered. It is geared toward uncovering the suffering of individuals 12 years old or older and the losses experienced by entire households. (Attempts to measure offenses committed against businesses, like burglaries or robberies directed at stores, were discontinued after a few years.)

The benefit of survey research is that it eliminates the futility of attempting the impossible: interviewing every one of the roughly 222 million people 12 years old or older living in the entire United States to find out how he or she fared in the past year. The collective experiences of the randomly selected 80,000 individuals in the sample (to the extent that they closely mirror the population as a whole in terms of important variables linked to victimization, like sex, age, race, income, marital status, and location of residency) can be projected to derive rough estimates of the total number of persons throughout the country who were robbed, raped, or badly beaten, or suffered burglaries or car thefts.

At its inception, the idea of surveying people about their recent misfortunes was hailed as a major breakthrough that would provide more accurate statistics than those found in the *UCR*. But, for a number of reasons, the technique of interviewing people about the offenses committed against them has not turned out to be the foolproof method for measuring the "actual" crime rate that some victimologists hoped it would be (for methodological criticisms see Levine, 1976; Garofalo, 1981; Skogan, 1981b, 1986; Lehnen and Skogan, 1981; Reiss, 1981, 1986; Schneider, 1981; O'Brien, 1985; Mayhew and Hough, 1988; and Fattah, 1991). First of all, the findings of this survey, like any other, are reliable only to the extent that the national sample is truly representative of the population of the whole country. If the sample is biased in terms of age, gender, race, class, geographical mix, or some other important factor, then the projections made about the experiences of the more than 200 million people who were not questioned will be either too high or too low. Because the *NCVS* is household-based, it might fail to fully capture the experiences of transients (such as homeless persons) or people who wish to keep a low profile (such as illegal immigrants).

Second, the credibility of what people tell pollsters is a constant subject of debate and a matter of continuing concern in this survey. Underreporting remains a problem because communication barriers can inhibit respondents from disclosing the details about certain crimes committed against them (that they probably also refused to bring to the attention of the police). Any systematic suppression of the facts, such as the unwillingness of wives to reveal that their husbands beat them, of teenage girls to divulge that they suffered date rapes, or of young men to admit that they were robbed while trying to buy illicit drugs or a prostitute's sexual services, will throw off the survey's projection of the true state of affairs.

Furthermore, crimes committed against children under 12 are not probed (so no information is forthcoming about physical and sexual abuse by caretakers, or molestations or kidnappings by acquaintances or strangers). Forgetting ("memory decay") also results in information losses, especially about minor offenses that did not involve serious injuries or expenses.

But overreporting can occur as well. Some respondents may exaggerate or deliberately lie for a host of personal motives. Experienced detectives filter out from police statistics accounts that do not sound believable (the charges are deemed to be "unfounded," and no further investigation is warranted). But there is no such quality control over what people tell *NCVS* interviewers. For example, if a person in the sample discusses a crime that was supposedly reported to the police, there is no attempt to check and see if the respondent's recollections coincide with the information in the case files. The police don't accept all reports of crimes at face value, but pollsters must. "Stolen" objects actually may have been misplaced, and an accidentally shattered window may be mistaken as evidence of an attempted break-in. **Forward telescoping**, the tendency to remember traumatic events and therefore believe that a serious crime occurred more recently than it did (within the reference period of the previous 6 months) and should be counted, when actually it was committed long before and ought to be excluded, can also contribute to overreporting.

Because being harmed within the previous 6 months is a relatively rare event, tens of thousands of people must be polled to find enough people with incidents worthy of discussion to meet the requirements for statistical soundness. (Estimates derived from small subsamples have large margins of error.) The surveys thus become very expensive to carry out. For example, about 1,000 people must be interviewed in order to locate a handful who were recently robbed. Over the years the survey has undergone a number of changes. To cut expenses the sample size was trimmed down on several occasions from about 60,000 households containing over 130,000 participants in the 1970s to 43,000 housing units with about 80,000 respondents aged 12 and older in 1998. To cut costs further, phone interviews assisted by computerized prompts increasingly substitute for time-consuming face-to-face home visits. Even with a relatively large and expensive sampling method, the findings of the survey only can describe the situation in the nation as a whole. The seriousness of the crime problem in a particular city, county, or state cannot be determined because the national sample is not large enough to break down into local subgroups of sufficient size for statistical analysis. Furthermore, the projected absolute number of incidents (offenses committed and victims harmed) and the relative rates (victims per 1,000 people) are really estimates at the midpoint of a range (confidence interval). These numbers should always be regarded as approximations, plus or minus a certain correction factor (margin of error) that depends mostly upon the size of the sample (all respondents) or subsample (such as low-income men living in cities who were robbed).

The *NCVS* has improved over the years as better ways were devised to draw representative samples, to determine which incidents fit or don't fit crime definitions, and to jog victims' memories. Beginning in 1986, questions probing several new subject areas were added: whether the victim thought the offender was high on drugs or alcohol at the time of the crime, how the victim behaved while under attack (self-protective measures), what the victim was doing when trouble struck (commuting to work or school, shopping, and so forth), and what contacts victims had with agents of the criminal justice system (Taylor, 1989). During the early 1990s the survey was fine-tuned once again. An advisory panel of criminal justice policymakers, social scientists, victim advocates, and statisticians redesigned some questions to provide cues that could help victims recall events and details, especially about incidents involving nonstrangers. Also, more explicit questions were added about sexual assaults (involving unwanted or coerced sexual contact) that fell short of the legal definition of rape and about outbreaks of domestic violence (simple assaults) (Hoover, 1994).

Comparing the *UCR* and the *NCVS* For victimologists the greater variety of statistics published in the *NCVS* offer many more possibilities for analysis and interpretation than the much more limited data in the *UCR*. But both official sources have their advantages and can be considered complements of each other.

The *UCR* is the only source to turn to for information about murder victims (other than public health statistics based on records maintained by local coroners' and medical examiners' offices, which are also valuable, detailed, and accurate). The *UCR* is also the place to look up geographically-based statistics, since it provides data about index crimes reported to the police in different cities, counties, states, and regions of the country. The *UCR* calculates the overall proportion of index crime cases that are solved by law enforcement agencies. Although some basic identifiers about arrestees are provided, the *UCR* doesn't provide any descriptions of the people harmed by rapists, robbers, burglars, and other thieves (until the NIBRS replaces current reporting methods). The incidents counted in the *UCR* can be considered as having passed through two sets of authenticity filters: victims felt what happened was serious enough to bring in the authorities shortly afterward, and officers who filled out the reports believed that the complainants were telling the truth as supported by evidence, statements by eyewitnesses, and maybe even confessions by offenders (accusations deemed to be **unfounded** are not counted).

On the other hand, the details collected during the *NCVS* interviews can be considered to be more inclusive and complete, since information is obtained about incidents that were not reported to the police. The yearly surveys are not affected by any changes in the degree of cooperation—or level of tension—between community residents and their local police, by improvements in record keeping by law enforcement agencies, or by temporary crackdowns in which all incidents are taken more seriously. But the *NCVS* interviewers must accept at face value the accounts respondents describe to them. Also, the *NCVS* annual report has nothing to offer about murders, bias crimes, line-of-duty assaults and deaths of police officers, offenses committed against children under 12, robberies and burglaries directed at commercial establishments, and injuries from fires that were intentionally set (arson). Statistics estimating the extent of the crime problem in particular cities and states are not available on a routine basis either.

When both official sources collect data about the same crimes, the findings may not be strictly comparable. First of all, the definitions of certain crimes (such as rape) can vary, so the numerators may not count the same incidents. In addition, the denominators differ. While the FBI computes incidents per 100,000 people, the BJS calculates incidents per 1,000 people aged 12 or older and for property crimes per 1,000 households, not individuals (the average household has between two and three people living within it). Therefore, when attempting comparisons several complications can arise. Furthermore, *NCVS* findings are estimates and are subject to sampling error, which means that the true value lies within a range (confidence interval) plus or minus a little correction factor (standard error) of the reported number.

Using Data to Bring the Big Picture Into Focus

The two official sources of government statistics can be examined to provide useful answers to the question "How often are people harmed by lawbreakers?" Crime rates, or more precisely **victimization rates**, are calculated and disseminated by the BJS in its yearly report of *NCVS* findings and by the FBI in its annual *UCR* compilation of information from police files. Estimates of the numbers of incidents yield an impression about the absolute size of the ranks of new crime victims. Relative rates indicate just how common or rare a particular kind of offense is during a given year. Rates are computed by constructing ratios whose numerators equal the number of incidents per year and whose denominators equal the number of potential targets. For example, in calculating the victimization rate for robberies committed in 1998, the 886,000 completed or attempted muggings and holdups disclosed to *NCVS* interviewers constitute the numerator. The denominator, 222,000,000, equals the U.S. population estimate of individuals 12 years old or older provided by the U.S. Census. Dividing the denominator into the numerator yields the decimal 0.00399. Multiplying this

Table 2.1 Estimated 1998 Victimization Rates from the *UCR* and the *NCVS*

Crime	*UCR* Definition	Incidents	Rate (per 100,000)
Murder	The willful (nonnegligent) killing of one human being by another; includes manslaughter and deaths due to recklessness; excludes deaths due to accidents, suicides, and justifiable homicides in self-defense.	16,914	6
Forcible Rape	The carnal knowledge of a female forcibly and against her will; includes attempts; excludes other sexual assaults and statutory rape.	93,103	34
Robbery	The taking or attempting to take anything of value from the care, custody, or control of a person or persons by force or threat of force; includes commercial establishments and carjackings, armed and unarmed.	446,625	165
Aggravated Assault	The unlawful attacking of one person by another for the purpose of inflicting severe bodily injury, often by use of a deadly weapon; includes attempted murder and severe beatings of family members; excludes simple, unarmed assaults.	974,402	363
Simple Assault	no weapon used, minor wounds inflicted	not measured	not computed
Personal Larceny	not a separate category	not measured	not computed
Burglary	The unlawful entry of a structure to commit a felony or theft; includes unlawful entry without applying force to residences and commercial and government premises.	2,329,950	862
Larceny-Theft	The unlawful taking, carrying, leading, or riding away of property from the possession of another; includes purse snatching, pocket picking, thefts from vehicles, thefts of parts of vehicles, and shoplifting; excludes the use of force or fraud to obtain possessions.	7,373,886	2,728
Motor Vehicle Theft	The theft or attempted driving away of a vehicle; includes automobiles, trucks, buses, motorcycles, snowmobiles, and commercially owned vehicles; excludes farm machinery and boats and planes.	1,240,754	459

tiny quotient by 1,000 (equivalent to moving the decimal place three digits to the right) produces a robbery rate of about 4 victims for every 1,000 teenagers and adults during 1998, according to *NCVS* data. However, according to *UCR* data, 466,625 robberies were reported to the police and 270,296,000 people of all ages were living in the United States during 1998, so the robbery rate was 165 per 100,000. Although the FBI definition is broader (it encompasses stickups of banks, for example), not all victims bring their problems to the attention of the police, so the *UCR* victimization rate is lower than the figure derived from the *NCVS* survey (165 compared to 400). The standard definitions used by police departments for *UCR* purposes and by *NCVS* interviewers and the estimated numbers of incidents and computed victimization rates for 1998 derived from both data collecting projects appear in Table 2.1.

Drawing upon the data from the *UCR* and the *NCVS* presented in Table 2.1, the big picture takes shape. The numbers of incidents and the victimization rates were higher from the *NCVS* than from the *UCR* for each type of offense. But both sources of data confirm that contrary to any impressions

Crime	*NCVS* Definition	Incidents	Rate (per 100,000)
Murder	not included in the survey	not measured	not computed
Rape	The carnal knowledge of a male or female through the use of force or threats of violence; includes attempts as well as verbal threats; excludes sexual contacts and statutory rape.	overall 200,000	90
		completed 110,000	50
		attempted 89,000	40
Sexual Assault	The imposition of unwanted sexual contact (grabbing, fondling) with or without force; includes attempts and threats; excludes molestations of children under 12.	overall 133,000	60
Robbery	The taking directly from a person of property or cash by force or threat of force, with or without a weapon; includes attempts; excludes commercial establishments.	overall 886,000	400
		completed 610,000	270
		completed (with injury) 170,000	80
		attempted 277,000	120
		attempted (with injury) 70,000	30
Aggravated Assault	The attacking of a person with a weapon, regardless of whether an injury is sustained; includes attempts as well as attacks without a weapon that result in serious injuries; excludes severe physical abuse of children under 12.	overall 1,674,000	750
		completed 547,000	250
		attempted 1,126,000	510
Simple Assault	The attacking of a person without a weapon resulting in minor wounds or no physical injury; includes attempts and intrafamily violence.	overall 5,224,000	2,350
		minor injury 1,175,000	530
		no injury 4,048,000	1,820
Personal Theft	The theft of cash or possessions from any place other than the victim's home or its immediate vicinity without the use of force or threats; includes pocket picking and purse snatching as well as attempts.	overall 296,000	130
Household Burglary	The unlawful entry of a residence, garage, or shed, usually but not always for the purpose of theft; includes attempts; excludes commercial or governmental premises.	overall 4,054,000	3,850 per 100,000 households
		completed 3,380,000	3,210
		attempted 674,000	640
Theft	The theft of property or cash without contact; includes attempts to take unguarded possessions as well as larcenies committed by persons invited into the home.	overall 17,703,000	16,810
		completed 17,074,000	16,200
		attempted 629,000	600
Motor Vehicle Theft	The driving away or taking without authorization of any motorized vehicle; includes attempts.	overall 1,138,000	1,080
		completed 822,000	780
		attempted 316,000	300

NOTE: Subcategories may not add up to totals because of rounding errors.
SOURCES: FBI's *UCR*, 1998, BJS's *NCVS*, 1998, Rennison, 1999.

gained from news media coverage and television or movie plots, victims suffer from property crimes much more frequently than from violent crimes. The *NCVS* findings reveal that the most common form of victimization (touching nearly 17% of all households each year) turns out to be the least serious of all: the stealing of property left unattended outdoors or of household possessions by someone invited into the home. (Most [more than 75%] of these incidents resulted in losses of less than $250.) *UCR* statistics confirm that larcenies of all kinds vastly outnumber all other types of crimes reported to the police. Of all the violent crimes disclosed to *NCVS* interviewers, simple assaults were the most common (far more likely than robberies, rapes, aggravated assaults, or murders). Most (77%) of these simple assaults left their victims uninjured. Aggravated assaults ranked second in terms of frequency, but fortunately in most of these incidents (67%), victims were just threatened with a weapon but did not actually sustain serious bodily harm (broken bones, loss of teeth, loss of consciousness, internal injuries, or wounds requiring medical attention in a hospital for two or more days). According to the *UCR,* aggravated (or felonious) assaults were the most common type of violent offense reported to the police, but that is because the *UCR* doesn't keep track of the number of simple assaults incidents in part I. (The number of arrests for misdemeanor assaults appears in part II.)

UCR figures indicate that about one quarter of all robberies were directed against gas stations, convenience stores, banks, and other businesses. *NCVS* findings don't include robberies of commercial establishments but do reveal that most robberies (69%) were successful from the offender's point of view. Fortunately, most robbery victims (73%) were not physically hurt. Unfortunately, more than half (55%) of the rapes disclosed to the *NCVS* interviewers were completed acts. The smaller *UCR* estimate of the total number of incidents indicates that many rape victims who disclosed their problems to interviewers were not willing to bring their plight to the attention of the police (also, the *UCR* only counts offenses against girls and women but not against boys or men). Both sources of data agree that rapes take place much less often than assaults or robberies.

The *NCVS* and *UCR* victimization rates derived from the estimates of incidents are not easily compared. The standard denominator for the *UCR* rates is "per 100,000 individuals" of any age. The denominators for *NCVS* violent victimization rates are "per 1,000 persons 12 years old or older." Furthermore, *NCVS* property crime rates are calculated as "per 1,000 households" and therefore do not correspond directly to the FBI's "per 100,000 individuals" (the typical household has between two and three persons living within it). To facilitate rough comparisons, *NCVS* rates were presented in Table 2.1 as "for every 100,000" simply by multiplying the published BJS rate by 100.

Victimization rates are easier to analyze and recall than the huge numbers of incidents and victimized individuals. These estimates of the rate of becoming a victim don't change much from year to year, so last year's rates closely resemble this year's risks of being harmed.

SEARCHING FOR CRIME WAVES: DETECTING VICTIMIZATION TRENDS

Each annual report from the *UCR* or the *NCVS* presents the latest findings about the current state of America's crime problem. But these are just snapshots that depict what went on during a relatively short period of time—one year. Trends refer to changes that occur over longer periods of time. Sharp increases in rates over several consecutive years are commonly known as "crime waves." Downward trends indicating reductions in the level of criminal activity can take place as well. To bring the big picture into focus, a key question that must be answered is whether the crime problem is becoming worse or getting better as the years roll by.

During the 1960s, a major crime wave swept across the country, according to the only annual source of nationwide data during that decade, the FBI's *UCR*s. Since 1973 the findings of the BJS's *NCVS* have provided an additional set of figures to monitor the upward and downward drifts in victimization rates.

Is the United States still in the midst of a crime wave? Few politicians or journalists dare to advance the argument that the sharp deterioration in public safety is over. But what do the statistics derived from the yearly government reports reveal? Are victimization rates rising, leveling off, or even dropping?

Changes Over Time in Violent Crime Rates

Graphs are particularly useful for spotting trends at a glance. Since two sources of official data can be tapped when looking for trends, the graphs can have two trend lines: one depicting changes over time in crime rates according to the *UCR* and the other according to the *NCVS*. The graphs shown in Figure 2.2 and Figure 2.3 depict the estimated rates for the violent crimes of robbery and aggravated assault committed across the country from 1973 to 1998.

Robbery is often cited as the offense most people worry about when they discuss their fears about street crime. Trends in robberies appear in the graph in Figure 2.2. The *UCR* trend line shows that robberies soared after 1977 and peaked in 1981, plunged until 1985, and then shot up again to record levels in the early 1990s. Then reports of muggings and holdups plummeted impressively. The *NCVS* trend line tells a similar story. It indicates that the robbery rate fell between 1974 and 1978, rebounded until 1981 when it hit an all-time high, dropped sharply during the early 1980s, but then climbed back up from 1985 until 1994. Then the robbery rate tumbled dramatically during the second half of the 1990s to its lowest levels since the *NCVS* surveys began.

Robbery and murder are the two crimes that continue to be the focus of this chapter, but a look at aggravated assault would be appropriate at this point. By definition, aggravated assaults result in serious injuries or involve the use or threatened use of a deadly weapon. Therefore, some aggravated assaults are attempted murders in which the victims barely survived (a bullet missed its mark, a knife wound was not fatal, or emergency medical care saved a life). The

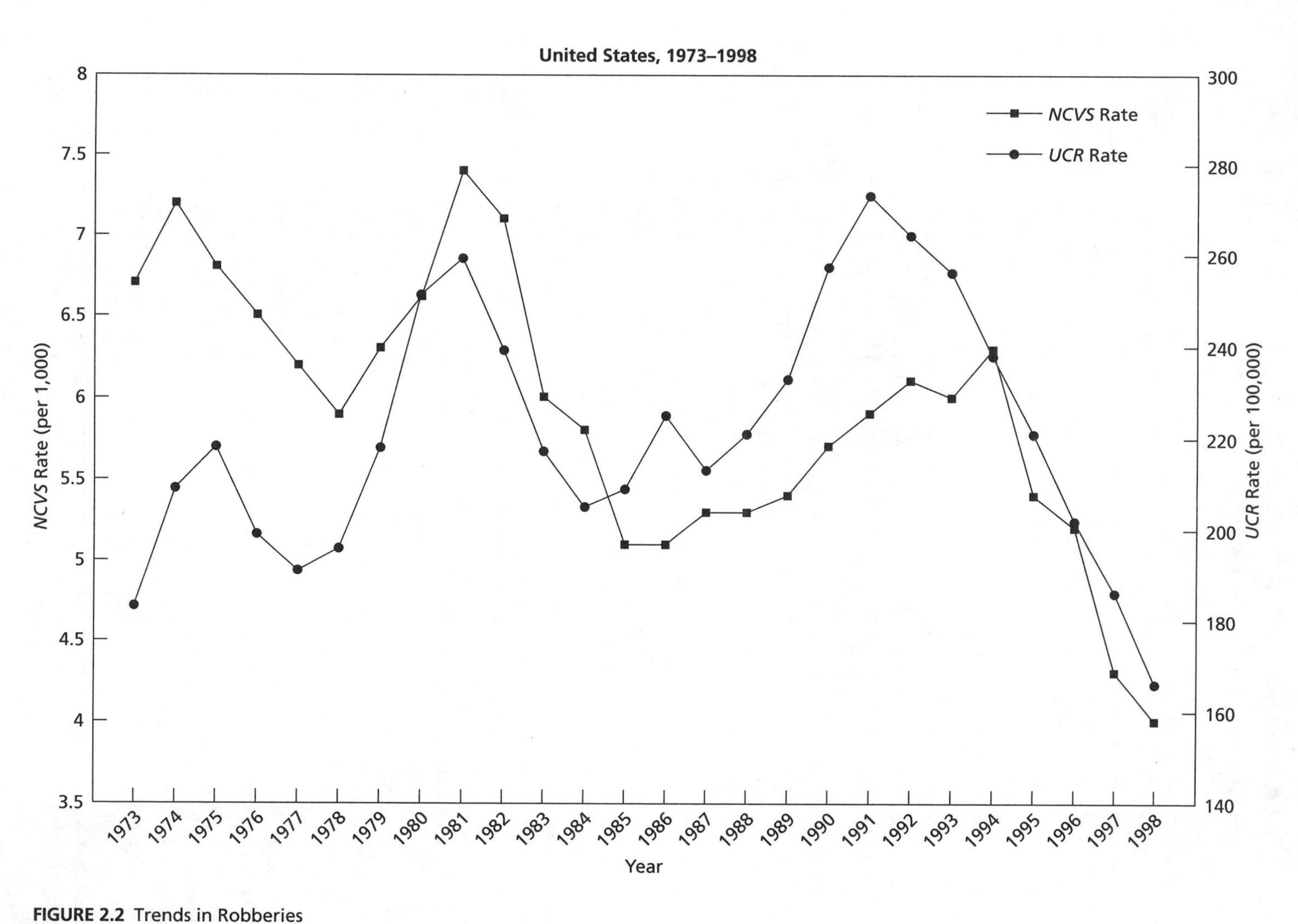

FIGURE 2.2 Trends in Robberies

NOTE: *UCR* includes reported commercial robberies. 1973–1991 *NCVS* findings adjusted for compatibility with the redesigned 1992 survey.
SOURCE: FBI's *UCRs*, 1973–1998; BJS's *NCVS*, 1973–1998

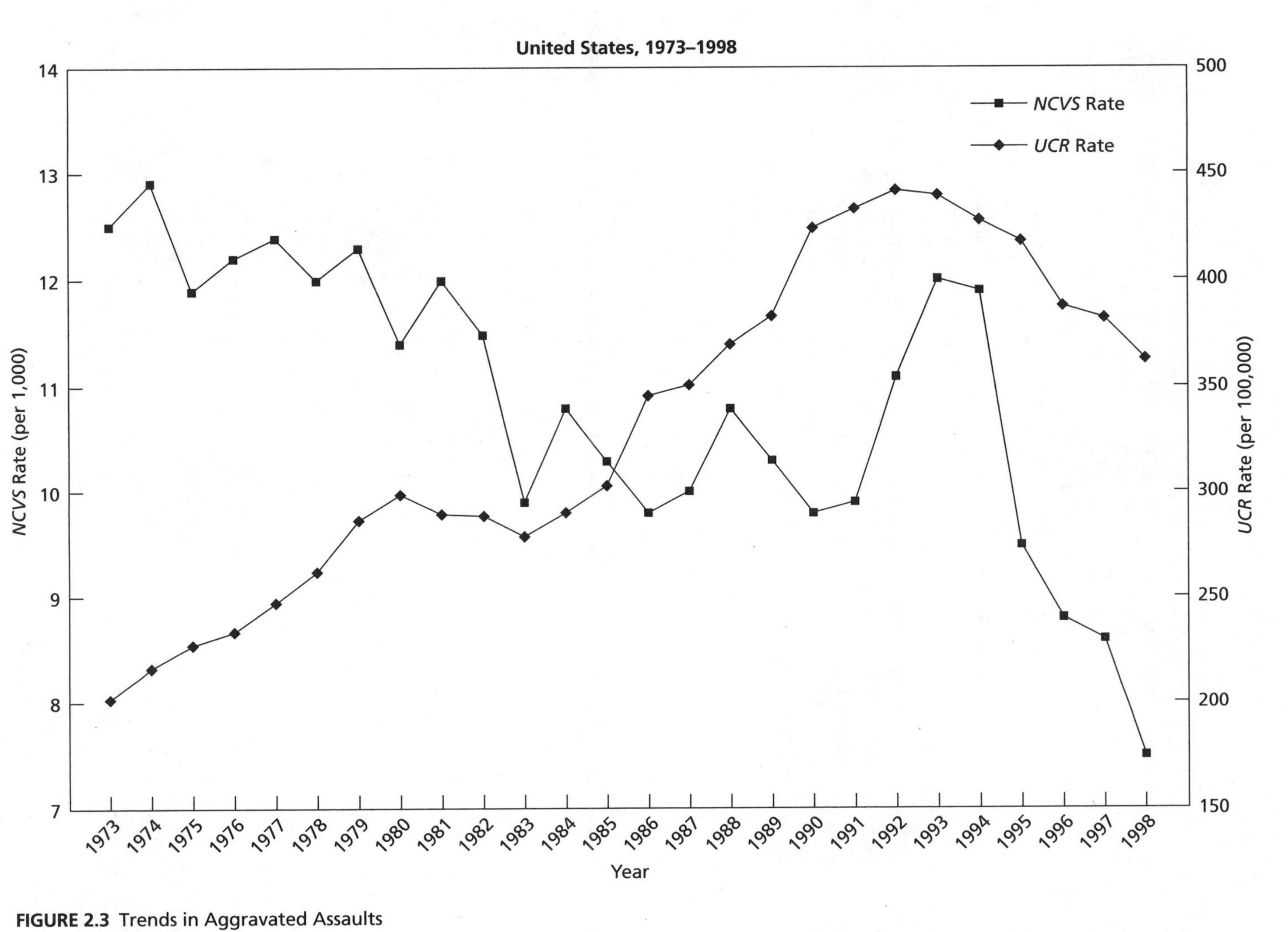

FIGURE 2.3 Trends in Aggravated Assaults

NOTE: *NCVS* 1973–1991 findings adjusted for compatibility with redesigned 1992 survey.
SOURCE: FBI's *UCRs*, 1973–1998; BJS's *NCVS*, 1973–1998

NCVS trend line graph in Figure 2.3 shows that close calls and near-death experiences of people shot or stabbed slightly declined in frequency over a 20-year period from the early 1970s until the early 1990s. Then the *NCVS* was redesigned, and the rate of aggravated assaults jumped in part because of the new measurement methods. However, by the end of the 1990s, a dramatic improvement in the level of serious interpersonal violence became evident from *NCVS* figures. *UCR* data shows a somewhat different pattern. After years of rising reports about serious attacks, complaints to the police about aggravated assaults peaked in the early 1990s. Then, just as the *NCVS* indicated, the level of violence subsided substantially during the second half of the 1990s.

Trends in homicide rates can be traced further back than changes over time in other crimes. The *UCR* has been monitoring murder since the beginning of the 1930s. But another source of data, drawn from death certificates by the National Center for Health Statistics, can be tapped to reconstruct what has happened since the start of the century. Graphing this data, as shown in Figure 2.4, facilitates the identification of steep rises and sharp drops in the murder rate over the years. Long-term trends can then be considered against a backdrop of major historical events affecting the nation as a whole.

As the trend line in Figure 2.4 indicates, homicide rates climbed rapidly soon after the statistical reporting system was initiated at the outset of the 1900s. In the three decades from 1903 to 1933, the murder rate soared from barely 1 person killed in every 100,000 each year to nearly 10 per 100,000 annually at the height of the Great Depression. Even though economic hardships continued throughout the 1930s, violent deaths plummeted, after Prohibition ended. Only 5 slayings took place per 100,000 inhabitants during the years of World War II. Following a brief surge in killings immediately after the war when most of the

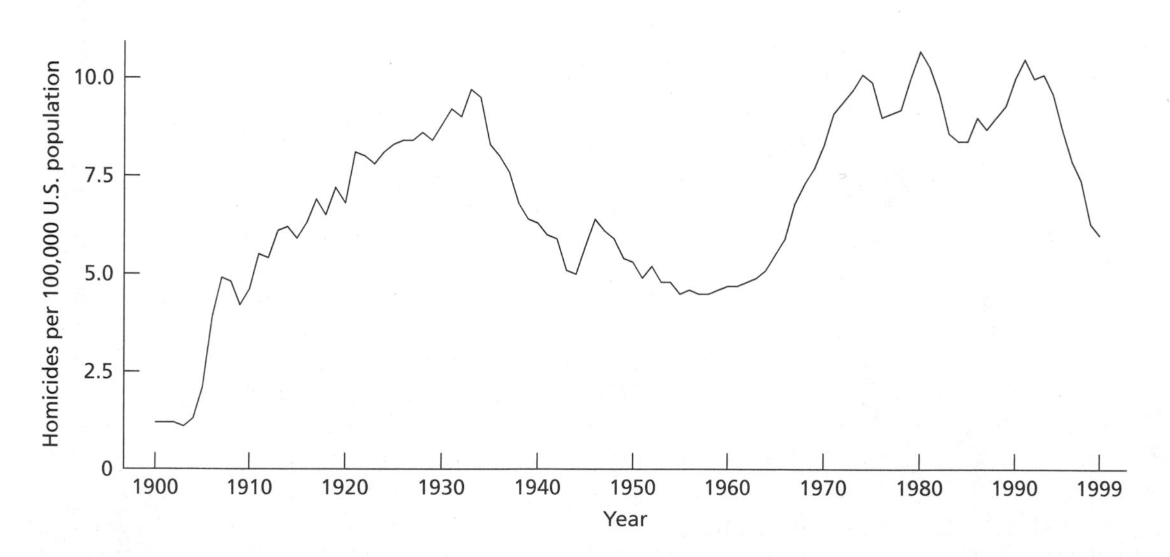

FIGURE 2.4 Trends in Murder Rates since 1900

SOURCE: National Center for Health Statistics, 1999

soldiers returned home, interpersonal violence continued to decline, reaching a low of about 4.5 victims per 100,000 persons by 1958. From the end of the 1950s to the late 1970s, slayings shot up again, reflecting the demographic impact of the baby boom generation passing through its most crime-prone teenage and young adult years, as well as the social turbulence that arose during the 1960s and lasted into the 1970s. An all-time high was recorded in 1980 when the homicide rate hit 11 deaths per 100,000 persons per year (BJS, 1988). After reaching that peak, murder rates dropped until the second half of the 1980s, when the crack epidemic touched off another escalation of bloodshed. By the start of the 1990s, murder rates once again were close to their highest levels for the century. But as the 1990s progressed, the fad of smoking crack and toting guns waned, the economy prospered, the proportion of the male population between 18 and 24 years old dwindled, and the murder rate plunged to close to 6 per 100,000 (Fox and Zawitz, 1999).

The graphs depicted in Figures 2.2, 2.3, and 2.4 surely indicate that violent crime rates have tumbled impressively from their historically high (and publicly intolerable) levels at the start of the 1990s. To conclude from this analysis of trends in murders, robberies, and aggravated assaults that the "worst is over" might be overly optimistic. Certainly, interpersonal violence is not "getting out of hand" or "spiraling out of control" (for the nation as a whole, although specific communities may be rocked by serious upsurges in lawlessness and bloodshed). No criminologist or victimologist knows for sure what the future holds. Predictions must be based on projected changes in a number of different variables, some very hard to anticipate and measure. Another crime wave could break out, or the dramatic improvement in America's crime problem that materialized as the century drew to a close might continue.

Checking Out Whether More Robberies Are Turning Into Murders

One more trend merits attention. How often do robberies escalate into murders? In other words, what are the chances of being killed by a robber? Robbers may fatally wound their victims inadvertently when quelling any resistance or wound them intentionally to prevent them from pressing charges and testifying in court.

A detailed study of over 100 criminal homicides occurring in Chicago during 1983 (that the police classified as robbery-related) revealed that different situations carried varying fatality risks. Whereas half of all robbery victims were accosted on the street, only about 20% of all slayings took place "right out in the open." Hence, being confined indoors during the confrontation seemed to heighten risks. Concerning resistance, the study revealed that a higher percentage of slain victims, compared to victims who were injured less severely or not at all, were actively resisting when they died. The researchers concluded that when confronted by an armed offender who growls "Your money or your life!" the correct response dictated by the data is to hand over the money (Zimring and Zuehl, 1986).

Researchers investigating trends in murders arising out of robberies in major U.S. cities concluded that from 1968 to 1973 the proportion of victims killed by robbers increased, remained roughly at the same level from 1973 until 1979, and then began to decline during the early 1980s (Cook, 1985). But some people have the impression that robbers kill their victims more readily "these days" than in the past. It is part of a despairing perception that American society is "falling apart," that "civilization is collapsing," and that offenders used to be of a "higher caliber" and today are more depraved and volatile than ever before.

In the aftermath of a vicious slaying, journalists sometimes play up this theme. This is nothing new. For example, in a news magazine cover story entitled "The Plague of Violent Crime" the following observation appeared: "Another frightening difference in the crime picture is that life is now pitifully cheap. Law enforcement officials think they have witnessed a shift toward gratuitous slaughter. 'It used to be "Your money or your life," says an assistant Bronx district attorney. . . . Now it's "Your money and your life" ' " (Press et al., 1981, p. 48).

When many older people discuss violence and theft "the way it used to be," they are referring to the 1940s and 1950s when street crime was not perceived to be a pressing problem or a major issue in electoral campaigns. Yet even during those "good old days," some people feared robbers would kill them even if they cooperated. A reporter at the time wrote

> The hoodlum will bash in your head with a brick for a dollar and ninety-eight cents. The police records of our cities are spotted with cases of "murder for peanuts" in which the victims, both men and women, have been slugged, stabbed, hit with iron pipes, hammers, or axes, and in a few cases kicked to death—the loot being no more than the carfare a woman carried in her purse or the small change in a man's pocket (Whitman, 1951, p. 5).

Is it true, as some people suspect, that more and more robberies are turning into murders? *UCR* statistics on murders and *NCVS* findings about robberies assembled in Box 2.1 can shed some light on this grisly question of whether there really is an upward trend in felony murders that started out as robberies.

Several tentative conclusions can be drawn from the data assembled in Table 2.2. In roughly 10% of all murders, the offender's motive was to take something of value and then escape. So getting away with a robbery is a common underlying motivation for taking a life. But, thankfully, slayings committed during the course of robberies are rare events. The number of robbery victims killed each year hovers around 2,000. But every year there are about a million confrontations in which a life could be lost. Hence, murdered victims constitute a tiny fraction—about one fifth of 1%—of all robbery victims (as few as 0.16% in 1984 and as many as 0.22% in 1991). That means that about 99.8% of all victims survive the ordeal of being robbed. Furthermore, there is no obvious upward trend, which means that there is no evidence to support the contention that, as time passes, robbers are becoming more inclined to snuff out the lives of their victims.

BOX 2.1 "Your Money or Your Life!"

The number of persons killed by robbers can be estimated from *UCR* figures on the numbers of murders and the motives of offenders, as surmised by the police. (A study of robbery-related homicides in Baltimore during 1983, however, revealed serious problems in the way deaths are classified. In a considerable proportion of murders, police investigations cannot uncover the motive for the slaying. And in some robbery-murders, the killer robbed the victim's corpse as an afterthought [see Loftin, 1986]). The number of robberies committed each year can be estimated from *NCVS* figures. (*UCR* figures are much smaller, representing only those robberies known to the police; however, because *NCVS* figures exclude robberies of commercial establishments, they are also underestimates of the actual but unknown grand total of personal and commercial robberies.)

Acknowledging the problems of uncertainty and incompatibility cited above, crude calculations can be performed to roughly estimate how often victims are murdered by robbers (see the computations in Table 2.2).

Table 2.2 Yearly Estimates of Murders Committed During Robberies

	1980	1982	1984	1986	
Number of persons murdered	23,040	21,010	18,690	20,610	
Percentage of murders where robbery was the motive	10.8	10.7	9.3	9.5	
Number of robbery victims killed	2,488	2,248	1,738	1,958	
Total number of robbery victims	1,179,000	1,334,000	1,117,000	1,009,000	
Murdered victims as a percentage of all robbery victims	0.21	0.17	0.16	0.19	
	1988	**1990**	**1991**	**1992**	**1993**
Number of persons murdered	20,675	23,440	24,700	23,760	24,520
Percentage of murders where robbery was the motive	8.3	9.2	10.2	10.0	9.9
Number of robbery victims killed	1,716	2,156	2,519	2,376	2,301
Total number of robbery victims	1,030,460	1,150,000	1,145,000	1,225,500	1,307,000
Murdered victims as a percentage of all robbery victims	0.17	0.19	0.22	0.19	0.18
	1994	**1995**	**1996**	**1997**	**1998**
Number of persons murdered	23,330	21,610	19,650	18,210	16,914
Percentage of murders where robbery was the motive	9.4	9.3	9.5	9.5	8.7
Number of robbery victims killed	2,193	2,010	1,867	1,730	1,472
Total number of robbery victims	1,299,000	1,142,000	1,134,000	944,000	886,000
Murdered victims as a percentage of all robbery victims	0.17	0.18	0.16	0.18	0.17

SOURCES: FBI's, *UCR* 1981–1998; BJS's, *NCVS* 1981–1998

USING THE *UCR* TO ANALYZE MURDERS

NCVS interviewers ask no questions about murder, but *UCR* reporting guidelines ask police officials to fill out a **Supplementary Homicide Report (SHR)** about each killing in their jurisdiction. The resulting *SHR* database provides information about the age, sex, and race of the victim and—if detectives solved the case by making an arrest—the accused person's age, sex, race, weapon, motive, and relationship to the victim.

Murder is the most terrible crime of all. The damage visited upon the victim cannot be undone. The loss suffered by the victim's survivors is total and irreparable. But the social reaction to the taking of a person's life varies dramatically. It is determined by a number of factors, including the offender's state of mind, the victim's possible contribution to the escalation of hostilities, the social standing of each party, where the crime was committed, how the victim was killed, and whether the killing attracted media coverage. Some homicides make headlines while others slip by virtually unnoticed except to the next of kin.

Homicide is defined as the willful (nonnegligent) killing of one human being by another. Not all homicides are punishable murders. Deaths caused by carelessness, accidents, and suicide are not classified as murders. Acts involving the legitimate use of deadly force in self-defense (justifiable homicides) are also excluded from the body counts, as are executions. The law takes into account whether the killing was carried out intentionally (malice aforethought), with deliberation (pros and cons weighed), and with premeditation (advance planning). Such first-degree murders carry the most severe punishments, including, depending upon the state, execution or life imprisonment without parole. Killing certain people—police officers; corrections officers; judges; witnesses; children; rape, kidnap, or robbery victims—may also be capital offenses. A homicide committed in the heat of passion, when the perpetrator intended to kill the victim (malice at the moment but with no advanced planning); or in response to the victim's provocations; or because of a reckless disregard for human life or gross negligence, is prosecuted as either a second-degree murder, a voluntary manslaughter, or an involuntary manslaughter. Offenders convicted of these deaths are punished less severely. Some types of slayings have special names (see Holmes, 1994): infanticide (of a newborn by a parent), parricide (of a parent by a child), domestic homicide (of a spouse), serial killing (several or more victims dispatched one at a time over an extended period), mass murder (several people killed at the same time and place), felony murder (committed as the culmination of another crime, like robbery or kidnapping), contract killing (a professional "hit" for a fee), and vehicular homicide (an accidental death caused by the driver of a car).

Murderers and Their Victims

The first criminologists who were attracted to victimology were drawn by the interaction between victims and offenders. They were especially curious about the relationship between the two parties in cases of interpersonal violence or theft. For example, they wondered whether the victim and the offender previously knew each other (as intimates, adversaries, or casual acquaintances), and whether the victims placed themselves in grave danger through their own actions. These issues are of particular importance in murder cases.

Data derived from the *SHRs* indicates that most murders can be categorized as male-on-male. About three quarters of the victims and 9 out of 10 offenders were boys or men. Most females (9 out of 10) also were murdered by males. When females kill they tend to slay the males in their lives rather than other females.

Most murders are intraracial. Focusing solely upon lone offender/single victim killings carried out during 1998, the *UCR* reported that 94% of black victims were slain by black offenders, and 87% of white victims were murdered by white perpetrators (note that most Hispanics were counted as whites on the *SHRs*).

During the 1990s the majority of murderers dispatched their victims by using firearms—handguns, rifles, and shotguns (rising from 64% in 1990 to just about 70% in 1993 before subsiding to 65% in 1998). Most of the bullets (about 80%) came from revolvers, with gunfire from shotguns and rifles taking a much smaller toll. Knives and other sharp instruments ran a distant second as the weapons of choice (accounting for less than 15% of all deaths). The rest of the victims were killed by blunt instruments, fists and feet, hands (largely via strangulation), and in assorted other ways (by explosions, from intentionally set fires, from poisons, by pushing, and other less frequent means).

The specific relationship between the victim and the offender can be broadly categorized to shed light on certain patterns within slayings. Three main categories can be distinguished. The victim and the offender were members of the same family (nuclear or extended), acquaintances or even close friends (including girlfriend or boyfriend) before the tragedy, or complete strangers brought together by fate. According to police investigations compiled in the FBI's *UCRs* during the 1990s, in the most common situation (ranging from 34 to 38%) the murder victim was killed by a friend or acquaintance. Killings of one family member by another added up to an additional 12 to 14% each year. Slayings by strangers accounted for about 13 to 15% of all the cases for which the relationship could be surmised by detectives. Unfortunately, homicides that were unsolved and thus "of unknown relationship" made up the largest category, hovering between 35 and 40%. If detectives could determine the victim-offender relationship in this residual grouping, the percentages due to family quarrels and confrontations with friends and strangers would be much larger and possibly of very different proportions. Proceeding on the basis only of solved cases, the old adage remains true that "a person is more likely to be killed by someone he or she knows than by a total stranger." But many of the murders that detectives fail to solve are suspected to have been killings committed by complete strangers, such as robbers. If the proportion of murders committed by strangers is rising, that would be a frightening development because it is more difficult to guard against attacks by unknown assailants (see Riedel, 1987). (*SHRs* are filled out shortly after killings take place. Police departments do not send in updated reports for cases that they solve months or years later.)

The relationship between the victim and the offender greatly influences how the case is handled within the criminal justice system. When victims are killed by complete strangers, prosecutors are inclined to indict them for the most serious charges allowed by law. If convicted, such offenders are likely to receive maximum sentences. In contrast, in cases of homicides arising out of quarrels between friends or acquaintances, prosecutors are likely to press charges that are less serious than first-degree murder. When former friends or acquaintances are convicted, they tend to receive lighter sentences. Perpetrators who were closely related to the dead victim usually receive even more lenient treatment. Discovered in a study of about 270 homicides in Houston, these patterns can be summarized as follows: The severity of the penalty for homicide varies with the distance within the victim-offender relationship (as closeness increases, punishment decreases) because of the way police, prosecutors, judges, and juries interpret and apply factors like malice, state of mind, intent, provocation, and self-defense (Lundsgaarde, 1977).

USING THE *NCVS* TO ANALYZE ROBBERIES

Robbers are usually complete strangers. Therfore, they are among the most feared and hated of all street criminals. Their offense combines stealing with extortion or outright violence (often including the use of deadly weapons), so it carries some of the stiffest prison sentences permissible under law. Throughout history, bandits were considered much more interesting than their victims, and their exploits were often romanticized. The highwaymen of Robin Hood's band, the pirates who plundered ships laden with treasure, the frontier outlaws who ambushed stagecoaches and trains, and the gangsters who held up banks during the Great Depression—all were the subjects of stories and songs sympathetic to, or at least understanding of, the impulse that drove their dramatic deeds. But the glitter has largely faded, and in its place is the image of the mugger or gunman as a vicious thug, a cruel predator, and an exploiter of weakness—one whose random violence casts a shadow over everyday life. This reversal in the imagery of robbers has sparked renewed concern for their victims.

Because nearly all robbery victims live to tell about their experiences, more details can be gathered about them than about people who were murdered. Some limited information about robberies that were reported to the police appears in the FBI's *UCR,* but the data describes the incidents and the arrestees—not the victims. The BJS's *NCVS* is the source to tap to find out about "who, how, where, when," plus losses, injuries, stolen property recovery rates, and reactions during the confrontations.

Robbers and Their Victims

All victim-offender interactions can be described in terms of a set of complementary roles. Each person plays a part. Robbers are the initiators and aggressors; victims are usually passive, at least at the start. But targeted individuals can refuse to play their "assigned" role, reject the "script," and overturn the scenario imposed on them. The intended prey might even gain the upper hand, switch roles, and disrupt the interaction or end it in a way dreaded by the aggressors. In other words, the incident may or may not proceed according to the offenders' plan.

Successful or completed robberies are those face-to-face confrontations in which perpetrators take something of value directly from victims against their will, either by force or by threats of violence. The law considers armed robberies more serious than unarmed ones ("strong-arm robberies," "muggings," or "yokings"). Successful robbers, whether armed or unarmed, must be skilled at what has been termed "target manipulation" or "victim management" (Letkemann, 1973).

When analyzed as a transaction based on "instrumental coercion" (applying force to accomplish a goal), a typical robbery proceeds through five stages, or phases: planning, establishing co-presence, developing co-orientation, transferring valuables, and leaving (Best and Luckenbill, 1982). During the planning stage the offenders prepare to strike by choosing accomplices, weapons, sites, and getaway routes. The robbers also choose their targets. They look for certain desirable characteristics, such as valuable possessions, vulnerability to attack, relative powerlessness to resist, and isolation from potential protectors. Strangers are preferred because they will have greater difficulty in providing descriptions to the police and in identifying suspects from pictures or lineups.

During the second phase of the interaction, the offenders establish co-presence by moving into striking distance. The robbers try not to arouse their victims' suspicion or to provoke either unmanageable opposition or fright and flight. Some offenders rely on speed and stealth to rush up to unsuspecting persons. Others employ deceit to trick people into letting down their guard.

When the one-sided transaction enters the third stage, the robbers announce their intentions to dominate the situation and exploit their advantages. They order victims to surrender valuables, and they demand compliance. Their intended prey either acquiesce or contest the robbers' bid to take charge, depending on their assessment of their aggressors' punitive resources (ability to inflict injury). Robbers who fail to develop co-orientation (secure compliance) through threats may resort to violence to subdue, incapacitate, or intimidate their targets.

If the robbers successfully gain and maintain the upper hand, the interaction moves into its fourth phase. Victims are searched and their valuables are seized. But the interaction is terminated prematurely (from the offenders' point of view) if the intended targets stubbornly resist, have no valuables, are unexpectedly rescued, or escape.

The fifth and final stage is marked by the robbers' attempts to break off the relationship at a time and under conditions of their choosing. As they prepare to leave the scene, they may inflict additional injuries in order to prevent interference with the getaway; or they may issue threats about the dangers of pursuing them or reporting the crime to the authorities (Best and Luckenbill, 1982).

This breakdown of robbery "transactions" into distinct stages and discrete steps facilitates the recognition of possible outcomes. Targeted individuals may or may not suffer financial losses from stolen (or damaged) property. Robbers may or may not injure their victims. Injured persons may or may not need medical attention and hospital care. The intended prey may or may not be able to resist their aggressors' advances and prevent successful completions. The police may or may not be brought in. And some victims who resist may be killed in incidents that escalate from robbery to homicide.

Findings From the *NCVS* That Shed Light on Robberies Respondents in the sample who confided that they had been recently robbed (within the past 6 months) provided *NCVS* interviewers with a wealth of data. They described the people who robbed them and the weapons used against them, and they disclosed whether the robbers got what they were after, where and when the crimes took place, if they resisted, whether they got hurt, and if so, how seriously. The answers from the individuals in the sample were used to derive projections about the experiences of all the Americans over the age of 11 who were robbed.

The primary motive behind robbery is theft. But offenders did not always get what they wanted. A little more than one third of all robberies were unsuccessful attempts to steal cash, valuables, or both. For the roughly two thirds of victims who were robbed of money or possessions, the mean loss averaged out to about $555 in 1992, a figure skewed by a relatively small number of huge hauls. If the median instead of the arithmetic mean is calculated, then in about half of all robberies the victims lost $90 or less (Klaus, 1994).

In 1992 victims told survey interviewers that about 80% of the individuals who used or threatened force were complete strangers that they had never seen before. Half of the incidents involved two or more persons working together. Almost all the perpetrators were males (96%), and most (62%) looked like they were younger than 29 years old. A little more than half (56%) were described as black. About 25% of all assailants were suspected of being high on drugs or alcohol at the time of the crime. The majority of the incidents (59%) took place between 6 P.M. and 6 A.M. As for the scene of the crime, the questionnaire category cited most often (40%) was "on the street" (but not near home or a friend's home). Other common locations were near home (11%); at home or in its immediate vicinity (10%); in a parking lot or garage (14%); and in a yard, park, playground, or field (6%). Very few victims were robbed on school grounds, on public transportation or in transit stations, or in bars or nightclubs. In answer to the question "What were you doing at the moment of the confrontation" victims most frequently responded that they were engaged in a leisure activity away from home (29%); another sizable category was "shopping or running errands" (11%). Only small percentages told interviewers they were on their way to school or work, or were attending school or at work when the robbers struck.

A little more than half (54%) of all the incidents were armed robberies. In about half of these armed robberies, offenders used knives, blunt instruments, and other weapons to intimidate and subdue their targets. The remainder (47%) involved a gun (mostly handguns). Therefore, victims faced the prospect of being shot in about one quarter of all robberies in 1992 (BJS, 1994d).

Robbers may hurt their victims for a number of reasons. They may do so initially to intimidate the target into submission. They may become violent during the holdup in reaction to any perceived resistance, noncooperation, or stalling. Offenders may relish taking advantage of a helpless person or may seize the opportunity to show off to accomplices. Injuring victims may be a sign of anger, scorn, contempt, sadism, fear, disappointment in the haul, or loss of self-control. It may also be instrumental: Wounding victims can render them incapable of later identifying the robbers, pursuing them, or even calling for help. Violent outbursts at the end of the interaction may be intended to shock, stun, or preoccupy victims, their associates, and any bystanders so that they will hesitate to call the police.

Despite all these possible motives for harming victims, most robbers didn't inflict injuries. A little more than one third of all robbery victims were wounded in 1992. (Some who escaped injuries were grabbed, shoved, and otherwise roughed up.) Among the wounded most victims experienced minor injuries, such as cuts, scratches, bruises, and swellings. About 1 in 12 suffered serious injuries, such as broken bones, lost teeth, loss of consciousness, or gunshot wounds that required medical care in a hospital emergency room. Just 3% of all robbery victims were hurt so badly that they had to remain in a hospital overnight or longer; 10% missed at least one day of work because of the consequences of the crime (BJS, 1994b).

The issue of resistance to attack is one of the more crucial subjects probed by interviewers carrying out the *National Crime Victimization Survey.* Different resistance strategies can lead to different outcomes. People targeted by robbers must make a split-second decision—whether to flee, fight, or otherwise resist, or to surrender and cooperate. *NCVS* interviewers asked victims about two sets of self-protective strategies: forceful means of repelling an attacker (including brandishing and using a gun, knife, or other weapon; or fighting back bare-handed to resist or capture the assailant) and nonviolent strategies (such as trying to escape, screaming to frighten off the offender and summon help, and threatening or reasoning with the offender). Of course, during a confrontation a victim might resort to more than one of these strategies. Combining the different kinds of self-protective measures, nearly 60% of robbery victims tried to defend themselves in 1992. The most common strategy was trying to physically resist or even capture the offender, followed by trying to run away or hide, trying to reason with or scare off the offender, or shouting for help. Fighting back bare-handed was also a common reaction, but drawing a weapon in self-defense was rare (BJS, 1994b).

Victims who were injured during a robbery were more likely to have taken some self-protective measures, as were victims who thwarted the robbers' intentions (the acts of theft were not successfully completed). The answers to the survey's questions cannot reveal whether victims who ended up injured started out by acquiescing to the robbers' demands or whether they resisted from the outset. The sequence of events cannot be reconstructed from the cross-sectional survey data. It cannot be established, for example, whether victims who resisted forcefully were fighting before, during, or after the robbers physically attacked them. The link between injury and resistance also depended on a number of other situational factors, especially the presence of weapons, other robbers, and other victims. Several researchers have tried to make sense of the complicated web of interconnections (three- and four-variable relationships) between the weapons brandished, the outcome in regard to theft, forms of resistance, and extent of injury. According to a study of cases reported to the *NCVS* between 1973 and 1979 (Cook, 1987), certain types of victims were more likely to be injured than other types, depending in part on the kind of robbers they faced (armed or unarmed, alone or in groups) and the form of resistance, if any, they offered (violent versus nonviolent tactics). Victims were more likely to be physically harmed and need medical attention if they were attacked by three or more robbers or by a complete stranger, or if they were alone when accosted and were older than 55.

The type of weapon wielded by the robber was the most significant factor determining whether or not a victim was wounded or killed. Although gunmen slay their victims 3 times as often as knife-wielding robbers, a different pattern prevailed in nonlethal confrontations. In several studies researchers concluded that an inverse relationship existed between the likelihood of victim injury and the use of deadly weaponry. That means that victims were more likely to be hurt by unarmed robbers. Apparently, weaponless "muggings," "yokings," or "strong-arm" robberies often began with an unprovoked attack meant to demonstrate the aggressors' determination to prevail. An alternative explanation is that victims might have resisted unarmed robbers until their assailants began to apply force. Armed robberies that unfolded with the brandishing of a gun or knife were less likely to escalate into bloodshed because the threat posed by the deadly weapon was sufficient to convince most victims to surrender without a struggle (Cook, 1987). A study of nearly 3,000 stranger-to-stranger incidents reported to *NCVS* interviewers between 1973 and 1979 yielded these observations: Nonforceful resistance (which included reasoning with, arguing with, and verbally threatening the offender, as well as yelling for help or trying to run away) was statistically linked to both lower monetary losses and reduced levels of physical attack and injury. Forceful resistance (fighting back bare-handed or with a weapon), though also associated with lower property losses, was tied to higher injury rates (Block and Skogan, 1986). Similarly, an analysis of over 4,500 incidents reported to interviewers from 1979 to 1985 resulted in these conclusions: Any form of self-protective tactic reduced the chances that the robber would get away with any valuables, armed resistance was a much more effective form of self-protection than unarmed resistance, and drawing a gun was the most effective response of all (in terms of thwarting the robbers' intentions and avoiding injuries) but it was very rarely possible or attempted. Fighting back without a weapon and calling for help (to attract attention and scare off the attacker) tended to lead to injuries. Facing a gun inhibited resistance, but since the weapon was rarely fired, most stickup victims wound up losing their possessions but escaping injury (Kleck and DeLone, 1993).

Starting in 1986, questions were added to the *National Crime Victimization Survey* about how victims judged the consequences of their self-protective measures. In 1992, 55% of all robbery victims told *NCVS* interviewers that their self-protective actions probably helped their situation, whereas about 9%

concluded their reactions hurt them. In the opinion of the remainder of the sample, victims said their actions both helped and hurt, neither helped nor hurt, or had an unknown effect on their offenders. Of those who believed their actions helped, nearly half judged that the beneficial impact was to minimize or prevent injuries to themselves. The rest answered that their resistance served to ward off their attackers, to facilitate their escape, and to safeguard the items the robbers sought. As for unwanted outcomes 59% of the victims who took self-protective measures felt, in retrospect, that their actions had made their assailants angrier and more aggressive (BJS, 1994).

It is tempting but dangerous to offer any advice based on the successes and failures of previous robbery victims. The outcomes of robberies in terms of both injuries and losses are determined by a complex web of interactions among offenders' initiatives (choice of weapon and target), victims' responses (unwillingness to cooperate), offenders' reactions to resistance (willingness to escalate or to give up and disengage), bystanders' initiatives (willingness to intervene), and other situational factors (number of offenders, number of victims, location, time, value of property at risk). Consequently, no simple rules of thumb or foolproof stratagems can be derived from the data. Since some studies indicated that victims who complied with robbers' demands were more likely to escape injury, criminal justice officials have tended to recommend trading valuables for personal safety. Some experts even have suggested that potential robbery targets should always carry sums of money they feel they can afford to lose and should hand over these "crime taxes" immediately to appease robbers' demands. But others have argued that victims can help deter crime by using various strategies, (depending on circumstances) to make robbery attempts unprofitable, frustrating, and even dangerous for aggressors (see Ziegenhagen and Brosnan, 1985; Kleck and DeLone, 1993).

MAKING INTERNATIONAL COMPARISONS

When bringing the big picture into focus, it is important to recognize that victimization rates vary from society to society, as well as from time to time and place to place within a country. Cross-national comparisons that reveal the magnitude of the crime problem in other societies can yield valuable clues about the causes of illegal behavior as well as innovative policies for prevention and control.

The two main sources of data about victimization rates in other countries are the United Nations (UN), which periodically surveys its members, and the International Police Organization (Interpol), which has cooperative relationships with law enforcement agencies around the world.

But for a number of reasons making international comparisons can be difficult and conclusions can be misleading. First of all, many governments do not disclose any reliable data on crime or they publish figures that seem unrealistically low, probably because they fear that high rates and rankings near the top will damage their nation's public image and scare off potential tourists and investors. Even when governments make an effort to be cooperative and to carry out accurate measurements, problems arise because of differences in definitions (for example, of rape, robbery, and burglary) and in reporting and record-keeping practices. One researcher who studied cross-national crime data came to these conclusions: Compared to other nations providing trustworthy statistics, U.S. victimization rates for violent crimes were very high, those for auto theft were fairly high, and those for burglary were near the middle of the range (Kalish, 1988). Violence is more of a problem in the United States than in other highly developed societies, but theft is not (Zimring and Hawkins, 1997).

Comparing the Murder Rates in Different Societies

The UN's World Health Organization (WHO) keeps track of homicides in most countries across the globe. But statistics on murder in various societies must be interpreted with great caution. Each country's definitions reflect laws and local customs that govern the way acts leading to death are classified. For international comparisons to be valid, definitions of which types of killings constitute murder must be consistent. For example, certain countries may count attempted murders, whereas cases in which victims survive are classified as aggravated assaults in the United States. Other inconsistencies arise if countries include deaths from legal interventions (such as the use of deadly force by police officers and executions), totally unintentional deaths (negligent manslaughter), and self-induced deaths (suicides)—all of which are excluded from U.S. figures (Kalish, 1988).

The Interpol data presented in Table 2.3 reveals that most technologically advanced Western societies—except for the United States—have relatively low murder rates. The developing nations of Asia, Africa, and Latin America show greater variation. Some report very low homicide rates even though the levels of interpersonal violence are much higher in neighboring countries. However, some of the killings that boost the murder rate in strife-torn societies across the globe are not the outgrowth of street crime but the result of intense political polarization, expressed as vigilantism, terrorism, and low intensity guerrila warfare.

Since some societies are strikingly different from others in terms of their economic systems, criminal justice systems, cultural traditions, and age distributions, it might make more sense to limit any comparisons of murder rates to fairly similar highly industrialized nations. Since a key determinant of the murder rate in any country is simply the proportion of the population that falls into the highest risk group (young males), one way to deal with variations is to calculate the homicide rate for every 100,000 teenage boys and young men in each society. Following this procedure and then restricting the comparison only to other highly industrialized societies, the United States stood out as having the worst murder rate during the late 1980s (Deane, 1987; Rosenthal, 1990).

When the murder rates in various countries are analyzed, higher rates tend to be associated with great economic inequality (huge gaps between the wealthy and the poor), limited government funding of social programs for the disadvantaged, cultural supports for "legitimate" violence by government officials and agencies (frequent executions and periodic warfare), family breakdown (high divorce rates), high rates of female participation in the labor force, and ethnic heterogeneity (see Gartner, 1990).

Table 2.3 Murder Rates Across the Globe: Selected Countries, 1998

Nation	Murder Rate, per 100,000 inhabitants	Nation	Murder Rate, per 100,000 inhabitants
Albania	17	Iceland	0
Argentina	3	Ireland	2
Australia	2	Israel	2
Austria	1	Italy	2
Bahamas	16	Jamaica	37
Bangladesh	3	Japan	1
Barbados	3	Korea (South)	2
Belgium	2	Kuwait	1
Brazil	21	Latvia	8
Bulgaria	5	Lithuania	9
Canada	2	Netherlands	1
Cameroon	0	Norway	1
Chile	4	Panama	2
Colombia	56	Philippines	13
Croatia	2	Poland	2
Czech Republic	3	Portugal	2
Denmark	1	Romania	2
Dominican Republic	16	Russia	18
Ecuador	12	Senegal	1
El Salvador	38	Singapore	1
Estonia	14	Spain	1
Fiji	2	Switzerland	1
Finland	0	Tanzania	6
France	2	Trinidad	7
Germany	1	Turkey	3
Ghana	2	Ukraine	8
Greece	1	United Kingdom	2
Guyana	15	United States	6
Hong Kong	1	Uruguay	7
Hungary	3	Zimbabwe	6

SOURCE: International Criminal Police Organization (Interpol), 1998

ASSESSING COMPARATIVE RISKS

Putting Crime Into Perspective

Another important way of discerning the big picture involves weighing the relative threats posed by different kinds of misfortunes. The chance of being harmed by a criminal needs to be compared to the odds of being hurt in an accident or of contracting a serious illness. The study of comparative risks rests on estimates of the likelihoods of experiencing various negative life events. One purpose of studying comparative risks is to determine which types of threats (crimes, accidents, or diseases) merit greater precautionary measures by both individuals and government-sponsored campaigns. (A more comprehensive list of calamities could be expanded to include fires and natural disasters such as floods, tornadoes, earthquakes, and hurricanes.) Once the chances of being stricken by an unwanted event are expressed in a standardized way (as rates per 100,000 people) different dangers can be compared, as they are in Table 2.4.

The nationwide data assembled in Table 2.4 for people of all ages, both sexes, and varying backgrounds indicates that in general, deaths from natural causes greatly exceeded losses of life from external causes. In particular, heart disease, cancer, and stroke were by far the leading causes of death in the United States as the 20th century drew to a close. As for other untimely demises, more people died from accidents of all kinds than from homicides (murders plus justifiable homicides by police officers and executions of death row prisoners). In fact, more people took their own lives than lost them due to lethal violence which ranked at the bottom of the list.

However, the usefulness of the comparison of the death rates shown in Table 2.4 is limited because these figures describe the risks faced by the "average American," a social construct that each person resembles to some extent. But the actual odds that a specific individual faces may differ tremendously from this fictitious norm. The most important determinants of mortality rates are age, sex, race/ethnicity, social class, and place of residence. To make more meaningful comparisons, some of these important variables must be controlled (held constant) (see

Table 2.4 Comparing the Risks of Death Posed by Crime, Accidents, and Certain Diseases

Cause of Death	Number of Deaths 1998	Death Rate per 100,000
All Causes	2,339,000	865
—Natural Causes—		
Heart Problems (cardiovascular diseases)	940,000	348
Cancers (malignant neoplasms)	539,000	199
Strokes (cerebrovascular diseases)	158,000	59
Lung Problems (pulmonary diseases)	114,000	42
Pneumonia	95,000	35
Diabetes	65,000	24
—External Causes—		
Accidents (excluding motor vehicles)	51,000	19
Motor Vehicle Accidents	42,000	16
Suicides	29,000	10
Homicides (and legal intervention)	17,000	6

NOTE: All deaths rounded to the nearest thousand.
SOURCE: U.S. CDC's National Center For Health Statistics, 1999

Fingerhut, Ingram, and Feldman, 1992a, 1992b). For example, for Americans between the ages of 15 and 24, homicide was the second leading cause of death. Accidents (including car crashes) claimed twice as many lives as homicides, but at the end of the 1990s many more teenagers and young adults died from violence than from suicide, heart attacks, cancer, strokes, AIDS, or any other diseases. Also, within every age group, being murdered loomed as much more of a danger to boys and men than to girls and women (see Kramgrow, et al., 1999).

Another obvious problem with risk comparisons is that the ranking represents a snapshot image of a fluid situation. Thus, Table 2.4 captures a moment frozen in time—the relative standing of the dangers of accidents, diseases, and crime in 1998. But it cannot depict underlying trends. For example, an encouraging downward trend in fatal accidents took place during the 1980s, according to a study by the National Safety Council. Deaths due to plane crashes, falls, drownings, fires, and poisonings all dropped during that decade (probably as a result of greater safety consciousness as well as new devices like smoke detectors and car seats for little children and new policies like mandatory seat belt laws and tougher penalties for drunk driving). By the 1990s, the risk of dying in a car crash had fallen to its lowest level since the 1920s (Hall, 1990). During the 1990s the chances of getting slain diminished impressively, as did the odds of perishing shortly after contracting full-blown AIDS. As the chances of dying accidentally, from a deadly disease, or from a violent attack rise and fall over time, any listing of comparative risks must undergo periodic revision.

To further complicate the picture, occupation must be taken into account when comparing the risks of becoming a crime victim to the risk of suffering a fatal injury at work. Naturally, risks are closely tied to tasks; some jobs are much more dangerous than others. Focusing on deaths in the workplace, studies conducted by the National Institute for Safety and Health and by the federal government's Bureau of Labor Statistics established that fatal accidents take place most often in construction (34 deaths per 100,000 workers per year), farming and forestry (26 deaths per 100,000), and transportation (23 deaths per 100,000). Putting accidents aside, researchers discovered that certain lines of work carry much greater risks of being murdered on the job. Taxi drivers and chauffeurs are the most vulnerable of all employees; 15 out of every 100,000 are killed while driving their vehicles each year (not counting traffic fatalities). Law enforcement officers have the second most dangerous occupation—9 slain per 100,000 per year. Compared to the national average of 0.7 homicides per 100,000 workers, other hazardous jobs (rate per 100,000 workers) include being a hotel clerk (5), a gas station attendant (nearly 5), a security guard (almost 4), a stock handler (3), a store owner or manager (nearly 3), and a bartender (a little more than 2). Throughout the 1980s about 750 people were murdered while doing their jobs each year; these shootings and stabbings accounted for 12% of all on-the-job deaths during that time period. During the first half of the 1990s, more than 1,000 people were slain while working each year, constituting about 17% of all occupational fatalities (the remaining deaths were attributed to motor vehicle collisions, falls, fires, explosions, exposure to harmful substances, and assorted other causes). Any valid study of comparative risks should conclude with recommendations for reducing and eliminating dangers. A variety of measures might bring down the number of workplace homicides: installing better lighting; minimizing the amount of cash an employee handles; making dangerous work sites visible to more people; installing alarms, bulletproof enclosures, and surveillance cameras; increasing the number of staff on duty; adopting policies that urge employees not to resist robbers; increasing police patrols of work sites; closing establishments late at night; and providing conflict-resolution training so that disgruntled employees who were fired do not retaliate by attacking supervisors and coworkers (Associated Press, 1993c; "The Feds Make It Official," 1993; Warchol, 1998).

These observations—that individuals face widely varying risks depending upon which groups they fall into—merits closer attention.

UNCOVERING VICTIMIZATION PATTERNS

Recognizing Differential Risks

Victimization rates for the entire population indicate how frequently murders, rapes, robberies, and assaults are committed against "average Americans," and how often "typical households" suffer burglaries and motor vehicle thefts. It is reasonable to suspect that the chance of becoming a victim is not uniform but more likely for some and less likely for others (just as different categories of people do not face the same odds of getting hurt accidentally, say from a skiing mishap, or of contracting a particular disease, such as AIDS). In terms of attributes like sex and age, certain categories of people may be burdened by crime much more or much less than others. If these suspicions can be documented, then overall rates projecting the risks for all Americans might mask important variations by subgroups. In other words, victimologists must disaggregate, or break down, general victimization rates to reveal the substantial differences faced by particular categories of people.

A pattern within a victimization rate is recognizable when one category suffers significantly more than another. (The most obvious example is the incidence of rape: Females are much more likely to be sexually violated than are males.) Searching for patterns means looking for regularities within a seemingly chaotic mass of information and finding predictability within apparently random events. To discover patterns, researchers must sort out the data collected each year into its component parts—the various groupings of people and households that participated in the survey. Patterns can emerge when rates are calculated separately for each grouping within a variable, especially sex, age, race, marital status, income class, and area of residence. Once a pattern has been established over the years, then differential risks observed in the past can be projected into the future. For example, since men have been assaulted more often than women (according to the annual surveys), it can be predicted that men face greater risks of being attacked than women next year and in the foreseeable future, unless major social changes affecting interpersonal violence take place.

The differential risks derived from victimization patterns will be investigated for the crimes of murder and robbery.

Differential Risks of Being Murdered

A number of striking patterns within homicides (which should be especially alarming for those who fall into some or all of the high-risk categories, and somewhat reassuring for all others) emerge when the FBI compiles statistics from *SHRs* and publishes them in the annual *UCRs*. The risks of being murdered vary greatly by geographic location (region of the country), area of residence (urban, suburban, or rural), sex, age, and race.

First of all, the murder rate varies substantially in different sections of the country. Over the decades, the highest homicide rates have been found in the South (8 out of every 100,000 southerners were killed in 1998). The risks of getting slain were half as bad in the Northeast (at 4 deaths for every 100,000 residents). The murder rate fell in between these two extremes in both the Midwest and the West (6 per 100,000 in each region).

The second factor of importance also is geographic in nature. People living in metropolitan areas faced higher risks of being murdered (7 per 100,000) than residents of rural counties (at 5) or of small cities beyond the fringe of metropolitan areas (at 4). A closer look at the FBI's data from municipal police departments confirms that some big cities were much more dangerous places to live than others. The map in Figure 2.5 indicates that in 1998, among the 10 largest cities in the country, violent deaths were much more common in Detroit, Chicago, Philadelphia, and Dallas than in New York, San Antonio, and San Diego (when size is taken into account, the only sound way to make such comparisons). Other big cities with high murder rates include New Orleans, Atlanta, and Washington, D.C. The disparities are not a function of size but seem to be determined by local conditions such as the area's population density, its local economy (including the poverty and unemployment rates, wage scales, and the gap between the rich and the poor), its special problems (such as the availability of handguns, the extent of drug trafficking, and outbreaks of "wars" between rival drug crews, street gangs, and mob families), local traditions and customs (including the persistence of a subculture of violence), and demographic factors (especially divorce rates and the proportion of the population that is poor, male, young, and of marginalized minority group background) (Tardiff, Gross, and Messner, 1986; Chilton, 1987; Land, McCall, and Cohen, 1990; Messner and Golden, 1992). Urban homicide rates can flare up or die down considerably from year to year as local conditions deteriorate or improve (see Karmen, 2000).

Sex is another crucial determinant of risks. More than three quarters of the people murdered were males (a proportion that has remained roughly the same since at least the early 1960s). Expressed as rates, boys and men were killed about 4 times as often as girls and women (14 per 100,000 compared to 3.5 per 100,000).

Besides geographical location and sex, murder rates vary dramatically by age (see Akiyama, 1981). Ten-year-olds are the least likely and 25-year-olds the most

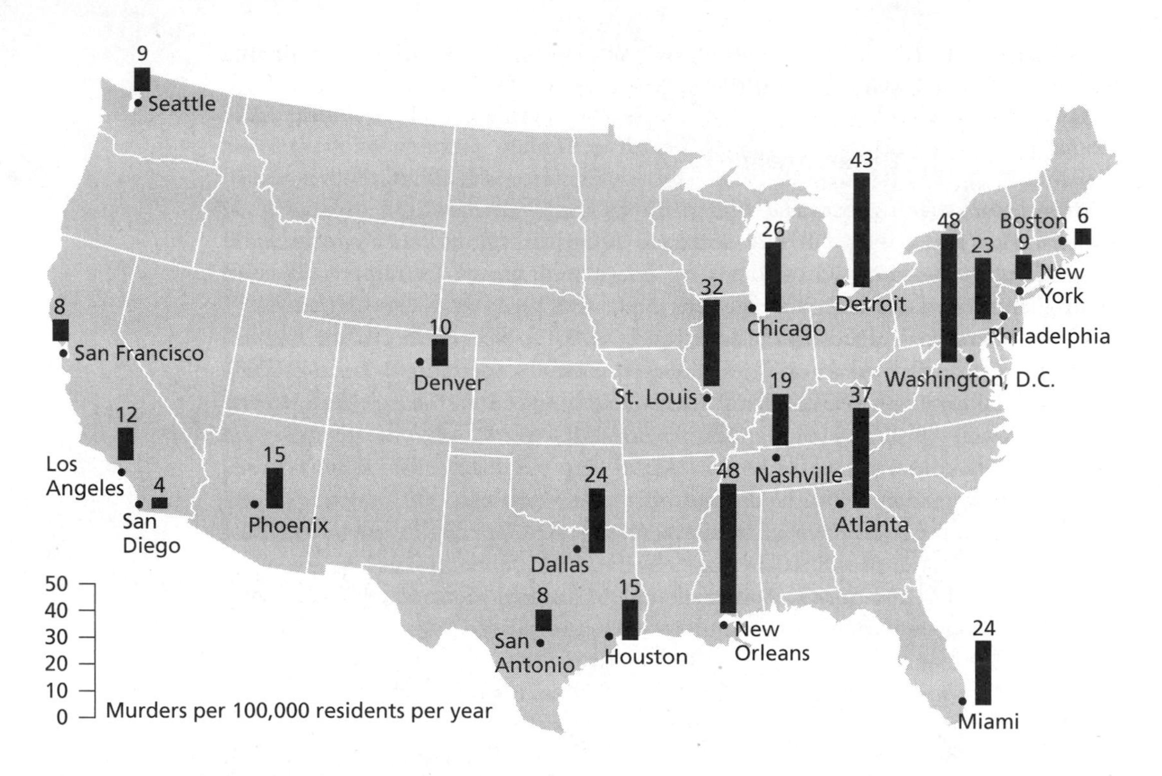

FIGURE 2.5 Murder Rates in Major Cities, 1998

NOTE: Murder rates were calculated on the basis of the population living within city limits and not for the entire metropolitan area of surrounding counties.
SOURCE: FBI's 1998 *UCR*

likely to be murdered. After rising during the teenage years and peaking during the mid-20s, the risks of dying violently drop rapidly.

Statistically, race turns out to be the most important of all the demographic factors associated with differential risks. African Americans confront much graver dangers of dying violently. Nearly half (48%) of all murder victims were African American in 1998, while an equal proportion were white (including most Hispanics); the remainder (2%) were of "other" races (mostly Asians). Since people who identified themselves as "black" on the 1990 census constituted about 12% of the U.S. population, black representation among the ranks of the dead was disproportionally high. Calculating homicide rates by race, 3 whites out of every 100,000 were slain in 1998 (6,931 victims out of a population of 223 million). The comparable figure for blacks was 19 per 100,000 (6,619 victims out of a population of 34.4 million)—more than 6 times higher.

From this review of the demographic factors that are correlated with murder rates, a profile can be derived of the groups of people who run the greatest risks of suddenly dying from an act of violence. They are southerners, urban residents, males, teenagers and young adults between 18 and 24, and African Americans. (Low-income persons are probably in this high-risk group as well, but police files and FBI compilations do not collect information about the victim's social class.) Those who fall into the opposite groups face the lowest risks of all: northeasterners, residents of rural areas, females, children and the elderly, and whites (and the wealthy).

Since World War II—and in particular between the mid-1980s and the mid-1990s—the most ominous change concerning homicides has been the trend toward the decreasing age of both killers and their victims. The escalation in the level of lethal violence among teenagers is largely attributed by criminologists to the revival of street gangs and the formation of drug-dealing crews, their willingness to resort to force to settle even minor disputes, their easier access to handguns, and their involvement with cocaine and alcohol. As the 1990s drew to a close, these pressing problems subsided (Blumstein and Rosenfeld, 1998).

Differential Risks of Being Robbed

When the respondents in the *NCVS* sample are broken down into subcategories according to various demographic attributes, sharp differences in robbery rates become evident. Certain groupings of people are robbed much more often than others, as Table 2.5 demonstrates.

Depending upon their attributes, certain individuals have much more to fear than others. Starting with sex, the first pattern that stands out is that robbers target males more often than females. As for race and ethnicity, the robbery rate suffered by black people was higher than the rates for white and Asian people. Hispanics also were burdened by much higher robbery rates. With regard to age, the analysis of the surveys' findings revealed that younger persons (between the ages of 12 and 24) get robbed much more often than older people. Individuals in their late teens ran the gravest risks of all. After those peak years, rates declined steadily with advancing age. Contrary to the impression that robbers prey primarily upon the frail, senior citizens were targeted the least often of any age group. Family income appeared to be negatively correlated with victimization rates: As income increased the chances of being robbed decreased (except for those earning from $25,000 to $35,000). In addition to sex, age, race/ethnicity, and income, marital status made a big difference: Single individuals who had never been married or who were separated or divorced endured much higher robbery rates than married or widowed persons (who generally were older and tended to be females). Residents of urban areas were targeted more often than suburbanites who in turn faced greater chances of being accosted than their rural, small-town counterparts. Regionally, robberies posed a graver problem for residents of the West and a lesser threat to inhabitants of the Northeast, with people living in the South and Midwest experiencing rates that were in between (Rennison, 1999).

To summarize the *NCVS* findings compiled in Table 2.5, higher risks were faced by men rather than women, minorities rather than members of the white majority, young persons more than middle-aged or elderly people, single or divorced individuals over married couples, poor people rather than those who are better off financially, city residents rather than people living in suburbs or small towns, and inhabitants of the West rather than the Northeast. Combining

Table 2.5 Robbery Rates for Various Groups, 1998

Victim Characteristics	1998 Rate
Overall rate	4.0
Sex	
Male	4.6
Female	3.5
Race	
White	3.7
Black	5.9
Other	4.4
Ethnicity	
Hispanic	6.3
Non-Hispanic	3.7
Age	
12–15	7.7
16–19	11.4
20–24	7.9
25–34	4.2
35–49	3.2
50–64	1.7
65 and older	0.5
Marital status	
Married	1.3
Widowed	1.2
Divorced or separated	6.8
Never married	8.0
Family income	
Less than $7,500	6.5
$7,500–$14,999	5.8
$15,000–$24,999	3.6
$25,000–34,999	6.9
$35,000–$49,999	3.1
$50,000–$74,999	2.8
$75,000 or more	2.9
Region	
Northeast	3.2
Midwest	3.8
South	3.8
West	5.2
Residence	
Urban	6.5
Suburban	3.2
Rural	2.6

NOTES: Rates are per 1,000 people with these characteristics per year.
SOURCE: BJS's *NCVS* of 1998; Rennison, 1999.

these factors, the profile of the person facing the gravest dangers of all is that of a poor, African-American or Hispanic-American teenage boy living in a western city. Affluent, elderly white ladies living in rural areas of the Northeast lead the safest lives. Unfortunately, the *NCVS* report does not calculate a victimization rate for comparison purposes for an individual who falls into all the high-risk or all the low-risk subcategories.

One additional variable is worthy of consideration—occupation. Robbery rates differ substantially by the victim's occupation. Statistics from the *NCVS* from the 1980s indicated that people holding the following (generally less desirable) jobs were much more likely to be robbed: taxi drivers, gardeners, busboys, dishwashers, carnival and amusement park workers, car wash attendants, messengers, newspaper carriers, peddlers, and certain kinds of construction workers. However, persons who were musicians and composers, painters and sculptors, and photographers also were victimized at above-average rates. Those least likely to be robbed worked as inspectors, line workers, bank tellers, opticians, farmers, professional athletes, elementary school teachers, engineers, and psychologists (Block, Felson, and Block, 1995). During the first half of the 1990s, retail sales workers, especially clerks at convenience stores and liquor stores, were robbed the most, along with cab drivers. Teachers, especially college professors, faced the lowest risks of being robbed or assaulted (Warchol, 1998).

PROJECTING CUMULATIVE RISKS

Estimating Lifetime Likelihoods

Yearly victimization rates might lull some people into a false sense of security. Annual rates give the impression that crime is a rare event. Only a handful of people out of every thousand fall prey to offenders; most people get through the year unscathed. But fears about victimizations do not conform to a January-to-December cycle; people worry that they will be robbed, raped, or murdered at some point in their lifetimes. For that reason the Bureau of Justice Statistics occasionally provides estimates of the likelihood of a person being harmed during the course of a lifetime. Estimates of the cumulative risks of victimization, viewed over a span of 60 or more years (from age 12 into the 70s, the average life expectancy in the United States today), yield a very different picture of the seriousness of the contemporary crime problem nationally. What appears to be a rare event in any given year looms as a real threat over the course of an entire lifetime (Koppel, 1987).

Over a span of about 60 years nearly everybody will experience at least one theft, and most people may eventually suffer three or more thefts, according to the projections made on the basis of rates that prevailed during the 1970s and 1980s, as presented in Table 2.6. Although the chance that a girl or woman will be raped in a given year is minuscule, it rises to a lifetime threat of 80 per 1,000, or 8%, (about 1 female in every 12). For black females the risks are somewhat greater (at 11% or nearly 1 in 9) over a lifetime. Robbery is a more common crime, so the projection is that about 30% of the population will be robbed at least once in a lifetime. Of this group 5% will be robbed twice, and 1% robbed three or more times over a 60 year period. Taking differential risks by sex and race into account, males are more likely to be robbed at least once in their lives (37%) than females (22%), and blacks are more likely to be robbed one or more times than whites (51% compared to 27%). When it comes to assault, the terms **likelihood** and **probability** take on their everyday meanings as well as their special statistical connotations. Being assaulted at least once is probable for most people—roughly 3 out of every 4 persons. (However, this alarming prediction includes failed attempts to inflict physical injury, threats of bodily harm that were not carried out, minor scuffles, and intrafamily violence.) Males face a greater likelihood of becoming embroiled in fights than females (82% compared to 62%). However, the mathematical and sociological assumptions underlying these crude projections are very complex and subject to challenge. The calculations

Table 2.6 Chances of Becoming a Victim Over a Lifetime

	Percentage of Persons Who Will Be Victimized			
Type of Victimization and Person's Race, Sex, and Age	Once or More	Once	Twice	Three or More Times
Rape				
All females age 12	8	8	—	—
White	8*	7	—	—
Black	11	10	1	—
Robbery				
All persons age 12	30*	25	5	1
Males	37	29	7	1
Females	22*	19	2	-
Whites	27	23	4	-
Blacks	51	35	12	4
Assaults				
All persons age 12	74	35	24	15
Males	82	31	26	25
Females	62	37	18	7
Whites	74*	35	24	16
Blacks	73*	35	25	12
Personal theft				
All persons age 12	99	4	8	87
All 40-year-olds	82*	31	19	33
All 60-year-olds	43	32	9	2

NOTE: Estimates are based on average victimization rates calculated by the *National Crime Survey* for the years 1975–1984; for rape, 1973–1982.
*Figures do not exactly add up to total shown because of rounding.
SOURCE: Adapted from Koppel, 1987

were based on constants derived by averaging victimization rates for the years 1975 to 1984. If crime rates drop substantially over the next 60 years or so, these estimates will turn out to be overly pessimistic; conversely, if the crime problem intensifies in the first few decades of the 21st century, the real odds will be much greater than these percentages (Koppel, 1987).

Lifetime likelihoods of being murdered also have been computed. Unlike the projections discussed above, which were based on *NCVS* findings, murder risk estimates were derived from *UCR* data. The risks vary tremendously depending on personal attributes, especially sex and race. Differential cumulative risks can be presented as ratios, such as "1 out of every x people will be murdered." All the $x - 1$ remaining individuals within this category are expected to die from accidents, diseases and other natural causes, or suicides. In general, males are more likely to die violently than are females and blacks more likely than whites. But when the effects of both sex and race were taken into account, black females turned out to be in greater danger of being slain (1 out of every 132) than white males (1 out of every 179). White females were in the least danger, relatively speaking, of the four groupings (1 out of every 495). But the prospects facing black males were frightening (1 out of every 30 black males, about 3%) would eventually become a victim of homicide if mid-1980s rates continued (BJS, 1988). (In the early 1980s the threat was even greater: 1 out of every 21 black males (nearly 5%) was likely to die violently [Langan, 1985].)

The recognition of differential risks as an important feature of the big picture touches off another round of questions for victimologists to grapple with as they analyze *UCR* and *NCVS* data. Why does the burden of victimization fall so heavily on some groups of people and not others? Have crime victims done something "wrong" or is victimization largely a matter of fate—being in the wrong place at the wrong time? What can potential victims do to cut down the risks they face? Is there anything that the government or society can do to help people lead safer lives? These issues are examined and debated in the next chapter.

CHAPTER SUMMARY

Statistics can convey important information about crimes and their victims but consumers of numerical data always must ascertain exactly what was counted, how accurate these measurements might be, and whether vested interests are promoting particular interpretations. The two leading sources of data about crime victims published annually by the U.S. Department of Justice are the FBI's *Uniform Crime Report* and the BJS's *National Crime Victimization Survey*. The *UCR* draws upon police files and is useful to victimologists who want to study murders but it is of limited value for research into other kinds of victimizations. The *NCVS* contains information about a wider range of violent and property crimes and gathers data directly from members of the large national sample who answer interviewers' questions.

Trends capture changes in victimization rates over time while patterns indicate connections between the attributes of victims and the frequency with which they are targeted. Victimization rates are expressed as per 1,000 (in the

NCVS) or per 100,000 (in the *UCR*) in order to make comparisons possible between groups, cities, or countries of different sizes.

Cumulative risks indicate the odds of being victimized over the course of a lifetime. Comparative risks reveal which kinds of misfortunes are more or less likely than others. International comparisons demonstrate that societal conditions and social traditions greatly affect crime rates. Differential risks show which categories of people are victimized more often than others. Studying the reasons for differential risks yields theories that explain why certain groups are very vulnerable to victimization.

DISCUSSION QUESTIONS

1. Choose some statistics presented in this chapter and interpret them in two ways: first, as alarming as possible; and second, as reassuring as possible.
2. What kinds of data about crime victims can be found in the FBI's annual *Uniform Crime Reports?* What are the sources of inaccuracies in these statistics?
3. What kinds of data about crime victims can be found in the BJS's annual *National Crime Victimization Survey?* What are the sources of inaccuracies in these statistics?
4. Explain the difference between comparative risks and differential risks.
5. Describe some trends in victimization that became evident during the 1990s.

3

The Victims' Contribution to the Crime Problem

Until victimology emerged, mainstream criminology had consistently ignored the role that victims might play in setting the stage for lawless behavior. Victimologists have pledged to correct this imbalance by examining all kinds of situations to see whether the people who were harmed might have played some part in their own downfall. Victimologists have thus departed from offender-oriented explanations which attribute lawbreaking solely to the exercise of free will by the wrongdoer. Victimologists have suggested that criminal incidents be viewed as the outgrowths of a process of interaction between two parties. What has emerged is a dynamic model that takes into account initiatives and responses, actions and reactions, and motives and intentions. Several expressions coined by the pioneers in victimology capture their enthusiasm for examining interactions: the "duet frame of reference" (Von Hentig, 1941), the "penal couple" (Mendelsohn, 1956), and the "doer-sufferer relationship" (Ellenberger, 1955). These situational reconstructions can provide a more balanced and complete picture of what happened and why, and thereby represent an improvement over earlier, static, one-sided, perpetrator-centered accounts (Fattah, 1979).

A well-known line of inquiry (albeit a controversial one) within criminology centers upon the differences, if any, between offenders and law-abiding people. Criminologists ask, "What distinguishes the offender from the nonoffender?" Why are some groups of people (for example, poor young men) more likely to get caught up in street crimes than other groups (say, wealthy elderly women)? In a similar vein, victimologists ask "What distinguishes victims from nonvictims? Do victims think or act differently than nonvictims? Furthermore, why are some groups of people (once more, poor young men) much more likely to be victimized (killed, shot, stabbed, beaten, or robbed) than other groups (again, wealthy elderly women)?"

Just posing these questions immediately raises the possibility of shared responsibility. Victimologists have borrowed the terminology of the legal system, traditionally used to describe criminals' behaviors, to describe the motives and actions of victims as well. The words *responsibility, culpability, guilt,* and *blame* crop up routinely in studies based on the dynamic, situational, interaction model. In the broadest sense, the concept of shared responsibility implies that certain victims as well as offenders did something "wrong." Some—but certainly not all—did not do all they could have done to reduce their odds or limit their exposure to dangerous persons or threatening situations. Some victims disregarded warning signs or failed to heed well-meaning advice and decided to take their chances. Worse yet, some acted carelessly and paid a price for their negligence. Those who acted foolishly later regretted their recklessness. Victims who behaved provocatively are blamed most of all, for without their instigation the attack may never have taken place. Instead of minimizing the risks they faced, certain victims maximized them by making bad choices. Following this line of thought, most victims can be faulted to some degree. The circumstances under which they were harmed were partly of their own making. The unfortunate events that befell them were avoidable.

Raising the question of shared responsibility touches off many controversies. Should victims, just like offenders, be held accountable for their actions? Is it unfair to blame victims after they have been harmed? How many precautions should prudent people be expected to take? How safe is safe enough? Should each individual worry only about his or her own personal safety and take protective measures to chase away prowlers and reduce risks, or should the entire community and society, largely through government-directed crime prevention strategies, attempt to eradicate the root causes of street crime?

THE SEARCH FOR RISK FACTORS

The data in the tables and graphs presented in chapter 2 from the *UCR* and the *NCVS* confirmed the long-held suspicion that certain groups of people were much more likely than others to be murdered, robbed, or assaulted, or to lose their valuables to burglars, car thieves, and other crooks. Why was that? What—if anything—was it they did or failed to do that caught the attention of criminals? What differentiated them from the rest of the population? In general, what risk factors heighten dangers and make people and their possessions more vulnerable to attack? Although victimologists cannot agree among themselves about exactly what behaviors and practices increase susceptibility, victimization definitely does not appear to be a random process, striking people just by chance. When victims ask "Why me?" victimologists suggest that the reason in most cases goes beyond simply "bad luck." The answers to these questions can be of great use to policymakers as well as to individuals in high-risk groups who face grave perils.

Theoretical explanations start off as hypotheses that answer questions that begin with *why*. Right after making an empirical generalization (an observation based on patterns or trends that emerged when the data was analyzed) theorists are inclined to ask "why?" For example, *NCVS* findings confirm earlier observations based on *UCR* statistics from police files that two types of crimes—unlawful entries (burglaries accomplished without using force to get in) and stranger rapes—are more frequent during the warmer months. This empirical generalization about the seasonality of certain victimizations requires an explanation. Why should burglary and rape exhibit a predictable cycle of increases and decreases during the course of a year? An offender-centered explanation might propose that burglars and rapists are more active during warmer weather for some reason. Another plausible line of thought could be that something about their intended targets changes with the seasons. Perhaps warm weather behavior patterns create greater opportunities for predators to strike against their prey. During the summertime, people spend more time outside and are more likely to leave windows open while they are away from home. As a result, strangers find more occasions to sexually assault girls and women, and prowlers find more unprotected homes to sneak into (Dodge, 1988). Robberies and personal larcenies (like purse snatching and pocket picking) do not show much seasonality, but they do peak in December when shopping for gifts reaches its height (BJS, 1993).

The first victimologist to zero in on risk factors (see Von Hentig, 1941) believed that certain personal attributes played a part in determining vulnerability.

The mentally retarded, newly arrived immigrants, less-educated people, and very inexperienced persons were pictured as attractive targets for exploitation by criminals employing deception and fraud. Con artists swindled the greedy, heartbroken, and lonesome with legendary ease. Physically handicapped people, the elderly and frail, the very young, and perhaps females in general were assumed to be easy prey for robbers. According to this early approach, a varied collection of psychological, biological, and social conditions set whole categories of people apart as particularly vulnerable.

Situational factors highlight how people and their possessions are more susceptible at certain times, periods, or stages than at others. For example, muggers may lie in wait as payday approaches or when social security checks arrive in the mail. Armed robbers might approach storekeepers at closing time. Prostitutes working the streets are particularly prone to robberies, rapes, beatings, and even murders (especially by serial killers). These young women are easy targets because they operate in the shadows, are willing to go off with complete strangers to isolated or desolate locations, and often abuse alcohol or other drugs that loosen their inhibitions, increase their desperation for money, and impair their judgment. Crimes committed against them are not taken very seriously by the public or the authorities, and witnesses in their behalf (usually other prostitutes, pimps, or johns) are often disreputable, unreliable, or uncooperative and therefore ineffective protectors of their legal interests (see Boyer and James, 1983). Similarly, tourists are the preferred prey of robbers, thieves, and pickpockets. Career criminals figure that even if they are caught by the police, few travelers on business trips or vacations will be willing and able to return to the jurisdiction of the crime to press charges and take part in legal proceedings because of time and money constraints. A tourist's average length of stay of a few days to a few weeks is invariably too brief to see a case through to its conclusion. As a result, charges against defendants who harm people on business trips or vacations are usually dropped or drastically reduced because of the absence of the complainant. To curtail the attractiveness of tourists as targets, extraordinary policies are needed. For instance, Waikiki Beach in Honolulu, Hawaii, was a haven for muggers and rapists until an apprehensive travel industry—convinced that crime was hurting business—began to pay for a victim-witness return project. Free airplane tickets, accommodations, and child care were furnished to visitors who flew back to Hawaii, pressed charges, and testified at trials. Government officials even interceded with victims' employers to assure them of the importance of the trip. As a result, prosecution and conviction rates went up, and tourists reportedly no longer suffered excessively high rates of robbery, theft, and assault ("Hawaii Return-Witness Program," 1982).

The Determinants of Differential Risks

Most victimologists are not satisfied with explanations that emphasize a single vulnerability factor that is biological (like gender, age, and race), psychological (such as loneliness or greediness), social (like income and occupation), or situational (for instance, being an immigrant or a tourist). A number of more elaborate explanations have been developed to account for differential risks.

From the offenders' standpoint, potential targets (such as individuals, homes, and cars) can be rated along several dimensions. One dimension is **attractiveness.** Teenage muggers assault their classmates to rob them of their stylish shoes or coats. Some people and things appear "ripe for the taking," while others present much more of a challenge to the robber of being thwarted or even captured. Certain prizes can easily be snatched, spirited off, and cashed in (like car stereos and airbags); others would take a long time and a lot of trouble to fence, and the net return might be minimal (such as used automobile tires). **Proximity** describes whether the offender can get within range of the target, geographically (direct contact) and socially (interaction). Offenders might have great difficulty getting within striking distance of certain very attractive targets, such as country mansions or millionaires. The proximity factor works to the disadvantage of those who must run into dangerous persons on a regular basis (see Garofalo, 1986; and Siegel, 1998). Victims might be chosen simply because they are handy. The most obvious examples would be nonviolent inmates who are locked in with hardened convicts in prisons, jails, holding cells, or mental institutions for the criminally insane. Similarly, elderly persons trapped in high-crime housing projects or well-behaved students stuck in troubled high schools also suffer grave dangers because they are readily available targets. A related concept, the **deviant place** factor, calls attention to exact locations rather than general proximity to particular individuals. Certain settings attract predators on the prowl and troublemakers looking for some action. "Hot spots" for crime tend to be concentrated in urban settings (Sherman, Gartin, and Buerger, 1989) and include crowded public spaces that serve as crossroads for a wide range of people (like downtown bus or train terminals), desolate areas where the police rarely patrol, or venues where heavy drinking and drug consumption regularly takes place (perhaps empty lots or park benches). Those who frequent these locations by necessity or choice expose themselves to greater risks. **Vulnerability** is a dimension that refers to a potential target's ability to resist attack: whether the target is well protected or largely undefended. Rare coins in a museum are attractive and can be viewed up close but usually are displayed in tightly guarded settings.

Weaving together several of these factors, victimologists often point to lifestyles and routine activities as explanatory concepts that account for observed differences in susceptibility to violence and theft. The sociological term **lifestyle** refers to how people spend their time and money at work and leisure, and the social roles they play (like business traveler, student, or homemaker). Lifestyles that place people in jeopardy may appear to be freely chosen but also are strongly influenced by structural constraints (such as the financial need to use public transportation) as well as role expectations (for example, how teenagers "ought" to spend their Saturday nights). The pursuit of certain forms of amusement and excitement boosts risk levels. Evening activities such as aimlessly cruising around, congregating in parks, partying with complete strangers, and frequenting bars and clubs late at night incorporate elements of uncertainty and volatility. Consequently, those who seek pleasure in daring, delinquent, and illicit activities bad luck or poor planning, some would-be killers wound up dead. For example, across the nation in 1998, 70 killings were classified as "organized-crime related" in terms of their "circumstances" or motives on the FBI's *Supplementary Homicide Reporting* (*SHR*) form. Some mobsters were "whacked" to settle a score, to depose a chieftain, to send a chilling message to informers or renegades, or as part of a power struggle. Many more slayings—roughly 625, or 4% of that year's total body count—took the form of drive-by shootings and resulted from warfare between members of rival street gangs because of real or imagined transgressions. An even greater number of quarrels escalating into murders—about 680, or 5%—took place between people involved in the drug trade, according to the information supplied on the *SHRs* by homicide detectives across the country. Of course, the death tolls due to mob hits, street gang wars, and drug-related conflicts would all be larger if the circumstances surrounding the thousands of unsolved killings were known to the authorities, and if the local police didn't submit thousands of *SHRs* with the reasons listed as "Other—not specified" or left blank.

Nationwide, slayings that were deemed to be "narcotics related" became a serious problem during the 1980s. They peaked in 1989 at about 1,400 (more than 7% of all murders) (Timrots and Snyder, 1994). Several distinct scenarios can result in deadly drug-connected showdowns: cutthroat competition between rival dealers (turf battles), conflicts between buyers and sellers (quarrels over high prices, money owed, misrepresentation of the contents, and scams surrounding inferior quality), and robberies of dealers or customers. Drug-related murders falling into these categories added up to much greater proportions in most metropolitan areas (see Zimring and Zuehl, 1986; Tardiff, Gross, and Messner, 1986; and Spunt et al., 1993). In Washington, D.C., drug-related murders boosted the overall homicide rate more strikingly than anywhere else during the late 1980s. About 20% of all murders in 1985 (in which the motive was known to the police) were drug related (either the coroner determined that the victim was under the influence of drugs, drug traces or paraphernalia were discovered at the crime scene, or the killing occurred in a drug hangout such as a "shooting gallery" or "crack house"), according to the Office of Criminal Justice in the District of Columbia. This proportion rose to 34% the following year, jumped to 51% in 1987, soared to 80% in 1988, and climbed to 85% during the first part of 1989 (Berke, 1989; Martz, et al., 1989). In New York City, drug-related killings also peaked at the close of the 1980s, but dropped by half to less than 17% by the end of the 1990s as the crack epidemic waned (see Karmen, 2000). The drug problem definitely fuels a substantial amount of interpersonal violence. However, it is possible to manipulate impressions about its impact by either including or excluding certain subcategories of murders (such as robbers killing drug dealers or robbers high on drugs slaying their victims) which can inflate or deflate the death toll. Larger or smaller estimates of drug-related killings can be used by various special-interest groups to prove or disprove something about the drug problem (making it appear more or less seriousness) or about the "war on drugs" (picturing it as succeeding or failing, as absolutely necessary, or causing more harm than good) (see Brownstein, 1996).

The violence that permeates street-level drug dealing caused the homicide rate among teenage boys to spiral upwards from the mid-1980s into the early 1990s. The overwhelming majority (about 85%) of these deaths were from gunfire. A self-perpetuating cycle of aggression and retaliation developed as growing numbers of poor young men in drug-ravaged communities armed themselves for self-protection and for prestige—whether or not they were involved in the crack or heroin trade—and fought each other, often over minor matters. The underlying causes of this teenage arms race were poverty, poor schooling, limited legitimate job opportunities, family instability, and immersion in a subculture of violence (Fingerhut, Ingram, and Feldman, 1992a; Blumstein and Rosenfeld, 1998).

Binge drinking is surely a dangerous practice that some people have made part of their lifestyle. Alcohol has been implicated even more consistently than illicit drugs in interpersonal violence leading to fatal outcomes (see Spunt et al., 1994; and Parker, 1995). The victim, the offender, or both were drinking before the killing took place in 64% of the cases, in Philadelphia around 1950, according to the first detailed study of murders (Wolfgang, 1958). Reports from medical examiners in eight cities in 1978 revealed that the percentage of corpses testing positive for alcohol ranged from a low of 38% to a high of 62% (Riedel and Mock, 1985). In a study of nearly 5,000 homicides committed in Los Angeles between 1970 and 1979, researchers reported that alcohol was detected in the blood of nearly half the bodies autopsied. The blood-alcohol content in about 30% of these 5,000 murder victims was high enough to classify the person as "intoxicated" by legal standards at the time of death. The typical alcohol-related slaying involved a young man who was stabbed to death in a bar on a weekend as the result of a fight with an acquaintance or friend (Goodman et al., 1986). Two mechanisms explain the linkage between consuming large quantities of alcohol and violence. The selective-disinhibition perspective predicts that if one or both parties have been drinking heavily, their judgment may become clouded, and they are more likely to misinterpret each other's actions, focus only on immediate concerns, and behave in a less restrained manner. The outlet-attractor perspective proposes that at certain alcohol-serving locations (like liquor stores, bars, and clubs) people gather with the expectation that they will seek "time out" from normal constraints and act "out of character" in an "anything goes" environment (Parker and Rebhun, 1995). These research findings raise the possibility that some victims may have been partly at fault for the escalation of tensions and the outbreak of lethal violence.

Besides a person's lifestyle, another explanation for differential risks centers upon **routine activities.** This theory stresses the interactions of three variables: the presence of motivated offenders (like drug addicts desperate for cash), the availability of suitable targets (people or their possessions), and the absence of capable guardians (ranging from police officers to burglar alarms). Would-be offenders seize opportunities to strike whenever attractive targets are not well protected. Everyday living arrangements that can have an impact upon victimization include patterns of commuting, shopping, attending school, and going to work. In recent decades, vulnerability to robbery and burglary increased as routine activities shifted away from the home and toward greater interaction with nonfamily members. Daily routines govern the **social ecology** of victimization: what kinds of people will be harmed, in what manner, at what time, and at which locations. For example, people who still spend most of their time at home are not in much danger of being murdered by strangers; if they do meet a violent end, it is likely to be at the hands of family members or close friends (Messner and Tardiff, 1985; Maxfield, 1987). The routine activities explanation for differential risks ties together several major themes within criminology and victimology: one is that social conditions continuously generate criminally inclined individuals, and another is that opportunities for committing thefts and robberies multiply as possessions proliferate. A third theme is that preventive measures in tandem with unofficial guardianship (informal mechanisms of social control in which relatives and neighbors assume responsibility for the well-being of others) may be more effective than stepped-up policing and punishment in discouraging offenders from striking. The fourth theme is that certain activities and circumstances expose people and their possessions to grave dangers (see Cohen and Felson, 1979; Cohen, Kluegal, and Land, 1981; Felson, 1994; Finkelhor and Asdigian, 1996; and Siegel, 1998).

What all these explanations of the victim selection process and of the illegal opportunity structure have in common is that they take on a collective, social orientation rather than an individualistic, psychological approach. They emphasize general patterns of behavior engaged in by entire groups of people instead of the peculiar propensities of specific individuals (to pick fights or treat valuable possessions carelessly, for instance) (Garofalo, 1986). All of these explanations take offender motivation as a "given" (it is assumed that some people are inclined to abuse and exploit other people) and focus attention upon informal and formal mechanisms of social control (the ways that potential offenders can be restrained). As a result, these explanations generate many strategies and tactics that can help to reduce risks or, even better, entirely prevent harm. However, observing safety tips and taking precautions may not be enough to meaningfully change the odds some very vulnerable people face (Miethe, Stafford, and Sloane, 1990).

Reducing Risks: How Safe Is Safe Enough?

Evaluating the effectiveness of specific precautions to prevent victimization is difficult. It is hard to identify particular instances when using avoidance strategies, practicing risk management tactics, and redesigning the environment have clearly prevented a crime by dissuading a potential offender from attacking his or her intended target. Certain risk reduction strategies do seem to work but not in ways that are readily quantifiable. Therefore, whether to sacrifice certain freedoms and pleasures for enhanced safety is a trade-off that each person must confront and weigh. Take, for example, the relatively low robbery rates of the elderly compared to other age groups, even though senior citizens are presumed to be extremely vulnerable. The apparent paradox can be explained by noting that older persons usually incorporate many risk reduction strategies into their lifestyles and routine activities to the point that these self-imposed restrictions become second nature. For example, to find young adults out late drinking in bars and clubs seems normal; to encounter elderly people in such settings at those hours is surprising. In general, it is safer to stay at home, especially late at night; travel in pairs or groups and use taxis; avoid public spaces, unfamiliar places, and complete strangers; steer clear of known hot spots and dangerous characters; and not let down one's guard by becoming intoxicated or distracted. Those precautions are a price that most older persons are willing to pay to avoid putting themselves in harm's way. But most teenagers and young adults tend to reject such severe restrictions on their quest for entertainment and nightlife (see Felson, 1997; and Mustaine and Tewksbury, 1998a).

Nonetheless, even the most sheltered lives can be marred by all sorts of unanticipated or dreaded events. When social scientists estimate risks, they are predicting how many people will experience unwanted incidents. The statistical concepts underlying risk estimates can be difficult to grasp. Only three distinct probabilities can be readily understood: "0," which signifies that an event is impossible; "1," which means that an event is inevitable; and "0.5," which indicates a toss-up, or a "50–50" chance (as in seeking "heads" when flipping a coin). But risks that are 0.1 (1 in 10) or 0.01 (1 in 100) or 0.001 (1 in 1,000) are harder to fathom or evaluate. If the odds of something happening were one in a million, statisticians would advise people not to worry about it (or not to count on it if the event is desirable). But when 4 people in every 1,000 are robbed each year, should the risk of robbery be taken into account when planning one's daily schedule? How much preparation and anxiety would be rational in the face of these odds? What sacrifices would be appropriate in terms of foregoing necessary or welcomed activities (like taking evening classes or watching the sun set on a deserted beach)? At what point does disregarding risks and ignoring precautions become foolhardy?

The proper balance between safety and risk is ultimately a personal decision. But it is also a matter of public debate. In general, more protection can be secured by greater expenditure. Dangers can be reduced if individuals and groups are willing to pay the price (for more police patrols, improved lighting, and other security measures). Any demand for absolute safety (zero risk), however, is irrational in statistical terms. Probabilities of unwanted events can be reduced but never entirely eliminated. "How safe is safe enough?" is strictly a value judgment. At some point, it is reasonable for a person to declare the odds an **acceptable risk** (Lynn, 1981). When performing a cost-benefit analysis, a point of **diminishing returns** eventually sets in. Additional efforts to increase safety are largely futile and wasteful (for example, adding more locks to the same door). Risk-benefit analyses seem scientifically sound and precise, but on close inspection they hinge on questionable assumptions and debatable value judgments. How much is a human life worth in monetary terms? Can the pain and suffering of victims or the public's fear of crime be converted by some formula into justifiable taxpayers' or consumers' expenditures?

From Crime Prevention to Victimization Prevention

The intense interest in the role of lifestyles and daily behavior routines has led to new strategies to reduce risks. Victimologists and criminologists have coined terms to describe the ways in which people try to diminish their odds of being run greater risks of being assaulted, robbed, raped, or murdered. Lifestyles largely determine the quantity and quality of the contacts between potential victims and criminally inclined individuals. Differences in lifestyles lead to variations in exposure to risks. In the long run, exposure is the primary determinant of a group's victimization rate (see Hindelang, Gottfredson, and Garofalo, 1978; Garofalo, 1986; Jensen and Brownfield, 1986; and Mustaine and Tewksbury, 1998b). For example, *NCVS* findings presented in chapter 2 indicated that single young men and women were robbed at a much higher rate than their married counterparts. Surely, muggers don't check for wedding bands before they strike. It must be the willingness of young singles to venture out alone at night to seek the company of acquaintances and even strangers that accounts for much of the difference in the dangers they face. The relatively low rates of robbery, rape, and assault by strangers for married young men and women with children can also best be understood as a function of lifestyle. In their daily routines, social companions, leisure activities, and family-centered obligations, young mothers and fathers are less exposed to dangerous persons and places than their counterparts without spouses or young children (Skogan, 1981a; Felson, 1997).

Some murders that arise from intense conflicts can be viewed as the outcome of a sequence of events in a transaction. The initial incident might be a personal affront, perhaps something as minor as a slur or gesture. Both the offender and the victim contribute to the escalation of a "character contest." As the confrontation unfolds at least one party, but usually both, attempts to "save face" at the other's expense by not backing down. The battle turns into a deadly showdown if both participants are steeped in a tradition that favors violence as the way to settle bitter disputes (Luckenbill, 1977).

The **equivalent group** explanation portrays victims who engage in certain high-risk lifestyles in a less than sympathetic light. It emphasizes the possibility that certain pairs of victims and victimizers shared the same interests, participated in the same activities, and were drawn from homogenous or overlapping lifestyle groups. Offenders selected their victims from their own circles of adversaries, acquaintances, and even former friends. Adherence to and participation in the norms of certain deviant subcultures can sharply raise the chances of becoming a casualty. Victims might have been viewed as "fair game" or "easy prey" because their own involvement in criminal behavior discourages them from turning to the authorities for help (see Fattah, 1991; and Siegel, 1998).

A considerable number of murders can be pointed to as illustrations of the explanation that both parties were drawn from equivalent groups. Most perpetrators and many of their victims had been in trouble with the law before their final showdowns, according to a survey of over 8,000 prosecutions carried out in the nation's 75 largest counties during 1988. About 45% of the deceased turned out to have criminal records (arrests or convictions for misdemeanors or felonies) as did 75% of all defendants (see Dawson and Langan, 1994). Entire categories of killings serve as a reminder that not all murder victims were totally innocent persons targeted by vicious killers for no logical reason and through no fault of their own. The most obvious examples of overlapping lifestyles include victims and offenders engaged in racketeering, gang fighting, and drug-dealing. Through harmed by incorporating risk reduction activities into their everyday activities. **Avoidance strategies** (Furstenberg, 1972) are actions people take to limit their personal exposure to dangerous persons and frightening situations (such as not allowing strangers into their homes, or ignoring passersby who attempt to strike up conversations on deserted streets). **Risk management tactics** (Skogan and Maxfield, 1981) minimize the chances of being harmed when exposure is unavoidable. Examples include walking home with other people rather than traveling alone, or carrying a weapon or weapons instead of going around unarmed. **Crime prevention through environmental design (CPTED)** stresses the importance of creating well-protected **defensible space** (Newman, 1972) by **target hardening** (adding locks, erecting fences) and maintaining effective surveillance (limiting the number of entrances, improving visibility by trimming down bushes and adding bright lights). Risk reduction actions are categorized as **individual** or **collective** (when arranged in cooperation with others) (Conklin, 1975) or as either **private-minded** or **public-minded** (Schneider and Schneider, 1978).

The term **crime prevention** refers to strategies that are pursued to head off the development of illegal activities as opposed to **crime control** measures that are taken in response to acts that have already been committed. Formerly, crime prevention strategies centered on government programs designed to eradicate the social roots of illegal behavior, such as desperation for money, job shortages, failing school systems, and racial discrimination. Community-based crime prevention campaigns focus on lowering the dropout rate in school systems, providing decent jobs for all those who want to work, and developing meaningful recreational outlets for otherwise idle youth. But crime prevention in a practical sense means "the anticipation, recognition, and appraisal of a crime risk, and the initiation of some action to remove or reduce it" (National Crime Prevention Institute, 1978). A better term than crime prevention for some of these preemptive measures is **victimization prevention** (Cohn, Kidder, and Harvey, 1978). Victimization prevention is much more modest in intent than crime prevention. Its goal is simply to discourage criminals from attacking particular targets, such as certain homes, warehouses, stores, cars, or persons. Like defensive driving, victimization prevention hinges on the dictum, "Watch the other guy and anticipate his possible moves."

The shift from crime prevention on a societal and governmental level to victimization prevention on a neighborhood, small-group, and individual level demands that potential victims become **crime conscious** ("street smart"). The responsibility for keeping out of trouble increasingly falls on the possible targets themselves who must outmaneuver and keep one step ahead of would-be offenders. Crime-conscious individuals are compelled to follow victimization prevention tips, which are long lists of "dos and don'ts" compiled from observations of other people's misfortunes. **Crime resistance** means making the offender's task more difficult through advanced planning.

The recommendation derived from routine activities theory is that measures should be taken to make people appear to be well-protected and property well-guarded so that criminally inclined prowlers will look elsewhere for easier pickings (Moore, 1985). If the findings of social experiments support this hypothesis, then the adoption of these victimization prevention measures might have far-reaching consequences. The "valve theory of crime shifts" predicts that the number of crimes committed will not drop when targets are hardened but that criminal activity will simply be displaced. If one area of illegal opportunity is shut off (for example, if robbing bus drivers is made unprofitable by the imposition of exact fare requirements), people desperate for cash will shift their attention to more vulnerable targets (such as cabdrivers or storekeepers) (National Commission on the Causes and Prevention of Violence, 1969a). When crime is displaced and criminals are deflected, the risk of victimization goes down for some but rises for others, assuming that offenders are intent on committing crimes and are flexible in terms of time, place, target, and tactics (Allen et al., 1981). In other words, the adoption of victimization prevention strategies by some very crime conscious persons might endanger other people who may be less cautious. Victimization will be redistributed, spatially, geographically, and socially. But that is a far cry from genuine crime prevention that would lower the risks everyone faces. For example, a pamphlet distributed by the country's largest police department frankly acknowledged that self-protective measures might merely redirect offenders elsewhere. "No vehicle is theft-proof. You must approach this problem with the attitude that it will not be my car that becomes part of the statistics. As selfish as it may sound, if the thief wants a car of your year, make, and model, let it be someone else's. If you follow these guidelines and take all the necessary precautions to protect your car, the chances are it will not be stolen" (New York Police Department, 1992).

Whether victimization prevention methods simply shift the burden on to others while alleviating the dangers some people and their possessions face, is a question researchers must examine. One thing is clear: Target-hardening strategies certainly lend themselves to commercial exploitation. Advertisements constantly proclaim that virtually foolproof new security-enhancing products are for sale. As these goods and services are purchased by a growing market share of people who desperately don't want to become statistics, victimologists can test the claims to see which devices work best, or if they have any appreciable impact at all.

Ambivalence About Risk Taking

Contradictory messages permeate American culture on the subject of risk taking. On the one hand, the entrepreneurial ideology extols risk taking and generously rewards those business ventures that defy conventional wisdom, survive financial hardships, and thrive in a highly competitive, adverse economic environment. Similarly, cultural heroes are invariably risk takers who overcome overwhelming odds: pioneers, explorers, inventors, private detectives, secret agents, soldiers of fortune, high-stakes gamblers, and other adventurers. On the other hand, middle-class values emphasize control over one's destiny and counsel prudence in the face of grave dangers. Conscientious, responsible, "mature adults" plan, build, invest, and save in order to be prepared for adversity, illness, old age, accidents, or devastating victimizations. They seek out safety, peace of mind, insurance, and protection to guard against unforeseen disasters and avoidable tragedies. The hallmarks of scientific achievement include mastery of events and domination over nature. Technological progress is recognized as the reduction of uncertainty and the attainment of reliable, predictable performance. Autonomy (personal independence) and security are highly desired goals. Underlying all these human aspirations and accomplishments are the notions of reducing or practically eliminating risks.

The ambivalent attitudes toward risks in American culture are mirrored by contradictory responses to victimizations. Some readily rush to the defense of victims while others impulsively criticize them, characterizing victims as risk takers who have lost or failed in their gambits. Their suffering evokes sympathy, but it also invites second-guessing about what might be altered in their attitudes and lifestyles to avoid future troubles. This line of inquiry leads to a close inspection of the specific acts that immediately preceded the crime. As the victim–offender interaction is deconstructed, reconstructed and scrutinized, exactly how the victim behaved becomes the focus of attention.

Victimologists have shown a keen interest in discovering what attitudes and actions increase rather than reduce risks.

Deterrence Theory As Applied to Victims

For over two centuries (ever since the time of Cesare Beccaria and Jeremy Bentham, the originators of the "classical school" of "free will," "choice," or "rational decision-making" theory), a fierce debate has raged over whether would-be offenders are deterred by the prospects of apprehension, conviction, and punishment. But rarely, if ever, is the debate redirected and focused on past and potential victims. Do victims also learn a lesson from their bad experiences, and does the public learn from the mistakes of victims?

Simply put, deterrence theory holds that swift and sure punishment is the solution to the crime problem. According to the tenets of specific deterrence, punishing offenders teaches them a lesson they won't forget, so they will not repeat the forbidden act again. According to the logic of general deterrence, publicly punishing offenders makes them into negative role models that serve as a warning to others to avoid similar misdeeds.

Proponents and opponents argue over whether offenders really learn the intended lesson (especially in jails and prisons, which might actually serve as "graduate schools" that churn out individuals with advanced degrees in criminality); whether would-be lawbreakers really mull over their decisions rationally, "think twice," and decide not to commit illegal acts (or instead often act impulsively, disregarding the possible consequences in the heat of passion); and whether others who hear about the crime and the punishment that followed truly make the connection, think "That could be me!" and are "scared straight" and dissuaded from violating the law.

Applying the principles of general deterrence to law-abiding people, do members of the public closely identify with victims who clearly made mistakes? Do they also make the connection "It could have been me!" and profit from someone else's misfortune? Does news media coverage of specific incidents strike fear in the hearts and minds of large numbers of would-be victims, making them think twice before engaging in some similar risky behavior? Does the frightening prospect of becoming a victim lead to constructive responses, such as incorporating risk avoidance and risk management precautions into lifestyles?

Bringing in the concept of specific deterrence, a parallel question arises. Do one-time victims learn their lessons? Do they realize their past mistakes, vow not to repeat these errors, take "dos and don'ts" tips more seriously, and change their ways? Or do they disregard the persistent threats, continue to take their chances, plow ahead recklessly, and become **repeat victims** and suffer **serial victimizations** (two or more incidents during a relatively short period of time)?

The answers to these queries require careful research. A reasonable hypothesis is that some potential victims are more likely to be deterred than others. Specifically, individuals who are middle class, middle-aged or older, and female are probably more inclined than others to respond to the fear of being harmed ("punishment") by thinking twice and concluding that the risks outweigh the benefits. They exercise their free will, rationally decide the activity isn't worth the risk, choose a more prudent course of action, and are deterred from behaving in a way that disregards the potential negative consequences.

The discovery of repeat victims who have suffered serial victimizations certainly draws attention to the possibility that some people are partly responsible for their own troubles. This issue of shared responsibility captivated the first criminologists who became interested in victimology and inspired considerable theorizing and research during victimology's first few decades. Leading figures in the field encouraged researchers to seek out evidence of shared responsibility. Some of their statements appear in Box 3.1.

THE CONTROVERSY OVER SHARED RESPONSIBILITY

A man pulls into his driveway, turns off his car's engine, and enters his home. A teenager walks by and spots the car's keys dangling in the ignition switch. He hops behind the wheel and drives off. Was the motorist partly responsible for the crime because he made the thief's task easier? Is victim facilitation a major reason for the high rate of auto theft?

A young woman tries to thumb a ride home from a local beach on a hot summer's day. A young man in a sports car picks up the hitchhiker and interprets her appreciation as a sign of sexual interest. He drives to a deserted parking lot and makes sexual advances. She resists, but he assumes her protests are feigned. When he tries to pin her down, she bolts from the car and runs screaming along the road. Did she contribute to the attempted rape by recklessly placing herself in a dangerous, sexually charged situation? Is victim precipitation a significant cause of sexual assaults?

A husband periodically beats his wife over the course of more than 20 years. After each episode he is contrite and vows to change his "evil ways." But one day he threatens to kill their daughter. When he falls asleep that

BOX 3.1 Expressions of Support for Inquiries into the Victim's Role

- A real mutuality frequently can be observed in the connection between the perpetrator and the victim, the killer and the killed, the duper and the duped. The victim in many instances leads the evildoer into temptation. The predator is, by varying means, prevailed upon to advance against the prey. (Von Hentig, 1941, p. 303)
- In a sense, the victim shapes and molds the criminal. Although the final outcome may appear to be one-sided, the victim and criminal profoundly work upon each other, right up until the last moment in the drama. Ultimately, the victim can assume the role of determinant in the event. (Von Hentig, 1948, p. 384)
- Criminologists should give as much attention to "victimogenesis" as to "criminogenesis." Every person should know exactly to what dangers he is exposed because of his occupation, social class, and psychological constitution. (Ellenberger, 1955, p. 258)
- The distinction between criminal and victim, which used to be considered as clear-cut as black and white, can become vague and blurred in individual cases. The longer and the more deeply the actions of the persons involved are scrutinized, the more difficult it occasionally will be to decide who is to blame for the tragic outcome. (Mannheim, 1965, p. 672)
- In some cases, the victim initiates the interaction, and sends out signals that the receiver (doer) decodes, triggering or generating criminal behavior in the doer. (Reckless, 1967, p.142)
- Probation and parole officers must understand victim-offender relationships. The personality of the victim, as a cause of the offense, is oftentimes more pertinent than that of the offender. (Schultz, 1968, p. 135)
- Responsibility for one's conduct is a changing concept, and its interpretation is a true mirror of the social, cutural, and political conditions of a given era. . . . Notions of criminal responsibility most often indicate the nature of societal inter-relationships and the ideology of the ruling group in the power structure. Many crimes don't just happen to be committed—the victim's negligence, precipitative actions, or provocations can contribute to the genesis of crime. . . . The victim's functional responsibility is to do nothing that will provoke others to injure him, and to actively seek to prevent criminals from harming him. (Schafer, 1968, pp. 4, 144, 152)
- Scholars have begun to see the victim not just as a passive object, as the innocent point of impact of crime on society, but as sometimes playing an active role and possibly contributing to some degree to his own victimization. During the last 30 years, there has been considerable debate, speculation, and research into the victim's role, the criminal-victim relationship, the concept of responsibility, and behaviors that could be considered provocative. Thus, the study of crime has taken on a more realistic and more complete outlook. (Viano, 1976, p. 1)
- There is much to be learned about victimization patterns and the factors that influence them. Associated with the question of relative risk is the more specific question (of considerable importance) of victim participation, since crime is an interactional process. (Parsonage, 1979, p. 10)
- Victimology also postulates that the roles of "victim" and "victimizer" are neither fixed nor assigned, but are mutable and interchangeable, with continous movement between the two roles. . . . This position, understandably, will not be welcomed by those who, for a variety of practical or utilitarian reasons, continue to promote the popular stereotypes of victims and victimizers, according to which the two populations are as different as black and white, night and day, wolves and lambs. (Fattah, 1991, p. xiv)

Calls for Research into the Victim's Role in Specific Crimes

- *Murder:* In many crimes, especially criminal homicide, which usually involves intense personal interaction, the victim is often a major contributor to the lawless act. . . . Except in cases in which the victim is an innocent

Continued

.1 continued

bystander and is killed in lieu of an intended victim, or in cases in which a pure accident is involved, the victim may be one of the major precipitating causes of his own demise. (Wolfgang, 1958, pp. 245, 264)

- *Rape:* The offender should not be viewed as the sole "cause" and reason for the offense, and the "virtuous" rape victim is not always the innocent and passive party. The role played by the victim and its contribution to the perpetration of the offense becomes one of the main interests of the emerging discipline of victimology. Furthermore, if penal justice is to be fair it must be attentive to these problems of degrees of victim responsibility for her own victimization. (Amir, 1971, pp. 275–276)
- *Theft:* Careless people set up temptation-opportunity situations when they carry their money or leave their valuables in a manner which virtually invites theft by pocket picking, burglary, or robbery. Carelessness in handling cash is so persistenly a part of everyday living that is must be deemed almost a national habit. . . . Because victim behavior today is conducive to criminality, it will be necessary to develop mass educational programs aimed at changing that behavior. (Fooner, 1971, pp. 313, 315)

Victims cause crime in the sense that they set up the opportunity for the crime to be committed. By changing the behavior of the victim and potential victim, the crime rate can be reduced. Holders of fire insurance policies must meet fire safety standards, so why not require holders of theft insurance to meet security standards? (Jeffrey, 1971, pp. 208–209)

- *Burglary:* In the same way that criminologists compare offenders with nonoffenders to understand why a person commits a crime, we examined how the burglary victim and nonvictim differ in an attempt to understand the extent to which a victim vicariously contributes to or precipitates a break-in. (Waller and Okihiro, 1978, p. 5)
- *Auto theft:* Unlike most personal property, which is preserved behind fences and walls, cars are constantly moved from one exposed location to another; and since autos contain their own means of locomotion, potential victims are particularly responsible for varying the degree of theft risk by where they park and by the occasions they provide for starting the engine. The role of the victim is especially consequential for this crime; many cases of auto theft appear to be essentially a matter of opportunity. They are victim facilitated. (McCaghy, Giordano, and Henson, 1977, p. 369)

night, his wife shoots him and then sets their house on fire. She is arrested and tried for first-degree murder. The jury rejects her contention that she was temporarily insane from terror and that she acted in self-defense to save herself and her daughter. The judge sentences her to life in prison even though she is permanently disabled from his beatings (Browne, 1987). Did the husband instigate his own murder? Is victim provocation a leading factor in the slayings of abusive spouses?

The first few criminologists drawn to the study of victims were enthusiastic about the concept of shared responsibility as an overlooked contributory "cause" of crime. By raising questions about victim proneness, vulnerability, and accountability, they put forward a more complete but also more controversial explanation about why laws are broken and people get hurt. While victimology has thus enriched criminology, it has also contributed to further schisms. Ever since the 1970s some criminologists and victimologists have expressed concern over the implications of studies into mutual interactions and reciprocal influences between the two parties. Those who raised doubts and voiced dissent might be seen as loosely constituting a different school of thought. Just as criminology (with a much longer, richer, and stormier history than victimology) has recognizable orientations and camps within it (for example, adherents of labeling theory and conflict models), so too does victimology have its rifts and factions. To put it bluntly, a victim-blaming tendency within victimology clashes repeatedly with a victim-defending tendency over a great many issues. However, victimologists cannot simply be divided up into victim blamers and victim defenders. The situation is much more complicated than that.

In the remainder of this chapter, the arguments of both sides in the debate over shared responsibility will be presented in a balanced manner. First, the concepts of facilitation, precipitation, and provocation will be introduced. Then, evidence from research into the issue of shared responsibility will be examined. After a general discussion of victim blaming and victim defending, the importance of fixing responsibility will be underscored. Next, the debate between these two schools of thought will be explored in three specific areas: whether some victims of car stealing facilitated the theft, whether some rape victims precipitated the attacks, and whether some abusive husbands provoked their wives to slay them. The chapter will conclude with a discussion of the strengths, weaknesses, and limitations of the victim-blaming and victim-defending perspectives.

Victim Facilitation, Precipitation, and Provocation

The notions of victim facilitation, precipitation, and provocation have been derived from the broader theme of shared responsibility to describe the specific, identifiable, blameworthy actions taken by certain individuals immediately before they were harmed. Unfortunately, these three terms have been used somewhat loosely and inconsistently by criminologists and victimologists to the point that important distinctions have been blurred or buried.

Victim Facilitation The term **facilitation** ought to be reserved for those situations in which victims unknowingly, carelessly, negligently, and inadvertently make it easier for the criminal to commit a theft. Facilitating victims unwillingly assist their offenders and therefore share a minor amount of blame. They increase the risks of losing their property by their own thoughtless actions. If it is assumed that the thieves who steal the possessions of careless owners were already on the prowl and looking for opportunities to grab and run, then victim facilitation is not a root cause of crime. Facilitation is more like a catalyst in a chemical reaction that, given the right ingredients and conditions, speeds up the interaction. Facilitating victims attract criminally inclined people to their poorly guarded possessions and thereby influence the spatial distribution of crime but not the number of incidents.

Auto theft and burglary are the property crimes most often cited by victimologists who study the problem of facilitation. A motorist who carelessly leaves the keys dangling in the car's ignition is considered blameworthy if a juvenile joyrider impulsively hops behind the wheel and drives off (see below). Similarly, a ransacked home is the price a person might pay for negligence. A residential burglary can be considered victim facilitated if the intruder did not need to break into the premises because a homeowner or apartment dweller left the door unlocked or ajar or a window wide open.

By definition, victim-facilitated burglaries are not break-ins but rather acts of trespass that don't require busting down doors or smashing windows. Details about victim-facilitated burglaries appear in the published findings of the yearly *National Crime Victimization Survey.* The survey keeps track of three categories of household (not commercial) burglaries: forcible entries, attempted forcible entries, and unlawful entries without force (attempts that were not successfully completed are not counted because survey respondents usually would be unaware of these close calls).

Throughout the 1990s about 50% of all completed burglaries reported to *NCVS* interviewers were unlawful entries without force. The immediate impulse is to speculate that the total number of successful burglaries could be cut practically in half if people would take greater care to lock up their homes (if they did, burglars would have to work harder and in some cases would be deterred, thwarted, scared off, or caught red-handed).

Some kinds of people are more likely to be "guilty" of victim facilitation than others, according to the breakdowns presented in *NCVS* annual reports. The age of the head of the household turned out to be the most important determinant of whether or not someone would be so careless as to facilitate a burglary. Younger persons were much less careful than older persons. Another key factor was the number of people in the household: The more people living under the same roof, the more likely carelessness would take its toll. People living alone experienced far fewer facilitated burglaries. The region of the country also turned out to be important. Unlawful entries without force were much more of a problem in the West than in the Northeast. Also, facilitated burglaries exacted more of a toll among city dwellers than among suburbanites and people living in the countryside. Renters were more likely than owners to leave doors and windows open or unlocked. The race and ethnicity of the head of the household hardly mattered. Finally, the income of the family did not seem to be correlated with the no-force entry rate either, although the lowest-income families in the survey may have been the most careless (BJS, 1994b).

Since people often talk about the "good old days" when they left their doors unlocked, data about changes that have taken place over time reveal some interesting insights. The findings from the *NCVS* over the years from 1973 to 1998 (BJS, 1994a; Rennison, 1999) appear in the graph in Figure 3.1. The graph shows a trend that the sellers of alarm systems probably do not want publicized: that (total) burglary rates have dropped substantially over the years. Completed forcible entries (break-ins) declined by 60% from about 30 per 1,000 dwellings in 1973 to about 12 per 1,000 in 1998. Unlawful entries without force also dropped sharply (by over 50%) from a little more than 40 per 1,000 to around 20 per 1,000 over the 25-year time interval. Apparently, security consciousness is more widespread these days: Burglars must work harder because fewer people are making it easy for intruders to come into their homes and spirit off their possessions.

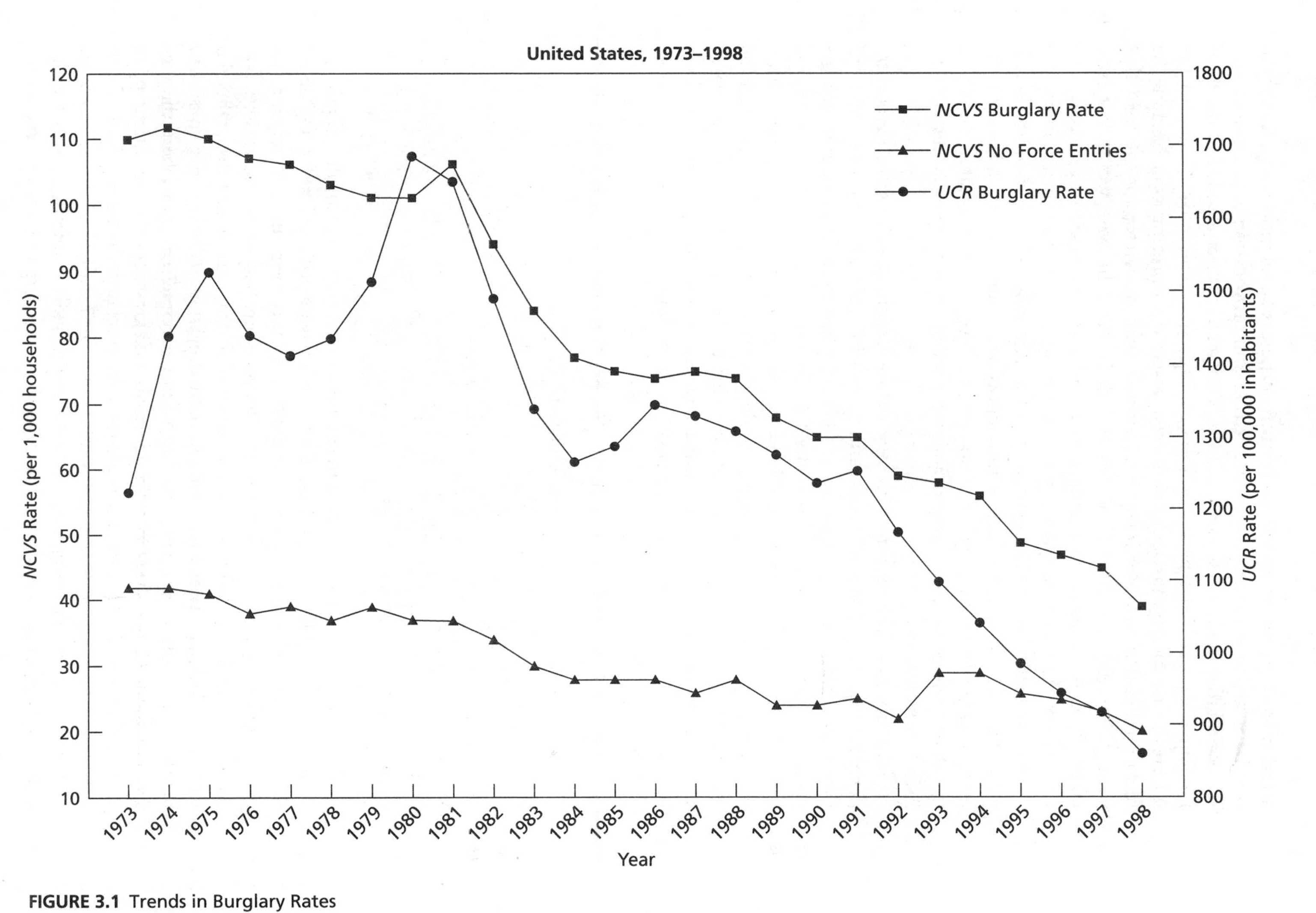

FIGURE 3.1 Trends in Burglary Rates

NOTE: 1973–1991 *NCVS* rates adjusted for compatibility with redesigned 1992 survey.
SOURCES: FBI's *UCR*, 1973–1998; BJS's *NCVS*, 1973–1998

Victim Precipitation and Provocation Whereas facilitation is a possibility in burglaries and thefts, charges of precipitation and provocation are hurled at victims of murder, robbery, assault, and rape. The accusation embedded in the term precipitation is that the person who gets hurt significantly contributed to the outbreak of violence. Provocation is even worse than precipitation because the term implies that the loser is more responsible than the victor for the fight that ensued. The injured party instigated an attack that otherwise would not have taken place. A provocative victim goaded, challenged, or incited a generally law-abiding person into taking defensive measures in reaction to forceful initiatives. When the battle ended the aggressor was the one who was wounded or killed. (Unfortunately, over the years, victimologists and criminologists have used the terms precipitation and provocation loosely, and even interchangeably, obscuring this distinction between less responsibility for precipitation and more responsibility for provocation).

The first in-depth investigation of what was deemed to be "victim precipitation" centered on homicides committed in Philadelphia from 1948 to 1952 (Wolfgang, 1958). Precipitation was the label applied to those cases in which the person who was killed had been the first to use force, either by drawing a weapon, striking the first physical blow during an argument, or in some other way initiating a resort to violence to settle a dispute. Often, the victim and the offender knew each other; some had quarreled previously. Situations that incited the participants to violence included charges of infidelity, arguments over money, drunken brawls, and confrontations over insults and "fighting words." Typical cases drawn from police reports were as follows:

> A husband threatened to kill his wife then attacked her with a knife. In the ensuing struggle he fell on his own weapon and bled to death.
>
> The person who ended up the victim was the one who had started a barroom shoving match. His friends tried to break up the fight, but he persisted. Finally the tide turned, and the aggressor was knocked down; he hit his head on the floor and died from his injuries.
>
> A man demanded money that he believed was owed to him. The other man maintained that he had repaid the debt and, incensed over the accusation, drew a knife. The creditor pulled out a gun and shot him as he lunged.

These victim-precipitated cases differed in a number of statistically significant ways from homicides in which the people who were slain did not bring about their own demise. Nearly all the precipitative victims were men, whereas a sizable minority of the totally innocent victims were women. Conversely, few women committed homicide, but a substantial proportion of those who did were provoked by the violence of the men they slew. Alcohol was consumed before most killings, especially prior to victim-precipitated ones where the victim was the one who had been doing the drinking rather than the offender. In cases of precipitation the victim was more likely to have had a previous run-in with the law than in cases of no precipitation. Over a third of the precipitative victims had a history of committing at least one violent offense, as opposed to only a fifth of the blameless victims. Overall, about 1 murder out of every 4 in

Philadelphia from 1948 to 1952 could be labeled as victim precipitated. Hence, widely held images of victims as weak and passive people shrinking from confrontations and of offenders as strong, brutal aggressors relentlessly pursuing their prey didn't fit the facts in a quarter of the cases, as reconstructed from the police department's files. In many of the victim-precipitated homicides, the characteristics of the victims closely resembled those of the offenders. In some cases two criminally inclined persons clashed, and chance alone determined which one would emerge as the winner or the loser in their final showdowns (Wolfgang, 1958).

Some precipitative victims actually may have wanted to die (Wolfgang, 1959). Their rash actions and foolhardy initiatives could be interpreted as attempts to commit suicide, as if they had a death wish but could not quite carry it through without help (Reckless, 1967). If the victim's outright dares and subliminal invitations are interpreted within this framework, victim-precipitated homicide is tantamount to suicide (Mueller, in Edelhertz and Geis, 1974). The term **subintentional death** can be applied to all situations in which victims play a contributory role in their own demise either by exercising poor judgment, taking excessive risks, or pursuing a self-destructive lifestyle (Allen, 1980). Obviously, this type of speculation, based on unverifiable interpretations of possible motives, is clearly unsympathetic to the dead victims who allegedly manipulated others to kill them. Coupled with the conclusion that a considerable proportion of slain people were largely responsible for their own fate, these outlooks foster a tendency to view some victims in a rather harsh light as troublemakers whose passing away is not a real tragedy.

This charge—that some people want to suffer and therefore consciously or unconsciously enter into risky situations or engineer tragic events that ultimately harm them—is leveled most commonly at repeat victims. In homicide cases the argument rests on a record of several "near misses" preceding the final violent outburst that claimed the victim's life. But an equally plausible explanation that is not psychologically based is that these precipitative victims didn't want to die, but instead thought they would emerge from their battles as winners, not losers. Their petty quarrels escalated into life-and-death struggles through a sequence of stages, or a series of transactions. The initial incident might be a personal affront, perhaps something as minor as a slur or gesture. Both the offender and the victim contribute to the escalation of a "character contest." As the confrontation spirals upward, each party attempts to "save face" at the other's expense by hurling taunts, insults, and threats, especially if onlookers are cheering them on (Luckenbill, 1977). Those who lost the showdowns didn't welcome their fate. What might be misinterpreted as their "death wish" was really their adherence to the norms of a **subculture of violence** (see Curtis, 1974; and Wolfgang and Ferracuti, 1967). In many serious assaults investigators often discover that both the victims and their assailants were mutual combatants immersed in lifestyles that championed a willingness to use force to resolve disputes (Singer, 1986). This readiness to resort to physical combat to settle arguments is not psychopathological but rather learned behavior. Lifestyles that require people to fight it out and not back down are reported to be most prevalent among southerners (Butterfield,

1999) and young men in poor urban neighborhoods who conform to "the code of the streets" in their quest to prove their manhood and gain their peers' respect (Anderson, 1999). But the reliance on force as a method of solving problems characterizes international politics as much as street-corner life.

Provocation is much worse than precipitation. In extreme cases the crime would not have occurred if a victim had not instigated or incited an otherwise law-abiding person into committing an illegal act, as the following example illustrates.

> **A** 23-year-old teacher befriends a 17-year-old high school student. She implores him to kill her because she is dying from a painful illness and is distraught over divorcing her husband. Reluctantly he agrees to shoot her, but she survives the botched job with a bullet to the shoulder. From her hospital bed she tries to turn the incident into an example of the need for greater school security, but detectives figure out what really happened, and the student is arrested for weapons possession and attempted murder. (Mitchell, 1992)

Note that according to the law, not all persons wounded or killed by shootings are victims. For example, an armed robber slain in a gun battle with the police would be classified as a dead offender, not a provocative victim. His demise would not be a murder but an act of justifiable homicide, provided that the officer used deadly force appropriately, according to state law and departmental regulations.

The Frequency of Shared Responsibility in Violent Crimes

The question of the victim's role in cases of street crime was systematically investigated for the first time in the late 1960s by the National Commission on the Causes and Prevention of Violence (NCCPV). As its name suggests, the blue-ribbon panel was searching for the roots of the crime problem and for practical remedies. If large numbers of victims were found to be partly at fault for what happened to them, then changing the behavior of the general public might be a promising crime prevention strategy. Social scientists working for the commission applied a definition of "victim precipitation" derived from previous studies by criminologists and victimologists to five types of crimes. Then they drew a sample of reports contained in police files from 17 cities and made a judgment about whether or not the victim shared responsibility with the offender in murders, aggravated assaults, forcible rapes, and robberies.

Victim-precipitated homicides (defined as situations in which the person who died was the first to resort to force) accounted for 22% of all murder cases in the 17 cities (not far off from the findings of other researchers), 26% in Philadelphia (Wolfgang, 1958), and 38% in Chicago (Voss and Hepburn, 1968). About 14% of all aggravated assaults (in which the seriously injured victim was the first to use physical force or offensive language and gestures) were deemed to be victim precipitated. Armed robberies were committed against precipitative victims "who clearly had not acted with reasonable self-protective behavior in handling money, jewelry, or other valuables" in 11% of all the holdups in the 17 cities, about the same as in a study of Philadelphia (Normandeau, 1968). Only 4% of the forcible rapes that led to arrests were designated as victim precipitated in which the woman "at first agreed to sexual relations, or clearly invited them verbally and through gestures, but then retracted before the act," although as many as 19% of all sexual assaults in Philadelphia were deemed to be precipitated (Amir, 1967) (see below). The commission concluded that instances of victim complicity were not uncommon in cases of homicide and aggravated assault, victim precipitation was less frequent but still empirically noteworthy in robbery, and the issue of shared responsibility was least relevant as a contributing factor in rapes (National Commission on the Causes and Prevention of Violence, 1969b; Curtis, 1974).

Recognizing Complete Innocence and Full Responsibility

Up to this point the degree of responsibility a victim might share with an offender has ranged from facilitation through precipitation to provocation. But the spectrum of possibilities extends further in each direction, from complete innocence to full responsibility.

Completely innocent individuals cannot be blamed for what happened to them. As crime-conscious persons, they tried to avoid trouble. They did what they reasonably could to reduce the risks they faced. (After the fact it can always be argued that they did not do enough.) In cases of property crimes, these victims took proactive steps to safeguard their possessions in anticipation of the possibility of burglary, larceny, or some other form of theft. They cannot be faulted for negligence or even passive indifference. In order to deter attacks, they sought ways to make the criminals' tasks more difficult. They "hardened their targets" by purchasing security devices like steering wheel locks, hidden ignition kill switches, and alarm systems for their cars. In cases of crimes of violence, they did nothing to instigate otherwise law-abiding people to attack them (no provocation) or to attract assailants to themselves; in fact, they were mindful of threatening situations and took precautions to limit their exposure to dangerous persons (no precipitation).

If taking precautions and adopting risk reduction strategies qualifies as the basis for blamelessness and complete innocence, then total complicity becomes the defining characteristic for full responsibility. Logically, a victim can be solely responsible only when there is no offender at all. Victims who bear total responsibility for what happened are by definition really not victims at all. They are offenders posing as victims for some ulterior motive. In cases of property crimes, phony victims usually seek either reimbursement from private insurance policies or government aid for imaginary losses. They file false claims and thereby commit fraud. Fake victims may have motives other than financial gain. Some people may claim to be victims to cover up what really occurred. For example, a husband who gambled away his paycheck may tell his wife and the police that he was robbed.

Typologies of Shared Responsibility

A typology is a classification scheme that aids in the understanding of what a group of people has in common and how it differs from others. Researchers have discussed and dismissed the possibility of "born victims" who are doomed from birth to become targets. They have also observed that the social reaction to victimization is not always outrage, empathy, and support but can range from indifference to tacit approval. Over the decades victimologists have devised many typologies to try to illustrate the degree of shared responsibility, if any, that victims bear in particular crimes. Some of the categories of persons identified in typologies include victims who are "ideal" (above criticism), "culturally legitimate and appropriate" (fair game, outcasts), "deserving" (asked for trouble), "consenting" (willing), and "recidivist" (chronic) (see Fattah, 1991; also Mendelsohn, 1956; Fattah, 1967; Lamborn, 1968; Schafer, 1977; and Sheley, 1979).

A Typology of Auto Theft Victims A typology of different kinds of victims of a single crime, such as auto theft, can be useful to illustrate the differences between complete innocence, facilitation, precipitation, provocation, and full responsibility. Such a typology also makes it possible to derive estimates about the relative proportions of various types or groupings of people—what they did "wrong," if anything, and how crime might be prevented (see Table 3.1).

Conscientiously resisting victims are totally blameless. They bear no responsibility because they tried to protect their autos by scrupulously following the crime-prevention tips suggested by security specialists and by purchasing antitheft devices. Yet the defensive measures they adopted proved futile, and they were preyed upon by professional thieves who knew how to disarm or circumvent the most sophisticated alarm systems and resistant locks.

Conventionally cautious victims relied upon the antitheft features provided by automobile manufacturers as standard equipment. They took the precautions of removing all valuables from sight, rolling up their cars' windows, locking all doors, and pocketing the keys. Even though they did all they were supposed to do, experienced thieves with the proper tools had no trouble driving off with their cars. These victims did nothing "wrong," but since they did not undertake the extra efforts to make their cars extra theft resistant, they can be faulted for not taking the threat of car stealing seriously enough. Thus, they can be considered largely blameless, although they are not above criticism.

Carelessly facilitating victims set the stage for crimes of opportunity through gross negligence. Their vehicles were taken by inexperienced thieves and teenage joyriders. They made the criminals' tasks easier by leaving their car doors unlocked, their windows rolled down, or, worst of all, their keys dangling in the ignition. They can be considered partly responsible precisely because their thoughtless behavior and indifferent attitudes contributed to their own losses. However, they were unintentional, unwilling, inadvertent victims who bear no guilt legally. (However, rental car companies might hold such customers financially liable for the cost of the lost vehicles if they left their keys in the cars [Marriott, 1991].)

Precipitative initiators were knowing and willing victims who intentionally singled out their vehicles for trouble. They wanted their cars to be stolen because they coldly calculated that they would be better off financially if they received the "blue book" value as reimbursement from the insurance company rather than if they kept their cars or tried to repair them or sell them. So they

Table 3.1 Types of Victims of Auto Theft

Type of Victim	Conscientiously Resisting	Conventionally Cautious	Carelessly Facilitating	Precipitative Initiators	Provocative Conspirators	Fabricating Simulators
Degree of responsibility	Totally blameless	Largely blameless	Partly responsible	Substantially responsible	Largely responsible	Fully responsible
Actions of victim	Takes special precautions	Takes conventional measures	Facilitates theft through negligence	Precipitates theft by leaving car exposed and vulnerable	Provokes theft by arrangements with criminals	Fabricates theft of nonexistent car
Motivations of victim	Determined to minimize risks	Concerned about risks	Indifferent to risks	Wants car to be stolen	Determined to have car stolen	Seeks to make it look as if car were stolen
Financial outcome after theft	Loses money	Loses money	Loses money	Gains money from insurance coverage	Gains money from insurance coverage	Makes large profit from false claim
Approximate proportion of all victims, currently	← 55% →		← 20% →	← 25% →		
Legal status	← Actual victims →			← Criminals posing as victims to commit insurance fraud →		
Extent of attention	← Overlooked →		← Objects of public education campaigns, sometimes scapegoated →	← Objects of investigations and new legislation →		

SOURCE: Adapted from Karmen, 1980.

took steps that went beyond carelessness. They deliberately left their cars unlocked with the keys in the ignition and parked invitingly in high-crime areas. By maximizing the vulnerability of their autos, they incited would-be thieves to strike. But the relationships between the precipitating victims and their criminals were impersonal; they never met each other despite the symbiosis between them. If challenged or investigated, these substantially responsible victims could conceal their dishonest motives and contend that they were merely negligent motorists who had accidentally left their keys in their cars.

Provocative conspirators are largely responsible for the stealing of their cars. These individuals pretended to be injured parties but actually were the accomplices of the thieves whom they hired to get rid of their cars. Without their instigations, the thefts would not have taken place. As part of a conspiracy to commit insurance fraud, these owners arranged to have their cars "splashed" (driven off a bridge or pier into deep water), "squished" (compacted, crushed, and then shredded beyond recognition), or "torched" (set on fire) to collect insurance reimbursement. Provocative conspirators share the same financial motives as substantially responsible victims, but they leave nothing to chance; they know and pay off the criminals who work with them (see Behar, 1993).

Fully responsible victims are really not victims at all because they never even owned cars. They insured a nonexistent vehicle (a "paper car," or "phantom car") and later reported it stolen to the authorities so that they could collect money by defrauding insurance companies. They simulated being a victim and fabricated the entire episode for their own dishonest purposes.

The relative mix of these six types of auto theft victims can be roughly estimated. Carelessly facilitating victims who leave their keys in their cars make up at most 20% of all victims in the 1990s (but constituted a higher proportion decades ago; see the discussion later in this chapter). Another 10% to 25% are suspected of engaging in insurance fraud (Baldwin, 1988; Sloane, 1991; Kerr, 1992). The percentage of conscientiously resisting motorists is more difficult to operationalize and measure, but it is growing as more cars on the road are protected by alarms and other built-in or after-market antitheft devices. If as many as 25% of all victims wanted their cars to be stolen (precipitative initiators, provocative conspirators, and fabricating simulators) and another 20% were careless facilitators, then conventionally cautious and conscientiously resisting motorists together add up to the remaining 55%. Therefore, the majority of auto theft victims (perhaps as many as 70%, assuming the lower national estimate for insurance fraud cases) are totally or basically innocent and should not be criticized in any way for their losses.

Victim Blaming Versus Victim Defending

Arguments that the victims of crime might share responsibility with their offenders for what happened due to facilitation, precipitation, and provocation have been characterized as **victim blaming. Victim defending** counters this approach by challenging whether it is accurate and fair to try to hold the injured party accountable to some degree for the injuries and losses that happened.

Since there are two opposing ideologies, it seems reasonable to presume that there are two distinct camps, victim blamers and victim defenders. But most people are not consistent when they analyze crime. They criticize specific individuals but defend others, or they find fault with certain groups of victims (for example, abusive husbands who get killed by their wives) but not other groups (such as women who have been raped by acquaintances).

Victim blaming casts doubt on the legal categories of "completely guilty" and "totally innocent." It states that they are potentially misleading descriptions of who did what to whom if precipitation or provocation took place. According to this view, applying such dichotomous labels to real people in actual situations often results in gross simplifications and distortions of the truth of why laws were violated. Victim blaming proceeds from the assumption that the offender and the victim are sometimes "partners in crime," that a degree of mutuality, symbiosis, or reciprocity may exist between them (Von Hentig, 1948). In such cases, investigating the past police record, possible motives, reputation, and actions of the victim as well as the offender can be justified (Schultz, 1968).

Victimology, despite its aspirations toward objectivity, may harbor an unavoidable tendency toward victim blaming. It is inevitable that a careful reconstruction of the behavior of a victim before, during, and after a crime will turn up rash decisions, foolish mistakes, errors in judgment, and inexcusable carelessness that with hindsight can be clearly seen to have shaped the unfortunate outcome. Step-by-step analyses of actions and reactions are sure to reveal evidence of what victims did (or failed to do) that contributed to their own losses and suffering.

Victim blaming follows a three-stage thought process (see Ryan, 1971). First, the assumption is made that there is something "wrong" with victims. They are thought to differ significantly from people who have never been singled out: Their attitudes, their behaviors, or both distinguish them from the unafflicted majority. Second, these presumed differences are said to be the source of the victims' plight. If they were like everyone else, the reasoning goes, they would never be targeted for attack. Finally, victims are warned that if they want to avoid trouble in the future, they must change how they think and act. They must abandon the careless, rash, or inciteful behaviors that brought about their downfall.

Arising from a microscopic, interpersonal, and interactionist analysis of a particular sequence of events, victim blaming is a widely held point of view for several reasons. It provides specific and straightforward answers to troubling questions like 'Why did it happen" and "Why him and not me?" Victim blaming also has great psychological appeal because it draws on deep philosophical and even theological beliefs concerning why "bad" things happen to seemingly "good" people. In addition, victim blaming readily comes to mind because it is a familiar theme, often voiced spontaneously by wrongdoers and presented even more convincingly by defense attorneys.

The widely held doctrine of personal accountability that underlies the legal system also encourages victim-blaming explanations. Just as criminals are condemned and punished for their wrongdoing, so too must victims answer for their behavior before, during, and after an incident. In retrospect, they may be faulted for errors in judgment that only made things worse or credited for minimizing the harm they experienced. Such assessments of praise or blame are grounded in the belief that people exercise a substantial degree of control over the course of events in their lives. They may not be totally in command, but they are not powerless or helpless and do not have to go around in resignation, waiting passively to become a statistic. Just as cautious motorists should study the techniques of defensive driving to minimize the risks of getting involved in an accident, crime-conscious individuals are obliged to review their lifestyles and routine activities to do what they reasonably can to enhance their personal safety. By following the advice of security experts about how to keep out of trouble, those who are cautious and concerned can find personal solutions to the social problem of crime in the streets.

Fervent believers in a "just world" outlook—that people get what they deserve during their lives—find victim blaming a comforting outlook. Bad things happen only to evil characters; good souls are rewarded for following the rules. Imagining a world governed by random events where senseless and brutal acts might be inflicted on anyone at any time is unnerving. The belief that victims must have done something neglectful, foolish, or provocative that brought about their misfortunes dispels feelings of helplessness and extreme vulnerability and gives the blamer peace of mind (Lerner, 1965; Symonds, 1975).

Victim blaming is also the view of offenders who are devoid of feelings of empathy and pity. Evidently, they have undergone a process of desensitization that reduces or even eliminates the guilt, shame, remorse, and moral inhibitions that would otherwise constrain their behavior. By derogating and denigrating the victim, juvenile delinquents or adult criminals can picture their harmful acts as justifiable. Outbursts of stark cruelty and savagery become possible when the victim is viewed as worthless, less than human, an appropriate target for venting hostility and aggression, or as an outcast deserving mistreatment (Fattah, 1976, 1979). To neutralize any pangs of concience, delinquents frequently disparage their intended victims as having negative traits ("He was asking for it," or "They are a bunch of thieves themselves"). In extreme cases youthful offenders picture the suffering they inflict as retaliatory justice that ought to be applauded ("We deserve a medal for doing that") (Sykes and Matza, 1957; Schwendinger and Schwendinger, 1967). Defense attorneys may persuasively articulate the victim-blaming views of their clients, especially in high-profile murder cases. A "trash-the-reputation" (demonization of the deceased) approach coupled with a "sympathy" (for the accused) defense might succeed in swaying a jury and securing an acquittal or in convincing a judge to hand down a lesser sentence. For example, in cases where children slay their parents, the dead fathers and mothers may be pictured as brutal abusers and perverse molesters, while their offspring are portrayed as the helpless targets of adult cruelty (see Estrich, 1993b; and Hoffman, 1994).

Victim defending rejects the premises of victim blaming (that victims are partly at fault) and challenges its recommendations (that victims must change their ways). First of all, victim blaming is criticized for overstating the extent to which facilitation, precipitation, or provocation explains the genesis of an illegal act. Motivated offenders would have struck their chosen targets even if the victims had not made their tasks easier, called attention to themselves, or aroused their anger. Second, victim blaming is condemned for confusing the exception with the rule and overestimating the actual proportion of cases in which facilitation, precipitation, or provocation occurred. Shared responsibility is unusual, not common. A few people's mistakes don't justify placing the attitudes and behaviors of most victims under a cloud of suspicion. Third, exhorting people to be more cautious and vigilant is no solution. This advice is unrealistic because it overlooks the cultural imperatives and social conditions that largely shape lifestyles. Most people lack the opportunities and resources to alter their means of travel, their hours of work, the company they keep, the schools their children attend, or the neighborhoods in which they live. Some of the sharpest attacks on victim blaming's notions of shared responsibility are presented in Box 3.2.

Victim defending is clear about what it opposes, but it is vague about what it supports in terms of who or what is to be faulted. Two tendencies within victim defending can be distinguished. The first can be called **offender blaming.** Offender blaming resists any attempt to shift the burden of full responsibility off of lawbreakers' backs and onto the victims' shoulders. Victim defending coupled with offender blaming represents an inconsistent and one-sided application of the doctrine of personal accountability because only the aggressors, not their targets, are held responsible for their misbehavior. The second tendency is to link victim defending with system blaming. According to the tenets of system blaming, neither the offender nor the victim is the real culprit; to varying degrees both are largely products of their culture and social environment. The attitudes and behaviors of both parties have been influenced by socialization—parental input, peer group pressures, school experiences, media images—along with criminal justice practices, economic imperatives, and many other social forces. Victim defending/system blaming is a more complex and sophisticated outlook than victim defending/offender blaming. According to this sociological type of analysis, the roots of the crime problem are to be found in the basic institutions upon which the social system is built (among many others, see Franklin, 1978; and Balkan, Berger, and Schmidt, 1980).

To illustrate the differences between victim blaming, victim defending/offender blaming, and victim defending/system blaming, three problem areas will be explored. First, charges of victim facilitation in automobile theft will be examined; then the controversy over whether or not some rapes are victim precipitated will be presented; and finally, the possibility that some murdered husbands provoked their wives to slay them will be investigated.

Victim Facilitation and Auto Theft: Is It the Careless Who Wind up Carless?

Some people mistakenly consider auto theft to be the "happy crime" in which no one loses and everyone gains (see Plate, 1975). The thief makes money, the owner gets reimbursed by the insurance company and then enjoys the pleasure

BOX 3.2 Criticisms of the Notion of Shared Responsibility

- The concept of victim precipitation has become confused because it has been operationalized in too many different, often incompatible ways. As a result, it has lost much of its usefulness as an empirical and explanatory tool. (Silverman, 1974, p. 99)
- The study of victim precipitation is the least exact of the sociological approaches; it is part a priori guesswork and part "armchair detective fun and games" because the interpretation rests in the final analysis on a set of arbitrary standards. (Brownmiller, 1975, p. 353)
- A tendency of investigators to assign responsibility for criminal acts to the victims' behavior reinforces similar beliefs and rationalizations held by most criminals themselves. . . . Scientific skepticism should be mantained regarding the concept of victim participation, especially for crimes of sudden, unexpected violence where the offender is a stranger to the victim. (Symonds, 1975, p. 22)
- Victims of crime, long ignored but now the object of special scholarly attention, had better temper their enthusiasm because they may be more maligned than lauded, and their plight may not receive sympathetic understanding. Some victimologists have departed from the humanitarian, helping orientation of the founders of the field and have turned victimology into the art of blaming the victim. If the impression of a "legitimate victim" is created, then part of the burden of guilt is relieved from the perpetrator, and some crimes, like rape for example, can emerge as without either victims or offenders. (Weis and Borges, 1973, p. 85)
- Victim precipitation explanations are plagued by the fallacy of circular reasoning about the cause of the crime, suffer from over-simplified stimulus-response models of human interaction, ignore incongruent facts that don't fit the theory, and inadequately explore the victim's intentions. (Franklin and Franklin, 1976, p. 134)
- An analytical framework must be found that salvages the positive contributions of the concept of victim precipitation, while avoiding its flaws—its tendency to consider a victim's provocations as both a necessary and sufficient condition for an offense to occur; its portrayal of some offenders as unrealistically passive; and its questionable moral and legal implications about who is the guilty party. (Sheley, 1979, pp. 126–127)
- Crime victimization is a neglected social problem in part because victim precipitation studies typically fail to articulate the distress of the victims and instead suggest that some may be to blame for their own plight. The inferences often drawn from these studies—that some individuals can steer clear of trouble by avoiding certain situations—suffer from the "post hoc ergo propter hoc" fallacy of treating the victims' behavior as both necessary and sufficient to cause the crime. (Teevan, 1979, p. 7)
- To accept precipitation and provocation as legitimate excuses for attenuating responsibility for violent crime is false, illogical, psychologically harmful to victims, and socially irresponsible. . . . Victim-blaming has been injected into the literature on crime by well-meaning but offender-oriented professionals. It becomes the basis and excuse for the indifference shown to supposedly "undeserving" victims. (Reiff, 1979, pp.12, 14)
- The eager acceptance of arguments about victim responsibility by scholars and the public alike is undeserved; these accounts of why the crime occurred often lack empirical verification, can lead to cruel insensitivity to the suffering of the victim, and tend to exonerate or even justify the acts of the offenders, especially rapists. (Anderson and Renzetti, 1980, p. 325)

of shopping for a new car, the manufacturer gains a customer who wasn't due back in the showroom for another couple of years, and the insurance company gets a chance to raise comprehensive fire and theft loss premiums and invest that money in profitable ventures. But in actuality, most victims of auto theft are quite upset for a number of reasons. Many motorists devote a great deal of time, effort, and loving care in keeping their vehicles in good shape. Second, the shock of discovering that the vehicle vanished touches off a sense of violation and insecurity that lingers for a long time. Third, not all owners purchase theft coverage, usually because they cannot afford it. Even those who are insured almost always must pay a hefty deductible out of their own pockets. Any personal items left in the trunk are lost as are any expensive add-ons, like stereos and radar detectors. The loss is always unanticipated, necessitating emergency measures like taking cabs, renting cars, and canceling important appointments. Finally, motorists who collect insurance reimbursement may find that either their premiums are raised or their policies are not renewed.

Car stealing is an old problem. As long ago as 1919, Congress passed the Dyer Act that authorized the FBI to investigate organized theft rings because professional thieves were driving stolen vehicles across state borders to evade local police forces with limited jurisdictions. Five different motives for car theft can be distinguished. Juvenile joyriding (which the law calls "unauthorized use of a motor vehicle" and treats as a minor offense) has been a craze among teenage boys ever since cars were marketed with the message that owning one is a sign of manhood. These amateurs—who seek the status, thrills, and challenge of "borrowing" cars to impress their friends—often prey upon careless motorists. But professional thieves don't need to rely on the negligence of drivers. It takes them just a few minutes with the right tools to disarm alarm systems and defeat standard security hardware like door, ignition, and steering wheel locks. These pros, working in league with commercial theft rings, steal cars either to sell or to strip. Steal-to-sell operations ("retagging") alter the registration and title documents and vehicle identification number, and then pass off the hot car as a used car. Steal-to-strip operations ("chop shops") dismantle vehicles and sell the crash-replacement parts (sheet metal components like the hood, trunk lid, fenders, and doors) to auto body repair shops as if they came from legitimate salvage and recycling pipelines. A fourth motive for stealing a vehicle is to use it for temporary or short-term travel, often as a getaway car after committing some other crime, such as a bank robbery. The fifth variety of auto theft is provided as a "service" to the victim as part of a conspiracy to commit insurance fraud. Some owners pay to have their cars disposed of without a trace so that they can collect insurance reimbursement for vehicles they no longer want or can afford to run or repair.

Changes in motor vehicle theft rates over the past few decades appear in Figure 3.2. One trend line portrays the yearly rates of all thefts of noncommercial vehicles disclosed to survey interviewers, whether successful completions or failed attempts, for every 1,000 households. The other trend line depicts the yearly rates per 100,000 people of completed or attempted thefts of all kinds of motorized vehicles reported to police departments across the country. Statistics derived from both the *NCVS* as well as the *UCR* indicate that rates of auto theft rose during the late 1980s, reached an all-time high at the start of the 1990s, and subsided as the century drew to a close. Also (not shown in Figure 3.2), stolen car recovery rates have dropped from over 90% in the 1940s and 1950s to about 73% in 1998 (according to *NCVS* nationwide figures) and are lower in some cities plagued by commercial

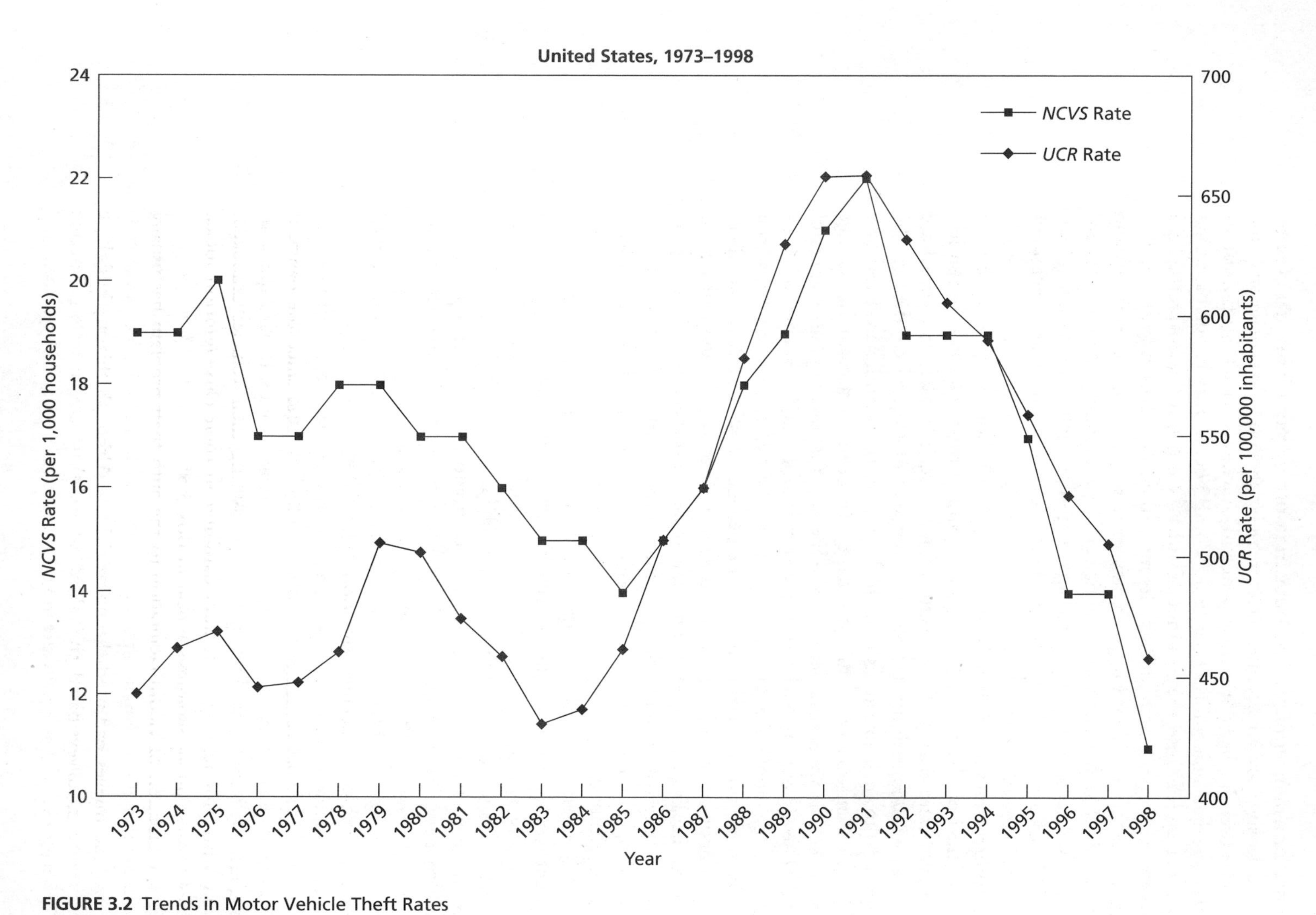

FIGURE 3.2 Trends in Motor Vehicle Theft Rates

NOTE: 1973–1991 *NCVS* rates adjusted for compatibility with redesigned 1992 survey.
SOURCES: FBI's *UCR* 1973–1998; BJS's *NCVS*, 1973–1998

rings. Even though a car is the kind of stolen property that is most likely to be returned to its rightful owner, about 25% of these "fortunate" motorists who get their vehicles back might be dismayed. What the police retrieve might be just an irreparable stripped hulk of what was formerly a source of pride and joy. The mean loss per motor vehicle theft was $6,800 in 1998 (BJS, 1999). This explains why car owners must pay such high insurance premiums for theft coverage.

As noted in chapter 2, all categories of people do not face the same chances of being harmed by criminals. In the case of auto theft, differential risks are determined by a number of factors. According to an analysis of over 12 million attempted and completed vehicle thefts disclosed to *NCVS* interviewers between 1973 and 1985, the categories of people who faced the greatest dangers of losing their cars were households headed by persons under the age of 25, apartment dwellers, residents of inner-city neighborhoods, African Americans and Hispanic Americans, and low-income families. The kinds of people whose cars were least likely to be stolen were residents of rural areas, those over 55, and homeowners (Harlow, 1988). Another risk factor was the make, model, and year of the car, since some types are more prized by thieves, are in greater demand in the market for stolen crash parts, or are easier to steal than others (see Clark and Harris, 1992; "NICB Study," 1993; Krauss, 1994). An analysis of insurance records revealed that for several reasons as cars age, they become more of a target for thieves, especially during their fourth, fifth, and sixth years on the road. If the model lines are not substantially redesigned, then the older cars can be stolen for parts to repair newer ones. Also middle-aged cars are less likely to be equipped with the latest state-of-the-art antitheft devices that thieves have not yet learned to defeat. Another reason is that as cars wear out their owners have less incentive to maintain security devices in good working order and to vigilantly observe precautions about where they park their less-valuable vehicles. Since most cars have a life expectancy of only 7 to 10 years, owners should never let their guard down, experts say ("NICB Study," 1993).

Blaming the Victim for Facilitating the Crime The question remains: Who or what is to blame for the theft and attempted theft of more than a million vehicles a year?

Car stealing seems to be the only crime for which there is an organized victim-blaming lobby, a peculiar situation that developed long ago. Composed of representatives of the automakers, insurance companies, and law enforcement agencies, this lobby has castigated motorist carelessness ever since the dawn of the automobile age. As their public pronouncements show, they are quick to fault negligent drivers for facilitating thefts by leaving their vehicles unlocked, and even worse for leaving their keys dangling in their cars' ignition locks. Examples of these public scoldings appear in Box 3.3.

The contribution of victim facilitation to the auto theft problem has usually been measured as the percentage of recovered stolen cars in which there was evidence that the thieves had used the owners' keys. Although this methodology has its limitations, surveys based on it show a trend that casts doubt on the continued relevance of negligence as a factor. Data derived from insurance company

BOX 3.3 Examples of "Motorist Blaming"

Source *Affiliation* *Date*	*Statement*
George Henderson Criminologist 1924	Careless owners of automobiles have their cars standing on the street with their engines running, with the magneto key in the locks or entirely unlocked on avenues of the city or in unprotected garages. And in so doing they make life a picnic for the car thief . . . Nine tenths of the loss by theft of automobiles is due to the carelessness of the owner (pp. 36, 38).
August Vollmer Police chief Berkeley, California 1936	No intelligent person would put from $1,000 to $5,000 in good money in the street and expect to find it there an hour later, yet that is exactly what a large number of people do when they leave an automobile in the street without locking it. Even more, not only are they leaving money at the curb but they are also putting four wheels under it to make it easier for the thief to take it (p. 65).
William Davis National Automobile Theft Bureau 1954	What is it about the American public that makes them so disrespectful of their own property as it applies to automobiles? . . . To us the greatest single cause of the theft of these cars is public indifference and irresponsibility (in U.S. Congress, 1954, pp. 383, 385).

records from the 1940s through the 1960s indicate that at least 40% and as many as about 90% of all thefts were facilitated by victims through carelessness about locks and keys. Since the 1970s, police, FBI, and insurance industry records estimate facilitation to be factor in from 13% to 20% of all thefts (Karmen, 1979; NIJ, 1984). In the early 1990s an insurance industry publication reported that only 13% of all vehicle thefts were still victim facilitated (National Insurance Crime Bureau, 1993).

These estimates support the following analysis: At one time, when the public was less concerned about crime, facilitation may have contributed substantially to the joyriding problem. But teenage amateurs no longer account for most of the car stealing that goes on in cities and suburbs. Professionals—often working for commercial rings that may be affiliated with organized crime syndicates—now represent the greater threat to car owners. As the years roll by, facilitation is declining in significance.

Even though the proportions of car thefts that are facilitated by motorists have been dropping over the decades, the absolute number remains high. (For example, if 13% of the roughly 820,000 completed thefts in 1998 were made easier by the thoughtless behavior of drivers, that means over 100,000 of these successful acts of car stealing were preventable.) According to a poll of 1,000 motorists commissioned by insurance companies, evidence persists that drivers are still not doing all they can to safeguard their prized possessions. Nearly 40% said they

BOX 3.3 *continued*

Source *Affiliation* *Date*	*Statement*
J. Edgar Hoover FBI director 1966	Yet through all this practical, emotional, and monetary attachment to the automobile, there emerges convincing evidence that it is one of the motorist's most carelessly neglected possessions.
John Roche President General Motors Corporation 1967	Carelessness by car owners is a major factor in car theft, and a strong educational effort will be required to alert the public to the dangers of theft (p. 7594).
Donald Wolfslayer Assistant chief engineer for security Chrysler Corporation 1975	All the security you put in a car is not going to do a darned bit of good if people are careless. People have to learn to take better care of their autos (in "Offenders Get Wrists Slapped," 1975, p. 2).
Travelers Insurance Company 1977	Will your car be next? It needn't be. Not if you follow these simple precautions. . . . if you're careless about these tips you may wind up carless (pp. 1–2).
U.S. News & World Report Magazine column 1992	Take the keys. Obvious? Sure. But 20% of stolen cars are all but given to thieves by owners who leave keys in the ignition ("Where's the Car?" March 30, p. 72).

were "not at all concerned" about having their cars stolen. As for taking precautions, about 75% of all owners had not installed an alarm or any other antitheft device in their vehicles. As many as 30% conceded that they did not always lock their car doors, and roughly 10% confessed that there were occasions when they left their keys in their parked cars (National Insurance Crime Bureau, 1995).

The clash in outlooks between victim blaming and victim defending is another example of the half-empty/half-full debate. Victim blaming focuses on the proportion of motorists who still have bad habits; victim defending emphasizes that the overwhelming majority of people whose cars were stolen did nothing wrong. The theft of their cars was not facilitated in any way. These drivers don't have self-defeating attitudes and don't act carelessly. According to victim defenders, the image of the absentminded owner that is frequently conjured up in victim-blaming arguments is an outmoded stereotype that no longer fits most motorists.

Victim Precipitation and Rape: Was It Somehow Her Fault?

Late one night a 22-year-old mother of two enters a bar filled with men. She has a few drinks and flirts with some of the patrons. Suddenly she finds herself held down on a pool table. Six young men force themselves upon her as onlookers cheer and she screams and curses. The six men are arrested and put on trial for aggravated rape. Their defense is that she acted seductively and "led them on." The prosecution argues that a sexual assault begins when a man continues after a woman has said no. The jury concludes that she did not consent to what they did to her and convicts four of the six. The judge sentences them to terms of from 6 to 12 years in prison. At a rally held on behalf of the victim, speakers hail the outcome as a symbol that gang rape will not be tolerated as a spectator sport. But at a demonstration protesting the verdicts and sentences, speakers sympathetic to the young men contend "She got herself raped" and "She should have known what she was getting herself into." They hold her largely responsible for enabling the men "to take advantage of her." (Schanberg, 1984, 1989)

A man is on trial for rape. His lawyer points out that the alleged victim was wearing a tank top, a lacy miniskirt, and no underpants. The defendant is found not guilty because, as one juror explains, "We felt she asked for it." The failed prosecution inspires the state legislature to amend the laws governing rape trials to bar defense attorneys from asking complainants about the clothes they were wearing at the time of the assaults. (Merrill, 1994)

A young man convinces a young woman to go back to his apartment after a date. They begin to kiss, but when he makes further sexual overtures she politely whispers "no." He persists, believing that the dating ritual requires the male to be the aggressor and the female to respond with ladylike "token resistance," at least at first. He assumes from past experience that "no" means "maybe" and "maybe" means "yes," unless he gets a slap in the face. When she says she's not ready for "that" yet, he misinterprets her protestation as an invitation to be even more assertive. As he climbs on top of her, she becomes petrified that further resistance will be met with violence. The evening ends with the young man perceiving that he ultimately "seduced" her, and the young woman feeling that she was violated against her will. She has him arrested. (Dershowitz, 1988)

A paradox surrounds the crime of rape. On the one hand, a victim's allegations may be sneered at and could become the subject of crude jokes. On the other hand, some rapists are punished so severely that sexual assaults can be considered one of the most terrible and strictly forbidden of all interpersonal crimes. (In the past, hundreds of accused rapists were lynched by angry mobs; between 1930 and 1968, 455 convicted rapists were executed in the United States. When the Supreme Court ruled in 1976 that capital punishment was an excessive penalty for rape, life imprisonment became the maximum sentence.) The wide range in reactions arises in part because accusations are subject to interpretations shaped by social attitudes as much as by legal codes, and both attitudes and laws have been changing. What "really happened" is interpreted first by the two people and then by the police, the prosecution, the judge, and the jury (as well as the media and the public). The confusion surrounding controversial cases stems from judgments about whether or not the victim bears any blame for the offender's sexual aggression. Charges about shared responsibility can arise in both kinds of forcible rapes: in **classic** (Williams, 1984) or **real** (in the public's mind) rapes (Estrich, 1986), epitomized by the knife-wielding stranger who leaps out of the darkness in a "blitz attack" to "ambush" and subdue his prey; and in **acquaintance rapes,** which arise out of interactions between people who know each other (as friends, relatives, neighbors, classmates, coworkers, or dates). A number of differences stand out when acquaintance rapes are compared to sexual assaults by strangers. Acquaintance rapes are more likely to take place in the victim's home or nearby, while ambushes by strangers are more likely to occur outdoors, in public places like parks. Strangers are more likely to brandish weapons and injure their victims; acquaintances are more likely to be drunk or high on drugs (Bachman, 1994a). (**Statutory rapes,** in contrast to **forcible rapes,** do not involve violence or threats but are exploitive seductions of minors below the age of consent.)

It is not clear from official statistics whether victims are assaulted more often by complete strangers or by assailants they know because so many victims don't want to disclose the incidents to anyone. The attacker was a stranger more than half the time (55%), according to an analysis of over 500,000 attempted and completed rapes discussed with *NCVS* interviewers from 1982 to 1984 (Timrots and Rand, 1987). However, a comparable analysis of *NCVS* data from 1987 to 1991 yielded a somewhat lower figure of 44% assaults by strangers (Bachman, 1994a). But in 3,800 cases reported to the police from three states in 1991, the girl or woman did not know the assailant in only 28% of the cases (Reaves, 1993). For a number of reasons, victims assaulted by someone they know may be more reluctant to report the crime to the police or even disclose the incident to survey interviewers. They may experience a greater sense of shame, guilt, embarrassment, and self-blame and may feel that they should have been able to prevent the attack. They may wish to protect the identity of the assailant if he is a relative, former friend, boss, or other powerful figure. They may fear reprisals for going to the authorities and may dread that if they do, their account will not be believed (Klaus, DeBerry, and Timrots, 1985). Another important consideration is that girls and women raped by acquaintances are much more likely to be blamed than those sexually assaulted by strangers.

The clash between victim blaming and victim defending is particularly sharp when it comes to rape. If auto theft provided a clear illustration of a crime for which there is a well-organized and well-financed group with a vested interest in promoting victim blaming, then rape serves as the best example of a crime for which there is a vocal and deeply committed victim-defending community. The controversy erupts over whether certain instances of rape should be viewed as victim-precipitated acts of uncontainable male sexual passion or whether all instances of forced sex are inexcusable acts of brutal domination always imposed upon unwilling, objectified targets.

A great deal is at stake in the battle between victim-blaming and victim-defending viewpoints for public support. The problem of rape forces people to choose between two very different courses of action. Who or what has to change: how women behave in the company of men, as victim blaming contends, or how boys are raised to treat girls and women, as victim defending emphasizes? Accepting victim-blaming arguments might lead to the acquittal of certain defendants, but the more socially significant consequence is that this line of thought "excuses" institutions and traditions that are now under attack for demeaning women. According to victim defenders who blame the system, to reduce the threat of rape it is necessary to root out the antifemale biases found within rigid sex roles, prevailing definitions of masculinity and femininity, existing laws and criminal justice practices, and popular culture (for example, see Hills, 1981).

Victim-Blaming Views The victim-blaming viewpoint contends that some rape victims differ in their attitudes and actions from other females who have never been subjected to a sexual assault. Victims who are "guilty" of precipitation singled themselves out for trouble through their own reckless deeds and "got themselves raped." They are condemned for showing poor judgment and failing to heed warnings about what they wore, said, or did. Their rash actions attracted violence-prone men and aroused irrepressible passions in them (MacDonald, 1971).

The most widely cited (and most heavily criticized) study of victim precipitation in rape was based on data drawn from the files of the Philadelphia police concerning cases reported in 1958 and 1960 (Amir, 1971). The researcher considered precipitation to have occurred whenever a girl's or woman's behavior was interpreted by a man or teenage boy either as a direct invitation to engage in sexual relations that was later retracted (she agreed and then changed her mind, according to him) or as a sign that she would be available if he persisted in his demands (she was saying *no* but meant *yes* in his opinion). Included in this researcher's working definition of a precipitated rape were acts of commission like drinking alcohol, hitchhiking a ride, or using what could be taken as indecent language or gestures; acts of omission, like failing to object strongly enough to his sexually charged overtures also counted against her. The offender's interpretation was considered to be the crucial element in recognizing instances of precipitation. Even if the offender was mistaken in his beliefs about her intentions, his perceptions led to actions and that is what mattered. In the police files the specific indicators of precipitation were statements by the offender, witnesses, or detectives claiming that "she behaved provocatively," "she acted seductively," "she was irresponsible and endangered herself," or "she had a bad reputation in the neighborhood." Using these criteria the researcher deemed 19% of Philadelphia's forcible rapes to be precipitated. Comparing precipitated rapes with nonprecipitated ones, it was found that consuming alcohol was more likely to have taken place, and that the offender was more inclined to sexually humiliate his victim. Precipitating victims included higher percentages of females who were white, teenagers, and casual acquaintances of the males they first met at bars or parties (Amir, 1971).

The victim-blaming perspective contends that some young women precipitate rapes because of their lifestyles. They do not understand (or choose to ignore) the risks involved in certain situations, such as going to bars unescorted or accepting rides home with men they hardly know. They are unaware, naive, or gullible in their dealings with males. They wear clothing or use language that men stereotype as signaling sexual availability. They ignore the dangers that might arise if they are suddenly confronted with a weapon or are overpowered while under the influence of alcohol or some other drug. For some teenage girls, their reckless behavior is considered a form of "acting out." These adolescents—especially if they come from poverty-stricken homes and suffer parental rejection—are said to be seeking protection, attention, love, intimacy, and status through precocious sexuality. As a result, they get involved with older male casual acquaintances and find themselves in situations in which they are forcibly exploited (see Amir, 1971; and Dean and de Bruyn-Kops, 1982).

Two sets of consequences follow the acceptance of victim-blaming arguments: first, if the female shares some responsibility, then the male can be considered less guilty and less deserving of severe punishment; and second, girls and women must be "educated" to behave more cautiously so as to prevent any "miscommunication" of their real desires.

If the victim's behavior can be criticized, then the "tragic misunderstanding" is not entirely the offender's fault. The legal principle involved is that the female "assumed the risk" of attack when she voluntarily participated in potentially dangerous events leading up to the rape, like heavy drinking or agreeing to enter a hotel room. Even though the male remains subject to arrest, her contributory behavior can provide grounds for granting him the benefit of the doubt. This line of reasoning can influence every stage of the criminal justice system's handling of these cases. Anticipation of harsh interrogation might discourage a victim from bringing her problem to the attention of the authorities. If after a thorough questioning of the complainant to determine her background, reputation, actions, and possible motives the police believe that she contributed to her own victimization, charges may not be pressed. If the police do make an arrest, the prosecutor may decide that the case is "unwinnable" and therefore may drop the charges. If the case is brought to trial, jurors may exercise their discretion in interpreting the facts and may find the assailant guilty of a lesser charge than forcible rape (assault, for example). If the defendant is convicted, the judge may hand down a lenient sentence in view of the mitigating circumstances—her misleading seductiveness might have been taken as a sign of "implied consent" (for references, see Schur, 1984; and Marciniak, 1998).

The other major consequence of accepting the victim-blaming point of view is that the burden of preventing rape is shifted away from aggressive males, the police, or any other third parties to the potential targets themselves. Girls and women are told that they may be unwittingly courting disaster and that it is their obligation to constantly review their lifestyles and do what they can to minimize their risks and maximize their safety. They are held personally accountable for their own security and are pressured to follow crime prevention tips derived from observations of other females' mistakes. Just as the threat of punishment is intended to make would-be rapists think twice before breaking the law, the public humiliation of victim blaming is meant to pressure females to think twice before stepping out of traditional, "sheltered" family roles and activities. Since controlling the actions of offenders is so difficult, victim blaming seeks to reduce the incidence of rape by constraining the behavior of the potential targets. Girls and women are warned about whom they associate with, what they say in conversations, where they go, and how they dress. They are urged to communicate clearly, to signal their true intentions, and to avoid teasing or taunting males.

Old-fashioned beliefs about the female's responsibility for precipitated rapes are widely held by teenagers. Surveys reveal that between one quarter and one half of all adolescents express agreement with some statements that pin blame on victims because of their demeanor, clothing, or prior actions (see Marciniak, 1998).

Victim-Defending Perspectives The traditional victim-blaming views presented above have become controversial since the 1970s. Victim-defending arguments developed by feminists in the women's movement challenge this "conventional wisdom" handed down from generation to generation and provide alternative explanations for why men force themselves upon women.

Victim defending rejects as a myth the notion that rapes are acts of lust or outpourings of uncontrollable passion. Rapes are seen as vicious assaults: physical attacks culminating in sexual acts that symbolize domination, conquest, subjugation, and humiliation. The aggression is not triggered by desire and arousal but is motivated by anger, hatred, and contempt for females as depersonalized objects. Using force to control an unwilling partner must never be confused with "making love."

Victim defending questions the applicability of the concept of precipitation, which was originally developed to describe the blameworthy, aggressive initiatives taken by people who start and then lose fights. Although some homicides might be deemed justifiable (cases of self-defense), there is no such thing as justifiable rape (Amir, 1971). In victim-precipitated homicides the person who died was the first to escalate the level of conflict by resorting to physical strength or a weapon; then the survivor reacted to the assault by fighting back with deadly force. Violence incited retaliatory violence. Since the woman does not physically assault the man before he attacks her, the only way to apply the concept of precipitation to rape is to consider the incident as primarily a sexually charged encounter. Only then can real or presumed sexual advances by the female be considered triggering mechanisms. But there is no justification for the resort to force, no matter what she wore, did, said, or promised. Furthermore, there is great confusion over what constitutes a sexual overture. Since the female's behavior can be subjected to a wide range of interpretations, whose perceptions should be accepted when deciding if there was precipitation on her part: his, hers, the police's, the jury's, or the researcher's? (see Silverman, 1974; Chappell, Geis, and Geis, 1977; and McCaghy, 1980). Therefore, the belief that certain rapes are victim precipitated has been dismissed as an ex post facto conclusion that fails to take into account the female's version (LeGrande, 1973), a personification and embodiment of rape mythology, cleverly stated in academic-scientific terms (Weis and Borges, 1973), and an academic endorsement of the rapist's point of view that provides an excuse for blaming the victim (Clark and Lewis, 1978).

Victim defending also rejects as ideologically tainted the crime prevention tips endorsed by victim blaming. A woman who abides by the long (and growing) list of recommended self-protection measures ends up resembling the "hysterical old maid armed with a hatpin and an umbrella who looks under the bed each night before retiring." For years a laughable stereotype of prudery, she became a model of prudence (Brownmiller, 1975). Following crime prevention tips means foregoing many of the small pleasures and privileges in life to which men are accustomed (like taking a walk alone at night). Warding off would-be rapists requires women to engage in an extraordinary amount of pretense and deception (like claiming that a boyfriend, husband, or father is nearby). Furthermore, seeking the protection of "trustworthy" men to fend off the unwanted advances of other males undermines the efforts of women to develop their own strengths, self-confidence, self-reliance, and independent networks of mutual support.

Antirape activists have sought not only to defend victims but also to place the burden of blame for recurring outbreaks of male sexual "terrorism" on key social institutions, especially the family, the economy, the military, religion, and the media. Asserting that "the personal is political," they have stressed that apparently private troubles need to be seen as aspects of larger social problems besetting millions of other people. Collective solutions that get at the social roots of male-against-female violence hold out greater promise in the long run than any reliance on individual strategies of risk reduction and self-defense. The cultural practices and traditions that encourage men to take the offensive in the "battle of the sexes" must be rejected. Attitudes that tacitly excuse acquaintance rape must be changed. The association of domination with eroticism must be discouraged. And men must realize that rape is their problem too.

Victim Provocation and Murder: When Is the Slaying of a Wife Beater Justified?

A woman employed by the Navy is married to a military recruiter. Demeaning her as "old, fat, crazy, and friendless," he often slams her up against doors, punches her in the face and kicks her in the stomach. Doctors treat her black eyes, bruises, and hemorrhages. After each beating, he apologizes, gives her gifts, and takes her on vacations. Envied by other wives, she feels ashamed for not appreciating him. As a career woman, she feels humiliated and tells no one why she often wears long sleeves and dark glasses. Eventually she files for a divorce, presses assault-and-battery charges, gets a restraining order, and evicts him from their retirement home. But night after night he comes back, banging on the windows and doors, trying to force his way in. Sympathizing with her plight, the police officers who repeatedly respond to her calls for help advise her to get a gun. One evening he barges in brandishing a knife, and she shoots him. Put on trial for first-degree murder, she is painted by the prosecutor as emotionally unstable and twisted by bitterness over the divorce. She is accused of luring her ex-husband to the house with a phone call as the culmination of a plot to kill him. A hung jury cannot decide her fate, but after another trial she is convicted of second-degree murder. Appeals of the conviction fail, and parole is denied; clemency remains her only hope. (Gibbs, 1993b)

A woman is raped on her way home from work. Twenty years later she marries a wealthy widower but soon discovers he served 2 years in prison for murdering his first wife. For 10 years, this jealous, possessive man controls her every movement, beats her, makes unreasonable sexual demands, and mocks her lingering rape trauma by repeatedly sneaking up from behind and grabbing her. One day he threatens to do to her what he did to his first wife. When he falls asleep she shoots him in the head. She is convicted of second-degree murder and sentenced to 5 years in prison. But with a new lawyer, she appeals, is granted a second trial, and presents a defense of extreme psychological impairment. After the jury becomes deadlocked, she pleads guilty to manslaughter and the judge sentences her to probation. (Abramson, 1994)

It seems hard to fathom at first that a significant part of the victims' rights movement would be deeply concerned about the plight of "murderers." Yet they have helped to raise money to pay attorneys' fees, packed courtrooms to demonstrate their solidarity with the accused, and held rallies outside prison gates demanding new trials, parole, pardons, or clemency for some of the killers within (Schechter, 1982; Johann and Osanka, 1989; Gross, 1992). This apparently strange twist of events can be easily explained: The cases that cause grave concerns for these otherwise pro-victim activists involve battered women who killed their violent mates. From the standpoint of the law the dead man is the victim, and the woman who took his life is the offender. But from the perspective of groups representing battered women, the official designations of "offender" and "victim" are misleading. The persons behind bars are not really criminals and don't belong in confinement. The assaultive husbands are not bona fide victims but actually are dead aggressors; the battered women are not the wrongdoers but the genuine victims.

Victim-blaming and victim-defending viewpoints lead to opposite conclusions regarding the tragic endings of these tortured love affairs. In these cases victim defending means siding with the dead man and arguing that his provocations, outrageous as they might have been, were not sufficient to justify the woman's overreactions, and that what she did cannot be condoned. Victim defending leads to offender blaming: She must be punished for the terrible crime she committed. On the other side of the issue, victim blaming leads to offender defending by excusing and justifying the actions of the woman: He instigated her to slay him.

If the battered woman is believed by the authorities to have acted in self-defense in a kill-or-be-killed showdown, then no charges will be pressed against her. However, if she appears to have shot or stabbed him after deliberation or premeditation at a time when she was not in imminent danger, then she can be indicted for first-degree murder. If there was no evidence of advanced planning, but she did act with malicious intent at the crucial moment, then she may be indicted for the lesser crime of second-degree murder. If the prosecution believes that his provocations caused her to kill him in a spontaneous fit of rage or in sheer terror, then she will face the less serious charge of voluntary manslaughter. If the death of the man appears to be merely the outgrowth of her recklessness, then the charge will probably be involuntary manslaughter, which carries the lowest penalty, perhaps just probation (Austern, 1987; Bannister, 1992). The possible outcomes in these cases range from no arrest, to no indictment, to an acquittal by a jury of all charges, to conviction for murder or manslaughter and a lengthy term of imprisonment. Usually, the case is resolved when the woman's lawyer strikes a deal with the prosecutor to allow her to plead guilty to a lesser charge with the understanding that the judge will hand down a reduced sentence. In a small proportion of cases, the women elect to stand trial; of those, most argue that they suffered from diminished capacity or temporary insanity at the time of the confrontation. But a growing number raise an affirmative defense against the murder or manslaughter charges and assert that they were compelled to lash out in self-preservation and should not be punished (Browne, 1987).

Wives might kill their husbands for many reasons; to put an end to physical abuse is just one possible motive. Similarly, men murder their wives for many different reasons. It is not known exactly how many homicides fall into the pattern of battered women slaying their violent mates, but the phenomena must be put into perspective. When it comes to lethal marital disputes, male-on-female violence is the more serious problem: Many more males (husbands and boyfriends) kill their lovers (wives and girlfriends) than the other way around (regardless of the motives). During the 1990s the ratio of female deaths to male deaths rose from 2:1 to roughly 3:1. During 1998, detectives determined that 1,078 women were murdered by their husbands or boyfriends, while only 372 men were slain by their wives or girlfriends. Considering that millions of women are beaten by the men in their lives (see chapter 5), only a tiny portion of these battered women (far less than 1% annually) kill their abusive mates. One obvious trend is that the number of cases of lethal violence between intimates subsided during the 1990s. But murders by women of the men they once loved have generally been dropping since the early 1980s. (See the death tolls in Table 3.2 from murders between "lovers" for all kinds of motives [jealousy, financial gain, revenge] compiled by the FBI from *SHRs* submitted by police departments nationwide; each year, in over one third of all murders, homicide detectives could not determine the motive or the relationship between the victim and the offender, so these body counts are minimal estimates.)

Put still another way, violence unleashed by intimates poses much more of a clear and present danger to females then to males. To illustrate, among all female murder victims in 1998, a considerable proportion (32%) were slain by husbands or boyfriends. Yet only a very small proportion (4%) of all male homicide victims were killed by the females they once were romantically involved with; most men were murdered by other men for some other reason, according to the *SHRs*.

Arguments Stressing That the Brutal Men Did Not Deserve to Die
Victim-defending arguments are advanced most clearly by the police who arrest the battered women and by the prosecutors who press charges against them. The reasoning goes as follows: His fits of temper and violent outbursts were wrong, even criminal in nature, but so was her escalation of the level of violence to lethal proportions. She went too far, using criminal violence to halt criminal violence. She did not explore and exhaust all other options open to her before she chose to resort to deadly force. In particular, she should have fled their

Table 3.2 Murders by Intimates

Year	Wives Killed By Husbands and Girlfriends Killed By Boyfriends	Husbands Killed By Wives and Boyfriends Killed By Girlfriends	Ratio of Female Victims to Male Victims
1977	1396	1185	1.2
1978	1428	1095	1.3
1979	1438	1137	1.3
1980	1498	1129	1.3
1981	1486	1149	1.3
1982	1408	1008	1.4
1983	1487	1043	1.4
1984	1420	897	1.6
1985	1480	835	1.8
1986	1525	866	1.8
1987	1508	824	1.8
1988	1592	765	2.1
1989	1441	817	1.8
1990	1524	797	1.9
1991	1528	714	2.1
1992	1510	657	2.3
1993	1531	591	2.6
1994	1348	574	2.3
1995	1214	458	2.7
1996	1103	369	3.0
1997	1109	339	3.0
1998	1078	372	2.9

NOTE: Relationships were often left blank on the *SHRs*.
SOURCE: Zavitz, 1994; FBI's *UCRs*, 1994–1998

home, escaped his clutches, and dissolved their relationship. The battered woman did not fulfill her duty to retreat (and flee) but instead engaged in mutual combat. Cases in which brutal men were shot while asleep or unconscious from too much drinking were clearly acts of vengeance, motivated more by fury than fear. Such actions in retaliation for alleged wrongs cannot be stretched to fit an expanded definition of self-defense predicated upon standards of a reasonable response to an imminent threat. In the final confrontations that ended their stormy relationships, these battered women retaliated in kind, getting even with their husbands for past abuses. They struck back to settle old scores and to punish their husbands for tormenting them. Such attempts by women to be the judge, jury, and executioner, by "taking the law into their own hands" to deliver a dose of "vigilante justice," cannot be permitted. His death must not go unpunished and she must not get away with murder (see Rittenmeyer, 1981; and Dershowitz, 1988).

Victim defending asserts that the truth about their relationship will never be known. The dead man's side of the story cannot be told, and the woman's version of the events stands largely unchallenged. Her account of what happened between them over the years is self-serving: He is depicted as uncontrollably, irrationally, chronically, and savagely violent. In her view the couple's problems were all his fault. This impression is reinforced by her use of the terms batterer, initiator, and aggressor to describe him, and target, object, and victim to refer to herself. The explanations of the survivor are partial, biased, imbalanced, and incomplete if the entire burden of responsibility is placed on the deceased party (see Neidig, 1984).

Victim defending concludes with several observations. First of all, courtroom testimony should focus on the woman who did the killing. The dead husband or boyfriend whose reputation is being vilified is not on trial and cannot counter the negative portrait of himself that she is painting. Second, there must be better ways for a decent society to express its outrage at the brutality some women are forced to endure than to symbolically condone homicide and excuse lethal preemptive strikes. Not prosecuting wrongdoers, acquitting defendants who clearly broke laws, or granting clemency to convicts only encourages others to pursue these drastic courses of action (see Caplan, 1991; Bannister, 1992; Frum, 1993; and Gibbs, 1993b).

Arguments Emphasizing That the Brutal Men Provoked the Lethal Responses Victim-blaming arguments proceed from the premise that the dead husband was responsible for his own demise. In cases of provocation the woman who emerged as the victor was reluctant to fight at the outset. In his final moments, however, the husband wound up as the victim because he incited his law-abiding mate through inflammatory insults, challenges, threats, gestures, and physical assaults that no longer could be ignored, endured, or evaded. Under attack and facing serious bodily harm, the wife repelled his aggression with self-protective measures. The husband died as a result of an act of self-defense. In these kinds of incidents, the party who should be faulted is the dead man who was the loser in a battle he started. He drove her to kill him in order to save her own life at a point when he was on the verge of murdering her. In a sense, the man got what he deserved by setting up a life-and-death struggle from which the woman could extricate herself only by resorting to lethal force.

Victim blaming asserts that these slain husbands are different from other married men and that their different attitudes and behaviors are the causes of their demise. If they had changed their ways when they had a chance, they would never have met such a fate. Specifically, the men who provoke their spouses to slay them are more abusive than the typical batterer. They attack their partners more often and more viciously and are more likely to carry out sexual assaults (that today are recognized as marital rapes). They tend to drink more heavily and to use illicit drugs more frequently than other batterers. Also, they are more inclined to threaten to kill their wives and to drive them to harbor suicidal fantasies and self-destructive impulses, according to an analysis of 41 cases (Browne, 1987). In a study of 100 battered women who killed their violent mates compared to 100 who didn't, those who struck back were more socially and economically isolated. They had suffered more severe beatings, their children were more likely to have been physically abused, and their partners were heavier drinkers and drug takers (Ewing, 1987).

In court, in the press, and among observers, the question that often arises is "Why didn't she leave him before the fatal showdown unfolded?" Husband blaming arguments point out that for many of these battered wives, escape was not a realistic option, or that they tried to leave and failed. The question presupposes that fleeing their home would put an end to the dangers she faced. But in many cases the husband would not let her escape his clutches. Often, a violence-prone man has a "you belong to me" mentality. Although she feels she can no longer live with him, he feels he can't live without her. He becomes infuriated by what he perceives to be rejection, abandonment, or desertion. With that mind-set, he is likely to stalk his wife, track her down if she is hiding, and use force to bring her back. As a result, the battered woman feels like a captive, trapped in a no-win situation she can't end. Practical considerations might also deter her from trying to escape. Shelters for battered women are few and far between, filled to capacity and with waiting lists and time limitations, and just temporary havens at best. Abruptly severing an intimate relationship is difficult when a couple has children, property in common, and intertwined families, friends, daily routines, and jobs. The woman may feel terrified at the thought of having to live on the run like a fugitive and of uprooting her children, and outraged at the "solution" of abandoning her home to the guilty party. And she may know of women who are separated or even divorced but still get beaten by their former husbands (Browne, 1987).

An understanding of "the battered woman syndrome" helps to explain why some women seem stuck in destructive relationships. The syndrome describes the predictable long-term consequences of repeated beatings. The assaults inflict a type of posttraumatic stress disorder of "learned helplessness" that undermines the self-esteem and sense of control of the demoralized and terrorized woman. Gripped by fear, with beatings following a predictable cyclical pattern (the syndrome of tension building/explosion/reconciliation), the woman can believe she is in constant danger, even when the man is not on the offensive (Walker, 1984). As a result, she might choose to fight back at a moment when he is not acting in a threatening manner. This can explain why she may seize the element of surprise and strike with whatever weapon is at her disposal when he is distracted, asleep, or has passed out from too much drinking or drug taking. The battered woman's syndrome is becoming recognized as a legitimate defense. Expert testimony about the cumulative psychological consequences of periodic beatings (explicitly permitted by laws passed in nine states and by Congress; admissible subject to the judge's discretion elsewhere) can help women on trial to explain why they killed a violent mate who was not advancing menacingly at the moment of his death (Kristal, 1991; Sargeant, 1991; Gibbs, 1993b).

In court some defendants claim they are "not guilty by reason of diminished capacity or temporary insanity." Pleading insanity means offering an excuse for the act. By using such a defense, the woman concedes that taking the man's life was wrong. But she argues that she should not be punished for the killing because her mental state was so impaired at the time that she was unable to form criminal intent. Temporary insanity pleas seem most appropriate in cases involving defendants who cannot recall their actions and who are found to be dazed and confused in the aftermath of the confrontation. If acquitted, she need not be confined in a mental institution, since she poses no danger to the community or to herself; the irritant that provoked her out-of-control response has been eliminated (see Bernat, 1992). However, legal strategies that rely on convincing a jury of the woman's irrational and pathological behavior shift attention away from the man's provocations and her right to self-preservation (Schneider, 1980).

Victim blaming interprets her resort to deadly force as defensive, even if it does not appear so by traditional standards. The legal doctrine of self-defense was developed by men to apply to fights between men and is usually debated and interpreted by men. The classical model posits a clash between two men of roughly equal strength who do not know each other. Self-defense is accordingly defined as the justifiable use of an appropriate amount of force against an adversary by an individual who reasonably believes that he is in imminent danger of unlawful bodily harm, and that the use of such force is necessary to prevent serious injuries from being inflicted. But this highly subjective male-oriented model with its assumptions and prescriptions needs to be modified when applied to clashes between males and females. For example, a woman can be considered to be acting in self-defense if she uses a weapon like a knife or gun against a man who is unarmed. The rationale is that his hands and feet can be viewed as deadly weapons, since women—especially battered wives—have been beaten to death by unarmed men. Because women are generally less skilled in combat and tend to be smaller in stature, the use of a lethal weapon is a way of matching but not exceeding his level of violence. A battered woman who resorts to deadly force during the phase of the cycle when the husband is just threatening harm but not yet physically attacking can also be considered to be acting in self-defense. Unlike a person confronted by a stranger, she is in a position to know from many bitter past experiences that his threats are real and will be carried out. The battered woman learns to recognize the small cues that signal that a beating is imminent, such as subtle changes in the tone of the man's voice or in his facial expressions. Similarly, the wife who strikes out against her assailant during a lull in the ordeal or after an outbreak has peaked can also be considered to be acting in self-defense because she knows the patterns in his attacks (see Fiora-Gormally, 1978; Jones, 1980; Schneider, 1980; Bochnak, 1981; Thyfault, 1984; Kuhl, 1986; Saunders, 1986; Browne, 1987; Ewing, 1987; Gillespie, 1989; and Bannister, 1992).

Victim-blaming arguments are most convincing to the police, prosecutors, and juries in cases where many of the following elements are present: The battered woman had been threatened many times, beaten repeatedly, rescued by the police from his wrath on several occasions, and granted an order of protection. It would also be held against him if she had testified in court after pressing charges, sought marital counseling, attempted to escape his clutches, separated from him and filed for divorce, had visible and severe injuries at the time of her arrest, and suffered permanent damage from her wounds after the final, deadly confrontation. If a "psychological autopsy" or courtroom reconstruction of the tormentor is presented effectively by a defense attorney using an expert witness, the jurors could become so inflamed that they will want to dig up the bully's corpse and kill him all over again (see Sargeant, 1991).

The clash between victim-blaming and victim-defending perspectives illustrates among other things that all crimes are socially defined. No act is inherently criminal, even the taking of a life. For example, not every homicide is a murder; each killing of one person by another must be examined and interpreted within its context. Some slayings can end up designated as noncrimes: enemy soldiers killed in battle during war, death penalties imposed on convicts and lawfully carried out by executioners, justifiable homicides of criminals engaged in shoot-outs with police officers, and, indeed, some deaths of wife beaters by the targets of their wrath.

Transcending Victim Blaming and Victim Defending

The above discussion of auto theft, rape, and murder uncovered some strengths and weaknesses of both victim blaming and victim defending.

Contrary to the sweeping characterizations made by some victimologists, victim blaming is not inherently an exercise in scapegoating, an example of twisted logic, or a sign of callousness. It all depends on which crime is the focus of attention, who the victims are, and why some people are condemning their behavior. Similarly, victim defending is not necessarily a "noble" enterprise engaged in solely by those who champion the cause of the downtrodden.

Hence, victim blamers are not necessarily liberal or conservative, rich or poor, young or old, or male or female. Sometimes victim blamers "switch sides" and become victim defenders; it depends on the facts of the case, the nature of the crime, and the parties involved. Individuals do not line up consistently on one side or the other. Nearly everyone blames certain victims and defends others.

The strengths of victim blaming and victim defending lie in their advocates' willingness to address specific criminal acts and real-life incidents. The two clashing perspectives dissect in great detail who said and did what to whom and under what circumstances. Victim-blaming and victim-defending arguments bridge the gap between theoretical propositions and abstractions on the one hand, and how people genuinely think and act on the other.

The most serious drawback of both perspectives is their tendency to be "microscopic" rather than "macroscopic." Victim-blaming and victim-defending arguments get so caught up (or bogged down) in the particularities of each case that they tend to ignore the larger social forces and environmental conditions that shape the ideas and behaviors of both criminals and victims. Thus, whenever partisans of the two perspectives clash, they inadvertently let the "system"—with its fundamental institutions (established ways of organizing people to accomplish tasks) and culture (way of life, traditions)—off the hook. Yet these outside influences compel the actors in the drama to play the well-rehearsed roles of offender and victim and to follow a well-known script in an all-too-familiar tragedy.

In the case of car stealing, victim-blaming and victim-defending arguments nearsightedly dwell on the actions of motorists and thieves. What is excluded from the analysis is as important as what is included. A comprehensive understanding of the roots of the problem would include a recognition of how sophisticated and organized commercial thievery has become, how profitable the market for "hot" cars and stolen parts is, how the practices of insurance companies provide incentives for thieves to steal crash parts and cars, how the way salvage yards operate makes it easier for thieves to infiltrate black-market parts into the flow of used parts to auto body repair shops, and how inadequacies in record keeping make it difficult for law enforcement officials to detect and prove thievery (see Karmen, 1980; and NIJ, 1984). Even more important, it is necessary to go beyond victim blaming and victim defending to realize that the manufacturers bear responsibility for the ease with which their products are taken away from their customers. Year after year, pros continue to brag that they need just a minute or two and an ordinary screwdriver to defeat the standard antitheft locks on the doors and ignitions of most makes and models of cars (see Kesler, 1992; Behar, 1993; "Auto Theft Alert," 1994; and S. Smith, 1994). Perhaps victim blaming for auto theft serves as a diversionary tactic, distracting attention away from engineering issues. The most virulent victim blaming has emanated from automobile industry spokespersons, insurance company representatives, and top law enforcement officials. Who or what are they protecting? Certainly, they are not apologists for the lawbreakers, either the joyriding juveniles or the professional criminals. Apparently, the condemnations of motorists who left their cars vulnerable to thieves are intended to draw attention away from the automobile manufacturers who design and sell cars that are so easily stolen! Considerable evidence exists to substantiate the charge that until recently vehicle security (like passenger safety) was assigned a low priority by automakers, probably because thefts stimulate new car sales (see Karmen, 1981a). Vehicle security is likely to remain a problem until manufacturers are compelled by law to post "theft resistance" ratings on new car stickers.

As for the terrible problem of forcible rape, victim blaming and victim defending focus too narrowly on the attitudes and actions of the female targets and their male aggressors. In the process both points of view tend to ignore crucial insights about the prevailing cultural themes that concern appropriate sex roles, romance, eroticism, violence, sadism, masochism, and seduction. The possibility that the roots of forced sex lie in the economic, political, and social inequalities between males and females gets lost when the analysis is limited to a deconstruction of the "he said/she said" interaction.

Similarly, when battered wives become widows by their own deeds, the parceling out of blame should not be limited to just one spouse or the other. If domestic disturbances are to be prevented from escalating to such explosive levels, then effective outside intervention is necessary. Murders within marriages reflect the failure of criminal justice and social service agencies to provide adequate protection for the victim who ultimately becomes the perpetrator and to provide timely treatment for the abuser who eventually loses his life. Some responsibility for these tragedies also falls on those officials who assign a low priority to cases of family violence, who cling to a "hands-off," "settle it yourselves" doctrine, and who discourage the development of adequate refuges to shelter battered women and therapy programs to rehabilitate abusive men. Additionally, cultural themes about marriage, wedding vows ("to honor and obey, till death do us part"), family values, and power relationships must be scrutinized, rethought, and then reformed.

Clearly, transcending the analytical confines of both victim blaming and victim defending requires that the researcher go beyond criminology and victimology and enter into the broader realm of social science: sociology, anthropology, psychology, economics, and political science. Only then can the influence of the whole social system on individuals be appreciated and understood.

Doling out the proper mix of exoneration and blame to just two people is of limited value because the influences of outside forces are eliminated from consideration. Given the limited choices of strategies derived from victim blaming versus victim defending, policymaking swings back and forth between attempts to control the behavior of either would-be predators or of their potential prey (but not their larger social environment, which flows from a system-blaming analysis). The frustrations of trying and failing to deter or rehabilitate criminals periodically propels public safety campaigns in the opposite, presumably easier, direction toward "crackdowns" on victim facilitation, precipitation, and provocation.

In the following satire a fictitious professor of victimology puts forward preposterous proposals in a laughable plan to solve the street crime problem. (See the spoof in Box 3.4.)

The Legal Importance of Determining Responsibility

The process of fixing responsibility for crime unavoidably rests on judgments that are subject to question and attack. These judgments are based on values, ethics, prejudices, and allegiances. And yet the crucial question is whether or not

BOX 3.4 Prof Calls for Crackdown on Crime Victims

There is so much talk about crime in the streets and the rights of the criminal that little attention is being paid to the victims of crime. But there is a current of opinion that our courts are being too soft on the victims, and many of them are going unpunished for allowing a crime to be committed against them.

One man who feels strongly about this is Prof. Heinrich Applebaum, a criminologist who feels that unless the police start cracking down on the victims of criminal acts, the crime rate in this country will continue to rise.

"The people who are responsible for crime in this country are the victims. If they didn't allow themselves to be robbed, the problem of crime in this country would be solved," Applebaum said.

"That makes sense, Professor. Why do you think the courts are soft on victims of crimes?"

"We're living in a permissive society and anything goes," Applebaum replied. "Victims of crimes don't seem to be concerned about the consequences of their acts. They walk down a street after dark, or they display jewelry in their store window, or they have their cash registers right out where everyone can see them. They seem to think that they can do this in the United States and get away with it."

"You speak as if all the legal machinery in this country was weighted in favor of the victim, instead of the person who committed the crime."

"It is," Applebaum said. "While everyone is worried about the victim, the poor criminal is dragged down to the police station, booked and arraigned, and if he's lucky he'll be let out on bail. He may lose his job if his boss hears about it and there is even a chance that if he has a police record, it may prejudice the judge when he's sentenced."

"I guess in this country people always feel sorrier for the victim than they do for the person who committed the crime."

"You can say that again. Do you know that in some states they are even compensating victims of crimes?"

"It's hard to believe," I said.

"Well, it's true. The do-gooders and the bleeding hearts all feel that victims of crimes are misunderstood, and if they were treated better, they would stop being victims. But the statistics don't bear this out. The easier you are on the victim, the higher the crime rate becomes."

"What is the solution, Professor?"

"I say throw the book at anybody who's been robbed. They knew what they were getting into when they decided to be robbed, and they should pay the penalty for it. Once a person has been a victim of crime and realizes he can't get away with it, the chances of his becoming a victim again will be slim."

"Why do people want to become victims of crime, Professor?"

"Who knows? They're probably looking for thrills. Boredom plays a part, but I would think the biggest factor is that victims think they can still walk around the streets of their cities and get away with it. Once they learn they can't, you'll see a big drop in crime statistics."

"You make a lot of sense, Professor. Do you believe the American people are ready to listen to you?"

"They'd better be, because the criminal element is getting pretty fed up with all the permissive coddling of victims that is going on in this country."

SOURCE: From "Victim Precipitation," by Art Buchwald, Copyright © *The Washington Post*, February 4, 1969. Reprinted by permission.

(and to what degree) the victim shares responsibility with the offender for a violation of the law. A number of important decisions that affect the fate of the criminal, the plight of the victim, and the public's perception of the crime problem hinge on determinations of victim responsibility. Whether or not the victim facilitated, precipitated, or provoked the offender is taken into account by policemen, prosecutors, juries, judges, compensation boards, insurance examiners, politicians, and crime control strategists. Victim responsibility is an issue at many stages in the criminal justice process: in applications for compensation; in demands for restitution and compensatory damages; in complaints about how crime victims are treated by family, friends, and strangers at home, in hospital emergency rooms, in court, and in the newspapers; and in the development of crime prevention programs and criminological theories.

At every juncture in the criminal justice process, judgments must be made about the degree of responsibility, if any, the victim bears for what happened. The police confront this issue first. For example, when called to the scene of a barroom brawl, officers must decide whether to arrest one or both or none of the participants and what charges to lodge if they do make arrests. Often the loser is declared the victim, and the combatant still on his feet is taken into custody for assault.

When prosecutors review the charges brought by the police against defendants, they must decide if the complainants were indeed totally innocent victims. If some degree of blame can be placed upon them, their credibility as witnesses for the prosecution becomes impaired. A district attorney may decide that the accused person would probably be viewed by a jury or a judge as less culpable and less deserving of punishment and therefore has less of a chance of being convicted. Since relatively few cases are ever brought to trial, the prosecution will engage in plea bargaining (accepting a guilty plea to a lesser charge) if a blameworthy victim would be an unconvincing witness. Such cases might even be screened out and charges dropped. For instance, a study of files in the District of Columbia during the early 1970s revealed that evidence of victim blameworthiness halved the chances that a case would be prosecuted (Williams, 1976).

Killings that resulted from extreme provocations by the deceased persons are likely to be considered justifiable homicides and won't be prosecuted. Different jurisdictions use different standards to determine what constitutes provocation and justification. For example, a study of slayings in Houston, Texas, turned up a figure of 12% deemed justifiable, whereas in Chicago only 3% of all killings were considered justifiable by the local authorities. It appears that the legal definition of justification was broader in Texas than in Illinois (Block, 1981). If the provocation by the dead victim is not considered sufficient to make a homicide justifiable, it might be treated as an extenuating circumstance. Evidence of victim provocation can persuade the district attorney to charge the defendant with manslaughter instead of murder. In a homicide or assault case, the victim's provocation must have been "adequate" in order for the charges to be reduced or for the defendant to be acquitted on the grounds of justifiable self-defense. In most states that means that the defendant's violent responses to the victim's provocations must have occurred during the heat of passion, before there had been a reasonable opportunity for intense emotions to cool (Wolfgang, 1958; Williams, 1978).

If the defendant is convicted, the judge may view the victim's provocation as a mitigating factor that makes a lesser sentence appropriate. In those jurisdictions where restitution by offenders to victims is permitted or even mandated, the culpability of victims can be a cause for reducing the amount of repayment that criminals must undertake. Similarly, the judge or the jury in civil court is likely to consider a victim's blameworthy actions as a reason for reducing the monetary damages a defendant must pay for causing loss, pain, and suffering. Parallel considerations arise when victims of violent crimes apply to a criminal injury compensation board for reimbursement. If the board members determine in a hearing that the victim bears some of the responsibility for the incident, they will reduce the amount of the award or may, in extreme cases of shared guilt and provocation, reject the victim's claims entirely (see chapter 6).

In some conflicts that erupt after extensive interaction between two mutually hostile parties, the designations "offender" and "victim" simply do not apply. When both people behaved illegally, adjudication under the adversary system may not be appropriate. Neighborhood justice centers have been set up to settle these shared responsibility cases through mediation and arbitration. Compromise solutions are appropriate when both disputants are to some degree "right" as well as "wrong" (see chapter 7).

In sum, widely held beliefs and stereotypes about the question of shared responsibility can profoundly shape the way a case is handled within the criminal justice process. How the legal system handles innocent victims is the focus of the next chapter.

CHAPTER SUMMARY

When victims ask "Why me?" victimologists suggest many possible explanations that range far beyond the notions of being in the wrong place at the wrong time as a result of either fate or just plain bad luck. But all explanations are debatable, especially for particular individuals, because they raise the possibility that the victim, along with the offender, shares some degree of responsibility for what happened.

Victims may have been targeted by their criminals because of the routine activities that shape their lives: where they work or attend school, how they get there, where they shop, and where they reside. Victims might not be able to do too much about their routine activities in order to reduce their risks, but they can modify their lifestyles, (leisure pursuits, friends, preferences, dislikes; and how they spend their free time and disposable income). Certainly, people engaged in illegal activities (like participation in the drug scene) heighten the dangers they face. The key factors that determine risk levels include proximity, exposure, target attractiveness, and guardianship (degree of protection). Some people temporarily may find themselves in unusually vulnerable arrangements because of their particular circumstances, such as being tourists in unfamiliar places. Other victims were not deterred by bad experiences and continue to place themselves in volatile situations because they fail to learn from their own mistakes or from the misfortunes of others.

Victim-blaming arguments focus upon facilitation through negligence, precipitation due to recklessness, and provocation because of instigation. Victim blaming insists that injured parties must change their ways if they want to live safer lives. Victim defending either places the entire blame for what happened on lawbreakers (offender blaming) or else finds fault with social institutions and cultural values that shape the lives of both offenders and victims (system blaming).

DISCUSSION QUESTIONS

1. Discuss how lifestyle choices and routine activities might account for an entire group's differential risks of being victimized.
2. What kinds of studies can victimologists undertake to test whether lifestyles and routine activities actually have an impact on a group's victimization rates?
3. Compare and contrast victim facilitation, victim precipitation, and victim provocation. Cite examples to illustrate the differences.
4. Explain victim blaming step-by-step and then argue that abusive husbands provoked their battered wives to kill them.
5. Describe the victim-defending point of view and then apply it to the problem of young women raped by casual acquaintances.
6. Explain system blaming and then apply this prespective to automobile theft.

4

Victims and the Criminal Justice System: Cooperation and Conflict

Criminologists study the operations of the criminal justice system (law enforcement agencies, prosecutors' offices, courts, probation and corrections departments, and parole authorities). They investigate how the system handles "offenders:" specifically suspects, defendants, convicts, probationers, inmates, and parolees. Victimologists explore how the system handles victims: how the police respond to complainants; how prosecutors, defense attorneys, and judges treat these witnesses for the state; and how corrections, probation, and parole officials react to special requests by victims. A fundamental question that will be addressed at the conclusion of this step-by-step walk through the system is, Are all victims handled the same, or are some treated much better than others?

Note that this chapter does not explore how victims fare within the juvenile justice system. This separate system handles cases in which minors are accused of committing crimes (against people of all ages). It operates according to other principles and treats victims differently (generally worse) because they are not permitted to play much of a role and can exercise fewer options and rights. During the 1990s about one third of all arrests for street crimes (*UCR* index crimes), particularly offenses against property, were of juveniles younger than 18. The victims of these delinquents face a separate set of problems that are beyond the scope of this chapter.

VICTIMS VERSUS THE CRIMINAL JUSTICE SYSTEM

The criminal justice system is one branch of government that comes under scathing attack from all political quarters. Conservatives, liberals, radicals, law-and-order advocates, civil libertarians, civil rights activists, and feminists all find fault with its rules and procedures. Even officials who run its agencies and shape its daily operations have joined the chorus of critics calling for change over the past few decades. Serious problems persist, and the indictment of the system still stands, as the excerpts collected in Box 4.1 demonstrate.

The consensus among the experts is that the criminal justice system does not measure up to expectations. It fails to deliver what it promises. It does not meet the needs and wants of victims as its "clients" or "consumers" of its services.

Suppose a person is robbed and injured. What could and should the system do to dispense "justice" in this case?

Law enforcement agencies are at the intake end of the legal system and are the criminal justice professionals that victims first encounter. Police officers could rush to help the victim and provide whatever physical and psychological first aid might be needed. They could catch the culprit and speedily return stolen goods to the rightful owner. The prosecutor could indict the defendant and press for a swift trial. After conviction, the victim's views about a fair resolution of this case could be fully aired. The judge could hand down a sentence that would balance the victim's wishes with the community's desires and the

BOX 4.1 Criticisms of the Way the Criminal Justice System Handles Victims

If there is one word that describes how the criminal justice system treats victims of crimes and witnesses to crimes, it is "badly." *(James Reilly, director of the Victim/Witness Assistance Project of the National District Attorney's Association, 1981, p. 8)*

Crimes that terrorize take many forms, from aggravated assault to petty thievery. But one crime goes largely unnoticed. It is a crime against which there is no protection. It is committed daily across our nation. It is the painful, wrongful insensitivity of the criminal justice system toward those who are the victims of crime. . . . The callousness with which the system again victimizes those who have already suffered at the hands of an assailant is tragic. *(Senator John Heinz, sponsor of the Omnibus Victims Protection Act passed by Congress, 1982, p. A19)*

Without the cooperation of victims and witnesses in reporting and testifying about crime, it is impossible in a free society to hold criminals accountable. When victims come forward to provide this vital service, however, they find little protection. They discover instead that they will be treated as appendages of a system appallingly out of balance. They learn that somewhere along the way the system has lost track of the simple truth that it is supposed to be fair and to protect those who obey the law while punishing those who break it. Somewhere along the way, the system began to serve lawyers and judges and defendants, treating the victim with institutionalized disinterest. . . . The neglect of crime victims is a national disgrace. *(Lois Herrington, chairperson of the President's Task Force on Victims of Crime, President's Task Force, 1982, pp. vi–vii)*

For too long, the rights and needs of crime victims and witnesses have been overlooked in the criminal justice system . . . we have begun to address this problem [through federal legislation passed in 1994 and 1996]. But those important measures are not enough. *(President Bill Clinton, 1996, p. 1)*

At the same time that they experience the impact of a crime, victims too often endure what has been called a "second victimization"—insensitive treatment at the hands of the criminal justice system. *(Julie Tomz and Daniel McGillis, authors of a National Institute of Justice guide about services for crime victims, 1997, p. 4)*

[According to a recent survey] . . . victims often feel that they are treated as a piece of evidence, helpful only when they help prove the prosecution's case and when they help a police officer find the bad guy. But they often feel disrespected and ignored and that their interests and concerns are irrelevant. *(Susan Herman, director of the National Center for Victims of Crime, 1999)*

offender's needs. Correctional authorities could make sure that the probationer, prisoner, or parolee doesn't harass or harm the person whose complaint set the machinery of criminal justice into motion.

But this "best-case scenario" frequently does not materialize. Instead of cooperation as the system handles "their" cases, victims might find themselves locked into conflicts with the police, prosecutors, judges, and parole boards.

The account presented in Box 4.2 illustrates how the system routinely mistreated victims in the "bad old days" before the victims' rights movement raised objections and brought about some meaningful reforms. This fictional composite sketch illustrates everything that could possibly go wrong. It was constructed from testimony about real-life ordeals brought to the attention of a presidential task force. Since this "worst-case scenario" provides a virtual checklist of nearly all the possible problems and abuses that can arise, it can serve as a standard for comparison with current cases to identify just how much progress has been made and exactly what remains to be accomplished. The narrative in Box 4.2

follows one woman's plight as her rape is processed as just another case winding its way through the system. The task force pinpointed the various reasons that victims find themselves pitted against the police, the prosecuting attorney working for the government, the defense lawyer acting on behalf of the accused, the judge presiding over the case, the jury sitting in judgment, and the parole board determining the convict's future. This excerpt accentuates the negative by focusing on rape victims because they were—and still are—the most mistreated of all.

WHAT DO VICTIMS WANT: PUNISHMENT? TREATMENT? OR RESTITUTION?

Why should victims bring their problems to the attention of justice officials? What do they want? What would they like to see done?

The victims' rights movement has sought **empowerment.** That means the ability to have some input into important decisions at every step along the way. But why demand inclusion? Why insist on having chances to participate at key junctures in the criminal justice process?

Victims can pursue one, or even a combination of, three distinct goals. The first is to see to it that a predator is punished. The second potential objective is to use the justice process as leverage to compel the lawbreaker to undergo rehabilitative treatment. The third possible aim is to get the court to order the convict to repay those he hurt for the costs arising from their injuries and losses.

It is punishment that comes first to most people's minds when considering what "justice" entails. Most deliberations concern questions of suffering: who, why, when, where, and how much? Throughout history, people have always punished one another. However, they may disagree about their reasons for subjecting someone considered to be a wrongdoer to pain and suffering. Punishment is usually justified on utilitarian grounds as a necessary evil. It is argued that punishing transgressors curbs future criminality in a number of ways. The offender who experiences unpleasant consequences learns a lesson and is discouraged from breaking the law again, assuming that the logic of specific deterrence is sound. Making an example of a convicted criminal also serves as a warning to would-be offenders contemplating the same act, provided that the doctrine of general deterrence really works. Punishment in the form of imprisonment has been defended as a method of incapacitating dangerous predators so that they can no longer prey upon innocents. Another rationale for punishment by the government is that it satisfies the thirst for revenge of angry victims and their supporters who otherwise may harbor an urge to engage in vigilantism and get even on their own.

Punishment has also been justified on nonutilitarian grounds as a morally sound practice, regardless of any value it has in deterring or incapacitating criminals. According to the theory of punishment as retribution, it is fair and just to make offenders suffer in proportion to the misery they inflicted on others. Since biblical times, people have believed in the formula of retaliation in kind,

BOX 4.2 The System's Shortcomings From a Victim's Point of View

The Crime

You are a fifty-year-old woman living alone. You are asleep one night when suddenly you awaken to find a man standing over you with a knife at your throat. As you start to scream, he beats and cuts you. He then rapes you. While you watch helplessly, he searches the house, taking your jewelry, other valuables, and money. He smashes furniture and windows in a display of senseless violence. His rampage ended, he rips out the telephone line, threatens you again, and disappears in the night.

At least you have survived. Terrified, you rush to the first lighted house on the block. While you wait for the police, you pray that your attacker was bluffing when he said he'd return if you called them. Finally, what you expect to be help arrives.

The police ask questions, take notes, dust for fingerprints, take photographs. When you tell them you were raped, they take you to the hospital. Bleeding from cuts, your front teeth knocked out, bruised and in pain, you are told that your wounds are superficial, that rape itself is not considered an injury. Awaiting treatment, you sit alone for hours, suffering the stares of curious passersby. You feel dirty, bruised, disheveled, and abandoned. When your turn comes for examination, the intern seems irritated because he has been called out to treat you. While he treats you, he says that he hates to get involved in rape cases because he doesn't like going to court. He asks if you "knew the man you had sex with."

The nurse says she wouldn't be out alone at this time of night. It seems pointless to explain that the attacker broke into your house and had a knife. An officer says you must go through this process, then the hospital sends you a bill for the examination that the investigators insist upon. They give you a box filled with test tubes and swabs and envelopes and tell you to hold onto it. They'll run some tests if they ever catch your rapist.

Finally, you get home somehow, in a cab you paid for and wearing a hospital gown because they took your clothes as evidence. Everything that the attacker touched seems soiled. You're afraid to be in your house alone. The one place where you were always safe, at home, is a sanctuary no longer. You are afraid to remain, yet terrified to leave your home unprotected.

You didn't realize when you gave the police your name and address that if would be given to the press and to the defendant through the police reports. Your friends call to say they saw this information in the paper, your picture on television. You haven't yet absorbed what's happened to you when you get calls from insurance companies and firms that sell security devices. But these calls pale in comparison to the threats that come from the defendant and his friends.

You're astonished to discover that your attacker has been arrested, yet while in custody he has free and unmonitored access to a phone. He can threaten you from jail. The judge orders him not to annoy you, but when the phone calls are brought to his attention, the judge does nothing.

At least you can be assured that the man who attacked you is in custody, or so you think. No one tells you when he is released on his promise to come to court. No one ever asks you if you've been threatened. The judge is never told that the defendant said he'd kill you if you told or that he'd get even if he went to jail. Horrified, you ask how he got out after what he did. You're told the judge can't consider whether he'll be dangerous, only whether he'll come back to court. He's been accused and convicted before, but he always came to court, so he must be released.

You learn only by accident that he's at large; this discovery comes when you turn a corner and confront him. He knows where you live. He's been there. Besides, your name and address were in the paper and in the reports he's seen. Now nowhere is safe. He watches you from across the street; he follows you on the bus. Will he come back in the night? What do you do? Give up your home? Lose your job? Assume a different name? Get your mail at the post office? Carry a weapon? Even it you wanted to, could you afford to do these things?

You try to return to normal. You don't want to talk about what happened, so you decide not to tell your co-workers about the attack. A few days go by and the police unexpectedly come to

Continued

BOX 4.2 *continued*

your place of work. They show their badges to the receptionist and ask to see you. They want you to look at some photographs, but they don't explain that to your co-workers. You try to explain later that you're the victim, not the accused.

The phone rings and the police want you to come to a line-up. It may be 1:00 A.M. or in the middle of your work day, but you have to go; the suspect and his lawyer are waiting. It will not be the last time you are forced to conform your life to their convenience. You appear at the police station and the line-up begins. The suspect's lawyer sits next to you, but he does not watch the stage; he stares at you. It will not be the last time you must endure his scrutiny.

Charges Are Pressed Against a Defendant

You have lived through the crime and made it through the initial investigation. They've caught the man who harmed you, and he's been charged with armed burglary, robbery, and rape. Now he'll be tried. Now you expect justice.

You receive a subpoena for a preliminary hearing. No one tells you what it will involve, how long it will take, or how you should prepare. You assume that this is the only time you will have to appear. But you are only beginning your initiation in a system that will grind away at you for months, disrupt your life, affect your emotional stability, and certainly cost you money; it may cost you your job, and, for the duration, will prevent you from putting the crime behind you and reconstructing your life.

Before the hearing, a defense investigator comes to talk to you. When he contacts you, he says he's "investigating your case," and that he "works for the county." You assume, as he intends you to, that he's from the police or the prosecutor's office. Only after you give him a statement do you discover that he works for the man who attacked you.

This same investigator may visit your neighbors and co-workers, asking questions about you. He discusses the case with them, always giving the defendant's side. Suddenly, some of the people who know you seem to be taking a different view of what happened to you and why.

It's the day of the hearing. You've never been to court before, never spoken in public. You're very nervous. You rush to arrive at 8 A.M. to talk to a prosecutor you've never met. You wait in a hallway with a number of other witnesses. It's now 8:45. Court starts at 9:00. No one has spoken to you. Finally, a man sticks his head out a door, calls out your name, and asks, "Are you the one who was raped?" You're aware of the stares as you stand and suddenly realize that this is the prosecutor, the person you expect will represent your interests.

You only speak to the prosecutor for a few minutes. You ask to read the statement you gave to the police but he says there isn't time. He asks you some questions that make you wonder if he's read it himself. He asks you other questions that make you wonder if he believes it.

The prosecutor tells you to sit on the bench outside the courtroom. Suddenly you see the man who raped you coming down the hall. No one has told you he would be here. He's with three friends. He points you out. They all laugh and jostle you a little as they pass. The defendant and two friends enter the courtroom; one friend sits on the bench across from you and stares. Suddenly, you feel abandoned, alone, afraid. Is this what it's like to come to court and seek justice?

You sit on the bench for an hour, then two. You don't see the prosecutor; he has disappeared into the courtroom. Finally, at noon he comes out and says, "Oh, you're still here? We continued that case to next month."

You repeat this process many times before you actually testify at the preliminary hearing. Each time you go to court, you hire a babysitter or take leave from work, pay for parking, wait for hours, and finally are told to go home. No one ever asks if the new dates are convenient to you. You miss vacations and medical appointments. You use up sick leave and vacation days to make your court apperances. Your employer is losing his patience. Every time you are gone his business is disrupted. But you are fortunate. If you were new at your job, or worked part-time, or didn't have an understanding boss, you could lose your job. Many victims do.

The preliminary hearing was an event for which you were completely unprepared. You learn later that the defense is ofter harder on a victim at the preliminary hearing than during the trial. In a trial, the defense attorney cannot risk

BOX 4.2 *continued*

alienating the jury. At this hearing there is only the judge—and he certainly doesn't seem concerned about you. One of the first questions you are asked is where you live. You finally moved after your attack; you've seen the defendant and his friends, and you're terrified of having them know where you now live. When you explain that you'd be happy to give your old address the judge says he'll dismiss the case or hold you in contempt of court if you don't answer the question. The prosecutor says nothing. During your testimony, you are also compelled to say where you work, how you get there, and what your schedule is.

Hours later you are released from the stand after reliving your attack in public, in intimate detail. You have been made to feel completely powerless. As you sat facing a smirking defendant and as you described his threats, you were accused of lying and inviting the "encounter." You have cried in front of these uncaring strangers. As you leave no one thanks you. When you get back to work they ask what took you so long.

You are stunned when you later learn that the defendant also raped five others; one victim was an eight-year-old girl. During her testimony she was asked to describe her attacker's anatomy. Spectators laughed when she said she did not understand the words being used. When she was asked to draw a picture of her attacker's genitalia the girl fled from the courtroom and ran sobbing to her mother, who had been subpoenaed by the defense and had to wait outside. The youngster was forced to sit alone and recount, as you did, each minute of the attack. You know how difficult it was for you to speak of these things; you cannot imagine how it was for a child.

Now the case is scheduled for trial. Again there are delays. When you call and ask to speak with the prosecutor, you are told the case has been reassigned. You tell your story in detail to five different prosecutors before the case is tried. Months go by and no one tells you what's happening. Periodically you are subpoenaed to appear. You leave your work, wait, and are finally told to go home.

Continuances are granted because the courts are filled, one of the lawyers is on another case, the judge has a meeting to attend or an early tennis match. You can't understand why they couldn't have discovered these problems before you came to court. When you ask if the next date could be set a week later so you can attend a family gathering out of state, you are told that the defendant has the right to a speedy trial. You stay home from the reunion and the case is continued.

The defense attorney continues to call. Will you change your story? Don't you want to drop the charges?

Time passes and you hear nothing. Your property is not returned. You learn that there are dozens of defense motions that can be filed before the trial. If denied, many of them can be appealed. Each motion, each court date means a new possibility for delay. If the defendant is out of custody and fails to come to court, nothing can happen until he is reapprehended. If he is successful in avoiding recapture, the case may be so compromised by months or years of delay that a successful prosecution is impossible. For as long as the case drags on, your life is on hold. You don't want to start a new assignment at work or move to an new city because you know that at any time the round of court appearances may begin again. The wounds of your attack will never heal as long as you know that you will be asked to relive those horrible moments.

No one tells you anything about the progress of the case. You want to be involved, consulted, and informed, but prosecutors often plea bargain without consulting victims. You're afraid someone will let the defendant plead guilty to a lesser charge and be sentenced to probation. You meet another victim at court who tells you that she and her family were kidnapped and her children molested. Even though the prosecutor assured her that he would not accept a plea bargain, after talking with the attorneys in his chambers, the judge allowed the defendant to plead guilty as charged with the promise of a much-reduced sentence. You hope that this won't happen in your case.

Continued

BOX 4.2 *continued*

The Trial

Finally the day of trial arrives. It is eighteen months since you were attacked. You've been trying for a week to prepare yourself. It is painful to dredge up the terror again, but you know that the outcome depends on you; the prosecutor has told you that the way you behave will make or break the case. You can't get too angry on the stand because then the jury might not like you. You can't break down and sob because then you will appear too emotional, possibly unstable. In addition to the tremendous pressure of having to relive the horrible details of the crime, you're expected to be an actress as well.

You go to court. The continuances are over; the jury has been selected. You sit in a waiting room with the defendant's family and friends. Again you feel threatened, vulnerable, and alone.

You expect the trial to be a search for the truth; you find that it is a performance orchestrated by lawyers and the judge, with the jury hearing only half the facts. The defendant was found with your watch in his pocket. The judge has suppressed this evidence because the officer who arrested him didn't have a warrant.

Your character is an open subject of discussion and innuendo. The defense is allowed to question you on incidents going back to your childhood. The jury is never told that the defendant has two prior convictions for the same offense and has been to prison three times for other crimes. You sought help from a counselor to deal with the shattering effect of this crime on your life. You told him about your intimate fears and feelings. Now he has been called by the defense and his notes and records have been subpoenaed.

You are on the stand for hours. The defense does its best to make you appear a liar, a seductress, or both. You know you cannot relax for a moment. Don't be embarrassed when everyone seems angry because you do not understand. Think ahead. Be responsive. Don't volunteer. Don't get tired.

Finally you are finished with this part of the nightmare. You would like to sit and listen to the rest of the trial but you cannot. You're a witness and must wait outside. The jury will decide the outcome of one of the major events of your life. You cannot hear the testimony that will guide their judgment.

The verdict is guilty. You now look to the judge to impose a just sentence.

The Sentence

You expect the sentence to reflect how terrible the crime was. You ask the prosecutor how this decision is reached, and are told that once a defendant is convicted he is interviewed at length by a probation officer. He gives his side of the story, which may be blatantly false in light of the proven facts. A report that delves into his upbringing, family relationships, education, physical and mental health, and employment and conviction history is prepared. The officer will ofter speak to the defendant's relatives and friends. Some judges will send the defendant to a facility where a complete psychiatric and sociological work-up is prepared. You're amazed that no one will ever ask you about the crime, or the effect it has had on you and your family. You took the defendant's blows, heard his threats, listened to him brag that he'd "beat the rap" or "con the judge." No one ever hears of these things. They never give you a chance to tell them.

At sentencing, the judge hears from the defendant, his lawyer, his mother, his minister, his friends. You learn by chance what day the hearing is. When you do attend, the defense attorney says you're vengeful and it's apparent that you overreacted to being raped and robbed because you chose to come and see the sentencing. You ask permission to address the judge and are told that you are not allowed to do so.

The judge sentences your attacker to three years in prison, less than one year for every hour he kept you in pain and terror. That seems very lenient to you. Only later do you discover that he'll probably serve less than half of his actual sentence in prison because of good-time and work-time credits that are given to him immediately. The man who broke into your home, threatened to slit your throat with a knife, and raped, beat, and robbed you will be out of custody in less than eighteen months. You are not told when he will actually be released, and you are not allowed to attend the parole release hearing anyway.

SOURCE: Excerpted from the report of the President's Task Force on Victims of Crime, 1982, pp. 3–11.

lex talionis, symbolized by the phrase "an eye for an eye." Wrongdoers must get their "just deserts." Retribution evens the score, rights a wrong, and restores balance to the moral order, as long as the severity of the punitive sanction is in proportion to the gravity of the offense, according to this point of view.

The quest for retribution has shaped history. Incorporated into the customs and consciousness of entire groups, classes, and nations, it is expressed in simmering hatreds, longstanding feuds, vendettas, and wars. Revenge fantasies can sustain individuals and even give purpose and direction to their lives. However, the thirst for vengeance can destroy victims as well by becoming an obsession. Even when fulfilled, acts of revenge are rarely as satisfying as had been imagined. Yet for victims to feel a sense of fury and rage toward those who have abused them is entirely human. In the hours and days following a crime, it is psychologically useful and even cathartic for victims to dream of inflicting pain on their offenders. But a chronic preoccupation with striking back and getting even endlessly and needlessly prolongs memories of the victimization. Vengeful victims never break free of the pernicious influence of their victimizers. Survivors learn that the best revenge is to transcend their offender's grip, put the experience behind them, and lead a fulfilling life (Halleck, 1980).

Sometimes, former victims can be found in the forefront of campaigns to deprive inmates of whatever comforts and privileges they enjoy behind bars so they will be even more miserable in bleak "no-frills" prisons (see Hanley, 1994a). However, despite the current popularity of punishment as the antidote to victimization and the cure for crime, the punitive approach remains controversial. Utilitarian opponents have documented how impractical, expensive, ineffective, and even counterproductive, high rates of imprisonment can be. Civil libertarians have condemned such harsh punishments as a tool of domination and oppression used by tyrants and totalitarian regimes to terrorize their subjects into submission (see Menninger, 1968; Wright, 1973; Prison Research, 1976; Pepinsky, 1991; Elias, 1993; and Mauer, 1999).

In some cases victims do not look to the criminal justice system to exact revenge in their name. Instead, they want professionals and experts to help wrongdoers become decent, productive, law-abiding citizens. Victims are most likely to endorse treatment if their offenders are not complete strangers but lovers, family members, other relatives, neighbors, classmates, or colleagues. Rehabilitation might take the form of counseling, behavior modification, intense psychotherapy, detoxification from addictive drugs, medical care, additional schooling, and job training. Despite the temporary ascendancy of a pessimistic, "nothing works" disenchantment with the ideal of rehabilitation (see Martinson, 1974), "helping" offenders remains as much a part of the system's mission as making them sorry for what they did. Rehabilitation followed by reintegration is a long-term strategy that is in the enlightened self-interest of both victims and society. Incapacitation of unrehabilitated predators is a short-term strategy that merely buys time and promotes a false sense of security. Victims who overcome their initial emotional outrage over what offenders did to them might become equally infuriated about heavy-handed punitive policies that backfire and drive offenders to new heights of antisocial conduct. Victims could also become dismayed by inept efforts to rehabilitate offenders while they are inmates in jails or prisons or on probation or parole.

As a third alternative, some victims seek restitution rather than retribution or rehabilitation. They want the legal system's help to recoup their losses and pay their bills—a necessary prerequisite for full recovery. Restitution collected from offenders can help to restore victims to the financial condition they were in before the crimes occurred. Once offenders make amends monetarily, reconciliation becomes a possibility (see chapter 7).

Whether they desire that something be done to the offender (punishment), for the offender (treatment), or for themselves (restitution), victims want the criminal justice system to react effectively to violations of law. What they don't want is inaction, lack of interest, neglect, empty promises, abuse, or manipulation.

VICTIMS AND THE POLICE

The police are the first representatives of the criminal justice system that victims encounter in the immediate aftermath of crimes, and they can help out in a number of ways. The police can respond quickly to calls for help and provide on-the-spot first aid. Detectives can launch thorough investigations and solve crimes by taking suspects into custody, recovering stolen property, and gathering evidence that will lead to convictions in court.

Victims can become bitterly disappointed with the police if officers are slow to arrive, disbelieve their accusations, conduct superficial investigations, don't make arrests, and fail to recover stolen property.

Reporting Incidents

Criminal justice authorities want people to "report, identify, and testify" and have launched periodic campaigns to promote this theme ("Crime Control Needs," 1985). Officials fear that if would-be offenders believe that victims won't complain about their depredations, then the deterrent effect of the risk of getting caught and punished will be undermined. Furthermore, if the public provided more complete information about where and when crimes were committed, then the police could more effectively anticipate where predators will strike next. Victims who fail to report incidents forfeit important rights and opportunities, such as eligibility for services and reimbursement of losses through compensation plans, tax deductions, and insurance policies.

Despite these appeals to civic responsibility and self-interest incentives, most individuals do not report incidents in which they were harmed to the police because of costs and risks. Less than half (46%) of all those who suffered acts of violence (rape, robbery, and aggravated and simple assaults) and just a little more than one third (35%) who experienced thefts of personal and household property (purse snatchings, pocketpickings, burglaries, larcenies, and stolen vehicles) informed the police about the incidents that they discussed with *NCVS* interviewers in 1998. The combined reporting rate for all the different types of crimes asked about on the survey was 38% (Rennison, 1999).

Reporting rates vary substantially by category of crime, and some go up or down over the years. Several overall patterns and trends are worth noting (see Table 4.1 for a summary of the findings about reporting rates since the *NCVS* began in 1973). Violent crimes are reported to the police at much higher rates than either personal thefts or household crimes. Victims are more likely to report incidents in which they sustain physical injuries or suffer considerable financial losses. Also, completed acts are brought to the attention of the police more often than mere attempts (according to figures not presented in the table).

Of all the crimes asked about on the *NCVS,* completed auto theft comes in each year as the category with the highest reporting rate (close to 90%). Most car theft victims inform the police for several well-founded reasons: There is a good chance their stolen vehicles will be recovered, filing a formal complaint is required for insurance reimbursement, and they do not want to be held responsible for any accidents or crimes involving their cars. (It could be assumed that they were behind the wheel of a getaway car used in a bank robbery, for example.) The lowest reporting rates surround attempted thefts of personal and household property (only about 12%). As for violent crimes, robberies were

Table 4.1 Trends in Reporting Crimes to the Police

	PERCENTAGE OF VICTIMIZATIONS DISCLOSED TO *NCVS* INTERVIEWERS THAT WERE ALSO REPORTED TO THE POLICE				
	1973	**1978**	**1983**	**1988**	**1990**
All crimes	32%	33%	35%	36%	38%
Rapes	49	49	47	45	54
Robberies	52	51	53	57	50
Aggravated assaults	52	53	56	54	59
Simple assaults	38	37	41	41	42
Burglaries	47	47	49	51	51
Household larcenies	25	24	25	26	27
Motor vehicle thefts	68	66	69	73	75
	1992	**1994**	**1996**	**1998**	
All crimes	39%	36%	37%	38%	
Rapes	53	32	31	32	
Robberies	51	55	54	62	
Aggravated assaults	62	52	55	58	
Simple assaults	43	36	37	40	
Burglaries	54	51	51	49	
Household larcenies	26	27	28	29	
Motor vehicle thefts	75	78	77	80	

NOTES: Figures include reports of both attempts and completed acts.
Survey redesign influenced rape reporting rates after 1992.
SOURCE: Bastian, 1993; BJS, 1994–1999.

reported the most and rapes the least. Overall, the police tend to find out about half of the more serious violent crimes in a community but do not learn about most of its minor property crimes (Harlow, 1985; Rennison, 1999).

Victimologists have long suspected that reporting rates vary from police department to police department, and those suspicions were confirmed when the *NCVS* carried out a comparative study of victims in 12 cities during 1998. Overall, the police forces in these 12 cities found out about a little more than one third of all the violent crimes committed in their jurisdictions and about the same fraction of property crimes. Fewer victims of violence called the cops in Spokane, Washington, (31%) and New York City (32%) than in Washington, D.C., (50%) or Springfield, Missouri, (58%). A smaller percentage of property crime victims informed the authorities in San Diego, California, (28%) and New York City (29%) than in Kansas City, Missouri, (45%) and Savannah, Georgia, (47%) (see Smith et. al., 1999). (Note that these differential reporting rates undercut the accuracy of city-by-city comparisons based on the FBI's *UCR* compilation of crimes "known to the police," except for murder rates.)

NCVS interviewers ask victims to explain why they did or did not report to the police the incidents they disclosed on the survey. When victims do report crimes to the police, their leading reasons are to recover their stolen property and to prevent the offender from harming them again. Victims who do not report crimes to the police tell *NCVS* interviewers that their main reasons are that the offender was unsuccessful and the property was recovered, that it was a private or personal matter (especially for simple assaults), or that they notified some other official. Only a small percentage of all nonreporting victims volunteered that they felt the police would probably be inefficient, ineffective, or insensitively biased (BJS, 1982–1999).

Reporting rates reflect rational calculations about advantages and disadvantages that can vary from group to group (see Biblarz, Barnowe, and Biblarz, 1984; Greenberg and Ruback, 1984; and Gottfredson and Gottfredson, 1988). Over the decades, *NCVS* findings reveal that females were somewhat more likely than males to bring their troubles to the attention of the authorities. As for race and ethnicity, African Americans (contrary to widespread impressions) were slightly more likely than whites and Hispanic Americans to call upon the police for help. In general, reporting rates increased with age; teenagers were much less inclined to complain about their misfortunes than were older persons. As for income, poor persons were a little more reluctant to call for help than middle-income people (BJS, 1982–1994; Rennison, 1999).

As for trends, Table 4.1 contains no single category showing steady or uninterrupted improvement over time. Slight gains are often followed by minor setbacks. Some reporting rates show considerable variations from year to year. The reporting rate for rapes, for instance, has dropped as low as 41% (in 1980) and risen as high as 61% (in 1985) (not shown). Motor vehicle thefts (both attempted and completed) are reported more often than in the past. Accentuating the positive, the data in Table 4.1 show that victims are now reporting a slightly greater proportion of crimes to the police than they did in the not-too-distant past. The figures in the row labeled "all crimes" combined show modest increases since the surveys were initiated in 1973. Stressing the negative, the data also indicate that police forces across the country have had only limited success over the last two decades in getting the public to cooperate more closely with law enforcement. This underreporting can be interpreted as a sign that many people remain alienated from a criminal justice system ostensibly set up to help them.

In most jurisdictions victims are not legally obliged to inform the authorities about violations of law committed against them or their property. But if they go beyond silence and inaction and conspire or collaborate in a cover-up to conceal a serious crime (like a shooting), they can be arrested themselves and charged with **misprison of a felony.** The failure of witnesses to report certain kinds of offenses, especially the abuse of a child or an elderly person, is a misdemeanor in many jurisdictions (Stark and Goldstein, 1985).

Responding Quickly

When victims call for help, they want officers to spring into action immediately. To meet this challenge most police departments have 911 emergency systems. But incoming calls have to be prioritized by dispatchers who determine each one's degree of urgency. Obviously, reports about critical situations—such as screams for help in the night or concerns about prowlers or shots fired—merit a higher priority than calls about cars that have disappeared from their parking spots. If officers reach crime scenes quickly, they have a better chance of rescuing a victim in grave peril, catching the culprit, recovering stolen property, gathering crucial evidence, and locating eyewitnesses.

For 50 years police departments have been experimenting with ways to reduce response times to emergency calls, but *NCVS* findings fuel suspicions that a substantial proportion of victims might be dissatisfied with the amount of time it took officers to arrive. In roughly 90% of all calls for help, an officer came within 60 minutes or less, but in some emergencies that track record was not good enough. Furthermore, no positive trend materialized during the 1990s (see Table 4.2 for the average nationwide response times from 1990 through 1994). Questions about this aspect of police performance were added to the

Table 4.2 Trends in Police Response Times to Violent Crimes

	POLICE RESPONSE TIMES			
Year	Within 5 Minutes	Within 6 to 10 Minutes	Within 11 to 60 Minutes	Total Within One Hour
1990	28%	31%	32%	91%
1992	29	28	32	89
1994	31	29	31	91
1996	31	25	32	88
1998	26	29	32	86

NOTE: Police response times to calls by rape victims are not available.
SOURCE: BJS, *Criminal Victimization in the United States,* 1990–2000.

NCVS at the close of the 1980s (Whitaker, 1989). As for trends, the data show no signs that local law enforcement agencies across the nation have been able to improve their response times to calls for help by victims of violence during the 1990s.

Travel time is only one reason for delays. Time is lost most often and more importantly when victims and witnesses hesitate before reporting a crime in progress. There are several reasons for such citizen delay: Onlookers and even participants might be unsure whether or not a crime really occurred; victims and witnesses might want to cope first with emotional conflicts, personal trauma, and physical injuries, and regain their composure before informing the authorities of what happened; or (less frequently) they couldn't locate a telephone (Spelman and Brown, 1984). However, with the proliferation of cell phones since the 1990s, reaching 911 becomes less of a problem and shortening response time takes on greater significance as a pro-victim priority.

Investigating Complaints

Police officials seek the cooperation of persons who have reported crimes, for without their help these cases are probably not going to be solved. But two areas of conflict between victims and the police can arise at the complaint investigation stage. First, the officers or detectives who respond to the calls for assistance might seem remote, uninterested, even unconcerned about the victims' plight. Second, the police may conclude that the complainants' charges lack credibility and may discontinue the investigations.

Some victims might be deterred from seeking assistance by their fear of a type of psychological "police brutality." After the first injury (the suffering inflicted by the criminal), victims are particularly susceptible to a "second wound." Expecting the police to comfort them and help solve their problems, they sometimes find that officers unwittingly make them feel worse. (These slights can also be delivered by care providers, like emergency room personnel, or by friends and relatives.) In the aftermath of a street crime, victims are likely to feel powerless, disoriented, and infuriated. Fear, guilt, depression, and revenge fantasies engulf them. Authority figures such as police officers are expected to calm and console the injured parties to help restore their sense of equilibrium and dispel any lingering feelings of helplessness they may have. But if officers act callously and prolong suffering needlessly, victims feel let down, rejected, and betrayed by those they counted on for support (Symonds, 1980b).

Studies of police work suggest that what victims are encountering is the protective coating of emotional detachment that officers develop to shield themselves from becoming overwhelmed by the misery they routinely see around them. To avoid "burnout," police officers (like others in "helping" professions) inhibit their impulses to get deeply involved in the cases they investigate. The paramilitary nature of police organizations and the bureaucratic imperatives of specialization and standardization reinforce the inclinations of officers to deal with tragedies as impersonally as possible. In addition, the "macho" norms of police subculture—with its emphasis on toughness, camaraderie, suspicion of outsiders, insider jokes, graveyard humor, and profound cynicism—put pressure on police officers to act businesslike when dealing with profoundly upsetting situations (Ahrens, Stein, and Young, 1980).

If individual officers appear surprisingly unmoved by the suffering that surrounds them, it might be that they fear "contamination" (Symonds, 1975). People who regularly come into close contact with the casualties of natural and social disasters tend to isolate and ostracize these victims as if they had a contagious disease. Such distancing is a defense mechanism to preserve the helper's faith that ultimately justice prevails: Misfortunes happen only to those who somehow deserve them.

Notifying the next of kin of murder victims is one of the most emotionally draining tasks in police work. Anecdotal evidence indicates that many officers are inept in delivering bad news in plain language and with compassion. To rectify this problem some departments have developed guidelines and manuals so that survivors are not further traumatized by memories of clumsy and uncaring behavior by officers carrying out these most unpleasant death notification obligations (Associated Press, 1994e).

Many departments have initiated training programs to prepare at least a portion of their force to act differently when they deal with victims with acute needs. Officers and detectives are taught how to administer "psychological first aid" to people in distress. They are instructed to respond swiftly, listen attentively, show concern, and refrain from challenging the victims' version of events or judging the wisdom of their reactions while the crime was in progress. Officers are told not to show skepticism because a rape victim is not badly bruised or bleeding, a child did not report a molestation immediately, an elderly person has trouble communicating, or a blind person offers to assist with the identification of a suspect. At the conclusion of the training sessions, the officers are informed that responsiveness to victims carries a high priority within the department and has become a criterion for evaluating performance and a consideration in granting promotions (Symonds, 1980b; President's Task Force, 1982; National Sheriff's Association, 1999).

Whether victims expect too much or receive too little, their grievances against the police can lead to a "community relations" problem. Administrators of the system have proposed police professionalism as the solution. This involves upgrading the caliber of academy recruits, using psychological tests to weed out potentially brutal or corrupt members of the force, devising regulations and procedures to cover every kind of anticipated emergency, monitoring on-the-job performance, and adding in-service training and specialized squads to handle problems addressed inadequately in the past. Satisfaction with police services is greater if officers act in a professional manner, if they arrive faster than expected, and if they make a serious effort to investigate property crimes, according to a survey of over 400 victims in a midwestern city (Brandl and Horvath, 1991). A survey carried out in 12 cities during 1998 revealed that 69% of the members of the community who have been victims of violent crime report that they are "satisfied" with the performance of their local police force; if they have never called upon the cops for help in the aftermath of violence, 86% are satisfied (Smith, et. al., 1999).

Judging Complaints to Be Unfounded

When people swear out a complaint, they want officers to accept without question their versions of what transpired. From the police officer's point of view, however, complainants are "presumptive" victims until they pass a credibility test. It is always possible that the person alleging to be a bona fide victim is making a fraudulent claim for some ulterior purpose. People might falsely swear they were harmed by criminals for a number of reasons. They may seek to exact revenge by getting an innocent person in trouble or to cover up the true circumstances surrounding an event (for example, when a husband claims he was robbed to account for the loss of his pay, which he actually spent on a prostitute or gambled away). Another motive is to commit insurance fraud. For example, tourists may dishonestly claim that they were robbed of their cash-filled wallets or expensive cameras as part of a scam to get reimbursement for nonexistent losses from policies sold to travellers (Associated Press, 1999). The police find it essential to screen people who say they have been victimized in order to weed out those whose charges are **unfounded.** The following examples demonstrate that occasionally individuals who tell the police a tall tale are up to something very serious. They may be manipulating the authorities and misleading investigators to conceal their roles in a major plot.

A prominent city official is found bleeding and dazed in his own car. He tells police that he was abducted, assaulted, and driven around by two unknown men. An investigation is launched, but no witnesses come forward. Then the official admits that his wounds were self-inflicted in a failed suicide attempt. When his role in a kickback scandal is revealed, he kills himself by plunging a knife into his chest. (Purnick, 1986)

A man calls 911 on his car phone and tells the police that a robber just shot him and his pregnant wife. She dies, as does her unborn baby, but he survives a serious bullet wound to the abdomen. Under great pressure to solve the case, the police round up scores of young black men fitting his sketchy description; eventually detectives make an arrest and announce that the case has been solved. But then the wounded man's brother comes forward and confesses that the shooting was staged: The man murdered his pregnant wife and stole her jewelry in order to collect insurance and then shot himself to make his story about an armed robbery more credible. As the police piece together what really happened, the man posing as a grieving widower commits suicide by jumping off a bridge. (Martz, Starr, and Barrett, 1990)

A distraught young mother tells the authorities that a black man with a gun barged into her car at a red light and forced her to drive 10 miles before ordering her out and speeding off with her two toddlers still strapped in the back seat. As the mother makes televised tearful appeals in which she prays along with her family for the safe return of her children, thousands of volunteers from her small southern hometown join state troopers and FBI agents in combing the countryside in search of the toddlers, her abandoned car, the offender, or any clues. But after she fails several lie detector tests, she breaks down and admits that she is not a victim of a carjacking but the murderer of her own two children, whom she drowned by rolling her car down a ramp into a lake. (Gibbs, 1994)

A 10-year-old who disobeyed his foster parents and went off to play touch football is discovered shoeless with his pants pulled down, tied to a fence post in an alley. As police officers free him, he tells them that a stranger lured him into a car and then raped him. He gives a description of the suspect. Soon, detectives announce that a man has been arrested and is being charged with kidnapping, criminal restraint, and sexual assault. But then the boy recants his allegations and admits he was tied up by three older playmates who were angry at him. He explains that he made up a story because he thought the police and his foster parents wouldn't be sympathetic unless he claimed he was harmed by an adult. The charges against the innocent man are dropped. (Associated Press, 1993a)

An armored car guard is found tied up. He claims that several robbers took the $8 million he was transporting and bound his wrists and ankles with wire. The police suspect it was an inside job and maintain around-the-clock surveillance on him, his relatives, and his close friends. Cracking under this pressure, one of the robbers confesses and implicates the security guard as a co-conspirator. (McFadden, 1993a)

The founder and leader of a nationwide civilian anticrime patrol tells reporters that he was injured when he tried to capture three rapists at a subway station. Years later, after a near-death experience (which remains an unsolved shooting), he admits that he conspired with other members of the newly formed group to stage a series of publicity stunts in order to further the organization's reputation. (Gonzalez, 1992)

People who knowingly fill out false complaints are breaking the law in most states if they "gratuitously" volunteer unsolicited incorrect information to the police. The laws against the misdemeanor of filing a false statement are intended to deter perjury and thereby protect innocent persons from the embarrassment and hardships caused by untrue accusations. A lying complainant who instigates a wrongful arrest for some improper motive (such as revenge) also can be sued in civil court for malicious prosecution. However, to encourage citizen cooperation with law enforcement, most jurisdictions have adopted a doctrine of witness immunity that shields complainants who furnish information to the police "in good faith" from any subsequent lawsuits by innocent individuals they mistakenly identified as suspects (Stark and Goldstein, 1985).

Unfounding is a process in which the police completely reject a person's claim about being the victim of a crime. **Defounding** means that detectives believe an offense really did occur but was not as serious as the complainant described it (Lundman, 1980). For example, what was initially reported as a burglary might upon further investigation be classified as an instance of criminal trespass—which is a misdemeanor rather than a felony—if nothing of value was stolen. Just as individuals might have a motive to lodge a false charge, police investigators might have an incentive to declare a report of a crime completely unfounded or to defound it down to a lesser offense. By defounding and unfounding complaints, detectives can reduce the number of serious crimes reported within their precincts and cut down the number of difficult cases they must try to solve.

Under pressure to meet departmental performance standards, some detectives might disregard legitimate pleas for help by abusing their authority and deeming complaints as totally unfounded or to defound charges. For example, in Chicago for more than 20 years, detectives were inclined to dismiss victims' accounts as unfounded because they would receive higher ratings and more promotions if they closed more cases. During this time the Chicago Police Department dismissed about 21% of their complaints about serious crimes as unfounded; the average rate for other big-city departments was less than 2%, according to the FBI. Auditors reviewing police files came to the conclusion that as many as 40% of the rape, robbery, burglary, and theft reports disregarded as unfounded probably did occur, just as the victims claimed. The kinds of cases that were prime candidates for official disbelief involved victims who were difficult to contact, knew their assailants, or did not lose much money ("Chicago Police," 1983; "Burying Crime in Chicago," 1983). In Oakland, California, overworked detectives in the late 1980s dismissed 24% of the rape complaints they received as unfounded. At that time the FBI reported that other departments across the country disbelieved about 9% of all rape charges. After a newspaper article questioned why there was such a disparity in the unfounding rate, the police chief conceded that perhaps 200 cases were written off too quickly and merited reexamination. But detectives in this California city advanced several arguments in their own defense. First, they asserted that the nationwide figure of 9% was a misleading standard for comparison, since many departments keep the unfounding rate artificially low by classifying cases as "filed pending further investigation" (not officially closed) rather than "closed due to baseless or false charges." Second, they pointed out that because of budget constraints the sexual assault unit's six investigators were so swamped with cases that they had to prioritize their workload. They felt pressured to disregard complaints from women who would appear uncooperative, untruthful, or unsympathetic in court, such as prostitutes and drug abusers who would be inclined to lie about the circumstances surrounding the assaults for fear of getting in trouble for solicitation or possession of controlled substances. Finally, the detectives insisted that many of the complainants refused to agree to medical examinations and failed to appear for follow-up interviews, making the investigation of their charges difficult, time consuming, and unlikely to ultimately lead to convictions (Gross, 1990).

Arresting Suspects

Victims expect thorough investigations, so dissatisfaction can arise whenever detectives deem a complainant's misfortunes to be too minor or too difficult to solve. In these cases it is hard to justify the expenditure of the department's limited human resources, time, and money. Some departments issue directives that specify cutoff points below which no action will be taken beyond simply making a formal note of the complaint. For example, in Dade County, which includes Miami, Florida, reports about stolen cars were taken solely over the telephone and only during certain hours (Combined News Services, 1993). In New York City during the 1980s, a detective from the burglary squad was assigned to a case only if the reported loss exceeded a figure of several thousand dollars (Gutis, 1988). Sometimes, the police might be reluctant to invest much effort if victims are likely to receive insurance reimbursement.

Many victims discover that with the passage of time their cases are closed even though they remain unsolved. How long an investigation remains open depends on the workload in the jurisdiction and the seriousness of the offense. If the police are unable to establish the identity of a suspect or cannot obtain sufficient evidence to justify an arrest, then they can exercise their discretion to discontinue any active effort to solve the crime. Victims have no formal means of compelling them to continue to work on it. Dissatisfied complainants have been unable to convince judges to intervene in matters of police discretion unless a pattern of noninvestigation reflects racial or religious discrimination (Austern, 1987).

Even when the trail of evidence leads to a suspect, an arrest is never automatic. Police officers exercise a great deal of personal and departmental discretion in deciding whom to take into custody and book and whom to let go. The factors that influence these decisions include pressures from colleagues and superiors, the individual predilections of officers, the nature of the offense, and the relationship of the victim to the suspect. Victims can become angry when officers don't arrest the persons they have accused of committing crimes.

One solution for victims is to convince judges to issue arrest warrants (which officers must then carry out) based on their sworn complaints. A second solution is to exercise the dangerous do-it-yourself option known as a "citizen's arrest." Private citizens are empowered to use whatever force is necessary to prevent a suspect from escaping until the police arrive to take charge of the situation. Civilians must apprehend their suspects immediately after a crime is committed and must turn their captives over to the authorities without delay. Police officers are generally obligated to accept custody of suspects taken prisoner by victims or bystanders. But citizen arrests are risky undertakings. Suspects are likely to resist being captured, endangering victims or bystanders who intervene on their behalf. In cases of mistaken identity, even victims who acted with probable cause and in good faith can be sued in civil court for false arrest and false imprisonment. Police officials generally discourage civilians from thinking of themselves as deputized to make arrests. They point to the lengthy training sworn officers receive in self-defense and the use of firearms and in the application of laws governing arrests and suspects' rights. Since acts of vigilantism can easily evolve out of attempts to make citizen's arrests, law enforcement officials encourage activist-oriented civilians to become involved in police auxiliary units or neighborhood anticrime patrols instead (Hall, 1975; Stark and Goldstein, 1985).

From the victims' point of view, the police have successfully completed their mission when, acting on solid evidence, they take a suspect into custody. Similarly, from the police department's standpoint, a case is closed when an arrest is made. The police consider the crime solved at that point even if the suspect is not ultimately convicted of the original charge or even any lesser charge. Police departments routinely compile and make public the percentages of cases that are closed by arrests (but do not track what happens to these cases at later stages of the criminal justice process). These **clearance rates** are used to evaluate the performance of individual officers, specialized squads (such as those concentrating on homicide, burglary, and sex crimes), and the department as a whole. But these same statistics can be interpreted from a different angle and for a different purpose. The proportion of cases that are solved can serve as an indicator of the percentage of complainants who have a solid basis for being satisfied or dissatisfied with the investigatory services provided by their local police force.

Each year in its *Uniform Crime Report,* the FBI calculates the average clearance rates for police departments across the country (see Table 4.3 for data from selected years over five decades). A glance at the figures for 1998 reveals that police forces nationwide are more successful at solving violent crimes than property crimes. Looking at these numbers from the victims' point of view, it is clear that the overwhelming majority of people who go to the trouble to report thefts to the police will not be pleased with the outcome of their cases; the investigations will be closed before any arrest is made. Put another way, 81% of larceny complainants and 86% of burglary and auto theft complainants will be frustrated because their offenders escaped the long arm of the law. Most individuals who report robberies (72%) will also suffer the aggravation of learning that no one was apprehended for accosting them. Just half of all females who have the courage to tell the authorities that they were raped can take comfort in knowing that their attackers have been arrested. More than half (59%) of those who were seriously wounded by assailants will be relieved to find out that arrests were made in their cases. The highest clearance rates of all are achieved by homicide squads, but even the best detectives who devote considerable time and effort to selected cases manage to figure out who did it in barely two thirds (69%) of all slayings. Accentuating the negative, that means that nearly 1 in 3 killers "gets away with murder!" Actually the situation is even worse. Just because a suspect is arrested doesn't mean that this individual is guilty or will be prosecuted or convicted of the original charges. The single most important factor in solving crimes—with the obvious exception of murder—is the ability of victims to furnish detectives with clues, leads, and descriptions, or even the names, of sus-

Table 4.3 Trends in Clearance Rates

	PERCENTAGE OF CASES SOLVED					
Type of Crime	**1953**	**1963**	**1973**	**1983**	**1993**	**1998**
Murder	93%	91%	79%	76%	66%	69%
Rape	78	69	51	52	53	50
Aggravated assault	75	76	63	61	56	59
Robbery	36	39	27	26	24	28
Burglary	27	27	18	15	13	14
Larceny	20	20	19	20	20	19
Vehicle theft*	26	26	16	15	14	14

*Since the 1970s, this category of the *Uniform Crime Report* has included the theft of all motorized vehicles, including trucks, vans, motorcycles, and buses.
SOURCE: FBI, *UCR,* 1954–1999.

pects. That's why crimes of interpersonal violence are more likely to be solved than offenses against property, which usually do not take place in front of eyewitnesses (Lundman, 1980).

The statistics presented in Table 4.3 summarizing the performance of police departments throughout the country during the second half of the 20th century reveal a disturbing trend. In every one of the seven index crimes (the eighth, arson, is excluded from this compilation because the numbers are considered incomplete by the FBI), a slow but steady downward drift is evident from the early 1950s until the early 1990s. During the 1950s practically all murders and most rapes and aggravated assaults were solved. Clearance rates for these three violent crimes and for robberies dropped sharply during the crime wave of the late 1960s. During the 1970s and 1980s, the solution rates for rapes and serious assaults remained stable, while the ability of the police to solve murders continued to decline. Burglaries and auto thefts were solved roughly twice as often in the 1950s as in the 1990s. Larcenies (thefts of all kinds) have always been difficult to solve. Overall, as the years pass, the police are becoming less and less able to close cases by making arrests. During the early 1990s, clearance rates hit new lows across the board, but then slightly improved (for murders, serious assaults, and robberies) as the century ended and crime rates (and detectives' caseloads) fell throughout the nation. Translating these statistical trends into human terms, most criminals are getting away with their crimes, and most victims have good reason to be dissatisfied with the performance of their local law enforcement agencies (since property crimes vastly outnumber violent offenses). Decades ago, long before the victims' rights movement began to demand improved services from law enforcement agencies, the police were much more effective at accomplishing their basic mission of catching culprits.

When police officers make arrests, they have a legal obligation to inform these suspects of their Miranda rights to remain silent and to be represented by a lawyer. When victims file complaints, they immediately discover that the police are under no comparable constitutional pressure to read them their "rights" about their obligations and opportunities. To start with, victims need to know the names and badge numbers of the officers and the detectives handling their cases, where and when they can be reached, case identification numbers, whether or not suspects have been apprehended, and, if so, whether they are being detained in jail or are out on bail. To guarantee these elemental rights endorsed by the President's Task Force (1982), a number of states have passed statutes that specify that the police must keep victims posted on the status of their cases. In the other states, victims must depend on departmental policies and the good will of individual officers.

Findings from the *NCVS* indicate that a large percentage of victims never find out if their cases were solved and arrests were made. For example, only 15% of all robbery victims in 1986 who reported their incidents to the police eventually learned that a suspect was arrested for robbing them. Yet police departments averaged a clearance rate of 25% for robberies that year. Similarly, only 34% of aggravated assault victims who reported the crimes to the police were informed about resulting arrests, although police departments solved about 59% of all aggravated assault cases brought to their attention that year. The neglect on the part of the police to tell burglary victims that someone was arrested for breaking into and stealing from their homes was even more dramatic: Only 7% of all victims were notified, although about 14% of all reported burglaries were solved. Motor vehicle theft victims were better informed; of the 15% whose cases were solved, 11% learned of an arrest (FBI, 1987; Whitaker, 1989).

Recovering Stolen Property

Besides catching the culprits, the police can satisfy victims' needs by getting back any possessions taken from them. Just as clearance rates indicate the approximate percentage of victims who receive optimum service in terms of arrests, recovery rates show how often the police succeed in retrieving stolen goods. Unfortunately, unlike clearance rates, recovery rates are not routinely tabulated and published by police departments or the FBI. (In the *UCR* the FBI does note the overall dollar value of recovered stolen goods for all reported incidents of a particular index crime.) However, interviewers for the *NCVS* ask respondents whether all or part of the money and property taken from them was recovered (not counting insurance reimbursement). The police recovery rates can then be estimated. But the figures will be biased upward because some victims are able to get back their stolen property through their own efforts (somehow they knew where to look for the missing items). Unfortunately, this statistic cannot be refined further to determine what percentage of victims recovered items by themselves and what percentage were given back their stolen goods by the police. Therefore, these rough approximations overestimate the ability of the police to retrieve goods taken from their rightful owners. Furthermore, these estimated rates combine partial and full recoveries, again biasing the statistics upward and presenting the ability of the police to accomplish recoveries as more efficient than it really is. Partial recoveries might not bring much satisfaction to victims. The discovery of a discarded wallet emptied of any valuables, for example, or the return of a badly stripped automobile with a traceable vehicle identification serial number on it would count as partial recoveries. With these reservations in mind, Table 4.4 shows a compilation of estimated police recovery rates during the 1980s and early 1990s.

The data reveal that this aspect of police work will leave most people who suffered robberies, burglaries, and household larcenies dissatisfied with the outcomes of their cases. The estimated recovery rates are very low, despite the fact that these percentages are overestimates. Only owners of stolen cars are likely to get back some or all of what was taken from them. As for changes over time, the data show mostly downward trends: Fewer victims are getting their stolen property back as the years go by. Motor vehicle recovery rates may have improved a little since the early 1980s.

Even if the police recover stolen property, some victims might not get it back, at least not for a while. Law enforcement agencies have the authority to hold seized items if they are of value in continuing investigations. Prosecutors are allowed to maintain custody of pieces of evidence until after the trial or even

Table 4.4 Trends in Stolen Property Recovery Rates

Type of Victimization	1980	1982	1983	1984	1985	1986	1987	1988
Robberies	24%	21%	24%	27%	26%	20%	20%	21%
Burglaries	12	13	10	10	11	11	10	9
Household larcenies	12	12	8	9	9	9	8	8
Motor vehicle thefts	65	63	69	70	70	71	72	73

Type of Victimization	1989	1990	1991	1992	1993	1994	1996	1998
Roberies	24%	20%	19%	18%	18%	20%	20%	19%
Burglaries	10	10	9	10	8	8	10	9
Household larcenies	8	8	7	8	9	9	9	9
Motor vehicle thefts	66	74	71	72	65	70	71	73

NOTES: Percentages represent the proportions of all cases in which victims get back some stolen items.
Recovery may be total or partial.
An unknown proportion of the recoveries were accomplished by the victims themselves, without the assistance of the police.
Figures were calculated from *NCVS* data on theft losses.
Only incidents that resulted in theft losses were considered.
SOURCE: BJS, *Criminal Victimization in the United States,* 1982–2000.

until those convicted have exhausted all appeals. Frustrated victims are now assisted in some states by statutes that compel the police to return stolen property to its rightful owner "expeditiously"—as soon as it is no longer needed for law enforcement purposes. In a growing number of jurisdictions, laws direct the police and prosecutors to promptly photograph the evidence and then return the actual item whenever it is feasible. But in states without these kinds of procedural directives, the release of property seized as evidence requires the explicit approval of the police department property clerk or the prosecutor's office or even the judge hearing the case. Victims who are denied prompt repossession might have to appeal the decision of the official maintaining custody of the property to some higher criminal justice authority. If the items are damaged, destroyed, or lost by the police property clerk's office or the prosecutor's office, victims can go to civil court to file claims for monetary compensation (Stark and Goldstein, 1985). Scattered studies suggest that many victims encountered this problem before new procedures were mandated. In a Wisconsin jurisdiction 31% of complainants who had been seriously harmed reported difficulties in getting back stolen property held as evidence (Knudten, Knudten, and Meade, 1978). In California a survey of victims determined that in 30% of the cases in which stolen property was recovered by the police and used in court as evidence, the items were never returned to their rightful owners (Lynch, 1976).

VICTIMS AND PROSECUTORS

Prosecutors are the chief law enforcement officers within their jurisdictions. They protect the interests of the county, state, or federal government. They also supply the lawyers that deal directly with victims. Therefore, prosecutors' offices can be viewed as public law firms offering free legal services to complainants who are willing to cooperate and testify as witnesses. (County prosecutors are elected officials who are usually referred to as **district attorneys.** The lawyers who actually handle criminal cases and personally work with victims are called **assistant district attorneys, [ADAs]**.)

Prosecutors' offices can and should serve victims in a number of different ways (President's Task Force, 1982). First, these lawyers can keep their clients informed of the status of their cases, from the initial charges lodged against defendants to the parole of convicts. Second, they can help victims to achieve justice by conveying to the attention of the judges their clients' views on questions of bail, continuances, negotiated pleas, dismissed cases and dropped charges, sentences, and restitution. Third, they can take steps to protect their clients from harassment, threats, injuries, and other forms of intimidation and reprisals. Fourth, they can try to resolve cases as quickly as possible without unnecessary delays and help their clients to minimize losses of time and money by notifying them of required court appearances and scheduling changes. Fifth, they can assist victims in getting back stolen property recovered by the police.

Sometimes, prosecutors are able to serve the interests of the government, their own agency, and their victimized client without any conflict. But frequently prosecutors cannot do what is best for all of their constituencies. Conflicts can arise between the interests of the government, plus the bureaucracy that employs them, as well as the "consumers" of their services, and certainly their own individual career aspirations. If they must sacrifice the interests of some party, it is likely to be the victim. Victims can feel betrayed if "their" lawyers do not look after their needs and wants. Or to put it another way, the lawyer assigned by the government automatically (without choice) and at no cost might not do a satisfactory job from the client's standpoint.

Assisting Victims and Other Witnesses for the State

The difficulties, inconveniences, and frustrations faced by victims serving as witnesses for the prosecution have been well known for decades (see McDonald, 1976). In 1931 the National Commission on Law Observance and Enforcement commented that the administration of justice was suffering because of the economic burdens imposed on citizens who participated in trials. In 1938 the American Bar Association noted that witness fees were deplorably low, courthouse accommodations were inadequate, intimidation went unchecked, and witness time was often wasted. The President's Commission on Law Enforcement and the Administration of Justice reached similar conclusions in 1967. In 1973 the Courts Task Force of the National Advisory Commission on Criminal Justice Standards and Goals noted that the failure of victims and witnesses to appear at judicial proceedings when summoned was a major reason for cases being dismissed. Noncooperation was attributed to the high personal costs of involvement incurred by citizens trying to meet their civic obligations.

In the past, victims serving as prosecution witnesses typically were mistreated in a number of ways. They would be ordered by subpoena to appear at some courtroom, grand jury room, or prosecutor's office. They would wait for hours in dingy corridors or in other grim surroundings. Busy officials would ignore them as they stood around bewildered and anxious. Often, they wouldn't be called to testify or make statements because of last-minute adjournments. Accomplishing nothing, they would miss work and lose wages, miss classes at school, or fail to meet their responsibilities at home. In most jurisdictions they would receive insultingly low witness fees for their time and trouble. In certain metropolitan areas they would receive no compensation at all because no official informed them of their eligibility and of the proper application procedures. Their experiences could thus be characterized as dreary, time consuming, depressing, exhausting, confusing, frustrating, and frightening (Ash, 1972).

In 1974 the National District Attorneys Association commissioned a survey to determine the extent to which victims and other witnesses for the prosecution encountered these kinds of problems. Conducted in Alameda County, California, the survey documented that about 12% of all victims were never notified that an arrest had been made in their case. Nearly 30% never got their stolen property back, even though it had been recovered and used as evidence. About 60% of injured victims who were eligible for financial reimbursement of losses under a state program were never informed of their right to file a claim. Roughly 45% reported that no one had explained to them what their court appearance would entail. Frustratingly, 27% of all witnesses (including victims) called to court were not subsequently asked to testify. Even though 78% lost pay to come to court, about 95% received no witness fees. As a final insult, 42% were never notified of the outcome of the case (Lynch, 1976).

To address these problems the Law Enforcement Assistance Administration (LEAA) funded the first Victim-Witness Assistance Projects (VWAPs) through the National District Attorneys Association. Pilot programs were set up in prosecutors' offices in California, Illinois, Utah, Colorado, Kentucky, Louisiana, Pennsylvania, and New York during the mid-1970s (Schneider and Schneider, 1981; Geis, 1983). Since then, most prosecutors' offices have followed suit. Several assumptions underlie the growth and development of these programs. One is that providing services will elicit greater cooperation from victims and other witnesses. Presumably, well-briefed, self-confident witnesses who have been in contact with and benefited from such programs will be more willing to put up with the hardships of testifying in court, leading to lower dismissal rates and higher conviction rates, the standards by which prosecutors' offices are judged. Also, offering services to a group perceived to be highly deserving of governmental aid will be good for community relations. Public confidence and faith in the criminal justice system will thus be restored, resulting in higher reporting rates within jurisdictions that have assistance programs (Rootsaert, 1987).

Most VWAPs are charged with the laudable but loosely defined mission of helping victims, aiding witnesses, and furthering the goals of law enforcement. In the best programs, agency personnel intervene as soon as possible after an offense is committed, providing immediate relief to the injured parties through services that include hot lines; crisis counseling; emergency shelter, food, and transportation; and immediate lock repairs. Some projects even provide translators, forms for replacing lost documents, and assistance in getting back stolen property recovered by the police. Most make referrals to social service and mental health agencies for those needing long-term care and counseling. All programs furnish information about opportunities for reimbursement of losses and eligibility for compensation benefits. A few offer mediation services for victims who seek to reconcile their differences with their offenders. To encourage witness cooperation, pamphlets about the adjudication process (with titles like "What Happens in Court?" and "Victims' Rights") are prepared and distributed. Through a case-monitoring and notification system (involving a series of form letters), the staff keeps victims and other witnesses advised of important developments, such as indictments, postponements and continuances, negotiated pleas, convictions, and acquittals. Linked to the notification system is a telephone alert or "on-call" system, intended to prevent unnecessary trips to court when dates are changed on short notice. (This is also used to save police officers who are needed as witnesses from wasting their time.) Some programs have also set up reception centers (waiting rooms exclusively for prosecution witnesses) in courthouses to provide a secure environment free from any last-minute opportunities for intimidation by offenders and their families and friends. Transportation to and from court, escorts, and child care are frequently available. Help in obtaining witness fees is provided. In some programs the staff may go so far as to intercede on behalf of victims with employers and landlords and other creditors who might not appreciate the stresses and financial difficulties faced by witnesses (Schneider and Schneider, 1981; Geis, 1983; Weigend, 1983; and Rootsaert, 1987).

Some signs that VWAPs are reducing the mistreatment of victims are evident. Whereas only 35% of the offices of district attorneys routinely notified victims of felonies of the outcomes in their cases in 1974, by 1992 97% of these offices did, according to the National Prosecutor Survey Program (Dawson, Smith, and DeFrances, 1993).

However, the establishment of victim-witness assistance programs has raised some constitutional and ethical questions. To deny services to a victim whose cooperation is not needed (or who desires to pursue a case that the prosecutor's office wants to drop) would be unfair but not illegal, since the aid is granted as a privilege rather than as a right. To deny similar services (free parking, child care, last-minute phone calls canceling a scheduled appearance) to witnesses for the defense would violate notions of fairness within the adversary system. As long as the defendant is presumed innocent unless proven guilty, evenhanded treatment of all witnesses should prevail. Rapport between victims and VWAP personnel that becomes too close can cause another problem: The testimony given in court can be considered coached or rehearsed if it departs from the original statements the witnesses have made and covers up contradictions in order to make the most convincing case against the defendant.

Protecting Victims Serving as Witnesses for the Prosecution

A man is robbed by three gunmen of $550. He reports the crime to the police and they round up three suspects. After he identifies them as the men who stole his money, he begins to receive death threats. The prosecutor's

> office suggests various measures to protect him, but he declines the offer. One night his doorbell rings and when he answers it, a stranger pulls out a gun and shoots him in the head. ("Warned Not to Testify," 1991)

Chilling tales like this could dissuade people who are unsure whether to report crimes, press charges, and testify in court. All victims who agree to serve as prosecution witnesses need to be protected from intimidation and reprisals; the gravest dangers are faced by defectors from street gangs, people harmed by drug-dealing crews, and battered women trying to break free from abusive mates. Intimidation can range from nuisance phone calls, stalking, and explicit threats of physical attacks to actual property damage (stone throwing, fire bombings) and assaults. Since the complainants' perceptions of the risk of cooperation determine whether they will testify in court, the primary responsibility for safeguarding their well-being falls to the prosecutor handling the case. When prosecutors don't react to acts of intimidation, one of the victim's worst fears is confirmed: Namely, that the criminal justice system can't provide protection from further harm and that the only way to avoid reprisals is to stop cooperating. Anonymous calls in the middle of the night or acts of vandalism are difficult to trace. But if left unaddressed, these incidents convey the message that complainants are on their own, and they signify to offenders that intimidation is worth a try: It may have the desired effect, and it carries little risk of additional penalties (see Docksai, 1979; President's Task Force, 1982; and Healey, 1995).

The actual extent of the intimidation problem is not known. Measuring intimidation is a difficult task, in part because successfully intimidated victims (and witnesses) are afraid to disclose their plight to researchers. Each year only a small percentage of respondents admit to *NCVS* interviewers that "fear of reprisal" stopped them from informing the police about crimes committed against them (see the rates of nonreporting due to fear of reprisal presented in Table 4.5). As might be expected the intimidation rate is higher for crimes of violence than for property crimes (not shown). Fear of reprisal prevents a significant fraction of rape victims from divulging information to the police. (The percentages fluctuate considerably from year to year because the number of respondents is small, statistically speaking.) Worries about offender retaliation pose less of a problem in cases of robbery and assault. As for changes over time, no clear trends are apparent. Police departments and prosecutors' offices certainly have not eliminated fear of reprisals as a genuine concern that holds down reporting rates.

Various studies have yielded contradictory findings about how often complainants are successfully intimidated by the people they accuse of harming them. In one survey of New Yorkers, about 13% of a sample of approximately 1,000 victims confided that their offenders or the defendants' friends or relatives had attempted to intimidate them, most commonly by verbally threatening them during face-to-face confrontations. Some victims had their property vandalized, but fewer than 1% were actually assaulted. The incidents occurred in police stations and courthouses, as well as in the neighborhoods and homes of the victims. The willingness of complainants to cooperate with prosecutors was not seriously

Table 4.5 Trends in Fear of Reprisal as a Cause of Nonreporting

	PERCENTAGE OF NONREPORTING VICTIMS WHO FEARED REPRISALS							
Type of Crime	**1980**	**1982**	**1983**	**1984**	**1985**	**1986**	**1987**	**1988**
Rape	12%	8%	8%	11%	17%	12%	21%	10%
Robbery	6	4	5	3	9	6	6	7
Aggravated assault	6	5	4	7	6	5	7	5
Simple assault	3	5	4	4	4	5	4	4
Type of Crime	**1989**	**1990**	**1991**	**1992**	**1993**	**1994**	**1996**	**1998**
Rape	12%	8%	11%	7%	12%	15%	12%	11%
Robbery	4	7	5	6	4	7	4	4
Aggravated assault	5	5	7	6	6	4	6	5
Simple assault	4	3	3	3	3	3	3	4

NOTE: Percentages represent the proportions of respondents citing "fear of reprisal" as their primary reason for not reporting to the police a crime that they were willing to disclose to *NCVS* interviewer.
SOURCE: BJS, *Criminal Victimization in the United States,* 1982–2000.

undermined by attempts at intimidation, and these attempts did not influence conviction rates to any statistically significant extent (Fried, 1982). But when the same agency conducted another study about 10 years later, the researchers came to a different conclusion: Attempts to intimidate often succeeded. New Yorkers who were threatened were more than twice as likely to ask that charges be dropped than those who were not contacted by defendants. Individuals who had close prior relations (romantic involvements or family ties) with the defendants were more likely to receive menacing looks, to be warned about bodily harm or damage to property, or to be assaulted than victims who accused complete strangers ("Study Shows Intimidation," 1990).

The intimidation problem goes beyond direct threats. Would-be complainants may experience strong pressures from their own families and friends not to come forward and tell the police what happened. Subjected to this kind of "cultural intimidation" by their community, they may be forced to either settle the score privately or let the matter rest. Another type of intimidation arises from perceptions rather than overt acts. Victims may be haunted by visions of what offenders might do, even though no specific threats have been made. The thought of sensationalized media exposure can also be chilling. Finally, intimidation can be directed against defense lawyers, defendants, and reluctant defense witnesses in the form of harassment by the authorities, especially in well-publicized and controversial cases. One-sided formulations of the intimidation problem imply that it is improper for anyone other than law enforcement agents to contact witnesses and victims. But defense attorneys must be allowed to, since a person accused of a crime has a constitutional right to confront his or her accusers, compel witnesses to testify, and put on a vigorous defense (ABA Committee on Victims, 1979).

Much of the intimidation problem can be traced to officials who have shirked their responsibilities to victims. Police officers might con victims into cooperating by making empty promises of added protection, knowing full well that their precincts don't have the resources to provide special attention. Because attrition lightens their workload, ADAs might allow cases to collapse when key witnesses and complainants fail to appear after being subpoenaed—perhaps due to intimidation. Judges may not be vigilant for the same reason: Intimidation leads to nonappearance and ultimately dismissals, which reduce caseloads. To reduce fears about reprisals, the American Bar Association Committee on Victims (1979) put forward the following recommendations: Legislatures should make attempts at intimidation a misdemeanor; police forces ought to set up victim-witness protection squads; judges should issue orders of protection and consider violations as grounds for contempt of court citations and revocations of bail; judges should grant continuances rather than drop all charges against defendants if complaining witnesses mysteriously fail to appear when subpoenaed; and prosecutors must avoid carelessly revealing information concerning the whereabouts of victims, even after cases are resolved.

Prosecutors always have had to coax victims and other witnesses to cooperate by offering them a number of protective services until the trial is over, or even longer. Victims need assistance to change their phone numbers and door locks, obtain orders of protection, move to new homes, hide out in safe houses or hotels, and in extreme cases get around-the-clock armed guards (Kleinfield, 1995). However, inadequate funding limits the ability of prosecutors' offices to offer these protective measures to all who need them (New York State Law Enforcement Council, 1994). The most extensive governmental response to the threat of reprisals has been the establishment of witness-protection programs on the state and county level. They provide tight security to victims, other witnesses, and their immediate families. These services are intended primarily to safeguard witnesses willing to testify against criminal organizations like mob families, street gangs, and drug trafficking networks. Many of the beneficiaries are not really victims but former lawbreakers. The federal Witness Security Program helps individuals who face reprisals for testifying on behalf of the government. The program promises relocation, new identities, new jobs, and payment of moving expenses (Associated Press, 1994i).

Dismissing Charges and Rejecting Cases

Crime victims, police officers, and prosecutors are all supposed to be on the same side within the adversary system. Yet their alliance—based in theory on a common commitment to convict people guilty of crimes—often unravels. Victims may feel rebuffed and abandoned when prosecutors dismiss or reduce charges and counts against suspects. A decision not to go forward means no further official action will be taken, and victims will not achieve the goals they sought when they reported the crime, whether they were looking for maximum punishment as revenge, compulsory treatment of the offender, or court-ordered restitution. To prosecutors these decisions, even if they infuriate victims, are unavoidable. It's impossible for prosecutors to fulfill their legal mandate to enforce every law and to seek the conviction of all lawbreakers.

When evaluating the cases brought before them by the police and deciding whether or not to go forward, ADAs must take into account other considerations besides the victims' wishes. The prosecution must weigh many factors. What are the chances of conviction rather than acquittal? Are there serious doubts about the guilt of the accused? How credible and how cooperative are the victim and other witnesses? Does the complainant have any improper motives for pressing charges? Was the evidence obtained according to constitutional guidelines, or will it be tossed out of court under the exclusionary rule? Is the effort worth the state's limited resources? (How much will it cost in time and money to resolve the matter?) Would indictment, prosecution, and conviction of the defendant serve as a general deterrent to others contemplating committing the same type of offense? Would punishment of the offender serve as a specific deterrent to discourage him or her from repeating this illegal act? Would pressing charges and seeking conviction enhance the community's sense of security and confidence in the criminal justice system? Could the accused serve as an informant for the police or as a key witness for the prosecution in other cases if his or her cooperation were secured by lenient treatment in this case? Would pressing or dropping charges set off protests from powerful interest groups in the community? If this office declines to prosecute, would the case be pursued by another branch of government or in a different jurisdiction? Are there appropriate pretrial diversion programs in operation in this jurisdiction that provide treatment to wrongdoers as an alternative to adjudication? How are cases of this kind routinely handled in this jurisdiction? And finally, would a victory in this case substantially advance the careers of the ADA handling the case and of the prosecutor heading the office? (see the National Advisory Commission, 1973; Sheley, 1979; and Boland and Sones, 1986).

When all these factors are taken into account, it is clear that the victim is only one of several key players who influence the decisions of prosecutors. Police officials, other persons in the prosecutor's office, defense attorneys, judges, community leaders, and vocal interest groups all affect prosecutorial decision making.

Cases that have been "solved" by arrests might not be pursued for a number of reasons. Prosecutors might screen out unwinnable cases because of perceived weaknesses that undercut the chances of conviction. Judges might dismiss charges on their own initiative if they feel that the evidence is lacking. In general, jurisdictions in which prosecutors weed out many cases before going to court have low case-dismissal rates at later stages of judicial proceedings. Where prosecutors toss out few cases, judges throw out many more. A periodic nationwide survey of case processing revealed that, overall, more than half of all cases in 1981 that were "solved" by arrest were not carried forward (23% were rejected at screening by prosecutors, 22% were dismissed in court by judges, and 6% were diverted out of court for a total of 51% not pursued) (Boland and Sones, 1986). By 1988 the percent of all felony arrests not carried forward had decreased to 45% because slightly smaller proportions of "solved" cases were rejected by prosecutors or dismissed by judges (Boland, Mahanna, and Sones, 1992). Clearly, the outcomes of these decisions give a great many victims reasons to be dissatisfied with the adjudication process.

Negotiating Pleas

The vast majority of cases that are carried forward (not diverted, screened out, or dismissed in court) are resolved through **plea negotiations.** Nationwide, most felony charges (67%) are resolved by guilty pleas. An overwhelming 97% of convictions are secured by the accused admitting guilt (possibly just to a misdemeanor instead of the original felony charge) rather than by a jury rendering a verdict of guilt, according to a study of cases adjudicated in the 75 busiest urban counties during 1994 (see Reaves, 1998). Plea negotiation refers to the process in which the ADA and the defense counsel meet to settle a case out of court without having to hold a trial. The typical outcome of the "bargaining" (as most observers and participants derisively refer to the offers and counteroffers) is that the defendant agrees to make a public confession in return for some **consideration** from the government. The concession the state agrees to could be the dropping of certain charges (often the most serious ones carrying the most severe penalties), the dismissal of particular counts (accusations of harm against specific victims), or a promise or recommendation about a lesser punishment, such as a suspended sentence, probation, a fine, or incarceration for an agreed-upon period of time below the maximum permitted by the law.

The expression **plea bargain** gives the erroneous impression that defendants who "cop a plea" invariably get a break or good deal that permits them to escape the punishment they deserve. Police officials and prosecutors routinely engage in "bedsheeting" and "overcharging" in anticipation of the negotiations that will follow. Bedsheeting refers to the practice of charging a defendant with every applicable crime committed during a single incident. For example, an armed intruder captured while burglarizing an occupied home can be held accountable for criminal trespass, breaking and entering, burglary, attempted grand larceny, and carrying a concealed weapon, in addition to the most serious charge of robbery. Overcharging means filing a criminal indictment for an offense that is more serious than the available evidence might support (for example, charging someone with attempted murder after a fistfight). Some of these charges could not be proven in court, but defendants and their lawyers might be too cautious to gamble and call the prosecutor's bluff. For these reasons and others, most accused persons who plead guilty in return for "concessions" receive substantially the same penalties that they probably would have received if convicted after a trial (Rhodes, 1978; Beall, 1980; Katz, 1980). Plea negotiation, even though it has been widely condemned for decades, appears to be the only practical way of handling a huge volume of cases. If all defendants demanded their constitutional right to be judged by a jury of their peers, the courts would be overwhelmed by trials.

Nevertheless, most victims are convinced that criminals are getting away with something when they accept plea bargains offered by the prosecution. Actually, resolving cases by negotiating pleas rather than by holding full-scale trials may be in the best interests of certain victims. Besides a sure conviction, plea bargaining spares victims the ordeal of testifying in court and undergoing hostile questioning (cross-examination) by defense attorneys. Concerns about the victim having to take the stand are voiced most often in cases of child abuse and rape. Other types of complainants may be particularly reluctant to undergo cross-examination if the facts of the case portray them in a negative light or reveal aspects of their lives that they do not want to make public and expose to the world through media coverage (especially in jurisdictions where trials can be televised, which includes most states).

Since doing away with deals and inducements is unrealistic, some victims want to play an active role in the plea negotiations that resolve their cases. Victims justify their quest for empowerment by emphasizing that they were the ones directly involved and personally harmed, but this demand has evoked considerable resistance.

It is often presumed that the adversarial model characterizes the actual workings of the adjudication process; that in the hard bargaining between prosecution and defense, the ADA must be able to produce a cooperative witness eager to testify in order to convince the defendant to cave in, negotiate a plea, and confess guilt to some of the charges. The reality of the situation might be that the **courtroom work group** (made up of the judge, ADA, and defense counsel) has a mutual interest in processing large numbers of cases expeditiously. Victims serving as witnesses for the prosecution are outsiders whose presence and involvement is often unwanted by these insiders because it will slow down their assembly-line practices that resolve cases quickly. Victims see their situations as unique events that deserve careful consideration, not as routine occurrences to be rapidly **disposed of** according to some formula based on that jurisdiction's current **going rate** (typical penalty or sentence currently merited by the type of crime in question, agreed upon by the insiders). Victim-witness programs have had little success in improving appearance rates and conviction rates because they have perpetuated the handling of victims as mere witnesses for the prosecution and not as the active participants some would like to be (Davis, 1983; Walker, 1994).

Predictably, defense attorneys, prosecutors, and judges make dire predictions about what would happen if victims (and police officers and defendants as well) joined them at the table at pretrial conferences. These insiders contend that the candid discussions necessary to foster settlements would be inhibited by the presence of outsiders, that volatile confrontations between victims and defendants would break out, that both victims and defendants would misconstrue the role of judges and accuse them of improper conduct, and that the dignity of judges would be diminished by their open involvement in negotiations in front of outsiders (Heinz and Kerstetter, 1979). Prosecutors in particular feel threatened by the inclusion of victims (whom they supposedly represent in addition to the state) at such meetings. They object because victims might try to use the administrative machinery as an instrument of personal revenge and might put forward unreasonable demands for the imposition of maximum penalties. Deals would fall through, and risky and costly trials would be necessitated (McDonald, 1976). In general, victims do not have a right to participate in or even be consulted during the process of plea negotiation. Only a few jurisdictions have granted victims a clearly defined role, and most state laws still do not provide them with any formal mechanisms to challenge the decisions of the prosecuting attorneys who act in their name as well as on behalf of "the people." The Supreme Court has issued several rulings that specifically deny complainants any right to challenge the decisions prosecutors make in their cases (see below).

VICTIMS AND DEFENSE ATTORNEYS

Victims and defense lawyers are natural enemies within the adversary system of criminal justice. Whether hired privately for a fee or provided free of charge to indigents, these attorneys have a duty to advise suspects, defendants, and convicts about their best interests, the risks they face, and the options they can exercise. Obliged to be vigorous advocates for their clients, they may staunchly deny guilt during plea negotiations or at a trial. In trying to cast doubt upon the government's version of events, they draw on all their skills and training to undermine the accusatory testimony of victims.

Conflicts often break out between victims and defense lawyers over two matters: how long the process takes (and how many court appearances are needed to resolve cases) and the line of questioning directed at victims who testify in court. From the victims' point of view, defense attorneys might engage in two kinds of abusive practices: asking judges for postponements of their clients' cases in order to wear victims down, and using unfair tactics to undermine their credibility when they appear as witnesses for the prosecution.

Postponing Hearings

The Sixth Amendment to the Constitution guarantees accused persons the right to a speedy trial. Hence, problems of court congestion and needless delays usually have been approached from the defendants' standpoint. Many states and the federal government have set limits on the amount of time that can elapse from arrest to trial (not counting continuances requested by defense attorneys). But victims also suffer from the uncertainty that envelops unresolved cases and share a common interest with defendants in having legal matters settled in as short a time as possible. However, if individuals accused of crimes are free on bail, defense lawyers may have an incentive to stall proceedings as much as possible to "buy time on the streets" and to wear the victims down. As the delays mount and victims appear in court unnecessarily, they (as well as other crucial prosecution witnesses) may lose patience with the slow deliberations of the legal system, and their commitment to see the case through to its conclusion may erode. The strategy succeeds if the victims (or other key witnesses) give up in disgust and fail to appear in court as required. For example, a victim who lost her handbag to an unarmed bandit may miss so many days from work that the lost wages far exceed what the robber took, so she may eventually drop out. Stalling for time may also pay off if victims (or other witnesses for the prosecution) forget crucial details, move away, get seriously ill, or die in the interim. At that point defense attorneys can move for a dismissal of all charges (Reiff, 1979). (Prosecutors can also manipulate continuance provisions for their own ends. If defendants are in jail rather than out on bail, then government attorneys may stretch out proceedings to keep them behind bars longer and to pressure them to accept unfavorable plea offers. In the process the defendants' right to a speedy trial could be violated.)

Postponements can prolong and intensify the suffering of victims. In order to be available if called to testify, they might have to repeatedly arrange for child care, miss school or work, cancel vacations, and break appointments, only to discover (often at the last minute) that the hearings have been rescheduled. To defeat this wear-the-victim-down strategy, some of the motions for postponements by defense attorneys could be opposed more vigorously by prosecutors sensitive to the needs and wants of their clients and rejected by judges if they suspect the requests for continuances are stalling tactics (President's Task Force, 1982). To prevent victims (and police officers) from showing up in court on days when hearings have been postponed, victim-witness assistance programs operate last-minute notification systems.

As a general rule, the more serious the charges against the defendant, the longer it takes to resolve the case. Cases resolved by negotiated pleas don't take as long as cases resolved by trials, of course. The average time it took to resolve a case from arrest to sentencing when defendants pled guilty was 114 days as compared to 241 days from arrest to sentencing after trials, according to data gathered from a national study of 30 jurisdictions in 1988 (Boland, Mahanna, and Sones, 1992). Researchers determined that murder cases in state courts took an average of 313 days to be resolved, rape cases required 133 days, and robbery cases went on for 108 days from arrest to sentencing, according to a study that used 1994 data about over 50,000 felonies handled in the nation's 75 largest counties (Reaves, 1998). However, in some high-crime areas huge backlogs cause even greater delays, prolonging the anxiety of both complainants and defendants waiting to discover the final outcome of their conflicts.

Cross-examining Witnesses During Trials

If they can't wear victims down through stalling tactics, defense attorneys may try to discredit them (and other prosecution witnesses) on the stand during the trial so that the jury won't give much weight to their testimony.

Under the adversary system each side puts forward its own best case and assails the version of events presented by the opposition. **Cross-examination** is the art of exposing the weaknesses of witnesses. The intent is to impeach their credibility by trapping them into revealing any hidden motives, lapses of memory, unsavory character traits, embarrassing indiscretions, prejudices, incompetencies, or dishonest inclinations. The Sixth Amendment to the U.S. Constitution gives defendants the right to confront their accusers. Since the burden of proof falls on the prosecution and the accused is innocent unless proven guilty, the accuser must be presumed mistaken until his or her credibility is established beyond a reasonable doubt. The defense attorney goes up against a formidable professional foe when the witness for the government is an expert or a police officer (although the credibility of police testimony has become the subject of much debate). But when the full brunt of the defense's well-honed counterattack is directed at the novice complainant, the potential for adding insult to injury reaches disturbing proportions. At its best the confrontation in the courtroom puts the victim-as-eyewitness to the test. At its worst the victim is set up as a target, to be injured again by being made to look like a liar, a fool, or an instigator who got what he or she deserved.

Trials are relatively rare events, so most victims will never be called upon to testify and undergo cross-examination. Since the outcomes of trials are uncertain and involve risks, both attorneys usually prefer to strike a deal out of court. However, statistically speaking, most trials are successful from the point of view of victims and prosecutors: Defendants are found guilty. The percentage of all criminal indictments that result in trials (either before juries or in **bench trials** before judges) varies according to two factors: the jurisdiction and the nature of the charges. Some prosecutors are more willing to put defendants on trial than others. Serious felonies such as murder, rape, aggravated assault, and robbery go to trial more often than cases involving lesser crimes like burglary or auto theft. Rape complainants are the most likely to be subjected to hostile cross-examination by defense attorneys. In 1992 about 18% of all rape convictions were achieved through trials with the help of the complainants' testimony (14% before juries and 4% in bench trials before judges alone); the remaining 82% of all convictions were secured through plea negotiations (Langan and Graziadei, 1995).

Cross-examinations can be ordeals for witnesses. But if defense attorneys were not allowed to sharply question prosecution witnesses, then the right of defendants to try (through their lawyers) to refute the charges against them would be undermined. The concerns of complainants and other witnesses (including witnesses for the defense who are cross-examined by prosecutors) about being embarrassed on the stand under oath must be balanced against the public humiliation suffered by defendants who are arrested and put on trial. Since defense attorneys have a duty to vigorously represent the best interests of their clients, their courtroom tactics might seem harsh from the victim's point of view. To rattle a witness, discredit damning testimony, and sow seeds of doubt and confusion among jurors, they may have to resort to theatrics and hyperbole. The Code of Professional Responsibility guiding legal strategies permits a zealous defense to gain an acquittal or a lenient sentence but prohibits any line of questioning whose sole aim is to harass or maliciously harm a witness. The experts and the public often disagree in specific trials over whether or not a defense attorney (or a prosecutor) crossed the line and acted unethically by badgering a witness during a cross-examination. The kinds of cases that provoke the greatest controversy are those in which defense attorneys cast aspersions on the character of victims or blame them for their own misfortunes (Shipp, 1987). In murder trials the families of the deceased find it particularly upsetting if defense attorneys attack the attitudes and actions of the dead persons to try to justify or exonerate the behavior of their clients. Unlike cross-examinations, these attempts to sully the reputation (or "trash the memory") of the dead are peculiarly one-sided affairs, since the subjects of the insinuations cannot rebut the accusations, as this case shows:

A young woman is strangled late at night in a public park by a young man she was dating. He tells police that she died accidentally as he protected himself during "rough sex play." His lawyer subpoenas her diary, which allegedly contains graphic descriptions of her aggressive sexual exploits with other men (later it turns out that it doesn't). Some members of the jury are swayed by the defense's arguments. The jury becomes deadlocked for days; before it can render a unanimous verdict, a last-minute plea is negotiated that permits the defendant to admit guilt to the lesser charge of manslaughter instead of murder. At a press conference the father denounces the defense's portrayal of his dead daughter, and calls it a bizarre pack of lies. (Hackett and Cerio, 1988; Lander, 1988)

VICTIMS AND JUDGES

Judges are supposed to act as referees within the adversary system. Defendants often consider them to be partisans representing the state and favoring the prosecution. Angry victims, however, frequently see judges as guardians of the rights of the accused rather than protectors of the innocent. Victims who have been mistreated by the offender, the police, the prosecutor, and the defense attorney expect that the judge will finally accord them the justice they seek. But conflicts between victims and judges can erupt over bail decisions and sentencing.

Granting Bail

Police officers often resent bail as a repudiation of the hard work and risks they have undertaken to apprehend perpetrators. To them, releasing defendants on bail is tantamount to turning dangerous criminals loose. If they are convinced that the defendants are indeed the culprits, victims can also be outraged by the decisions of judges to grant bail.

The Eighth Amendment to the Constitution prohibits the setting of excessive bail. Whether or not it establishes a chance to be bailed out as an affirmative right, however, is a subject of scholarly debate and considerable public concern. State and federal courts routinely deny bail to defendants accused of first-degree murder. In noncapital cases bail can be denied to jailed suspects who have a history of flight to avoid prosecution or who have tried to interfere with the administration of justice by intimidating a witness or a juror, for example. Otherwise, defendants generally are given a chance to raise money or post bond to guarantee that they will show up for their hearings and trials. The amount of bail is usually determined by the judge and is set according to the nature of the offense and the record of the defendant; the prosecutor can recommend a figure. Making bail is a major problem for defendants who are poor and have no prosperous friends or relatives. Across the nation, houses of detention are crammed full with people unable to raise a few hundred dollars to purchase their freedom until their cases are resolved.

Nationwide, about one third of all victims of serious crimes face the prospect that the person accused of harming them will be let out on bail before the case is resolved (7% of all felony defendants were denied any chance at bail and 57% who had an amount set by a judge couldn't raise the necessary money and property required to secure their release in the 75 largest counties during 1994) (Reaves, 1998).

The question of bail versus jail raises a number of troubling issues. When accused people are denied bail (and subjected to preventive detention) or are unable to raise the necessary amount, they are sent to jail and thereby immediately undergo punishment before conviction. The living conditions in houses of detention are usually far worse than in prisons, which hold convicted felons. Yet the release of a defendant who is genuinely guilty and also prone to strike again poses a direct threat to the victim who will serve as a witness for the state and an immediate danger to the entire community. One partial resolution of this dilemma is for the judge to state that a condition of bail will be that the defendant must avoid all contacts with the complainant or else forfeit the privilege of pretrial release.

Sentencing Offenders

After a defendant has been convicted by an admission of guilt as part of a negotiated plea or by a jury verdict after a trial, the judge has the responsibility of imposing an appropriate sentence. Judges can exercise a considerable amount of discretion when pronouncing sentences unless there are mandatory minimums or explicit guidelines. Sentences can involve incarceration, fines, enrollment in treatment programs, community service, and obligations to repay victims. The main objectives that guide sentencing are specific deterrence, general deterrence, incapacitation, retribution, rehabilitation, and restitution.

The substantial variation between judges in the severity of the punishments meted out in comparable cases is termed **sentence disparity.** Civil libertarians find great disparities troubling because judges might be expressing their social prejudices, to the extent that they deal more harshly with certain kinds of offenders than with others. Convicts might view sentence disparities as a sign of unjustifiable arbitrariness. Law-and-order advocates consider wide ranges as evidence that judges on the low end are too "soft" or "permissive" toward offenders. Activists in the victims' rights movement find the spectrum of possible punishments that might be handed down as an inspiration to press for greater input in sentencing.

Historically, the exclusion of victims from the sentencing process has been justified on several grounds. If the purpose of punishing offenders is to deter others from committing the same acts, then sanctions must be swift, sure, and predictable, and not subject to uncertainty and modification by the injured parties. If the objective is retribution, then lawbreakers must receive the punishments they deserve, not the penalties their victims request. If the goal of sentencing is to rehabilitate offenders, then the punitive urges of the people they harmed cannot be allowed to interfere with the length and type of treatment prescribed by experts (McDonald, 1979).

The potential impact of victims' desires on sentencing outcomes is limited because many different parties have input. Victims who want to try to determine their offenders' sentences have to compete for influence with other individuals and groups who routinely affect the exercise of judicial discretion. State legislatures pass laws that set maximum and minimum limits for periods of confinement and for fines. Prosecutors make recommendations based on deals arrived at during plea negotiations and draw upon the courtroom workgroup's mutual understandings of the appropriate penalty for specific crimes in that jurisdiction at that time (the going rate). Defense attorneys use whatever leverage they have on behalf of their clients. Defendants determine to some degree their own sentences by their demeanor, degree of remorse, prior record of convictions, and other mitigating or aggravating personal characteristics. Probation officers conduct presentence investigations and make recommendations to guide judges. Parole boards determine the actual time served when they decide to let convicted felons out of prison ahead of schedule or keep them confined until their maximum sentences expire. By filing reports corrections officers influence whether or not convicts earn "good-time" reductions and parole. The news media can shape outcomes by their coverage or lack of it. The public's reactions can affect the handling of cases, prompting either harshness or leniency. And ultimately, state governors can shorten terms of imprisonment (or even stop executions) by issuing pardons or commuting sentences.

Victims can attempt to directly influence sentences in two ways: either by conveying their requests to judges in writing or by expressing their views orally in person at sentencing hearings (**allocution**). Written **victim impact statements (VIS)** enable judges to learn about the actual physical, emotional, and financial effects of crimes on the injured parties and their families. Written questionnaires ask (with the threat of penalties for perjury) about any wounds, medical bills, counseling costs, other expenses, insurance reimbursements, and lifestyle changes. **Statements of opinion** ask victims what they would consider to be appropriate sentences. In most jurisdictions, the victim impact statement is incorporated into the **presentence investigation report (PSIR)** prepared by a probation officer.

The invention and adoption of impact statements and the granting of the allocution privilege represented important gains for the victims' rights movement. Prior to their acceptance and implementation, victims had to rely on prosecutors to present their views and to fully describe their plight. Direct appeals to judges were thought to undermine the judiciary's professional objectivity by injecting inflammatory emotional considerations into the proceedings. But advocates of victims' rights argued that the situation was unbalanced. Convicted persons did not have to depend solely on their lawyers to speak for them. They were permitted to directly address the court before their sentences were handed down. Yet two lives—the offender's and the victim's—were profoundly shaped by the sentence, which represented an official evaluation of the seriousness of the harm inflicted. Judges couldn't make informed decisions if they heard from only one side: the defendants themselves and their lawyers, families, friends, and other character witnesses. Notions of fairness dictated that suffering individuals also be allowed to write or speak about their experiences before sentences were determined (President's Task Force, 1982).

A nationwide study of how criminal justice officials find out about the harm offenders inflicted on their victims concluded that for judges the most important source of information was the presentence investigation report, not the prosecutor or the trial testimony. However, the probation officers who prepared the PSIR usually obtained much of their information about how seriously victims were harmed from secondhand sources, such as police reports and medical records, and not directly from victims through impact statements (Forst and Hernon, 1984).

Just because activists in the victims' rights movement succeeded in securing the right to submit an impact statement or to speak in person at a sentencing hearing does not mean that this practice has become widespread and effective. On the contrary, a study carried out in California in 1982 concluded that very few victims took advantage of these opportunities, and when they did their participation seemed to have very little influence (Villmoare and Neto, 1987).

When a sentence is handed down, it is possible that the victim is misled into thinking that it is more severe than it really is. Therefore, the victims' rights movement has urged states to impose a **truth-in-sentencing** rule which would require judges to calculate and announce the earliest possible date (actual time served) that a convict could be released from confinement, taking into account time off for good behavior behind bars and parole immediately upon eligibility (Associated Press, 1994c). For example, during the 1980s, felons sent to prison by state court judges across the country served an estimated 38% of their maximum sentences. A federal truth-in-sentencing law, passed in 1987 and adopted since then in many states, requires felons to serve at least 85% of their court-imposed sentences (parole has been abolished, and the maximum allowable good-time credit is 15%) (Langan, Perkins, and Chaiken, 1994).

A study of more than 300 victims of felonies in eight jurisdictions across the country established that most victims were dissatisfied with the sentences judges handed down in their cases. Eighty-six percent agreed with the statement that "guilty offenders are not punished enough" (Forst and Hernon, 1984). This perception that many judges are too lenient is shared by the public at large. Annual nationwide polls ask, "In general, do you think the courts in this area deal too harshly or not harshly enough with criminals?" In 1972, 66% of those polled answered "not harshly enough", by 1976 the number had risen to 81%, in 1986 the figure peaked at 85%, and by 1993 the percentage had declined to 81% (Maguire and Pastore, 1994).

This widespread impression raises a crucial question: Just how much punishment is enough? Victims might feel that the offenders convicted of harming them don't stay in prison long enough. But no formula or equation exists to calculate the gravity of an offense and translate this rating into the "proper" amount of time the perpetrator should be incarcerated. The profound disagreements that divide people over the issue of whether murder should carry the death penalty or life imprisonment are well known. Usually overlooked, however, are the dramatic differences in maximum penalties from state to state for lesser crimes like rape, robbery, or burglary. Clearly, legislators who have the authority to set the upper limits for penalties can't agree on the maximum length of prison time that one person who harms another really deserves. It is impossible to conclude with any degree of objectivity that a particular offender "got off too lightly" when the maximum sentences differ so sharply from one jurisdiction to another (see Katz, 1980).

A bitter controversy erupted over whether victim impact statements should be allowed and whether allocution by survivors in the victims' immediate family should be permitted during the penalty phase of murder trials (after the defendants have been convicted and face the possibility of execution, in most states). The following case was brought before the Supreme Court and was at the core of the debate over the admissibility of victim impact information.

> Caught up in a drug-induced frenzy, a man stabs to death the mother of two toddlers, as well as her 2-year-old daughter. During the penalty phase of the trial, the grandmother describes to the jury how the 3-year-old boy who survived the attack still cries mournfully for his mother and little sister. The jury sentences the convict to die in the electric chair. (Clark and Block, 1992)

Victims' rights groups and prosecutors' organizations argued that it was illogical to demand that a jury focus all of its attention on the defendant's difficult circumstances and other mitigating factors and then ignore the suffering of the deceased's survivors. But civil rights and civil liberties groups argued that the introduction of impact statements could be highly inflammatory and prejudicial in capital cases, diverting the jury's attention toward the victim's character (how much or how little the dead person will be missed and mourned) and away from its duty of evaluating the defendant's blameworthiness and the circumstances surrounding the crime. The first time the high court considered a case that raised the issue, it voted to exclude impact statements; but when the issue came up again, the majority of justices ruled that survivors could testify during the penalty phase of a capital case (Clark and Block, 1992).

Appealing to the Supreme Court

The U.S. Supreme Court is the highest appellate body in the judicial system. It hears only those cases on appeal from federal and state courts that appear to raise important principles of constitutional law. Its nine justices are appointed for life by the president (with the approval of the Senate) so that they can feel independent of outside pressures. When a majority of Supreme Court justices (five or more) agree on a decision in a case chosen for review, their ruling sets a precedent that must be followed in all lower courts throughout the nation. These **landmark decisions** also guide the procedures followed by the police, prosecutors, trial judges, corrections officials, and other agencies within the criminal justice system. Over the past several decades, a number of decisions handed down by the Supreme Court have affected the rights and interests of crime victims (see O'Neill, 1984). Some of these far-reaching rulings are briefly summarized in Box 4.3.

BOX 4.3 Supreme Court Decisions Directly Affecting Victims

Victims Cannot Compel Prosecutors to Take Action Against Suspects
A number of decisions handed down in 1967, 1973, 1977, 1981, and 1983 have established that attorneys general and district attorneys have absolute discretion over whether or not to charge defendants with crimes and what charges to press or drop. Victims cannot compel prosecutors to take particular actions, and courts cannot intervene in this decision-making process (see Stark and Goldstein, 1985).

Victim Impact Statements Can Be Used in Capital Cases
In 1987 *(Booth v. Maryland),* the Supreme Court overturned a death sentence because during the penalty phase of the trial, the jury heard a particularly heart-rending impact statement about how the murder of an elderly couple shattered the lives of three generations of their family. The majority ruled that the use of such "inflammatory" impact statements created a constitutionally unacceptable risk that juries might impose the death penalty in an arbitrary and capricious manner, swayed by the standing and reputation of the murdered victims in their communities. The majority believed that the victim's "worth" was not an appropriate factor for a jury to consider when weighing the killer's fate—imprisonment or execution—because it would undermine the guarantee of equal protection (Triebwasser, 1987b).

But in 1991 *(Payne v. Tennessee),* the Court reversed itself and ruled that prosecutors could introduce victim impact statements and that the survivors of murder victims could testify. The majority held that courts have always taken into account the harm done by defendants when determining appropriate sentences (Clark and Block, 1992).

Insufficient Proof That the Lives of Murdered Black Victims Count for Less
In 1987 *(McCleskey v. Kemp),* in upholding a death penalty conviction, the Supreme Court rejected a statistical analysis that seemed to show that the deaths of black victims were not taken as seriously as the deaths of white victims by criminal justice decision makers—prosecutors, juries, and judges. The court ruled that a pattern in which persons convicted of killing white victims were 11 times more likely to be sentenced to die than those convicted of murdering black victims was not compelling evidence of intentional discrimination in violation of the Eighth and Fourteenth Amendments (Triebwasser, 1987a).

Offenders Can Escape Paying Restitution to Victims
In 1989 (*Pennsylvania Dept. of Public Welfare v. Davenport),* the Court ruled 7–2 that if convicts declare bankruptcy, they can avoid paying court-ordered restitution, since restitution obligations are dischargeable debts.

In another case in 1990 *(Hughey v. United States),* the Court ruled that a federal judge cannot order a defendant to pay restitution to a victim if the charge involving that victim was dropped as part of a negotiated plea. The Court based its ruling on a provision of the federal Victim and Witness Protection Act of 1982 (Eddy, 1990).

Government Has No Constitutional Duty to Protect Individuals
In 1989 *(De Shaney v. Winnebago County Dept. of Social Services),* six of the nine justices decided that a government agency could not be sued for failing to intervene (on behalf of a child repeatedly beaten and permanently injured by his father) because the state does not have a special obligation to protect individuals from harm by other private persons ("U.S. Supreme Court," 1989).

Newspapers Can Publish the Lawfully Obtained Names of Rape Victims
In 1989 a majority of six justices argued that the First Amendment's guarantee of freedom of the press protected a newspaper from liability for printing the name of a woman who already was identified as a rape victim in publicly available police reports. However, the decision did not declare unconstitutional state laws in Florida, Georgia, and South Carolina that prohibit the publishing of a rape victim's name as an invasion of privacy (Greenhouse, 1989).

Continued

BOX 4.3 ***continued***

Victimized Children Can Testify Via Closed-Circuit Television
In 1990 *(Maryland v. Craig)* in a 5–4 decision, the Court held that it was constitutional for a state to pass a law that shields a child who accuses an adult of sexual abuse from a face-to-face confrontation during a trial. The child's testimony and the defense attorney's cross-examination can take place in another room and can be shown to the jury over closed-circuit television if the prosecutor can convince the judge that the young witness would be traumatized by having to testify in the defendant's presence. The majority felt that the state's interest in the physical and psychological well-being of the abused child may outweigh the defendant's Sixth Amendment right to face his or her accuser in person (Greenhouse, 1990).

Rape Victims' Past Can Be Kept Out of Court
In 1991 the Supreme Court ruled by a 7–2 vote that the rape shield laws passed in all 50 states were constitutional. The laws allow judges to suppress as irrelevant attempts by the defense to introduce allegations about the past sexual experiences of rape victims (Rauber, 1991).

Victims Can't Easily Claim Income Gained by Notorious Offenders
In 1991 *(Simon & Schuster v. New York Crime Victims Board),* the Supreme Court struck down New York's 1977 "Son-of-Sam" statute, which served as a model for 41 other state laws. The law confiscated fees and royalties offenders gained from selling their inside stories to book publishers or moviemakers and permitted victims to claim that money. The unanimous opinion held that the state's worthwhile goals of ensuring that criminals do not profit from their crimes, and of transferring the proceeds to victims, did not justify infringements on the First Amendment right of free speech (Greenhouse, 1991).

Victims of Rape and Domestic Violence Can't Sue Attackers in Federal Court
In 2000 *(U.S. v. Morrison),* the Supreme Court by a 5-4 margin struck down a provision of the 1984 Violence Against Women Act which had granted injured parties in domestic violence and rape cases the additional option of suing their assailants for monetary damages in federal court. The majority voted to uphold the doctrine of state sovereignty over gender-based violence rather than extend federal authority via the interstate commerce clause (Biskupic, 2000).

VICTIMS AND CORRECTIONS OFFICIALS

Corrections officials include jail and prison staffs and probation and parole officers. Victims whose cases led to successful prosecutions seek the cooperation of these corrections professionals but may find themselves in conflict over issues of safety and money. Victims are more likely to have contacts with county probation departments than with county jail, state prison, or state parole authorities. Of all felons found guilty in state courts, offenders sentenced to probation for up to several years make up the bulk (about 50%) and thereby outnumber convicts sent to jail for up to a year (10%) or to prison for longer stretches (37%), in 75 urban jurisdictions in 1994 (Brown and Langan, 1998).

Victims want two things from probation and parole officers. When offenders are placed on probation or are released on parole after serving time in prison, victims want to be protected from any harassment or further harm. They can feel especially endangered by a vengeful, violent ex-offender if their cooperation and testimony was a crucial factor leading to conviction. And if making restitution is a condition of probation or parole, victims want to receive the payments they are entitled to right on schedule. Probation and parole officers share these goals but often find their caseloads so overwhelming that they cannot effectively keep offenders away from their former victims or see to it that restitution payments arrive on time.

According to legislation enacted in most states, corrections officials are supposed to safeguard the well-being of victims by keeping them notified of the inmates' whereabouts. Correctional agencies can go further and make sure that prisoners on temporary leave from confinement (on furlough, work release, or educational release) or who escape from an institution do not threaten, track down, stalk, and injure their former victims (see National Victim Center, 1990). Whenever victims are shocked to discover that their offenders (especially those guilty of aggravated assault, armed robbery, rape, or sexual molestation) are back on the streets, conflicts can erupt with corrections officials who did not meet their notification obligations. Computer technology now allows corrections officials to send registered victims a phone message or letter informing them about a prisoner's release or escape from custody.

Contacting Parole Boards

Statistically speaking, relatively few victims ever deal with members of parole boards because small percentages of offenders are caught, convicted, and sent to prison for several years. However, this group of corrections officials has received a great deal of attention from the victims' rights movement because they determine the fates of inmates who have inflicted serious injuries.

By definition, parole means an early release before the maximum or upper limit of the judge's sentence has been served. Parole is the earned privilege of conditional liberty, with restrictions on conduct. Prisoners become eligible for parole after serving a specified proportion of their sentences. Of course, parole is not automatic, and many convicts are turned down by parole boards and kept incarcerated after hearings. (However, even without parole, early release is still possible because most correctional institutions subtract time for good behavior.) Rule violators and parolees accused of committing new crimes (recidivists) can be arrested and reimprisoned for the remainder of their unexpired full sentences at the discretion of administrative judges after revocation hearings.

Parole has become an extremely controversial practice, even though its origins date back to the mid-1800s. The rationales for setting up boards to grant the privilege of early release to selected prisoners are that ex-convicts can make a smoother transition from a prison regimen to civilian life with the guidance of parole officers; corrections authorities can control inmates better as long as the possibility of early release looms as a reward for good behavior; and that parole enables authorities to manage the flow of prisoners into and out of institutions, ensuring that sufficient cell space is available for the steady waves of new arrivals sent by the courts.

Prisoners' rights groups have rejected the image of parole as a form of benevolence and as an incentive for rehabilitation. They have criticized the practice as a way of extending the length of time ex-convicts are under governmental control, as a device to prolong punishment, and as a source of anxiety and uncertainty for prisoners. These groups have called for the abolition of the practice of parole and have suggested determinate or fixed sentences of shorter duration as a replacement for indefinite sentences with widely varying minimums and maximums (Shelden, 1982). Law-and-order groups have also demanded an end to the parole system, perceiving it, however, as a source of unwarranted leniency because it allows dangerous criminals to be let out prematurely. They want parole ended and replaced with definite sentences of longer duration (President's Task Force, 1982). Victims, too, may bitterly resent the practice of parole, since it further reduces sentences of incarceration that they may originally have considered too short.

As a result of the widespread dissatisfaction with parole, the federal prison system and a number of state systems have phased it out. In other jurisdictions parole is being granted less often. The reliance on parole reached its peak in 1977, when as many as 72% of all prisoners returning to society were granted conditional liberty with community supervision. By 1986 the proportion of released prisoners who were let out on parole had dropped to 43% (Hester, 1987), and by 1990 the figure stood at 41% (Jankowski, 1991). Of the nearly 500,000 inmates released from state prisons in 1998 (see Beck and Mumola, 1999), roughly 177,000 were granted discretionary parole (see Bonczar and Glaze, 1999). Since about 35% of all prisoners did not serve out their maximum terms as the 20th century ended, victims retain an interest in exercising their rights before parole boards. Board members can serve victims by inviting them to participate in the decision-making process, by warning them in advance that the persons they helped send to prison are being let go, and by ordering the convicts to pay restitution as a condition of release.

Legislation in most states expressly grants victims the right to personally attend parole hearings (usually held in faraway prisons) and voice their views or submit written or videotaped impact statements (National Victim Center, 1990). Through these channels they might oppose early release on the grounds that, in their opinion, the offender has not been punished sufficiently. Information about the physical, emotional, and financial harm inflicted by the offender could convince members of the board about the severity of the crime. Alternatively, victims might support early release but demand that restitution be one of the conditions in addition to the usual terms, such as refraining from further illegal activity, avoiding the company of known criminals, abstaining from drinking, and reporting to the authorities regularly. In some states, restitution is a mandatory requirement for parolees, unless the board excuses them from this obligation.

As with sentencing, the potential impact of victim input into parole board decision making is limited. The boards review statements from victims, prosecutors, judges, and other concerned parties. They interview the inmates themselves and review their criminal records and files describing their behavior while in prison. Boards are often subject to intense pressures either to keep convicts confined longer or to let some out ahead of schedule to make room for new arrivals.

AND JUSTICE FOR ALL

The Fourteenth Amendment to the Constitution promises equal protection under the law for all citizens. The standard interpretation of this pledge is that federal and state criminal justice systems ought to regard social factors like class, race, nationality, religion, and sex as irrelevant to the administration of the law. Traditionally, criminologists and political activists have applied this important principle of equal protection to the way suspects, defendants, and convicts are handled by officials and agencies. The main focus of concern has been whether offenders who are poor or members of a minority group are subjected to discriminatory treatment. Until recently, the equally significant question of whether certain kinds of victims are handled in a discriminatory manner has escaped notice.

It is often said that the United States is a country "ruled by laws, not men." This maxim implies that the principles of due process and equal protection limit the considerable discretionary powers of criminal justice officials. Due process means procedural regularity, and equal protection requires that different categories of people be treated similarly. Yet enough discretion remains at each step in the criminal justice process to generate unequal outcomes. Of course, those who exercise discretion can and do justify their actions. The explanations range from pragmatic considerations about time and money to philosophical rationales about the true meaning of justice. Nevertheless, the actions they take generate, maintain, and reveal double standards, or more accurately (since sometimes more than just two distinct groups are involved), **differential handling.**

Recognizing "Second-class" Treatment

Many social institutions have two or more tracks and deliver unequal services to their clients or consumers. For instance, the health care system does not treat all patients the same: Some get much higher quality medical attention than others. The school system does not provide all students with equal educational opportunities: Some are challenged and nurtured and they excel, while others are discouraged and neglected and they fail to reach their potential. A review of how cases are processed by the criminal justice system leads to an inevitable question. Now that victims have rights and are no longer routinely overlooked, do some get much better service than others?

Criminologists have documented the discrepancy between official dogma and actual practices. For example, race and class are supposed to be extraneous factors in a system of "blind justice," but in reality they turn out to be predictors of how officials respond to offenders. When victimologists pieced together scattered research findings about how different categories of victims are treated, a comparable picture emerged. Certain victims were more likely to be given what might be termed "VIP," "red carpet," or "first-class" treatment, while others tended to be neglected or abused and dealt with as second-class complainants by the same agencies and officials. In other words, how a case was handled was determined by who the victim was as well as who the offender was (in addition to the particular circumstances of the crime).

According to a number of independent studies, victims who were totally innocent and from "respectable" backgrounds and privileged groups were more likely to receive better service from police officers, prosecutors, juries, and judges. Individuals whose backgrounds were "tarnished" or who came from disadvantaged groups were less likely to get favorable responses from the constituent agencies and officials of the justice system (see Box 4.4 for a profile of the people who in the past tended to be treated better than others).

It should come as no surprise that many of the social handicaps that held people back in other aspects of everyday life also impeded their ability to receive fair treatment as crime victims. The same discretionary powers that resulted in "overzealous" law enforcement in some neighborhoods contributed to "underzealous" enforcement in other neighborhoods. Apparently, calls for help from victims from discriminated-against groups were not perceived as being entirely legitimate or as compelling by those at the helm of the criminal justice system. The credibility of disadvantaged victims was eroded by a belief that these same people were offenders in other incidents. Such stereotypical responses by the authorities poisoned relations between the two camps. From bitter experience, victims from outgroups, the lower strata, and marginal lifestyles anticipated that their requests for intervention would be greeted with suspicion or even hostility. They expected perfunctory treatment at best. As a consequence, they turned to the criminal justice system only under the most desperate circumstances (Ziegenhagen, 1977).

The way that police and prosecutors responded to murders provides some of the clearest examples of differential handling. When an "important" victim was murdered, the police department came under tremendous pressure from the media, elected officials, and powerful constituencies within the general public to solve the crime. To give an illustration, a highly publicized robbery and murder of a foreign visitor was so threatening to the multibillion-dollar tourist trade that local business interests and the chamber of commerce generated tremendous pressure to apprehend whoever was preying upon tourists (see Rohter, 1993b; Boyle, 1994). But when an "ordinary" or even "expendable" person was slain, the overworked and understaffed homicide squad detectives carried out only a superficial, routine investigation. For example, the fatal shooting of a street-level drug dealer would attract little public notice or official concern and would not receive high priority handling (see Simon, 1991; and Maple, 1999). But when a member of the police force is slain, homicide detectives work day and night following up every possible lead in order to catch the killer and send out the message that the death of an officer will not go unpunished. To illustrate how law enforcement agencies give the killing of "one of their own" VIP treatment, consider this comparison: In 1992, police departments across the country were able to solve 65% of all murders; that same year they managed to solve 91% of the killings of fellow officers (FBI, 1993). Similarly, during 1998, 93% of line-of-duty officer killings were solved, compared to 69% of civilian murders across the nation (FBI, 1999).

BOX 4.4 Which Victims Get Better Treatment?

Arrests

Suspects are more likely to be taken into custody if the victims:

- request that the police make an arrest in a deferential, nonantagonistic manner (Black, 1968).
- convince the police officer that they were not involved in any illegal activity themselves before the incident (La Fáve, 1965).
- prove to the officer that they are not a friend, relative, or neighbor of the suspect (Black, 1968; Giacinti, 1973; Goldstein, 1960; La Fave, 1965; Reiss, 1971).

Prosecutions

Charges are more likely to be lodged against defendants if the victims:

- are middle-aged or elderly, white, and employed (Myers and Hagan, 1979).
- have high status in the community ("Prosecutorial discretion," 1969).
- are women, and the offender is a male stranger (Myers, 1977).
- are women without a reputation for promiscuity (Newman, 1966).
- are not known to be homosexual (Newman, 1966).
- are not alcoholics or drug addicts (Williams, 1976).
- have no prior arrest record (Williams, 1976).
- can establish that they weren't engaged in misconduct themselves at the time of the crime (Miller, 1970; Neubauer, 1974; Williams, 1976).
- can prove that they didn't provoke the offender (Neubauer, 1974; Newman, 1966; Williams, 1976).
- can show that it wasn't a "private matter" between themselves and a relative, lover, friend, or acquaintance (McIntyre, 1968; Williams, 1976).
- and the offenders are not both black, and the incident is not viewed as "conforming to neighborhood subcultural norms" (McIntyre, 1968; Miller, 1970; Myers and Hagan, 1979; Newman, 1966).

Convictions

Judges or juries are more likely to find defendants guilty if the victims:

- are employed in a high-status job (Myers, 1977).
- are perceived as being young and helpless (Myers, 1977).
- appear "reputable," with no prior arrest record (Kalven and Zeisel, 1966; Newman, 1966).
- had no prior illegal relationship with the defendant (Newman, 1966).
- in no way are thought to have provoked the offender (Kalven and Zeisel, 1966; Newman, 1966; Wolfgang, 1958).
- are white, and the defendants are black (Allredge, 1942; Bensing and Schroeder, 1960; Garfinkle, 1949; Johnson, 1941).
- and offenders are not both black and are not viewed as acting "in conformity to subcultural norms" (Mcltyre, 1968; Miller, 1970; Myers and Hagan, 1979; Newman, 1966).

Punishments

Judges will hand down stiffer sentences to defendants if the victims:

- are employed in a high-status occupation (Myers, 1977; Farrell and Swigert, 1986).
- did not know the offender (Myers, 1977).
- were injured and didn't provoke the attack (Dawson, 1969; Neubauer, 1974).
- are white and the offenders are black (Green, 1964; Southern Regional Council, 1969; Wolfgang and Riedel, 1973; Paternoster, 1984).
- are females killed by either males or females (Farrell and Swigert, 1986).

Most of the research uncovering evidence of differential handling was conducted before the victims' rights movement scored sweeping legislative victories. Therefore, victimologists need to carry out a new round of investigations to discover whether the past inequity of differential handling persists or the lofty goals of "equal protection under the law" and "justice for all" are becoming a reality in state criminal justice systems across America these days.

CHAPTER SUMMARY

In their pursuit of justice—whether that means punishment, treatment, or restitution—victims might find themselves in conflict rather than in cooperative relationships with the police, prosecutors, judges, and corrections officials.

If they report crimes, victims want the police to come quickly, administer psychological and physical first aid, believe their accounts, apprehend the perpetrators, gather evidence that is admissible in court, and get back any property taken from them. However, the police might take a while to arrive, handle them insensitively, consider their versions of events unbelievable or exaggerated, fail to solve their cases, and be unable to recover their stolen goods.

Victims want prosecutors' offices to provide them with lawyers who will faithfully represent their interests, but they may be disappointed if the assistant district attorneys assigned to them can't take steps to protect them from reprisals and don't consult with them during plea negotiations. Victims expect defense attorneys to try to wear them down by stalling tactics and asking hostile questions intended to undermine their credibility during cross-examination at trials.

Victims hope that judges will be evenhanded but may become upset if judges set bail low enough that defendants are released and threaten them, and if judges impose sentences that do not reflect the gravity of the offenses that harmed them. Victims want corrections officials to keep them posted concerning the whereabouts of convicts, protect them from reprisals after release, and effectively supervise any restitution arrangements that were imposed as conditions of probation or parole.

In the distant past just about all victims were mistreated by agencies and officials within the criminal justice process. In the recent past some victims were treated much better than others. Researchers need to document whether the system now delivers equal justice for all or if the problem of differential handling persists.

DISCUSSION QUESTIONS

1. Explain why victims might be dissatisfied with the services they receive from their local police departments.
2. Explain why victims might disagree with the way "their" lawyers are handling their cases.
3. What do victims want from judges?
4. What kinds of cooperation do victims want from probation officers, corrections officials, and parole boards?
5. Summarize the impact of Supreme Court decisions on the rights of victims.
6. How can victimologists determine if differential handling is still a problem within the legal system?

5

Special Kinds of Victims: Problems and Solutions

Continued

The previous chapter looked at the way the criminal justice system handled "ordinary" victims (those harmed by street crimes like robberies, assaults, burglaries, and car thefts). This chapter will analyze the special vulnerabilities and needs of particular groups: kidnapped children; physically and sexually abused youngsters; financially, physically, and emotionally abused elders; battered wives and other casualties of violence between intimates; and sexually assaulted individuals. How the criminal justice system accords them (or is supposed to grant them) special considerations and extra-sensitive treatment will be the focus of attention.

One line of inquiry that arises repeatedly when the special problems of particular groups are examined is "How many people are suffering in this way?" An ongoing debate rages between the **maximalist alarmist** point of view and the **minimalist skeptical** perspective over the seriousness of each problem. In general, the maximalist position argues that an overlooked problem is reaching epidemic proportions. Dire consequences will follow unless drastic steps are taken. This outlook can be characterized as "maximalist" because it assumes the worst and tries to mobilize people and resources to combat a coming crisis. Frightening claims about a dangerous situation that is spiraling out of control provoke a predictable opposite reaction that can be termed "minimalist." It is marked by a skeptical stance that considers "maximalist" estimates to be grossly inflated for self-serving purposes. The minimalist assessment that massive expenditures and emergency measures are not warranted sparks bitter clashes with maximalists. They take the form of acrimonious debates at conferences and hearings, strident denunciations in reports and books, and angry letters to the editors of newspapers and magazines that carried articles espousing the views of the other side. The estimates that have generated the most heated exchanges concern the actual fate of missing children, the real extent of child abuse, the genuine prevalence of incest and child molestation, and the frequency of date rape on college campuses. Victimologists can enter into these controversies as objective "claims investigators" applying the tools of social science research to determine where the truth lies—which is usually in between the high-end estimates put forward by maximalist alarmists and the low-end estimates offered by minimalist skeptics. Like victim blaming and victim defending, maximalist and minimalist viewpoints are ideologies. Individuals accepting these views are alarmists or skeptics. But alarmists on one issue might be skeptics on another, so, as with victim blaming and defending, it is best not to personalize the matters as disputes between individuals but rather to view the controversies as outgrowths of the opposing assumptions and outlooks of special-interest groups.

MISSING CHILDREN

A 6-year-old boy wanders over to the toy counter in a department store. A few minutes later his mother realizes he has disappeared. The police launch an intensive search. Two weeks later and 100 miles away, a fisherman discovers the boy's severed head. The boy's father sets up a group to help locate missing children and becomes a leading figure in the child-find movement. But his son's murder is never solved because the local police misplace crucial evidence implicating a serial killer as the prime suspect. (Spitzer, 1986; Reuters, 1996)

A child molester lures a 7-year-old boy into a car by offering him a lift home. He pretends to call the boy's family to secure their permission for the boy to stay with him overnight. Then he convinces the child that his parents don't want him back. For the next 7 years the boy lives with this man, who exploits him sexually. He goes to school under a false name but is too scared of a beating to tell his teachers about his plight. But when the kidnapper brings home another young captive, he summons up the courage to go to the police. (Andrews, 1986)

A man rings the bell of a home on the pretext of looking for a lost dog. He barges in, pushes a baby-sitter aside, and drives off with a 7-year-old girl. Even though her hands are taped together, she manages to put on her seat belt. After a 100-mile ride and a high-speed chase, the kidnapper's car flips over. Inside the overturned vehicle, he holds a gun to her head for over an hour while he negotiates with the police. A sharpshooter kills him and rescues the little girl. (Associated Press, 1996d)

Taking and holding a person against his or her will for some nefarious purpose was recognized hundreds of years ago as a vicious act under English common law. In state and federal statutes today, force is not a necessary element of the crime. The victim can be detained through trickery or manipulation (what is called "inveiglement"). Besides extorting a ransom, the kidnapper may intend to rob the captive (for example, compel an adult to withdraw money from an automated teller machine), exploit the person as a mere sex object, keep and raise a very young child, or cruelly snuff out a life. If the kidnapper makes a ransom demand or transports the hostage across state lines, federal statutes are violated and the FBI can enter the manhunt.

At the start of the 1980s, amidst deep-seated concerns about the disintegration of traditional families, children who were thought to have vanished were rediscovered by reporters, politicians, and crusading members of the victims movement. Very rapidly, **missing children** became a household term and a subject of intense concern, if not widespread panic. The phrase actually was a media invention that lumped together disappearances for all kinds of reasons. Frantic parents feared the worst: Youngsters who disappeared had met with foul play and would never be seen or heard from again. The question "What really happened to these children?" was answered differently in sensationalized media coverage, in dramatic books and films, and eventually in social research studies. The highlights of this rediscovery process appear in Box 5.1.

Estimates of the Incidence and Seriousness of the Problem

Statistics about kidnappings of youngsters measure one of the most heinous crimes imaginable. Yet no organization or government agency was monitoring this problem at the beginning of the 1980s when the issue of missing children was rediscovered. No records were kept about the number of cases in which parents told the police that they did not know where their young children were. Because that situation did not neatly fit any standard legal category, no one knew how many innocent, helpless children were seized and carried off each year.

One official source of data about crimes known to the police, the FBI's *Uniform Crime Report,* was of little use because arrests for kidnappings were mixed in with lesser crimes under the headings "offenses against family and children" and "all other offenses" in Part II. In the other official source, the *National Crime Victimization Survey,* respondents were not asked about kidnappings of members of their households. In fact, the interviewers did not count any crimes committed against persons under 12. The only estimates about the number of missing children presumed to be victims of foul play were derived from very limited studies of police files or projections from surveys based on small samples. As a result, throughout the 1980s a heated debate erupted between maximalist alarmists and minimalist skeptics over what had happened to all those youngsters whose whereabouts were not known to their parents.

Maximalists believed that kidnapping had become frighteningly common and that a complacent public needed to become aroused and mobilized. Assuming the worst about these disappearances, alarmists called for emergency measures to halt the surge in abductions by strangers. They warned that child snatchers were everywhere, no youngster was ever completely safe, and parents could never be too careful about taking precautions and restricting their children's activities. Two remarks illustrate the near-hysteria of the times: a Congressman offered "the most

BOX 5.1 Highlights of the Rediscovery of the Missing Children Problem

1932 The child of a famous aviator is kidnapped and killed. A man caught with some of the ransom money is executed. State and federal laws are strengthened.

1955 The National Child Safety Council is established as the first private and voluntary organization in the field.

1974 Congress passes the Juvenile Justice and Delinquency Prevention Act, which mandates that runaways be sheltered but not arrested and confined.

1977 California becomes the first state to make violating a child custody agreement a felony.

1980 Congress amends the Juvenile Justice and Delinquency Prevention Act to permit the police to detain chronic runaways under court order to return home. Congress passes the Federal Parental Kidnapping Prevention Act, which prohibits state courts from modifying original custody decrees issued after divorces and establishes a locator service that tracks down "fugitive parents" by tracing social security numbers.

1981 A Senate subcommittee holds the first hearings on the problem of missing children.

Child safety groups form a Child Tragedies Coalition.

The mysterious disappearances of 28 youngsters in Atlanta over a 2-year period are solved when a young man is convicted of murder.

1982 Congress declares May 25 National Missing Children's Day and passes the Missing Children's Act, which grants searching parents new rights in their dealings with law enforcement agencies.

1983 A TV docudrama about the abduction and murder of a boy named Adam is viewed by an estimated 55 million people (approximately 1 out of every 4 Americans).

1984 Congress passes the Missing Children's Assistance Act, which sets up a National Center for Missing and Exploited Children as a resource base and establishes an advisory board to guide, plan, and coordinate federal efforts.

1985 After a televised documentary President Reagan appeals to viewers to help find missing children; 60 photos are shown and three youths are quickly recovered.

1986 The first annual National Conference on Missing and Exploited Children is held.

1987 A National Association of Missing Child Organizations is formed to share information and maintain professional standards.

A National Resource Facility is opened for public use.

A National Endowment for the Protection of Children is created to raise money for public education, professional training, and services.

1988 Congress amends the Missing Children's Assistance Act to allocate money for establishing and operating clearinghouses on the state level to coordinate local law enforcement, social services, and educational activities.

1990 Congress passes the National Child Search Assistance Act, which requires the police to immediately enter information about a disappearance into their computer networks.

1993 In response to the kidnap-murder of a 12-year-old girl by a parolee, federal and state lawmakers pass "three strikes and you're out" provisions to incarcerate repeat offenders for life.

SOURCES: *Davidson, 1986; NCMEC, 1987; Howell, 1989; Aunapu et. al., 1993.*

conservative estimate you will get anywhere" that 50,000 children were abducted by strangers a year (see Best, 1989a); and a father of a murdered child told a congressional hearing, "This country is littered with mutilated, decapitated, raped, and strangled children" (see Spitzer, 1986).

Minimalists suspected the true scope of the problem was blown all out of proportion by frantic parents who meant well but were unduly alarmed; by businesses that sought to profit from selling products and services to panicky adults; by journalists willing to sensationalize stories to attract larger audiences; by politicians looking for a pristine issue that would gain them publicity and votes; and by child-search organizations seeking recognition, contributions, and government funding. Minimalists charged that maximalists were using the most inclusive definitions to generate the largest possible numbers (see Schneider, 1987). A child-welfare advocate summed up the minimalist position when he charged that inflated statistics were being circulated by "merchants of fear" and "proponents of hype and hysteria" who "have foisted on a concerned but gullible American public" what he termed "one of the most outrageous scare campaigns in modern American history" (Treanor, 1986).

As concerns escalated during the 1980s, the estimates disseminated from maximalist and minimalist sources differed strikingly (see Best, 1989a; Forst and Blomquist, 1991; and Kappeler, Blumberg, and Potter, 1993). Several factors having to do with police department practices, vague definitions, and opposing assumptions account for the sharp divergence. Some departments were less inclined than others to request outside assistance and federal intervention; consequently, the FBI did not investigate all the kidnapping cases in which a stranger might have been involved. The definitions that a police department used in classifying crimes determined the number of stranger-abduction cases in its files. For example, if a child was lured into a car, sexually molested, and then abandoned hours later, most law enforcement agencies would categorize the incident as a sexual assault for record-keeping purposes, thus inadvertently obscuring the fact that an abduction took place, albeit for a relatively short period of time. Assumptions about unsolved cases colored the estimates as well. The disappearance of a teenager might be the tragic result of a stranger-abduction. But a much more likely explanation is that a missing adolescent is a runaway who will eventually return home voluntarily. (Such youth may be victims in a different sense, not of abduction but of parental sexual or physical abuse. Further, while on the run they are very vulnerable to exploitation.) Other missing teens are not runaways but "throwaways" expelled from their homes by angry or neglectful parents. Furthermore, some of the children grabbed by adults were not snatched by strangers but were taken by parents who disregarded court orders after bitter custody battles following separations or divorces. (Parental abductions, of course, can easily be ruled out in many disappearances.) In some of the remaining cases, especially those involving very young children, the missing youth may be simply lost for a while. Minimalists suspect that many missing children are merely temporarily lost, were spirited off by an angry ex-spouse, are runaways or throwaways who will eventually return on their own, or are in the clutches of molesters who will soon release them. Maximalists assume that many of these missing children were victims of foul play and will never be reunited with their distraught parents. Their debate demonstrates how important statistics are in bringing social problems to the attention of the media, the public, and policymakers, and in assessing the seriousness of the problems.

Many worthy causes compete for media coverage, public concern, and governmental action. The first few crusaders to alert people to the danger of kidnappings by strangers issued press releases with shockingly huge estimates that generated widespread fears. They were the only experts on the subject, since no officials or agencies were authorized to analyze mysterious disappearances of children across the country. But some journalists and social scientists became skeptical of these statistical projections. Soon, members of the media adopted misleadingly low official estimates with the same uncritical enthusiasm with which they had earlier accepted the activists' overestimates. This capsule history of the controversy confirms these suspicions: Large numbers call attention to neglected social problems more readily than small numbers, figures from official sources carry greater weight than unofficial estimates, and large official estimates are the best of all to galvanize public support and governmental action (Best, 1988, 1989a).

In an effort to try to resolve the maximalist-minimalist debate, the Department of Justice, as mandated by the 1984 Missing Children's Assistance Act, funded a 5-year National Incidence Study of Missing, Abducted, Runaway, and Throwaway Children (*NISMART*). Researchers collected data in several ways: by conducting a telephone survey of nearly 35,000 randomly selected households, by analyzing FBI homicide records and the case files of nonfamily abductions in 83 law enforcement agencies in 21 randomly selected counties across the nation, and by interviewing runaways and the professionals who dealt with them in social service agencies and juvenile facilities. These social scientists clarified definitions, consulted with experts, and generated numbers that led them to the conclusion that the term "missing children" caused endless confusion by mixing together five distinct problems that had very different victims, causes, dynamics, and remedies. The worst-case scenario that fit the stereotype of a kidnapping by a stranger with evil intentions thankfully turned out to be a rare occurrence. Family abduction was found to be a much bigger problem than policymakers realized. The number of missing children who turned out to be runaways was about the same in 1988 as it had been in 1975, but up to 20% of these homeless youngsters had actually been "thrown out." Finally, the researchers discovered a formerly ill-defined category of apparently missing children who got lost, were injured and couldn't reach their parents, or failed to clearly tell their caretakers where they were going and when they would return home (Finkelhor, Hotaling, and Sedlak, 1990). The report's findings indicate that adherents of the maximalist position were overestimating the real scope of the "stranger-danger" threat to young people, while those who took the minimalist approach were underestimating it. The probable numbers of missing children who really were crime victims appear in Box 5.2.

A research project that zeroed in on kidnappings of children under 18 resulting in homicide yielded an estimate of about 100 stranger killings a year (about 0.5% of all murders nationwide). More than 7 out of every 10 victims were white girls. Their average age was 11. The typical assailant was a single white man about 27 years old, often with a history of past sexual assaults and abductions. Roughly three fifths of the abductions were characterized as crimes of

BOX 5.2 How Often Are Children Kidnapped, and What Happens to Them?

The NISMART study of patterns observed across the nation in 1988 yielded the following estimates of the number of different kinds of victim-offender relationships and the characteristics of abducted children:

200–300 Kidnappings of Children by Adults per Year
(These cases fit the stereotype of a kidnapping: The youngster is detained overnight or longer and/or is transported 50 miles or more. The abductor intends to permanently keep the child, extort a ransom, or commit some other crime, including murder. In most of these extremely serious offenses, the kidnapper is not a complete stranger, but instead is a disgruntled former boyfriend of the child's mother, a friend of the family, a neighbor, a baby-sitter, or someone else known by the victim.)

Between 1976 and 1987 as few as about 50 children and as many as around 150 were murdered by kidnappers each year. There was no discernible trend over the 12-year period. The victims of these kidnappings that ended in homicides tended to be older (ages 14 to 17), female, and from racial minority groups. Overall, a teenager's chances of being kidnapped and murdered during this period were calculated to be 7 out of every million; the chances for younger children were 1 out of a million, per year.

3,200–4,600 Short-Term Abductions by a Nonfamily Member per Year
(These cases meet all the legal elements of kidnapping: A crime by an acquaintance or by a complete stranger who takes the child by force or by deceit into a building, vehicle, or some other place, and/or detains the child for more than an hour, perhaps to commit a sexual assault or molestation.)

About half the victims were 12 years old, or older, and three quarters were girls. In more than two thirds of the cases, the youngsters were abducted for sexual purposes. The majority of incidents began in a street setting, involved the use of force (often the brandishing of a weapon), and the ordeal lasted less than a whole day. Black and Hispanic children were disproportionately victimized in these ways.

About 11,500 attempted abductions by strangers per year were reported by caretakers to survey interviewers. In most of these attempts, a passing motorist tried to lure a child into a car, without the use of coercion and without inflicting physical injuries. Most attempts—and probably a substantial number of completed abductions for the purpose of sexual assault—were not reported to the police, generally because the children were ashamed or intimidated.

163,000 Long-Term Abductions by a Family Member per Year
(In these cases a family member, usually a parent, takes the child in violation of a family court

Continued

opportunity. But nearly two fifths of the offenders were the victims' friends or acquaintances. About 7 out of 10 had been sexually assaulted or raped before they were slain. Almost half of all victims had been dispatched within the first hour; within 4 hours almost three quarters had been murdered, according to an analysis of 562 child killings carried out in 44 states between the late 1970s and the mid-1990s ("Study Puts Facts," 1997).

Hunting for Children Who Have Vanished

A 12-year-old girl and her two friends are enjoying a slumber party when they hear a knock on the bedroom door. The girl opens her door and a tall, bearded man wielding a large knife barges in. As her two friends giggle, thinking it is a practical joke, the intruder ties them all up and then

BOX 5.2 ***continued***

decree and tries to conceal the taking and/or the whereabouts of the child and/or moves the child to another state and/or intends to keep the child permanently or alter the custodial arrangements.)

These abductions were most likely to occur during January and August, when school vacations and parental visits end. Most incidents lasted from a few days to up to a week. In about 60% of these unlawful detentions, the parent with custody rights did not inform the police; lawyers were contacted in 50% of the cases. In about 50% of these power struggles, the caretaking parent knew where the child was being held but was unable to recover the child from the lawbreaking ex-partner (Finkelhor, Hotaling, and Sedlak, 1990; Forst and Blomquist, 1991).

Patterns from Police Files

An intensive study of police department records for 1984 in Houston, Texas, and Jacksonville, Florida, provided tentative answers to several key questions: What kinds of children are typically the targets of nonfamily abductions? Are they lured or captured by force? When and where are they approached, and where are they taken? How long are they held? What additional crimes are committed against them?

According to the researchers who analyzed more than 200 cases reported to the police in those two cities that year, girls are targeted much more often (in 88% of the cases) than boys (although many young males may not tell their parents about the abduction and subsequent molestation, and their parents may not report the incidents to the police). The typical captive was between 11 and 14 years old. A little more than half (57%) of the youngsters were forced to go with their captors (they were intimidated by the sight of a weapon or were physically overpowered), while the remainder were lured or tricked into accompanying their abductors. Most of the victims were taken to secluded spots, either indoors (empty apartments, garages) or outdoors (woods, fields), but a sizable number were kept in a vehicle. Nearly all (98%) were released within 24 hours. In the majority of the cases (72%), the abductor molested the child; in most of the remaining cases (22%), the child escaped unharmed from an attempted kidnapping; 4% were simply held and then let go; and, tragically, 2% were murdered after being sexually assaulted.

The researchers discovered that only 15% of the cases involving an abduction were classified by the police as primarily a kidnapping. Most of the cases were filed under the heading of sexual assault and were so categorized on the FBI's *Uniform Crime Report* form (NCMEC, 1986).

carries the 12-year-old off into the night. The kidnapping galvanizes a sleepy community into action. Waves of volunteers flock to a storefront command center. Thousands of people beg to be assigned some task, like answering telephones or circulating posters with a picture of the victim and a police artist's sketch of the suspect. Shopkeepers close down their stores, and workers give up their vacations to assist the search. A well-known actress donates a huge reward for information leading to an arrest or the safe return of the abducted child ("Kidnapping Summons City to Action," 1993). Two months later the police arrest a suspect. A crowd gathers for a vigil outside the jail, chanting "Tell the truth and set your conscience free." Shortly afterward the suspect, who was out on parole after spending 15 of his last 20 years behind bars for abductions, assaults, and burglaries, confesses that he strangled the girl and leads police to her body. An outraged

> community demands that a "three strikes and you're out" law is needed to prevent hardened convicts like him from ever being released. (Gross, 1993)

Kidnapping symbolizes the ultimate clash between good and evil: innocent and defenseless little victims in the clutches of ruthless adults. No other group of crime victims has so captured the attention and hearts of the public. Rarely has the citizenry's involvement been solicited on such a grand scale as in the campaign to prevent abductions and recover stolen children. Few victims' rights organizations have been so instrumental in the drafting of new laws and the early reforming of criminal justice procedures as the child-search movement. Even though the platitude "children are our most precious resource" was frequently voiced in the early 1980s, there were only a few groups geared to help locate missing children, staffed by a handful of people with an annual budget of less than $30,000. By the late 1990s a federally sponsored national center operated a network linking 30 federal agencies, 50 state clearinghouses, and more than 60 private and nonprofit organizations (Gill, 1989; Aunapu et al., 1993; OJJDP, 1998a).

Before the advent of child-search organizations, parents were totally dependent on the police to locate and recover their missing children. But the working relationships between frantic parents and the law enforcement agencies that were supposed to be carrying out the manhunt were frequently strained. The issues that divided them were delays in police response, restricted access to law enforcement computer files, and a reluctance by local authorities to call for nationwide assistance.

When distraught parents turned to missing persons bureaus for help, they expected the police to spring into action by issuing an all-points bulletin describing the child who had disappeared and by launching an intensive search. But many departments followed procedures that dictated that a youngster had to be missing for 24, 48, or even 72 hours before an official investigation could be initiated. These waiting periods were based on experiences that indicated the overwhelming majority of cases were not life threatening and would "solve themselves." The missing youths would turn out to be runaways who would soon return home tired, hungry, and broke. But agitated parents condemned such arbitrary delays as endangering the lives of their children. They claimed that it enabled abductors to escape from the local area to other jurisdictions where any call for a manhunt would receive an even lower priority and interest in the case would be difficult to sustain. The crux of the problem for parents was that the burden of proof fell on them to somehow demonstrate that their children were victims of foul play. In 1990, responding to parental appeals for reform, Congress passed the National Child Search Assistance Act. The legislation prohibited law enforcement agencies from imposing waiting periods before entering the child's description into computer networks linking the FBI's National Crime Information Center, police departments, and state clearinghouses that helped to locate and recover missing children (Girdner and Hoff, 1994). A family survival guide written by parents who have been through this ordeal suggests that immediate steps include putting out a "Be On the Look Out" (BOLO) bulletin to other police departments, faxing a photo to the National Center for Missing and Exploited Children, and searching with bloodhounds. Many states now require police officers to take in-service training courses on how to investigate missing children cases, to interact with their families, and to follow the FBI's Child Abduction Response Plan (OJJDP, 1998a).

Victimization Prevention Measures

As parents and their children have become more conscious of "stranger-danger," they have incorporated preventive steps into their daily routines in a myriad of ways. Youngsters are instructed by police officers, teachers, and parents—as well as through comic book characters, board games, songs, and books—"What to do if. . . ." The training that the children receive in recognizing and rejecting "child lures,"—the deceitful tricks abductors use to entice them into their clutches—far exceeds the old warning of "Don't accept candy from strangers." They are taught to distinguish between "good touches" and "bad touches" and to be wary of certain situations and behaviors as well as specific kinds of persons. The aim is to build self-confidence rather than to instill unreasonable fears. Some risk-reduction strategies involve planning, products, and services. At the height of the near panic that gripped many families during the mid-1980s, so many new products flooded the market that department stores set up child safety displays. Today, high-tech outlets sell homing devices that trigger alarms when children stray or are taken beyond a certain range. Dentists offer to bond microchips containing identifying information to children's teeth. Computer firms can be hired to generate "video portraits" that project how a missing child might look after several years. Shopping centers attract crowds by offering fingerprinting for infants and toddlers. Playgrounds, schoolyards, and large stores are designed to limit access and escape routes. The shadow cast by the ominous stranger has eclipsed the mushroom shaped cloud that haunted the imaginations of previous generations (Wooden, 1984; "Teaching Children," 1999).

Understandably, child-safety campaigns have provoked a backlash. Some skeptics are concerned about the questionable performance of expensive products and services. They take a dim view of commercial outfits that charge for information, devices, and forms of assistance that can be obtained for free from nonprofit child-find organizations or the police. They are suspicious of the motives of the many corporations that have made tax-deductible contributions to child-search projects; amidst the hoopla over staged events, they get free publicity and cultivate good public relations. Civil libertarians fear that the intense concern about stranger-danger will erode the public's healthy reluctance to allow government bureaucracies to maintain fingerprints and photographs on file, which could be another step toward a "big brother" police state. Other critics worry about the potential social and psychological costs of certain victimization prevention measures. They wonder whether an anxious, suspicious, and dependent generation will be cheated out of a carefree childhood and will grow up obsessed by security considerations and burdened by adult responsibilities prematurely. Victimologists can conduct research to determine whether the child safety measures really work as intended, fail to be effective, or, worse yet, have unanticipated negative social and emotional side effects (see Karlen et al., 1985; Andrews, 1986; Gill, 1987, 1989; and Adler, 1994).

PHYSICALLY AND SEXUALLY ABUSED CHILDREN

The Rediscovery of Child Abuse

For centuries parents were permitted to beat their children as they saw fit in the name of imposing discipline. Legal notions of progeny as the property of their parents and religious traditions (of "honor thy father and mother" and "spare the rod and spoil the child") legitimized corporal punishment of youngsters as a necessary, even essential, technique of child rearing. Only if permanent injury or death resulted were adults in danger of being held responsible for going too far, a problem labeled "cruelty to children."

The "House of Refuge" movement of the early 1800s intervened on behalf of beaten and neglected children. Its priority was to prevent abused children from growing up to be delinquents. Youngsters were removed from their dysfunctional homes but they were thrown into environments where they mingled with young vagrants and lawbreakers. Similarly, the Society for the Prevention of Cruelty to Animals (SPCA) undertook responsibility for rescuing children from uncaring foster parents and heartless employers in the late 1800s. Its offshoot, the Society for the Prevention of Cruelty to Children, used the police powers it was granted to place abused youngsters from big-city slums into institutions in a misguided attempt to head off delinquency. During the early 1900s the "child savers" movement was motivated by the same fear: that neglect and abuse caused lawbreaking later in life. It designed a special court system and developed reform schools strictly for juveniles (see Platt, 1968; and Pfohl, 1984). (This concern about abused children growing up to become abusers and victimizers themselves continues to inspire a great deal of theorizing and research; see, for example, Gray, 1986; Wyatt and Powell, 1988; Barringer, 1989; and Widom, 1989.)

In the early 1960s, pediatric radiologists (doctors who study X rays of childhood injuries) sparked the rediscovery of physical abuse. Apparently, other physicians (pediatricians and emergency room doctors) were inhibited from exposing the consequences of severe beatings by their face-to-face dealings with the victims' parents, by the norm of confidentiality between doctors and patients, and by their reluctance to get embroiled in the criminal justice process. Pediatric radiologists, on the other hand, had few direct contacts with parents and desired greater recognition within the medical profession. Therefore, they were willing to set into motion the process of exposing brutality, labeling it as a deviant behavior and encouraging legislation against it by alerting colleagues and the public to the "battered child syndrome" (Pfohl, 1984). This syndrome was identified as a cyclical pattern in which excessive physical punishment was perpetrated by parents who had been beaten themselves as children. In the typical case the victim was younger than 3 years old and suffered traumatic injuries to the head and limbs, and the caretakers claimed that the wounds were caused by an accident and not a beating. News media coverage of "horror stories" that described particular viciousness, severe injuries, and disturbing circumstances evoked strong condemnations and helped to galvanize a social movement. Initially, journalists focused on battering, but they soon broadened their inquiries to include cases of gross neglect, emotional cruelty, and eventually sexual exploitation and incest. Coverage of these human interest stories fit the organizational needs not only of the news media to attract readers and viewers but also of professional and occupational groups and private and nonprofit agencies seeking increased funding and more recognition for their missions (Johnson, 1989).

Social workers, women's organizations, public health associations, and law enforcement groups joined doctors to help raise public consciousness about the suspected dimensions of the problem. Between 1962 and 1966, laws forbidding parents from abusing their children were passed in all 50 states (Pfohl, 1984). Since the victims usually were too young or frightened to complain, requirements for reporting cases of apparent abuse to child-welfare and protection agencies were imposed on doctors, teachers, and others who routinely came into contact with youngsters.

In 1974, Congress passed the Child Abuse Prevention and Treatment Act and amended it in 1978. The law prohibited **maltreatment** in all its guises (acts of omission as well as commission), including neglect, physical abuse, sexual abuse, and emotional abuse. **Neglect** ranged from abandonment to failure to meet a child's basic requirements in three areas: physical (including inadequate supervision and medical care), emotional (denial of nurturing and affection, tolerance of a child's drug or alcohol abuse, or spouse abuse in the child's presence), and educational (tolerance of chronic truancy). **Physical abuse** involved assaults (punching, kicking, scalding, suffocating, shaking, and extended confinement, even if unintended as the consequence of excessive punishment). **Sexual abuse** was recognized as incest, fondling, sodomy, intercourse, rape, and commercial exploitation (impairment of morals, use for pornographic purposes or prostitution). In addition, maltreatment could take the form of **emotional abuse** (leading to serious behavioral or mental disorders) (see Irwin, 1980; and National Clearinghouse, 1997). During the 1980s the focus of researchers, practitioners, and an indignant public shifted from physical maltreatment to sexual abuse (Milner, 1991).

In 1989 the United Nations amended earlier international declarations (dating back to 1924 and 1959) and adopted "The Convention on the Rights of the Child." The member states that ratified the convention pledged to take all appropriate legislative, administrative, social, and educational measures to protect youngsters less than 18 years old from all forms of physical and mental violence, injury, or abuse. The convention promised that governments would promote the physical and psychological recovery and social reintegration of victimized children, and would enable them to be heard at any judicial and administrative proceedings affecting their welfare (NOVA, 1991).

The problem of child abuse has always been of great concern to victimologists, who want to know: what percentages of cases go unreported and unattended? What are the short-term and long-term consequences? How are abused youngsters handled by the authorities? And are existing mandatory reporting requirements and treatments effective? To anticipate and thereby prevent future cases of abuse, victimologists want to discover the risk factors that indicate which children face the gravest dangers. For example, an inquiry carried out by the National Center on Child Abuse and Neglect verified the suspicion that children with physical, emotional, and mental disabilities are maltreated by their primary caretakers (generally their mothers) at an unusually high rate. Disabled children are physically abused at twice the rate of other youngsters, sexually abused nearly twice as often, and emotionally neglected almost three times as frequently (Associated Press, 1993b). Research into the backgrounds of physically abused children indicates that beatings are more likely to occur in dysfunctional families racked by a combination of symptoms of marital discord: where the two parents fight viciously (partner abuse), one or both of the parents are currently substance abusers (drug takers and/or alcoholics), the mother was raised by a substance-abusing parent, and the mother was often beaten while she was growing up (Salzinger, Feldman, and Hammer, 1991). As for sexual abuse (which is imposed most often on boys and girls between the ages of 7 and 13) inadequate parenting, poor parent-child communication, parental unavailability, and father-mother conflict seem to be risk factors (Finkelhor, 1994). It is widely believed that children from poverty-stricken families face the greatest risk of being neglected and/or physically abused and/or sexually abused (DeConcini, 1989; Garbarino, 1989). However, the apparent concentration of abuse cases in lower socioeconomic neighborhoods that is indicated by official statistics and agency files might be misleading because the problems of poor families are more likely to come to the attention of social welfare agencies and the police. Therefore, some researchers have concluded that there is no substantial difference in victimization rates among children of different social classes or races (Finkelhor, 1994). In fact a study of how police officers exercised their discretion about whether to report suspected cases of child abuse concluded that officers were more likely to overlook signs of possible abuse in low-income minority families because of prejudicial beliefs that violence and promiscuity are "normal" among the poor and that minority youths need sterner discipline (Willis and Wells, 1988).

The consequences of being abused greatly concern victimologists. Studies of sexually exploited youngsters indicate that they may suffer complicated, far-reaching, and long-lasting problems. A review of the literature written by therapists turned up seven groupings of adverse effects. Affective problems were evidenced by guilt, shame, anxiety, fear, depression, anger, low self-esteem, concerns about secrecy, feelings of helplessness, and an inordinate need to please others. Physical repercussions included genital injuries, unwanted pregnancies, venereal diseases, loss of appetite, sleep disruptions, and bed-wetting. Cognitive effects took the form of shortened attention spans and troubles concentrating. Behavioral symptoms materialized as hostile-aggressive acting out, tantrums, drug taking, delinquency, withdrawal, and repetitions of the abusive relationship.

Self-destructive impulses were manifested as suicidal thoughts, near-death experiences, and self-mutilations. Psychopathological repercussions showed up as neuroses, character disorders, psychotic thought patterns, and multiple personalities. Finally, sexual disorders took the form of age-inappropriate sexual knowledge, talk, and involvements. Since sexual abuse can range from a single molestation to an ongoing incestuous relationship, each youngster may exhibit a different mix of symptoms, and no specific problem or repertoire of behaviors definitively and conclusively indicates that a child has been abused (Yapko and Powell, 1988; Whitcomb, 1992). Many women on public assistance because of multiple problems—especially addiction to alcohol or drugs, disabling bouts of anxiety and depression, and injuries from their violent mates—were sexually abused when they were girls (de Parle, 1999). Worse yet, being neglected and/or physically abused and/or sexually abused as a youngster becomes a risk factor for entering into a cycle of delinquency, crime, and violence later in life. Those who were physically abused face the gravest risks of becoming lawbreakers (aside from prostitutes), more than those who were sexually abused or grossly neglected. However, illegal behavior as a grown-up is not an inevitable side-effect; most adults who were abused as children don't have arrest records (Widom, 1992, 1995; Turman, 1999). An intergenerational transmission of poor parenting skills takes place when victims grow up and abuse their own children in the same ways that they were mistreated. Children socialized into a subculture of violence that is very much on display in their own homes are being taught to use force to settle disagreements in much the same imitative way that they learn other behaviors.

Estimates of the Incidence, Prevalence, and Seriousness of Child Abuse

The two official sources of crime statistics, the FBI's *UCR* and the BJS's *NCVS,* contain no data about child maltreatment's **incidence** (new cases that come to light each year) and **prevalence** (proportion of people in some population being studied who have ever suffered this form of victimization). The *UCR* monitors the age of murder victims, but not all homicides against youngsters were carried out by abusive parents or other caretakers. The *NCVS* does not ask respondents about any illegal acts committed against persons younger than 12. Therefore, another source of official statistics must be tapped: the reports collected from child-protection services (child-welfare agencies) in the 50 states.

In 1997 this data collection system noted that all the state agencies combined investigated about 2 million reports alleging maltreatment of almost 3 million children. Although the majority of the allegations (almost 60%) were not proven, just under 1 million children were deemed to be victims of indicated or substantiated acts of neglect and abuse. That means that 43 out of every 1,000 children were suspected of being abused, and 14 out of every 1,000 youngsters less than 18 years of age were victimized. Cases involving boys were as numerous as those about girls. More than 50% were 7 years old or younger. Parents were the abusers in 80% of all cases. Complaints from teachers, police officers, social workers, child-care providers, and medical personnel (who are mandated to report their suspicions) triggered more than 50% of all the investigations. The children themselves or their relatives were the source of about 25% of the charges looked into by state agencies. Complaints about neglect accounted for 56% of all investigations, 25% concerned allegations about physical abuse, just 13% centered on charges of sexual abuse, and the remainder were about other kinds of maltreatment (some cases involved more than one type of abuse). Nearly 1,000 children were known to have died as a result of the severe physical beatings or gross neglect inflicted upon them. More than 75% of these deaths claimed the lives of infants and toddlers up to the age of 3, according to the state child-welfare agencies sending data to the U.S. Department of Health and Human Services in 1999.

The maximalist and minimalist perspectives disagree sharply when it comes to interpreting official statistics like these (see Gardner, 1990, 1994; Mash and Wolfe, 1991; Feher, 1992; and de Koster and Swisher, 1994). The maximalist point of view contends that the time has come to reject the reluctance of earlier generations to face the facts and recognize the enormity of the crisis. Parents are abusing and neglecting their children in record numbers, and exploitive adolescents, pedophiles (child molesters), and other abusers are preying upon youngsters like never before. This alarmist perspective puts forward strong arguments to support its case that child abuse is all too common (see Finkelhor, 1990; Whitcomb, 1992; and Ceci and Bruck, 1993).

- The maximilist perspective proceeds from the assumption that incidence rates based on statistics from official sources are probably gross underestimates. Presumably, a great (but unknown) number of episodes are never reported to the authorities—not by the child, the other parent, another relative, or a neighbor. Underreporting is a serious problem because many victimized children are too young to know their rights or to be taken seriously or too terrorized to tell anyone. Most abuse and neglect takes place behind closed doors without witnesses, and unless obvious physical injuries or venereal diseases appear, tangible evidence is lacking. Many professionals who are supposed to err on the side of caution fail to file mandatory official reports when they suspect abuse, preferring instead to pressure adults in troubled families to enter counseling, drug treatment, or other programs. The professionals responsible for intervening in child abuse cases hold cherished beliefs about family privacy and parental rights and are therefore reluctant to become enmeshed in court cases. This overshadows any concerns they have about the well-being of very young children.
- Many reports of abuse are mistakenly screened out and dismissed by child-welfare agencies that simply do not have sufficient time, money, and staff to do the thorough investigations necessary to verify the charges. Just because a report is deemed to be "unsubstantiated" due to a lack of sufficient evidence to meet stringent legal standards of proof does not mean it is untrue; classifying a report as "unfounded" certainly does not mean it is completely baseless or intentionally and maliciously false.

- Alarmists cite additional statistics from unofficial sources that reveal shocking incidence and prevalence rates. Violence against children (ranging from minor acts like throwing an object to extreme outbursts like using a knife or gun) seems to be the norm, occurring in more than 60% of all intact (two-parent) American families each year, according to the findings of a telephone survey of over 1,400 parents (Straus and Gelles, 1986). As for physical abuse prevalence rates, as many as 30% of very poor children are beaten or grossly neglected at least once (and often chronically) while they are growing up (Garbarino, 1989). As for sexual abuse prevalence rates, the percentage of girls who are molested during their childhood might be as high as 38% (if peer exploitation is included) (Russell, 1984) or even 62% (counting being subjected to male exhibitionism) (Wyatt, 1985). Between 4% and 16% of women in various surveys reported a childhood sexual experience with a relative, and about 1 girl in every 100 endured sexual contacts with her father or stepfather (Herman, 1981; Russell, 1986). As many as 31% of boys may have been sexually abused (see Peters, Wyatt, and Finkelhor, 1986).

The minimalist point of view makes the following arguments to back up its contention that child abuse is much less widespread than the maximalist alarmist perspective would have the public believe (see Besharov, 1990; Wexler, 1990; and Ceci and Bruck, 1993):

- The definition of child maltreatment has been expanding and diluting over the years. Minor instances of bad parenting that were justifiably overlooked in the past are now being routinely reported. All forms of physical discipline (slaps, spankings) do not automatically qualify as child abuse. For example, in a 1977 ruling (*Ingram vs. Wright*), the Supreme Court held that corporal punishment in school (within reasonable limits, by designated personnel, and with parental approval) is permissible under the Constitution. In many studies it is not clear which definition is being applied to real-life cases—the law's, the reporter's, the researcher's, or the children's (especially once they have grown up). Some research applies the label "abuse" to acts that most consider "normal discipline" involving corporal punishment instead of reserving it for clearly inappropriate and excessive force. No state prohibits, and five states expressly permit, parents to use "reasonable corporal punishment" when disciplining their children (see Pagelow, 1989). Various ethnic and religious subcultures have dramatically different notions of where to draw the line between appropriate parenting and maltreatment, but some protection agencies blindly apply a rigid "one standard fits all" approach.
- Child abuse may not be increasing; it is just reports of abuse that are going up, skeptics charge. Heightened public awareness and mandatory reporting regulations are producing this apparent crime wave. Professionals face civil and criminal penalties if they cover up or are grossly negligent in overlooking abuse. In many states, mandatory reporting requirements are imposed on all adults—not just those who routinely come into contact with children as part of their occupation—leading to baseless charges. And in all jurisdictions any

person can easily file a report (often anonymously) to a "tip" hotline. When failure to report occurs, children face grave dangers; but when unwarranted allegations come in, agencies waste their limited resources, and the reputations of innocent parents are called into question. Large numbers of honestly mistaken allegations, as well as maliciously false ones, are mixed in with true disclosures, making the problem seem much worse than it really is. Caseloads from official sources are grossly inflated overestimates, since many allegations are never "validated" conclusively. "Unfounded" reports (also called "unsubstantiated" or "not indicated" cases) are dismissed or closed when, after an investigation, there is insufficient legally admissible evidence on which to proceed. Unproven allegations about child abuse should not be counted in official statistics. The public's emotionally driven desire to "do something," coupled with the media's sensationalistic coverage of a formerly taboo topic, plus the "take no chances" overzealousness of professionals subjected to mandatory reporting requirements, accounts for the rise in unproven complaints. The high rate of unsubstantiated claims (more than half of all allegations) recorded by many child protection agencies is due in part to a lack of screening of calls to hotlines; a willingness to follow up anonymous tips, some of which may be deliberately false and vengeful to get an adult in trouble (estimated at 3%); an acceptance of complaints from estranged spouses locked in custody battles; and a reliance on "behavioral indicators" as possible symptoms of abuse (in the absence of corroboration in the form of statements by the victim or eyewitnesses, or physical evidence) (Besharov, 1987; also see Snyder and Sickmund, 1995).

- As for incidence rates, skeptics point out that fewer than 1% of all children in the United States were sexually abused in 1991 (Robin, 1991). As for prevalence rates, the percentage of females who suffer childhood sexual abuse could be as low as 7% (Siegel et al., 1987); and for males, it might be as low as 3% (see Peters, Wyatt, and Finkelhor, 1986).
- The label "child sexual abuse" covers a wide range of forbidden activities. The long-term consequences of adults forcing children to submit to sexual demands may be severe for the victims, but the willing sexual involvement of adolescents with adults, although exploitive, may not be as harmful, according to an analysis of studies of college students who reported that they were sexually involved while in their early teens (see Goode, 1999).
- Concerning trends, the alarmist view fueled the impression that abuse is spiraling out of control. But the skeptical position is that the problem is stubbornly persistent but not getting out of hand. Data from official sources furnishes some evidence that the rising tide of reports from the 1970s to the early 1990s actually may be ebbing in the late 1990s. Nationally, allegations of abuse increased 50% between 1985 (30 reports for every 1,000 children) and 1993 (45 reports per 1,000). But in 1997 that figure slipped back down to the 1992 level (of 43 reports per 1,000 youngsters under the age of 18). Furthermore, a more reliable statistic, fatalities due to extreme abuse and neglect (as determined in many jurisdictions by a child death review team

made up of coroners, detectives, prosecutors, and social workers) dropped slightly from about 1,260 during 1992 to just under 1,200 in 1997 (McCurdy and Daro, 1994; U.S. HHS, 1999). Also, the frequency of parents resorting to force may have been diminishing during a period when the maximalist position thought it was growing. Researchers carrying out a National Family Violence Re-Survey in 1985 noted a substantial decline from 1975 in disclosures of "very severe violence" (biting, kicking, punching, beating up, using weapons like a knife or gun) by parents against their children. The incidence rate dropped from 36 cases of "very severe violence" to 19 cases for every 1,000 families in the 10-year period, a nearly 50% drop (Straus and Gelles, 1986).

In general, the societal factors that contribute to child abuse are alcohol and drug problems among adults, teenage motherhood, and impoverishment ("Child Abuse Reports," 1988). The social conditions that decrease maltreatment are upturns in the nation's economy, a trend toward marrying later in life and having fewer children, greater public awareness and condemnation of abuse, improved treatment and prevention programs, and more shelters for battered women and their offspring (Jennings, 1986; Straus and Gelles, 1986).

More Controversies Surrounding Childhood Sexual Abuse

Two intense controversies have broken out over the real extent of sexual abuse during childhood. One surrounds charges of parent-child incest, especially allegations of father-daughter sexual contacts. These accusations usually arise during divorce proceedings or shortly afterward. Other molestation charges sometimes are leveled by children many years later against their parents or other trusted adults (see MacDonald and Michard, 1995; and Beckett, 1996).

The incest taboo, which prevails in nearly all societies, forbids reproductive sexual relations between members of the same family (other than husband and wife). Incest was traditionally viewed as an activity that was so repulsive and heinous that it must be extremely rare, occurring perhaps in one family out of a million (Weinberg, 1955). But a careful review of the records maintained by child-protection agencies in Boston from 1880 to 1930 revealed that, in 10% of the violence-scarred, troubled families, incest was taking place. Almost all the perpetrators were older male relatives, usually fathers but also stepfathers, uncles, and older brothers; nearly all the victims were young girls (Gordon, 1988). Ever since the 1980s, adult-child incest, (and in particular, man-girl sexual contact) has been rediscovered as a problem and acknowledged to be more widespread than was ever thought or feared.

Accusations Made During Divorce Proceedings and Custody Battles

When allegations surface during the height of a divorce and a tug-of-war over a child, two camps quickly emerge. People on one side argue that since there are no outsiders who witness violations of the incest taboo within the home, these "family secrets" usually are not exposed unless the parents break up. People on the other side contend that baseless allegations are being taken too seriously, and the resulting investigations ruin the lives of innocent parents, usually fathers.

In the mid-1980s an organization was formed to provide support to adults who insisted that they were falsely accused. They nicknamed their predicament the "SAID syndrome": sexual allegations in divorce ("False Accusations," 1989). Their contention was that in most of these cases a spiteful mother pressured her daughter to echo a fictitious story about molestations that never occurred. Spreading this vicious lie was a wife's vindictive ploy to discredit her former husband so that the court would issue an order to prevent the girl's father from having further contact with her as she grew up (Fahn, 1991; Sheridan, 1994).

Charges are deemed to be "unsubstantiated" in these civil proceedings if the preponderance of the evidence is insufficient to affirmatively conclude that the girl was sexually molested by the defendant. The investigators for the child-protection agency who interview the girl and her parents in order to evaluate the family dynamics and home environment often feel a need to quickly resolve the matter and minimize the strain on all three parties. In many jurisdictions they are too overburdened by huge caseloads to carry out a thorough investigation. The caseworkers may lack the assessment skills and interviewing techniques necessary to elicit crucial testimony. Faced with a father who vehemently denies everything, an intimidated and confused child torn by divided loyalties, and a lack of corroboration by witnesses, the investigators may have little choice but to conclude that it was unlikely that abuse occurred. However, their verdict might be attributed more to the constraints of time, money, and training than to the merits of the case. An "unproved" charge is not necessarily "untrue" (Fahn, 1991).

Although feelings run high on both sides of this controversy, it is usually not an issue in divorce proceedings. In one study of over 6,000 cases in seven family court jurisdictions, allegations of sexual abuse lodged by one parent against the other were raised in only 2% to 10% of all disputes over custody and visitation rights (Nicholson, 1988).

The Furor Over Recalling Repressed Memories of Childhood Sexual Abuse Sigmund Freud, the founder of modern psychology, originally believed that many of his adult patients diagnosed as suffering from "hysteria" were desperately trying to repress memories of childhood sexual abuse. But after several years of psychoanalyzing his clients, he arrived at the conclusion that his female patients' suspicions about being molested when they were very young were actually just fantasies of incestuous desires, which were strictly taboo. Ever since then the question of memory loss and recovery (amnesia and delayed recall) has been controversial, and grown-ups who claim they were molested as infants, toddlers, or very young children generally have not been believed.

> **A** prosecutor cross-examining a man accused of molesting his three-year-old daughter suddenly becomes nauseous and dizzy. Fragmented memories flash before her. She begins to pound on the witness stand and screams, "These men just get away with it! The law never does anything!" After the judge

jails her for two days for contempt, she enters therapy. She begins to remember being repeatedly molested by both her older brother and her father, although they deny it. To break the conspiracy of silence around childhood incest, she teams up with several other lawyers to draft new legislation to enable grown children to sue their molesters many years after the alleged incident occurred. (Mithers, 1990)

During the 1980s a memory-recovery movement emerged to support adult "survivors" (as they prefer to be called) of childhood incest and molestations. The movement forged a coalition of victims, support groups, authors of self-help handbooks, and therapists who practice what might be called memory-retrieval techniques. In this sense, it took a maximalist stance. It proclaimed that new treatment methods made it possible for many sufferers of certain common symptoms to discover that they actually had been incest and molestation victims; their efforts to try to forget these traumatic events were burdening them with deep-seated emotional problems. The possibility of repressed memories was addressed in incest support groups, the recovery movement, confessions and revelations by well-known figures, tabloid exposés and talk show conversations, made-for-television movies, magazine cover stories, popular psychology best sellers, family therapy journals, computer bulletin boards, and in the testimony of expert witnesses during civil lawsuits. The thousands of people recalling childhood sexual abuse (including celebrities and other public figures) represented just the "tip of the iceberg," according to alarmist assumptions. Unfortunately, many sexual abuse victims will never become aware of the true source of their misery and anguish and will go through life blaming themselves for their emotional distress (Maltz and Holman, 1986; Bass and Davis, 1992; Herman, 1992).

The aftershocks of childhood incest can be devastating. Youngsters reportedly suffer from clinginess, loss of appetite, nightmares, bed-wetting, inappropriate sexual preoccupations and knowledge, and posttraumatic stress disorder. As they grow older, they are more prone than others to alcohol and drug abuse, reckless promiscuity, sexual dysfunctions, eating disorders, depression, guilt, self-hatred, self-mutilation, and suicidal impulses. However, there is no single symptom that crops up in a majority of sexually abused children. Also, although these symptoms are consistent with abuse, they don't constitute legal proof that incest definitely occurred; other problems can bring about these same disorders (Kendall-Tackett, Williams, and Finkelhor, 1993).

Maximalists believe that when adults suspect unspeakable acts were foisted on them as children, these unsettling hunches are usually well-founded. They have been expending great mental energy to unconsciously block, blot out, or deny any recollection of their "terrible secrets," but with the help of new therapeutic techniques, a flood of these submerged memories eventually is unleashed. The therapy involves hypnosis, psychoactive drugs that serve as truth serums, age regression, guided fantasy, and automatic writing. Successful patients progress through several stages, proceeding from initial denial, to suspicions, to realization (after considerable self-examination, probing, dredging up, and digging). Survivors come to recognize that many others have shared their fate, speak openly about their past tribulations, and join self-help support groups to further the healing process (Bass and Davis, 1992; Terr, 1994).

Incest is always difficult to prosecute because the case usually lacks eyewitnesses or tangible evidence and therefore hinges entirely on the child's contentions against the adult's denials. When children grow older it is usually too late to bring criminal charges. In most states the statute of limitations for felonies runs out 5 to 7 years after the crime is committed. Therefore, adults who think they can recall memories of incest are seeking to punish their tormentors in a different arena (civil court) via lawsuits for monetary damages for pain and suffering. Many state legislatures have recognized the possibility of "delayed discovery" and the legitimacy of the demands by incest victims for some avenue of redress. In these jurisdictions the lawmakers lengthened the statute of limitations for filing civil lawsuits (which previously expired a few years after the youth reached the age of majority, generally at 18) to several years after the victim recalls the abuse (which could be as long as 20 or 30 years or more after the crime). This reform can be considered pro-plaintiff (pro-victim, but antidefendant) because the purpose of a statute of limitation is to protect defendants from having to fight allegations from the distant past. Accused persons may not remember where they were and what they did—and witnesses in their defense may have moved away or died (Mithers, 1990). Thousands of lawsuits have been filed, encouraged by a national center for civilly prosecuting cases of child sexual abuse. Some suits arise from claims that boys were molested by men other than their fathers. But in the typical case, the plaintiff is a woman who believes she was forced to endure incestuous acts imposed by her father. In about a quarter of these suits, both parents stand accused of wrongdoing and complicity.

In reaction to the emergence of the repressed memory movement and its maximalist outlook, a countermovement has emerged which takes a minimalist position. Its skeptical perspective concedes that until the 1980s the sexual abuse of children, particularly by parents, went largely underreported and unprosecuted. But this movement questions whether a genuine medical breakthrough and a new, sound method of psychological diagnosis really has been developed. The suspicion is that certain intervention techniques do not unearth buried memories but actually invent "pseudomemories" that are delusions arising from the therapist's repetition of persuasive suggestions. As a result, certain practitioners who are so intent on unlocking repressed memories are misguiding some of their highly vulnerable and confused patients. The minimalist perspective charges that the maximalist alarmist definition of what behaviors constitute "violations," which are then characterized as "childhood sexual abuse," is much too inclusive (for example, unwanted kisses and hugs, or lack of respect for personal privacy). Similarly, too many of the vague symptoms on the lengthy checklists in self-help manuals are interpreted as likely signs of childhood sexual abuse—everything from ordinary physical ailments (headaches, stomach pains, dizziness) and common emotional problems (general malaise, alienation, low self-esteem, and phobias) to specific attitudes and behaviors (like feeling powerless or having difficulties in maintaining long-term relationships). As a result of these overly broad definitions and unwarranted assumptions about the origins of these symptoms, many therapy patients end up deceiving themselves. They come to believe that they can remember awful events that never really happened (Goldstein, 1993; Ofshe and Watters, 1993; Loftus and Ketcham, 1994; Pendergrast, 1994; and Yapko, 1994).

The debate over claims of therapeutic breakthroughs on the one hand versus charges of planted suggestions and intense coaxing on the other became unusually acrimonious during the early 1990s. Maximalists denounced skeptics who questioned the authenticity of some claims as "enemies" of incest survivors. Minimalists dismissed the many testimonials about long-forgotten episodes of childhood sexual abuse as part of a modern-day "witch hunt" reflecting a jump-on-the-bandwagon phenomenon and a passing fad. Some psychologists and psychiatrists voiced concerns that the furor surrounding symptom-producing traumatic memories was undermining the reputation of the entire profession of clinical therapy and causing genuine victims to be scoffed at as misguided. Some feminists supported the memory recovery movement as a socio-political force that could help put an end to the sexual exploitation of children and the subordination of women. They interpreted the resistance as a backlash, just another tactic in the long-standing tradition of silencing, denying, dismissing, belittling, and deriding what women say about their oppression within the family. But other feminists argued that the tendency of the incest survivor movement to blame so many problems that crop up in women's lives on some clearly identifiable villain who might have committed sexual offenses long ago has the counterproductive political consequence of shifting the focus of activism from seeking sweeping social changes to pursuing individual recovery and private retribution (see Darnton, 1991; Chira, 1993; Horn, 1993; Tavris, 1993; and Ofshe, 1994).

Parents and others targeted by these suits have organized a foundation to defend themselves against what they brand as a "false memory syndrome." Somc convictions based on recalled memories have been overturned. Some defendants have filed countersuits against their accusers for defamation of character. Some former patients who recanted their exhumed "memories" have brought malpractice suits against the therapists who persuaded them to view themselves as incest victims (see Horn, 1993; and Sugarman and McCoy, 1997).

In 1989 a 29-year-old-woman is watching her daughter play when she suddenly has a flashback of her father killing her 8-year-old playmate by hitting her head with a rock 20 years earlier. She presses charges and testifies against him. The retired firefighter is convicted of murder and sentenced to life behind bars. But after serving 6 years, his conviction is overturned and he is released from prison. The prosecution decides not to retry the case for two reasons: His daughter lied about not being hypnotized before the flood of memories she recounted at the trial, and DNA tests cleared him of another murder she accused him of committing. (Associated Press, 1996b)

A woman claims that 6 years of therapy convinced her that she was part of a satanic cult that engaged in cannibalism, that she was sexually abused by numerous men, and that she abused her own two sons. When she files a civil lawsuit, insurance companies representing the doctors and the mental hospital agree to an out-of-court settlement that awards her over $10 million. (Belluck, 1997)

Strange Allegations of Ritualistic Abuse by Satanic Cults

Four members of a family that runs a preschool, plus three teachers who work there, are accused of subjecting 42 children to satanic rituals that involved sexual abuse. Charges are quickly dropped against five of the defendants. The mother is kept in jail for 2 years but is acquitted after a lengthy trial. After 5 years in detention and two trials, charges are dismissed against her son in 1990. Jurors are divided over the issue of whether the overzealous officials who interviewed the children suggested much of their testimony. (Goldberg, 1998)

A deputy sheriff is arrested and charged with sexually abusing his two daughters, now 18 and 22. Soon the charges emanating from the devoutly religious 22-year-old (who has a history of making unsubstantiated complaints about sexual abuse) grow to alarming proportions: She claims to have attended 850 satanic rituals and to have watched 25 babies being sacrificed and then cannibalized. Eventually, both daughters, the mother, and then even the father, can visualize being present at these ceremonies where members of a sadistic devil-worshiping cult forced the women to perform sexual acts with goats and dogs. The father is grilled by his police department colleagues and quickly confesses, but then hires a new lawyer and tries to withdraw his guilty plea. However, it is too late, and he is convicted of six counts of child molestation. His older daughter demands that he receive the stiffest punishment possible, and the judge sentences him to 20 years in prison. (Wright, 1994)

One of the most peculiar debates between the maximalist and minimalist viewpoints reached a feverish pitch during the late 1980s and early 1990s. It incorporated elements of great concern at the time: child abuse, sexual exploitation, kidnapping, and repressed memories.

The maximalist position was that thousands of people disappeared each year because they were dispatched by secret cults. Believers in the existence of a satanic conspiracy circulated frightening accounts about bizarre "wedding" ceremonies in which covens of witches and devil worshipers chanted, wore costumes, took drugs, sacrificed animals, and even mutilated, tortured, and murdered newborn infants or kidnapped children. In its most extreme form, the charge was that satanic cults engaged in baby breeding and in kidnapping in order to maintain a supply of victims for human sacrifices and cannibalism. The people who came forward and said that they survived ritual abuse were often young women who made these claims after undergoing psychotherapy. They told tales of being fondled, raped, sodomized, and exploited as objects in sexual games and pornographic films. Usually, the scenarios they recalled involved groups of adults, sometimes including members of their own families, abusing very young children. Although the alleged victims complained that they encountered resistance or even outright disbelief when they reported the crimes to the police, some law enforcement agencies took their charges seriously. Newsletters, conferences, and training sessions were organized for detectives, social workers, child welfare investigators, and therapists. Responding to a public outcry, several state legislatures outlawed the "ritual mutilation" of innocents during religious initiation rites (see Bromley, 1991; Richardson, Best, and Bromley, 1991; Lanning, 1992; Shapiro et al., 1993; and Sinason, 1994).

The minimalist position pointed out that the scare developed after bizarre charges about teachers practicing witchcraft at a California preschool generated one of the longest and costliest trials in American history (but no convictions). To investigate the deluge of claims about ritual abuse, researchers sponsored by the National Center on Child Abuse and Neglect surveyed more than 11,000 psychiatrists, psychologists, clinical social workers, district attorneys, police executives, and social service agency administrators during 1993. The respondents told the survey interviewers that over 12,000 accusations of ritual abuse had been brought to their attention, but that not a single case had been proven in which a well-organized, intergenerational ring of satanic followers had sexually molested, tortured, or killed children in their homes or schools. The study could only find some cases in which lone individuals or couples carried out abusive rituals or perpetrated crimes in the name of religion (Goleman, 1994). The minimalist view attributed the panic to sensationalism by the tabloid press and irresponsible talk shows that fed a climate of rumors and fears. The time was ripe because of widespread and deep-seated anxieties concerning new brainwashing techniques of mind control, the growth of cult-like religious groups, the breakdown of traditionally structured families, the redefinition of male and female roles, youthful experimentation with sex and drugs, increased conflict over abortion as "baby-killing," and greater reliance on day-care services for preschoolers. Fears about well-financed, hidden cells of satanic infiltrators seemed to have replaced "communist subversives" as the forces of an "evil underworld" in these versions of conspiracy theories. Although many people claimed to have witnessed, participated in, and survived these devilish ordeals, the skeptical stance concluded that their credibility was as questionable as that of the hundreds of people who swore they had been abducted by aliens from outer space or who said they remembered events from their "past lives" as different people (see Bromley, 1991; Richardson, Best, and Bromley, 1991; Lanning, 1992; Sakheim and Devine, 1992; Nathan and Snedeker, 1995; and LaFontaine, 1997).

Abused Children and Legal Proceedings

Intrafamily abuse cases traditionally were handled by child-welfare protective services, family courts, and the juvenile justice system. As more cases involving very serious charges were brought to criminal courts, a long-standing dilemma became acute: In trying to protect the child from further abuse, the judicial proceedings could inadvertently compound the youngster's trauma. It became clear that the adult-oriented criminal justice system was not designed to address the emotional, psychological, and physical needs of victimized youth. As key witnesses for the prosecution, they often found the setting to be hostile and the proceedings to be confusing, hard to fathom, and frightening (Munson, 1989).

Taking the Best Interests of the Child into Account It is clear that a victimized child needs a "friend" or "advocate" who will provide support and advice during legal proceedings, especially when the accused offender is a parent. The law has recognized the inability of the government's prosecutor to play this role and has created a special position, called the **guardian ad litem (GAL),** to look after "the best interests of the child." The Child Abuse Prevention and Treatment Act passed by Congress in 1974 required that youngsters be provided with GALs if their cases were heard in family court. The Victims of Child Abuse Act of 1990 went further and recommended the provision of GALs to young complainants whenever their serious allegations channeled their cases to criminal court. By 1997 nearly 650 advocacy programs operated in jurisdictions across the country. Usually, these court-appointed advocates are attorneys, but in some states they can be specially trained volunteers. Their duties include accompanying the child to legal proceedings and helping him or her get needed social, mental health, and medical services. In criminal proceedings against an abuser, the GAL is supposed to serve as counselor, interpreter, defender against system-induced trauma (insensitive handling), monitor, coordinator, advocate (of rights to privacy and protection from harassment), and spokesperson (about wishes, fears, and needs). In some states GALs assist the child in preparing a victim impact statement and can submit their own recommendations to the court about what would be best for the child's welfare (Whitcomb, 1992; and Lawry, 1997).

Handling Charges of Abuse The creation of the role of guardian ad litem dramatized the importance of a much larger question: What are the victim's best interests? When victims are too young to be capable of defining for themselves what they consider to be to their advantage, it is up to GALs to advocate in their behalf. But what are the options, opportunities, perils, and pitfalls of various courses of action?

Two official responses are possible in cases of physical or sexual abuse. One is to view parental wrongdoers as dysfunctional people in need of treatment and rehabilitation. The other is to react to them as criminals who deserve punishment. These two alternatives reflect opposing philosophies. Mental health professionals (psychiatrists, psychologists, counselors, and social workers) tend to see criminal proceedings as unproductive, inhumane, damaging to both victims and perpetrators, and inappropriate in all but the most horrendous cases. Police officials and prosecutors tend to resent therapeutic approaches that, in their view, coddle offenders and excuse their antisocial conduct. But in recent years the alternatives have become intertwined, as criminal proceedings have been used to compel abusers to undergo court-mandated and supervised treatment programs as a condition of pretrial diversion or probation (see Berliner, 1987; Harshbarger, 1987; and Newberger, 1987).

Children as Witnesses Historically, when children were drawn into the adult court system as prosecution witnesses, the proceedings were inherently biased against their participation. Their testimony was automatically suspect, and their unique and legitimate needs were routinely overlooked. Now, it is widely recognized that young complainants have special problems and require special handling. An estimated 20,000 children are called upon each year to testify in legal proceedings stemming from allegations of sexual abuse, and as many as 80,000 more are questioned by investigators annually about possible molestations (Goleman, 1993). As a result, whether or not children tend to tell the truth or are prone to concoct stories has become an emotionally charged issue with significant legal repercussions. Should youngsters have an automatic credibility problem simply by virtue of their age? Would children lie about important matters? Is there a kernel of truth to most revelations, whether spontaneously volunteered or coaxed out of children, or do hysterical parents and overzealous investigators set off witch hunts and fall for hoaxes? Researchers estimate that around 500 studies have examined the issue of children's "suggestibility" since a bitter controversy erupted during the late 1980s (Goldberg, 1998).

Nineteen children between the ages of 3 and 5 testify at the trial of their nursery school teacher. They tell the jury that over a period of 7 months, during nap time, this 22-year-old woman (who received an excellent evaluation and a promotion) inserted knives, forks, spoons, and Lego blocks into them. Some testify that they all played games naked and she made them drink urine, eat feces, and defecate on her. Although no staff members saw, heard, smelled, or suspected anything suspicious, and no parent ever detected any evidence of strange behavior, the jury believes the children. Three years after the alleged incidents, the 10-month trial ends, and the teacher is convicted on 115 counts of sexual abuse and sentenced to 47 years in prison. But 5 years later, the conviction is overturned on appeal when a three-judge panel rules that prosecution interviewers pressured the little complainants to confirm the charges with bribes and threats; and that the judge shed his mantle of impartiality when he coaxed the young witnesses to testify against the teacher over closed-circuit TV in his chambers while they were sitting on his lap and whispering into each other's ears. The prosecution decides not to retry the case, in part because some parents conclude that putting their now teenage children back on the witness stand would be too stressful. (Manshel, 1990; Nieves, 1994)

The testimony of children has been viewed with skepticism ever since the Salem witch trials of 1692 (in which a number of girls made fantastic claims that they publicly recanted several years later after the "witches" were executed). Now, social scientists are conducting experiments to determine the accuracy of the memories children acquire, retain, and retrieve. Because of their immaturity very young children suffer from cognitive limitations that can undermine their credibility. They think in very concrete terms and have trouble understanding generalizations. They do not organize their thoughts logically or recount stories sequentially. They may be unable to properly locate events in space, distance, and time, making it difficult for them to be sure about "where" and "when" something happened. They may tend to assume that adults know the whole story, and think that their partial answers are satisfactory. They also have short attention spans. Finally, they may be uncomfortable confiding in strangers who intimidate them (Whitcomb, 1992).

Two distinct points of view characterize the debate over the issue of credibility (see Ceci and Bruck, 1993). At one extreme is the pro-prosecution/pro-victim "believe the children" position that says that youngsters are generally competent witnesses about events that happened to them weeks or months earlier, are resistant to suggestions, and do not make up charges about abuse, especially sexual molestations and assaults that didn't happen. In fact, children might even retract accusations that ring true if the social reaction to their disclosure threatens to cause chaos. For example, a girl who reveals an incestuous relationship might recant her original testimony if she fears that she will be rejected and branded as a liar by her father, who faces disgrace and imprisonment; that her mother will become hysterical and enraged; that her siblings will be furious about the disruption of their family life; and that caseworkers and detectives will become more intrusive. The girl could feel she is being blamed for provoking the crisis and might back down in a vain attempt to restore some semblance of normality (Whitcomb, 1992).

At the other extreme is the pro-defendant position that questions the trustworthiness of the testimony of children who serve as witnesses for the prosecution. Their versions of events should be viewed with skepticism because children are extremely vulnerable to coaching and manipulation by adults. The testimony of very young witnesses loses credibility once they have been subjected to intensive questioning by caseworkers, detectives, prosecutors, and parents who strongly believe that abuse has taken place. If authority figures attempt to "validate" their preconceived notion of what may have happened, the youngsters may keep repeating the "right answers" to the leading questions adults ask. Then the youngsters may eventually be swayed and regurgitate the adults' suspicions back to them, as if these events actually occurred. When a high-pressure interviewing technique is imposed upon a hyper-suggestible youngster, the result can be the creation of a "false memory." A baseless charge against an innocent adult ultimately could lead to a wrongful conviction.

Contradictory findings about the reliability of children's claims have filled the forensic literature since the mid-1970s. Some studies conclude that youngsters can be swayed only about minor details, but others indicate that repeated interrogations can coerce children to make up tales that they believe are memories. Professionals who look into and report about instances of suspected maltreatment must be scrupulous about carrying out two legal obligations simultaneously: promoting the best interests of their young clients while safeguarding the legal rights of the grown-ups they investigate (Ceci and Bruck, 1993; Hewitt, 1998).

Ever since the landmark decision of the Supreme Court in 1895 (*Wheeler v. United States*), children have had to pass pretrial competency tests before testifying (unless they were over the age of 14). Nearly 100 years later the Victims of Child Abuse Act of 1990 reversed that presumption; now children are considered competent witnesses unless there is evidence to the contrary. However, in most state courtrooms across the country, before the trial begins the judge evaluates whether children understand the difference between truth and falsehood, appreciate the seriousness of the oath to swear to tell the truth, and can remember details of past events. Child-welfare advocates welcome these reforms because they believe most children in abuse cases don't lie (Whitcomb, 1992). But civil libertarians are concerned that the presumption of competency might undermine a defendant's right to a fair trial (Austern, 1987; Dershowitz, 1988).

Besides credibility, another special problem requires special solutions: testifying in legal proceedings can add to the suffering of victimized children. To avoid further traumatizing these youngsters, the idea of developing a child-friendly courtroom setting and protocol quickly caught on (see Libai, 1969).

The right to a public trial always has protected defendants against judicial misconduct and governmental persecution. However, the prospect of testifying in front of a crowd of strangers can deter a youthful complainant from pressing charges. In particular, the spectacle of describing in intimate detail what happened during an episode of sexual abuse is so potentially disturbing to a sensitive youngster that exceptions to the public nature of a trial have been legislated. Some states grant judges the authority to bar spectators from the courtroom during the testimony of a child who claims to have been sexually abused. In more than half of the states, the release of identifying information by the news media about a complainant in a sexual abuse case is severely limited (Whitcomb, 1992).

The Sixth Amendment guarantees all defendants in criminal trials the right to confront their accusers. In theory, looking the defendant in the eye in court as an accusation is repeated has traditionally been considered a test of a complaining witness's truthfulness. But when very young children are the complainants, they often dread seeing the defendant in person. For many years what prosecutors did to avoid last-minute intimidation when the youngster took the stand was to position themselves in such a way as to block the small witness' view of the defendant. Other prosecutors simply instructed the child to look at someone in the spectator section during the testimony, preferably toward a supportive person like a family member or victim advocate. More overt physical methods to shield frightened complainants from the direct gaze of defendants, such as using a screen or one-way glass or having the children turn their backs, were considered to violate the face-to-face requirement of the confrontation clause's concerns for truthfulness. With the advent of closed-circuit television and videotaping, more options developed. To avoid intimidation and the heightened anxiety caused by the presence of jurors and other courtroom personnel, nearly all states allow youngsters to be questioned in another room using two-way, live closed-circuit television. To spare the child the ordeal of reliving unpleasant experiences in front of strangers, most of these states permit testimony and cross-examination previously videotaped at depositions, grand jury proceedings, or preliminary hearings to be used in trials. In 1990 the Supreme

Court ruled (in *Maryland v. Craig*) that these alternatives to direct confrontation were constitutionally permissible under certain circumstances (Whitcomb, 1992).

Hearsay is usually not admissible during trials because statements uttered outside the courtroom are not made under oath or subject to cross-examination. Yet in child-abuse cases, what the youngster said before legal proceedings were initiated may be very compelling evidence. For example, the casual, innocent remark of a very young and immature girl might be a surprisingly graphic description of a sexual act that should be unfamiliar to her. Therefore, in the "interest of justice" in more than half the states, special exceptions to the hearsay rule enable witnesses to tell the court what allegedly sexually abused children have told them. In 1980 the Supreme Court ruled (in *Ohio v. Roberts*) that a statement made by a complainant who does not testify at the trial can be used as evidence if it falls under one of the rules for hearsay exceptions or meets a reliability test (Whitcomb, 1992).

In the late 1970s, investigators began to use anatomically detailed dolls (with prominent genitalia) to facilitate and enhance interviews with children who might have been sexually abused. The rationale was that the presence of a doll would make the interview seem less formal and stressful, enable children with limited vocabularies or suffering from great embarrassment to demonstrate what happened to them, and permit the information to be disclosed without any reliance on leading questions. The Victims of Child Abuse Act of 1990 endorsed the use of dolls as demonstrative aids during interviews and court proceedings, and some states have followed suit. But some critics point out that experiments have shown that even children with no suspected history of abuse play with the anatomically intriguing dolls in a suggestive way that could falsely imply inordinate interest in sexuality (see Whitcomb, 1992).

Other reforms that are less controversial and more often implemented include allowing children to use drawings to describe what happened to them, interviewing victims in decorated playrooms at police stations rather than in dingy, bare-walled interrogation rooms, modifying the courtroom's protocol and seating arrangements to make the setting less imposing, giving child witnesses an orientation tour of the courthouse, enrolling them in brief "court schools" that explain the role of key figures and the procedures that will be followed, permitting them to have a supportive person at their side, and using a single trained interviewer to elicit all their testimony. To limit the length of the ordeal of going to trial, some jurisdictions give child abuse cases a high priority in scheduling and try to avoid continuances that cause upsetting delays. To minimize stress the medical, mental health, treatment, and legal aspects of abuse cases are now coordinated by child-protection teams composed of professionals from different disciplines. Information-sharing procedures eliminate unnecessary interviews. Public funds cover the costs of physical and mental health examinations. Caseworkers from protective services agencies and law enforcement officers are empowered to take children endangered by their situations into emergency custody. Because confused and intimidated youngsters often do not inform anyone of their plight for years, many states have extended their statutes of limitations so they do not begin to run until the victim reaches a more mature age (see Whitcomb, 1986; "Child Abuse Victims," 1989; Howell, 1989; and Myers, 1998).

A survey revealed that the following percentages of judges have used these approaches to minimize the stress on child victims who testified in their courtrooms: adjusted questions to the child's comprehension level (88%), excluded the public during the child's testimony (55%), child testified in judge's chambers (46%), judge posed questions (45%), child testified while on adult's lap (41%), courtroom furniture rearranged (31%), testimony videotaped (27%), defendant removed from child's view (16%), therapist posed questions (13%), child testified over closed-circuit television (11%), and one-way mirror used (3%) (Hafemeister, 1996).

The "funnel" model of the criminal justice system best describes what happens to child abuse cases. Although the system potentially has a huge caseload to tackle, cases are "lost" or "weeded out" at each stage until there are very few left at the end of the process. Children testifying and parents getting convicted and punished turns out to be a relatively rare event (see Chapman and Smith, 1987; and Whitcomb, 1988, 1992).

Proactive Versus Reactive Strategies

Strategies to prevent children from being abused take many forms. They range from screening potential child-care workers for known molesters, or setting up "help lines" and crisis nurseries where parents can drop off their children if they feel they are about to lose control, to organizing self-help Parents Anonymous support groups for abusers, and offering child-rearing courses for new parents (Irwin, 1980).

The problem of child maltreatment raises many profound issues. Although proactive and preventive strategies are as important as reactive criminal justice responses, sharp differences of opinion erupt over the proper role of government in the balance between social nurturance and social control. In reply to the question "Whose children are they?" one long-standing answer is that children belong to, or are the property of, their parents. But another way of looking at youngsters is to see them as "junior" citizens: Parents have custody of them, but the larger community has "visiting rights." In extreme cases the community might even assert "joint custody" and violate the privacy of the family and the rights of parents. Government agencies step in as the parents of last resort when children face a clear and present danger. Yet in an age when the social conditions experienced by children are generally deteriorating (in terms of reduced parental involvement and support, increased exposure to violence, and persistent poverty during childhood in female-headed households), stepped-up efforts to criminalize the maltreatment of children may not do much to stem the growth of the problem (Garbarino, 1989). On the other hand, the price for inaction or minimal reaction in the name of family preservation on the part of child protection agencies and family courts can be serious injury or death.

MORE CASUALTIES OF DOMESTIC VIOLENCE

Besides child maltreatment, several other victim-offender relationships falling within the realm of intrafamily violence have been rediscovered and now are being explored. Victimologists are carrying out research into adolescent abuse by parents, parent abuse by adolescents, sibling abuse, elder abuse by grown children, and partner abuse (by a spouse or live-in lover).

Abuse of Adolescents by Parents

The realization that teenagers still can be abused by their parents used to be overlooked entirely or else was subsumed under the heading "child abuse" and then neglected in favor of a focus on the very young and totally helpless. Attempts to define and measure abuse become confusing because of cultural ambivalence about the thin line between physical abuse and physical discipline. Many adults consider the venting of parental wrath to be justifiable if there is "sufficient provocation" (if a teenager is argumentative, defiant, "incorrigible," or "out of control"). Adolescents are not viewed as particularly vulnerable or defenseless as are infants, toddlers, and children under 12. The same force that could injure a little child might not seriously wound a teenager. The overt consequences of psychological abuse and emotional neglect become less detectable as adolescents mature into independent young adults (see Lourie, 1977; Libbey and Bybee, 1979; and Pagelow, 1989).

Attempts to measure the frequency of adolescent abuse have yielded estimates that from one fifth to almost one half of all cases of child maltreatment known to social service agencies involved youths between 12 and 17 (measurements were taken at various times during the 1970s and 1980s). Parents tend to use greater force against their older children. As a result, battered teenagers can suffer serious wounds just like younger children. Their injuries usually come to light when they are reported by their parents or their teachers to the authorities for disobedience or "acting out" behavior or are referred to counselors for "emotional problems." Girls are more likely than boys to be physically, sexually, and emotionally abused; boys are more often emotionally and educationally neglected. As boys grow older the power differential between parents and their sons decreases and physical abuse declines. As girls become sexually mature and seek greater independence, the power differential between parents and their daughters diminishes more incrementally, leading to conflicts as parents attempt to impose restraints backed up by force. Sons who strike back get into legal trouble for assault. Girls generally do not fight back physically, but they seek to escape a repressive household by running away, acting promiscuously, or taking drugs. The majority of abused teenagers are white and from lower-income families where they are either the only child or 1 of 4 or more children. Their abusive parents tend to be middle-aged, are often stepparents, and are going through their own mid-life crises. Excessive parental forcefulness takes the form of hair pulling, slapping, choking, beating, threatening with a knife or gun, and using a weapon (see Pagelow, 1989).

Abuse of Parents by Adolescents

When teenagers batter their parents, their fathers and mothers tend to feel ashamed and wish to keep the matters private, so the underreporting rate remains high. In many cases the use of force directed at parents can be seen as a reaction to the violence these caretakers previously visited upon their children. In that sense, an intergenerational cycle of violence has been set into motion. Mothers and stepmothers are more likely to be the injured parties than fathers or stepfathers. But male parents are more likely to be the targets of extreme violence, perhaps in retaliation for abuse or in self-defense against an attack. Physically aggressive fathers with drinking problems are the most common victims of severe injuries or even lethal force by sons who view themselves as protectors of their mothers and siblings. In the rare cases in which a daughter is involved in the murder of a parent, the actual killer is usually a male she recruited for the deed (see Steinmetz, 1978b; Straus, Gelles, and Steinmetz, 1980; Lubenow, 1983; Pagelow, 1989; Mones, 1991; and Ewing, 1997).

Sibling Abuse

When brothers and sisters fight each other, their roughhousing is often disregarded as a "normal" expression of sibling rivalry. Sons are more violent than daughters, and all-boy families are the most violent of all. The use of force to resolve quarrels breaks out more often between siblings than between parents or between parents and children. Older youths may not only physically assault but also sexually abuse younger siblings. The younger child generally does not tell anyone about the incidents for fear of being blamed, of not being believed, or of suffering reprisals (see Straus, Gelles, and Steinmetz, 1980; Pagelow, 1989; and Wiehe, 1990, 1997, 1998).

Sibling-on-sibling violence stands out because it is the most frequent type of assault and yet the least studied, which evidently reflects the difference between the priorities of researchers and the concerns of youngsters. In terms of a typology of victimization during childhood, violence between siblings can be classified as "pandemic" (occurs in the lives of a majority of children as they grow up), more common than the incidence of robbery, theft, vandalism of a possession, assault by a peer, and physical punishment by a parent (Finkelhor and Leatherman, 1994).

Elder Abuse

According to *NCVS* data, elderly people are the least likely of all age groups to become victims of violence, personal theft, and household crimes, largely because of the precautions they take (Klaus, 1999). But starting in the 1970s, victimologists and senior citizen advocates began to delve into other ways that older people are made to suffer by younger people (see Goldsmith and Goldsmith, 1976; Boston, 1977; Center, 1980; and Hochstedler, 1981). Therefore, elder abuse was rediscovered right after child abuse and spouse abuse. Many obvious parallels facilitated the rediscovery process. Once the term was coined, the problem began to receive the attention it merited from geriatric social workers, care providers, and law enforcement professionals, as well as researchers (see Quinn and Tomita, 1986; Breckman and Adelman, 1988; and Steinmetz, 1988).

Definitions of elder abuse vary but usually include both acts of commission (assaults, unreasonable confinement, financial exploitation in the form of outright theft, extortion, fraud, embezzlement, or misuse of income or savings) as well as acts of omission (failure to provide medical care, food, clothing, and shelter; failure to protect from health and safety hazards; and failure to assist with personal hygiene) by caretakers responsible for the older person's well-being. Therefore, abuse encompasses gross neglect as well as acts of intentional harm (House Subcommittee, 1992).

Domestic elder abuse is perpetrated by persons who provide care to elderly people who live at home. Institutional elder abuse is committed by individuals (such as employees of nursing homes) who have a contractual obligation to tend to the needs of older persons (McGrath and Osborne, 1989). The offender is most commonly a close relative, especially a grown child, spouse, or sibling. Less often the abuser is a son- or daughter-in-law, grandchild, niece, nephew, or friend and neighbor. The typical target is a frail, ailing woman more than 70 years old. In most cases the victim and the abuser live in the same household in social isolation from friends, neighbors, and kin who might otherwise informally deter the wrongdoing. The abusers usually are overburdened care givers who become depressed and hostile at the long-term prospects of tending to a mentally and physically impaired, isolated, and dependent individual. When homebound parents are physically beaten or financially exploited, sons are the most likely culprits; when daughters and daughters-in-law are abusive, their maltreatment usually takes the form of emotional and physical neglect. Mistreatment by home health aides and nursing home staff members is also suspected to be commonplace (Pagelow, 1989).

An estimated 1.5 million older Americans (about 5% of all senior citizens) were subjected to physical, psychological, or financial abuse or suffered serious, even life-threatening, neglect in 1992 (House Subcommittee, 1992). Depending upon the definition the problem may be even more serious (according to a maximalist perspective), since the underreporting of incidents of elder abuse undermines attempts to collect reliable data. Congressional investigators estimated that only about 16% of abused elders dared to bring their plight to the attention of the proper authorities. Many reasons explain the reluctance of victims to complain about their situations. The offender is most likely a family member who is depended upon for daily care. Victims might regard their situations as a cause for shame or as private family matters. Some victims might feel they have provoked the abuse, while others may not even be aware of the wrongdoing (particularly financial exploitation). Mandatory reporting laws similar to those that require disclosure of suspected cases of child abuse have been imposed on health-care professionals, especially doctors, generating upwardly spiraling statistics and overwhelming caseloads for geriatric social workers. However, as in child abuse cases, many allegations are never substantiated (Wolf and Pillemer, 1989; Editors, New York Times, 1991; Tatara, 1993).

VIOLENCE BETWEEN INTIMATES

The Rediscovery of Wife Beating

In her autobiography the daughter of a prominent political figure reveals that she endured many vicious beatings by her first husband, a police officer, shortly after they got married. During fits of jealous rage, he punches and kicks her in the head so brutally that she fantasizes about killing him. But when she picks up his service revolver, she finds she is incapable of pulling the trigger. She tells her coworkers, friends, and parents that her cuts and swellings are due to accidents. Her father, a former president of the United States, finally discovers the truth about her "bruises from accidents" when he reads her book. (Bruni, 1989)

The rediscovery of the plight of battered wives during the 1970s shattered the illusion of "domestic tranquillity"—that women were safe from harm as long as they remained at home, protected by their husbands from the vicious dog-eat-dog world raging outside. Once it was realized that a "silent crisis" marred the lives of many women and that the perpetrators were the men they married, not menacing strangers, the "look-the-other-way," "mind-your-own-business," and "hands-off" policy toward "lovers' spats" that took place "behind closed doors" could no longer be justified (see Straus, 1978; Pagelow, 1984a, 1984b; Gelles and Cornell, 1990; Straus and Gelles, 1990; and Dobash and Dobash, 1992).

For centuries, legal traditions granted the man, as "head of the household" whose "home was his castle," the "right" to "discipline" his wife and children "as he saw fit," since they were regarded as his "property" or "chattel." This prescription became the basis in English common law (which was accepted into American jurisprudence) for a nonintervention stance that denied women equal protection under law. Such institutionalized indifference was legally permissible because it was a wife's duty to "love, honor, and obey" her husband. Indeed, many battered wives did not even define their beatings as crimes and did not consider themselves to be victims because they accepted the prevailing ideology (echoed by authority figures, friends, and parents) that they had "stepped out of line" and "had it coming" and therefore "got what they deserved." Such traditional thinking made the marriage license into a "hitting license" for husbands.

A mistaken impression prevails that the issue of spouse abuse was raised during the 1970s for the first time, primarily by feminists intent on exposing the weaknesses and cruelties of the system of male dominance known as "patriarchy." Actually, there had been two previous periods of concern about family violence in American history (Pleck, 1989).

As early as the mid-1600s, the Pilgrims who settled in New England officially recognized the possibility that wives could be victims of assault by their husbands, that husbands could be brutalized by their wives, that children could be harshly mistreated by their parents, and that incestuous sexual relations could be imposed upon youngsters. Guided by religious teachings about the virtues of harmonious family life and the sins of disobeying authority, the Puritans in

Plymouth Colony and Massachusetts Bay Colony passed the first laws anywhere in the world forbidding verbal or physical abuse between family members. Wife beating was punishable by a fine or a whipping. However, the sentence for husband abuse was up to the judge; child abuse (called "unnatural severity") carried a fine, but if incest was discovered it could result in execution by hanging, as the Bible recommended. Even though conformity to all laws was insisted upon and intervening into a neighboring family's affairs was expected, none of these laws were vigorously enforced. Only on very rare occasions were wives brought to court for verbally abusing ("nagging") their husbands. Husbands rarely were fined and almost never whipped for beating their wives (some charges were dropped when judges decided wives had provoked their husbands' wrath). Wives who complained that their husbands beat them often recanted their accusations when they got to court. No case of child abuse was ever prosecuted, and no one was ever put to death for incest, according to court records from these New England colonies. Apparently, these laws merely served a symbolic function, outlining rights and responsibilities and setting limits. Puritan teachings held that God ruled the state, the state supervised the family, and the husband headed the household. The occasional use of force to discipline a wife (what they called "moderate correction" within "domestic chastisement") was permissible within reasonable limits (as long as the beating caused no permanent damage). The expression "rule of thumb" in those days was a guideline that prohibited men from using sticks thicker than their thumbs to beat their wives whose "provocations" included "passionate language" (scolding) or refusing to engage in sexual relations. The desire to reinforce patriarchal control, uphold parental rights, and shore up the nuclear family necessitated that laws criminalizing abuse within families would be rarely enforced and that "sinners" would receive lenient sentences. The most effective restraints on male violence were informal means of social control: community disapproval, pressures from the wife's parents, and in extreme cases divorce (Rhode, 1989; Pleck, 1989).

As agriculture as a way of life gave way to industrialization and urbanization, a second wave of concern about family violence developed in the late 1800s. Reformers argued in favor of the principle that the government had a responsibility to enforce morality as codified in law. Fears of immigrants, drifters, and the growing "dangerous classes" of criminals and delinquents in the large cities fueled this movement for change. Societies for the Prevention of Cruelty to Children (SPCC) were set up across the country. Temperance advocates hammered away at the evils of drinking by emphasizing how wives and children were abused by drunkards who wasted their time and money in saloons. Some women's rights activists contended that fines and jail terms were insufficient to deter wife beating, and called for the restoration of the whipping post. (Public flogging had been abandoned in most states about 100 years earlier as an uncivilized and barbaric form of corporal punishment.) Other feminists sought ways to help battered wives get orders of protection and divorces (Pleck, 1989).

The third wave of reform focused on victim-support activities and was spearheaded by feminists in the women's liberation movement in the early 1970s. Wife beating symbolized women's oppression within the family, and the lack of responsiveness on the part of the men who ran the criminal justice system demonstrated the institutionalized discrimination women faced in everyday life. Projects such as setting up shelters for battered women typified the tangible aid, victim empowerment, and self-help that women could achieve if they acted collectively. A battered women's movement developed out of this third wave of concern about family violence.

The battered women's movement encountered resistance and opposition because of the widespread acceptance of victim-blaming arguments that portrayed beaten wives in an unsympathetic light. Many people, including some counselors and family therapists, believed that a high proportion of beatings were unconsciously precipitated or even intentionally provoked. Those wives who were said to be responsible for stirring up their husbands' wrath were negatively stereotyped as "aggressive," "masculine," and "sexually frigid." Their husbands were categorized as "shy," "sexually ineffectual," "dependent and passive," and even as "mothers' boys." The dynamics of their conflict was thought to start when a badgered husband tried to please and pacify his querulous and demanding wife. But eventually her taunts and challenges provoked an explosion, and he lost his self-control (see Snell, Rosenwald, and Roby, 1964; and Faulk, 1977). Activists in the battered women's movement stated that this victim-blaming outlook failed to condemn the violence and implied that it was not a matter for the police and courts. The husband's main problem appeared to be his weakness rather than his assaultiveness. Victim blaming pictured the wife's main problems as her domineering nature, her coldness, and her secret masochistic cravings for suffering. It placed the entire burden of change on the woman and not the man, the community, and the culture that encouraged male dominance (see Schechter, 1982; and Beirne and Messerschmidt, 1991).

The battered women's movement succeeded in replacing this victim-blaming outlook with a victim-defending one. Therapists working with victims and couples began to recognize a cycle of violence accompanied by "learned helplessness," which they termed "the battered woman's syndrome." It contended that beatings often follow a pattern and escalate in frequency and intensity unless the couple receives help. Shortly after courtship a three-phase cycle begins: tension building; the battering; and the tranquil, loving aftermath (Walker, 1984).

During the tension-building phase the aggressor hurls insults and even breaks objects while his docile target tries to appease him in a vain attempt to stave off a blow-up and preserve their relationship. She attempts to cope with her mate's bad behavior and conceal it from others, inadvertently isolating herself from potential rescuers.

When her sacrifices in search of marital bliss fail, the second stage of acute violence erupts. He goes on a rampage and savagely assaults her. Feeling trapped she acts submissively as part of a defense mechanism to avoid his wrath. The injuries that he inflicts shock and confuse her.

When he becomes fearful of driving her away, he begins to show shame and remorse and the third reconciliation or "honeymoon" phase commences. He apologizes, pledges it won't happen again, and acts tenderly. Unwilling to confront the seriousness of her plight, she blames herself for his loss of control and forgives him. Believing she can head off his next round of assaults, she becomes protective of him, covers up what really happened, and decides not to seek outside help or try to leave him. An illusion of normalcy prevails for a while. But nothing has been resolved or corrected, and soon tensions rise and the cycle begins to repeat itself.

But his next round of attacks increases in ferocity. He expresses less contrition and she feels less confident about being able to defuse his anger. He rachets up his efforts to dominate her life, and she finds herself more isolated, trapped, vulnerable, and endangered than before (Walker, 1984).

Early on in the rediscovery process during the 1970s, journalists depicted wife beating in ways surprisingly favorable to a pro-victim, pro-feminist analysis, according to a content analysis of stories and reports in widely read magazines during the 1970s and 1980s (Loseke, 1989). Abusers usually were depicted as "supermacho types" who felt that following conventional sex-based roles gave them a right to discipline and control their wives and to beat back any challenges to their manly privileges. The targets of their wrath were pictured as stereotypically "feminine" women who believed that a wife's place was in the home, and that she should be selflessly devoted to her husband, dependent upon him as a breadwinner, and deferential to his rightful authority. Several themes ran through most of the articles: that wife beating is a social problem afflicting millions and not just a personal trouble burdening only a few unfortunate women; that the victims did not deserve or provoke the abuse heaped upon them; that the consequences were serious, even life threatening; that this crisis in a fundamental social institution, the family, should concern everyone because it broke out at all levels of society even if it was harder to detect in affluent, high-status families; and that governmental action could bring it under control with social programs and criminal justice solutions. Most articles identified the root causes as unjust gender relations, buttressed by an ideology which proclaimed that men were superior to women, and perpetuated by socialization practices that exhorted boys to be aggressive, tough, and powerful and girls to be passive, submissive, and supportive.

Before the 1970s, wife beating received very little attention in the journals read by counselors and social workers and others in the helping professions. Now the problem of woman battering is probably the most studied victim-offender relationship of all.

Estimates of the Incidence, Prevalence, and Seriousness of Spouse Abuse

> I never reported it. . . . I was intimidated, ashamed. I had nowhere to go. I had five children to raise. I was told that if I ever left, he would find me and kill me," said the police chief of a small rural department, who suffered broken bones, burns, and stab wounds in a series of beatings that began 2 weeks after she got married. ("Police Chief," 1993)

As the terms **spouse abuse, wife beating,** and **woman battering** became part of everyday vocabulary, a number of questions arose but the most basic was "How widespread was the problem?" The myth that very few husbands beat their wives was hard to dispel because official statistics had no such breakdown under the general heading "assault." When the battered women's movement organized "speakouts," where victims revealed their plight to audiences of sympathetic strangers, it became evident from these true confessions that violence between lovers was all too common. But anecdotal evidence would not suffice to document the true dimensions of the problem. The emerging maximalist perspective was that the visible victims were just the tip of the iceberg of a hidden, "silent crisis" (see Langley and Levy, 1977). Shortly afterward a minimalist reaction began to challenge the maximalist assumption that because fierce fighting poisoned so many outwardly loving relationships, battering constituted a low-profile epidemic. The opposing viewpoints sharply disagreed in part because basic methodological issues surrounding efforts to estimate the seriousness of the problem were not resolved.

The first and most basic issue concerns which victim-offender relationships should be included and excluded. Several terms with similar and overlapping but not identical meanings can cause endless confusion and create inconsistencies from one study to another. Choosing one definition over another can make the scope of the problem seem much larger or much smaller. Restricting attention only to wife abuse (only beatings of married females) will yield the lowest estimates. Counting all instances of partner abuse (the broadest term, which refers to all male and female initiated violence arising from intimate romantic relationships, including couples who are just dating or are living together, whether heterosexual or homosexual) will generate the highest estimates. Measuring spouse abuse (which technically refers only to male or female victims who are legally married) will lead to medium size estimates. Hunting for statistics about domestic disturbances (a police expression) will turn up only cases known to the authorities, but involving any members of the same household, including grandparents and siblings, not just intimates. Domestic violence refers to the broadest grouping of all, since it embraces physical fights that may or may not be reported to the police, between children, parents, siblings, elders, and other relatives living under the same roof (as well as intimates). Another inclusive definition would count all assaults committed by persons who are currently romantically involved (whether legally married or not) plus attacks by ex-spouses and former lovers who are no longer part of the household. Finally, woman battering only focuses on female victims, whether married or not.

Additional fuel for the maximalist-minimalist debate arises from vague notions of which specific behaviors constitute "abuse," "violence," "battering," or beatings. There are differences among these terms and different shades of meaning, connotations, and ambiguities that permit observers to draw very different conclusions. For example, if abuse is recognized only when a victim is physically injured and not just "attacked," then very different estimates of the incidence rate can result. Since most physical assaults do not bring about visible injuries, partners may attack each other but not inflict tangible injuries. If "physical injury" is taken to be the defining criterion, then domestic violence is overwhelmingly a male-on-female crime. But if "attacks" are counted, then females act aggressively against their male partners almost as often as males assault their female lovers (Straus, 1991). (Put succinctly, many men who are attacked are not wounded; assaults by males tend to result in injuries more often than assaults by females.) Clearly, which definition is used by the researcher profoundly shapes the numbers and the interpretation of the statistical findings.

Social workers, family therapists, feminists, psychologists, criminologists, victimologists, police officers, and prosecutors have tried but failed to reach a consensus about where to draw the line between inclusion and exclusion of actions labeled abusive, violent, or assaultive. Many people approve of, tolerate, or are resigned to some "normal" level of quarreling and fighting among partners in romantic relationships. Although there is no standard definition, a good working definition would take into account the seriousness of the assault, the assailant's intentions, the actual physical injury inflicted, the depth of psychological trauma, and the nature of the threat. These behaviors can cover the entire gamut of specific acts comprising simple and aggravated physical assaults, including pushing, shoving, pulling, dragging, shaking, ripping clothing, hitting with an open hand, punching with a closed fist, choking, kicking, stomping, throwing an object, threatening with a weapon, and wounding with a weapon like a knife or gun. The full continuum of physical injuries sustained by victims ranges from bruises and swellings, cuts and scratches, dizziness, sprains, and burns to loss of vision or hearing, fractures, concussions, and even more serious internal wounds. Emotional harm, on the other hand, is not so easily characterized (see Loseke, 1989; and Rhodes, 1992).

A related issue concerns whether "minor violence" constitutes "criminal violence." Beating one's partner with a weapon (baseball bat) surely is criminal violence; using a lesser object (stick, belt) is also criminal by most definitions; but what about punching with a closed fist or just slapping with an open hand? The lack of public consensus can be called "normative ambiguity" (Straus, 1991), and it reflects the distinction some would make between conflicts that occur within the family and fights between strangers. The cultural support that still exists for using force to settle family quarrels has important policy implications. If all physical attacks between spouses were criminalized—judged by the same standards (rules, expectations) as those used to identify assaults between nonfamily members—many more outbursts of spouse abuse (if reported) would trigger arrest.

Reliable sources of data about the incidence and prevalence of spouse abuse are difficult to find. For cases of child abuse, compulsory reporting laws have been passed in every state, and data-gathering clearinghouses have been established. But for spouse abuse no comparable reporting and compiling systems yet exist. The FBI's *Uniform Crime Report* is of little use because assaults between intimates are not recorded in a separate category from other assaults. The BJS's *National Crime Victimization Survey* attempts to measure the disclosure by household members of assaults committed against them by partners. But it produces a serious undercount because most "victims" don't consider themselves to have been "criminally" harmed by an "offender" in the legal sense unless they were seriously injured or the perpetrator was a former partner (after separation or divorce). Of course, many incidents are not disclosed if the assailant is present when the victim is being interviewed. Researchers studying *NCVS* findings from 1978 to 1982 determined that only about half of all batterings were reported to the police. The main reasons cited for informing the authorities were to end the attack, to keep it from happening again, and to get the offender in trouble so that he would be punished. The leading reasons for not calling for help were the women's beliefs that these incidents were private and personal matters, that the crime wasn't important enough, that the police wouldn't or couldn't assist them, and that they would be subject to reprisals if they dared to seek outside protection. *NCVS* data indicate that women who report being assaulted by a mate one year are likely to report being physically abused again when they are interviewed in later years. Police files confirm that the cycle of violence tends to escalate in frequency and severity over time (Langan and Innes, 1986).

Given the limitations of these two official sources of crime statistics, researchers have had to devise their own measurement scales and carry out their own surveys or turn to fragmentary sources (like records kept by hospital emergency rooms and police departments). However, using a biased source can strongly skew the results of a study. For example, any findings based on files about women seeking treatment cannot be generalized ("the clinical fallacy") because the sample is not representative of the entire population (Straus, 1991).

Despite all these methodological problems, a number of statistical findings support the maximalist contention that domestic violence is an extremely serious problem:

- At least 6 million women are physically abused one or more times each year (using the criterion of even just one incident of minor violence, such as being slapped). Using a more restrictive definition of serious assaults (being kicked, punched, choked, or attacked with a weapon), at least 1.8 million women are targets of severe aggression annually. The average victim was assaulted six times during the year, according to projections from a 1985 national family violence survey (Straus, 1991).
- Although simple assaults are most common, about one third of the violent outbursts described to *NCVS* interviewers would be classified by the police as more serious felonies—aggravated assaults, rapes, and even robberies (Langan and Innes, 1986). About half of all incidents of battering are not reported to the police, partly because of fear of reprisals and previous negative experiences with officers answering domestic disturbance calls (Fleury, et al., 1998).
- About 1.5% of women in a survey disclosed that they were physically assaulted and/or even forcibly raped by a current or former spouse, cohabiting partner, or date within a year; 25% had suffered this kind of an attack by an intimate during the course of a lifetime (Tjaden and Thoennes, 1998).
- About 1 million women each year seek medical attention for wounds inflicted by a male partner—husband, ex-husband, boyfriend, or former lover. Somewhere between 22% and 35% of all visits by women to hospital emergency rooms are to treat injuries resulting from a partner's assault (Gibbs, 1993b).

- Domestic violence poses the single greatest threat of injury to women between the ages of 15 and 44, taking a greater toll than automobile accidents, robberies, and cancer combined. About one third of all female murder victims are killed by "intimates" (their spouses, former husbands, or lovers). The social costs of domestic violence—in terms of health care, social services, and criminal justice outlays—add up to between $5 and $10 billion dollars a year (Senate Committee on the Judiciary, 1993; Gibbs, 1993b).
- About 6% of 13,000 new mothers in four states conceded to interviewers that they were physically injured by their husbands or partners during their pregnancy. The beatings pregnant women receive cause more birth defects than all diseases combined for which children are immunized. The greatest risks are faced by younger women who are not formally married and are poorly educated, living in crowded households, and unable to get prenatal care (Hilts, 1994).
- The rate of domestic violence in military families (about 18 confirmed cases of spouse abuse per 1,000 couples per year) is about double that of civilians, according to a survey of 55,000 soldiers at 47 bases (Schmitt, 1994).
- Only about half of all violent attacks by intimates were reported by women to the police. About one third of all these victims suffered more than one violent attack during the 6 months preceding their *NCVS* interview during the mid-1990s (Greenfeld et al., 1998).

The minimalist position is that violence between intimates, while serious, is not as much of a threat as alarmist calls to action make it seem. Only about 20 out of every 1,000 (1 in 50) young women in their early 20s are victimized by an intimate each year, according to *NCVS* surveys (Greenfeld et al., 1998). Many minor "assaults" that are registered on surveys don't lead to physical injuries and should not be lumped in with aggravated assaults that inflict severe bodily harm. Some incidents that are counted in studies were just threats or attempted assaults that failed. Furthermore, some researchers use an expanded definition of abuse that includes vicious name-calling, which may cause psychological damage but not physical wounds. Finally, some of the fighting is initiated by women and involve acts of retaliation by women, who are not always automatically the passive victims of aggression (see Straus, 1999).

As a trend, domestic violence may be declining in frequency, skeptics point out. Researchers found in a 1975 survey of 2,000 married couples that over one fourth (28%) admitted that one partner (usually the husband) had physically assaulted the other at least once since their wedding. A decade later, however, researchers using the same definitions in interviews (but this time with a larger representative sample of over 6,000 married and cohabiting couples) uncovered evidence that serious incidents of spouse abuse may be subsiding rather than intensifying. In the 1975 survey roughly 4 couples out of every 100 admitted having at least one serious outbreak of violence within the year; by 1985 the rate had declined to about 3 couples per 100. Serious incidents were defined as those involving kicking, hitting with a fist, biting, beating up, or using or threatening to use a gun or knife during a dispute. The overall incidence rate, which included less serious instances of slapping, shoving, pushing, and throwing things, was estimated to be about 16% of all married and cohabiting couples. The prevalence rate was 33% for one or more incidents involving violence during the lifetime of the marriage or cohabiting relationship (Straus and Gelles, 1986).

Aiding Victims Who Feel Trapped

Victimologists wonder "What kinds of families are wracked by these problems?" At first there were only media images and personal revelations (true confessions), but this kind of anecdotal evidence might be very unrepresentative and misleading. Atypical cases make the news, but what kinds of women are usually the objects of their lovers' wrath?

The statistical profile of a couple in which the woman is at risk for a severe beating is as follows (the more factors that fit, the higher the risk): The family income is low. She is young, unemployed, poorly educated, and lives with but is not married to a man of a different religious or ethnic background. He is between the ages of 18 and 30, is unemployed or working in a blue-collar job, did not graduate from high school, beats his children, and abuses alcohol and illicit drugs. His parents were violent toward each other, and he grew up in a rough neighborhood. She suffers from isolation, low self-esteem, passivity, dependence, and an inordinate need for attention, affection, and approval. He is impulsive, jealous, and possessive and also suffers from a low sense of self-worth. His violent outbursts are often triggered by feelings of rejection and abandonment. He threatens to harm or torture the family pet if she tries to leave. Threats of a separation or her moving out are interpreted as "provocations" because he feels he is losing control of her. If he owns a gun, goes on drinking binges, disregards restraining orders, and stalks her, she may be in very grave danger (Ingrassia and Beck, 1994; Goleman, 1995a; Healey and Smith, 1998; "Domestic Abusers," 1999).

The highest-risk groups for intimate violence, as identified by their responses on the *National Crime Victimization Survey,* are women who are young (between the ages of 16 and 24), black, and living in low-income households in urban areas (Greenfeld et al., 1998).

Another question that often comes to mind is "Why does she stay if he is so brutal?" Until the 1970s it was dismissed with the victim-blaming rejoinder that being regularly beaten must somehow fulfill a pathological need of hers. For example, battered women have been accused of being masochistic and enjoying feeling miserable or of looking forward to the passionate sex that supposedly follows a violent outburst when a "repentant" husband asks her for forgiveness (see Paglia, 1994).

Researchers have discovered a number of plausible reasons why women stay with their violent mates, repeatedly enduring the cycle of battering/reconciliation/battering. Some feel dependent, dread being alone, and despair that they have nowhere to go and no one to turn to for aid and comfort. They are intimidated, even terrorized, and fear reprisals if they dare to try to escape their possessive and controlling husbands obsessed with a "You belong to me!" and "If I can't have you, no one can!" mentality. They worry about their children's welfare (psychological damage, loss of financial support, and custody and visitation issues). Some still love their tormentors and invoke higher loyalties (a commitment to the institution of marriage and to the vows they took "for better or worse, in good times and in bad") and because of cultural and religious traditions are ashamed of the stigma (of "abandoning or deserting a husband" and of a "failed marriage"). Many believe they should stand by their men and try to help to cure them (attributing their whole "mess" to external causes, like alcoholism, unemployment, or job-related stress). Finally, trying to escape from a batterer's clutches is a risky course of action. Some find themselves stalked and beaten more viciously when they try to break up or after they separate from their abusive partners (Frieze and Browne, 1991; Steinman, 1991; Barnett and LaViolette, 1993; Kirkwood, 1993).

From its inception the battered women's movement's first priority was to provide tangible aid at a time of great need. To offer immediate support to victims during a crisis, activists established shelters as places of refuge. In 1974, following the lead of feminists in England a few years earlier, a group in St. Paul, Minnesota, transformed an old meetinghouse into the first of many women's shelters in the United States (Martin, 1976). These "safe houses" offer a number of services to their temporary residents. First and foremost, they provide short-term room and board in a secure setting for victims who are in continuing physical danger. Most also furnish emergency clothing and transportation. Through self-help groups the women can give one another emotional support when grappling with transitional issues, particularly about whether to try to sever or salvage their relationships with abusers. Counselors discuss legal issues (such as pressing charges; obtaining court orders of protection; and the complexities of separation, divorce, child custody, and alimony), educational matters (such as, for displaced homemakers, returning to school and retraining, and job hunting). Hotline staffers instruct victims where to go, since the locations of shelters are kept secret to protect the residents from stalking. Through outreach activities staff members raise public awareness about the needs for empowering these otherwise dependent women and for reforming the criminal justice and social service systems (Warrior, 1977; Neidig, 1984; Dutton-Douglas and Dionne, 1991; OJP, 1998).

Although the first safe houses were initially set up as independent self-help projects and were staffed by volunteers, many people quickly agreed that local governments had a responsibility to establish permanent shelters run by social service agencies. By 1987 approximately 1,200 battered women's shelters were operating across the country. Most were overcrowded, underfunded, and understaffed, according to the National Coalition Against Domestic Violence (Abrams, 1987). Those who were turned away or whose time ran out faced the same limited choices that battered women confronted before there was a movement to shelter them: to return home and face renewed attacks or seek temporary respite with friends, relatives, or parents. As government-sponsored shelters spread during the 1980s, a backlash against them emerged. "Pro-family" organizations sought to limit local, state, and federal funding for shelters, and police referrals of victims to them. These critics contended that shelter workers tended to be "homewreckers" who contributed to the breakup of marriages by encouraging victims to divorce their abusive husbands (see Stone, 1984; and Pleck, 1989). Actually most women who took refuge in a shelter eventually returned to live with their abusive mates again, and many of them suffered additional beatings, according to limited follow-up studies by researchers attempting to assess the effectiveness of this method of intervention (Dutton-Douglas and Dionne, 1991). About 1,900 shelters were operating around the country at the end of the 1990s ("Domestic Abusers," 1999).

As might be anticipated the battered women who flee their violent mates and seek refuge in government-sponsored shelters tend to be the poorest and most desperate of all. Two surveys of women seeking emergency housing estimated that these women were suffering between 60 and 70 beatings per year, whereas the average victim endured 6 per year. They also differed from the "norm" in another way: These targets of routine beatings rarely dared to fight back (see Straus, 1991).

Battered Women and the Criminal Justice System: Violence Is Violence, or Is It?

> **A** woman is beaten by her husband hundreds of times. She divorces him and then testifies against him in court. He is sent to prison and vows to get even with her some day. A note is placed in his file that she must be warned before he is released from custody. One day he is let out for a brief furlough but she is not contacted. He catches her by surprise at home and murders her. (Pollitt, 1989)

Historically, battered women seeking help from the criminal justice system were regularly maltreated, discouraged, disappointed, and repeatedly injured as the authorities stood idly by because a double standard prevailed. Battering was treated as special (in a negative sense) by police departments, prosecutors, and courts. These assaults were not considered to be "real" crimes because the violence was not unleashed by strangers. The dominant noninterventionist ideology recommended that the long arm of the law shouldn't reach into the sanctuary of the home and intrude into private family squabbles between spouses unless the fighting approached life-threatening levels. Otherwise, battered women were urged to endure their lot and preserve their marriages by forgiving and forgetting.

The consciousness-raising efforts undertaken by activists in the battered women's movement have successfully convinced many people that a hands-off policy endangers victims who feel trapped in abusive relationships. Women in distress needed, and were entitled to, the constitution's pledge of "equal protection under the law." The marriage license did not grant husbands a license to hit their wives. Fights between partners could have grave consequences when left to fester and smolder. Instead of fading away the conflicts could escalate in intensity and lead to severe injuries—usually for the woman, less often for the tormentor (see Schechter, 1982).

Once the public as well as criminal justice officials became convinced that intervention was the proper course of action, the question arose "What type of response would lead to the desired results—that the violent men would cease and desist and change their ways?" Three longstanding options were explored: merely separate the combatants, arrest the assailant, or refer the couple to marital counseling. Each choice had its possibilities and shortcomings. Battered women, their advocates, and victimologists are still divided over how best to respond to the problem: whether to pursue a legalistic course of action that depends on a quick resort to criminal justice solutions or to follow a social service approach that relies on counseling and reconciliation (see Sherman, 1986; Fagan, 1988; Gondolf, 1988; Ohlin and Tonry, 1989; Pleck, 1989; Buzawa and Buzawa, 1990; Roberts, 1990; Bouza, 1991; Bowman, 1992; Hilton, 1993; Klein et al., 1997; Healey and Smith, 1998; Jasinski and Williams, 1998; and Malefyt et al., 1998).

The "preserve the family" way of handling domestic violence was the favored approach during the 1950s and 1960s. It proposes that the primary objective of any outside intervention should be to restore harmony to the marriage. That means salvage the relationship, keep the family intact, heal its wounds, and foster its nurturing potentials. Couples locked into ongoing bitter conflicts need to see counselors who can mediate their disputes and build on the underlying strengths of their relationship. Advocates of this therapeutic, nonadversarial, pro-reconciliation approach presume that many battered women are not totally innocent victims. They are partly to blame for being the first to resort to force or at least for provoking their husbands' ire. Such cases of shared responsibility are not well handled by the courts with their emphasis on total guilt or complete innocence, conviction or acquittal, and victory or defeat. But seeking professional assistance is a long-term approach that seems promising only if a strong underlying bond persists, if the victims are not afraid to be candid during therapy sessions, and only if the aggressors are motivated and committed to voluntarily participating and to reforming their behaviors. Also, this reliance on social service agencies and mediation has been criticized for trivializing or condoning what might be serious criminal violence, for assuming shared responsibility, and for disregarding glaring inequalities in power relations between the two parties in their "negotiations." Because their instability is deemed to be "individual," "personal," and "peculiar," this approach downplays the seriousness and pervasiveness of wife beating as a social problem inextricably connected to family life, contemporary culture, and gender relations.

The legalistic approach has been in favor since the 1980s. It argues that violence is violence, regardless of who the offender is and what his relationship with the victim might be. Criminalizing spouse abuse entails arresting the wrongdoer, and if convicted following up with a fine and/or a jail term coupled with compulsory treatment in a batterers' anger management therapy group during a period of probation. The approach rests on these tenets: Separate the parties, rescue and protect the injured, and punish but also rehabilitate the aggressor. The philosophical underpinnings of the legalistic approach are that the state has a responsibility to enforce public morality as codified in law, and that the government has a duty to intervene when vulnerable individuals are in danger and reach out to the authorities for help. Adherents of this approach fault the criminal justice system for not taking violence between intimates as seriously as violence between strangers. Too often assailants are not arrested; or if the police take them into custody, charges are not filed or are later dropped; or if prosecutors achieve convictions, judges impose very lenient sentences. Proponents of the legalistic approach advocate reliance on the civil remedy of an order of protection (also called a restraining order) backed by criminal penalties to discourage a batterer from harassing, stalking, and striking again until he has undergone a cure or accepted a divorce. Arresting the aggressor might serve as a deterrent to further abuse, provided that the man learns the intended lesson from a night in a police holding cell and a day in court. But it is considered a risky strategy that could turn out to be counterproductive. Once he returns home infuriated, he might escalate the ferocity of his attacks against his partner who has gotten him in trouble. Prosecution could be a waste of precious resources and court time, especially if the victim changes her mind about pressing charges, forgives her mate, and bails him out of jail. Incarceration can be self-defeating because locking up the breadwinner means he cannot provide a steady income for his economically dependent wife and children.

Just temporarily separating the two parties might not have any lasting impact. If officers summoned by the neighbors or by the victim simply demand of the aggressor that he leave the premises and not return until he has regained his temper, nothing much might come out of this brush with the law. Only if the man was acting out of character (perhaps due to unusual disinhibition from heavy drinking) would a brief cooling-off period resolve matters (see Davies et al., 1998).

The Police Response Police officers always have found breaking up fights between husbands and wives to be an unpleasant, thankless, and dangerous assignment. In the past, departmental policies governing domestic disturbances stressed preserving the peace. The preferred course of action for officers who responded to calls about lovers' quarrels was to pressure the participants to call a halt and then "kiss and make up." If that failed, the officer might have insisted that the enraged man vacate the premises until he regained his composure. If the family was known to have been the site of a ruckus in the past, the couple might have been referred to counseling. Officers routinely failed to advise victims of their rights to file complaints because they identified with their male counterparts and assumed that the females either provoked the fights or subconsciously enjoyed the beatings. Only as a last resort—if the women's injuries were so severe as to require surgical sutures (the "stitch rule")—would officers make an arrest (Rhode, 1989).

A field experiment conducted in Minneapolis, Minnesota, during the early 1980s aimed to find out which course of action produced the lowest recidivism rate. Officers followed a randomly selected option—either compel the batterer to take a walk and cool off, refer the couple to counseling, or arrest the aggressor—before they rang the doorbell (unless they discovered clear evidence of a felonious assault). For the next 6 months, researchers surveyed the victims by telephone about any further fighting and monitored that address for additional domestic disturbance calls. The social experiment's findings indicated that arrested offenders were about half as likely to assault their partners again (13% did during the follow-up period) as those men who only were forced to leave their homes to cool off (26% of them were recidivists). Those couples who were referred to counseling suffered a relapse rate in between these two extremes (18% had another violent fight). These results led the researchers to conclude that police departments should adopt a "presumption of arrest" policy unless good reasons convinced the officers at the scene that taking the assailant into custody would be counterproductive (Sherman and Berk, 1984).

As the findings of this social experiment became widely publicized, many police departments shifted away from their past practice of selective enforcement based on the officers' exercise of discretion toward an officially announced policy of full enforcement without discretion. They issued mandatory, or "pro-arrest" directives, even though the researchers had recommended a presumptive or preference for arrest stance. Furthermore, the same lower recidivism rate for arrested men did not materialize when the experiment was replicated in other cities (as it must be in social science to establish external validity, which means that the findings can be generalized with confidence to other situations). In fact, the results from five replication sites suggested that arresting certain men (who were poor, unemployed, and without much of a stake in conforming to societal standards) may cause them to behave worse toward their mates in the future. Only batterers who were employed, well educated, and married to their partners (not just living together) seemed to be shaken and deterred by being arrested (see Sherman, Berk, and Smith, 1992; and Berk, Campbell, Klap, and Western, 1992).

The widespread adoption of pro-arrest policies required retraining and a change in state laws. Police officers are empowered to make a probable cause warrantless arrest for a domestic violence misdemeanor not committed in their presence only if there are visible signs of injury, if a dangerous weapon was involved, if the officers believe the violence will continue after they depart, if the police have prior knowledge of the offender's predilection for violence, or if an order of protection was violated (Bouza, 1991). In many states, officers must write up a complete report, transport injured victims to a nearby hospital, supervise the eviction of abusers from their strife-torn homes, and inform victims of their legal rights by reading or presenting a written list. In most places the victim does not have to be married to the offender to receive these forms of protection (Hendricks, 1992).

Although the law is now supposed to be on the side of battered women, in some jurisdictions glaring problems remain. Evaluations of actual practices showed that the local police often were not arresting violent men (Bouza, 1991; Steinman, 1991; Ferraro, 1992; Miller, 1992; Senate Committee on the Judiciary, 1993).

The Prosecutorial Response After deciding whether or not to call the police, the next dilemma a battered woman faces concerns prosecution: Should she keep up the pressure and get him into further trouble, thereby jeopardizing the continuation of the relationship? Or should she withdraw her complaint and permit her violent mate to come home? Historically, many prosecutors have discouraged women from pressing charges because they are concerned about their office's conviction rates and don't want to be committed to pursuing cases that are difficult to prove. They also have viewed domestic violence cases as minor disputes that are private matters that don't merit expenditures from their tight budgets and ought to be diverted into mediation (since many victims presumably share responsibility or want to try to salvage the relationship). A woman might anticipate that punishing her mate will be counterproductive, harming her and their children as well, or she may fear his fury when he is released or prefer that he receive treatment rather than punishment.

In some jurisdictions where spouse abuse is taken more seriously, prosecutors have simplified procedures for filing complaints, set up special units staffed with trained assistant district attorneys, provided supportive victim-witness assistance programs and advocates, and devised more sentencing options. In other jurisdictions most domestic violence cases are dismissed; of the remainder, most are bargained down to lesser offenses, and most of these convictions result in a sentence of probation, perhaps coupled with mandatory participation in some aggression-control program. Because many women change their minds about pressing charges or are manipulated or intimidated by their violent mates to drop the charges, some jurisdictions have established procedures to go forward without the victim's testimony by relying solely on the evidence (911 tapes of calls for help, eyewitness accounts, hospital reports, incriminating statements by the defendants). Other jurisdictions adopting this "no-drop"approach have gone as far as mandating victim cooperation and threatening women with contempt-of-court proceedings if they set the legal machinery into motion and then decide they don't want to follow through and testify. However, the absence of the accuser usually results in dropped charges, dismissed cases, or the acquittal of the accused (Bouza, 1991; Cahn and Lerman, 1991; Ferraro, 1992; and Davis and Smith, 1995).

The Judicial Response The final set of obstacles facing victims arises from their attempts to get the courts to act in their best interests. Judges seeking to dispose of cases and clear their calendars are reluctant to clog up the system with long and drawn-out spouse abuse cases. But there are a number of steps dedicated judges can take to assist victims: accede to their wishes that bail either be made low or kept high, or revoked if reprisals occur; speed up case processing by avoiding continuances; and exercise their judicial authority to issue **orders of protection** or **restraining orders,** which are intended to shield victims from further attacks. These court orders are supposed to grant victims immediate relief by enjoining abusers from entering the battered women's sphere of activity. A judge's order can evict and bar an assailant from their shared residence; prohibit any contacts, threats, harassment, or stalking; limit his supervised child visitation rights; require him to pay child support; and compel him to enter treatment. In the interest of the victim's immediate safety, a temporary order of protection can be handed down in the defendant's absence if there is insufficient time to grant notice and hold a hearing. (After a proceeding where both parties have an opportunity to present their versions of events, the temporary order may become permanent for up to a year.)

Since the orders are issued in civil court, the aim is separation of the disputants and not punishment, and the standard of proof is a preponderance of the evidence, not guilt beyond a reasonable doubt. Violating a court order of protection can be a civil or criminal offense that subjects the trespasser to immediate arrest. However, criminal justice officials and advocates for battered women have serious doubts about whether orders of protection are now, or can ever be, truly effective. In theory, stay-away orders straddle the middle ground between inaction (no arrest, dropped charges, probation) and overreaction (incarceration that results in escalating tensions, a criminal record, diminished job opportunities, and reduced financial support for the family). In practice, the greatest problem is that civil orders are not vigorously enforced by many police departments, especially in high-crime urban areas (Finn, 1991; Ferraro, 1992; Buzawa and Buzawa, 1996). However, the overwhelming majority of victims who had received a temporary or permanent order of protection reported that they felt better about themselves and felt safer when surveyed in the mid-1990s (Keilitz, et al., 1997). The stay-away stipulation of restraining orders is enforced using cell phones, electronic ankle bracelets, and alarm systems in some jurisdictions (Herszenhorn, 1999).

Preventing Battering

As always, reliance on criminal justice solutions may bring about temporary relief in specific cases and may even resolve particular conflicts among certain couples, but working with abusers and their victims does not address the root causes of the problem.

According to activists in the battered women's movement, it is a mistake to attempt to "pathologize" spouse abuse as a problem that burdens just a limited number of emotionally unstable couples. But it is also incorrect to try to normalize family violence as an inevitable by-product of unavoidable conflicts that occasionally arise in every intimate relationship.

Social scientists have developed a variety of competing explanations to account for the widespread problem of partner abuse (see Gelles, 1987; Hotaling et al., 1988). Those who apply exchange theory start out with the explanation that in a couple each partner supplies the other with valued services and benefits. The problem arises when a domineering person employs force to obtain his goals and discovers that the gains outweigh the losses (rough treatment pays off). In nuclear families where couples live in isolation from the scrutiny and support of others, the benefits of violence can exceed the costs because the authorities are reluctant to violate the privacy of intimates. Similarly, a resource theory analysis proposes that decision-making power within a family flows from the income, property, contacts, and prestige that each partner contributes to the relationship. Because men have advantages in the outside economy, they command much more power in most families, leaving the women in a subordinate and therefore vulnerable position. According to the subculture-of-violence theory, battering occurs more often in poverty-stricken families where the ready resort to physical force to settle disputes is more acceptable than among the middle classes, who purportedly believe in negotiation and compromise. The problem of male violence, according to social learning theory, arises because acting aggressively is generally taught and encouraged, along with female passivity and resignation, as part of sex-role socialization. Intergenerational transmission of wife beating occurs when boys grow up watching their fathers beat their mothers during times of stress or bouts of heavy drinking. The root causes lie in the traditions of patriarchy (a system of male dominance), according to feminist theory. The division of domestic labor in families places the husband in the dominant role, assigning him male prerogatives, and the wife in a subordinate position, burdening her with female duties. These distinctions are legitimized by religion and the state, as symbolized by the wife's marriage vows to "love, honor, and obey" her husband. Some couples are on a collision course whenever the "head of the household" feels that his wife's assertions of independence are threatening his privileges and social status as protector and provider, and he may hit her in order to regain control. In other couples, overly dependent, passive, and submissive wives serve as inviting targets for displaced aggression and misplaced blame. They seem resigned, crushed, and defeated and have learned to feel helpless and trapped because escape seems impossible: emotionally destructive to the children, economically disastrous, and likely to trigger more violence. In a society controlled by giant corporations and large government bureaucracies, some men seize upon domination over their wives and children as a substitute for real autonomy in their personal lives. As long as women with children are financially dependent upon men and both sexes are raised to expect male aggression and female passivity, woman battering will persist as a serious social problem (see Dobash and Dobash, 1979; Schechter, 1982; Walker, 1984; Yllo and Bograd, 1988; Rhode, 1989; Viano, 1992; and Healey and Smith, 1998).

The Rediscovery of Other Victims of Beatings

Once wife beating was recognized as a pervasive problem, two other rediscoveries became inevitable. First, partner abuse is not limited to heterosexual couples. It can also break out in intimate relations between members of the same sex. Second, in some couples the presumed victim-offender relationship is reversed: The woman is the aggressor and the man is the injured party.

Battering Within Same-Sex Relationships A predictable rediscovery was that physical fighting can mar the intimate relationships between gay men and between lesbians as well. Understandably there was initial reluctance and resistance within the homosexual community to publicly concede that partner abuse took place in same-sex love affairs, for two reasons. Some feared that it would be exploited to fuel homophobia. Others were concerned that the discovery of violence in male-male or female-female relationships would cause wife beating to be reconceptualized. Battering would be considered to be an outgrowth of the way power and privilege are exercised in any and all intimate relationships; domestic violence would no longer be viewed as strictly the result of patriarchal male dominance over females. Partner abuse in gay and lesbian couples is suspected to occur about as frequently as within heterosexual relationships.

However, gay and lesbian victims have fewer options and legal rights than do their heterosexual counterparts. As a result, they often turn to programs intended to assist victims of hate crimes such as gay bashings committed by strangers (see Island and Letellier, 1991; Renzetti, 1992; King, 1993; Haugrud, Gratch, and Magruder, 1997; Burke, 1998; Cruz and Firestone, 1998; and Jackson, 1998).

The Controversy Surrounding Battered Husbands The attention paid to wife beating led inevitably to the rediscovery of husband beating. Starting in the late 1970s, several social scientists began to challenge the assumption that men were virtually always the initiators and the victors in lovers' quarrels. They reported that their data on family violence had uncovered an overlooked problem within spouse abuse—man battering. Survey findings revealed that there was some truth to the old cartoon images of women slapping men's faces, or wives chasing husbands with rolling pins or throwing dishes at them. Research indicated that women attacked the men in their lives (by slapping, kicking, biting, punching, throwing something, or threatening with a weapon) about as often as the men assaulted the women they professed to love (see Steinmetz, 1978a; Straus and Gelles, 1986; Mignon, 1998; and Straus, 1999).

But skeptics argued that the sequence of events was not recorded in the surveys cited above and that much of the self-reported "violence" by women was probably unleashed in response to male provocations or carried out in self-defense, and did not qualify as aggressive initiatives. Because men tend to be bigger and stronger than their mates, their use of physical force is far more likely to bring about serious injuries. Perhaps for every battered woman there exists an abused man when it comes to minor uses of force (pushing and shoving). But the overwhelming majority of instances of "severe aggression" in which someone winds up in a hospital emergency room are male-on-female offenses. Therefore, husband abuse should not be mistakenly "equated" with wife abuse, and a recognition that men can be injured too should not be used to undercut the urgency of tackling the much more pressing issue of women battering (see Pleck et al., 1978; Lewin, 1992; and Cose, 1994).

Battered men face several unique problems. First of all, most are reluctant to report their plight to the authorities. If they call the police, they face either disbelief or mockery. The disbelief can cause officers to stereotypically presume they were the initiators and aggressors and to arrest them. They face ridicule for not being able to "control" their mates (unless the battered men are elderly or physically infirm). Since men traditionally are supposed to be physically adept and to "take charge of situations," for battered husbands to publicly admit that their wives get the best of them in family fights is to confess that they are not living up to these "manly" standards. Their failure to measure up to the "head of the household" stereotype might add to their confusion and emotional distress. This special stigma may inhibit them from seeking help and can only contribute to their sense of isolation. Second, if they overcome their feelings of inadequacy, self-loathing, and shame, and dare to come forward, they do not have access to the same resources now available to battered women, especially support groups, professional counseling, and temporary shelters. The first sanctuary for battered men was established in 1993 in St. Paul, Minnesota, (where the first women's shelter was set up over 20 years earlier). It housed more than 50 men in its first 6 months. However, these battered husbands had one crucial advantage compared to battered wives: Their ability to support themselves financially probably encouraged many of them to leave the troubled relationship. And when they separated they were rarely stalked, brought back, and beaten again (Chavez, 1992; Lewin, 1992; Cose, 1994; Straus, 1999). As a result of gender-neutral laws targeting the "primary aggressor" and mandatory arrest policies, women make up one quarter or more of all arrestees for domestic violence in some jurisdictions (Goldberg, 1999; Young, 1999).

VICTIMS OF SEXUAL ASSAULT

The Rediscovery of the Plight of Rape Victims

Forcible rape is surely one of the most heinous violent crimes imaginable, and yet for centuries the social reaction to this offense showed little regard for the well-being of the victim. Rape was handled as an offense that harmed the interests of a father or husband rather than the emotional and physical health of the daughter or wife herself. Some rapists were punished severely, but others went unprosecuted, depending on the status of the victim and the accused offender. In biblical times a man could be put to death for the rape of a virgin; but if a married woman was raped, she could be executed too because she was considered blameworthy (unless her husband intervened on her behalf). During medieval times a man seeking upward mobility might engage in "heiress stealing"—abduct and then rape a young woman from a wealthy family in order to compel her to agree to be his bride. As feudalism evolved only the rape of a woman from the nobility was punishable; forcing a peasant woman to submit was not considered a crime. In the Old South a black man merely accused of raping a white woman faced the prospect of execution, or even a lynching without a trial. In wartime the enemy's women are enjoyed by the conquering soldiers as the spoils of victory (see Brownmiller, 1975; and Siegel, 1998).

At the start of the 1970s, feminists fighting for the rights of women to control their own bodies (reproductive rights via contraception and abortion) contributed to the rediscovery of rape victims. Instead of being regarded as some man's "damaged goods," they were recognized as individuals suffering from terrible violations of their personhood who deserved respect, support, assistance, and protection from further harm. The pro-victim antirape movement exposed a legacy of injustice, routine abuse, and systematic neglect: Because of class, race, and gender discrimination, most women did not report the offenses to the authorities, and of the incidents that were reported most went unpunished. Rape was more than a personal tragedy, it was a social problem and a political issue, feminists argued. They interpreted sexual assaults as skirmishes in what had been traditionally referred to as the "unending battle of the sexes." Forcible rapes functioned as acts of terrorism that intimidated all women and served to keep them in their "proper place"—outside of male territorial preserves and yet subordinate to males (dependent upon "good" men for protection against "bad" men). A sexual assault symbolized how a male could exploit his power differential (his superior physical force) to have his way in a "man's world." The handling of rape cases dramatized how the men who ran the criminal justice system could not be trusted to act in behalf of the interests of victimized women. Invariably, the all-male (until recently) police, prosecution, judiciary, and juries became preoccupied with the relationship between the two parties (especially their social class, race/ethnicity, prior contacts, and her alleged blameworthiness) rather than the violence surrounding the sexual assault (see Russell, 1975; Griffin, 1979; Rhode, 1989; and Muehlenhard et al., 1992).

Through consciousness-raising groups and public speakouts, the antirape movement redefined the prevailing image of the crime and of its victims. Over the ages, rape had been pictured as an act of lust and an outpouring of uncontrollable sexual urges. This old view seems plausible only if the physical injuries sustained by these "objects of desire" are totally ignored. The violence surrounding the sexual assault—before, during, and after it ends—betrays its true nature: an attack upon the victim's dignity and personhood for the purpose of domination and subjugation. The assailant reveals his hatred and contempt for all females and certainly not his "passion" or "love" for a particular girl or woman, according to the view that rape is really all about power and control.

The word **rape** comes from the Latin **rapere,** which means "to take by force." In English common law the crime was called "carnal knowledge" but the unwanted intrusion could be committed by a male only against a female who was not his wife or cohabiting lover. Recent laws in each state go beyond the limitations of the old common-law definition. The crime is now gender-neutral, so men can be victims too (usually of other men). Forced intercourse is not the only punishable type of violation. Other unwanted invasions of the body or forced participation in sexual acts are covered by statutes prohibiting "sexual assaults" and "sexual battery." The phrase "forcible rape" implies that the target reasonably fears bodily harm if she (or he) refuses to acquiesce. Lack of consent therefore is the key factor that distinguishes a sexual assault from a merely unpleasant sexual experience. "Aggravated" rape is penalized more severely since it involves more than one assailant, and/or the use of a weapon, and/or the infliction of additional wounds besides the unwanted penetration. Sexual assaults short of rape (for example, unwelcomed sexual contacts like fondling) carry a lesser penalty. Taking sexual advantage of a person who is mentally retarded or unable to give meaningful consent because she (or he) is drugged, drunk, or unconscious (whether or not this altered state was induced by the offender) is illegal as well. (Statutory rape is an unlawful, exploitive act in which a minor below the legal age of consent voluntarily engages in sexual intercourse.)

"Real Rapes" and "Date Rapes"

Although all sexual violations involve coercion of an unwilling person in terms of the law, not all of these assaults qualify as "real rapes" in terms of public opinion. Surely, widespread confusion over what constitutes "real rape" accounts for some of the controversy that still surrounds the handling of certain cases. Many people have trouble distinguishing forced intercourse from "engaging in sex." As a result, when a woman summons up the courage to go public and claims to have been penetrated against her will, some people might conjure up images of "lovemaking" rather than "forcible bodily invasion."

"Real rapes" (in the language of sociology, "ideal types" in the sense that they are the clearest examples) are readily identifiable without question or doubt. Real rapes are perpetrated against unsuspecting females who are ambushed in blitz attacks. Real rapes have several features. The offender is a complete stranger to the victim. He is heavily armed and leaps out of the darkness to surprise his prey. The victim is completely virtuous and above reproach—perhaps too young, too old, or too inexperienced to be faulted in any way for attracting his attention. At the time, she is engaged in some "wholesome" activity that can't be criticized. Even though she faces grave dangers, she dares to fight back, resists to her utmost, and suffers severe physical injuries in a futile attempt to fend him off. Eyewitnesses glimpse parts of the struggle and hear her cries for help. As soon as she escapes from his clutches, she reports the crime to the police. Detectives find forensic evidence that backs up all her charges that she was caught off guard, confronted with a weapon, brutally assaulted, overpowered, and compelled to submit to his demands. Finally, the assailant, who is obviously a deeply disturbed predator, quickly confesses when captured (see Estrich, 1986). Few people would have any difficulty conceding that a "real rape" that mirrors many of these characteristics is one of the worst experiences that a woman can suffer. Detectives, prosecutors, juries, and judges agree that victims of such heinous crimes deserve to be treated with dignity and sensitivity within the criminal justice process and that such vicious assailants must be removed from society and severely punished.

The problem for most rape victims is that the facts in their cases usually fall short, in one way or another, of the unambiguous standards that characterize a "real rape." As a result, the accusers' versions of events are likely to be questioned when essential elements are missing (for example, no brandishing of a weapon, no infliction of physical injuries, no ferocious struggle or desperate screams, and/or no corroboration by eyewitnesses or forensic tests). Doubts quickly surface if some crucial defining features of "real rapes" are missing (perhaps the victim knows the accused or she fails to meet the old-fashioned criterion of being "virtuous" or she does not report the attack for days or weeks). As a consequence of these ambiguities, the man she accuses is less likely to be arrested, prosecuted, and convicted.

The following real-life, headline-generating story was not considered a "real rape" by many people, including jurors who acquitted the alleged assailant:

> **A** young man from a prominent family meets a woman late at night at a fashionable cocktail lounge. They share some drinks, dance, and flirt. She returns to the oceanfront home where he is vacationing and they take a walk on the deserted moonlit beach at three in the morning. They embrace, he sheds his clothes, takes a brief swim, and then . . . throws her down on the sand, overpowers her, and violates her, she insists. (Gibbs, 1991)

Some would argue that if forced intercourse is preceded by a series of consensual acts with sexual overtones, her "contributory behavior" makes the nature of the crime less serious and it should be penalized less severely than an ambush attack on an unsuspecting depersonalized target. Others insist that it makes no difference if the victim and the offender knew each other and interacted warmly, even passionately, prior to the incident. The encounter cannot be written off as a case of miscommunication, a terrible misunderstanding, or an instance of a woman having regrets for the way she behaved the night before. What counts is that she was stripped of control, denied the right to make a crucial decision, and compelled to submit to someone else's sexual demands (Gibbs, 1991). Until the late 1980s most prosecutors were very reluctant to move forward, press charges, and go to trial on a date rape case in which there were no eyewitnesses, no bruises from a beating, and no signs of a fierce struggle. Yet forced sex arising out of a romantic encounter meets the legal definition of rape, which hinges on the use of physical coercion against a nonconsenting person, and not on the previous relationship between the accuser and the accused (see Estrich, 1993a; and Spears and Spohn, 1997).

The Consequences of Being Sexually Assaulted

Victimologists have studied the plight of rape victims intensively for several decades. Researchers aim to assess the nature of the suffering and to discover ways of speeding up the recovery process (see McCahill, Williams, and Fischman, 1979; APA Task Force, 1984; Girelli et al., 1986; Burt and Katz, 1987; Allison and Wrightsman, 1993; Wiehe and Richards, 1995; and Giannelli, 1997). Being raped is almost always shattering to the victim, at least for a time. The ordeal challenges and may even transform her identity and the assumptions she makes about the world. The emotional impact is manifested largely as fear, anxiety, depression, sexual dysfunction, and feelings of isolation. The social impact shows up as the loss of illusions about invulnerability and immortality: the destruction of any sense of predictability within her environment and of the meaningfulness of events in her life, and a decline in her own sense of self-worth. The tribulation of being treated as an object instead of a person may plunge her into a "rape crisis syndrome." The acute initial phase of this syndrome lasts for about 2 or 3 weeks immediately following the sexual attack. The typical short-term reactions to being violated and humiliated are revulsion, shock, anger, fury, self-recrimination, fear, sorrow, and total disorientation. Victims often suffer from nausea, tension headaches, and an inability to sleep. The second phase, in which the victim's personality reintegrates, can last much longer and is characterized by recurring nightmares, defensive reactions, and strains in relationships with men. Many victims try to reorganize their daily lives by changing jobs, moving to a new location, dropping out of college, and limiting personal contacts. Lingering effects often include loss of sexual desire and the development of phobias: fear of being indoors as well as going outdoors, of being alone as well as part of crowds, and of persons approaching stealthily from behind (Burgess and Holmstrom, 1974; Giannelli, 1997; Resick and Nishith, 1997).

Like others who are stunned by an unexpected life-threatening ordeal, rape victims can suffer from a condition called posttraumatic stress disorder (PTSD) during the crime's immediate aftermath. They may reexperience the attack over and over again in daydreams, flashbacks, or nightmares. Other symptoms include feeling different, a desire to avoid things that serve as reminders of the trauma, a general lack of interest or enthusiasm, an inability to concentrate, and increased irritability (Williams, 1987). Recognizing the severe consequences of the crime for the person turned into a sex object should dispel any notions that rape is an act of passion rather than of subjugation, and demolish any beliefs that the unwilling target somehow invited, secretly desired, or deserved such rough handling.

Even though most rapes are not completed (according to the yearly *NCVS* surveys, about two thirds are not), females who thwart their assailants' intentions still suffer serious psychological scars. In fact, women who endured attempted rapes were more likely to contemplate suicide and to try to kill themselves than women who suffered completed rapes, according to the results of a telephone survey carried out in South Carolina (Kilpatrick, 1985).

Estimates of the Incidence, Prevalence, and Seriousness of Rape

Victimologists and criminologists routinely point out that official statistics usually do not accurately indicate how many crimes of a specific kind are committed each year because many victims do not report incidents to the police. When it comes to rape, it is particularly likely that even the most carefully derived estimates could be way off. Figures from the two government sources, the FBI's *UCR* and the BJS's *NCVS,* are both indisputably incomplete. The *UCR* statistics are gross underestimates because a large percentage of sexual assault victims do not tell the authorities about their plight. Roughly half of all victims who were willing to discuss incidents with *NCVS* survey interviewers did not inform the police, annual BJS findings reveal. The statistics compiled by the *NCVS* were supposed to circumvent this problem of nonreporting by counting all disclosed incidents, whether or not a complaint was filed with the local police (Bachman, 1998).

But another methodological question arose: What percent of people who are raped are willing to reveal this information to government interviewers? Even though it was more accurate than the *UCR,* the *NCVS* underestimated the true dimensions of the problem, many victimologists suspected. The manner in which the data was gathered for the *NCVS* discouraged some individuals from discussing what happened to them. Although confidentiality was pledged, anonymity was compromised by face-to-face questioning. Surely, some girls and women were very reluctant to speak openly about such incidents, especially in the presence of other family members. Some respondents might feel uncomfortable delving into such a sensitive subject with any stranger, especially a male interviewer, particularly if his age, class, or ethnicity differ from that of the respondent. Some incidents that could legally be classified as rapes may not be defined as crimes by the females who experienced them, especially if the aggressor was an acquaintance and he used force or made threats but was not brutally violent. Screening questions were worded in roundabout ways; the term "sexual attack" was used but not spelled out graphically with examples. The survey's working definition excluded disclosures about marital rapes; acts of forcible sodomy to other parts of the body; and incidents in which the perpetrator took advantage of a person's intoxicated state, mental illness, or mental retardation. Finally, "series victimizations" (repeated rapes, generally by an intimate or acquaintance) were not counted as separate incidents (Koss, 1992).

In 1992, the BJS redesigned the survey's questionnaire (and changed its name from the *National Crime Survey* to the *National Crime Victimization Survey*). The original set of questions (used from 1973 until 1992) never bluntly asked about rapes because the subject was considered too personal, delicate, and sensitive to address directly. Interviewers only found out about these incidents if the respondent volunteered the information while thinking about physical attacks and threatened assaults. But in the redesigned questionnaire, the interviewer asks, "Has anyone attacked or threatened you in any of these ways . . . —any rape, attempted rape, or other type of sexual assault?" The interviewer follows up by saying, "Please mention it even if you were not certain it was a crime. . . . Incidents involving forced or unwanted sexual acts are often difficult to talk about. Have you been forced or coerced to engage in unwanted sexual activity by someone you didn't know before; or a casual acquaintance; or someone you know well?" Once this battery of questions was implemented (used on half of the sample), the *NCVS* estimate of the number of rapes jumped 157% for 1992 (Kindermann and Lynch, 1997).

To address some of the methodological criticisms leveled by researchers against the way the FBI's *UCR* measured rape, its data-collecting systems were changed. In 1991 a new National Incident Based Reporting System (NIBRS) definition of rape replaced the old, narrow *UCR* guideline of "carnal knowledge of a female forcibly and against her will." The FBI's NIBRS now counts sexual assaults directed against males and broadens the definition to keep track of incidents in which the person was not violated by force but was unable to give consent because of either a temporary or permanent mental or physical incapacity (due, for example, to drug-induced unconsciousness). In addition, acts of forcible sodomy that don't involve intercourse, sexual assaults carried out with an object, and forcible fondling are counted. However, most police departments across the country had not switched over to the NIBRS computerized system by the end of the 1990s, so the older ways of recording rape incidents still prevailed in the *UCR*s.

When the estimated number of rapes committed each year as measured by the *NCVS* and the *UCR* are plotted on the same set of axes, the trend lines diverge and become a source of some confusing and contradictory impressions. According to the FBI's *UCR,* the data showed an alarming, fairly steady upward trend from the early 1970s (which actually began in the mid-1960s) until the early 1990s. After the sexual violence unleashed by men against women reached an all-time high in 1992 (of 43 reported rapes for every 100,000 females in the

U.S. population), the situation reversed. For the remainder of the 1990s, the rape rate declined, as did the rate of all the other index crimes, like murder, robbery, assault, burglary, and motor vehicle theft. Therefore, after worsening for several decades, this problem also peaked and then subsided during the 1990s (see Figure 5.1).

But, according to the *NCVS,* the number of rapes disclosed to survey interviewers (as opposed to local police departments) varied from year to year in a rather choppy and unpredictable way from 1973 until 1992, although the direction of drift was clearly downward. Therefore, prior to 1992 the impressions from the two sources were exactly opposite. Rapes were becoming more frequent according to police reports and less frequent according to survey disclosures. After 1991, *NCVS* rape rates trended generally downward during the remainder of the 1990s, mirroring the decline indicated by *UCR* figures (refer back to Figure 5.1). Therefore, both monitoring systems indicated that sexual violence was becoming less of a threat to girls and women as the century drew to a close.

The discrepancy between *NCVS* and *UCR* trends until 1992 puzzled criminologists and victimologists. Some suspected that the *UCR* statistics showed an upward trend because more women were coming forward over the years to report rapes that in the past would not have been brought to the attention of the police. In particular, public attitudes toward women raped by nonstrangers were improving, so the police were learning about more assaults by dates and acquaintances (Orcutt and Faison, 1988). (However, rape reporting rates did not increase steadily until the early 1990s, according to *NCVS* figures; refer back to Table 4.1, which presents the percentages of rapes revealed to interviewers that were also reported to the police since the early 1970s.) It was also suggested that police departments were hiring female detectives who were taking the allegations of rape complainants more seriously and were investigating, documenting, and recording these kinds of incidents more carefully than in the past (Jensen and Karpos, 1993).

Although the *NCVS* figures remain underestimates, the differential risks of being raped derived from the yearly surveys are worth analyzing. The findings confirm the suspicion that various categories of girls and women face different levels of risk. The statistical portrait painted by the data indicates that the highest risks of being raped are faced by females who are in their late teens or early 20s, unmarried, living in low-income families, unemployed, black, and residing in large cities (see the first column of victimization rates in Table 5.1) (Harlow, 1991). Figures from the late 1990s reveal that the importance of these same risk factors have not changed much over the decades (see the second column in Table 5.1) (see Rennison, 1999).

As for prevalence estimates, about 15% of all women reported they had endured a completed rape, and an additional 3% had suffered an attempted rape, according to a government sponsored survey of 8,000 women and 8,000 men during the mid-1990s (Tjaden and Thoennes, 1998). That finding was higher than the 8% lifetime likelihood projected during the mid-1980s (Koppel, 1987).

One issue that many people speculate about and that has received attention from victimologists concerns whether strangers or nonstrangers pose the gravest

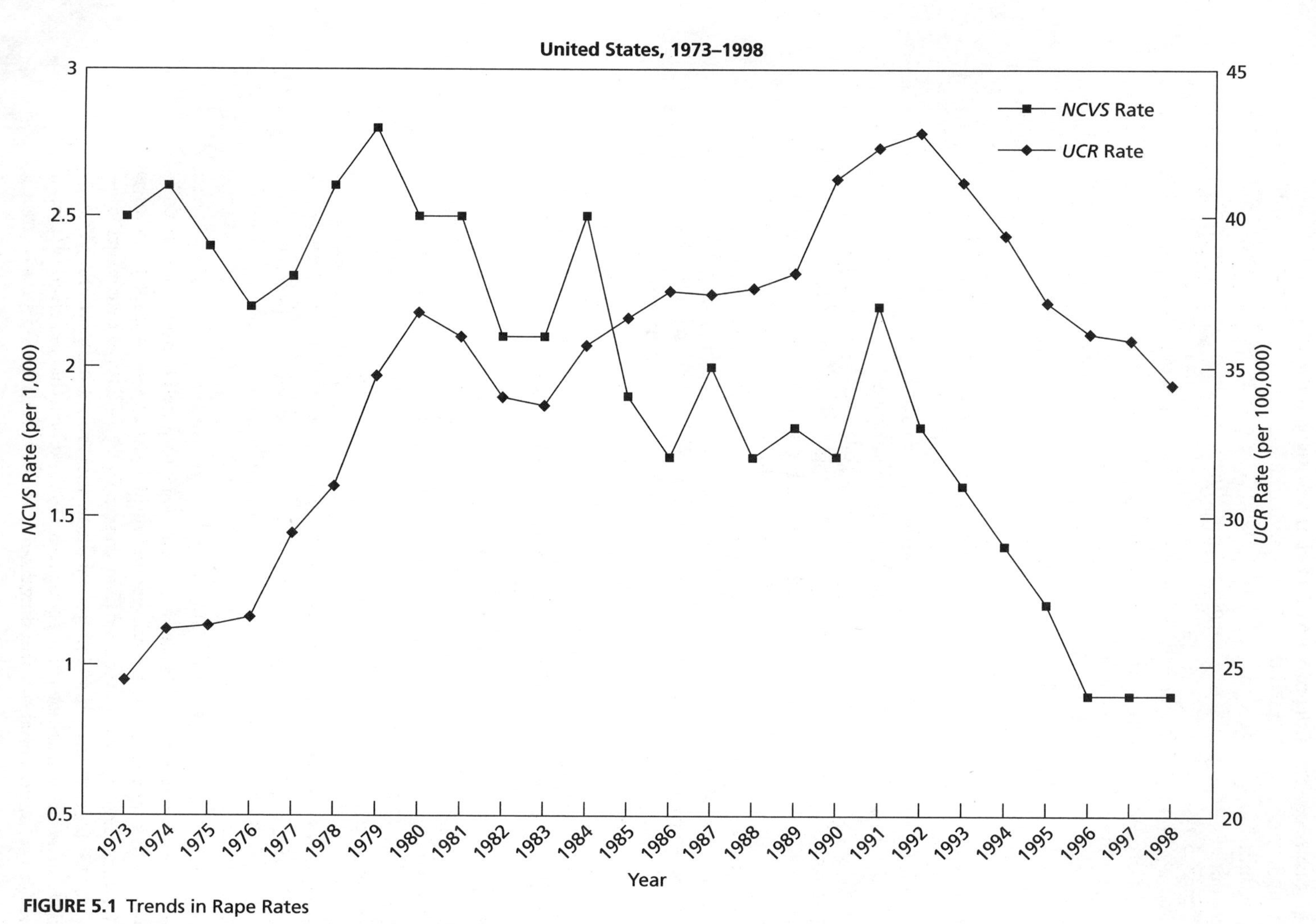

FIGURE 5.1 Trends in Rape Rates

NOTE: *UCR* counts female victims only. 1973–1991 *NCVS* rates adjusted for compatibility with redesigned 1992 survey.
SOURCES: FBI's *UCR*, 1973–1998; BJS's *NCVS*, 1973–1998

Table 5.1 Differential Risks of Being Raped and Sexually Assaulted

	Annual Rape Rate Per 1,000 Females 1973–1987	1998 Annual Rate Per 1,000 Persons
All Females	**1.6 for every 1,000**	**1.5 for every 1,000**
By age:		
12–15	2.3	3.5
16–19	4.8	5.0
20–24	4.1	4.6
25–34	2.3	1.7
35–49	0.6	0.7
50–64	0.2	0.2
65 and over	0.1	0.0
By race and ethnicity:		
White	1.5	1.5
Black	2.7	2.0
Other	1.8	0.7
Hispanic	1.5	0.8
By marital status:		
Married	0.5	0.5
Widowed	0.4	0.3
Divorced or separated	4.3	2.6
Never married	3.5	3.1
By employment status:		
Employed	1.7	N/A
Unemployed	6.2	N/A
Keeping house	0.8	N/A
Going to school	3.8	N/A
By income:		
Low	2.7	2.7*
Middle	1.2	1.5*
High	0.8	1.2*
By area of residence:		
Central cities	2.5	1.7
Suburbs	1.4	1.4
Nonmetropolitan areas	1.1	1.5

NOTES: Estimated rates were derived from an analysis of 2,515,200 rapes (832,200 completed and 1,683,000 attempted) reported by respondents to *NCVS* interviewers from 1973 until 1987. After 1992, sexual assaults are included. 1998 includes male victims; * = estimated; N/A = not available.
SOURCES: Harlow, 1991; Rennison, 1999.

threat to girls and women. Sexual assaults were somewhat more likely to be committed by someone known to the victim (55%) than by a complete stranger (44%), according to an analysis of rapes reported to *NCVS* interviewers from 1987 to 1991 (Bachman, 1994a). However, strangers were responsible for only 25% of all attacks disclosed in 1998, possibly because the redesigned survey elicited more responses about the illegal behavior of intimates (Rennison, 1999).

Statistically speaking, acquaintances, intimates, and dates seem to be the offenders much more often than sinister stalkers, intruders, and other assailants whose identities were unknown to the girls and women they ambushed.

The Controversy Over Date Rape on College Campuses

A bitter controversy broke out over the actual incidence of date rape, especially on college campuses, during the early 1990s (see Warshaw, 1988; Schreiber, 1990; Bohmer and Parrot, 1993; Faludi, 1993; and Leone and de Koster, 1995). Anti-rape activists took a maximalist stance and launched educational campaigns alerting students, college administrators, and parents to what they perceived to be an epidemic of sexual assaults in dorms, fraternity houses, and off-campus apartments. But minimalist critics pointed out that despite widespread rape awareness programs, FBI statistics monitoring crime on college campuses revealed that very few students ever filed complaints about being raped after a date. "Real" rapes by young men appeared to be rare and isolated events, skeptics insisted.

Advocates of the maximalist position argued that a date rape crisis was raging but it went unrecognized because these offenses are reported even less often than sexual assaults by strangers. Young women feel humiliated, don't want their former dates to be severely punished, anticipate that they won't be believed, and dread that they will be harshly judged, condemned, and slandered for allegedly "precipitating" the young man's out-of-control outpouring of "lust." The only way to accurately estimate the true dimensions of the problem is by administering anonymous questionnaires in which respondents who disclose intimate details about their upsetting confrontations are assured of confidentiality. For example, in one widely cited survey, over 3,000 women students at 32 colleges were presented with scenarios that described what recently reformed state statutes would designate as sexual assaults. Respondents could identify elements of the crime that resembled their own experiences, such as being plied with liquor until their judgment was so impaired that "consent" was meaningless, being physically held down, or being forced to submit after painful arm twisting. From the survey's findings, the researcher estimated that about 166 out of every 1,000 female students (a shocking 17%) suffered one or more attempted or completed rapes per year. Fewer than 5% reported the assault to the police, about 5% sought solace at a rape crisis center, and almost half told no one at all about what happened. In 84% of the cases, the victim knew the offender; in 57% of these non-stranger assaults, he was a date. Projecting a yearly incidence estimate into a lifetime prevalence estimate suggested that as many as 1 in 4 college-aged young women might have experienced an attempted rape or a completed rape since she was 14 years old (Koss, Gidyez, and Wisniewski, 1987; Koss and Harvey, 1991; Koss and Cook, 1998). Part of the date rape problem was traced back to some campus fraternities and some college athletic teams. These organizations fostered a pro-rape hypermasculine subculture among their members that devalued and degraded young women as mere faceless objects to be toyed with, sexually exploited, and then discarded (see Schwartz and DeKeseredy, 1997; Benedict, 1998; Benedict and Klein, 1998; and Martin and Hummer, 1998).

Skeptics charged that alarmists were disseminating inflated risk estimates by loosely applying the very serious term *rape* to regrettable sexual encounters that involved coercion or deceit but not force or threats of bodily harm. Cases in which a young woman felt pressured into agreeing to engage in sex (out of guilt), had lost good judgment because of drinking or drug taking, or wanted to say "No!" but was not assertive enough to stop the young man's advances were classified as rapes by maximalists adopting a definition that was too broad and vague. If the woman was "given" alcohol or drugs by the man prior to intercourse, that does not mean she was "intentionally incapacitated" as the law requires for prosecution and conviction. Verbal coercion, manipulation, deception (about being in love), false promises (of marriage), and betrayal of trust—all of which are nonviolent tactics in the male arsenal of "seduction"—are erroneously equated with "being forced to give in" but are not the same as physical assault, the use of a weapon, or a credible threat of bodily harm. These "date rapes" included in the count by maximalists actually fell into a gray area between sexual assault and consensual sex and should have been excluded, minimalists contended. Most of the women deemed victims by the maximalist researchers did not consider themselves to have been raped, and over 40% of them dated their supposed assailants again and engaged in intercourse again with them. The *NCVS* survey figure that roughly 1 female in 1,000 is raped or fends off a would-be rapist each year is much closer to the truth and puts the problem in its proper perspective. By overestimating the date rape problem, maximalists were manufacturing a crisis in order to further their social agenda of unfairly portraying all male-female relationships as inherently antagonistic and fraught with danger. Promoting such a negative image of sexuality stigmatized normal heterosexual intercourse as bordering on criminal conduct unless explicit, unambiguous consent is secured from the female partner before each escalation in intimacy. The presumed adversarial model of bold male initiatives and timid female resistance denies the reality of female desires and portrays women as naive, helpless, vulnerable, and more in need of strictly enforced protective codes of appropriate sexual behavior than of equal rights. Overestimates unnecessarily alarmed young women, trivialized those "real" rapes that are genuinely brutal, and undermined the credibility of "real" complainants. The underlying politics of the "anti–date-rape movement" actually sets back the cause of women's equality, adherents of the minimalist position contended (see Eigenberg, 1990; Gilbert, 1991; Podhoretz, 1991; Crichton, 1993; Hellman, 1993; and Roiphe, 1993).

Regardless of the actual dimensions of the threat, the tactics to discourage date rapes (like sensitizing college men to the issue) must be different from those employed to prevent stranger rapes (for example, guarding campus buildings against intruders). Efforts undertaken by college administrations include holding dating workshops during freshman orientation week, complete with reenactments of dangerous situations and role-playing exercises led by seniors; setting up rape crisis centers and fostering a climate of openness on campus that encourages students to report offenses and seek help; and issuing student-government approved guidelines and handbooks for completely consensual sexual conduct, with violations punishable by expulsion by a campus judicial committee (Crichton, 1993; Bohmer and Parrot, 1993).

How the Criminal Justice System Handles Rape Victims

Before public consciousness was raised by the antirape movement, complainants who courageously reported sex crimes were socially stigmatized. The old-fashioned notion was that good girls don't get raped, so those who do must have somehow done something to deserve their fate. Even if an unquestionably innocent victim was taken against her will, she was callously looked down upon as being "defiled" and "devalued" by the experience. Those who dared to press charges were often told that their cases were unprosecutable or unwinnable, given the unreasonably stringent legal standards required for conviction. However, as the public grew alarmed about an apparent upsurge in sexual violence, legislators became more willing to change sexist practices that reflected the moralistic assumptions of the distant past. Beginning with Minnesota and Michigan in 1974, statutes were rewritten state by state as the analysis put forward by feminists gained acceptance and as more women became lawyers and legislators and reformed the legal system from within as well as pressuring it from without (Largen, 1987).

The laws passed over the centuries and amended by judges' case-by-case decisions (common law) were not intended, and never functioned, to guarantee the safety, freedom of movement, and peace of mind of women. The choice of terms like "fallen," "ravaged," and "despoiled" to describe rape victims betrayed the antiquated attitudes of men toward girls and women: that they were the "property" of their fathers or husbands who lost "market value" if they were "violated." Rape laws reflected and reinforced the prevailing double standards regarding appropriate forms of sexual conduct and sex-based roles for females and males (LeGrande, 1973). Built-in antivictim biases that shaped the way cases were investigated and prosecuted were most evident in the corroboration rule, the resistance requirement, and the practice of inquiring into the victim's sexual history.

Over the decades the pro-victim antirape movement has tried to eliminate these unfair roadblocks on the path to justice. Today, cautious optimists emphasize how much progress has been made in dismantling the institutionalized discrimination that put victims at such an unusual disadvantage in the not-too-distant past (see Fairstein, 1993). Critics point out how many traditional antivictim practices persist within the justice system. The degree of success of efforts by the antirape movement can be evaluated with reference to the following criteria: improvements in public attitudes regarding a woman's right to sexual autonomy, free from coercion; gains in the willingness of victims to report the crimes and press charges; declines in the perceptions of complainants that the entire fact-finding and decision-making process is emotionally painful and degrading; and increases in the rates of arrest, prosecution, conviction, and incarceration of rapists (see Goldberg-Ambrose, 1992; Spohn and Horney, 1992; and Bachman and Paternoster, 1993).

The Controversy Over Unfounded Accusations Rape has always been in a class by itself in one peculiar way: The complainant immediately confronts a credibility issue. Both the law and public opinion show great concern about the danger of false accusations. Knowingly and maliciously filing a false complaint with the police and testifying falsely are punishable acts no matter what the crime, but these fears about baseless charges arise almost automatically in rape cases. Special safeguards to protect male defendants—which female accusers had to surmount—were built right into the law (see MacDonald and Michaud, 1995). Two types of errors are always possible: honest mistakes and deliberate acts of perjury intended to hide the truth. A complainant acting in good faith in any kind of criminal case can make a terrible mistake and identify the wrong person—some innocent stranger—as the perpetrator (this would not be a problem in acquaintance rapes). New forensic tests for DNA matches make it possible to eliminate some male suspects and even to rectify some miscarriages of justice by overturning convictions and freeing innocent prisoners from their cells. But problems of victim misidentification of the assailant still can crop up.

> **A** college student tells the police that she was raped outside her dormitory late one night. She identifies a graduating senior in engineering who is a basketball star as her attacker by selecting his picture from the school yearbook and then pointing him out in a police lineup. The rape charge polarizes the campus, in part because he is black and she is white. His supporters view him as a victim of an injustice; at rallies, they argue that the woman and the police are having trouble distinguishing one black man from another in their rush to find the culprit. Her supporters march in solidarity with all women who have been assaulted and then disbelieved when they come forward and ask for help. He is arrested then released on bail, but is barred from the campus except to attend classes and use the library. She returns to her home to study for her final exams. When a number of credible alibi witnesses testify that the accused was far away from the campus that night, the prosecutor drops the charges against him and closes the case for lack of additional evidence or investigatory leads. (Lyall, 1989)

> **A** hitchhiker is picked up by a man with a beard wearing a three-piece suit. He drives the young woman down a dirt road, pulls over, overpowers and rapes her, and then kicks her out. She goes to the police and identifies her attacker from a "photo lineup"—a collection of mug shots that the detectives show her. The young arrestee insists he is innocent but is convicted largely on the basis of her testimony. But several months after the trial, the police uncover evidence that links someone else to a series of rapes, including this one. When detectives show the complainant the new suspect's picture, she immediately recognizes him and then breaks into tears, crying "Oh my God, what have I done?" The mistakenly accused and convicted man is soon released from prison but his life is in shambles: He has no money left because of legal fees; he has lost his job and good reputation; and his fiancé has broken off their engagement. He sues the authorities but dies from a heart attack shortly before being awarded a settlement of $2.8 million. (Goleman, 1995b)

Fraudulent accusations are even more of a concern than honest misidentifications. A dishonest girl or woman could attempt to deceive the authorities and knowingly lodge a fake charge against an innocent boy or man for some ulterior purpose—perhaps to arouse sympathy and gain attention, to punish a former lover, to provide an alibi, to give a "don't blame me" explanation for contracting an embarrassing pregnancy or venereal disease, or to hide the truth for some other reason. Widely held negative stereotypes and suspicions about manipulative or vengeful women obviously fuel these fears. To justify the routine skepticism that many rape complainants receive in press accounts, police stations, prosecutors' offices, and courtrooms, cases like the following are often cited:

> **A** secretary working for a prominent law firm goes to the sex crimes squad and tells detectives in a calm and forthright manner that a senior partner raped her when they were working alone in the office late one night. When questioned, the attorney denies he raped her but admits to carrying on a discreet affair with her, telling his wife he was working late or traveling overnight on business trips. He claims that when she demanded that he leave his family and move in with her, his refusal provoked her to threaten to kill herself, kill his wife, or kill him. Confronted by detectives with his version of events—that a "scorned woman" was making up terrible accusations to get even with him for dashing her dreams of upward mobility—she initially denies the charges. But when the police dig up hotel bills and airline ticket receipts documenting their secret trysts together, she confesses that her vengeful claim was intended to cost him his prestigious job and his marriage. (Fairstein, 1993)

> **A** 15-year-old black girl is discovered in an apparent state of shock curled up in a plastic garbage bag. She does not say much to police officers or doctors but according to her relatives and her advisors, she had been kidnapped and repeatedly raped for several days by four white men who appeared to have law enforcement affiliations. Her explosive charges divide the public along racial lines. A special grand jury is impaneled by the state's attorney general to look into the inflammatory accusations and to explore the possibility of an official cover-up. It concludes that there is insufficient evidence to charge anyone with a crime. Months later the girl's boyfriend claims that she told him that she and her mother made up the whole story so that her violence-prone stepfather would not beat her for staying out late. Unfortunately, an aunt who believed the story contacted the news media, which sensationalized the concocted allegations into headlines for months. Years later, one of the maligned men, an assistant district attorney, sues the supposed victim and her advisors in civil court for defamation of character and wins a monetary judgment against them. (Payne, 1989; Taibbi and Sims-Phillips, 1989; Schaye, 1998)

The 1931 "Scottsboro Boys" case stands out in history as the most notorious example of a false accusation of rape for some malicious purpose. The trumped-up charges were made for political reasons. In the Old South, white women were often pressured by white men to falsely accuse black men of rape so that the alleged suffering of the victims could be seized upon to justify the execution or lynching of the accused individuals and by extension to legitimize the segregation and repression of all black men (Sagarin, 1975). The controversy surrounding the way the defendants in this case of "southern racial justice" were "railroaded in a kangaroo court" without lawyers and sentenced to die led to a Supreme Court decision (*Powell v. Alabama,* 1932) that established the right of persons accused of capital crimes to be represented by competent counsel.

The task confronting detectives and prosecutors is to weed out the very few false claims (about a consensual act that is later characterized as forced or about a totally fabricated incident that never took place) from the overwhelming majority of genuine charges. The dishonesty of a few does not justify systematically mistreating all complainants as liars (Fairstein, 1993). The task for criminologists and victimologists is to determine how often baseless charges are lodged and whether false accusations are really more of a problem in rape cases than in other crimes like robberies or car thefts (see MacDonald and Michaud, 1995).

Credible statistics about the percentage of complaints that turn out to be "definitely" baseless are hard to find. Social workers at a hospital and a police sex crime unit have estimated their false complaint rates to be less than about 2% (Bode, 1978). However, about 40% of over 100 formally filed complaints turned out to be false—the woman recanted her original charges when told that she faced a stiff fine and a jail sentence—according to a study based on the records from 1978 to 1987 of a police department in a small midwestern city (Kanin, 1994). The FBI's *UCR* reported that in 1966, police forces across the country, after a preliminary investigation, had declared 20% of all rape complaints unfounded; and 19% were declared unfounded in 1976. Throughout the 1990s the annual *UCR*s stated that only about 8% of all rape complaints were classified as unfounded by local police departments across the nation (compared to about 2% of all complaints about other index crimes). However, the designation "unfounded" is not synonymous with "false accusation." Some of the cases in this category were deemed to be unprovable in court, but that doesn't mean that the complainants were deliberately committing perjury or imagining things.

Detectives often operated on the presumption that false cries of forcible rape were the rule and not the exception. For example, many police departments routinely administered lie detector tests to check a complainant's credibility. The prospect of submitting to a polygraph test of questionable reliability loomed as an added indignity and served as a further deterrent to reporting crimes and pressing charges. Therefore, groups in the antirape movement (who are convinced the problem of false allegations is greatly exaggerated) went to court to get injunctions against the practice. The President's Task Force on Victims of Crime (1982) recommended that procedures that reflected automatic distrust of complainants be abandoned, and a number of states have specifically outlawed polygraph testing of complainants.

Because of the credibility issue, unusually stringent standards of proof were intentionally crafted decades ago into rape laws in order to make it particularly difficult to secure convictions. The men who wrote the laws and administered the legal system considered these difficult-to-surmount hurdles to be safeguards against miscarriages of justice. But from the genuine innocent victim's standpoint, these "safeguards" loomed as major obstacles that discouraged and thwarted her pursuit of justice. From a feminist perspective these obstacles represented a clear case of institutionalized discrimination against all female complainants. The exceptionally high standards of proof took several forms: demands for evidence that the accuser did not willingly consent to engage in sex, a requirement that her testimony be corroborated (backed up in some independent way), and a tradition that she undergo particularly vigorous cross-examination by a defense attorney at the trial. At the end of a trial, a judge often delivered a "cautionary instruction" to the jurors before they began their deliberations, paraphrasing an English judge's warnings from 1671 that it is easy to accuse a man of rape but hard to prove the charge, but it is even harder for an innocent man to defend himself and clear his name.

False accusations about sexual assaults lodged by dishonest complainants posing as victims send out shock waves within the criminal justice process, which threaten to undermine much of the progress made by the antirape movement. Highly publicized instances give renewed life to traditional doubts that cast a cloud of suspicion over the credibility of all genuine victims who demand to be taken seriously. The belief that the woman's word alone should not be enough to secure a conviction in court is based on several legitimate concerns: that certain individuals might somehow gain something by committing perjury; that defendants charged with rape are socially stigmatized immediately—and possibly permanently—even if they are acquitted of all charges; and that conviction carries severe penalties including, until the 1970s, execution.

The Accuser Versus the Accused Rape prosecutions directly pit the rights of the accused male against the rights of the female complainant. He has a Sixth Amendment right to wage a vigorous defense through his attorney. According to recent victims' rights legislation and rewritten rape laws, she has a right to be taken seriously and treated with respect on and off the witness stand. Observing the rights of both parties requires a delicate balancing act that has not been resolved yet.

The accused can pursue one of several possible defense strategies. The first is to argue that the complaining witness has made a terrible but honest error, picking an innocent man out of a lineup (the "mistaken identity" defense). The second is to deny that he engaged in sexual acts with her (the "it-never-happened" defense). This requires a direct attack on the alleged victim's credibility and motivation by charging that she made up a completely false story for some deceptive reason. The third defense is to concede that he had sexual intercourse with her, but that she agreed at the time; afterward, she changed her mind, considered it a rape, and had him arrested (the "consent" defense).

The issue of consent is central to any rape complaint, since "willingness" or at least "voluntary compliance" is what distinguishes "making love" (or "engaging in sexual relations") from being sexually assaulted. The victim must convince the police, the prosecution, and ultimately a jury that she did not freely agree to participate in sex but was forced to submit by her attacker. The burden of proof shifts onto the woman, who must present a compelling account that she was violated "against her will." The prosecution must establish beyond a reasonable doubt that she was forced—hit, knocked down, pinned down, overpowered, or threatened with serious bodily harm. The prosecution must also show that she is a person to be believed and a woman of integrity and good character, who has no motive to distort the truth. To stir up reasonable doubts, the defense will pursue a strategy of impeaching her credibility by attacking her virtue. The goal is to sow the seeds of doubt among jurors by asserting that she consented at the time but later regretted her decision and then lodged false charges. To undermine her credibility as the star witness for the prosecution, the defense attorney often pursues a "nuts and sluts" strategy, portraying her as a mentally unstable liar and/or as a sexually promiscuous willing partner.

To counter such personal attacks, the prosecution must argue that the defense attorney is turning the tables and is putting the victim on trial and humiliating her once again, this time in front of the jury. From the complainant's point of view, some reasonable limits should be placed on the defense's cross-examination so it doesn't become a degrading spectacle. But from the defendant's point of view, it is only fair that she answer probing questions about her sexual involvements in the past and her mental health. Only then can he have a fighting chance in this credibility contest to clear his name and expose the falseness of her charges against him (see Estrich, 1993b; and Vachss, 1993).

Rape Shield Laws The antirape movement successfully convinced legislatures in almost every state in the mid-1970s to the mid-1980s to pass laws prohibiting improper cross-examinations. Generally, shield laws stipulate that the defense cannot introduce evidence about an accuser's past sexual conduct unless the woman has previously been convicted of prostitution, has had consensual sex before with the defendant, or has an obvious incentive to lie. Procedural guidelines provide for a hearing to be held in the absence of the jury, spectators, and the press. The aim is to permit the judge to determine whether or not the defense counsel's allegations about the woman's past should be aired in open court. Staunch supporters of shield laws want more restrictions to be placed on the ability of defense attorneys to assassinate the complainant's character as a way of impeaching her credibility. They cite several justifications: to encourage victims to go to the authorities for help by assuring them that their privacy will be respected, to spare complainants the embarrassment of having the most intimate details of their sex lives made public and used against them in court, to dispel the fallacy that "if she consented in the past she probably consented this time too," and to prevent juries and judges from being distracted by allegations about the complainant's past affairs when they should be focusing on the issue of the defendant's use of force. Critics of shield laws want fewer restrictions and argue that the laws deny the accused the right to effectively confront his accuser and therefore to have a fair trial on a "level playing field." Higher-court decisions have held that most inquiries into the woman's reputation for "chastity" have little relevance for determining consent (Stark and Goldstein, 1985; Austern, 1987; and Lewin, 1993). But prosecutors may not object strenuously enough about irrelevancy on behalf of their clients' reputations, and judges may err on the side of the defendants in order to prevent subsequent convictions from being overturned on appeal (Spohn and Horney, 1992).

Force and Resistance In the not-so-distant past in order to convict a rapist, a woman had to convince a jury that she forcefully resisted "to her utmost" and ceased struggling only because she feared she would be killed or seriously injured. The justification cited for requiring such proof of fierce resistance was that it indicated the victim's state of mind (unwillingness) and refuted the defendant's claims that he reasonably believed his partner was just feigning reluctance and was actually willing to engage in sex. Most state laws no longer require that the woman who wants to press charges has to prove that she risked her life to fend off her attacker. A "reasonableness standard" stipulates that the degree of resistance that expresses nonconsent can depend on the circumstances. A strong statement or an unambiguous act is sufficient to show lack of consent in the face of overwhelming force or an intimidating weapon. The woman does not even have to fight back, scream, or try to flee. Evidence that the accused possessed a weapon or that the victim was physically injured also is sufficient to establish nonconsent (Robin, 1977; Stark and Goldstein, 1985; Austern, 1987).

Although they may be emotionally devastated, most rape victims were not physically wounded, according to a survey of 4,000 women. About 70% of those who endured completed rapes reported no additional physical injuries; 24% said they suffered additional minor injuries; and 4% sustained serious wounds in addition to being penetrated against their will (Kilpatrick, 1992). Although the proportion of women who are killed after being raped is believed to be extremely small, the proportion of murdered women who were raped before they were killed is not negligible. About 7% of the deceased had been sexually assaulted before they were murdered, an analysis of female homicide victims in California during 1988 revealed (Sorenson and White, 1992). Nationally, FBI *SHRs* indicate that a declining proportion (about 2% in the mid-1970s to less than 1% in the mid-1990s) of all murder victims were raped or sexually assaulted before they were killed (Greenfield, 1997).

How the victim reacts during the sexual assault can profoundly influence the outcome in terms of her injuries. Her behavior—either submission or resistance—affects the attacker's decisions about whether to try to complete the act and about how much force to use to subdue her. Most assailants are unarmed (about 21% had guns, knives, or other sharp instruments), according to an analysis of *NCVS* data from 1987 until 1992. Most of the victims who took some type of self-protective action, such as yelling for help or fighting back, told survey interviewers that they believed it helped the situation (61%) rather than made it worse (17%) (Bachman, 1994a). Victims who resisted improved their chances of thwarting the rapists' aims of completing the act, but they also increased their risks of suffering additional injuries. One third of the nonresisting victims were wounded in addition to being sexually assaulted, whereas two thirds of the victims who applied self-defense measures were physically hurt—

bruised, cut, scratched, even stabbed or shot—according to a study of *NCVS* data from the late 1970s (McDermott, 1979). The best strategy turned out to be a "dual verbal defense" of calling out for help while simultaneously attempting to reason with, plead with, or threaten the attacker, a study of 125 victims concluded. Nearly all of the women who physically resisted their assailants reported that their actions only made the men angrier, more vicious, and more violent (Cohen, 1984).

Studies assessing the relative effectiveness of various responses have generated mixed, confusing, and perhaps impractical recommendations. It is impossible to predict the outcome of a particular assault, given the complex web of factors involving the offender, his intended victim, and their situation at that moment. Criminologists report that there are different types of rapists who react to resistance differently. Girls and women under attack and rape defense strategists face an unavoidable dilemma: Resistance may foil a rape but may further endanger their physical well-being. But at least one factor in the equation has changed to the advantage of victims. Whether or not fiercely resisting "within reason" is the best strategy under all circumstances, it is no longer required to justify an arrest and prosecution.

The apparent acquiescence of some victims can be readily explained. The primary reaction of nearly all rape victims is to fear for their lives, according to interviews conducted at a hospital emergency room (Burgess and Holmstrom, 1974). Therefore, some victims are simply immobilized by terror, shock, and disbelief. Faced with the prospect of death or severe physical injury, many conclude that their only way out is to "strike a bargain" or work out a tacit "understanding" with the attacker and trade submission for survival (to exchange sexual violation for some sort of pledge that they won't be killed, savagely beaten, or cruelly disfigured). There is, of course, no guarantee that compliance will minimize physical injury. The rapists do not have to keep their promises (Brownmiller, 1975).

Corroboration In the past one aspect of the law that made rape charges very difficult to prove beyond a reasonable doubt in most states was the corroboration requirement, which demanded that the prosecution discover independent evidence to back up the key elements of the victim's account. Derived hundreds of years ago from the evolution of English common law, the corroboration requirement assumed that the complainant's accusations alone were not credible without some other form of substantiation. Corroboration could take the form of obvious physical injuries; medical and forensic evidence gathered by a doctor; torn clothing; other signs of a struggle; or the testimony of an eyewitness or a third party like a police officer, family member, or friend who had been promptly told about the assault. But the corroboration requirement was criticized as being patently unfair for putting rape victims in the unique position (compared to complainants of other kinds of assaults) of being automatically distrusted without additional "real proof." To strike a balance most state laws have been reformed and no longer require corroboration, unless the victim is a minor, was previously intimate with the accused, did not promptly report the crime to the authorities, or provides a version of events that is inherently improbable and self-contradictory (Robin, 1977; Stark and Goldstein, 1985; Austern, 1987).

Arrest, Prosecution, and Adjudication In order for a crime to be solved, it must first be reported. But most rapes are not reported to the police, according to the annual findings from the *National Crime Victimization Survey.* Close to half of all victims tell *NCVS* interviewers about sexual assaults which were never brought to the attention of the police. The reasons females cite most often for not informing the authorities are that they fear reprisals, consider the incident to be a private or personal matter, or feel that they lack proof to make the charges stick. Women who report the offenses to the police most often say that they do so to be rescued, to prevent the rapist from harming them again or from attacking someone else, and to get him in trouble so that he will be punished. Women are more likely to go to the authorities if the assailant used a weapon or if they are physically wounded and require medical care for their injuries. Surprisingly, whether or not the offender was a complete stranger, an acquaintance, or an intimate does not seem to affect the decision to report or not report the crime to the police, according to *NCVS* findings (BJS, 1994b). No pronounced upward trend toward higher rates of reporting appears in annual *NCVS* findings (as Table 4.1 showed), despite many public relations efforts to encourage more victims to come forward (such as poster campaigns and special hotline numbers) and several reforms (like safeguarding a woman's privacy by not publicly identifying her, and providing intermediaries and advocates to turn to at rape crisis centers at hospitals and on campuses).

Similarly, rape clearance rates for police departments across the nation show no improvement in recent years (refer back to Table 4.3). This lack of progress in improving the solution rate is disappointing, considering that more acquaintance rape cases (where the suspect's identity and whereabouts are known) presumably are being brought to the attention of the local authorities (see Kanin, 1984; and Estrich, 1986). Also, to prevent victims from being deterred from pressing charges by the prospect of insensitive handling, some police departments have set up sex crimes squads with specially trained female detectives. Despite these new measures the percentages of cases that were solved each year were much higher in the past, even though most of the reported rapes in those days involved attacks by strangers. Although acquaintance rape cases are solved more easily, convictions are more difficult to secure than in cases of stranger rapes. Attrition rates for acquaintance rape cases are substantially higher. Victims are more inclined to ask that charges be dropped, and prosecutors are less willing to press forward because they fear juries will find "reasonable doubts" and not convict defendants (Mansnerus, 1989; LaFree, 1989; Bachman, 1998). In an effort to increase the conviction rate, some district attorneys have established sex crimes prosecution units with specially trained lawyers. Traditionally, prosecutors whose performance was judged on the basis of their won/lost records preferred offering lenient pleas rather than going to trial. Unless the complainant fit their narrow stereotype of the kinds of victims who are believed by jurors and arouse their sympathy—wives and mothers who are well educated, articulate, visibly upset but not hysterical while testifying, and attractive but not too "sexy"—prosecutors preferred to negotiate an out-of-court settlement (Vachss, 1993). Even though more rape cases go to trial than any other type of charge except murder and aggravated assault, the overwhelming majority of cases are still resolved through plea negotiations. The percentage of rape cases that go to trial varies greatly by jurisdiction (Boland and Sones, 1986). About 10% of all rape cases were resolved by a trial, with the prosecution victorious about 70% of the time, in the 75 largest counties during 1994 (Reaves, 1998).

Besides the creation of special investigation and prosecution squads, a number of other reforms have been enacted to try to increase arrest, prosecution, conviction, and incarceration rates. In most jurisdictions the chances of conviction in sexual assault cases have been enhanced by new legal codes and sentencing structures which specify gradational levels of seriousness (from improper sexual contact to forcible rape), each carrying a corresponding penalty (Bienen, 1983; Largen, 1987). In many courtrooms, evidence of rape trauma syndrome can be introduced during trials to account for questionable behavior on the victim's part (concerning reporting delays or failure to actively resist) that in the past would have undermined her credibility.

And yet despite these many reforms and attempts at improving the criminal justice system's handling of rape cases, most attackers are never arrested, prosecuted, convicted, and certainly not incarcerated (see Lisefski and Manson, 1988; and Senate Judiciary Committee, 1993). According to one nationwide study (Reaves, 1998), 35% of all defendants find the charges against them dropped; 3% are acquitted at a trial; and only 61% are convicted, mostly of felonies (but 3% of merely a misdemeanor). By the end of the adjudication process in state courts, only about 35% of all accused rapists were sentenced to prison and another 10% wound up in jail for up to one year (plus a slightly larger percentage were placed on probation).

Crisis Centers: Providing Emergency Assistance

No matter how poorly (or how well) the criminal justice system handles rape cases in the long run, sexual assault victims need immediate aid in the short run. Starting in 1972, feminist activists began to provide concrete emergency assistance to women who had just been raped. The first crisis centers (also known as distress or relief centers) were set up in Berkeley, California, and Washington, D.C. These independent self-help projects were intended to provide an alternative to the very limited services available at that time through the police, at hospital emergency rooms, and through mental health centers. They also became organizing bases for the nationwide antirape movement.

Rape crisis centers provide a variety of services. Usually, a 24-hour telephone hotline puts victims in contact with advocates who are standing by to help. The center's staff members are available to accompany women to hospital emergency rooms where forensic evidence is collected and first aid is received, and to police stations or prosecutor's offices where complaints are filed and statements are made. Individuals may receive peer counseling and are invited to participate in support groups. Referrals are made to other community agencies that provide social services. Some centers conduct in-service training to sensitize doctors, nurses, police officers, and assistant district attorneys about the needs and problems of the rape victims they encounter. Most undertake educational campaigns to raise public consciousness about the myths and realities surrounding sex crimes and the victims' plight. Frequently, centers offer self-defense courses for women and children.

Many staff members at the original crisis centers were former victims who shared a commitment to most of the themes embodied in the protest movements of the 1960s and early 1970s. Feminist activists put forward the analysis that rape was primarily a women's issue, best understood and more effectively dealt with by women than by male authorities. A distrust of remote bureaucracies and control by professionals who claim to know what is best for their clients was derived from the youthful counterculture with its "crash pads" (emergency shelters), drop-in centers (for counseling and advocacy), and free clinics (for drug-related health crises) in "hippie" neighborhoods. The New Left's emphasis on egalitarianism, volunteerism, and collective action led to grassroots, community-based projects stressing self-help and peer support, and to symbolic confrontations with the power structure (pro-victim demonstrations at police stations and courtrooms).

With the passage of time, however, rifts developed within many rape crisis centers. More pragmatic and less ideological staffers softened the staunch stands taken by these nonprofit, nonbureaucratic, nonhierarchical, nonprofessional, and nongovernmental organizations. They pressed for a more service-oriented approach that would avoid militancy and radical critiques, improve chances for funding, increase referrals from hospitals and police departments, and permit closer cooperation with prosecutors. To the founders of the centers, such changes represented a co-optation by the establishment and a retreat from the original mission (see Amir and Amir, 1979; and Largen, 1981).

Unwanted Publicity and Negative Media Protrayal

Fears of public exposure and of being blamed discourage some women from turning to the criminal justice system for help. From the victims' point of view, reporters and editors have trouble covering rape cases without inflicting further harm.

Since the middle of the 1800s, newspapers have regularly featured stories about violent crimes but they rarely covered rapes until the two "Scottsboro Boys" trials in the 1930s. For a number of years the only cases that aroused media interest were those that resulted in lynchings where a black man accused of raping a white woman was murdered by a white mob. The mainstream media outlets remain preoccupied with the rape of white women, continue to sensationalize interracial cases involving a black defendant and a white victim, and rarely devote attention to sexual assaults upon black women. Journalists tend to stereotype victims as either "virgins" (pure and innocent, who are ravaged by bestial males) or "vamps" (wanton and sexually provocative, who arouse male lust). The victim is likely to be portrayed as a vamp if the defendant is an acquaintance, no weapon is brandished, the persons involved are both from the same ethnic group and social class, and the victim is young, considered attractive and doesn't live with her family. By assigning blame to one party or the other, crime reporters assume the responsibilities of judges and juries, according to a content analysis of the way the news media covered several highly publicized rape cases (Benedict, 1992).

When a girl or woman lodges charges of sexual assault against a man, like any other complainant of any other crime her name appears in police files and court documents. The question then arises whether her identity should be revealed in media accounts of the case.

Laws prohibit the press from publishing the name of the victim in a sex crime in a number of states. Elsewhere, most newspapers, magazines, and radio and television stations have adopted a policy of self-restraint that shields the injured person from unwanted public exposure.

The arguments in favor of keeping the victim's name out of the media center on the potential for additional harm to the victim and the chilling effect on other women who are considering going to the authorities for help. The long-standing ethical norm of concealing the name of a complainant who wishes to remain anonymous developed out of a realization that rapes are not like other crimes. Victims are more likely to be in an emotionally fragile state and afflicted by posttraumatic stress, nervous breakdowns, and suicidal impulses. Publicly identified rape victims have always been discredited, stigmatized, scandalized, mocked, scorned, and even harassed. Harsh victim-blaming accusations are particularly likely and especially painful psychologically. Therefore, revealing a victim's name against her will is a humiliating second violation that is likely to prolong her suffering. Furthermore, other rape victims who see how powerless another victim was to prevent her name and intimate details about her life from being broadcasted might be discouraged from reporting similar incidents to the police. Therefore, media self-censorship is a way to respect a victim's privacy rights unless she chooses to go public and speak out about the attack (Pollitt, 1991; Young, 1991).

The arguments in favor of disclosing victims' names appeal to the principles of the public's right to know, the defendant's right to a fair trial, and the news media's right to be free from censorship. Media outlets have an obligation to disseminate all relevant and newsworthy facts. Accusations from anonymous sources are contrary to American jurisprudence. The accused who is presumed to be innocent unless proven guilty endures humiliation from the publicity. The accuser's name should be revealed as well to deter untrue allegations. Potential witnesses with knowledge about her credibility might come forward with information about her background and character that could aid the defense of a falsely accused man. Finally, shielding victims from exposure implies that being forced to submit to a sexual act is a "dirty secret" to be ashamed of, when it should not be a cause of public humiliation. In the long run, routinely giving faceless victims a human identity might diminish the persisting stigma surrounding being raped (see Dershowitz, 1988; Cohen, 1991; and Kantrowitz, Starr, and Friday, 1991).

Reducing the Threat of Rape

Over the years three approaches have been developed to cut down the problem of sexual assaults. The oldest (and now subject to vehement denunciation) is the "blame the victim" approach that faults the attitudes, words, and actions of the girl or woman attacked by the violent boy or man. Following the logic of this approach, women must stop precipitating rape through careless, reckless, or even provocative behavior. Instead, these would-be targets must learn to take precautions to reduce the risks they face in a dangerous male-dominated world. One alternative perspective is the "blame the offender" approach that views sexual assaults as pathological acts by mentally disturbed individuals. If deranged sexual predators are the source of the problem, then criminal justice strategies that remove these dangerous deviants from circulation (incapacitation via incarceration, followed by rehabilitation) are the solution. Since the public can't be sure a released "sexual predator" has been completely cured, neighbors should be informed whenever an ex-convict moves in (community notification laws) so their female family members can remain vigilant and take defensive measures.

But a third approach—more sociologically based because it emphasizes the wide variety of offenders, motives, targets, and victim-offender relationships—considers rape to be the outgrowth of social conditions, especially patriarchy (rule by men); exploitive cultural themes about females as sex objects for male gratification; traditional gender-based roles emphasizing male sexual aggressiveness and female passivity; and prevailing patterns of socialization (how children are raised). If this analysis is correct, then criminal justice "solutions" can only keep a lid on a potentially explosive situation. Deterrence through punishment attempts to teach offenders who are not mentally deranged a lesson they won't forget and make negative role models out of transgressors to serve as a warning to other men contemplating similar sexual assaults (so they will "think twice," consider the likelihood of imprisonment, and decide not to act out their oppressive fantasies). But many rapists escape the punishment they deserve; at best an efficient criminal justice system weeds out assailants and brings them under control one at a time, after they have struck and harmed the targets of their wrath. If social conditions breed generation after generation of sexually exploitive males, then the only viable strategy is to eradicate the root causes of the problem. That means doing something about the encouragements to commit rape that pervade contemporary culture: the glorification of the coupling of sex and violence in popular music lyrics, movies, pornography, and other forms of entertainment, as well as advertising (promoting violence as "sexy" and sexual desire as something to be expressed forcefully rather than tenderly); and the general indoctrination of boys and men to look disdainfully at girls and women as little more than objects for gratifying sexual urges (see Buchwald, Fletcher, and Roth, 1993).

The Rediscovery of More Rape Victims

Because of the renewed attention paid to rape by the antirape movement, the plight of two other groups soon was rediscovered: wives raped by their husbands and males subjected to sexual assaults by other men.

Wives Raped by Their Husbands The antirape movement argued that all kinds of forced sex should be outlawed, regardless of who the aggressor is and what his relationship to the victim might be. This understanding of abuse within intimate relationships led to the rediscovery that rape can occur even between husbands and wives. Despite religious teachings about submission, the license issued by the government, and marriage vows recited at weddings, a wife retains the right to say "No!" to her husband. The forcible rape of a spouse first became explicitly recognized as a crime in 1975, when South Dakota legislators rewrote the state's statutes and rejected the common-law "exception" (or exemption from arrest) that granted husbands the right to virtually unlimited sexual access (Russell, 1982). By 1990 in every state, the immunity extended to a husband no longer applied if his wife had separated from him and filed for divorce. In many states a sexually assaultive husband could be arrested and prosecuted even if the couple was living together (if he used a weapon or took advantage of his mentally or physically incapacitated wife who was unable to give meaningful consent) (Russell, 1990).

More than one million women who are currently married may have been forced to perform unwanted sexual acts one or more times by their husbands, according to projections from a telephone survey (Crime Victims Research and Treatment Center, 1992). The prevalence rate during the lifetime of a marriage is thought to range from as low as 8% (Russell, 1990) to as high as 25% (Bergen, 1998). An equally troubling proportion of women, 15% to 25% percent, report that they were raped by an estranged or ex-husband or former live-in lover (Finkelhor and Yllo, 1985). Raped wives are also battered wives in most cases. They are beaten periodically and raped repeatedly over the years, and many beatings include acts of sexual abuse as well (Peacock, 1998). Raped wives endure many of the same problems that burden women who were sexually assaulted by nonintimates. They are physically injured, psychologically scarred, and personally humiliated (Bowker, 1983). Wives whose husbands force them to submit to unwanted degrading acts are the least likely of all sexual assault victims to report the incidents, to be believed by the authorities, to have their cases adjudicated, and to secure convictions. Between 1978 and 1985 only 118 husbands were prosecuted across the country, although 104 of them (90%) were convicted, according to a report by a national clearinghouse on marital rape (Barden, 1987). If they could devise ways of convincing victims to fully disclose their plight, researchers suspect that forced sexual participation (without consent) by a spouse would take place about as frequently as rapes by dates, acquaintances, and strangers (see Beirne and Messerschmidt, 2000).

Sexually Assaulted Males The rape of a male by a female or of a female by a female is presumed to be extremely rare, and the imagery usually arouses smirks rather than alarm. When women are arrested in sexual assault cases, it is usually as the accomplices of domineering men. But the molestation of little boys by men (discussed above under the heading of sexual abuse of children) has been of great concern for a long time (see Maghan and Sagarin, 1983; Porter, 1986; and the discussion earlier in this chapter). More recently, the rape of a male by another male (or by a gang of males) was recognized as more than just a theoretical possibility. Yet this had been such a taboo subject that many state laws had ignored this victim-offender relationship and had defined rape strictly as a crime perpetrated by males against females. In 1986, however, Congress passed a bill revising federal rape statutes (which govern the handling of sexual assaults committed on federal property). Among other changes the law redefined rape as a gender-neutral offense so victims and perpetrators both could be of either sex ("Federal Rape Laws," 1986). This official recognition that males could be rape victims too paved the way for their rediscovery, including efforts to estimate the scope of the problem and to devise effective ways of easing their suffering.

The first rough estimates about sexual assaults attempted or completed against males (teenagers and adults) were derived from the findings of annual *National Crime Victimization Surveys.* Between 1973 and 1982 almost 125,000 male rape victims were projected, adding up to about one twelfth of the problem females faced, numerically speaking (Klaus, DeBerry, and Timrots, 1985). In 1998, males suffered about the same proportion of all rapes (about one thirteenth, or nearly 8%; a rate of 0.2 per 1,000), as reported to interviewers for the redesigned *NCVS* (that more effectively probed for sexual assault incidents) (Rennison, 1999). Similarly, about 9% of all rapes reported to the local police in three states during 1991 were male-on-male (0.8% were female-on-female and 0.2% were female-on-male), according to the first analysis of more detailed data gathered by the FBI's new National Incident Based Reporting System (NIBRS) method (Reaves, 1993). Records kept by rape crisis centers indicated that about 1 caller out of every 10 was a victimized male. But these measures of the incidence of male-on-male rapes are probably gross underestimates because they exclude the thousands of sexual assaults committed in the most dangerous places of all—institutional settings like jails, prisons, and reform schools. Sexual violence among inmates has been documented as a serious problem (see Lockwood, 1980) that now is routinely dramatized in movies about life behind bars. Older and stronger "wolves" compel younger and weaker inmates to be their sex slaves in return for protection from gang rapes that would stigmatize them as easy pickings and as the "girl" of the institution. In the pumped-up, muscled, tatooed, violent same-sex world of prison life, men who are stripped of their autonomy and are forced to obey orders like little boys try to regain their sense of masculinity by forcing weaker inmates to submit to sexual demands like females (Sabo, 1992; Beirne and Messerschmidt, 2000).

Male rape victims are subjected to the same kind of disbelief, scorn, and insensitive treatment today that female victims endured routinely in the not-so-distant past. They are often blamed for their own misfortunes, stereotyped as homosexual (the majority are exclusively heterosexual), disparaged as not being "real men" for not resisting to the utmost and for not thwarting their attackers, and accused of secretly enjoying the experience. Although males and females suffer in similar ways, experiencing bouts of depression, flashbacks, recriminations, nightmares, and an overwhelming sense of vulnerability, males are more visibly angry and more preoccupied with fantasies of revenge. In a few large cities, they have set up self-help support groups. Impressionistic evidence indicates that male rape victims experience more force and brutality, are held captive for a longer period, and are subjected to more acts of sexual humiliation. Evidently, sexual assaults against both males and females are expressions of culturally induced drives toward domination and subjugation within a society that prizes exercising power over other people (Krueger, 1985; White and Wesley, 1987).

CHAPTER SUMMARY

Many groups of victims face special problems that require special solutions.

The distraught parents of missing children need to convince the authorities that their youngsters were truly victims of foul play and to take immediate action. Child-search organizations run by volunteers can help to mobilize manhunts, and state clearinghouses for information about missing children can coordinate activities.

Infants, toddlers, and little children are vulnerable to maltreatment in the form of physical or sexual abuse or gross neglect. Since they can't speak out on their own behalf, mandatory reporting laws compel those with knowledge to come forward to child-protection agencies so investigations can be launched. Children old enough to testify need to establish their credibility and must be shielded from emotionally distressing cross-examinations as well as overzealous coaching that plants ideas in their minds.

All victims of violence by intimates who live in the same household need special forms of protection from reprisals, including restraining orders and shelters. Domestic violence is no longer a private matter.

Sexual assault victims face special credibility tests when they come forward as complainants and witnesses for the prosecution. Rape shield laws concerning cross-examination on the witness stand, revised rules about corroboration, crisis centers, and restraints against intrusive media coverage lessen the burdens they face.

DISCUSSION QUESTIONS

1. Outline the maximalist and minimalist positions and apply these perspectives to missing children, child abuse, spouse abuse, and date rape.
2. Describe the special problems faced by abused siblings, teenagers beaten by their parents, and abused elders.
3. Describe the special solutions already implemented by the criminal justice system to help the parents of missing children, physically and sexually abused children, battered women, and raped women.
4. Speculate about the reasons why the following controversies suddenly

emerged, reached great intensity, and then died down: a) charges raised by alleged survivors about physical and sexual abuse, and even human sacrifices, by satanic cults; b) charges made by little children about sexual abuse by workers at day-care centers; c) charges raised by wives during divorce proceedings about the alleged sexual abuse of their children by their husbands; and d) charges raised by grown children who have recovered memories about alleged molestations when they were much younger.

5. Based on the materials presented in this chapter, extend the analysis and speculate about the special problems and the special solutions of a) victims of hate crimes and b) of collisions caused by drunk drivers.
6. Discuss how and why the following groups with special problems were rediscovered: battered husbands, homosexuals beaten in same-sex relationships, women raped by dates, and women raped by their husbands.

6

Repaying Victims

The costs imposed by crime cannot be measured in dollars and cents. Receiving financial reimbursement can't erase the mental anguish and physical wounds imposed upon victims. Nevertheless, restoring financial health is an achievable goal and a necessary first step toward recovery.

Victims suffer monetarily when offenders take cash, vandalize or steal property, inflict injuries that require medical attention and interfere with work, and cause trauma that necessitates psychological care. Victims can seek to recover their financial losses in a number of ways. Making the offender pay is everyone's first choice, as it embodies the most elemental notion of justice. Judges in criminal court can order convicts to make restitution; judges and juries in civil court can compel defendants to pay damages. Another possible source of reparations might be a grossly negligent third party, such as an enterprise or a governmental agency, that bears some responsibility for the criminal incident. Insurance coverage can also be a source of repayment. In some cases, financial aid can be forthcoming from state compensation programs that may cover certain expenses and losses. Restitution and compensation are alternative methods of repaying losses. **Restitution** is the responsibility of offenders; **compensation** is the financial obligation of government-run funds or private insurance companies. Finally, in rare instances victims might be able to deprive offenders of any profits accrued from telling a sensationalized "inside story" of their shocking exploits. This chapter explores all of these means of monetary recovery: court-ordered restitution, lawsuits for damages, third-party civil suits, private insurance policies, government compensation plans, and acts prohibiting criminals from cashing in on their notoriety.

GAINING RESTITUTION FROM OFFENDERS

Back to Basics

> **T**hree teenagers break into an ice skating rink. They steal money from a concession stand cash register and start a fire that results in damages exceeding $20,000. Charged with larceny, wanton destruction of property, and arson, they get 2-year suspended sentences. In addition, the judge orders them to work full time for up to 4 months repairing and repainting the property they destroyed. (Klein, 1988)

The growing use of "alternative," "creative," or "constructive" sentences heralds a renewed interest in restitution. Advocates of restitution argue that it's time to get back to basics. The financial health of victims shouldn't be neglected or sacrificed by a system ostensibly set up to deliver justice for all. Criminal acts are more than symbolic assaults against abstractions like the social order or public safety; real flesh-and-blood people suffer losses. Offenders shouldn't be prosecuted solely on behalf of the state or "the people." They don't only owe a "debt to society." They have incurred a debt to their victims. Fairness demands that victims be "made whole again" by being restored to the financial condition they were in before the crime occurred (see Abel and Marsh, 1984).

Restitution takes place whenever offenders return stolen goods to their rightful owners, hand over equivalent amounts of money to cover out-of-pocket expenses, or perform direct personal services to those they have harmed. Community service is designed to make amends to society as a whole by benefiting some worthy cause or group. "Symbolic restitution" to substitute victims seems appropriate when society as a whole has been menaced, when the immediate casualties can't be found, or when the victims don't want to accept the offenders' aid (Harris, 1979). "Creative restitution," the ideal solution, comes about when offenders, on their own initiative, go beyond what the law or their sentences require, exceed other people's expectations, and leave their victims better off than they were before the crimes took place (Eglash, 1977).

Usually, wrongs are righted in a straightforward manner. Litterbugs clean up the mess they have made. Adolescent graffiti artists scrub off their spray painted signatures. Burglars repay cash for the loot they have carted away. Embezzlers return stolen funds to the company. Occasionally, "client-specific" punishments are imposed, tailored to fit the crime, the criminal, and unmet community needs. For example, a drunk driver does several months of voluntary labor in a hospital emergency room to see the consequences of her kind of recklessness. A lawyer caught defrauding his clients avoids disbarment by spending time giving legal advice to needy individuals too poor to pay for it. A young purse snatcher who preys on the elderly is ordered to work weekends at a nursing home. Such sentences anger those who are convinced that imprisonment is the answer and fervently believe "If you do the crime, you must do the time." But imaginative dispositions that substitute restitution and community service for confinement are favored by reformers who want to reduce jail and prison overcrowding, cut the tax burden of incarceration, and shield first-time and minor offenders from the corrupting influences of the prison subculture ("Fitting Justice?" 1978; "When Judges Make the Punishment Fit the Crime," 1978; Seligmann and Maor, 1980).

The Rise, Fall, and Revival of Restitution

The idea of making criminals repay their victims is an ancient one. Spontaneous acts of revenge predated the invention of restitution. During the centuries before governments, laws, and criminal justice systems, the gut reaction of victims was to seek to "get even" with aggressors by injuring them physically in counterattacks and by taking back things of value. But as wealth accumulated and primitive societies established rules of conduct, the tradition of retaliatory violence gave way to negotiation and reparation. For the sake of community harmony and stability, compulsory restitution was institutionalized in ancient societies. Reimbursement practices went beyond the simplistic formula of "an eye for an eye and a tooth for a tooth." Restitution was intended to satisfy any thirst for vengeance, as well as to repay losses. These transactions involving goods and money were designed to encourage lasting settlements ("composition") between the parties that would head off any further strife (Schafer, 1970).

As handed down by Moses, the law of the Hebrews stated that an assailant repay the person he injured for any losses due to recuperation from a serious wound. Mosaic law also required that a captured thief give back five oxen for every one stolen. The Code of Hammurabi granted a victim as much as 30 times the value of any goods stolen or damaged. Under Roman law a thief had to pay the victim double the value of what he stole if he was caught in the act; if he escaped and was caught later, he owed the victim 3 times the value of what he took; and if he used force to commit the theft, the robber had to repay the injured party 4 times as much as he stole. Under the ninth century "Dooms" of King Alfred of England, each tooth knocked out of a person's mouth by an aggressor required a different payment, depending upon its location (Peak, 1986).

Also by this time in England, an offender was supposed to restore peace and harmony by offering two separate payments: a "bot" (or "bote") to the victim and a "wer" (or "wergild") to the victim's kin. An official list spelled out exact penalties for specified acts. Private retaliation was permissible only if the offender refused to hand over payments. Anyone in the community could kill such an outlaw who rejected the chance to make amends. But fragmentary historical records confirm the suspicion that in a society with sharply defined classes, restitution worked to the advantage of the upper classes. If they were powerful enough, guilty parties could scoff at the claims of their social "inferiors." If compelled to settle accounts, the affluent could easily make fiscal atonement for even the most outrageous breaches of law through relatively inconsequential composition payments of gold, cattle, land, or other valuables. On the other hand, offenses by the marginal against the mighty were not so readily resolved. The amounts specified were often beyond the resources of the common folk. Those commoners who could not meet their obligations were branded as outlaws or were forced to sell themselves into virtual slavery. Restitution functioned as one of many mechanisms that made the rich richer and the poor poorer (Schafer, 1970; Geis, 1977; Peak, 1986).

Restitution practices changed as the power of the feudal aristocracy and nation-states consolidated. Royal officials drew up regulations to formalize the process of redressing grievances between subjects. Public involvement in what were formerly considered private matters was justified on several grounds: to more effectively preserve the peace; to curb brutality, extortion, and exploitation of the weak by the strong; and to raise revenue for the Crown. Offenders found themselves obligated to repay the state for its services, as well as reimburse victims for their losses. The nobility extracted a "wite" as a fee for supervising reconciliation between the two parties and for guaranteeing protection to the offenders from any retaliation by the victims or their kin. By the 12th century the victim's bot and the kin's wer were shrinking, while the wite paid to the treasury was growing. The expansion of the state's interest in resolving criminal matters was solidified with the emergence of a category of "bootless" crimes considered so heinous that no transfer of money could restore social equilibrium; the offender had to pay in blood. As the concept evolved, representatives of the government (as protectors of the "king's peace" and "public order") began to consider the state as the injured party in most crimes. Governmental demands to punish and collect fines from transgressors soon crowded out the victim's right to recover damages, especially after the Crown proclaimed a forfeiture law that enabled it to seize whatever property a felon owned (Mueller and Cooper, 1973; Younger, 1977).

In colonial America before the Revolution, criminal acts were viewed primarily as private conflicts between individuals. Police departments and public prosecutors did not exist yet. A victim in a city could call upon night watchmen for help, but they might not be on duty, or the offender might flee beyond their jurisdiction. If a victim sought the aid of a sheriff, he had to pay a fee. If the sheriff located the alleged perpetrator, he would charge extra to serve a warrant against the defendant. With the suspect in custody, the victim had to hire a lawyer to draw up an indictment. Then the victim either prosecuted the case personally or hired an attorney for an additional fee to handle the private prosecution. If the accused was found guilty, the victim could gain substantial benefits. Convicted thieves were required to repay their victims 3 times as much as they had stolen. If the thieves could not hand over such large amounts, they were assigned to their victims as servants until their debts were paid off. If the victims wished, they could sell these indentured servants for a hefty price, and they had 1 month in which to find a buyer. After that they were responsible for the costs of maintaining the offenders in jail; if they didn't pay, the convicts were released (McDonald, 1977; Hillenbrand, 1990).

In the years following the American Revolution, the procedures set up by the British in the 13 colonies were substantially reorganized. Reformers were concerned about the built-in injustices afflicting a system in which only wealthy victims could afford to purchase "justice" by posting rewards and hiring sheriffs, private detectives, bounty hunters, and prosecuting attorneys. Crimes were redefined as acts against the state. The redress of individual grievances was no longer regarded as the primary function of court proceedings. To promote equality, local governments hired public prosecutors. State agencies built prison systems to house offenders. A distinction developed between crimes and torts. Crimes were offenses against the public ("the people") as represented by the state, and torts were the corresponding wrongful acts against specific persons. Criminals were forced to "pay their debt to society" through fines and periods of confinement. Victims who wanted to compel offenders to repay their personal expenses were shunted away from criminal court to civil court, a separate arena where lawsuits were resolved (McDonald, 1977).

As the notion of restitution faded over the centuries, leading figures in legal philosophy and criminology called for its revival. Sir Thomas More proposed in his book *Utopia* that offenders labor on public works projects. The English utilitarian philosopher Jeremy Bentham advocated mandatory restitution for property offenses. A French jurist developed a plan in 1847 that combined restitution with compensation from state funds. A number of criminologists introduced restitution resolutions at international "prison congresses" around 1900. Prominent figures raised the issue in Italy in the 1920s and in England during the 1950s (Jacob, 1977; Schafer, 1970).

In 1967 the President's Commission on Law Enforcement and the Administration of Justice recommended that restitution obligations be imposed on convicts more frequently and that laws passed during the Great Depression that restricted the sale of products made by prisoners (and thereby limited inmate earnings) be repealed. Since the 1970s, opinion polls have indicated public support for the revival of this ancient practice. A greater reliance on restitution also received an endorsement from the American Law Institute, the American Bar Association, the American Correctional Association, the National Advisory Commission on Criminal Justice Standards and Goals, the U.S. Supreme Court, the National Association of Attorneys General, the Office for Victims of Crime of the U.S. Justice Department, and from reform groups like the National Moratorium on Prison Construction. The Federal Victim/Witness Protection Act of 1982 removed restrictions that had limited restitution solely to a condition of probation within the federal judicial system. Also in 1982 the President's Task Force on Victims of Crime noted that it was unfair that people suffering serious injuries had to liquidate their assets, mortgage their homes, make do without adequate health care, or cut back on tuition expenses while criminals escaped financial responsibility for the hardships they imposed. The task force recommended that judges routinely impose restitution or else state for the record the specific reasons for not doing so. The Violent Crime Control and Law Enforcement Act passed by Congress in 1994 made restitution mandatory in federal cases of sexual assault or domestic violence. The enactment of the Mandatory Victim Restitution Act of 1996 imposed repayment obligations on all violent offenders in the federal system. The Federal Bureau of Prisons created a collection program in the late 1980s that many state correctional authorities have copied. Payments can be derived from inmates' wages from prison labor, state and federal income tax refunds, lottery winnings, inheritances, trust accounts, and collateral used for bail. More than half of all state legislatures have passed laws that presume restitution will be imposed on every convict unless the presiding judge offers a compelling reason not to do so. But in the remaining states, restitution is required either only from violent offenders or only from the perpetrators of property crimes. In many jurisdictions, victims must wait until offenders are placed on probation or parole, and juvenile delinquents may be excused from any obligations (McDonald, 1988; Leepson, 1982; Harland, 1983; Herrington, 1986; Galaway, 1992; National Victim Center, 1992b; OJP, 1997).

Restitution has been ordered more often and for a longer period of time in the juvenile justice system. The oldest existing repayment program for victims harmed by delinquents was initiated in Florida in 1945; the earliest community service program was set up in South Dakota in 1965. A Minnesota program established in 1972 was the first to allow youthful offenders to perform direct services for victims instead of paying them cash; it also pioneered the use of mediation sessions between the two parties to foster a spirit of reconciliation. Hundreds of juvenile restitution projects were set up during the 1970s and 1980s (Warner and Burke, 1987; Klein, 1997; Roberts, 1998; Bradshaw and Umbreit, 1998).

The ground swell of support for restoring restitution is due to the glaring inadequacies of the other ways of recovering losses: private insurance coverage, governmental compensation plans, and civil lawsuits. Yet the principles underlying offender repayment are deceptively simple. They sound good in theory, but thorny problems arise when they are translated into practice.

Divergent Goals, Clashing Philosophies

The use of community service obligations as a form of restitution benefiting agencies, organizations, institutions, and whole neighborhoods has drawn criticism as an abuse of judicial activism. Guidelines in most jurisdictions specify that community service obligations cannot be imposed to enrich profit-making enterprises. But beyond that, judges can force people on probation or parole to labor on behalf of what judges consider to be noble causes, worthy charities, or deserving individuals. In the process of defining and assigning such "good works," judges may go beyond their legitimate mission and jeopardize their neutrality within the political patronage process (Czajkoski and Wollan, 1986). Also, through their ingenuity in devising individualized "creative sentences," some judges thwart guidelines intended to make sentences more consistent, predictable, and proportionate (Von Hirsch, 1988).

The major argument against the centrality of victim reimbursement is that the operations of the criminal justice system are intended to benefit society as a whole, not just the injured party. Other considerations should come first: punishing criminals harshly to teach them a lesson and to deter would-be lawbreakers from following their example, treating offenders in residential programs so that they can be released back as rehabilitated and productive members of the community, or incapacitating dangerous persons by confining them for long periods of time. Subordinating these other sentencing objectives to restitution would reduce the legal system to a mere debt collection agency catering to victims, according to a 1986 Supreme Court decision (Triebwasser, 1986). For these reasons restitution is often overlooked. But when restitution receives the attention it deserves, its supporters cannot agree among themselves about priorities. Some advocates have been promoting this ancient practice as an additional form of punishment, while others tout it as a better method of rehabilitation. Still other champions of restitution emphasize its beneficial impact on the financial well-being of victims and its potential for resolving interpersonal conflicts. As a result, groups with divergent aims and philosophies are pushing restitution, but are pulling at established programs from different directions (Galaway, 1977; Klein, 1997; Outlaw and Ruback, 1999).

Restitution as a Means of Repaying Victims Those who advance the idea that restitution is primarily a way of helping victims (see Barnett, 1977; and McDonald, 1978) argue that the punitively-oriented criminal justice system offers victims few incentives to get involved. Victims who cooperate with the police and prosecutors incur additional losses of time and money for their trouble (for example, for missing work while appearing in court). They also run the risk of suffering reprisals from offenders. In return they get nothing tangible, only the sense that they have discharged their civic duty by assisting in the apprehension, prosecution, and conviction of a dangerous person—a social obligation that goes largely unappreciated. The only satisfaction the system provides is revenge. But when restitution is incorporated into the criminal justice process, cooperation really pays off.

If the primary goal of restitution is to see to it that victims get repaid, then they should be able to directly negotiate their own arrangements, in terms of the total amount of money and the schedule of payments on an installment plan. Reimbursement should be as comprehensive as possible. The criminal ought to pay back all stolen cash plus the current replacement value of any lost or damaged property, any outstanding medical bills stemming from crime-related injuries (including psychological wounds attended to by therapists), any wages lost because of absence from work (including sick days or vacation time used during recuperation or while cooperating with the investigation and prosecution), plus any crime-related miscellaneous expenses (such as the cost of renting a car to replace one that was stolen or the cost of child care when a parent is testifying in court). Repayment should be as prompt as possible, since victims foot the bill in the interim.

Restitution as a Means of Rehabilitating Offenders Advocates of restitution as a means of rehabilitation (see Prison Research, 1976; and Keve, 1978) argue that instead of being punished, wrongdoers must be sensitized to the disruption and distress that their illegal actions have caused. By learning about their victims' plight, they come to realize the injurious consequences of their deeds. By expending effort, sacrificing time and convenience, and performing meaningful tasks, they begin to understand their personal responsibilities and social obligations. By making fiscal atonement or doing community service, they can feel cleared of guilt, morally redeemed, and reaccepted into the fold. Through their hard work to defray their victims' losses, offenders can develop a sense of accomplishment and self-respect from their legitimate achievements. They may also gain marketable skills, good work habits (like being punctual), self-discipline, and valuable on-the-job experience as they earn their way back into the community.

If restitution is to be therapeutic, offenders must perceive their obligations as logical, relevant, just, and fair. They must be convinced to voluntarily shoulder the burden of reimbursement because it is in their own best interest as well as being "the right thing to do." However, offenders probably will define their best interest as minimizing any penalty for their lawbreaking. This includes minimizing restitution, even if it is offered as a substitute for serving time behind bars. Offenders most likely will underestimate the suffering they have caused, while victims may tend to overestimate their losses and want to extract as much as they can (see McKnight, 1981). The sensibilities of wrongdoers must be taken into account, since their willingness to make amends is the key to the success of this "treatment."

Restitution as a Means of Reconciling Offenders and Their Victims Some advocates of restitution view the process primarily as a vehicle for reconciliation. After offenders have fully repaid their victims, hard feelings can dissipate. Also, reconciliation between two parties who share responsibility can be achieved after face-to-face negotiations. In situations without a clearly designated wrongdoer, restitution might be mutual, with each of the disputants reimbursing the other for damages inflicted during their period of hostility. Both parties have to consider the restitution agreement to be fair and constructive if a lasting, peaceful settlement is to emerge. (The philosophy and operating principles of "restorative justice," which relies heavily on restitution, are discussed in chapter 7.)

Restitution as a Means of Punishing Offenders Those who view restitution primarily as an additional penalty (see Schafer, 1977; and Tittle, 1978) argue that for too long offenders have been able to shirk this financial obligation to their victims. First, convicts should suffer incarceration to pay their debt to society. Next, they should undertake strenuous efforts to repay the specific individuals they harmed. Only then can their entanglement with the criminal justice system come to an end.

Reformers who promote restitution as a means of repaying victims, as a way of rehabilitating offenders, or as the basis for bringing about mutual reconciliation can come into conflict with hard-liners who view restitution as an additional means of punishment and deterrence. The problem with imposing restitution as an extra penalty following incarceration is that it delays repayment for many years. Since few convicts can earn decent wages while behind prison walls, the slow process of reimbursement cannot begin until their period of confinement is over, either when the sentence expires or upon the granting of parole. When punishment takes priority over reimbursement, the victims' financial needs, the offenders' therapeutic needs, and the community's need for harmony are subordinated to the punitive interests of the state. As long as prison labor remains poorly paid, restitution and incarceration will be incompatible.

Opportunities Versus Obstacles

Restitution is an extremely flexible sanction that is not being used to its full potential. It could arise at every juncture, from the immediate aftermath of the crime up until the final moments of parole supervision following a period of imprisonment (see Figure 6.1, which illustrates how restitution can be introduced at each stage in the criminal justice process).

As soon as a suspect is apprehended, an informal restitution arrangement can settle the matter. For example, a storekeeper might order a shoplifter to put the stolen item back on the shelf and never return to the premises. Parents might offer to pay for their son's spray painting on a neighbor's fence. In most states, however, serious offenses cannot be resolved informally. It is a felony for an injured party to demand or accept any payment as "hush money" to cover up a major violation of the law, in return for not pressing charges, or as a motive for discontinuing cooperation with the authorities in an investigation or prosecution. A criminal act is an offense against the state in addition to a particular person and cannot be settled privately (Laster, 1970).

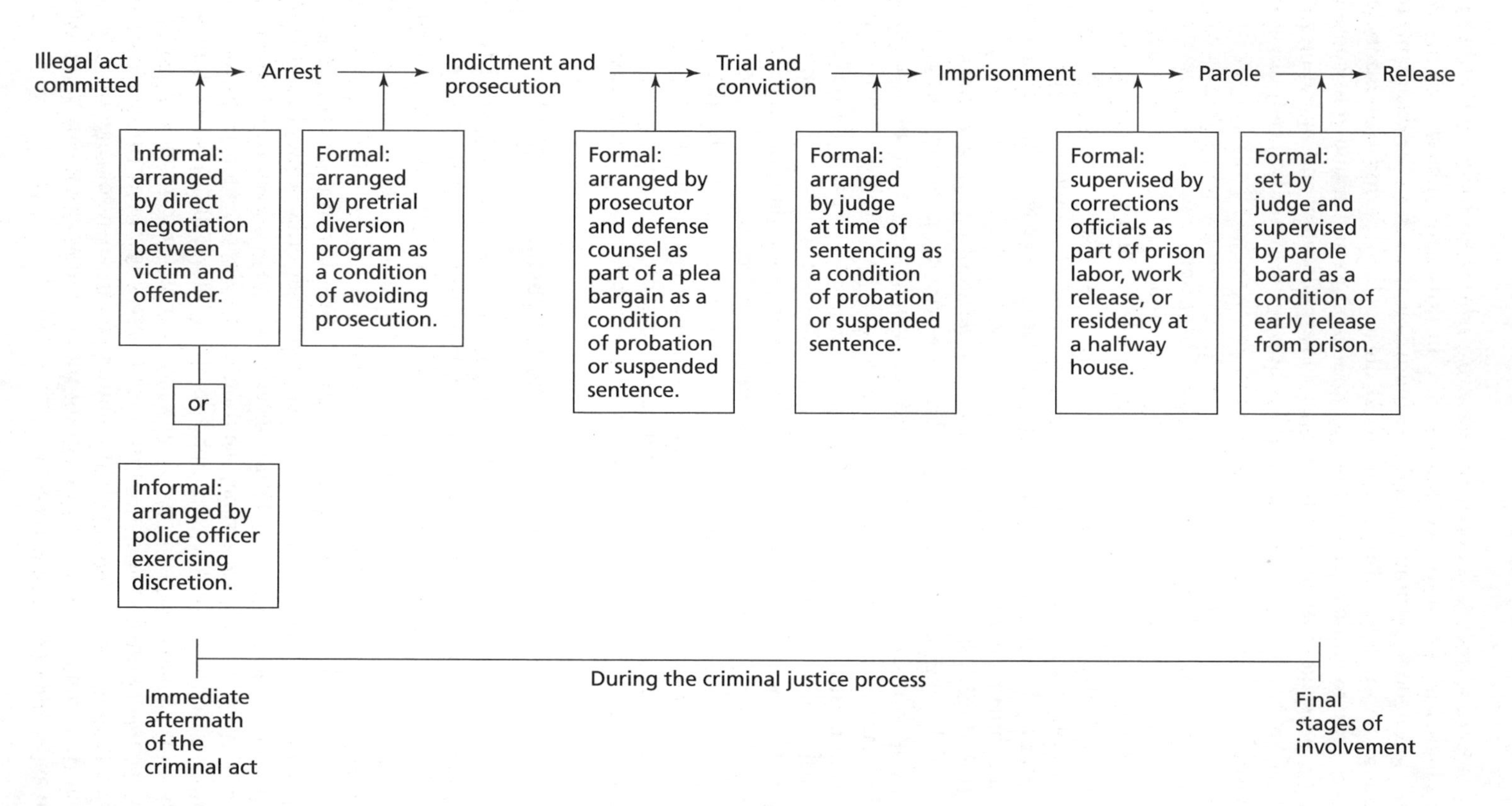

FIGURE 6.1 Opportunities for Restitution

After a suspect is arrested, a restitution agreement can be worked out as an alternative to prosecution (diversion). If a defendant is indicted, the district attorney's office can make restitution a condition for dismissing formal criminal charges. Once prosecution is initiated, restitution can be part of a plea bargain struck by the defense lawyer and the district attorney, wherein the accused concedes guilt in return for lesser penalties. Restitution is particularly appropriate as a condition of probation or of a suspended sentence. If incarcerated, an inmate can begin to repay the victim from wages earned from labor in prison or from a real job while on work release or residing at a halfway house. After serving time, restitution can be included as a condition of parole. Restitution contracts can be administered and supervised by various parties concerned about the crime problem: community groups, private and nonprofit charitable and religious organizations, juvenile courts, adult criminal courts, probation departments, corrections departments, and parole boards.

Yet as promising as restitution seems to be, it is not the answer for most victims. Only a small percentage will ever collect anything. The problem is directly comparable to the quest for emotional satisfaction from retribution. Just as most criminals escape punishment, most also evade restitution. The phenomenon of case attrition has been labeled "funneling," or "shrinkage," and has been likened to a "leaky net." At the outset many cases seem appropriate. But at the end of the criminal justice process, only a relative handful of victims receive even partial restitution. All the other cases (and offenders) have slipped through holes in the net (see Figure 6.2 for an explanation of how and why so many "escape" their financial obligations).

A large number of offenders will never have to make amends because their victims do not report the incidents to the police (refer back to Table 4.1). Also, the majority of offenders get away with their crimes because the police cannot figure out who the perpetrators are (clearance rates are especially low for the most numerous property crimes: burglaries, car thefts, and other forms of stealing; refer back to Table 4.2). Hence, right away most victims already have been eliminated from any chance of receiving reimbursement. For example, only about one half of all robberies are reported and only one quarter are solved, so only 1 out of every 8 robbery victim-offender relationships enters the system.

Of the relatively small number of crimes that are solved, additional problems can arise during the adjudication process. The overwhelming majority of cases (upwards of 90% in many jurisdictions) are resolved through plea negotiations that involve dropping charges or counts. Many victims are eliminated from consideration for these reasons. Some cases that go to trial result in acquittals, and some convictions are reversed on appeal. Of those who are convicted or who plead guilty, many are unwilling or unable to shoulder financial obligations. Prisoners granted parole have trouble finding any work, let alone a job that pays enough to allow them to make meaningful payments after all their other deductions. Finally, many jurisdictions lack both a tradition of ordering restitution and a mechanism for monitoring and enforcing such arrangements. Actually collecting the funds remains a major challenge for victims (Harland, 1983; McGillis, 1986; Davis and Bannister, 1995).

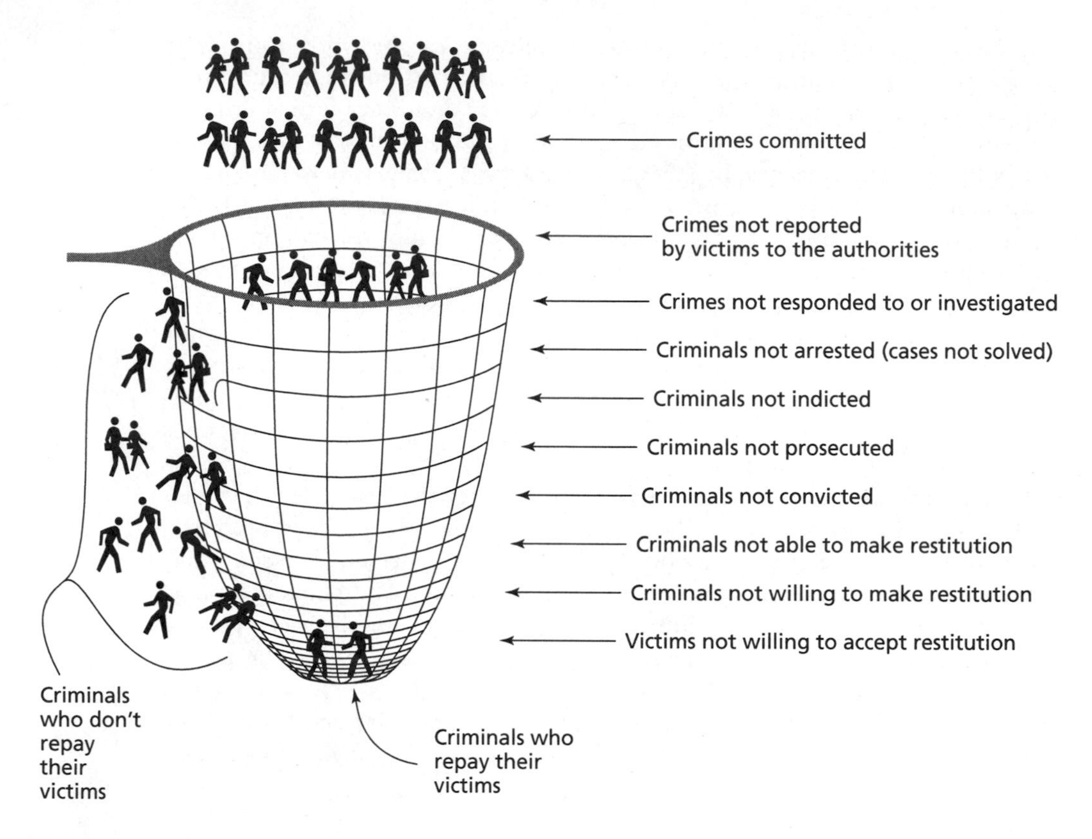

FIGURE 6.2 Funneling or Shrinkage: The Leaky Net

Economic realities also limit the ability of many convicts to meaningfully meet their restitution obligations. Since the street crime problem is in large part an outgrowth of poverty and the desperation it breeds, restitution obligations collide with economic realities. Restitution is predicated on work. Offenders must have, must be assisted to find, or must be given jobs. These jobs need to pay far more than the minimum wage to permit installments to be deducted from total earnings. But the U.S. economy cannot provide decent jobs for all who want to earn a living, even during the best of times. Besides chronic unemployment in some depressed communities, there is a permanent shortage of positions in government and industry paying adequate wages that would allow meaningful amounts to be deducted monthly and sent to victims.

Many dilemmas arise when restitution programs are considered within this context of intense competition and relative scarcity: If a job is found or created for an offender, then the prospects for the successful completion of the restitution obligation are increased. Otherwise, the victims of down-and-out street criminals are denied a chance to get repaid. If the job pays low wages, then the repayment cannot be completed within a reasonable amount of time. If nearly all of the offender's earnings are confiscated and handed over to the victim, then commitment to the job and to repaying the debt is jeopardized. If the job is demeaning, then its therapeutic value as a first step in the direction of a new lifestyle built on productive employment is lost. If the job is temporary and only lasts for the duration of the restitution obligation, then the risk of returning to a career of crime is heightened. But if the job found or created for the offender is permanent and pays well, then some observers might object that criminals are being rewarded, not punished, for their misdeeds. Law-abiding people desperately seeking decent jobs will resent any policy that seems to put offenders at the front of the line. Trade union members rightfully will fear that convict labor could replace civilian labor over the long run. But if offenders are put to work in large-scale prison industries, then business interests and labor unions justifiably will complain about unfair competition. If adolescents owing restitution are too young to receive working papers, then a job in private industry would violate child labor laws. Only unpaid community service would be permissible, but then victims get nothing. When victims are hard-pressed to make ends meet, restitution seems most appropriate. But if indigent offenders must hand over money to affluent victims, then restitution smacks of exploitation—taking from the poor and giving to the rich. Conversely, if offenders are allowed to pay off their obligations from their bank accounts instead of by hard work, it will appear that they are "buying their way out of trouble." If poor people without marketable job skills are kept behind bars and denied the opportunity to make restitution as a condition of probation or parole, such discrimination against an entire class of criminals would be a violation of the equal protection clause of the Fourteenth Amendment. Yet when the criterion "perceived ability to repay" determined eligibility for release from confinement, the typical participant in a restitution program turned out to be a white, middle-class, first-time property offender, and the most common recipient of reimbursement was a business (see Galaway and Hudson, 1975; Edelhertz, 1977; Hudson and Chesney, 1978; Gottesman and Mountz, 1979; Harland, 1979, 1981a; and Outlaw and Ruback, 1999).

In sum, although restitution is often morally appropriate and theoretically possible, given all these difficulties it is not statistically probable. Restitution was ordered in addition to a prison sentence in a small proportion of all convictions for violent crimes (for murder, 8%; rape and robbery, 12%; and aggravated assault, 18%); and in a larger proportion of all convictions for property crimes (for burglaries, 24%; and for fraud, 35%), according to a study of felony sentences handed down in state courts during 1992 (Langan and Graziadei, 1995). Of convicted felons who were fortunate enough to be sentenced to probation for violent acts, only 15% had to make restitution; and for property crimes just 34% had to try to repay their victims, during 1994 in the nation's 75 largest counties (Reaves, 1998). By 1996 the proportion of property crime offenders on probation who were ordered to pay restitution rose to 40%, but for perpetrators of violent crimes, the figure remained stuck at a mere 15% or so (Brown, Langan, and Levin, 1999; Hart and Reaves, 1999).

Evaluating Restitution Programs

Despite the limitations, conflicting priorities, dilemmas, and ironies discussed above, restitution is under way in many jurisdictions. Most supervision and collection programs (75%) are run by probation departments (OJJDP, 1998b). When criminologists and victimologists evaluate the effectiveness of these programs, the challenge is to properly identify the specific goals and to devise appropriate criteria to measure degrees of success and failure. Victim-oriented goals involve making the injured parties "whole again" by enabling them to collect full reimbursement and regain peace of mind (restoration of victims' psychological well-being and recovery from emotional stress and trauma). Offender-oriented goals involve identifying signs of rehabilitation and lowered recidivism. System-oriented goals include reducing case processing costs, relieving taxpayers of the financial burden of compensating victims, alleviating jail and prison overcrowding through alternative sentences, and improving citizen cooperation by providing material incentives to injured parties for participating in the criminal justice process (McGillis, 1986).

So many different aims and touted benefits coexist that no sweeping conclusions about the effectiveness of the programs now in operation can be drawn. Two offender-oriented evaluations found lower rates of recidivism among those delinquents who successfully complied with restitution orders imposed by juvenile courts (Butts and Snyder, 1992; Jacobs and Moore, 1994). One victim-centered evaluation of four programs with reputations for being successful uncovered considerable dissatisfaction with the amount imposed, the rate of repayment, and the total actually handed over. Most of the recipients believed that officials in the two probation departments, the prosecutor's office, and the victim service agency that administered the programs could have done more to involve them in determining the size of the award, to keep them posted about developments, and to help them collect the full amount due. The average reimbursement owed was about $250. The losses stemmed primarily from larcenies and burglaries, but also from robberies and assaults, some traffic-related offenses, and acts of fraud like passing bad checks. Unfortunately, the compliance rate with restitution orders was low. Even if probationers knowingly and willingly failed to keep up with the agreed-upon payment schedule, their conditional liberty was not likely to be taken away. Judges were not inclined to revoke probation, since they were more concerned with jail overcrowding and with being fair toward probationers (Davis, Smith, and Hillenbrand, 1992). If probationers make good-faith efforts to meet their obligations (by seeking employment, borrowing money, or selling off assets) but fail to pay off their debts in full, revocation would violate their Fourteenth Amendment rights, according to a Supreme Court ruling. If convicts can demonstrate an "inability to pay" an "unreasonable" or "unduly burdensome" restitution order, judges can reduce the amount due, stretch out the installments, or suspend the payment schedule entirely (National Victim Center, 1992b). Some states place limits on the total amount that can be extracted (for example, $5,000 for felonies, $1,000 for misdemeanors, and $2,500 for parental responsibility for damages inflicted by juveniles) (Roy, 1990).

Victims who have become impatient and dissatisfied with criminal court-ordered restitution can pursue another avenue for reimbursement: lawsuits in civil court.

WINNING JUDGMENTS IN CIVIL COURT

The Revival of Interest in Civil Lawsuits

> **A** 16-year-old exchange student from Japan, dressed up as a disco dancer, is looking for a Halloween costume party in a suburban neighborhood, but he rings the wrong doorbell. A woman opens the door, becomes frightened by the sight of the stranger, and slams the door shut, yelling to her husband to get his gun. He grabs his revolver, opens a side door and shouts "Freeze!" Apparently not understanding the meaning of the colloquialism, the foreign student moves forward and is shot and killed. A jury, understanding how the man might have felt he was under attack and in imminent danger, acquits the homeowner of manslaughter, deeming the killing a justifiable homicide. After the disappointing verdict is handed down in criminal court, the boy's parents sue the homeowner in civil court. The civil judge who hears the case (without a jury) rules that there was no justification whatsoever for the shooting and awards more than $650,000 in damages and funeral costs to the student's parents. (Nossiter, 1994b)
>
> **A** young black man is accosted by members of the Ku Klux Klan, kidnapped at gunpoint, beaten, and then hung from a tree. Two Klansmen are convicted of the racially motivated lynching. The victim's mother hires a lawyer experienced in civil rights cases to sue the Klan, not for money or even for revenge, but to shut it down by taking away its resources. A civil jury awards her $7 million, entitling her to ownership of the Klan chapter's headquarters building. (Kornbluth, 1987)
>
> **A** famous retired football player is put on trial for the murder of his ex-wife and her friend, but he is acquitted by a jury that is not convinced by the prosecution's extensive yet complicated forensic evidence. The outraged families of the murder victims sue him in civil court. A jury finds him liable for the wrongful deaths and awards the families millions of dollars in compensatory and punitive damages. (Ayres, 1997)

A growing number of victims are no longer content to simply let prosecutors handle their cases in criminal court, especially if convictions are not secured. They have discovered that they can go after their alleged wrongdoers and pursue their interests in another arena: civil court. Criminal proceedings are intended to redress "public wrongs" that threaten society as a whole. As a result, the economic interests of victims seeking restitution from convicts routinely are subordinated to the government's priorities, whether they concern probation, incarceration, or execution. Injured parties seeking financial redress are directed to civil court. There they can launch lawsuits designed to remedy "torts" (private wrongs) arising from violations of criminal law. Under tort law, plaintiffs (victims) can sue defendants and win judgments for punitive damages (money extracted to punish wrongdoers and deter others) as well as compensatory damages (to repay expenses).

Activists in the victims' movement want to call attention to these often overlooked legal rights and opportunities. Guilty verdicts in criminal courts cost offenders their freedom; successful judgments in civil courts cost offenders their money. Lawsuits can be successful even if charges are not pressed, or if the alleged perpetrator is found "not guilty" after a trial in criminal court. To make lawsuits an occupational hazard and a deterrent for habitual criminals, centers for legal advocacy and technical assistance have sprung up in a number of cities (Barbash, 1979; Carrington, 1986; Carson, 1986; National Victim Center, 1993).

The Litigation Process

Civil suits can involve claims for punitive damages as well as compensatory and pecuniary damages. Awards for compensatory damages (repayment of expenses) and pecuniary damages (to cover lost income) are supposed to restore victims to their former financial condition (make them "whole" again). They can receive the monetary equivalent of stolen or vandalized property, wages from missed work, projected future earnings that won't materialize because of injuries inflicted by the offender, and outlays for medical and psychiatric care (hospital bills, counseling expenses) plus recompense for physical pain and mental suffering (resulting from loss of enjoyment, fright, nervousness, grief, humiliation, and disfigurement). Punitive damages might be levied by the court to make negative examples out of lawbreakers who deliberately acted maliciously, oppressively, and recklessly (Stark and Goldstein, 1985; Brien, 1992).

In civil courts, victims can sue offenders for a number of "intentional torts": wrongful death, which enables survivors to collect compensation for the loss of a loved one without justification or legitimate excuse; assault, which covers intentionally threatening acts sufficient to cause fear of immediate bodily harm; battery, which involves intentional, harmful, physical contact that is painful, injurious, or offensive; trespass, which refers to the intentional invasion of another person's land; conversion of chattel (knowingly stealing or destroying someone's possessions or property); false imprisonment occurring against the person's will, like during a hostage-taking or rape; and infliction of emotional distress through extreme or outrageous conduct (Stark and Goldstein, 1985; Brien, 1992).

Civil actions commence when the **plaintiff** (also called the second party) formally files a complaint (also referred to as a "pleading"). This document includes a brief statement of the legal jurisdictional issues, a summary of the relevant facts of the case (the "causes of action" that show how the harm to the victim was a "direct and proximate result" of the alleged wrongdoer's behavior), and a request for relief for the injuries and damages sustained (monetary compensation). The victim's attorney brings the complaint to civil court and pays a fee. A deputy sheriff (or a privately retained process server) must physically hand this written document to the defendant (also called the first party) along with a summons requiring a response to the allegations within a stated period of time (usually 1 month). The accused wrongdoer submits an answer either admitting to the charges or, more likely, contesting them and issuing a defense (or perhaps even launching a countersuit). In preparing for a trial to resolve the competing claims, both parties engage in a process called discovery, in which they exchange written replies to questions (interrogatories), documents, and sworn statements of eyewitnesses (including police officers). Just as in criminal proceedings, the typical outcome is a negotiated compromise agreement. But if an out-of-court settlement cannot be reached, the accused exercises his or her Seventh Amendment right to a trial, and the victim has to prove the allegations in court. After considerable delays because of congested court calendars, the trial is held before 12 (or in some states 6) jurors or perhaps only in front of a judge. Following opening statements presented by attorneys for each side, witnesses testify and are cross-examined, and physical evidence is introduced. Then each party's attorney sums up, and the jury retires to deliberate. The jury votes and then renders its verdict about which of the two versions of events seems most truthful. The jury awards compensatory and perhaps punitive damages if it finds for the plaintiff and rejects the defendant's arguments. The losing party is likely to appeal the decision, and a higher court can overturn the trial court's verdict if errors in procedural law are discovered, or if the jury acted contrary to the evidence. Appeals may take many years to be resolved (Stark and Goldstein, 1985).

Litigation in civil court usually follows rather than precedes adjudication in criminal court. Victims usually wait to proceed with litigation because the evidence that is introduced during the criminal proceedings can be used again in the lawsuit and generally is sufficient to establish that a tort occurred. Furthermore, if the civil action is filed too early, the defense attorney will use this fact to try to undermine the victim's credibility as a witness for the prosecution, claiming that the testimony is motivated by potential financial gain. But if the civil action is not filed for years, the statute of limitations might run out, and it will be too late to sue the defendant. For example, in most states lawsuits alleging assault must be filed within 2 years, before victims' and offenders' memories fade and material evidence is lost or destroyed (Brien, 1992).

Possibilities and Pitfalls

Victims considering civil litigation must weigh the advantages and disadvantages of this course of action. One reason civil lawsuits are relatively uncommon is that most victims conclude that the benefits are not worth the costs. In addition, many injured parties are unfamiliar with this option.

Civil lawsuits have several attractions (see Stark and Goldstein, 1985; and Brien, 1992). First and foremost, victims can seize the initiative, haul their assailants into court, bring them to the bar of justice, and sue them for all they can get. In criminal cases, prosecutors exercise considerable discretion and make all the important decisions, even in jurisdictions where victims have the right to be informed and consulted. In civil cases, victims can regain a sense of control and feel empowered. It is up to them whether to sue and whether to accept a defendant's offer of an out-of-court settlement. Plaintiffs can present their own cases in small-claims courts, which have simplified procedures designed to expedite trials. Plaintiffs seeking larger amounts of money can hire attorneys of their own choosing and can participate in developing a strategy and preparing the case in anticipation of the trial. Victims can achieve full reimbursement through lawsuits. They can collect punitive damages far in excess of their actual out-of-pocket expenses. Defendants' assets—including homes, cars, savings accounts, investments, and inheritances—can be attached (confiscated), and their wages can be garnished (seized). Most attorneys practicing civil law accept cases on a **contingency basis** and don't charge victims unless they win.

Winning a judgment in civil court is easier than securing a conviction in criminal court because the standard of proof is lower and less demanding. In lawsuits, conflicting claims are decided by a **preponderance of the evidence** (the winning side is the one that presents the more convincing arguments, translated as "more likely than not" or "51%"), not by guilt beyond a reasonable doubt (proving the charges to a moral certainty). Therefore, a civil suit following a conviction in criminal court is likely to succeed because the same evidence and testimony can be used again in front of a second jury that does not have to reach an unanimous agreement and does not have to be convinced beyond a reasonable doubt. An acquittal in criminal court does not rule out civil action, since a jury still might decide in favor of a plaintiff who presents a more persuasive case than the defendant. Even if the prosecutor drops the criminal charges that were initially lodged by the police, a plaintiff might win if the evidence that came to light during the police investigation is presented in civil court. Since defendants in civil court do not face imprisonment or execution, constitutional protections are less stringent than in criminal court. Defendants cannot ignore lawsuits for more than 30 days or else they automatically lose (a "default" judgment). Nor can the accused wrongdoers "plead the Fifth Amendment" and refuse to testify on the grounds of self-incrimination; they must reply to the questions put to them or else risk a quick defeat. Rules of evidence are more flexible and, for example, allow the plaintiff to reveal the defendant's prior convictions for similar acts, a disclosure that usually wouldn't be permissible in criminal court. If plaintiffs win awards but defendants are unwilling to pay up voluntarily, sheriffs and marshals can be enlisted to enforce the courts' judgments by seizing contested assets or property (which can be sold at public auctions to raise cash).

Successful suits can make victims feel vindicated: The judges and jurors sided with them, accepted their version of events, and rejected the defendants' denials, excuses, or justifications. Victims teach perpetrators the lesson that crime does not pay and that wrongdoers ultimately will be held liable for their misdeeds. Reimbursement is soothing and revenge is sweet. Civil suits are the only means of redress when the entire injury and loss is intangible and subsumed under the heading of "pain and suffering."

> **A** 14-year-old boy tells his father that he was sexually molested on a number of occasions by a rock music superstar. The family sues the performer in civil court for sexual battery, seduction, willful misconduct, intentional infliction of emotional distress, fraud, and negligence. At first the entertainer's lawyers contend that the father is trying to extort money, but then they work out an out-of-court settlement involving millions of dollars. In return the family of the unidentified boy drops the lawsuit. Although the district attorney vows that the criminal investigation will go on, and the family says the teenager is cooperating with the authorities, without his testimony there is no prosecution. (Weinraub, 1994)

Despite the prospect of financial reimbursements, a number of drawbacks deter most victims from pursuing civil actions (see Stark and Goldstein, 1985; and Brien, 1992). Civil proceedings are independent of criminal proceedings. The entire case must be fought all over again in the courtroom, this time at the victim's expense without the backing of the government and its enormous resources. Victims have to put their lives on hold for years while the litigation process slowly drags on. Cases involve motions, hearings, conferences, depositions, interrogatories, negotiations, trials, and appeals. In the meantime, plaintiffs (and defendants as well) undergo a long drawn-out ordeal punctuated by moments of suspense, anxiety, frustration, despair, and humiliation. Despite their opposing interests and simmering mutual hostility, the warring parties must keep in contact with each other (at least through their respective lawyers) for months or even years after criminal proceedings end. If negotiations fail and last-minute out-of-court settlements are beyond reach, victims must relive the crime once again on the stand. After testifying, victims must submit to a withering cross-examination by the defense attorney that could raise questions of shared responsibility, damage the victims' reputation, and expose the most intimate details about lifestyles, injuries, losses, and suffering. The backlogs and delays in civil court are worse than those in criminal court because litigation has become such a popular way to settle disputes. Win or lose, civil suits drag on for years before they are resolved, forestalling closure for victims who want to get on with their lives.

Furthermore, the injured parties run the risk of being sued themselves. Countersuits by defendants against plaintiffs fit into a strategy of harassment and intimidation intended to force victims to drop charges or accept unfavorable out-of-court settlements. The defendants are likely to allege contributory negligence (the injured party was partly responsible for what happened), victim provocation, or even consent by the plaintiff to the action causing harm (that is, the plaintiff assumed the risk; for example, a woman alleging rape was drinking heavily and agreed to go to the man's apartment).

In the adversary system of civil proceedings, top-notch lawyers are said to be as important a factor as the facts of the case. Unfortunately, they probably won't be interested unless great sums of money are at stake. If they are victorious, their contingency fees may range as high as one third to one half of the money awarded to plaintiffs. Even victims who win may have to pay for most litigation expenses other than their attorney's fees, such as filing fees, deposition costs, and expert witness fees. Most discouraging of all is the problem of collection. Even in victory there can be defeat. If the offenders have spent or hidden the spoils of their crimes, it will be difficult for the victims' attorneys to recover any money without incurring great expenses. Most street criminals don't have what lawyers call "deep pockets" (assets like homes, cars, jewelry, bank accounts, investments in stocks and bonds, or business interests). On the contrary, many are virtually "judgment-proof"—broke and with no prospects of coming into money from work or inheritances.

Records about the successes and failures of victims who have sued offenders in civil courts have not been systematically compiled. The actual dollar amounts of some out-of-court settlements are kept confidential. However, advocacy groups are urging victims to consider exercising the civil court option if the identity and whereabouts of the offender are known, if restitution is not forthcoming from criminal court proceedings, and if compensation is not available from insurance companies or government-administered funds. Recognizing that few street criminals who commit acts of violence or theft have substantial assets or incomes, attorneys within the victims' rights movement have developed a strategic alternative: lawsuits against financially sound third parties.

Collecting Damages From Third Parties

Even when the perpetrators of a crime are known to be judgment-proof, victims still have a chance to recover their losses. Instead of suing those who directly and intentionally inflicted their injuries, plaintiffs can go after **third parties:** individuals, or entities such as businesses, institutions, or government agencies. The twist in these civil suits is to allege that a third party is partly to blame for the victim's misfortunes. The legal theory behind third-party suits parallels traditional notions of "negligence." The plaintiff argues that the defendant (the third party) had a duty or obligation, that there was a breach of this duty, and that this breach proximately caused injury to the plaintiff. The plaintiff tries to prove that the third party's gross negligence put the criminal in a position to single out the plaintiff for harm (Carrington, 1977).

Third-party suits can be of two types. The first is directed against enterprises like private businesses (for example, firearms distributors that fail to take adequate steps to prevent their handguns from being sold illegally to teenage gang members). The second type is aimed at custodial agencies and officials of the criminal justice system (such as parole boards, prison wardens, probation officers, and directors of mental institutions). Whereas suing offenders is reactive, third-party civil suits can be both reactive and proactive. If for no other motive than their own enlightened self-interest, the private enterprises and governmental bodies that are the targets of these kinds of suits are compelled to take reasonable and necessary precautions to prevent further incidents for which they could be sued again. By discouraging the indifference and negligence that facilitate predatory acts, third-party civil suits contribute to security consciousness and crime prevention (Carrington, 1986).

Suing Private Enterprises Several successful suits during the 1970s served as landmark cases for many subsequent claims.

> **A** well-known singer is raped in a motel by an unknown assailant who has entered her room by jiggling the lock on the sliding glass terrace doors. Badly shaken by the experience and unable to appear on stage, the singer sues the motel chain for loss of earnings. Her attorney argues that the motel has shown gross negligence by failing to maintain secure premises for its guests. A jury renders a verdict in her favor of $2.5 million. The motel chain agrees to a settlement by not appealing the verdict and pays her $1.5 million. (Barbash, 1979; Rottenberg, 1980)

> **A** security guard at a drive-in hamburger stand is shot in the head during a robbery. He doesn't sue the offender or his employer (the restaurant). Instead, his attorney argues successfully that the chain store that sold the robber the bullet is guilty of gross negligence. The guns and ammunition department routinely ignored an obscure state law that requires two citizens to vouch for the identity of the purchaser of bullets. (Barbash, 1979; Rottenberg, 1980)

Third-party lawsuits against businesses have established new definitions of corporate responsibility and financial liability. The suits never accuse the defendant (business) of intentionally harming the plaintiff, since the executives in charge probably never met either the victim or the offender and were two or three steps removed from the criminal action. What is alleged is that the defendant's gross negligence and breach of responsibility created a climate that made the criminal's task easier and the incident predictable (Carrington, 1977, 1978). Third-party suits against private enterprises can take several forms. Lawsuits can allege that landlords are responsible for crimes committed against their tenants because of inadequate lighting or locks; that hotels and motels are liable for assaults and thefts committed against guests because of lax security measures (such as failure to install closed-circuit television monitors, store room keys safely, or hire guards); that banks, stores, shopping malls, and theaters can be held accountable for failure to provide ordinary care to protect customers from robbers and thieves; that common carriers (bus, train, or airplane companies) are liable for failure to furnish customary forms of protection for passengers on vehicles or at stations and platforms; that employers who negligently hire known felons and put them in positions of trust and responsibility are liable if they commit crimes during the course of their work; and that college administrations are responsible for failing to correct security lapses that reasonable and prudent persons would realize endanger students in campus buildings and dormitories (Austern, 1987).

Victims can win if they can prove in civil court that the third party did not act to prevent a reasonably foreseeable crime. To prevail, the attorney must convincingly demonstrate that the defendant chronically disregarded complaints, did not post warnings, chose not to rectify conditions and improve security, and did not offer the degree of protection expected by community standards. Most claims fail to meet this test, but the few that successfully do can contribute to the improvement of public safety in places like shopping centers, bus terminals, parking lots, hotels, and apartment complexes (Brien, 1992).

While attorneys are honing their skills at "security litigation" seminars, landlords and businesses are attempting to make their premises "suit-proof" even if they cannot be crime-proof (Purdy, 1994). Since many lawsuits against property owners are settled out of court, reliable figures about their rate of occurrence and success are hard to find. One estimate from a sample of court records turned up 186 suits against property owners from 1958 to 1982. A later study established that the rate has increased, locating 267 third-party suits from 1983 to 1992. Almost half of all the suits were launched by rape victims (Deutsch, 1994).

Suing Governmental Bodies Successful third-party lawsuits against criminal justice agencies and custodial officials, like the two 1970s landmark cases described below, are less common than suits against private enterprises.

> **A** 14-year-old girl is abducted from a private school, tied to a tree, molested, and then left to freeze to death. The man who kills her had previously attacked another girl from the same school in the same way. He had been committed for treatment while under confinement at a nearby psychiatric institute. The victim's parents sue the mental hospital, a psychiatrist, and a probation officer for arranging the release of the offender into an outpatient program without first receiving court approval. They win a judgment of $25,000. (Carrington, 1977, 1978)

> **An** inmate with a record of 40 felony convictions and 17 escape attempts is permitted to participate in a "take-a-lifer to dinner" program. After eating at the home of the prison's baker, he breaks loose, commits an armed robbery, and kills a man. The victim's widow sues the warden both personally and in his official capacity, in addition to the state prison system, for gross negligence. Her attorney argues that the warden didn't have legislative authority or administrative permission from his superiors to let the inmate out that night. She wins a judgment of $186,000, which the state does not appeal. (Barbash, 1979; Rottenberg, 1980)

The basic charge in civil actions against the government also is gross negligence. The plaintiffs allege that officials severely abused their discretionary authority. The crimes are said to have happened because official inaction or incompetence facilitated the offenders' inclinations to harm innocent parties. In a few states, governmental bodies cannot be sued even when the negligence of officials clearly contributed to the commission of crimes; the agents and agencies are protected by the English common law doctrine of "sovereign immunity." Most states and the federal government permit citizens to sue but impose limitations (like financial caps and exemption from punitive damages) and invoke special procedures (Austern, 1987; Carrington, 1978).

The specific charges in third-party liability lawsuits against governmental agencies and officials fit under a number of headings (Austern, 1987). Claims against the police can allege nonfeasance: that officers failed to act to protect individuals to whom they owed a special duty, such as witnesses for the prosecution. Claims can also allege police malfeasance: that officers acted carelessly or inattentively as victims got hurt.

> **A** husband stabs his wife 13 times. Nearly 30 minutes later, the police arrive in response to her earlier call for help. He wanders around screaming, kicks her in the head, then drops their son on her unconscious body and kicks her again. Finally, the police restrain him and take him into custody. After 8 days in a coma and several months in a hospital, she sues the city, three police chiefs, and 29 officers. Her lawsuit alleges that because the assailant was her husband the police failed to provide her with equal protection under the law (as guaranteed by the Fourteenth Amendment) by handling her numerous calls for help over the years differently than stranger assaults. A jury finds the police negligent for failing to protect her and awards her $2.3 million. The city appeals, and she settles for $1.9 million out of court. (Gelles and Straus, 1988)

When prisoners are not adequately supervised or are let go as the result of an administrative error and then inflict harm, suits can allege "wrongful escape." When dangerous convicts are released and then injure persons whom they had previously publicly threatened, suits can be filed for "failure to warn." Claims can also allege "wrongful release" when through gross negligence on the part of officials a high-risk inmate is granted conditional release (like probation, parole, or furlough) from a jail, prison, or mental institution and then commits a foreseeable crime.

> **A** mental patient walks out of a minimum-security state psychiatric hospital and wanders into a small town. He buys a hunting knife and then for no apparent reason seizes a 9-year-old-girl walking down the street with her family and stabs her more than 30 times. He is found not guilty of murder by reason of insanity. The girl's parents sue the state for failing to protect their daughter from this madman. The state agrees to a $1.5 million out-of-court settlement, compensating the mother for the emotional harm of witnessing her daughter's murder and pledging to improve security at state mental hospitals. (Hays, 1992)

Suits against custodial officials and agencies raise important issues. The U.S. Supreme Court ruled in 1980 (Martinez case) that neither the Constitution nor the Civil Rights Act of 1964 gave the survivors of a murder victim the right to sue a state parole board (Carrington, 1980). In upholding the doctrine of sovereign immunity from liability, the justices of the Court argued that government has a legitimate interest in seeking to rehabilitate criminals. All the treatment alternatives to totally incapacitating convicts through maximum-security confinement involve a gamble with the public's safety. Halfway houses, therapeutic communities, work release, educational release, furloughs, probation, and parole all grant conditional liberty to known offenders who may pose a continuing threat to community safety. Underlying a charge of "abuse of discretionary authority" and "gross negligence" is the assumption that dangerousness can be predicted. It usually can't be with any statistical certainty. Some patients and inmates thought to be dangerous turn out to be well-behaved, and some individuals on conditional liberty who were rated as posing a low risk may suddenly act viciously.

What is predictable is that successful third-party lawsuits by victims against custodial officials and agencies will have a chilling effect on wardens, psychiatrists, parole boards, and others who make decisions regarding confinement versus release. What might develop in these therapeutic relationships is a type of defensiveness comparable to the defensive medicine practiced by doctors afraid of malpractice suits. Fear of legal and financial repercussions could dominate professional judgments and record keeping. Rehabilitation programs could be severely constrained. Eligible convicts could be barred from such programs because administrators wouldn't want to jeopardize their own careers by releasing them from total confinement. Qualified professionals could be deterred from taking jobs as custodial officials because of exposure to personal liability lawsuits, unless states protect such employees under a doctrine of sovereign immunity.

On the other hand, vulnerable members of the general public need lawsuits as a vehicle to exert some leverage over justice officials and unresponsive bureaucracies. And aggrieved parties need a way to hold grossly negligent agency officials accountable, as well as a mechanism to recover losses inflicted by dangerous persons who should not have been left unsupervised. Some victim advocates see third-party lawsuits as the appropriate remedy to establish a proper balance between two conflicting policy objectives: lowering the crime rate in the long run by rehabilitating offenders through the judicious granting of conditional liberty, and maintaining public safety in the short run by incapacitating and incarcerating individuals believed to be dangerous to the community.

COLLECTING INSURANCE REIMBURSEMENTS

Private Crime Insurance

Private insurance companies are innocent third parties that can quickly and routinely reimburse victims for their losses. The positive aspect is that a prudent policyholder can be repaid without too many complications (as long as a formal complaint is filed with the police). The drawbacks are that a potential target must have the foresight to purchase protection in advance, that a company must be willing to issue a policy (some people and businesses in high-crime areas have trouble finding an insurer), that the premiums for the coverage must be affordable (many people are aware of life's dangers but do not have the disposable income to pay for the "luxury" of insurance), and that exclusions of losses (because of "deductible clauses") considered to be relatively minor by the company loom as serious financial blows for low-income families (Sarnoff, 1996).

Cautious individuals can protect themselves against a wide variety of hazards (see Miller, Cohen, and Wiersema, 1996). Life insurance policies can pay sizable sums to survivors of murder victims. Some policies (which cost more) contain a "double indemnity" clause that grants survivors twice as much if the policyholder dies unexpectedly from an accident or a criminally inflicted injury. Coverage can also be purchased to offset lost earnings (income maintenance) and expenses due to medical bills (health insurance). Property can be insured against loss or damage. Car and boat insurance covers costs imposed by theft, vandalism, and arson. Home insurance covers losses due to burglary, some larcenies (of items left on porches or in yards, for example), vandalism, arson, and robbery (if the confrontation occurs within the dwelling). Some companies sell robbery insurance that reimburses losses of valuables like jewelry or cameras no matter where the crime occurs. A few companies offer protection to businesses whose executives might be kidnapped and held for ransom.

Patterns of Loss, Recovery, and Reimbursement Statistics derived from the *National Crime Victimization Survey* confirm some commonsense predictions about insurance coverage and recovery. First, some types of coverage are more common than others. More people are insured against medical expenses than against property losses. Medical costs are potentially more devastating than theft or vandalism of tangible goods, and health coverage often is provided by an employer as a fringe benefit of full-time jobs. Second, higher-income individuals are more likely to buy crime insurance than lower-income people (even though the poor are exposed to more risks and suffer higher victimization rates). Third, large losses are more likely than small ones to be reimbursed through insurance claims; the victims most likely to receive cash settlements are those whose cars are stolen. Only a small proportion of families who suffer burglaries and larcenies are reimbursed. An even smaller fraction of persons who are robbed or victims of pickpockets are insured against such losses. Most policies have "deductible" clauses that stipulate the victim must bear the first $100 (or some other sum) of the losses and cannot file a claim unless the out-of-pocket expenses exceed this figure. Hence, most crime-imposed losses (which add up to minor amounts) cannot be recovered (Harland, 1981a).

Studies concerning patterns of burglary loss, coverage, and recovery reveal that both the average amount stolen and the percentage of victims who are insured are positively correlated with family income. That means that wealthier families lose more to burglars but also are more likely to be insured than lower-income households. In one study during the 1970s, only 1 family in 10 was insured in the lowest income category, whereas about half of all families in the higher-income category were covered. (Presumably, the rich were fully insured, but that data was unavailable.) In sum, although a small number of families recover substantial amounts, insurance provides relief for relatively few burglary victims (Skogan, 1978; Harland, 1981a).

Federal Crime Insurance

Insurance companies make profits in two ways: They adjust their rates continuously so that they take in more in premiums than they pay out in claims, and these enterprises invest the money paid in by policyholders in order to collect interest, dividends, and rents. To contain costs and limit payouts, companies raise their rates, place caps on reimbursements, impose sizable deductibles, and exclude certain kinds of common losses. One irony of the for-profit insurance business is that those who face the greatest risks are sometimes denied coverage outright or can't afford the exorbitant premiums. The insufficiency and unfairness of private insurance underwriting practices first received public attention during the late 1960s. The National Advisory Panel on Insurance in Riot-Affected Areas (part of the National Advisory Commission on Civil Disorders) was appointed by President Johnson in 1967 to examine the plight of inner-city residents and businesses that had suffered losses during ghetto rebellions. The panel cited a general lack of insurance availability as a contributing factor in urban decay: the closing of businesses, the loss of jobs, the abandonment of buildings, and the exodus of residents from high-crime areas.

In 1968, Congress followed some of the panel's recommendations and granted relief to victims of insurance "redlining" (an illegal, discriminatory practice that results in denial of coverage). The Department of Housing and Urban Development Act set up Fair Access to Insurance Requirements (FAIR) plans to make sure that property owners were not denied fire damage coverage solely because the neighborhood had a high rate of arson cases. In 1970, Congress amended the 1968 act to permit the federal government to offer "affordable" burglary and robbery insurance directly to urban homeowners, tenants, and businesses in locales where such coverage from private companies was either unavailable or unreasonably expensive. Federal intervention into the insurance market to assist actual and potential crime victims was viewed as a last resort (Bernstein, 1972). The Federal Emergency Management Agency (FEMA) currently runs the Federal Insurance Administration.

Once the government began to sell insurance coverage, it became reasonable to ask whether public funds could be set up to bail out families that faced economic ruin because they were not willing or able to take out insurance or were not adequately protected, especially against huge medical bills and lost earnings. Public insurance plans have been devised to aid such persons. They are called victim compensation programs.

RECOVERING LOSSES BY TURNING TO COMPENSATION PROGRAMS

Reimbursement From Government Funds

Most street crime victims never receive criminal court-ordered restitution for one obvious reason: Their offenders were not caught and convicted. For a parallel reason most victims never collect court-ordered civil judgments: Their perpetrators cannot be identified or located and successfully sued. Furthermore, rarely can any third party be held partly responsible for the incident and sued for its liability. Given the inadequacy of most people's private insurance coverage when major disasters strike, the only remaining hope for monetary recovery lies with a different sort of third party, a state compensation fund. Reimbursement from a government fund appears to be the only realistic method for routinely restoring individuals to the financial condition they were in before the crime occurred.

> **A** middle-aged man is blinded by assailants, who are later caught, convicted, and imprisoned. Upon their release they are ordered by the court to pay restitution to their victim for the loss of his eyesight. Under the arrangement it will take 442 years for the man who lost his sight to collect the full amount due him. (Fry, 1957)
>
> **A** Good Samaritan comes to the aid of two elderly women who are being harassed by a drunken youth on a subway train. As his wife and child watch in horror, the man is stabbed to death by the drunk. The killer is captured and sentenced to 20 years to life in prison. The widow is forced to send her child to live with her mother while she goes to work to pay off bills. ("The Good Samaritans," 1965)
>
> **A** man shot during the course of a robbery is awarded $30,000 for unpaid medical bills and $12,000 for wages lost because of his injuries. He receives $600 a month until he is able to go back to work. (New York State Crime Victims Board, 1988)
>
> **T**he widow of a murder victim is granted $1,500 for funeral expenses and $15,000 for loss of support. She collects $1,000 a month in death benefits until a maximum of $20,000 in payments is reached. (New York State Crime Victims Board, 1988)

The first two cases, which took place respectively in England in 1951 and in New York City in 1965, dramatized the need for special funds to compensate victims for devastating losses. The remaining two cases, from a state-run compensation program, illustrate the kinds of aid that these government-run boards now provide. Money can't erase painful memories or cure lingering emotional and physical wounds. Payments are stopgap measures that counteract the effects of crime without touching its roots. Yet reimbursement can ease the suffering of victims. It is the easiest, simplest, and most direct way of speeding a victim's recovery and of institutionalizing the notion of lending a helping hand to someone in need.

The History of Victim Compensation by Governments

The earliest reference to governmental compensation for crime victims can be found in the ancient Babylonian Code of Hammurabi (about 1775 B.C.), which is considered to be the oldest written body of criminal law. The code instructed territorial governors to replace a robbery victim's lost property if the criminal was not captured; in the case of a murder, the governor was to pay the heirs a specific sum in silver from the treasury. In the centuries that followed, restitution by the offender replaced compensation by the state. But during the Middle Ages, restitution also faded away. Victims had no avenue of redress except to try to recover losses by suing offenders in civil court.

Interest in compensation revived during the 1800s when the prison reform movement in Europe focused attention on the suffering of convicts and in doing so indirectly called attention to the plight of their victims. A major figure in the classical school of criminology (Jeremy Bentham) argued that those who had been victimized in their person or their fortune should not be abandoned to their fate. The society to which they had contributed and which ought to have protected them owed them an indemnity. The three leading criminologists of the positivist school of thought (Cesare Lombroso, Enrico Ferri, and Raffaele Garofalo) also endorsed compensation (and restitution) at several International Penal Congress meetings held at the turn of the century. But these resolutions did not lead to any concrete actions. Legal historians have uncovered only a few scattered instances of special funds set aside for crime victims: one in Tuscany after 1786, another in Mexico starting in 1871, and one beginning in France in 1934. Switzerland and Cuba also experimented with victim compensation (MacNamara and Sullivan, 1974; Schafer, 1970; Silving, 1959).

An English magistrate (Margery Fry) is widely acknowledged as the prison reformer who sparked the revival of interest in compensation in Anglo-Saxon legal systems in the late 1950s. Because of her efforts, a government commission investigated different reparations proposals and set up a fund in 1964 in Great Britain. Several Australian states and Canadian provinces followed suit during the next few years. New Zealand offered the most complete protection in the Western world. In 1972 it abolished the victim compensation program it had pioneered in 1963 and absorbed it within a universal accident insurance system. Everyone in New Zealand was covered for losses arising from any kind of misfortune, including crimes. The nature of the event, the reason it occurred, and the responsibility for it did not affect compensation decisions (European Committee on Crime Problems, 1978; Meiners, 1978).

The Debate Over Compensation in the United States

In the late 1950s the question of compensation surfaced in American law journals. Initially, distinguished scholars raised many objections to the idea of government aid to crime victims. But support for the notion of compensation grew when a Supreme Court Justice (Arthur Goldberg) argued that society should assume some responsibility for making whole again those whom the law had failed to protect. Soon, some well-known political figures of the period came to accept the proposition that special funds to repay victims should be set up. Their enthusiasm was in accord with the liberal political philosophy embodied in President Kennedy's "New Frontier" and President Johnson's "Great Society": that government programs should be designed to try to solve persistent social problems.

The proposals of elected officials, the suggestions of legal scholars and criminologists, and the pressures of coalitions of interest groups were necessary but not sufficient to trigger legislatures into action. Widely publicized incidents of brutality and tragedy supplied the missing ingredient of public support in the first few states to experiment with compensation schemes. In 1965, California initiated a repayment process as part of its public assistance system. In 1966, New York created a special board to allocate reimbursements. In 1967, Massachusetts designated certain courts and the state attorney general's office as granters of financial aid to victims.

Starting in 1965, Congress began to debate the question of federal encouragement of and assistance to state compensation programs. No lobby emerged to pressure elected officials to vote against compensation plans. Even private insurance companies did not feel threatened by the potential loss of business. At the hearings the idea of compensation was endorsed by the American Bar Association, the International Association of Chiefs of Police, the National District Attorneys' Association, the U.S. Conference of Mayors, the National League of Cities, the National Conference of State Legislatures, existing state compensation boards, judges' organizations, senior citizens' groups, and the National Council on Crime and Delinquency ("Crime Control Amendments," 1973; Edelhertz and Geis, 1974; "Crime Victims' Aid," 1978; Meiners, 1978). The arguments over the pros and cons of governmental compensation raised many important political, philosophical, and pragmatic issues (see Childres, 1964; Schultz, 1965; Wolfgang, 1965; Brooks, 1972; Geis, 1976; Meiners, 1978; Carrow, 1980; U.S. House Committee on the Judiciary, 1980; Gaynes, 1981; and Elias, 1983a).

The most compelling rationales advanced by advocates presented compensation as an additional type of social insurance, as a way of meeting an overlooked governmental obligation to all citizens, or as a means of assisting individuals facing financial ruin. Proponents of the "shared risk" rationale viewed compensation as part of the safety net of the comprehensive social insurance system that had been developing in the United States since the Great Depression. All public welfare insurance programs are intended to enable people to cope with the hazards that threaten stability and security in everyday life. Health expenses are addressed by Medicaid and Medicare, disability and untimely death by Social Security, on-the-job accidents by workers' compensation, and loss of work and earnings by unemployment compensation. The premiums for these state-run compulsory insurance plans are derived from taxation. Criminal injury insurance, like the other types of coverage, provides "equal protection" against dangers that are reasonably certain to harm some members of society but that are unpredictable for any given individual. All taxpayers contribute to the pool to spread the costs, and therefore everyone is entitled to reimbursement.

The "government liability" rationale argued that the state is responsible for the safety of its citizens because it monopolizes, or reserves for itself, the right to use force to suppress crime and to punish offenders. Since individuals are not allowed to routinely carry deadly weapons around for their own defense, and settling serious criminal matters privately is forbidden, the government has made it difficult for victims to protect themselves and to recover their losses. Therefore, within the social contract, the state becomes liable for damages when its criminal justice system fails to fulfill its public safety obligation to its citizens. By the logic of this argument, all victims ought to have a right to compensation, regardless of their economic standing and the type of loss they have suffered.

Those taking the "social welfare" approach held that the state has a humanitarian responsibility to assist victims, just as it helps other needy and disadvantaged groups. The aid is given as a symbolic act of mercy, compassion, and charity (and not as universal insurance coverage or because of any legal obligation). According to this theory, receiving compensation is a privilege, not a right, so eligibility and payment amounts can be limited.

Besides these three rationales several additional arguments were advanced to encourage public acceptance of compensation. Some sociologists and criminologists contended that the "system" (the social institutions, economic and political arrangements, and prevailing relationships within society) generates crime by perpetuating bitter competition, poverty, discrimination, unemployment, and financial insecurity, which in turn breed greed, desperation, and violence. Therefore through its governmental bodies, society owes crime victims compensation as a matter of social justice. Other advocates contrasted the attention accorded to criminals with the neglect shown toward their innocent victims. They charged that it was blatantly unfair to attend to many of the medical, educational, vocational, legal, and emotional needs of wrongdoers (albeit minimally and sometimes against their will) at public expense and yet leave injured victims to fend for themselves. Compensation partly corrected this "imbalance." Finally, some pragmatists anticipated that the prospect of monetary reward would induce more victims to cooperate with the authorities by reporting incidents, pressing charges, and testifying against their assailants.

Some skeptics and critics objected to the notion of government intervention on both philosophical and practical grounds. The earliest opponents of importing this British Commonwealth practice to America denounced what they considered to be the spread of "governmental paternalism" and "creeping socialism." They contended that taxpayer-funded crime insurance undermined the virtues of rugged individualism, self-reliance, personal responsibility, independence, saving for emergencies, and calculated risk taking. They considered any expansion of the welfare state and the growth of new, expensive, and remote bureaucracies to be greater evils than the fiscal neglect of victims. They contended that, unlike governmental bodies, private enterprise could write more effective and efficient policies for individuals and families who had enough prudence and foresight to purchase protection before tragedy struck. Other opponents worried that criminal-injury insurance—like fire, auto, and theft coverage—was vulnerable to fraud. Deserving applicants would be hard to distinguish from manipulators who staged incidents, inflicted their own wounds, and padded their bills. Finally, certain critics did not dispute the merits of compensation programs but objected to their establishment and expansion on financial grounds. They argued that it was unfair to compel taxpayers to repay the losses of victims as well as foot the bill for the costs of the police, courts, and prisons. (To accommodate this objection, state programs have come to rely more heavily on raising money from penalties imposed on lawbreakers of all kinds, including traffic law violators.)

A statistical analysis of congressional votes on bills between 1965 and 1980 revealed that Democrats (particularly liberal Democrats) tended to favor allocating federal aid to reimburse crime victims; Republicans (especially conservative Republicans) tended to oppose spending federal tax dollars on state compensation programs. The usual exceptions to these patterns were conservative Democrats (generally from southern states) who sided with conservative Republicans against compensation plans and some liberal Republicans (often from northern states) who joined with liberal Democrats in support of these pro-victim legislative initiatives. In other words, ideology proved to be a better predictor of voting behavior than party affiliation (Karmen, 1981b).

In 1984, Congress finally reached a consensus about the appropriate role for the federal government on the question of compensation and passed a Victims of Crime Act (VOCA), ending nearly 20 years of floor debates, lobbying, political posturing, maneuvering, and last-minute compromises. VOCA established a fund within the U.S. Treasury, collected from fines, penalties, and forfeitures. Administered by the attorney general, the money was earmarked to subsidize state compensation funds and victim assistance services, and to aid victims of federal crimes (Peak, 1986). In 1989, VOCA guidelines were revised to encourage state programs to expand their coverage and to resemble each other more closely. Providing federal matching funds worked out as intended: Every state had set up a compensation program by 1993 (Maine and South Dakota were the last to join in).

How Programs Operate: Similarities and Differences

In all of the 50 states plus the District of Columbia, the question of whether to compensate victims or not has been resolved for the time being. But the programs vary in a number of ways, reflecting the diversity in the traditions, populations, crime rates, and resources of the states and the differing rationales on which the programs were based.

Certain requirements are the same in each state (see Parent, Auerbach, and Carlson, 1992). All of the programs grant reimbursements only to "innocent" victims. Compensation board investigators always look for evidence of "contributory misconduct." If it is established that the individual was partly to blame for getting hurt, the grant can be reduced in size or disallowed entirely. For example, applicants would not be repaid if they were engaging in an illegal activity when they were injured (such as getting shot while holding up a liquor store, getting robbed while buying drugs, or being beaten after agreeing to perform an act of prostitution). Most boards would rule victims of barroom brawls as ineligible if they had been drinking, uttered "fighting words," and thereby provoked the fracas in which they got seriously injured. However, applicants can appeal claims that were denied.

Another common feature is that the programs deal only with the most serious crimes that result in physical injury, psychological trauma, or death: murder, rape, assault, robbery, child sexual abuse, child physical abuse, spouse abuse, other types of domestic violence, and also hit-and-run motor vehicle collisions and crashes caused by drunk drivers. Most do not repay people for property that is damaged or lost in thefts, burglaries, or robberies (unless they are elderly or the possessions are "essential," like hearing aids or wheelchairs). Only "out-of-pocket expenses" (bills not paid by collateral sources [such as Medicaid] or private insurance [like Blue Cross]) are reimbursed. The payments can be for medical expenses (to doctors, nurses, emergency rooms, clinics, hospitals), for mental health services (to psychiatrists, counselors, therapists), and for earnings lost because of missed work. The families of murder victims are eligible for assistance with reasonable funeral and burial costs; surviving dependents can qualify for a death benefit or pension to compensate for their loss of financial support. Each program requires that all parts of a claim be fully documented with bills and receipts. All the programs prohibit double recoveries. Any money collected from insurance policies or other government sources is deducted (subrogated) from the compensation board's final award. In the statistically unusual cases in which offenders are caught, found guilty, and forced to pay restitution, this money is also subtracted from the award. For a victim to get repaid, the assailant does not have to be caught and convicted. But in every state the applicant must report the crime promptly to the police and cooperate fully with any investigation and prosecution to remain eligible.

Despite sharing these basic features, the 50 state programs differ in a number of ways: how long victims can wait before telling the police about the crime (from 1 day to 3 months, with a mode of 3 days), how long victims can take before applying for reimbursement (from 6 months to 3 years, with a mode of 1 year), how much victims can collect (maximum awards of $1,000 to $50,000 plus limitless medical expenses, with modes at $10,000 and $25,000), whether the program will grant an emergency loan before fully investigating a case, and whether lawyers can be hired to help present cases and collect fees. Eligibility rules differ slightly from state to state. For example, survivors of murder victims (who can apply for reimbursements of customary funeral costs and perhaps loss of financial support) include parents, siblings, and in-laws in some programs, but most limit coverage to children and spouses. In 1988, amendments to the Victims of Crimes Act mandated that eligibility in all states be extended to innocent family members injured by domestic violence, people hurt by drunk driving crashes, and nonresidents (visitors and commuters). On the other hand, whole groups of people can be automatically ruled ineligible. In each state the list varies. Law enforcement officers and fire fighters injured in the line-of-duty are generally excluded because they are covered by workers' compensation. In some jurisdictions, prison inmates, parolees, probationers, ex-convicts, and members of organized crime are automatically eliminated from consideration (NIJ, 1998).

A number of trends in compensation regulations are worth noting. Initially, the money given out by compensation programs came from general revenues, which essentially means from taxpayers. The trend since the 1970s is to rely more heavily on funds derived from "penalty assessments" or "abusers' taxes" (more than half of the programs get all or part of their money this way). These funds are raised from fines and surcharges levied on persons convicted of traffic violations, misdemeanors, and felonies plus, in some states, taxes imposed on the earnings of offenders on work release and from collateral forfeited by defendants who jump bail. Offender-funded compensation programs reflect a larger trend that compels convicts to shoulder all kinds of financial obligations, including restitution, charges for room and board, fines, court costs, and supervision fees. Before the 1980s, in about one third of the states, only claimants who faced severe financial hardships would pass a "means test" to become eligible for reimbursement; the others were told they could afford to absorb their losses. By the end of the 1980s, only 11 programs still required their applicants to establish a dire fiscal need before granting an award. Another change over time has been to extend coverage to include losses resulting from pain and suffering, child care, cleaning up the crime scene, and replacing essential personal property like eyeglasses and false teeth. Some programs are broadening eligibility to include incest victims, victims of sexual assault who escaped without physical injuries, elderly victims of burglaries, and parents of missing children. Encouraged by VOCA's financial support, some states have recognized the need to raise the upper limits for awards because of substantial hikes in the cost of living over the years. In the other states with frozen maximum benefits, compensation payments are failing to keep up with the rate of inflation. Minimum loss requirements and deductible provisions (usually of $100) designed to eliminate minor claims are being scrapped and persist in less than half the states (NOVA, 1988; Parent, Auerbach, and Carlson, 1992; NIJ, 1998).

Monitoring and Evaluating Compensation Programs

Many of the arguments about the "rightness" of compensation hinge on judgments about what type of financial help victims require and on assumptions about the ability of programs to meet these needs. Since a number of states have operated programs for several decades, a substantial body of data has become available for analysis. The differences between state programs can be considered an asset. Each jurisdiction can be regarded as a "social laboratory" where an experiment is in progress. From this viewpoint various approaches to achieving the same ends are being tested to determine which works best. Evaluation is especially important as a means of improving service delivery during periods when the public clamors for additional government aid but is unwilling to pay higher taxes for it.

Program evaluations reveal how well compensation boards are meeting their goals. But assessing whether they are succeeding or failing in their mission requires that their goals be stated clearly and precisely. In the 1960s the early advocates of reimbursing victims from government-administered funds had ambitious expectations and made optimistic (and perhaps unrealistic) pronouncements. Their noble, charitable, and humanitarian aims of substantially alleviating the economic suffering of injured parties generally have not been realized. Statistics that either support or refute other contentions can be derived from two kinds of assessments: process evaluations and impact evaluations.

Uncovering How Programs Work Process evaluations are focused on the programs' internal operations and monitor variables like productivity, overhead costs, and decision-making patterns. Assessments of the efficiency of administrative practices contribute to efforts to eliminate delays, minimize overhead, and iron out inequities. Process evaluators also develop profiles of the typical claimants and recipients of awards. Analyzing data bearing on these questions allows evaluators to provide useful feedback to administrators and board members about the trends and patterns that characterize their efforts.

Two process evaluations of a sample of the 50 state funds in operation at the end of the 1980s (Parent, Auerbach, and Carlson, 1992) and the start of the 1990s (Sarnoff, 1993) shed some light on various aspects of how compensation programs really work. During fiscal year 1988 the programs in the survey's sample received over 92,000 claims and granted aid to nearly 66,000 people. Most (62%) of the funds' revenue was raised from fines and penalty assessments levied on law violators of all kinds (including traffic infractions), 22% of the income was derived from general appropriations (taxes), and the remaining 15% came from the federal government in accordance with the Victims of Crime Act. Most of the claims concerned drunk driving crashes, homicides, rapes, robberies, aggravated assaults, and child abuse cases. Very few claims arose from spouse abuse. The volume of cases handled per year varied dramatically by population size and crime rate. Workloads ranged from 62 claims (Wyoming) to over 33,000 (California) during fiscal 1988. Case processing time (how long it took to resolve a claim) ranged from 1 month (Utah, Washington, West Virginia) to 2 years (Rhode Island), with a mean of 18 weeks. In the interim these applicants probably suffered bouts of anxiety from uncertainty and felt strong pressures from creditors. In most states, small emergency awards between a few hundred and a few thousand dollars were permissible. Some programs seemed to be run a lot more efficiently than others. Administrative costs as a percentage of total expenditures averaged about 16%, but ranged from a low of 3% (in Missouri) to a high of 31% (in Wyoming, with its small caseload; however, New York with the second-highest workload had the second-highest overhead, spending 26 cents of every dollar on administration).

As for decision-making patterns, denial rates indicated that some boards are much stricter than others. The proportion of applicants who were turned down ranged from a low of 11% (Pennsylvania) to a high of 76% (Virginia); overall, about 36% got nothing and 64% received some financial assistance. Denials can be for "technical reasons," such as failure to supply sufficient documentation of expenses; and for "fault," such as the stigmatizing moral judgment that the victim was "guilty" of contributory misconduct. Fault denials that rejected victims' assertions of complete innocence ranged from 0% (Wyoming) to 48% (Virginia). Some boards seem more generous, while others are determined to refute the charges that they "give money away" and are vulnerable to fraud and abuse. The average award ranged from a low of nearly $700 (Arizona) to a high of roughly $9,000 (Rhode Island, where attorney's fees are covered). The rate of compensation, calculated as a proportion (crimes actually compensated compared to all reported crimes committed in that state that year that potentially would have been eligible for compensation) also showed tremendous variation and ranged from a low of 1% (Michigan) to a high of 91% (Minnesota) and averaged out at

19%. The total number of unserved victims a year in the late 1980s was estimated to be about 90,000, or about 55% of the almost 170,000 potentially eligible persons (innocent, injured, facing expenses, uninsured). In other words, despite outreach efforts (such as public service announcements and posters in police stations and hospital emergency rooms), more than half of all possible beneficiaries did not know their rights and/or did not even file a claim. Some state program administrators estimated that 67%, maybe even 95%, of eligible victims did not apply for financial aid. Of course, if more eligible persons were aware of their rights and did seek reimbursement, the state funds would take even longer to process their claims and either would have to cut back on the average size of awards or turn down a greater proportion of applicants, unless the directors could somehow raise more money (Parent, Auerbach, and Carlson, 1992; Sarnoff, 1993). Setting up storefront offices to accept claims from people living in high-crime areas might help to achieve the objective of reaching the maximum number of deserving individuals in the most effective and efficient manner possible (McCormack, 1991).

The findings from process evaluations about insufficient funding and inadequate outreach confirm that compensation plans are failing to live up to their humanitarian commitments. Because of their limited budgets, many boards maintain low profiles or even face prohibitions against advertising. Lack of interest on the part of police, prosecutors, and hospital emergency room personnel might also be a continuing problem. Some injured parties might be deterred by complex filing procedures and detailed probes into their personal finances (to prevent fraud). Others are discouraged when they hear about high rejection rates, long waits, and disappointingly small awards. Even with low rates of applications and awards, underfunded programs can run out of money before the year is over (McGillis and Smith, 1983; Sanderson, 1994).

In 1995, state crime victim compensation programs across the country paid out nearly $250 million to about 120,000 victims of violent crimes. Victims of assault (47%) and child sexual abuse (12%) were the most numerous. Almost half of the money went to cover medical expenses, and most of the rest was reimbursement for lost wages, mental health treatment, and funeral expenses. The national average for an award was close to $2,000 (OJP, 1997).

Measuring the Effects of Programs Impact evaluations are carried out to compare a program's intentions with its actual accomplishments. These studies reveal the consequences of a program for its clients and the community. To determine whether or not compensation really eases the financial stress experienced by crime victims, the ratio of award payments to submitted losses can be calculated. To assess a program's impact on the participation of compensated victims in the criminal justice system, those who did and did not receive aid can be compared with regard to their attendance rates as witnesses in police lineups and court proceedings.

The diversity of structures and procedures in different state programs provides opportunities to test which arrangements work best under what conditions. The findings of research and evaluation studies can have important consequences for the future of compensation. Determining successes and failures can help to resolve the ongoing debates over the pros and cons of compensating crime victims with public funds and the merits and demerits of particular rules and practices (Chappell and Sutton, 1974; Carrow, 1980; NIJ, 1998).

The findings of several impact evaluations do not support the hypothesis that the prospect of reimbursement would increase the public's degree of cooperation with law enforcement. In the 1970s when the reporting rates for violent crimes in states with programs were compared with the rates in states without programs, no appreciable differences were found in the extent to which victims in cities told the police about their misfortunes (Doerner, 1978). A comparison of the attitudes of claimants in Florida who were granted awards versus those whose requests were denied revealed that getting repaid did not significantly improve victims' ratings of the quality of performance of the police, prosecutors, or judges (Doerner and Lab, 1980).

More information is needed about the impact of board decisions on the psychological and economic well-being of victims. Applicants who were rejected because of what they perceived as mere "technicalities" (like waiting too long before filing) might feel cheated. Insensitive treatment, lengthy background investigations, extensive delays, and partial reimbursements can make even successful claimants feel victimized once again (McGillis and Smith, 1983). One researcher who evaluated the New York and New Jersey programs concluded that claimants ended up more alienated from the criminal justice system than nonclaimants. Instead of reducing public discontent with the police and courts, compensation programs provoked additional frustrations. Applicants' expectations probably rose when they first learned about the chance of reimbursement, but these hopes were consistently frustrated when most claimants, for a variety of reasons, were turned down entirely or awarded insufficient funds to cover all their documented expenses. Three quarters indicated that they would not apply for compensation again if they were victimized a second time, largely because of their displeasure over delays, eligibility requirements, incidental expenses, inconveniences, their treatment by program administrators, and ultimately the inadequacy of their reimbursements (Elias, 1983a).

The enactment of victim compensation programs might have been merely an exercise in "symbolic politics" (Elias, 1983b, 1986), a judgment that accuses certain manipulative politicians of voting for programs that look impressive on paper because they want to appear to be doing something for victims but won't allocate the necessary resources to make the promise a reality. Nevertheless, the public is favorably impressed by the foresight and concern shown by policymakers and legislators toward victims. Unaware that the majority of claimants are turned down and that the remainder are largely dissatisfied with the extent of reimbursement, people are led to believe that an effective safety net has been set up to cushion the blows of violent crime. As long as their levels of funding remain woefully insufficient, compensation programs serve more to pacify public opinion than to genuinely restore victims to their previous financial condition.

CONFISCATING PROFITS FROM NOTORIOUS CRIMINALS

> **A** lone gunman terrorizes New Yorkers, carrying out ambushes that leave six people dead and a number of others wounded. Dubbed the "Son of Sam" as well as the "44-Caliber Killer" by the media, he is eventually caught, convicted, and sentenced to a lifetime behind bars. From his cell, he grants interviews to writers and accumulates about $90,000 in royalties from publishers. The victims he shot and the families of the people he killed sue him to prevent him from profiting from his notoriety. Eight years later his attorneys arrive at a settlement: All the money will be divided among those he harmed, and they will share any additional earnings he might receive. (Associated Press, 1984a)
>
> **A** robber enters a bank but bungles the job and winds up taking four employees hostage when his escape route is blocked by police. After a siege they are released, and he is captured, convicted, and imprisoned. Hollywood producers pay him $100,000 for the rights to depict his exploits in a movie entitled, "Dog Day Afternoon." The money is seized by the New York State Crime Victims Board and apportioned out to his kidnap victims, his lawyers (to whom he owed fees), and his former wife (for alimony and child support payments). (Roberts, 1987)

One additional option for recovering losses remains open to just a handful of victims or their survivors: going after the profits made by offenders who sell their firsthand accounts of how and why they committed their crimes. In a few cases each year, offenders cash in on the sensationalism surrounding their highly publicized crimes. The question that arises is whether victims can take these "fruits of crime" away from offenders.

In 1977 the New York State legislature passed a forfeiture of assets bill to prevent a vicious serial killer (cited in the first example above) from being showered with lucrative offers for book contracts, movie rights, and paid appearances to tell his inside story. Afterward, nearly all states and the federal government enacted similar "Son of Sam" laws to head off the financial exploitation of crimes by their perpetrators. Public opinion backed this legislative trend; in one poll 86% of the respondents favored laws that took profits from notoriety away from criminals and distributed the money to victims (National Victim Center, 1991a). These statutes went after financial gains in the form of fees, advances, and royalties from any reenactments of the heinous deeds in movies, memoirs, books, magazine articles, tape recordings, phonograph records, radio programs, television shows, or other forms of entertainment. If offenders (accused or convicted) were paid for expressing their thoughts, opinions, or feelings about their depredations, or for giving graphic descriptions about these acts, their income could be seized by the government and placed in an escrow account before they could spend it. For up to 5 years individuals who had incurred direct physical or mental injuries, or financial losses could argue in civil court that they were entitled to a portion of that money. In some states any leftover funds not awarded in damage lawsuits could revert back to the offenders. But in other jurisdictions the remaining money could have been used to cover unpaid attorneys' fees plus the court costs of the prosecution or to replenish the state's victim compensation fund (Stark and Goldstein, 1985; NOVA, 1988). The legal issue of just who was the victim became very complicated when the offenders were not guilty of predatory street crimes but of political crimes, white-collar crimes, or vice offenses like running prostitution rings or trafficking in drugs.

Notoriety-for-profit laws were primarily symbolic gestures to drive home the message that "crime doesn't pay," but they also were intended to facilitate the handing over of money to innocent victims. Yet from the outset these laws were controversial. Critics argued that the confiscation of payments by government had a chilling effect on the First Amendment's guarantee of freedom of expression. In 1991 all of the justices of the Supreme Court agreed and by a vote of 8 to 0 struck down New York's law and all others like it. In a unanimous opinion (*Simon and Schuster v. New York State Crime Victims Board*), the Court recognized that states had an undisputed compelling interest in depriving offenders of the fruits of crime and were pursuing a worthwhile goal in trying to transfer the proceeds from criminals to their victims. However, the justices argued that enacting these overly broad state laws unfairly singled out a convict's "speech-derived income" for a special tax burden and thereby established an inhibiting financial disincentive to create or publish works with a particular content. Publishers, moviemakers, and civil libertarians hailed the Court's landmark ruling as a victory for authors and their audiences and noted that a substantial body of worthwhile literature and redeeming commentary by notable prisoners might never had been written if these laws were on the books. Victim advocates denounced the Court's decision as a blow to victims' rights and undertook the task of redrafting provisions about lawsuits, statutes of limitation, fines, forfeitures, and escrow accounts so that they would meet constitutional standards. State legislatures passed revised "Son of Sam" laws that do not single out royalties from books or movies but target any and all assets these offenders accrue (Fein, 1991; Alexander, 1992).

CHAPTER SUMMARY

Victims can try to recover their financial losses in several different ways. Restitution payments directly from the offender's earnings seem to be a fair and appropriate method of reimbursement and may provide a solid foundation for eventual reconciliation. Restitution may be viewed as an additional penalty but also as a way to sensitize and rehabilitate lawbreakers. Unfortunately, many victims never receive any money because their offenders are not caught, convicted, and sentenced to restitution, or are unable or unwilling to earn and hand over sufficient funds.

Victims can attempt to sue their offenders in civil court for compensatory and punitive damages. As plaintiffs they have a better chance of winning against defendants than in criminal court because the standard of proof—a preponderance of the evidence—is easier to meet than guilt beyond a reasonable doubt. However, only offenders who are identified and who have substantial exposed assets can be successfully sued. If criminals are not caught or have no tangible assets, victims might be able to launch lawsuits against third parties such as businesses or criminal justice agencies that acted with such gross negligence that innocent parties were targeted by dangerous individuals.

Private insurance coverage can repay losses from assaults, car thefts, burglaries, and robberies. But many victims cannot afford the premiums, do not have the foresight to take out a policy, or cannot find a company that will sell them coverage.

Victim compensation funds have been set up in most states since the 1960s, although they initially met considerable political resistance. To get reimbursement it is not necessary that the perpetrator be caught and convicted. However, only innocent victims of violent crimes, not property crimes, are eligible for financial aid to cover lost earnings and out-of-pocket medical expenses. Many state funds do not have enough money from penalty assessments and the general treasury to quickly and adequately reimburse violent crime victims.

A small number of victims might be able to claim a portion of the money certain convicts make by cashing in on their notoriety.

DISCUSSION QUESTIONS

1. Explain how restitution can serve a number of different purposes.
2. Discuss the complications that can arise when restitution programs place offenders in jobs so that they can repay their victims.
3. Describe the advantages and disadvantages victims face when they sue offenders in civil court.
4. Why are third-party lawsuits potentially lucrative to victims but also controversial?
5. Summarize the different arguments that support the establishment of victim compensation funds by state governments. Then present arguments that the government should not provide financial reimbursement to crime victims.
6. Why are laws that compel criminals to repay their victims from profits gained by notoriety controversial?
7. Even though a number of possible sources of reimbursement exist—court-ordered restitution, private insurance coverage, state compensation funds, civil lawsuits, and "Son-of-Sam" laws—why do so many victims fail to receive any repayment of their losses and expenses?

7

Victims in the 21st Century: Alternative Directions

How will victims fare during the 21st century? The answer to that question depends upon how several contradictory tendencies that characterize the current period work themselves out. On the one hand, the victims' movement is waging a successful campaign to gain additional formal legal rights within the criminal justice system. Activists and advocacy groups want to empower victims so they can exercise greater influence over how their cases are resolved and be treated with fundamental fairness. On the other hand, some individuals and groups are moving away from the arena of formal legal rights to explore "informal" alternatives. Within this tendency toward informalism are two opposite currents. One leads participants on a quest for nonlegalistic and nonadversarial ways to settle differences between people embroiled in conflicts. In this new paradigm of **restorative justice,** victim-offender **reconciliation** is the goal, restitution arranged through mediation is the method, and a neighborhood justice center or community-based program is the setting.

This search for another forum to resolve interpersonal disputes is spurred on by a belief that it is hopelessly unrealistic to attempt to compel an intransigent criminal justice system to become more responsive and accountable to the ostensible "clients" or "consumers" of its services. But an opposite current within informalism rejects this peacemaking approach and reverts to earlier, more violent methods of resolving matters. But forceful "solutions" embody vigilantism, in which victims and their allies retaliate against their alleged offenders to make sure they get punished. The situation of victims in the years ahead will be shaped by the interaction of these three tendencies.

TOWARD GREATER FORMAL LEGAL RIGHTS WITHIN THE CRIMINAL JUSTICE SYSTEM

The struggle to gain formal rights has been a powerful motivation throughout history. Legal rights serve as a remedy for injustice and abuse as well as a basis for independent and autonomous action. A number of social movements seeking freedom, liberation, empowerment, equality, and fairness have sought greater rights for their constituencies. The most well-known include the civil rights, women's rights, workers' rights, students' rights, children's rights, gay rights, patients' rights, and prisoners' rights movements. The victims' rights movement that arose during the 1970s falls within this reformist tradition.

The legal rights of journalists, political activists, criminal defendants, and convicts have been derived from the safeguards specified in the first ten amendments to the U.S. Constitution, which taken together are referred to as the Bill of Rights. But the framers of the Constitution, the ultimate arbiter of conflicting claims, did not enumerate any rights for crime victims. The pledges, guarantees, entitlements, privileges, benefits, options, practices, and opportunities for redress commonly subsumed under the heading of "victims' rights" flow from several different sources. A few rights originated as idiosyncratic policies adopted by certain caring and innovative officials, such as police chiefs, district attorneys, trial judges, and probation officers. Other rights were derived from case law based on court decisions. The remainder were established by laws passed by city and county governments, statutes enacted by state legislatures, acts approved by Congress, and referenda placed on the ballot by advocacy groups and endorsed by voters. As a result, an inconsistent, nonuniform "crazy quilt" of rights has developed that varies markedly from state to state, jurisdiction (county or municipality) to jurisdiction, and even courthouse to courthouse. However, one trend is certain: Since the 1960s, victims' rights have been proliferating and expanding geographically. A self-reinforcing cycle is operating: As more victims become aware of their rights and begin to exercise them, these rights become accepted and honored within the criminal justice system. These victories encourage victims and their allies to raise new demands for further rights (Stark and Goldstein, 1985; Viano, 1987).

Activists and advocacy groups first raised the possibility of adding pro-victim language to the Sixth Amendment after a presidential task force recommended rewording it in 1982. But in 1986, reformers decided to postpone this plan in favor of a strategy of securing amendments to state constitutions. An opinion poll administered in the early 1990s showed overwhelming public support: 90% of the respondents said they would probably or definitely support an amendment to their state's constitution (NVC, 1991b). By the end of the 1990s, this approach had succeeded in 33 states, although the percentage of the voters that ratified the amendment was usually considerably below 90% (NVC, 1992a; News Wire Services, 2000). The common threads running through these amendments were that victims should be treated with fairness, compassion, and respect and should have the right to be informed about, be present at, and be heard at all critical stages of the criminal justice process. Also, since 1980 almost every state legislature has passed packages of statutes termed a "Victim's Bill of Rights." These packages most often promise these rights: to be handled with fairness, respect, and dignity; to be notified about, be present at, and heard at important judicial proceedings; to promptly get back stolen property that was recovered and held as evidence; to get protection from intimidation and harassment; and to receive restitution or compensation (NCVC, 1996).

The National Victim Constitutional Amendment Network's campaign to insert additional phrases into the Sixth Amendment reignited during 1996 when Republicans and Democrats co-sponsored a bill in both houses of Congress that many elected officials quickly attached their names to—one that also received President Clinton's endorsement. The proposal needs to secure the approval of two thirds of the members of both the House of Representatives and the Senate and then must be ratified by three fourths of the state legislatures. It would grant victims of violent crimes the right to reasonable notice of, access to, and opportunities to speak out or submit written statements at proceedings that determine conditional release from custody (bail), acceptance of a negotiated plea, a sentence upon conviction, and parole. It also pledges a speedy trial free from unreasonable delays, restitution from convicts, notification about a release or escape of a prisoner, and timely information about all these rights (Crime Victims Report, 1999; News Wire Services, 2000). Proponents of this drive to update the Bill of

Rights argued that these federally backed promises would rectify a Constitutional imbalance—its enumeration of many rights for suspects, defendants, and inmates versus its silence on victim issues. The reworded Sixth Amendment would serve as an equalizer that could end institutionalized second-class treatment. However, opposition quickly surfaced, even from pro-victim quarters. Some critics noted that restricting participatory rights to just individuals harmed by violent acts but not by property crimes was an unprincipled cost-saving compromise that would officially disenfranchise the overwhelming majority of victims, since theft is so much more common than violence. Furthermore, the language of the proposed amendment eliminated any chances for meaningful redress for victims whose rights were violated. Lawsuits could not be filed for damages against the United States, a state, a political subdivision, or a public official. Nor were victims given any grounds to halt or reopen any proceedings or rulings. The rights pledged in the proposed amendment would be virtually unenforceable, merely symbolic, and practically meaningless. Yet other opponents feared that adding pro-victim phrases to the Sixth Amendment would strengthen the coercive power of the government, could open the door to further federal involvement in hearings and trials in state courts, and would impose heavy expenses on local criminal justice systems. Critics contended that the Seventh Amendment already enabled victims to exercise their most important right, to sue offenders in civil court in order to get restitution (Gahr, 1997; Pilon, 1998; NCVC, 1999). Because of a lack of political support, backers of the victims' rights amendment pulled the measure from the Senate floor in 2000 (Associated Press, 2000).

The rights that crime victims have fought for and secured are so numerous and varied that they must be grouped for comparison and analysis. One way to categorize these newly achieved rights is to note which groups of victims directly need, want, and benefit from a specific right. For example, in 1984, Wisconsin was the first state to adopt a Child Victim's Bill of Rights. Among other provisions it stipulated that all legal proceedings must be carefully explained to the young complainant in language he or she can understand. Another way to keep track of rights is to note at which stage of the criminal justice process these options can be exercised. For example, the right to be present at all court proceedings (as long as the presiding judge approves) begins at arraignment when bail is considered. At the other end of the spectrum, the right to address the parole board arises years after the convict has been imprisoned. Still another way to classify victims' rights is to note "at whose expense" they were gained. Conflicts between individuals, groups, and classes permeate society. Rights gained by one group or class enhance its position vis-à-vis its competitors or adversaries. If this group conflict "zero sum game" model is accepted, then three categories of victims' rights can be discerned: those gained at the direct expense of "criminals" (more precisely: suspects, defendants, and convicts); those gained at the expense of the criminal justice system (agency budgets and the privileges and convenience of law enforcement, judicial, and corrections officials); and those gained at the expense of either offenders or officials, depending upon how victims exercise their newly authorized influence.

Rights Gained at the Expense of Offenders

Some advocates insist that victims' rights ought to be gained at the expense of offenders' rights; too much concern has been shown for the "rights of criminals," they say, and not enough for the plight of the innocent people they harm. In the unending battle between lawbreakers and law-abiding citizens, the "bad guys" have gained certain advantages within the legal system over the "good guys." To restore some semblance of evenhandedness to the scales of justice that have been tipped or tilted in favor of the wrong side, victims need rights to match, counter, or even "trump" the rights of offenders. In this context, reform means reversing certain court decisions and legal trends and shifting the balance of power away from wrongdoers and toward the parties they injured (see Hook, 1972; Carrington, 1975; and the President's Task Force, 1982).

Collisions between the rights of victims versus suspects, defendants, and prisoners can arise over many issues. For example, in the aftermath of completed sexual assaults, victims understandably fear the prospect of contracting AIDS, so they want to discover whether they were exposed to a deadly and incurable disease by infected assailants. But HIV positive attackers don't want their health status to become known because of fear of social discrimination and extra legal penalties. In most states, legislators predictably have sided with distraught victims who want to find out: judges can compel convicted offenders (and in some jurisdictions even defendants before they go to trial) to submit to blood tests, even if that undermines their privacy rights and confidentiality laws. (However, the screening for antibodies cannot indicate if a molester or rapist contracted the disease after the sexual assault but before the test or determine whether the infection was actually transmitted during the spread of bodily fluids. To be certain the victim must undergo periodic testing [Infolink, 1999]). Conversely, victims of sexual assaults want their privacy rights to prevail over any demands by defendants (through defense attorneys) that the records from counseling sessions maintained by rape crisis centers be turned over during the discovery phase of pretrial proceedings. Defendants hope to find exculpatory statements that might indicate consent or concerns about misidentification in these files about frank conversations and intimate disclosures. In many jurisdictions, judges will order the release of these otherwise privileged and confidential patient-counselor discussions, but only if the defense attorney can argue persuasively that these records probably contain relevant information. (Counselors who choose to respect victims' privacy rights rather than accede to defendants' rights to exculpatory evidence and refuse to hand over their notes have been found in contempt of court) ("Victim's Counseling Records," 1999).

Those who emphasize punishing the offender as a way of vindicating the victim assume that the interests of victims and government officials largely coincide: apprehension, prosecution, conviction, and imprisonment. Victims' rights gained at the expense of their offenders would include provisions that facilitate conviction of the accused, close any legal loopholes that enable these defendants to escape their "just deserts," increase the likelihood of incarceration, and eliminate any "unwarranted" acts of leniency toward these prisoners. The President's

Task Force on Victims of Crime (1982) proposed a number of recommendations of this nature, and some were enacted in California in 1982 when voters passed Proposition 8, which its sponsors called a Victim's Bill of Rights. (Some provisions that fit within this punitive/retributory framework and have been characterized as "pro-victim" reforms are listed in Table 7.1.)

Critics of this approach of enhancing victims' rights at the expense of suspects, defendants, and convicts raise a number of objections. First, making inmates suffer more does not mean victims suffer any less. Second, many of these measures do not really empower victims but simply strengthen the government's ability to control its citizens. Civil libertarians who fear the development of a repressive police state warn that the implementation of antidefendant, pro-police, and pro-prosecutor measures undermines cherished principles: the presumption of innocence and the state's burden of proof. These due process safeguards are subverted when defendants are denied pretrial release, when improperly obtained evidence is used against them, and when the victims' desire for revenge (for example, as expressed in impact statements) is manipulated by the government to enhance its punitive powers (see Henderson, 1985; Fattah, 1986; Hellerstein, 1989; Hall, 1991; Abramovsky, 1992; and Simonson, 1994). Finally, these opportunities to press for ritualized revenge benefit only a small proportion of all victims: only those fortunate ones whose reported cases were solved and then prosecuted vigorously and successfully.

Table 7.1 Victims' Rights Gained at the Expense of Suspects, Defendants, and Prisoners

Subject	Right of Victims
Denial of bail	To be protected from suspects whose pretrial release on bail might endanger them
Protection from further harm	To be reasonably protected during the pretrial release period from the accused through orders of protection and by increased penalities for acts of harassment and intimidation
Defenses	To be assured that defendants cannot avoid imprisonment by pleading "not guilty by reason of insanity," through the substitution of "guilty and mentally ill," which requires treatment in a mental institution followed by incarceration in prison
Counseling	To be assured that statements divulged to counselors remain confidential if requested by the defense during the discovery phase of court proceedings
Evidence	To be assured that defendants cannot benefit from the exclusion of illegally gathered evidence by having all evidence obtained by the police in good faith declared admissible in trials
Offender's age	To be assured that juvenile offenders do not escape full responsbility for serious crimes by having such cases transferred from juvenile court to adult criminal court
Restitution	To receive mandatory repayments from convicts who are put on probation or parole unless a judge explains in writing the reasons for not imposing this obligation
Appeals	To appeal sentences that seem too lenient
Notoriety for profit	To have any royalties and fees paid to notorious criminals confiscated and used to repay victims or to fund victim services
Abuser's tax	To have penalty assessments collected from felons, misdemeanants, and traffic law violators to pay for victim services, compensation, and assistance programs

SOURCES: BJS, 1988; MADD, 1988; NOVA, 1988.

Rights Gained at the Expense of the System

Some rights that victims gain can come at the expense of justice system officials and agencies that have neglected the needs and wants of their ostensible clients for far too long, advocates say. Society, or more precisely the social system, is partly at fault for the crime problem that plagues many communities. The state therefore is obligated to minimize suffering and to help innocent injured parties recover and become "whole again" through government intervention, even if offenders cannot be caught or convicted. A preoccupation with punishing law-breakers must not overshadow the need for assisting and supporting the people they harmed. New laws must guarantee that standards of fair treatment be met that respect the dignity and privacy of victims. Since extra effort, time, and money must be expended to provide services that were not formerly available on a routine basis, these rights can be considered to have been gained by victims at the expense of the prerogatives of officials (like detectives, assistant district attorneys, and probation officers) and the budgets of agencies (such as court systems and parole boards). For example, in many states sexual assault victims no longer are charged for the costs of medical examinations to collect evidence ("rape kits"); the police department or the district attorney's office now pay that bill.

Rights gained at the expense of officials and agencies first were enacted in 1980, when Wisconsin's state legislature passed the nation's first comprehensive "bill of rights" for victims and witnesses. The President's Task Force (1982) endorsed similar proposals which were incorporated into federal statutes when Congress approved of the Victim/Witness Protection Act. Many states have proclaimed similar assurances, either through specific laws or via more comprehensive legislative packages (see the provisions listed in Table 7.2, p. 314).

Some critics of these rights gained at the expense of officials and agencies contend that requirements about notification, protection (such as separate waiting areas in courthouses), and intercession (with employers and creditors) increase the justice system's workloads and costs and thus interfere with its public safety priorities. Yet some advocates believe that mere pledges of fair treatment do not go far enough. For example, being notified about the results of a bail hearing, plea negotiation session, sentencing hearing, or parole board meeting falls far short of actually participating to advance one's perceived best interests; and attending and speaking out is no guarantee of being taken seriously and truly having an impact.

Rights Gained at the Expense of Either Offenders or the System or Both

A 60-year-old convict serving a life sentence for gunning down two policemen during a robbery of a bar is in front of the parole board for the eighth time. The victims' survivors and their supporters in law enforcement organizations vow to continue to appear before the board every few years when it reviews his status to make sure he remains behind bars until he dies. (Hanley, 1999)

Table 7.2 Victims' Rights Gained at the Expense of Criminal Justice Agencies and Officials

Subject	Right of Victims
General rights	To be "read their rights" as soon as a crime is reported, or to be provided with written information about all obligations, services, and opportunities for protection and reimbursement
Case status	To be kept posted about any progress in their cases; to be advised when arrest warrants are issued or suspects are taken into custody
Court appearances	To be notified in advance of all court proceedings and of changes in required court appearances
Secure waiting areas	To be provided with courthouse waiting rooms separate from those used by defendants, defense witnesses, and spectators
Employer intercession	To have the prosecutor explain to the complaining witness's employer that the victim should not be penalized for missing work because of court appearances
Creditor intercession	To have the prosecutor explain to creditors like banks and landlords that crime-inflicted financial losses necessitate delays in paying bills
Suspect out on bail	To be notified that a suspect arrested for the crime has been released on bail
Negotiated plea	To be notified that both sides have agreed to a plea of guilty in return for some consideration
Sentence and final disposition	To be notified of the verdict and sentence after a trial, and the final disposition after appeals
Work release	To be notified if the convict will be permitted to leave the prison to perform a job during specified hours
Parole hearings	To be notified when a prisoner will be appearing before a parole board to seek early release
Pardon	To be notified if the governor is considering pardoning the convict
Release of a felon	To be notified when a prisoner is to be released on parole or because the sentence has expired
Prison escape	To be notified if the convict has escaped from confinement
Return of stolen property	To have recovered stolen property that has been held as evidence returned expeditiously by the police or prosecution
Compensation	To be reimbursed for out-of-pocket expenses for medical bills and lost wages arising from injuries inflicted during a violent crime

SOURCES: BJS, 1988; MADD, 1988; NOVA, 1988.

The boldest demands raised by advocacy groups within the victims' rights movement concern the question of power. Some victims want to influence the outcome of the criminal justice process at key stages. Instead of being relegated to the role of passive observers, they want to be active participants in the events that shape their lives. This point of view leads to the formulation that victims should be present and heard whenever suspects, defendants, and convicts are present and heard.

Any participatory rights victims gain may come at the expense of offenders, agency officials, or both, depending upon how victims actually use their leverage. They can be seen as allies of the government and as junior partners "on the same side" as the police and the prosecution in the adversarial system. Therefore, empowering them means strengthening the ability of the government to arrest, detain, convict, and punish persons accused of wrongdoing. Enhancing the powers of a potentially repressive state apparatus will provoke opposition from civil libertarians concerned about safeguarding constitutional rights and maintaining checks and balances. But if victims are visualized as independent actors, then they may not agree with the course of action taken by their ostensible governmental allies. Calls to empower them might provoke resistance from criminal justice professionals who fear that their personal privileges will be jeopardized or their agency's mission will be compromised and its budget strained (see Karmen, 1992).

It is often asserted or assumed that victims primarily want retribution. If retribution is their highest priority, then they are likely to seize every opportunity to press for harsher handling of offenders. Vengeful victims might insist that defendants not be offered low bail or generous concessions in return for guilty pleas, that sentences imposed on convicts be as severe as the law allows, and that parole boards reject prisoners' petitions for early release. On the other hand, victims may have different priorities and find themselves at odds with the authorities over how to handle particular cases. For instance, a battered woman's greatest concern may be securing treatment for a violence-prone lover. If so, she might favor diversion of the case from the criminal justice system to allow the wrongdoer to enter a rehabilitation program. Burglary victims concerned about receiving full and prompt reimbursement of their financial losses might favor an alternative to incarceration, such as restitution as a condition of probation. Thus, the involvement of the victim as an additional party in the decision-making process constrains the free exercise of discretion formerly enjoyed by prosecutors' offices, judges, probation departments, and parole boards.

The critical junctures for victim input are at bail-setting arraignments, during plea negotiations, at sentencing hearings, and at parole board appearances. At arraignments victims can argue that "no contact" be a condition of bail. As for plea negotiations, victims have never been granted veto power over the compromises worked out by assistant district attorneys (ADAs) and defense lawyers. But in many states they are offered a chance to consult with "their" ADA and voice their opinions as the out-of-court settlements are hammered out. Opportunities for victims to influence the outcome of sentencing decisions take two forms. In the less active approach, victims are allowed to submit a written statement. Victim impact statements are objective assessments of the crime's economic, medical, and emotional consequences. They are prepared by probation officers and presented to judges as part of the presentencing investigation report in all states. Victim statements of opinion—written recommendations regarding appropriate sentences—also can be submitted to judges in most states. Allocution is the more active alternative. This opportunity to speak out before the judge sentences the offender is now permitted in most states. Similarly, victims can make their views known to parole boards in three ways: by submitting an impact statement, through allocution during the hearing, or via a videotaped message (NOVA, 1988; NCVC, 1996; and Curran, 1999).

Pledges about the chance to participate in crucial decisions raise several policy questions. Should such formal rights also be extended to individuals who do not fit the profile of the innocent, law-abiding, mature victim of a serious crime? For example, should assault victims from "unsavory backgrounds" (who in previous cases were arrested as street gang members, drug dealers, mobsters, and prostitutes) be permitted a say in plea negotiations and sentencing? If so, should their requests carry less weight? Should victimized children have input? Should people who represent the victim (in their capacity as survivor of a killing, executor of the estate of the deceased, the legal guardian of a minor, lawyer for the family, or volunteer advocate) be granted consultive rights during plea negotiations and allocution rights before sentencing and parole decisions? Should participatory rights be restricted to victims of serious crimes like felonies or, even more narrowly, only to persons injured by violence? And what happens when these participatory rights are violated? What remedies do victims have when criminal justice agencies fail to involve them in the decision-making process or don't live up to the standards for fair treatment? Anticipating this issue, legislation usually contains clauses that bar lawsuits by victims whose rights were not respected to secure money damages or to overturn unfavorable decisions. Under the separation-of-powers doctrine, however, judges could grant injunctive relief and order executive agencies and officials to comply in the future with policies created by legislative bodies (Stark and Goldstein, 1985; NOVA, 1988; and NCVC, 1996).

The lack of enforcement mechanisms highlights another related problem: the absence of clear lines of responsibility for implementation. Which officials or agencies can be held accountable for keeping victims informed of their rights? For example, does the duty of notifying the victim about the right to allocution before sentencing fall to the police officer who records the initial complaint, to the assistant district attorney who prosecutes the case, to the probation officer who prepares the presentence report, or to the clerk in the office of court administration who schedules the postconviction hearing? And how many times must the responsible official attempt to contact a victim before giving up and declaring that a good-faith effort was made?

Providing all complainants with advocates from the outset would be one way to make sure that victims find out about all their rights and options and exercise them as best they can. Rape crisis centers and shelters for battered women were the first to empower their clients by furnishing them with the services of dedicated and knowledgeable consultants who understood how the criminal justice process really worked and how to make the system responsive to their clients' needs. These pioneers in advocacy usually were former victims who knew from firsthand experience just what injured parties were going through. Shortly afterwards, prosecutors' victim-witness assistance programs (VWAPS) and family courts (assigning guardians ad litem to abused children) hired professionally trained advocates. But as yet no jurisdiction has institutionalized and universalized the practice by assigning an advisor to every complainant who wants one, in the same way that lawyers are routinely provided to all suspects, defendants, and convicts. Furthermore, imagine if victims were "read their rights" the same way officers read suspects their Miranda warning prior to interrogation. Complainants would be told that they have a right to remain vocal about how they are treated and what they believe should happen at bail hearings, plea negotiations, sentencing hearings, and parole board meetings (see Karmen, 1995). Complainants would also be informed that they had the right to consult with a lawyer and to refuse to answer questions or disclose any personal information (that was not directly relevant to the investigation and usually is protected by privacy privileges) about such subjects as sexual history, sexual orientation, medical or mental health records, or conversations with doctors, therapists, spouses, attorneys, or religious counselors. At the outset, victims would be warned that any disclosures about personal matters would come to the attention of not only the prosecutor but also the defense counsel, the defendant, expert witnesses, and the judge, in addition to the media and the public, during court proceedings (Murphy, 1999).

Another measure that would substantially empower complainants would be to permit them to hire their own private attorneys to act as prosecutors—to initiate charges, to handle plea negotiations, and to present the case at trials. This option is allowed in other countries, and used to be standard procedure in colonial America. By the end of the 1990s, only a few jurisdictions still authorized a victim's attorney to directly ask a judge or grand jury to start proceedings against a defendant (see Beloof, 1999). (However, if this reform were implemented, only the prosperous would be able to afford this "personalized" justice, thereby intensifying an existing double standard compared to the treatment of indigents.)

Social scientists have just begun to evaluate the effectiveness of most of the informational and participatory rights that have been granted in recent decades. Criminologists and victimologists are sure to discover evidence of "differential handling" or "differential access to justice": that certain groups of people are more likely than others to be informed of their rights, to exercise them, and to use them effectively to influence the decision-making process (see Karmen, 1990). Even with all the new options, does institutionalized indifference toward the victims' plight still pervade the justice system? The answer seems to be a qualified "yes," according to some preliminary findings gathered from evaluation studies. Only 3% of victims who reported offenses to the police in 1991 told *NCVS* interviewers that they had contact with or received advice or help from any office, agency, or program set up to serve them (Dawson, Smith, and DeFrances, 1993). Several studies discovered that many victims were never informed of their right to be kept posted about progress in their cases and about court dates (Webster, 1988), about filing impact statements that might influence sentences (Wells, 1990) and parole board decisions (NVC, 1991b), and about the release of the felons they helped to send to prison (Cuomo, 1992; Dawson, Smith, and DeFrances, 1993). Most failed to appear and speak out at sentencing hearings (Forer, 1980). Those who did exercise their allocution rights to voice their opinions in person exerted very little influence, especially when convicts faced determinate (fixed) sentences (Villmoare and Neto, 1987; Walsh, 1992). A survey of New Yorkers turned up no evidence that those who filed victim impact statements experienced a greater sense of involvement or were more satisfied with the city's justice system and the disposition in their cases (Davis and

Smith, 1994). However, when victims submitted impact statements to Pennsylvania parole boards, inmates were less likely to subsequently be granted early release (Parsonage, Bernat, and Helfgott, 1994). And when California prosecutors introduced victim impact statements during the penalty phase in capital murder trials, the additional evidence raised the likelihood that the jury would impose execution rather than sentence the killer to life in prison without the possibility of parole (Aguirre et al., 1999).

Even though many legislatures have passed a victims' "bill of rights" and their electorates have ratified victims' rights amendments to their state constitutions, a study conducted by the National Center for Victims of Crime (NCVC) concluded that much educational work needs to be done. It surveyed victims in two states considered to have strong pro-victim protections and in two states where their rights on paper were limited. Overall, those whose cases were processed by the justice systems of states with strong protection fared better, but even they were not afforded all the opportunities they were supposed to get. In the two states that theoretically guaranteed many rights, more than 60% of all interviewed victims were not notified that the defendant was released on bail, more than 40% never were told about the date of the sentencing hearing, and nearly 40% never were informed that they were entitled to file an impact statement at the convict's parole hearing. Of those who found out in time, most (72%) attended the sentencing hearing and submitted an impact statement, but relatively few went to bail or parole hearings to exercise their rights to make recommendations. Only about 40% of the local officials surveyed in the two strong protection states were cognizant of the new laws enumerating victims' rights (Brienza, 1999; and NCVC, 1999).

One explanation for the resistance that thwarts the implementation of victims' rights is that the courtroom work group of "insiders"—prosecutors, defense attorneys, and judges—tends to frustrate attempts by "outsiders" (victims, their advocates, and lawmakers) to influence their rapid, assembly-line processing of cases. These key courtroom figures usually have developed a firm consensus about the appropriate "going rate" (sentence) for various crimes at particular times and places (Walker, 1994). To the extent that the courtroom insiders are able to resist the "interference" by outsiders to alter the going rate, victims will find the use of their participatory rights an exercise in futility (see Ranish and Shichor, 1985).

In fact, some activists within the victims' rights movement are pessimistic and cynical about the much-heralded "reforms" that supposedly have empowered victims. Victims still have no constitutional standing, which means that they cannot go to civil court and sue for monetary damages if their rights are ignored or violated, and they cannot veto decisions about bail, sentences, and parole that are made in their absence without their knowledge and consent (Gewurz and Mercurio, 1992). Pledges that the rights of victims to fair treatment will be carefully carried out by officials might prove to be mere "lip service," "paper promises," and "cosmetic changes" without much substance (Gegan and Rodriguez, 1992; Elias, 1993). This frustrating situation causes some victim activists to redirect their efforts in an entirely different direction.

TOWARD RESTORATIVE JUSTICE

Peacemaking

A 16-year-old girl has an affair with a 38-year-old man who owns an auto body shop. The lovestruck teenager shoots the man's wife in the face. The young assailant is quickly captured, pleads guilty to first-degree assault, and is sentenced to a 5 to 15 year prison term. The wife survives but the bullet remains lodged in her brain, interfering with her eating and drinking and causing her constant pain and suffering. The husband pleads guilty to statutory rape and serves 6 months in jail before becoming a talk show host. Nearly 7 years later the shooter comes up for parole. She tells the woman she tried to kill, "It was my fault and I'm sorry." The wife recommends to the parole board that they release her, and they do. (Associated Press, 1999)

An 11-year-old boy selling candy door-to-door to raise money for his school is lured into the home of a 15-year-old boy, who sexually assaults and then strangles him. The teenager is convicted of first-degree murder and is sentenced to 70 years in prison. The child's father, a lawyer, becomes an advocate for victims' rights and a candidate for the state assembly. The killer's parents reach the brink of bankruptcy after financing their son's unsuccessful legal defense, but they are named in a civil lawsuit aimed mostly at the psychiatric institutions that ineffectively and negligently treated the disturbed teen. But after their minister intercedes, both sets of parents end 2 years worth of icy stares and mutual recriminations. The two fathers hug each other and "cry like babies." "The anger has to stop," the victim's father declares. "It's a miracle. It's such a burden lifted," the prisoner's father adds. (Mansnerus, 1999)

Even in these cynical times when calls for rehabilitating criminals are greeted with skepticism while demands for severe punishment receive enthusiastic support, a new approach that assumes the best about people is gaining ground. It is attracting a growing proportion of victims who don't want to use their leverage within the legal system to make their offenders suffer. They are taking advantage of the chance to actively participate in a process whose goals are offender sensitization, victim recovery, a cessation of mutual hostilities, and a sense of closure, in which both parties put the incident behind them and rebuild their lives. These are the aims of restorative justice, a rapidly evolving way of reconceptualizing and contextualizing the crime problem that many enthusiastic adherents find promising. It draws upon nonpunitive methods of peacemaking, mediation, negotiation, dispute resolution, conflict management, and constructive engagement. These tactics are employed to bring about mutual understanding, offender empathy for the victim's plight, victim sensitivity for the cause of offender's crime-inducing problems, and lasting settlements that reconcile tensions between the two parties as well as within their community. Restorative justice embraces themes important to the victims rights movement, especially empowerment, notification, direct involvement, offender accountability, and making restitution.

This emerging challenge to the prevailing punitive paradigm incorporates some traditions that helped repair crime's negative repercussions centuries ago, before the state asserted its authority to dominate the justice process. In the distant past, legal systems were victim-focused and restitution-oriented. Detailed "price lists" had been worked out specifying how much the wrongdoer had to pay the injured party for every kind of loss imaginable. But priorities shifted dramatically in most societies when the upper class discovered that the legal apparatus could be used to control the populace. The government symbolically displaced the wounded person as the injured party, and the courts were transformed from a forum to settle disputes between specific individuals into an arena for ritualized combat between representatives of the state and of the accused. If the prosecution succeeded, the state inflicted pain upon its vanquished opponents in order to teach them not to break the law again (specific deterrence) and to make negative examples of them to serve as a warning to others (general deterrence). Later, prisons were invented to serve these purposes, as well as to take troublemakers out of circulation to protect the public (incapacitation) and to force maladjusted persons to undergo compulsory treatment (rehabilitation). In addition to the suffering caused by the deprivation of liberty and the imposition of harsh conditions (retribution), the government often extracted a fine or seized property from convicts, but it never shared the spoils with victims. The overriding concern of the authorities was to impose the appropriate punishment, not to restore the victims' emotional and economic well-being. This paradigm shift to retributive justice resulted in a process that was state-centered, offender-focused, and punishment-oriented, rather than injury-centered, victim-focused, and reparation-oriented.

Centuries later, reformers are trying to revive the ancient insight that achieving "genuine justice" requires that something be done *for* the victim and not simply *to* the offender. They point out that street crimes are best viewed as conflicts between individuals rather than as affronts to an abstraction like society's norms or the state's authority. Making restitution (in the form of monetary payments from earnings or performing direct personal services) is a symbolic gesture that is a prerequisite for reconciliation and reacceptance into the community. Reparations not only help victims recover from the aftershocks of predatory incidents but also provide the basis for forgiveness. The government—through its criminal justice agencies—can strive to maintain order and protect lives and property, but only the community—through its local institutions and traditions—can encourage reintegration. A neutral third party can facilitate and oversee the process of restoring harmonious relations better than an agent of the state (such as a prosecutor, judge, or probation officer) who coerces both parties to agree to certain terms (Umbreit, 1989, 1990; Van Ness, 1990; Wright, 1991). The differences between retributive justice and restorative justice are highlighted in Table 7.3.

Some restorative justice projects are experimenting with two traditional ways of bringing the various estranged parties together, **peacemaking circles** and **family group conferencing.** The use of overlapping peacemaking circles composed of the victim and his or her support system, the offender and his or

Table 7.3 Comparing and Contrasting Retributive Justice and Restorative Justice

Issue	Retributive Justice	Restorative Justice
Nature of street crime	A violation of the state's rules	An act that harms specific individuals
Jurisdiction	Handled by the criminal justice system's agencies and officials	Resolved by community members
Goals	Conviction and punishment for the purpose of retribution, deterrence, and incapacitation	Recovery of victim, rehabilitation of offender, restoration of harmony
Methods	Adversary system, establish guilt according to strict rules of evidence	Mediation, negotiation, frank discussion, consensus, restitution
Victim's role	Limited to complainant and witness for the prosecution	Central figure, direct participant
Offender's role	Must accept blame, suffer consequences	Must accept responsibility, make amends
Orientation	Past wrongful acts, prevention via fear of consequences	Past harm and future recovery, rehabilitation

SOURCES: Adapted from OJP, 1997; Crowe, 1998; and Zehr, 1998.

her family, and community members is derived from Native American tribal culture in the United States and Canada. After frank discussions about what caused the problem, the groups merge into a disposition circle that develops a consensus about how to restore harmony to the afflicted individuals, their relationships, and their neighbors. A follow-up circle monitors the wrongdoer's progress in making amends (OJJDP, 1998; Zehr, 1998; Pranis, 1999). Family group conferencing is a means of conflict resolution developed by the Maori, the indigenous people of New Zealand. It has been adapted to resolve juvenile delinquency cases in that country as well as Australia. Run by a trained facilitator, the conference begins with the wrongdoer undergoing **reintegrative shaming** by describing the incident to an assemblage of relatives, friends, and neighbors. Then the victim explains how this event caused distress, injuries, and losses. Other members of the community fill in details about the impact on their lives. The offender begins to realize how his or her actions harmed other people and how he or she ought to repair the damage. After the victim suggests desired outcomes, the entire group discusses possible ways to solve the problem. By the conclusion of the conference, a written settlement is worked out that sets forth the community's expectations about the constructive actions the wrongdoer is obliged to undertake to undo the harm he or she caused (Bradshaw and Umbreit, 1998; Zehr, 1998).

The development of methods of "alternative dispute resolution" (ADR) has furthered interest in reconciliation programs. Mediation is usually the key. One of several techniques for resolving disputes, it lies in the middle of a continuum bounded by conciliation and arbitration. Conciliation simply requires a go-between to facilitate the flow of information from one disputant to another. Arbitration is a process in which a neutral individual is called in to break a deadlock. The arbitrator plays an active role as fact finder and then after hearing presentations from both sides imposes a fair, final, legally binding decision. Mediation requires direct negotiations between disputants. As a neutral person the mediator helps the feuding parties arrive at a mutually acceptable compromise by promoting discussion, soliciting viewpoints, and helping uncover areas of common interest. Dispute resolution was embraced in the 1970s as a way of resolving interpersonal conflicts that involved shared responsibility. Calling the police, pressing charges, prosecuting in court, and seeking vindication through conviction was considered to be an inappropriate procedure for handling minor violations of the law, especially if they stemmed from ongoing relationships in which each person did something "wrong" to antagonize, provoke, and harm the other. The adversary system that underlies both criminal and civil proceedings is essentially a "zero sum game." At each stage one party gains points at the expense of the other. Strict rules of evidence may prevent the disputants and witnesses from telling the whole story. Both sides are preoccupied with issues of blame, guilt, and liability. At the end of the contest, there must always be a winner and a loser. The victorious side is pleased with the outcome, while the defeated side is angry and disappointed. The two parties may leave court just as they arrived, locked in conflict and hostile toward each other, and sometimes even more alienated, bitter, and polarized than at the outset (Wright, 1989). Using ADR was viewed as preferable to adjudication, since it could lead to a compromise settlement that might satisfy both parties and resolve their dispute with some degree of finality.

A **multidoor courthouse** or a **neighborhood justice center** is a place where these alternative ways of settling conflicts are made available. Disputants take their cases to an intake/diagnosis/referral unit, where a screening specialist decides upon the most appropriate method of resolving the matter: conciliation, mediation, arbitration, or adjudication within the criminal justice system. At neighborhood justice centers practicing ADR techniques, hearings are scheduled at the convenience of the participants, not the staff. The use of private attorneys is discouraged. The rules governing the introduction of evidence are minimized. Witnesses are not sworn in. Mediators do not wear robes or sit above and apart from the others. Nontechnical language is used, and only limited records of the proceedings are kept. The **moot model** of informal justice avoids the constraints of a guilty-innocent, wrong-right, pin-the-blame/deny-responsibility framework. With the mediator acting as a referee, the disputants educate each other by presenting their own versions of their conflict. The intent is to look to the future rather than to dwell on the past. The ultimate goals are to reconcile the estranged parties and repair rifts within their community (Prison Research, 1976; Wright, 1985; Roehl and Ray, 1986).

Neighborhood justice centers were not sought by activists when the victims' rights movement first emerged during the 1970s. Originally, the idea of relying upon informal negotiations to settle criminal matters conjured up the unfavorable image of an unwilling, trembling victim being forced to shake hands with a smirking, unrepentant offender. The impetus for developing this additional forum came from other constituencies. Attempting to streamline the judicial process, court administrators sought ways of removing the minor criminal cases that clogged their calendars. Judges, including the justices of the Supreme Court, encouraged experiments in conflict resolution, hoping to find a way to make working problems out in court at great public expense a last resort. Police and prosecutors endorsed the weeding out of what they considered "junk" cases from their workloads. From their point of view, too many people wasted the time of public agencies trying to resolve private matters. They argued that the complex machinery of criminal justice should be reserved for real crimes involving large financial losses and serious injuries inflicted by strangers and should not be used to attempt to settle petty squabbles between people with prior relationships. Prosecutors complained that a great many complainants decided to drop charges or failed to appear in court to testify when their offenders were family members, lovers, former friends, classmates, colleagues, or neighbors. Anticipating that these complainants would change their minds shortly after an arrest, prosecutors disposed of their "garbage" cases quickly, either by dropping the charges completely or by plea bargaining them down (Silberman, 1978; Ray, 1984; and Umbreit, 1987).

The first experiments with ADR techniques for resolving conflicts of both a civil and a criminal nature were launched at the start of the 1970s in Philadelphia and Columbus, Ohio. The Law Enforcement Assistance Administration (LEAA) provided seed money to cover the start-up costs of other programs. The majority were sponsored by and attached to a criminal justice agency (such as a court or prosecutor's office); the others were run by private nonprofit organizations (like the American Arbitration Association or the Institute for Mediation and Conflict Resolution), by a community group (like the local bar association), or by some county or municipal governmental body. The kind of sponsorship behind a center shaped the way it conducted its business and the types of cases it accepted (Alper and Nichols, 1981; Freedman and Ray, 1982; McGillis, 1982; Goldberg, Green, and Sander, 1985; Harrington, 1985).

In 1980, Congress passed the Dispute Resolution Act authorizing the creation of a national clearinghouse to conduct research and disseminate information about "storefront" justice. In 1981, New York became the first state to fund new and existing programs. The entire branch of social science known as conflict resolution received much-needed recognition, legitimation, and support in 1984 when Congress earmarked money within the military budget for the establishment of a United States Institute of Peace. Courses on the techniques, strategies, and philosophies of conflict resolution and peacemaking are now routinely offered in schools and colleges and in training programs for lawyers, police officers, and other criminal justice personnel (Volpe, 1989).

Pilot programs to test whether mediated restitution arrangements could lay the groundwork for reconciliation were pioneered in Canada in the mid-1970s and Elkhart, Indiana, in 1978. Members of the Mennonite religious sect were among the first enthusiastic supporters of this healing process. Their experimental project served as a model for others to replicate and modify, just as the penitentiary (initially invented by the Quakers as a nonviolent alternative to corporal and capital punishment in the early 1800s) was copied by governments worldwide. At the start of the 1990s, over 125 Victim Offender Reconciliation Programs (VORPs) were operating in 20 states, handling about 16,000 cases a year. By the close of the 1990s, in nearly all the states, about 300 of these programs brought victims and offenders together (Coates, 1990; Umbreit and Coates, 1993; Umbreit, 1994, 1995; Umbreit and Greenwood, 1998).

How Reconciliation Programs Work

The kinds of cases considered appropriate for mediation and conflict resolution have grown steadily since the first projects were initiated. Originally, guidelines restricted the types of matters referred to neighborhood justice centers to noncriminal quarrels between people with ongoing relationships. Then the scope of eligible cases was broadened to include such misdemeanors as harassment, simple assault, petty larceny, and vandalism, in which the disputants had committed retaliatory acts against each other as part of a simmering feud. Such cases of shared responsibility were not suitable for criminal justice processing because the adversary framework imposed a "winner take all" format that resulted in an undeserved victory for one party and an unjust defeat for the other. Over the years the nature of the relationship between the victim and the offender rather than the nature of the offense became the single most important criterion for diverting cases out of the criminal justice system. Neighborhood justice centers began to handle acts of violence unleashed by offenders who knew their victims. Eventually, even violent incidents perpetrated by complete strangers were considered appropriate cases for face-to-face meetings. Some programs go so far as to bring together for group sessions victims whose cases were never solved and offenders convicted of harming people who don't wish to participate (Wright, 1985, 1989; Umbreit, 1989).

Most programs treat reconciliation as the desired outcome of a process with four distinct phases: case selection, preparation, mediation and negotiation, and monitoring during the follow-up period. The healing process begins when a case manager sorts out ones that seem suitable. Next, a trained mediator (either a staff member or a volunteer) contacts the complainant and then the accused in order to explain the mechanics of the program, discuss the nature of the charges, and test their willingness to participate in a face-to-face encounter. If they both agree, the mediator meets with each side separately and then brings the two disputants together (perhaps at the victim's home, at the jail where the defendant is being detained, or at the program's office). At their **conference** or **dialogue,** both parties vent their emotions and share their reactions to the crime and the way it was handled by the criminal justice system. After that they focus on the damage that was done. They attempt to hammer out a mutually acceptable arrangement in which the offender pledges restitution to cover the victim's expenses. After the meeting the mediator remains in contact with both parties, supervising and verifying that the written contract is being completely fulfilled. The agreement usually requires that the wrongdoer make payments from earnings, perform useful and needed personal services, or undertake community service work to benefit some charity (Galaway, 1987; Coates, 1990; Umbreit, 1990, 1994; OJJDP, 1998).

The heart of the process is the encounter between the victim and the offender in a structured and secure setting, often at the program's headquarters or in a community center, library, or house of worship, but occasionally in a courtroom or the victim's home. Usually, each side has already met separately with the mediator. The mediator, typically an uncertified volunteer with at least 30 hours of training and experience, tries to make both parties feel comfortable, facilitates their dialogue, and assists them to find common ground. At the outset the victim describes how the illegal act inflicted emotional, physical and financial harm, and gets answers to nagging questions like "Why me? What did I ever do to you?" and "How could I have avoided this?" The wrongdoer then tells his or her side of the story, often in the presence of his or her parents. Hopefully, at the conclusion the wrongdoer comes to appreciate the error of his or her ways, accepts responsibility, expresses genuine remorse, apologizes, and agrees to try to restore the victim to the condition he or she was in before the crime occurred. The mediator, the program's staff, or a probation officer supervises the repayment process during the follow-up period. In cases where compliance lags, continued contacts and renegotiation of the settlement may become necessary. After restitution obligations have been fulfilled, reconciliation becomes a real possibility (see Umbreit and Greenwood, 1998).

The majority of victim-offender reconciliation programs are run by private nonprofit organizations rather than criminal justice agencies, according to a survey carried out during the mid-1990s. Programs administered by private, community-based groups made up the largest single category (more than 40% of the total). Nearly 25% of the programs were overseen by religious organizations. Criminal justice agencies ran the remainder: probation departments (about 15%), corrections departments (nearly 10%), and police forces and prosecutor's offices (a few percent each). Almost half of all programs dealt with both juvenile and adult offenders, about 45% only handled delinquency cases, and nearly 10% only supervised adult lawbreakers. Local and state governments were the most frequent primary sources of funding. The federal government, religious organizations, foundations, private charities (like the United Way), and individual contributors also helped to pay for operating expenses. The typical program had a relatively small budget of just over $50,000, employed only two full-time staff members, and relied on 35 or more volunteers to carry out their mission. The average program handled about 135 cases concerning juvenile offenders and supervised around 75 involving adults.

Roughly 33% of the offenses were felonies, and the remaining 67% arose from misdemeanors. The most common crimes were vandalism, minor assaults, thefts, and burglaries. But around 33% of the programs reported that they occasionally handled more serious offenses, such as attacks leading to physical injuries and assaults with a deadly weapon. Some programs even dealt with sexual assaults by strangers, attempted murders, negligent homicides, and manslaughter. Probation officers, judges, and prosecutors referred all kinds of cases to mediation.

In every program, victims participated voluntarily, and they could quit at any time. Offenders, however, had to take part if their victims wanted them to in about 20% of the programs and had to admit their guilt in 65% of them before proceeding. About 33% of all wrongdoers were participating as a condition of diversion before adjudication. A little more than 25% had been found guilty in court but had not been sentenced yet, and an equal percentage were attending as part of their sentence. Of the cases in which victims and offenders met in the presence of a mediator, nearly 90% led to a written agreement, and the overwhelming majority of offenders successfully completed their obligations (Umbreit and Greenwood, 1998).

Program directors report that a variety of problems plague their operations. Securing adequate funding from private and public sources presents a continuing challenge. Receiving a steady flow of appropriate referrals from criminal justice agencies requires that good working relationships be maintained. Cultivating support within the community demands an ongoing dialogue with the advocates of retributive justice. Similarly, convincing angry victims to give restorative justice a chance requires patience to overcome their initial resistance (see Umbreit and Greenwood, 1998).

Evaluating Efforts at Reconciliation

In theory, victim-offender reconciliation offers advantages to both parties and their crime-plagued communities. In the presence of skilled intermediaries, victims get an opportunity to release pent-up feelings and get answers to troubling questions. In addition to emotional catharsis, victims ought to be able to leave the negotiations with a satisfactory restitution agreement in hand. For offenders the encounter offers an occasion to accept responsibility, express remorse, and ask for forgiveness. Probably more important to most perpetrators is the chance to substitute restitution obligations for time behind bars. For the community the pragmatic benefit is that negotiated settlements relieve court backlogs and jail and prison overcrowding, and eliminate the need to build more cells to confine greater numbers of convicts at the taxpayers' expense. A less tangible but significant spiritual dividend is the fostering of an atmosphere of tolerance, understanding, and redemption within the community (Coates, 1990; Umbreit, 1990; Viano, 1990).

Evaluations of different programs nationwide highlight a number of important issues. Offender recidivism rates may not be any lower for adult participants in restorative justice experiments (see Niemeyer and Shichor, 1996; and Hansen,

1997), but juveniles may benefit from making restitution. Youthful offenders who passed through mediation committed fewer and less serious offenses than a control group of their peers during the one-year follow-up period (Umbreit, 1994). As for the willingness of victims to meet with their perpetrators (juveniles placed on probation for property crimes), the percentages ranged from 54% to 90%. Reportedly, nearly 95% of the meetings led to a mutually acceptable agreement. The average amount of money the adolescents pledged to pay to their victims ranged from about $175 to $250. The proportion of the contracts that were carried out to the victims' satisfaction ranged from a low of 52% in one program to a high of 91% in another. In general, the research findings showed that many victims volunteer to participate in face-to-face confrontations, very few mediation sessions become emotionally explosive, and most victims are not vindictive and do not make unreasonable demands (Galaway, 1987). Another evaluation of four mediation projects attached to juvenile courts uncovered high levels of client satisfaction, approaching 80% of the victims and nearly 90% of the offenders. Roughly 85% of the participants felt that the process of mediation was fair to both parties. Before meeting their offenders in person, nearly 25% of the victims confided that they were afraid of being preyed upon again by the same individual; after the mediation session ended, only 10% still harbored that fear. Over 80% of the delinquents successfully completed their negotiated restitution arrangements, compared to 58% of similar offenders ordered to make restitution by juvenile court judges who didn't directly involve victims or use mediation (Umbreit, 1994). Victim dissatisfaction surfaces in those programs that fail to follow up to see to it that restitution pledges are fulfilled (Coates and Gehm, 1989).

Mediators received higher ratings for "fairness" than judges, according to several evaluations that compared cases handled at selected ADR programs to similar cases adjudicated in court. Most disputants reported that they left the neighborhood justice centers believing that their differences had been settled. The compromise solutions worked out at centers were adhered to more faithfully than dispositions imposed by criminal or civil court judges (Cook, Roehl, and Sheppard, 1980; Davis, Tichane, and Grayson, 1980; Garofalo and Connelly, 1980). Proponents of mediation in pursuit of reconciliation interpret these findings as evidence of a solid, positive track record. They conclude that the experimental stage can be judged a success and that the time has come for a substantial reallocation of resources that would enable these programs to handle many more cases. They point to polls which demonstrate that considerable public support favors restitution as an alternative to imprisonment, at least for cases involving property crimes and minor assaults (Galaway, 1987, 1989).

Pros and Cons From the Victim's Point of View

For victims of minor offenses who are embroiled in ongoing conflicts for which they admittedly bear some responsibility, alternative dispute resolution offers several advantages over adjudication in criminal or civil court. If victims don't want an arrest to be made or charges to be pressed, they now have the additional option of bringing their problems to a neighborhood justice center. Incidents that otherwise would be too trivial to interest the police or prosecutors can be addressed. Smoldering tensions that might flare up again and result in a spiral of violence and retaliation can be smothered. Individuals who dread the public spectacle of testifying and of being cross-examined in open court can choose to hold low-key hearings behind closed doors. They can represent themselves rather than accept the services of a prosecutor who primarily looks after the state's interests or, in civil court, a private attorney who is after a share of the money. Informal justice has proven to be speedier, cheaper, and more accessible than formal proceedings. Cases are handled sooner, are heard at times and places convenient to the participants, and cost less in terms of time, money, and emotion. The settlement can be seen as a vindication if the other party apologizes in writing and undertakes restitution as an admission of responsibility. Such agreements can provide a sound basis for reconciliation for people who want to—or have to learn to—get along with each other in the future within their community.

From a civil liberties standpoint, several issues raise concerns. Suspects and defendants are being pressured to give up their due process rights and readily admit guilt in order to get on with the healing process and get out of the grip of the punitive system. Sentence disparity grows because the consequences for committing the same crime vary substantially, depending entirely upon the input from the particular victim and community members who take part in the unstructured process. Also, the willingness of programs to deal with even the most minor infractions stimulates the criminal justice system's appetite for "widening the net"—intervening more intrusively in private matters.

But from the victims' point of view, other drawbacks persist. As with criminal court-ordered restitution, the opportunity for ADR arises only in cases where a suspect has been apprehended (but not necessarily formally convicted). Statistically, that prerequisite excludes most property crime victims. As for violent crimes the harm inflicted in a moment can last a lifetime. Injuries and losses may be so great that they add up to expenses that far exceed what the offender is able to repay and what a small community can afford to reimburse. The limited capacity of the offender and the community to provide resources should not serve as a cap that impedes a seriously wounded victim's full recovery (Herman, 1998). Furthermore, a completely innocent victim might find informal justice unsatisfactory. If the process consciously abandons the presumptions of guilt and innocence that underlie the labels "offender" and "victim" and terms both parties "disputants," then the complainant's conduct is open to scrutiny, especially in the absence of rules governing evidence and cross-examination. The notion of shared responsibility is frequently invoked by mediators, who view disputes as outgrowths of misunderstandings and the pursuit of narrow self-interest by both parties. To reach a compromise, complainants might be pressured to concede more responsibility, fault, or involvement than they feel they should. The entire notion of a compromise solution as a means of achieving reconciliation rests on the practice of both parties giving in, to varying degrees, from their original demands. Complainants who insist that they are absolutely blameless can feel cheated. When their case was diverted from the criminal justice system, that reassignment symbolized a withdrawal of governmental support (prosecutorial backing) from their side. They may feel that they were coerced to give in to a preordained outcome—reconciliation—even if their legitimate feelings of anger and hostility have not dissipated.

For victims intent on revenge, the greatest drawbacks of mediation and restitution are that these processes are not punishment oriented. Neighborhood justice centers and victim-offender reconciliation programs are not authorized to convict offenders, publicly humiliate them with the stigma of the label of "criminal," impose stiff fines, or confine them in a penal institution (Garofalo and Connelly, 1980).

Several potential problems could plague ADR and VORP programs in the near future. Overly enthusiastic staff members and mediators might pressure victims to participate and make them feel that they must end up forgiving and reconciling with their offenders. If caseloads grow too large, mediators might be inclined to adopt an assembly-line approach to speed up the process and avoid backlogs. Worse yet, overworked staff members might be tempted to eliminate the face-to-face mediation session entirely in order to more quickly dispose of a large caseload. Originally, the cases considered suitable for mediation, restitution, and reconciliation involved petty nonviolent offenses against property. Program staff members acceded to this limitation in order to perfect their techniques, avoid controversy, and maintain funding and referral sources. But now legislators and judges seem increasingly willing to send conflicts marred by violence to mediation. Some of these more serious cases don't fit the mediation format, and the harm cannot be repaired through restitution. And other tough cases will require more time to resolve, more professionally trained mediators, a greater commitment of resources, and more support from social service and criminal justice agencies (Coates, 1990; Umbreit, 1990).

The number of cases directed to neighborhood justice centers and victim-offender reconciliation programs will grow because there is a movement toward informality throughout the criminal justice system. In practice, informality is marked by a preference for unwritten, flexible, commonsense, discretionary procedures tailored to fit particular cases. As an ideology informality is characterized by an antipathy toward rigid hierarchy, bureaucratic impersonality, and professional domination. The growing interest in informal justice is fostered by several beliefs: that centralized governmental coercion has failed as an instrument of social change; that people must solve their own problems in decentralized, community-controlled settings; that nonstranger conflicts ought to be diverted from the formal adjudication process whenever possible; that both punishment and rehabilitation efforts behind bars have failed to "cure" offenders; and that criminal justice officials and agencies primarily serve the state's interests (or their own) to the detriment of both offenders and victims. Enthusiasm for informal alternatives is fed by perceptions that the criminal courts are paralyzed, civil courts are swamped with frivolous lawsuits, and prisons and jails are dangerously overcrowded. As a pragmatic response to such economic and political realities, informality beckons as a solution to the government's fiscal crisis. Neighborhood justice centers and victim-offender reconciliation programs can relieve the overburdened criminal justice system at a time when calls for more services are clashing with demands for less taxation (Able, 1982; Van Ness and Strong, 1997).

Restorative justice can be oversold as a cure-all. Enthusiasm for other sweeping reforms in the past quickly led to disillusionment as they failed to live up to their promises. Unfounded optimism greeted the substitution of supposedly rehabilitative *reform*atories, *penitent*iaries and houses of *correction* for harsh corporal and capital punishment, and the setting up of an ostensibly treatment-oriented juvenile justice system to supplant a punitive adult court and prison system. Other major changes have also disappointed their advocates: the replacement of fixed terms of incarceration with indeterminate sentences that provided incentives for self-improvement, the use of scared-straight visits to local jails and prisons to shock delinquents into changing their ways before it was too late, and the proliferation of boot camps as places to break youthful offenders of their bad habits and build self-disciplined, law-abiding young men. Restorative justice programs may fall short too, but they certainly merit more of a role in crime-ridden metropolitan areas.

TOWARD RETALIATORY JUSTICE

The owner of a grocery parks his car outside his store. Later, he spies a man breaking into it, so he grabs a pistol and, joined by an employee with a bat, runs outside. They beat the unarmed car thief and then shoot him. The grocer and his clerk are arrested for murder. ("Car Thief Slain," 1988)

A teenager waiting for a train is robbed of his gold jewelry by six young men. The next night the adolescent spots the gang of robbers at the same station. He comes up to them and says cryptically, "Remember me?" They don't recognize him and look puzzled, until he pulls out a revolver and starts shooting. He wounds three and then flees. When the injured youths tell the police the full story about why they were shot, they are arrested for confessing to the robbery that apparently provoked the victim's wrath. He is never found. (Marriott, 1989)

A young man accused of killing a teenage boy at a party is in court for his 11th pretrial hearing. Infuriated by what he considers to be the slow pace of justice, the father of the slain adolescent enters the courthouse and shoots the defendant in the back in plain view of a crowd of lawyers and off-duty detectives. Put on trial for attempted murder, the father is acquitted because the jurors agree with him that the defendant posed a threat to him and his remaining children. But the jury convicts the father of the misdemeanor of illegally possessing a handgun. (Tomasson, 1991)

Two robbers barge into a family's apartment in a drug-ridden, high-crime area. They hit the husband on the head with the butt of a gun and flee with some jewelry as his wife screams for help, alerting neighbors. The husband recovers and races after them. Ten other men join in the chase. The husband tackles the robber holding the stolen valuables, and they wrestle each other to the ground. The robber pulls a knife and slashes the husband, but the crowd closes in, kicking, punching, and stabbing the robber to death. Then the participants melt away into the evening and when detectives arrive, they get no help from silent and uncooperative eyewitnesses. Local residents tell reporters that they have lost faith in the justice system and that this killing of a "bad guy" might be a good thing for the neighborhood's reputation. (Lorch, 1990)

There is another kind of "informal justice" that has little in common with the peacemaking that is offered at mediation programs. It is an entirely different type of conflict resolution that relies on the use of force, not negotiation and compromise. It has a long and bloody history, and its goal is not reconciliation but retaliation. This outlawed alternative to formal case processing within the criminal justice system embodies a "do-it-yourself" approach. In common parlance it is dubbed "back-alley justice," "curbstone justice," "street justice," or "frontier justice." To government officials, criminologists, and victimologists, it is the modern-day expression of that old-fashioned impulse called **vigilantism.**

Clear-cut examples usually attract extensive media coverage and become well known. Most reported incidents fit into one of four categories (see Shotland, 1976): victims unleashing more force than the law permits under the doctrine of self-defense (first example above) or avenging an earlier incident (second example), retaliatory actions carried out on behalf of victims by family members or close friends (third example), or spontaneous mob actions in which a crowd responds to a victim's plea for help and gets carried away (fourth example).

Vigilantism's Frontier Origins

Vigilantism has a long and violent history, especially in the Old West and the Deep South. It began in colonial times as a frontier reaction to marauding bands of desperadoes. In Virginia in the late 1700s, a "vigilance committee" led by a Colonel Lynch developed a reputation for the public whippings it staged. Its escalating violence against lawbreakers gave rise to the terms **lynch law** and **lynchings.** From 1767 to 1909, 326 short-lived vigilante movements peppered American history (mostly as western frontier phenomena), claiming 729 lives (Brown, 1975). From 1882 until as recently as 1951, spontaneously formed lynch mobs killed 4,730 people. Many of the victims were black men accused of harming white women, particularly in rural areas (Hofstadter and Wallace, 1970).

Over the course of American history, vigilantism has often arisen as a response to victimization. Vigilantes called for action whenever "honest, upright citizens" became enraged and terrified about what they considered to be an upsurge of criminality and a breakdown of law and order. Pointing to the plight of victims, vigilantes feared that they were next if they didn't take drastic measures. Hence, "red-blooded, able-bodied, law-abiding" men banded together and pursued outlaws who were threatening their families, property, and way of life. Vigilance committees led by individuals from the local power elite (with a solid middle-class membership) tended to go after people at the bottom of the hierarchy and the margins of society. They lashed out at alleged cutthroats, bushwhackers, road agents (robbers), cattle rustlers, horse thieves, and desperadoes of all kinds. They also crusaded against people they branded as parasites, drifters, idlers, sinners, "loose" women, "uppity" members of subjugated groups, "outside agitators," and "subversives" with anarchist and communist leanings. The targets of their wrath were blacklisted, banished (run out of town), flogged (whipped), tarred and feathered, mutilated, and in some instances slaughtered (Burrows, 1976).

Very few of these self-appointed guardians of virtue ever got into legal trouble for their lawless deeds. Vigilantes portrayed themselves as true patriots and dedicated upholders of moral codes and sacred traditions. The manifestos of vigilance committees were crowned with references to "the right to revolution," "popular sovereignty," and personal survival as "the first law of nature." Just as they held criminals fully accountable for their transgressions, these rugged individualists held themselves personally responsible for their own security. If duly constituted authority could not be relied on for protection, they would shoulder the burden of law enforcement and the obligation to punish offenders. The vigilante credo boiled down to a variation on "the end justifies the means:" breaking the law is necessary in order to preserve the rule of law. Most vigilantes defended their violence in terms of avenging victims and punishing common criminals. But in retrospect other reasons may have been paramount. Teaching lawbreakers a lesson and making an example out of them to deter other would-be offenders was the goal the men in the mob attacks cited to rationalize their own criminality. But vigilantes had ulterior motives as well: to quash rebellions; to reassert control over rival racial, ethnic, religious, or political groups; to intimidate subordinates back into submission; and to impose the dominant group's moral standards on outsiders, newcomers, and defiant members of the community (Brown, 1975).

Currently, vigilantism is argued about much more than it is carried out. The label "vigilante"—a term formerly accepted with pride but now hurled as an epithet—crops up frequently. Usually, the word is used for shock value by journalists and public officials. When "survivalists" fortify their homes and stockpile weapons, that is not vigilantism (although some extremists warn that they will resort to violence if a crisis develops and the government becomes paralyzed or collapses). When neighbors organize citizen patrols and serve as additional eyes and ears for the police, that's not vigilantism either. (The first such crime-watch patrol in 1964 in a Brooklyn community was quickly dubbed a "vigilante group," but the concerns of the authorities quickly subsided. Federal money has sponsored such local efforts to supplement law enforcement, and police departments have provided training and equipment to civilian patrols.) Tenant and subway patrols (like the Guardian Angels) also have been mischaracterized as vigilante groups. They are not as long as they confine their activities to reporting incidents, attending to injured victims, and making citizen's arrests of suspects. If they do not cross the line and dish out "back-alley justice," then they are not vigilantes (Marx and Archer, 1976).

Vigilantism Versus Legitimate Use of Force in Self-defense

> **A** sixth-grader is going door to door, selling chocolates for a school fund-raiser. A man sitting on his porch agrees to buy some candy and invites the girl inside while he gets some money. But then he whips out a knife and threatens to kill the 11-year-old if she doesn't undress. As he throws her on a couch, she snatches the knife away from him, slashes him on the hand, kicks him in the stomach, and bolts out the front door. Within minutes the man (who previously served time for raping a 10-year-old relative) is placed under arrest for attempted aggravated sexual assault, assault with a deadly weapon, and kidnapping. (Smith, 1994)

> **A** businessman shoots a reputed member of organized crime who is trying to extort protection money from him. Placed on trial for murder, the businessman is condemned by the prosecutor for firing an "outrageously excessive" number of shots (18 in all) leaving the alleged gangster "perforated like a piece of Swiss cheese." But a jury acquits him of all charges, accepting his lawyer's contention that he acted in self-defense and was "on automatic pilot." (Fraser, 1991)

The ultimate right for any individual is to resist victimization. People under attack are entitled by law to protect themselves. Self-preservation should not be confused with vigilantism.

The statutes governing fighting back in self-defense are not worded the same in each state because they have been shaped by four different rationales. According to a **punitive** rationale, using force against an attacker is permissible because any injuries the aggressor suffers are deserved. Under the rationale of **necessity,** the use of violence is excused when a victim fearing great harm has no choice but to resort to force as a means of self-protection. According to the **individualist** rationale, a citizen does not have to yield or concede any territory to those who would encroach on his or her autonomy. Under the **social** rationale for self-defense, resistance to attack is justified as a way of preserving order (Fletcher, 1988a).

In general, the right to self-defense is formulated as the permissible use of reasonable force to protect one's life (or that of an innocent third party) from an adversary whom one reasonably believes is threatening harm. Several qualifications within the law are intended to restrain victims in order to discourage needless escalations of hostilities that can place them in greater danger or imperil bystanders and to prevent terrible misunderstandings that can cause innocent people to be mistaken for dangerous offenders. If a person who meant no harm is hurt or killed, the individual who made the mistake can be held responsible for assault or murder. The first restriction is that the threat posed by an aggressor must be imminent. The intended victim may not use force if the would-be aggressor issues a conditional threat ("If I ever catch you . . . then . . .") or a future threat ("The next time I catch you . . ."). The second qualification is that if the assailant retreats, removing the victim from imminent danger, force may no longer be used. (In some states the victim must try to evade a confrontation or attempt to escape before resorting to deadly force.) Third, the victim's belief that harm is imminent must be reasonable. A "reasonable person" takes into account the size of the adversary, the time of day, the location, the presence or absence of a weapon, and similar factors. Fourth, the degree of force the victim uses to repel the attack must be in proportion to the threat of injury or death posed by the aggressor. Finally, the timing of the victim's action must be appropriate. A preemptive strike initiated (too soon) before the presumed attacker makes his or her intentions known is illegal. A retaliatory strike made (too late) after the clash is over also exceeds the limits of self-defense (see Austern, 1987; and Fletcher, 1988a).

In every state the law permits innocent victims to use deadly force to protect themselves from serious bodily harm and also spells out the circumstances under which victims of particular crimes can try to wound or kill their adversaries. For example, whether or not citizens are entitled by law to unleash deadly force to protect their homes and property varies dramatically from state to state. In most jurisdictions, intruders guilty of forcible entries into dwellings can be shot; in some states, however, victims must be threatened or actually attacked before they can use lethal force against criminals who invade their homes. Trespassers are generally not considered to pose a grave peril and therefore cannot be shot on sight. Only a few states authorize citizens to use some degree of physical force to safeguard their property from thieves (BJS, 1988).

In fact, most victims of violent attacks took measures to protect themselves (in 60% of all robberies, 74% of all assaults, and 80% of all rapes). However, their self-defense tactics did not necessarily involve violence. Their reactions included screaming for help, running away, reasoning with or threatening the offender, resisting and trying to capture the assailant, and counterattacking with or without a weapon. Willingness to take self-protective measures did not seem to vary by race, sex, or prior relationship (stranger or nonstranger) but was dependent upon age (older victims were less likely to put up a struggle). Males were more likely to try to fight back to resist and capture an assailant, while females were more inclined to call for help or threaten the attacker verbally. More victims reported that their self-protective measures helped the situation (by enabling them to avoid injury altogether or at least to prevent further injury) rather than hurt it (by making the attacker angrier and more aggressive). Only about 1% of all victims reported that they counterattacked by drawing their own weapon, according to responses provided to *NCVS* interviewers in 1992 (BJS, 1994b).

Would Potential Victims Be Better Off if They Were Armed?

In response to the threat posed by offenders, many people have armed themselves in self-defense, believing that they are improving their odds of surviving a felonious assault. Surveys going back to 1959 have confirmed that almost half of all American households own at least one gun. During the 1990s an estimated 44 million Americans owned over 190 million firearms, of which 65 million were handguns. This private arsenal was more than double the total number of firearms in nonpolice/nonmilitary hands in 1970, when federal gun control laws first became a major political issue. (However, the proportion of armed households may be declining.) Nearly one half (46%) of all gun owners cite self-protection as one of the main reasons for acquiring firearms (Morganthau and Shenitz, 1994; Witkin, 1994; Cook and Ludwig, 1997). In response to an "arm yourself in self-defense" movement, a growing number of state legislatures (31 by the end of the 1990s) passed **right-to-carry** statutes that enable ordinary citizens to pack concealed handguns as they go about their everyday lives. In these states, pistol permits are easily obtainable, provided that the applicant is "of good character" and doesn't have a record of arrests and convictions or a documented history of mental illness. In the other states, citizens have to prove that they have a compelling need to be armed, and local police chiefs, sheriffs, and judges decide who gets the limited number of permits (Verhovek, 1995; Ratnesar, 1998).

Public opinion is sharply divided over the issue of armed self-defense. The debate is centered around the question of whether intended victims would be better-off or worse-off if they were in a position to draw their own guns when threatened or under attack. One side sees guns as "equalizers" that can save innocent lives and pushes for policies that provide ready access to firearms for responsible, law-abiding adults. The other side seeks to further restrict gun availability because firearms are seen as "facilitators" that cause minor conflicts to escalate into deadly confrontations. These weapons are considered more dangerous to the individuals who wield them than to their opponents at whom they take aim. Both sides in the debate admit there is a trade-off between appropriate self-defense uses and improper uses (accidental shootings, shootings of the wrong person by mistake, using firearms to commit suicide, and using guns for criminal purposes), but differ on whether the costs on balance outweigh the benefits (see Kleck, 1997).

Advocates of armed self-defense like to cite examples like the following that indicate how guns can be used successfully to protect life and property:

> **A** man breaks into a home and badly beats a teenage girl. Emotionally devastated, she drops out of school. Many years later another intruder enters her home and threatens her family. This time she gets her semiautomatic rifle out of the closet. Hearing the sound of the weapon being loaded, the intruder curses and runs away. (Seelye, 1995)
>
> **T**wo customers enter a jewelry store and suddenly pull guns and announce a stickup. As one robber holds a gun to the owner's head, the shopkeeper's son emerges from the back room with his licensed pistol. The robbers turn and fire at him but miss; he shoots back, mortally wounding one and frightening off the other. ("The Armed Citizen," 1991)

The defenders of gun ownership consider keeping a firearm at home and carrying a legally registered handgun to be a rational response or antidote to the threat of violent crime. Besides citing the Second Amendment to the Constitution, they offer several arguments in favor of arming for self-protection. First, the likelihood that intended targets would be prepared for battle might dissuade some potential predators from trying to start trouble. Second, the mere sight of a firearm in the hands of the target may abort the plans of a would-be offender. Third, when a crime is in progress, recourse to a firearm may enable a victim to drive off an attacker and thwart his criminal intentions. Fourth, an armed, law-abiding citizen could capture and hold an assailant at bay until the police arrive. Finally, in a life-or-death struggle, a gun can improve the victim's odds of surviving a confrontation with a dangerous, more physically powerful foe.

Some advocates of armed self-defense as well as self-reliance go so far as to argue that intended victims have a "moral responsibility" to fight back if their property, lives, families, and communities are in danger. To do this effectively, law-abiding citizens need to be trained and to be equipped with guns as equalizers. The existence of police departments does not relieve individuals of their obligation to protect themselves, and officers cannot reasonably be depended upon to serve as personal bodyguards. Readiness to resist an assault on one's dignity is a prerequisite for self-respect, as well as a deterrent to crime (see Snyder, 1993; and Will, 1993).

Gun advocates believe that firearms are used by intended victims for self-defense more often than they are used by predators to commit crimes. They suspect that the number of lives saved by guns might exceed the number of lives lost to bullet wounds annually. The crime-inhibiting effect of gun ownership by potential victims might counterbalance the crime-generating impulse of gun ownership by criminally inclined persons (Kleck, 1991, 1997; Will, 1993; and Witkin, 1994). Some gun proponents even claim that the spread of right-to-carry laws helped to bring down the crime rate in certain states during the second half of the 1990s (see Lott, 1998).

On the other side of the gun ownership issue stand the critics of this domestic arms race. They believe that although many people conjure up fantasies about how drawing a gun will save them, the reality is that gunfire claims many innocent lives. Advocates of gun control bring up horror stories like the following incidents that illustrate how individuals who mistakenly perceive themselves to be in grave danger might fire their guns in error, causing avoidable tragedies and needless suffering:

> **L**ate one night a toddler crawls out of his bed and goes into the living room to watch the blinking colored lights on his family's Christmas tree. His actions set off an alarm on a motion detector. His stepmother awakens, grabs a handgun, and fires at what she believes is a burglar. The 3-year-old boy is shot in the head under the tree and dies. His death is ruled an accident. (Associated Press, 1994f)

> **T**wo teenage boys play hooky from high school. When the father of one of the boys returns home unexpectedly in the early afternoon, they quickly hide in a closet. The father hears muffled noises, mistakes the boys for burglars, grabs his gun, and fires through the closet door. After the 15-year-old friend dies from his wounds, the father is arrested and charged with assault, reckless endangerment, and criminal possession of a weapon, even though the victim's parents did not want to press charges. (Freifeld, 2000)

> **A** shopkeeper and his two relatives hide in the darkness with guns drawn, lying in wait as once again a burglar dares to enter their store after it closes, this time by climbing in through a broken window. Meanwhile, out on the street, plainclothes detectives spot the illegal entry and burst in through the back door. Mistaking the detectives for more criminals, the store owner opens fire. Believing they have stumbled upon a gang of well-armed burglars, the police fire back. When the shooting stops both the shopkeeper and the burglar are dead. The officers arrest the two surviving relatives for possession of unlicensed firearms. (McKinley, 1991)

Gun control advocates argue that owning a firearm for self-defense actually heightens risks and leads to a false sense of security. They point to studies that seem to show that keeping a gun at home, instead of protecting the members of a household, increases the likelihood that someone will be killed there. According to an analysis of 420 homicides committed in the homes of victims who had access to guns, the majority (77%) were slain by a spouse, other family member, or someone else they knew; only a small proportion (4%) were murdered by complete strangers (the remaining cases [19%] were not solved). The highest risks of being shot to death at home are faced by people who keep one or more guns handy, reside in a rental unit, and either live alone or with someone who was previously arrested, uses illicit drugs, hits others, or was hurt in a family fight (see Leary, 1993). Similar studies have concluded that loaded guns are more likely to be used to slay family members than intruders. The availability of handguns causes ordinary fights between family members, former friends, and neighbors to escalate into deadly encounters. More people die in one year from handgun accidents than are killed over several years by home-invading burglars and robbers. In shoot-outs with armed offenders, victims lose more often than they win. In some confrontations attackers may wrest the gun away and shoot victims with their own weapons (this even happens to well-trained, physically fit police officers). Firearms also facilitate suicides by deeply depressed individuals. During 1997, guns were used in over 17,500 suicides (about 60% of the total), compared to about 13,500 homicides (about 67% of all murders), according to health department records from around the country. Skeptics conclude that the gravest threats to members of a household come from within, not from outside; and therefore, on balance, the risks that arise from access to guns substantially outweigh the benefits (see Wright, Rossi, and Daly, 1983; Kates, 1986; Zimring, 1986; Green, 1987; Witkin, 1994; and Butterfield, 1999).

How often victims pull guns to protect themselves in confrontations is a matter of great controversy. Defensive uses number just about 100,000 in a year, according to *NCVS* findings. But gun ownership advocates dismiss this official estimate as misleadingly low and suspect that many respondents are reluctant to tell the full story to interviewers working for the government about how they repelled the attacker. A 1994 telephone survey projected a nationwide figure of as much as 2.5 million, an entirely different order of magnitude. So the real number of attempted assaults, robberies, thefts, and break-ins warded off by armed victims is a subject for conjecture. But even if the larger figure is accepted, more is not necessarily

Table 7.4 Justifiable Homicides by Police Officers and Private Citizens

	Number of Killings in Self-defense	
Year	**By Police Officers**	**By Private Citizens**
1988	343	238
1989	363	273
1990	385	328
1991	367	331
1992	418	351
1993	455	356
1994	462	353
1995	389	268
1996	358	261
1997	366	280
1998	365	194

SOURCE: FBI, *UCR*, 1989–1998

better. Some who drew their weapons against perceived threats really may not have been innocent, unprovoked victims. Also, the threat posed by armed citizens may touch off another round in an escalating arms race, motivating predatory street criminals to get more powerful guns and shoot first during confrontations (see Kleck and Gertz, 1995; and Cook and Ludwig, 1997).

One way to measure how frequently Americans resort to deadly force in self-defense is to monitor the justifiable homicide body count. The FBI's *UCR* has been keeping track of the number of justifiable homicides (killings of criminals committing felonies by law enforcement officers and by private citizens in self-defense) since 1989. The yearly data show a pattern in which officers slay more criminals than civilians do each year. During the 1990s, people under attack (officers and civilians combined) put an end to the lives of hundreds of apparent offenders annually. Taking into consideration the number of Americans who were slain each year, justifiable homicides (which are not classified by the FBI as murders because they are legally excusable) account for about 3% of all crime-related violent deaths. Most of these nonpunishable killings result from gunfire. When the level of lethal violence rose throughout the United States during the first half of the 1990s, the number of justifiable homicides climbed as well. As murders dropped at the close of the century, the death toll from defensive violence unleashed by officers and civilians subsided too (see Table 7.4).

The Drift Back Toward Retaliatory Violence

As she leaves her apartment building to go to work, a mother of nine children is robbed of her jewelry by two men. Shaken and crying she runs back upstairs to describe her assailants to her family. Three of her teenage sons rush out and spot a suspect lounging on a park bench. They confront him and a struggle ensues. As the suspect apparently reaches for a weapon, one of the brothers fatally stabs him. Although the dead man has a reputation as a person who robbed to get money for drugs, the police find no weapon of his at the crime scene. When the 18-year-old brother is arrested for first-degree manslaughter, his neighbors sign petitions on his behalf and take up a collection to hire a good lawyer for him. But after a grand jury refuses to indict the brother, the district attorney feels compelled to warn the public not to interpret this decision "as a green light for people to take the law into their own hands." (James, 1990)

A 10-year-old girl is abducted from her bedroom at four in the morning. Twelve hours later she comes running back to her apartment and tells her father that a notorious neighbor kidnapped and raped her. The father and some friends surround the accused man and begin to pummel and stomp him. In a fit of rage, the father stabs him. When the police arrive the father is arrested along with the suspect. The district attorney presses charges to demonstrate that vigilantism will not be tolerated. But while the father is held overnight in the police station, officers visit his cell to shake his hand. When he is released on very low bail by a sympathetic judge, his neighbors hail him as a hero and solicit donations to pay for his legal expenses. Complete strangers who saw him on television stop him on the street to express their approval of what he did. ("Street Sentence," 1983; Winerip, 1983)

A man is in court accused of molesting several young boys. Detecting a smirk on his face as he walks forward to take the witness stand, the mother of one of the boys pulls out a gun and shoots him in the back of the head five times. When she is put on trial for murder, some people rally to her side. Picturing her as a heroic figure who rose up in righteous indignation in defense of her child, they send telegrams offering their support and raise money for her defense. But others are skeptical of her portrayal as an anguished parent pushed to the breaking point by an arrogant offender who was about to be coddled by an ineffectual judicial system. When they learn that she waited 2 years for the chance to shoot the alleged molester, was high on methamphetamine that day, and had a past conviction for auto theft herself, they view her more like a drug-addled ex-con with a score to settle. Convicted of voluntary manslaughter she is sentenced to 10 years in prison by a judge who categorizes her courtroom gunplay as an "execution" that was an intentional and intolerable assault on the justice system. The sentence is hailed by the prosecutor who interprets it as affirming the message that victims must not take the law into their own hands. But her supporters urge clemency so she can be freed to lead a crusade to toughen the way child molesters are handled by the legal system. (Kincaid, 1993; Associated Press, 1994d)

A 48-year-old, heavily tattooed auto body repairman harasses and bullies his neighbors for years with taunts like, "I know where you live." One day he warns a retired Navy commander, "You and your family are as good as dead." Those are the last words he ever utters because the man he threatens

> pulls out a pistol, starts shooting, reloads, and fires a total of 13 rounds, killing the widely-feared, high on methamphetamine, but unarmed loudmouth. Although about 8 out of 10 callers to a talk radio show support his actions, saying things like, "He should get a medal" and "Put me on that jury and he'd get off," the retired commander is convicted of second-degree murder. But the judge, declaring that the deceased was a "jerk" and a "ne'er-do-well" who got what was coming to him, overturns the verdict, reduces the conviction to manslaughter, and cuts the shooter's sentence in half. (Goldberg, 1996; Associated Press, 1997)

Self-defense involves the use of force to prevent a crime from being completed or to rescue an intended victim from harm. Retaliatory "justice" employs force to punish an offender after a crime has been completed. Once the threat has passed, the victim may not use violence to exact revenge. But such distinctions are more easily drawn in classrooms and textbooks than in real-life confrontations. In actual cases difficult questions must be resolved: Was the victim still in imminent danger? Did the victim still reasonably fear serious bodily harm or even death? Was the response proportionate to the perceived threat, or did the victim overreact?

Police officers grapple with these questions first when they decide whether or not to make an arrest. Prosecutors confront these issues when they determine what charges, if any, to lodge against an intended victim who has emerged victorious from a battle with an aggressor. If the case goes to trial, jurors, acting as the conscience of the community, must arrive at a verdict by answering such hypothetical questions as "What would I have done under similar circumstances?" "Does the abuse the victim endured excuse his or her violent reaction?" "Did the assailant get what was coming to him or her?" and "What message does the verdict send to the public?" Juries retain the right to **nullify** legal principles, disregard the limits imposed by the law, and render a collective decision based on their own interpretations of what is reasonable and appropriate under particular circumstances (Dershowitz, 1988). The acceptance by juries of "abuse excuse" defenses (that the person on trial is more a victim than a perpetrator and therefore should not be punished) reflects both a growing intolerance toward crime and a yearning to regain control over the immediate environment—by drastic measures if necessary—especially when the criminal justice system appears to be incapable of providing adequate protection (Dershowitz, 1994).

When individuals accused of retaliatory violence are not arrested, are not vigorously prosecuted, or are acquitted by a jury after a trial, commentators try to decipher the meaning or symbolism: Was the person who was accused of dispensing street justice vindicated by public opinion as doing the right thing? Was the prosecution, representing the criminal justice system and the government, repudiated? Were the laws restraining the use of force rejected? Various interpretations are possible when persons charged with retaliatory violence are not punished for their questionable deeds (see Bahr, 1985; Zimring, 1987; and Dershowitz, 1988).

Retaliation seems to appeal to many people on a gut level. A steady stream of extremely popular movies have capitalized on the theme of personal vendettas and getting even. Even though the plots are transparent and the thirst for revenge is quenched by the end of the story, audiences stand up and cheer victims who strike back and make vicious thugs pay in blood for their cruel misdeeds.

In public opinion polls conducted during the early 1990s, from about one quarter to about one third of the people who were questioned expressed support for frontier-style justice. When asked in a survey (NVC, 1991a) whether vigilantism is ever justified, 33% answered yes, while 61% said no, and 6% were not sure. In another public opinion poll (Roper, in Maguire, Pastore, and Flanagan, 1993), respondents were asked whether or not the situation (for example, police not being around when innocent victims need them) has reached the point at which it is necessary for citizens to take the law into their own hands to protect themselves from attack in any way they can. Overall, 26% replied, "Yes, it is necessary," while 66% declared, "No, it is wrong," with 8% saying they didn't know.

No statistics purporting to measure the prevalence of retaliatory violence are available (no government agency or private research group keeps track of such outbreaks). The FBI's *UCR* does not have a category for "revenge killings" in its *Supplementary Homicide Reports.* Cases of vigilante violence seemed to be relatively infrequent during the 1990s. But if vigilantism is defined broadly as "taking the law into one's own hands" by physically punishing suspected transgressors, then it may be more common than initially realized. Many, if not most, instances of vigilantism are never detected, recorded, investigated, or prosecuted because victims and their allies (relatives, accomplices, or members of a crowd) don't want the authorities to find out their real motives. Bystanders who spontaneously intervene to break up a crime in progress to rescue a person in trouble and catch an assailant might get swept away by a mob mentality or crowd psychology and feel compelled to "get in a few good licks" to punish the offender right then and there. When innocent victims gain the upper hand during confrontations, they too may overreact and use more force than the law allows, not only to subdue their attackers but also to make them pay on the spot for their attempted crimes. Additionally, many schoolyard fistfights and barroom brawls probably are touched off by a victim's desire to settle a score with some bully or aggressor. Surely, some incidents of domestic violence are fueled by a yearning for personal vengeance. Some battered wives who fight back or even kill their tormentors go beyond the legal limits of self-defense by launching preemptive strikes to forestall another beating or unleashing retaliatory violence to get back for a previous one. A few cases even have come to light in which physically and sexually abused children grow up and slay their parents. Perhaps some incidents in which officers use excessive force to take resisting or unruly suspects into custody (which are commonly referred to as cases of "police brutality") might really be outbreaks of **police vigilantism** (Kotecha and Walker, 1976). Criminals can act as vigilantes too: They routinely resort to brute force to settle their disputes, precisely because they cannot bring their personal problems and business quarrels to the police, prosecutors, and courts without incriminating themselves. Vigilantism breaks out whenever street gangs engage in drive-by shootings to retaliate for an ambushing of one of their members, when mobsters hire hit men to "whack" some rival, or when drug dealers eliminate someone who cheated or stole from them.

Vigilantism also has its overtly political side. It has been part of the ideology of right-wing extremist groups—such as the Ku Klux Klan, neo-Nazis, racist skinheads, and certain militia groups—that openly proclaim their intention to revive the "night rider" tradition to "rid society of undesirable elements," "troublemakers," and "traitors" (see Madison, 1973; Burrows, 1976; Lasch, 1982; King, 1989; and Dees and Corcoran, 1997).

Episodes of old-fashioned vigilantism of the Western Frontier and Deep South varieties are unlikely to make a comeback unless large numbers of victims and their supporters conclude that only civilian violence can quell criminal violence. But opportunistic politicians seeking to ride the pro-victim and anticrime vote to higher office run the risk of rekindling the vigilante impulse with their inflammatory rhetoric. Their use of the metaphor of "waging war on crime" has become a household phrase. In this "war" victims are obviously the casualties, the "criminal element" is cast as the enemy, the streets are the battlefields, and criminal justice personnel serve as the troops. Alarmist pronouncements that the "war" is being "lost" because the criminal justice system has "broken down" can spread panic. Charges that the government is "paralyzed" and unwilling to act, that police are "handcuffed" by needless rules, that judges are "too soft," and that prisoners are "coddled" can prompt distraught victims and their allies to mobilize their own forces lest they be overrun. If the situation appears to grow desperate, violent actions may loom as reasonable solutions to stave off military defeat and rout the enemy.

The emotional attraction of the vigilante "solution" to the street crime problem rests on the notion that retaliation-in-kind is what "justice" is all about. Offender rehabilitation, restitution, and reconciliation are out of the question. Because the legal system cannot impose far-ranging punishments that directly match the suffering inflicted by offenders, it consistently fails to deliver payment-in-blood. As the gulf widens between the harsh punishments some people are calling for and the actual incarceration penalties that the system metes out, street justice gains appeal in some circles as being more appropriate than official justice.

The impulse toward vigilantism is held in check by two counterideologies. Law enforcement officials and responsible figures in government, embracing the tenets of professionalism, reject vigilantism out of a conviction that experts, not ordinary citizens, ought to control the criminal justice process. They urge citizens to allow the proper authorities and courts to handle cases and to reject any do-it-yourself impulses. Civil libertarians marshal even stronger arguments. They insist that due process safeguards and constitutional guarantees must be adhered to faithfully to make sure that innocent individuals are not falsely accused and then subjected to the passions of mob rule, as in the following cases:

A woman holding her hand over her bruised eye is accompanied by a crowd of men who are looking for the person who assaulted her. They come upon a fellow drinking a bottle of beer, begin to question him, and then rough him up. Although the woman screams to them "That's not the guy!" they continue to pummel him and then break the bottle over his head. As they drift away, realizing they attacked the wrong man, he dies from his wounds. Later, neighbors discover that the original fight stemmed from a drug deal that went sour. (Newman, 1992)

A furious father corners a 17-year-old boy whom his 14-year-old daughter claims raped her on the roof of their apartment building. The father shoots the teenager and then bashes his head with a hammer. But then the girl admits she lied about key parts of her unfounded rape charge. The father is convicted of first-degree manslaughter and is sentenced to 7 to 14 years in prison for his terrible mistake. (Barrett, 1998)

A crowd of 50 teenagers masses in response to a rumor (which later proves false) that a girl from their suburban high school has been raped. Intent on retaliating, they pile into cars and cruise around an adjoining neighborhood, spoiling for a fight. Several fistfights break out, and some youths are injured by rocks and bottles. Then the suburban teenagers break out baseball bats, corner about 15 parochial high school boys, and beat one 16-year-old to death. Six students from the mob who really don't know each other and have not been in serious trouble before are arrested, charged with murder, and tried as adults. All six are convicted of conspiracy to commit murder, and three are found guilty of third-degree murder. (Janofsky, 1994; "Mixed Verdict," 1996)

"Do-it-yourself justice" has been criticized as too swift, too sure, and too informal. Victims and their accomplices dispense with all the rules of the criminal justice "game" and assume the roles normally played by the police, prosecutor, judge, jury, and ultimately, executioner. The delicate balance between the rights of victims and of accused persons, hammered out through centuries of competition and compromise, is overturned, and suspects are presumed to be guilty no matter how much they assert their innocence. The history of vigilantism is filled with cases of mistaken identity, in which the wrong person was made to pay for someone else's misdeeds.

Street justice has also been denounced as too harsh. Physical punishments, including death, are imposed in the heat of the moment for offenses that merit lesser penalties under the law. Unlike restorative justice, which is also informal but arrived at through mediation and restitution at reconciliation programs, street justice is not directed toward a peaceful resolution of an antagonistic relationship through negotiation and compromise. On the contrary, the vigilante's intent is to forcefully settle matters in a manner that mirrors the original act but with the roles reversed.

The widely used phrase "taking the law into one's own hands" does not capture the essence of this reaction to crime. Vigilantes don't "take" the law; they break the law. They don't use force in self-defense, which is legal; they unleash retaliatory violence in order to inflict physical punishment, which is illegal. Their disdain for the "technicalities" of due process mocks the entire criminal justice system. Unleashed in the name of restoring law and order, vigilantism undermines the legal system and sends shock waves through the social order by trampling on the Bill of Rights. In trying to vindicate victims, vigilantes create new ones.

From an academic standpoint the study of revenge killings and other acts of vigilantism leads victimology full circle, back to its ancestral origins in criminology. Through vigilantism's role reversals, victims become lawbreakers, physically harming individuals whom they suspect previously made them suffer. Offenders, formerly enjoying the advantage within the oppressive relationship, are compelled to experience firsthand what it is like to be on the receiving end of criminal violence. But trading places—transforming victims into offenders and offenders into victims—is no solution to the crime problem. In an ironic twist, by retaliating against the wrong person or unleashing excessive force, vengeful victims open themselves up to the risk of being sued in civil court and prosecuted in criminal court. There are too many offenders already. Encouraging vigilantism and retaliatory violence would just add to their ranks.

CHAPTER SUMMARY

As the 21st century unfolds, victims will pursue three very different courses of action. Most will seek to exercise their recently granted rights within the formal criminal justice process. Some will explore the possibilities that are opening up in a new approach called restorative justice. A relative few will turn to retaliatory violence to try to get even with the offenders who harmed them.

The victims' movement has secured important new rights that pledge information, protection, and opportunities to participate in decision making. As the movement seeks to make further inroads at the expense of suspects, defendants, convicts, and prisoners, it will encounter resistance from civil libertarians who fear that the government will use victims to enhance its powers over individuals. As victims seek more rights from justice system agencies, officials will try to defend their privileges and fend off outside interference and imposed costs. Victim advocacy may become institutionalized as the options and obligations become more extensive, complicated, and contested.

Some victims will direct their attention towards developing more restorative justice programs, which at the end of the 20th century handled only a small (but growing) fraction of cases. Restorative justice rejects retributive justice's emphasis on conviction and punishment, and instead substitutes mediation, restitution, and reconciliation. Its goal is to enable the two parties to work out a lasting settlement that fosters harmony within the community.

The third course of action that some will continue to pursue can best be described as vigilantism. This do-it-yourself approach has a long and bloody history. It arises from a preoccupation with exacting revenge and a frustration with the cumbersome criminal justice process. As opposed to legitimate self-defense, retaliatory violence visited upon suspected predators causes a role reversal: victims become offenders, and offenders become victims.

DISCUSSION QUESTIONS

1. Which victims' rights might be considered to be gained at the expense of either "criminals" or of "criminal justice officials," depending upon the way victims exercise them?
2. Why hasn't a victims' rights amendment been added to the U.S. Constitution?
3. Compare and contrast retributive justice and restorative justice.
4. From a victim's point of view, what are the promises and drawbacks of participating in a victim-offender reconciliation program?
5. What is the difference between using deadly force in self-defense and vigilante violence by victims?
6. Should victims be encouraged to "seek retaliatory justice"?

References

Abel, C., and Marsh, F. (1984). *Punishment and restitution: A restitutionary approach to crime and the criminal.* Westport, CT: Greenwood Press.

Able, R. (1982). *The politics of informal justice: Vol. 1. The American experience.* New York: Academic Press.

Abramovsky, A. (1992). "Victim impact statements: Adversely impacting upon judicial fairness." *St. John's Journal of Legal Commentary* 8(1) (Fall): 21–35.

Abrams, A. (1987). "Sharing sorrow: Shelter helps turn victims into survivors." *New York Newsday,* December 21, pp. 2, 40.

Abramson, L. (1994). "Unequal justice." *Newsweek,* July 25, p. 25.

Acker, J. (1992). "Social sciences and the criminal law: Victims of crime—plight vs. rights." *Criminal Law Bulletin* 28: 64–77.

Adler, J. (1994). "Kids growing up scared." *Newsweek,* January 10, pp. 43–50.

Aguirre, A., Davin, R., Baker, D., and Konrad, L. (1999). "Sentencing outcomes, race, and victim impact evidence in California." *The Justice Professional* 11(3): 297–310.

Ahrens, J., Stein, J., and Young, M. (1980). *Law enforcement and victim services.* Washington, DC: Aurora Associates.

"AIDS tests for rapists." (1993). *Crime Victims Digest* 4 (April): 9.

Akiyama, Y. (1981). "Murder victimization: A statistical analysis." *FBI Law Enforcement Bulletin* (March) 8–11.

Alexander, R. (1992). "Victim's rights and the Son of Sam law: Implications for free speech and research on offenders." *Criminal Justice Policy Review* 6: 275–290.

Allbritten, R., and Allbritten, W. (1985). "The hidden victims: Courtship violence among college students." *Journal of College Student Personnel* 26: 201–204.

Allen, H., Friday, P., Roebuck, J., and Sagarin, E. (1981). *Crime and punishment: An introduction to criminology.* New York: Free Press.

Allen, N. (1980). *Homicide: Perspectives on prevention.* New York: Human Sciences Press.

Allison, J., and Wrightsman, L. (1993). *Rape: The misunderstood crime*. Newbury Park, CA: Sage.

Allredge, E. (1942). "Why the South leads the nation in murder and manslaughter." *Quarterly Review* 2: 123–134.

Alper, B., and Nichols, L. (1981). *Beyond the courtroom*. Lexington, MA: Lexington Books.

American Academy of Pediatrics (AAP). (1985). *Child sexual abuse*. Elk Grove Village, IL: Author.

American Bar Association (ABA). (1987). *Dispute resolution program directory*. Washington, DC: Author.

American Bar Association (ABA) Committee on Victims. (1979). *Reducing victim/witness intimidation: A package*. Washington, DC: ABA.

American Psychological Association (APA) Task Force on Victims of Crime and Violence. (1984). *Final report*. Hyattsville, MD: APA.

Amnesty International, USA (AIUSA). (1999). *United States of America: Race, rights, and police brutality*. New York: Amnesty International.

Amir, D., and Amir, M. (1979). "Rape crisis centers: An arena for ideological conflicts." *Victimology* 4(2): 247–257.

Amir, M. (1967). "Victim precipitated forcible rape." *Journal of Criminal Law, Criminology, and Police Science* 58: 493–502.

———. (1971). *Patterns in forcible rape*. Chicago: University of Chicago Press.

Anderson, M., and Renzetti, C. (1980). "Rape crisis counseling and the culture of individualism." *Contemporary Crises* 4(3) (July): 323–341.

Andrews, L. (1986). "Are we raising a terrified generation?" *Parents Magazine*, December, pp. 139–142, 228–230.

"The armed citizen." (1991). *American Rifleman* (September) 6.

Ash, M. (1972). "On witnesses: A radical critique of criminal court procedures." *Notre Dame Lawyer* 48 (December): 386–425.

Associated Press. (1984a). "Victims to get 'Son of Sam' cash." *New York Times,* September 20, p. B3.

———. (1984b). "Wounded ice cream vendor robbed by children." *New York Times,* July 15, p. A21.

———. (1993a). "Boy recants rape account, freeing suspect." *New York Times,* May 28, p. B6.

———. (1993b). "A disabled child is seen more likely to be abused." *New York Times,* October 7, p. A21.

———. (1993c). "High murder rate for women on job." *New York Times,* October 3, p. A29.

———. (1994a). "As cities reach record numbers of killings, youths play grim role." *New York Times,* January 1, p. A7.

———. (1994b). "Author's mugging one for the book." *Long Island Newsday,* June 12, p. A10.

———. (1994c). "Courts in New Jersey adopt 'truth in sentencing' rule." *New York Times,* April 26, p. B7.

———. (1994d). "Mother gets 10 years for slaying molester suspect." *New York Times,* January 8, p. A7.

———. (1994e). "Notifying the next of kin: The worst job is often poorly done." *New York Times,* June 12, p. A35.

———. (1994f). "A parent kills child mistaken for a burglar." *New York Times,* December 6, p. A18.

———. (1994i). "Witness intimidation is called a growing problem." *New York Times,* August 7, p. A30.

———. (1996a). "Menendez brothers sentenced to life in prison." *New York Times,* July 3, p. A15.

———. (1996b). "Repressed memory case won't be retried." *New York Times,* July 3, p. A15.

———. (1996c). "Found memory murder case won't be retried." *Long Island Newsday,* July 3, p. A44.

———. (1996d). "7-year-old Oregon girl escapes as sharpshooter kills kidnapper." *New York Times*, October 5, p. A8.

———. (1997). "Judge reduces term for man who killed bully." *New York Times,* April 18, p. 8.

———. (1999a). "Amy Fisher wins parole after 6 years in prison for shooting." *New York Times,* May 7, p. B12.

———. (1999b). "Some park visitors stroll safely, then claim robbery." *New York Times,* October 15, p. B4.

———. (2000). "Victims' rights issue shelved." *Long Island Newsday,* April 28, p. A24.

Aunapu, G., Epperson, S., Kramer, S., Lafferty, E., and Martin, K. (1993). "Robbing the innocents." *Time,* December 27, p. 31.

Austern, D. (1987). *The crime victim's handbook.* New York: Penguin.

"Auto theft alert." (1994). *CAR (Citizens for Auto-Theft Responsibility) Newsletter* (Fall): 7.

Ayres, B. (1994). "Big gains are seen in battle to stem drunk driving." *New York Times,* May 22, pp. A1, A24.

———. (1997). "Civil jury finds Simpson liable in pair of killings." *New York Times,* February 5, pp. A1, A16.

Bachman, R. (1992). *Crime victimization in city, suburban, and rural areas: A National Crime Victimization Survey report.* Washington, DC: U.S. Department of Justice.

———. (1994a). *Violence against women: A National Crime Victimization Survey Report.* Bureau of Justice Statistics. Washington, DC: U.S. Department of Justice.

———. (1994b). *Violence and theft in the workplace. BJS Crime Data Brief.* Washington, DC: U.S. Department of Justice.

———. (1998). "The factors related to rape reporting behavior and arrest: New evidence from the National Crime Victimization Survey." *Criminal Justice and Behavior* 25(1): 8–29.

Bachman, R., and Paternoster, R. (1993). "A contemporary look at the effects of rape law reform: how far have we really come?" *Journal of Criminal Law and Criminology* 84 (3): 554–574.

Bahr, R. (1985). "The threat of vigilantism." *Kiwanis* (May): 20–24.

Baldwin, J. (1988). "Car thefts (33 a day) becoming an ugly fact of life." *New York Times,* May 8, sec. 12, p. 2.

Balkan, S., Berger, R., and Schmidt, J. (1980). *Crime and deviance in America: A critical approach.* Belmont, CA: Wadsworth.

Bannister, S. (1992). "Battered women who kill their abusers: Their courtroom battles." In R. Muraskin and T. Alleman (Eds.), *It's a crime: Women and justice* (pp. 316–333). Englewood Cliffs, NJ: Regents/Prentice Hall.

Barbash, F. (1979). "Victim's rights: New legal weapon." *Washington Post,* December 17, p. 1.

Barden, J. (1987). "Marital rape: Drive for tougher laws is pressed." *New York Times,* May 13, p. A16.

Barnett, O., and LaViolette, A. (1993). *It could happen to anyone: Why battered women stay.* Newbury Park, CA: Sage.

Barnett, R. (1977). "Restitution: A new paradigm of criminal justice." In R. Barnett and J. Hagel (Eds.), *Assessing the criminal: Restitution, retribution, and the criminal process* (pp. 1–35). Cambridge, MA: Ballinger.

Barrett, D. (1998). "Vigilante dad sentenced in mistaken rapist slay." *New York Post,* July 28, p. 6.

Barringer, F. (1989). "Children as sexual prey, and predators." *New York Times,* May 30, pp. 1, A16.

Bass, E., and Davis, L. (1992). The courage to heal: A guide for women survivors of child sexual abuse (3rd ed.). New York: Harper Collins.

Bastian, L. (1993). *Criminal victimization 1992. Bureau of Justice Statistics Bulletin.* Washington, DC: U.S. Department of Justice.

Bastian, L., and Taylor, B. (1991). *School crime: A National Crime Victimization Survey Report.* Washington, DC: U.S. Department of Justice.

Beall, G. (1980). "Negotiating the disposition of criminal charges." *Trial* (October): 10–13.

Beck, A., and Mumola, C. (1999). *BJS Bulletin: Prisoners in 1998*. Washington, DC: U.S. Department of Justice.

Beck, M., Rosenberg, D., Chideya, F., Miller, S., Foote, D., Manly, H., and Katel, P. (1992). "Murderous obsession." *Newsweek,* July 13, pp. 60–62.

Beckett, K. (1996). "Culture and the politics of signification: The case of child sexual abuse." *Social Problems* 43 (1): 57–76.

Behar, R. (1993). "Car thief at large." *Time,* August 16, pp. 47–48.

Beirne, P., and Messerschmidt, J. (1991). *Criminology*. San Diego, CA: Harcourt Brace Jovanovich.

———. (2000). *Criminology,* 3rd edition. Boulder, CO: Westview.

Belluck, P. (1997). "Memory therapy leads to a lawsuit and big settlement." *New York Times,* November 6, p. A1, A14.

Beloof, D. (1999). *Victims in criminal procedure*. Raleigh, NC: Carolina Academic Press.

Benedict, H. (1992). *Virgin or vamp: How the press covers sex crimes*. New York: Oxford University Press.

Benedict, J. (1998). *Athletes and acquaintance rape*. Thousand Oaks, CA: Sage.

Benedict, J., and Klein, A. (1998). "Arrests and conviction rates for athletes accused of sexual assaults." In R. Bergen (Ed.), *Issues in intimate violence*. (pp. 169–179) Thousand Oaks, CA: Sage.

Bensing, R., and Schroeder, O. (1960). *Homicide in an urban community*. Springfield, IL: Charles C Thomas.

Bergen, R. (Ed.) (1998). *Issues in intimate violence*. Thousand Oaks, CA: Sage.

Berk, R., Campbell, A., Klap, R., and Western, B. (1992). "The deterrent effect of arrest in incidents of domestic violence: A Bayesian analysis of four field experiments." *American Sociological Review* 57 (October): 698–708.

Berke, R. (1989). "Capital offers unlimited turf to drug dealers." *New York Times,* March 28, pp. 1, A16.

Berliner, L. (1987). "Commentary: Editor's introduction." *Journal of Interpersonal Violence* (March): 107–108.

Bernat, F. (1992). "Book review: 'Representing . . . battered women who kill' by Johann and Osanka." *Justice Quarterly* 9(1) (March): 169–172.

Berns, W. (1994). "Getting away with murder." *Commentary* 97(4) (April): 25–29.

Bernstein, G. (1972). "Statement." In U.S. Senate, *Report on the federal crime insurance program*. Committee on the Judiciary, Subcommittee on Criminal Laws and Procedures, 1st sess. (pp. 521–529). Washington, DC: U.S. Government Printing Office.

Berreby, D. (1988). "The ordeal of the credit fraud victim." *New York Times,* September 4, Sec. 3, p. 4.

Berry, J. (1992). *Lead us not into temptation*. New York: Doubleday.

Besharov, D. (1987). "Federal action urged to protect rights of parents accused of child abuse." *Crime Victims Digest* (November): 5–6.

———. (1990). *Recognizing child abuse: A guide for the concerned*. New York: Free Press.

Best, J. (1988). "Missing children, misleading statistics." *Public Interest* (Summer): 84–92.

———. (1989a). "Dark figures and child victims: Statistical claims about missing children." In J. Best (Ed.), *Images of issues: Imagining contemporary social problems* (pp. 21–37). New York: Aldine de Gruyter.

———. (Ed.). (1989b). *Images of issues: Imagining contemporary social problems*. New York: Aldine de Gruyter.

———. (1997). "Victimization and the victim industry." *Society* (May–June): 8–10.

Best, J., and Luckenbill, D. (1982). *Organizing deviance*. Englewood Cliffs, NJ: Prentice-Hall.

Biblarz, A., Barnowe, J., and Biblarz, D. (1984). "To tell or not to tell: Differences between victims who report crimes and victims who do not." *Victimology* 9(1): 153–158.

Bienen, L. (1983). "Rape reform legislation in the United States: A look at some practical effects." *Victimology* 8(1): 139–151.

Birkbeck, C. (1983). " 'Victimology is what victimologists do.' But what should they do?" *Victimology* 8(3–4): 270–275.

Biskupic, J. (2000). "Justices reject lawsuits for rapes." *Washington Post*, May 16, p. A1.

Black, D. (1968). *Police encounters and social organization*. Unpublished doctoral dissertation, University of Michigan, Ann Arbor, MI.

Block, R. (1981). "Victim-offender dynamics in violent crime." *Journal of Criminal Law and Criminology* 72: 743–761.

Block, R., and Skogan, W. (1986). "Resistance and nonfatal outcomes in stranger-to-stranger predatory crime." *Violence and Victims* 1(4) (Winter): 241–254.

Block, R., Felson, M., and Block, C. (1985). "Crime victimization rates for incumbents of 246 occupations." *Sociology and Social Research* 69(3): 442–449.

Blumstein, A. (1995). "Violence by young people: Why the deadly nexus?" *National Institute of Justice Journal* 229 (August): 2–9.

Blumstein, A., and Rosenfeld, R. (1998). "Explaining recent trends in U.S. homicide rates." *Journal of Criminal Law and Criminology* 88(4) (Summer): 1175–1216.

Bochnak, E. (Ed.). (1981). *Women's self-defense cases: Theory and practice*. Charlottesville, VA: Michie Co. Law Publishers.

Bode, J. (1978). *Fighting back*. New York: MacMillan.

Bohmer, C., and Parrot, A. (1993). *Sexual assault on campus: The problem and the solution*. New York: Lexington Books.

Boland, B., Mahanna, P., and Sones, R. (1992). *The prosecution of felony arrests, 1988. BJS Report*. Washington, DC: U.S. Department of Justice.

Boland, B., and Sones, R. (1986). *BJS special report: Prosecution of felony arrests, 1981*. Washington, DC: U.S. Department of Justice.

Bonczar, T., and Glaze, L. (1999). *BJS Bulletin: Probation and parole in the United States, 1998*. Washington, DC: U.S. Department of Justice.

Boston, G. (1977). *Crimes against the elderly: A selected bibliography*. Washington, DC: National Criminal Justice Reference Service.

Bouza, A. (1991). "Responding to domestic violence." In M. Steinman (Ed.), *Woman battering: Policy responses* (pp. 191–203). Cincinnati, OH: Anderson.

Bowker, L. (1983). "Marital rape: A distinct syndrome?" *Social Casework* (June): 340–350.

Bowman, C. (1992). "The arrest experiments: A feminist critique." *The Journal of Criminal Law and Criminology* 83(1): 201–208.

Boyer, D., and James, J. (1983). "Prostitutes as victims." In D. MacNamara and A. Karmen (Eds.), *Deviants: Victims or victimizers?* (pp. 109–146). Newbury Park, CA: Sage.

Boyle, P. (1994). "Travel industry launches drive to protect tourists." *New York AAA Motorist* (April): 1, 18.

Bradshaw, W., and Umbreit, M. (1998). "Crime victims meet juvenile offenders: Contributing factors to victim satisfaction with mediated dialogue." *Juvenile and Family Court Journal* 49(3): 17–25.

Brandl, S., and Horvath, F. (1991). "Crime victim evaluation of police investigative performance." *Journal of Criminal Justice* 19: 109–121.

Breckman, R., and Adelman, R. (1988). *Strategies for helping victims of elder mistreatment*. Newbury Park, CA: Sage.

Brien, V. (1992). *Civil legal remedies for crime victims*. (Office for Victims of Crime bulletin). Washington, DC: U.S. Department of Justice.

Brienza, J. (1999). "Crime victims laws sometimes ignored." *Trial* 35(5) (May):103–105.

Briere, J. (1992). *Child abuse trauma: Theory and treatment of the lasting effects*. Newbury Park, CA: Sage.

Bromley, D. (1991). "The satanic cult scare." *Society* (May–June): 55–66.

Brooks, J. (1972). *Criminal injury compensation programs: An analysis of their development and administration*. Unpublished doctoral dissertation. Ann Arbor, MI: University Microfilms.

Brown, J., and Langan, P. (1998). *BJS Report: State court sentencing of convicted felons, 1994*. Washington, DC: U.S. Department of Justice.

Brown, J., Langan, P., and Levin, D. (1999). *BJS Bulletin: Felony sentences in state courts, 1996*. Washington, DC: U.S. Department of Justice.

Brown, R. (1975). *Strains of violence: Historical studies of American violence and vigilantism*. New York: Oxford University Press.

Browne, A. (1987). *When battered women kill*. New York: Free Press.

Brownmiller, S. (1975). *Against our will: Men, women, and rape*. New York: Simon & Schuster.

Brownstein, H. (1996). *The rise and fall of a violent crime wave*. Guilderland, NY: Harrow and Heston.

Bruni, F. (1989). "Maureen Reagan reveals husband beat her." *New York Post,* April 3, p. 9.

Buchwald, A. (1969). "Victim precipitation." *Washington Post,* February 4, p. 23.

Buchwald, E., Fletcher, P., and Roth, M. (1993). *Transforming a rape culture*. Minneapolis, MN: Milkwood Editions.

Buckley, W. (1994). "Excelsior the counterculture." *On the Right* (syndicated column). *Islamorada* (Florida) *Free Press,* December 21, p. 30A.

Bulger, J. (1933). "Automobile thefts." *Journal of Criminal Law, Criminology, and Police Science* 23: 806–810.

Bureau of Justice Statistics (BJS). (1974–1999). *Criminal victimization in the United States, 1973–1998.* (Annual Reports) Washington, DC: U.S. Department of Justice.

———. (1988). *Report to the nation on crime and justice* (2nd ed.). Washington, DC: U.S. Department of Justice.

———. (1994a). *Criminal victimization in the United States: 1973–1992 trends*. Washington, DC: U.S. Department of Justice.

———. (1994b). *Criminal victimization in the United States,1992*. Washington, DC: U.S. Department of Justice.

———. (1994c). *Elderly crime victims*. Washington, DC: U.S. Department of Justice.

———. (1994d). *Firearms and crimes of violence: Selected findings from a national statistical series*. Washington, DC: U.S. Department of Justice.

Burgess, A., and Holmstrom, L. (1974). "Rape trauma syndrome." *American Journal of Nursing* 131: 981–986.

Burke, T. (1998). "Male-to-male gay domestic violence: The dark closet." In N. Jackson and G. Oates (Eds.), *Violence in intimate relationships: Examining sociological and psychological issues* (pp. 161–180). Woburn, MA: Butterworth-Heinemann.

Burrows, W. (1976). *Vigilante!* New York: Harcourt Brace Jovanovich.

Burt, M. (1983). "A conceptual framework for victimological research." *Victimology* 8(3–4): 261–268.

Burt, M., and Katz, R. (1987). "Dimensions of recovery from rape." *Journal of Interpersonal Violence* 2(1) (March): 57–81.

"Burying crime in Chicago." (1983). *Newsweek,* May 16, p. 63.

Butterfield, F. (1999). "Guns used more for suicide than homicide." *New York Times,* October 17, p. A16.

Butts, J., and Snyder, H. (1992). *Restitution and juvenile recidivism: OJJDP Update on Research*. Washington, DC: U.S. Department of Justice.

Buzawa, E., and Buzawa, C. (1990). *Domestic violence: The criminal justice response*. Newbury Park, CA: Sage.

———. (1996). *Do arrests and restraining orders work?* Thousand Oaks, CA: Sage.

Cahn, N., and Lerman, L. (1991). "Prosecuting woman abuse." In M. Steinman (Ed.), *Woman battering: Policy responses* (pp. 95–113). Cincinnati, OH: Anderson.

"California study finds victims' rights bill has not put an end to all plea bargaining." (1985). *Crime Victims Digest* (November): 5.

Campbell, G. (1999). "N.Y. needs a stalking law." *New York Daily News,* May 27, p. 53.

Caplan, G. (1991). "Battered wives, battered justice." *National Review,* February 25, pp. 15–20.

Carrington, F. (1975). *The victims.* New Rochelle, NY: Arlington House.

———. (1977). "Victim's rights litigation: A wave of the future?" *University of Richmond Law Review* 11(3): 447–470.

———. (1978). "Victim's rights: A new tort." *Trial* (June): 39–41.

———. (1980). "Martinez ruling won't bar suits on negligent custodial releases." *National Law Journal,* February 11, p. 26.

———. (1986). "Preventing victimization through third-party victims' rights litigation." *Networks* (newsletter of the National Victims Center, Fort Worth, Texas) 1(1) (June): 7.

Carrow, D. (1980). *Crime victim compensation: Program model.* Washington, DC: U.S. Department of Justice.

Carson, E. (1986). "Crime victims strike back with civil lawsuits for compensation." *NOVA Newsletter* (September): 1–2, 4.

"Car thief slain—pair charged." (1988). *New York Post,* April 19, p. 10.

Ceci, S., and Bruck, M. (1993). "Suggestibility of the child witness: A historical review and synthesis." *Psychological Bulletin* 113(3): 403–439.

Center, L. (1980). "Victim assistance for the elderly." *Victimology* 5(2): 374–390.

Chapman, J., and Smith, B. (1987). *Child sexual abuse: An analysis of case processing.* Washington, DC: American Bar Association.

Chappell, D., Geis, R., and Geis, G. (1977). *Forcible rape: The crime, the victim, and the offender.* New York: Columbia University Press.

Chappell, D., and Sutton, P. (1974). "Evaluating the effectiveness of programs to compensate victims of crime." In I. Drapkin and E. Viano (Eds.), *Victimology: A new focus,* vol. 2 (pp. 207–220). Lexington, MA: D. C. Heath.

Chavez, J. (1992). "Battered men and the California law." *Southwestern University Law Review* 22: 239–256.

"Chicago police found to dismiss cases erroneously." (1983). *New York Times,* May 2, p. A20.

"Child abuse reports rise 2%." (1988). *Law Enforcement News,* May 15, pp. 1, 12.

"Child abuse victims get help through interior decor." (1989). *Law Enforcement News,* May 15, pp. 1, 12.

Childres, R. (1964). "Compensation for criminally inflicted personal injury." *New York University Law Review* 39: 455–471.

Chilton, R. (1987). "Twenty years of homicide and robbery in Chicago: The impact of the city's changing racial and age composition." *Journal of Quantitative Criminology* 3(3): 195–206.

Chilton, R., Major, V., and Propheter, S. (1998). "Victims and offenders: A New *UCR* Supplement." Paper presented at the 1998 annual meeting of the American Society of Criminology, Washington, DC.

Chira, S. (1993). "Sexual abuse: The coil of truth and memory." *New York Times,* December 5, p. E3.

Clark, C., and Block, T. (1992). "Victim's voices and constitutional quandries: Life after *Payne v. Tennessee.*" *St. John's Journal of Legal Commentary* 8(1) (Fall): 35–64.

Clark, L., and Lewis, D. (1978). *Rape: The price of coercive sexuality.* Toronto: Women's Press.

Clark, R., and Harris, P. (1992). "Auto theft and its prevention." In M. Tonry (Ed.), *Crime and justice: A review of research, vol. 16* (pp. 1–54). Chicago: University of Chicago Press.

Clement, H. (1946). "Stealing your own car." *FBI Law Enforcement Bulletin* (April): 21–34.

Clinton, W. (1996). "President Clinton's memorandum to attorney general Janet Reno." White House Press Release, June 27.

Coates, R. (1990). "Victim-offender reconciliation programs in North America: An assessment." In B. Galaway and J. Hudson, (Eds.), *Criminal justice, restitution and reconciliation* (pp. 125–134). Monsey, NY: Willow Tree Press.

Coates, R., and Gehm, J. (1989). "An empirical assessment." In M. Wright and B. Galaway (Eds.), *Mediation and criminal justice: Victims, offenders, and community* (pp. 251–263). Newbury Park, CA: Sage.

Cohen, L., and Felson, M. (1979). "Social change and crime rate trends: A routine activity approach." *American Sociological Review* 44: 588–607.

Cohen, L., Kluegal, J., and Land, K. (1981). "Social inequality and criminal victimization." *American Sociological Review* 46: 505–524.

Cohen, P. (1984). "Resistance during sexual assaults: Avoiding rape and injury." *Victimology* 9(1): 120–129.

Cohen, R. (1991). "Should the media name the accuser when the crime being charged is rape?" *New York Times,* April 21, p. E4.

Cohn, E., Kidder, L., and Harvey, J. (1978). "Crime prevention vs. victimization prevention: The psychology of two different reactions." *Victimology* 3(3): 285–296.

Collins, J., McCalla, M., Powers, L., and Stutts, E. (1988). *OJJDP update on research: The police and missing children—Findings from a national survey.* Washington, DC: U.S. Department of Justice.

Combined News Services. (1993). "NYC man slain on Florida highway." *New York Newsday,* September 27, p. 17.

Conklin, J. (1975). *The impact of crime.* New York: Macmillan.

Cook, P. (1985). "Is robbery becoming more violent? An analysis of robbery murder trends since 1968." *Journal of Criminal Law and Criminology* 76(2): 480–490.

———. (1987). "Robbery violence." *Journal of Criminal Law and Criminology* 78(2): 357–377.

Cook, P., and Ludwig, J. (1997). *NIJ Research in Brief: Guns in America—National survey on private ownership and use of firearms.* Washington, DC: U.S. Department of Justice.

Cook, R., Roehl, J., and Sheppard, D. (1980). *Neighborhood justice centers field test.* Washington, DC: U.S. Department of Justice.

Cose, E. (1994). "Truths about spouse abuse." *Newsweek,* August 8, p. 49.

Cox, M. (1998). "Kendra's law ready to pass." *Long Island Newsday,* August 4, p. A5.

Crichton, S. (1993). "Sexual correctness: Has it gone too far?" *Newsweek,* October 25, pp. 52–56.

"Crime control amendments." (1973). *Congressional Quarterly Almanac* 29: 370–372.

"Crime control needs citizens to do their part in helping." (1985). *Crime Victims Digest* (August): 1–2.

"Crime victims' aid." (1978). *Congressional Quarterly Almanac* 34: 196–198.

Crime Victims Research and Treatment Center. (1992). *The national women's study.* Charleston, SC: Medical University of South Carolina.

Crowe, A. (1998). "Restorative justice and offender rehabilitation: A meeting of the minds." *Perspectives: the Journal of the American Probation and Parole Association,* (Summer): 28–40.

Cruz, J., and Firestone, J. (1998). "Exploring violence and abuse in gay male relationships." *Violence and Victims* 13(2) (Summer): 159–174.

Crystal, S. (1988). "Elder abuse: the latest 'crisis.' " *Public Interest,* 88 (Summer): 56–65.

Cuomo, M. (1992). "The crime victim in a system of criminal justice." *St. John's Journal of Legal Commentary* 8(1) (Fall): 1–20.

Curran, J. (1999). "Crime victims' families can testify via videotape before parole board." *Associated Press,* December 29.

Curtis, L. (1974). "Victim precipitation and violent crime." *Social Problems* 21: 594–605.

Czajkoski, E., and Wollan, L. (1986). "Creative sentencing: A critical analysis." *Justice Quarterly* 3(2) (June): 215–229.

Darnton, N. (1991). "The pain of the last taboo." *Newsweek,* October 7, pp. 70–72.

Davidson, H. (1986). "Missing children: A close look at the issue." *Children Today* (July–August): 26–30.

Davies, J., Lyon, E., and Catania, D. (1998). *Safety planning with battered women: Complex lives/Difficult choices.* Thousand Oaks, CA: Sage.

Davis, R. (1983). "Victim/witness noncooperation: A second look at a persistent phenomenon." *Journal of Criminal Justice* 11: 287–299.

Davis, R., and Banniser, P. (1995). "Improving the collection of court ordered restitution." *Judicature* 79(1): 30–33.

Davis, R., Erez, E., and Avitabile, N. (1998). "Immigrants and the criminal justice system: An exploratory study." *Violence and Victims.*

Davis, R., Kunreuther, F., and Connick, E. (1984). "Expanding the victim's role in the criminal court dispositional process: The results of an experiment." *Journal of Criminal Law and Criminology* 75(2): 491–505.

Davis, R., and Murray, D. (1995). *Immigrant populations as victims: Towards a multicultural criminal justice system.* New York: Victim Services Agency.

Davis, R., and Smith, B. (1994). "Victim impact statements and victim satisfaction: An unfulfilled promise?" *Journal of Criminal Justice* 22: 1–12.

———. (1995). "Domestic violence reforms: Empty promises or unfulfilled expectations." *Crime and Delinquency* 41: 541–552.

Davis, R., Smith, B., and Hillenbrand, S. (1992). "Restitution: The victim's viewpoint." *The Justice System Journal* 15(3): 746–758.

Davis, R., Taylor, B., and Lurigio, A. (1996). "Adjusting to criminal victimization: The correlates of postcrime distress." *Violence and Victims* 11(1) (Spring): 21–38.

Davis, R., Tichane, M., and Grayson, D. (1980). *Mediation and arbitration as alternatives to criminal prosecution in felony arrest cases: An evaluation of the Brooklyn Dispute Resolution Center (first year).* New York: Vera Institute of Justice.

Dawson, J., and Langan, P. (1994). *Murder in families: BJS Special Report.* Washington, DC: U.S. Department of Justice.

Dawson, J., Smith, S., and DeFrances, C. (1993). *Prosecutors in state courts, 1992. Bureau of Justice Statistics Bulletin.* Washington, DC: U.S. Department of Justice.

Dawson, R. (1969). *Sentencing: The decision as to type, length, and conditions of sentence.* Boston: Little, Brown.

Dean, C., and de Bruyn-Kops, M. (1982). *The crime and the consequences of rape.* Springfield, IL: Charles C Thomas.

Deane, G. (1987). "Cross-national comparison of homicide: Age/sex-adjusted rates using the 1980 U.S. homicide experience as a standard." *Journal of Quantitative Criminology* 3(3): 215–227.

DeConcini, D. (1989). "National child abuse prevention month." *Crime Victims Digest* 6(2): 4–5.

Dees, M., and Corcoran, J. (1997). *America's militia threat.* New York: Harper Collins.

Del Castillo, V., and Lindner, C. (1994). "Staff safety issues in probation." *The Justice Professional* 8(2): 37–54.

De Koster, K., and Swisher, K. (Eds.). (1994). *Child abuse: Opposing viewpoints.* San Diego: Greenhaven Press.

Demaris, A. (1992). "Male versus female initiation of aggression: The case of courtship violence." In E. Viano (Ed.), *Intimate violence: Interdisciplinary perspectives* (pp. 111–120). Washington, DC: Hemisphere Publishing.

De Parle, J. (1999). "Early sex abuse hinders many women on welfare." *New York Times,* November 28, p. A1, A28.

Dershowitz, A. (1988). *Taking liberties: A decade of hard cases, bad laws, and bum raps.* Chicago: Contemporary Books.

———. (1994). *The abuse excuse and other cop-outs, sob stories, and evasions of responsibility.* Boston: Little, Brown.

Deutsch, C. (1994). "Victims of violence increasingly hold landlords liable for crimes." *New York Times,* June 3, p. B8.

Dillon, S. (1994). "Report finds more violence in the schools." *New York Times,* July 7, pp. B1, B7.

Dobash, R. P., and Dobash, R. E. (1979). *Violence against wives: The case against patriarchy.* New York: Free Press.

———. (1992). *Women, violence, and social change.* New York: Routledge.

Docksai, M. (1979). "Victim/witness intimidation: What it means." *Trial* (August): 51–54.

Dodge, R. (1988). *BJS bulletin: The seasonality of crime.* Washington, DC: U.S. Department of Justice.

Doerner, W. (1978). "An examination of the alleged latent effects of victim compensation programs upon crime reporting." *LAE Journal* 41: 71–80.

Doerner, W., and Lab, S. (1980). "Impact of crime compensation on victim attitudes toward the criminal justice system." *Victimology* 5(2): 61–77.

"Does your agency measure up?" (1999) *Rap Sheet, newsletter of Concerns of Police Survivors* 6 (November): 4.

"Domestic abusers take it out on pets, too." (1999). *Law Enforcement News,* February 28, p. 6.

Dutton-Douglas, M., and Dionne, D. (1991). "Counseling and shelter services for battered women." In M. Steinman (Ed.), *Woman battering: Policy responses* (pp. 113–130). Cincinnati, OH: Anderson.

Ebony Magazine. (1979). *Black on black crime* (Special issue) (August).

Eddy, D. (1990). "Supreme Court decides cases involving VOCA, restitution, child witnesses, sobriety checkpoints." *NOVA Newsletter* 14(3): 6.

Edelhertz, H. (1977). "Legal and operational issues in the implementation of restitution in the criminal justice system." In J. Hudson and B. Galaway (Eds.), *Restitution in criminal justice* (pp. 63–76). Lexington, MA: Lexington Books.

Edelhertz, H., and Geis, G. (1974). *Public compensation to victims of crime.* New York: Praeger.

Editors, *New York Times.* (1987). "Paying victims, freeing prisoners." *New York Times,* July 7, p. A26.

Eglash, A. (1977). "Beyond restitution: Creative restitution." In J. Hudson and B. Galaway (Eds.), *Restitution in criminal justice* (pp. 91–100). Lexington, MA: Lexington Books.

Ehrenreich, B. (1997). "Silence of the beltway feminists." *New York Times,* January 17, p. A31.

Eigenberg, H. (1990). "The *National Crime Survey* and rape: The case of the missing question." *Justice Quarterly* 7: 655–671.

Elias, R. (1983a). *Victims of the system: Crime victims and compensation in American politics and criminal justice.* New Brunswick, NJ: Transaction Books.

———. (1983b). "The symbolic politics of victim compensation." *Victimology* 8(1): 210–219.

———. (1986). *The politics of victimization: Victims, victimology and human rights.* New York: Oxford University Press.

———. (1993). *Victims still: The political manipulation of crime victims.* Newbury Park, CA: Sage.

Ellenberger, H. (1955). "Psychological relationships between the criminal and his victim." *Archives of Criminal Psychodynamics* 2: 257–290.

Endo, E. (1999). "Anti-stalking bill stalled by budget." *Long Island Newsday,* July 21, p. A45.

Estrich, S. (1986). *Real rape.* Cambridge, MA: Harvard University Press.

———. (1993a). "Balancing act." *Newsweek,* October 25, p. 64.

———. (1993b). "The sympathy defense." *New York Times,* October 24, p. E15.

European Committee on Crime Problems. (1978). *Compensation of victims of crime.* Strasbourg, Austria: Author.

Ewing, C. (1997). *Fatal families: The dynamics of intrafamilial homicide.* Thousand Oaks, CA: Sage.

Ewing, P. (1987). *Battered women who kill: Psychological self-defense as legal justification.* Lexington, MA: D.C. Heath.

Fagan, J. (1988). "Contributions of family violence research to criminal justice policy on wife assault: Paradigms of science and social control." *Violence and Victims* 3(3): 159–186.

Fagan, J., Piper, E., and Cheng, Y. (1987). "Contributions of victimization to delinquency in inner cities." *Journal of Criminal Law and Criminology* 78(3): 586–611.

Fahn, M. (1991). "Allegations of child sexual abuse in custody disputes: Getting to the truth of the matter." *Family Law Quarterly* (Summer): 16–21.

Fairstein, L. (1993). *Sexual violence: Our war against rape.* New York: William Morrow.

"False accusations of abuse devastating to families." (1989). *Crime Victims Digest* 6(2): 4–5.

Faludi, S. (1993). "Whose hype?" *Newsweek,* October 25, p. 61.

Farrell, R., and Swigert, V. (1986). "Adjudication in homicide: An interpretive analysis of the effects of defendant and victim social characteristics." *Journal of Research in Crime and Delinquency* 23(4) (November): 349–369.

Fattah, E. (1967). "Towards a criminological classification of victims." *International Criminal Police Review* 209: 162–169.

———. (1976). "The use of the victim as an agent of self-legitimation: Toward a dynamic explanation of criminal behavior." In Emilio Viano (Ed.), *Victims and society* (pp. 105–129). Washington, DC: Visage.

———. (1979). "Some recent theoretical developments in victimology." *Victimology* 4(2): 198–213.

———. (1986). *From crime policy to victim policy.* New York: St. Martin's Press.

———. (1990). "Victims and victimology: The facts and the rhetoric." *International Review of Victimology* 1(1): 43–66.

———. (1991). *Understanding criminal victimization: An introduction to theoretical victimology.* Scarborough, Ontario: Prentice-Hall Canada.

———. (1992a). *Towards a critical victimology.* New York: St. Martin's Press.

———. (1992b). "The need for a critical victimology." In E. Fattah (Ed.), *Towards a critical victimology* (pp. 3–28). New York: St. Martin's Press.

Faulk, M. (1977). "Men who assault their wives." In M. Roy (Ed.), *Battered women: A psycho-sociological study of domestic violence* (pp. 119–126). New York: Van Nostrand.

Federal Bureau of Investigation (FBI). (1954–1999). *Uniform crime report: Crime in the United States* (selected years, 1953–1998). Washington, DC: U.S. Government Printing Office.

———. (1993). *Law enforcement officers killed and assaulted, 1992.* Washington, DC: U.S. Department of Justice.

———. (1999). *National incident-based reporting system.* Washington, DC: U.S. Department of Justice.

Federal File. (1994). "Bureau of Justice Statistics report." *Law Enforcement News,* April 30, p. 7.

"Federal rape laws revised: Now apply to male victims." (1986). *Crime Victims Digest* (November): 10.

"The Feds make it official: For many, the workplace is a dangerous place to be." (1993). *Law Enforcement News,* December 15, p. 5.

Feher, T. (1992). "The alleged molestation victim, the rules of evidence and the Constitution: Should children really be seen and not heard?" In E. Fattah (Ed.), *Toward a critical victimology* (pp. 260–282). Englewood Cliffs, NJ: Prentice-Hall.

Fein, E. (1991). "Decision praised as a victory for free speech rights." *New York Times,* December 11, p. B8.

Felson, M. (1994). *Crime and everyday life.* Thousand Oaks, CA: Pine Forge Press.

———. (1997). "Routine activities and involvement in violence as actor, witness, or target." *Violence and Victims* 12(5): 209–220.

Ferraro, K. (1992). "Cops, courts, and woman battering." In P. Bart and E. Moran (Eds.), *Violence against women: The bloody footprints* (pp. 165–176). Newbury Park, CA: Sage.

Ferrigno, R. (1987). "How foreign diplomats get away with crime." *New York Newsday,* October 2, p. 81.

Fingerhut, L., Ingram, D., and Feldman, J. (1992a). "Firearm and non-firearm homicide among persons 15 through 19 years of age." *Journal of the American Medical Association* 267(22) (June 10): 3048–3053.

———. (1992b). "Firearm homicide among black teenage males in metropolitan counties: Comparison of death rates in two periods, 1983 through 1985 and 1987 through 1989." *Journal of the American Medical Association* 267: 3054–3058.

Finkelhor, D. (1990). "Is child abuse overreported?" *Public Welfare* 48(1) (Winter): 20–30.

———. (1994). "Current information on the scope and nature of child sexual abuse." *The Future of Children* 4(2): 31, 46, 48.

Finkelhor, D., and Asdigian, N. (1996). "Risk factors for youth victimization: Beyond a lifestyle/routine activities theory approach." *Violence and Victims* 11(1) (Spring): 3–20.

Finkelhor, D., Hotaling, G., and Sedlak, A. (1990). *Missing, abducted, runaway, and thrownaway children in America: First report.* Washington, DC: U.S. Department of Justice, Office of Juvenile Justice and Delinquency Prevention.

Finkelhor, D., and Leatherman, J. (1994). "Victimization of children." *American Psychologist* 49(3) (March): 173–183.

Finkelhor, D., and Yllo, K. (1985). *License to rape: Sexual abuse of wives.* New York: Holt, Rinehart & Winston.

Finn, P. (1991). "Civil protection orders: A flawed opportunity for intervention." In M. Steinman (Ed.), *Woman battering: Policy responses* (pp. 155–190). Cincinnati, OH: Anderson.

Fiora-Gormally, N. (1978). "Battered wives who kill: Double standard out of court, single standard in?" *Law and Human Behavior* 2(2): 133–136.

"Fitting justice? Judges try 'creative' sentences." (1978). *Time,* April 24, p. 56.

Fletcher, G. (1988a). *Bernhard Goetz and the law on trial.* New York: Free Press.

———. (1988b). *A crime of self-defense: Bernhard Goetz and the law on trial.* Chicago: University of Chicago Press.

Fleury, R., Sullivan, C., Bybee, D., and Davidson, W. (1998). "Why don't they just call the cops?" *Violence and Victims,* 13(4): 333–340.

Flynn, E. (1982). "Theory development in victimology: An assessment of recent progress and of continuing challenges." In H. Schneider (Ed.), *The victim in international perspective* (pp. 96–104). Berlin: de Gruyter.

Follingstad, D., Rutledge, L., McNeill-Harkins, K., and Polek, D. (1992). "Factors related to physical violence in dating relationships." In E. Viano (Ed.), *Intimate violence: Interdisciplinary perspectives* (pp. 121–135). Washington, DC: Hemisphere Publishing.

Fooner, M. (1971). "Money and economic factors in crime and delinquency." *Criminology* 8(4) (February): 311–320.

Forer, L. (1980). *Criminals and victims: A trial judge reflects on crime and punishment.* New York: Norton.

Forst, G., and Hernon, J. (1984). *NIJ research in brief—The criminal justice response to victim harm.* Washington, DC: U.S. Department of Justice.

Forst, M., and Blomquist, M. (1991). *Missing children: Rhetoric and reality.* New York: Lexington Books.

Franklin, B. (1978). *The victim as criminal and artist: Literature from the American prison.* New York: Oxford University Press.

Franklin, C., and Franklin, A. (1976). "Victimology revisited." *Criminology* 14(1): 125–136.

Fraser, C. (1991). "18-shot killing is ruled by jury as self-defense." *New York Times,* July 5, p. B3.

Freedman, L., and Ray, L. (1982). *State legislation on dispute resolution.* Washington, DC: American Bar Association.

Fried, J. (1982). "Intimidation of witnesses called widespread." *New York Times,* May 2, p. S1.

Friedman, L. (1985). "The crime victim movement at its first decade." *Public Administration Review* 45 (November): 790–794.

Friedrichs, D. (1983). "Victimology: A consideration of the radical critique." *Crime and Delinquency* 29(2) (April): 280–290.

Friefeld, K. (2000). "Man charged in shooting of son's hooky partner." *Long Island Newsday,* February 11, p. A35.

Frieze, I., and Browne, A. (1991). "Violence in marriage." In L. Ohlin and M. Tonry (Eds.), *Crime and justice: A review of research, Volume 11: Family violence* (pp. 163–218). Chicago: University of Chicago Press.

Frum, D. (1993). "Women who kill." *Forbes Magazine,* January 18, pp. 20–24.

Fry, M. (1957). "Justice for victims." *London Observer,* November 10, p. 8. Reprinted in *Journal of Public Law* 8 (1959): 191–194.

Fuller, R., and Myers, R. (1941). "The natural history of a social problem." *American Sociological Review* 6 (June): 320–328.

Furstenberg, F. (1972). "Fear of crime and its effect on citizen behavior." In A. Biderman (Ed.), *Crime and justice* (pp. 52–65). New York: Justice Institute.

Gahr, E. (1997). "Advocates raise wide support for victims rights amendment." *Insight on the News,* March 10, p. 42.

Galaway, B. (1977). "The uses of restitution." *Crime and Delinquency* 23(1): 57–67.

———. (1987). "Victim-offender mediation as the preferred response to property offenses." In E. Viano (Ed.), *Crime and its victims: International research and public policy issues* (pp. 101–111). New York: Hemisphere.

———. (1989). "Prospects." In M. Wright and B. Galaway (Eds.), *Mediation and criminal justice: Victims, offenders and community* (pp. 270–275). Newbury Park, CA: Sage.

———. (1992). "Restitution as innovation or unfilled promise?" In E. Fattah (Ed.), *Toward a critical victimology* (pp. 347–371). New York: St. Martin's Press.

Galaway, B., and Hudson, J. (1975). "Issues in the correctional implementation of restitution to victims of crime." In J. Hudson and B. Galaway (Eds.), *Considering the victim: Readings in restitution and victim compensation* (pp. 351–360). Springfield, IL: Charles C Thomas.

———. (Eds.) (1981). *Perspectives on crime victims.* St. Louis, MO: C.V. Mosby.

Galliher, J., Kunkel, K., and Hobbs, D. (1986). "Media explanations of small-town vigilante murder." *Contemporary Crises* 10: 125–136.

Garbarino, J. (1989). "The incidence and prevalence of child maltreatment." In L. Ohlin and M. Tonry (Eds.), *Crime and justice: A review of research, Volume 11: Family violence* (pp. 219–262). Chicago: University of Chicago Press.

Gardner, R. (1990). *Sex abuse hysteria: Salem witch trials revisited.* Cresskill, NJ: Creative Therapeutics.

———. (1994). "Belated realization of child sex abuse by an adult." In K. de Koster and K. Swisher (Eds.), *Child abuse: Opposing viewpoints* (pp. 217–223). San Diego, CA: Greenhaven Press.

Garfinkle, H. (1949). "Research note on inter- and intra-racial homicides." *Social Forces* 27 (May): 370–381.

Garofalo, J. (1981). "Victimization surveys: An overview." In B. Galaway and J. Hudson (Eds.), *Perspectives on crime victims* (pp. 98–103). St. Louis, MO: C. V. Mosby.

———. (1986). "Lifestyles and victimization: An update." In E. Fattah (Ed.), *From crime policy to victim policy* (pp. 135–155). New York: St. Martin's Press.

Garofalo, J., and Connelly, K. (1980). "Dispute resolution centers: Part 1—Major features and processes; Part 2—Outcomes, issues, and future directions." *Criminal Justice Abstracts* (September): 416–610.

Gartner, A., and Riessman, F. (1980). "Lots of helping hands." *New York Times,* February 19, p. A22.

Gartner, R. (1990). "The victims of homicide: A temporal and cross-national comparison." *American Sociological Review* 55(1) (February): 92–106.

Gaynes, M. (1981). "New roads to justice: Compensating the victim." *State Legislatures* (November–December): 11–17.

Gegan, S., and Rodriguez, N. (1992). "Victims' roles in the criminal justice system: A fallacy of empowerment." *St. John's Journal of Legal Commentary* 8(1) (Fall): 225–250.

Geis, G. (1976). "Compensation to victims of violent crime." In R. Gerber (Ed.), *Contemporary issues in criminal justice* (pp. 90–115). Port Washington, NY: Kennikat.

———. (1977). "Restitution by criminal offenders: A summary and overview." In J. Hudson and B. Galaway (Eds.), *Restitution in criminal justice* (pp. 147–164). Lexington, MA: Lexington Books.

———. (1983). "Victim and witness assistance programs." In *Encyclopedia of Crime and Justice* (pp. 1600–1604). New York: Free Press.

Geller, W. (1992). "Put friendly-fire shooting in perspective." *Law Enforcement News,* December 31, p. 9.

Gelles, R. (1987). *The violent home.* Newbury Park, CA: Sage.

Gelles, R., and Cornell, C. (1990). *Intimate violence in families* (2nd ed.). Newbury Park, CA: Sage.

Gelles, R., and Straus, M. (1988). *Intimate violence.* New York: Touchstone Books.

Gewurz, D., and Mercurio, M. (1992). "The victims' bill of rights: Are victims all dressed up with no place to go?" *St. John's Journal of Legal Commentary* 8(1) (Fall): 251–278.

Giacinti, T. (1973). *Forcible rape: The offender and his victim.* Unpublished master's thesis. Ann Arbor, MI: University Microfilms.

Giannelli, P. (1997). "Rape trauma syndrome." *Criminal Law Bulletin* 33: 270–279.

Gibbs, N. (1991). "When is it rape?" *Time,* June 3, pp. 38–40.

———. (1993a). "Hell on wheels." *Time,* August 16, pp. 44–46.

———. (1993b). "Til death do us part." *Time,* January 18, pp. 38–45.

———. (1994). "Death and deceit." *Time,* November 14, pp. 43–48.

Gilbert, N. (1991). "The phantom epidemic of sexual assault." *The Public Interest* 103 (Spring): 54–65.

Gill, J. (1987). "Let's stop fingerprinting kids." *New York Newsday,* August 14, p. 94.

———. (1989). "Missing-kids' groups foster fear rather than facts." *New York Newsday,* April 11, p. 65.

Gillespie, C. (1989). *Battered women, self-defense, and the law.* Columbus, OH: Ohio State University Press.

Girdner, L., and Hoff, P. (1994). *Obstacles to the recovery and return of parentally abducted children: Research summary.* Washington, DC: U.S. Department of Justice.

Girelli, S., Resick, P., Dvorak, S., and Hutter, C. (1986). "Subjective distress and violence during rape: Their effects on long term fear." *Victims and Violence* 1(1): 35–46.

Goldberg, C. (1996). "Support builds for killer who broke cycle of fear." *New York Times,* June 18, p. A14.

———. (1998). "Getting to the truth in child abuse cases: New methods." *New York Times,* September 8, pp. C1, C5.

———. (1999). "Spouse abuse crackdown, surprisingly, nets many women." *New York Times,* November 23, p. A16.

Goldberg, S., Green, E., and Sander, F. (1985). *Dispute resolution.* Boston: Little, Brown.

Goldberg-Ambrose, C. (1992). "Unfinished business in rape law reform." *Journal of Social Issues* 48(1): 173–185.

Goldsmith, J., and Goldsmith, S. (1976). *Crime and the elderly: Challenge and response.* Lexington, MA: D. C. Heath.

Goldstein, E. (1993). *Confabulations: Creating false memories, destroying families.* Boca Raton, FL: SIRS Books.

Goldstein, J. (1960). "Police discretion not to invoke the criminal process." *Yale Law Journal* 69 (March): 543–594.

Goleman, D. (1993). "Studies reveal suggestibility of very young as witnesses." *New York Times,* June 11, pp. A1, A23.

———. (1994). "Proof lacking for ritual abuse by satanists." *New York Times,* October 31, p. A13.

———. (1995a). "An elusive picture of violent men who kill their mates." *New York Times,* January 15, p. A22.

———. (1995b). "Studies point to flaws in lineups of suspects." *New York Times,* January 17, pp. C1, C7.

Gondolf, E. (1988). "The state of the debate: A review essay on woman battering." *Response* 11(3): 3–8.

Gonzalez, D. (1992). "Sliwa admits faking crimes for publicity." *New York Times,* November 25, pp. B1, B2.

Goodman, R., Mercy, J., Loya, F., Rosenberg, M., Smith, J., Allen, N., Vargas, L., and Kolts, B. (1986). "Alcohol use and interpersonal violence: Alcohol detected in homicide victims." *American Journal of Public Health* 76(2): 144–148.

"The Good Samaritans." (1965). *New York Times,* November 20, p. 34.

Goode, E. (1999). "Study of child sex abuse provokes a political furor." *New York Times,* June 13, p. A33.

Gordon, L. (1988). *Heroes of their own lives: The politics and history of family violence, Boston, 1880–1960.* New York: Viking.

Gottesman, R., and Mountz, L. (1979). *Restitution: Legal analysis.* Reno, NV: National Council of Juvenile and Family Court Judges.

Gottfredson, M., and Gottfredson, D. (1988). *Decision making in criminal justice: Toward the rational exercise of discretion* (2nd ed.). New York: Plenum.

Governor's Task Force on Bias-Related Violence. (1988). *Final Report.* Albany, NY: Author.

Graham, E. (1993). "Education: Fortress academia sells security." *Wall Street Journal,* October 25, p. B1.

Gray, E. (1986). *Child abuse: Prelude to delinquency?* Washington, DC: U.S. Department of Justice.

Gray, J. (1993). "New Jersey court says victims of car chases cannot sue police." *New York Times,* July 29, pp. B1, B6.

Grayson, B., and Stein, M. (1981). "Attracting assault: Victims' nonverbal clues." *Journal of Communications* 31: 65–70.

Green, E. (1964). "Inter- and intra-racial crime relative to sentencing." *Journal of Criminal Law, Criminology, and Police Science* 55 (September): 348–358.

Green, G. (1987). "Citizen gun ownership and crime deterrence: Theory, research, and policy." *Criminology* 25(1) (February): 63–82.

Greenberg, M., and Ruback, R. (1984). "Elements of crime victim decision making." *Victimology* 10(1): pp. 600–616.

Greenfeld, L. (1997). *BJS Report: Sex offenses and offenders.* Washington, DC: U.S. Department of Justice.

Greenfeld, L., Rand, M., and Craven, D. (1998). *BJS Report: Violence by intimates: Analysis of data on crimes by current or former spouses, boyfriends, and girlfriends.* Washington, DC: U.S. Department of Justice.

Greenhouse, L. (1989). "Supreme court roundup: First Amendment protects paper that named rape victim, justices rule." *New York Times,* June 22, p. B9.

———. (1990). "Child abuse trials can shield witness." *New York Times,* June 28, pp. A1, B8.

———. (1991). "High court upsets seizing of profits of convict's books." *New York Times,* December 11, pp. A1, B8.

———. (1993). "Justices uphold stiffer sentences for hate crimes." *New York Times,* June 12, pp. A1, A8.

Griffin, S. (1979). *Rape: The power of consciousness.* New York: Harper & Row.

Gross, J. (1990). "203 rape cases reopened in Oakland as the police chief admits mistakes." *New York Times,* September 20, p. A13.

———. (1992). "Abused women who kill now seek way out of cells." *New York Times,* September 15, p. A16.

———. (1993). "California town mourns abducted girl." *New York Times,* December 6, p. A12.

Gutis, P. (1988). "New head of police speaks out." *New York Times,* April 10, sec. 12, p. 2.

Hackett, G., and Cerio, G. (1988). "When the victim goes on trial." *Newsweek,* January 18, p. 31.

Hafemeister, T. (1996). "Protecting child witnesses: Judicial efforts to minimize trauma and reduce evidentiary barriers." *Violence and Victims* 11(1) (Spring): 71–92.

Hall, D. (1975). "The role of the victim in the prosecution and conviction of a criminal case." *Vanderbilt Law Review* 28(5): 932–985.

———. (1991). "Victims' voices in criminal court: The need for restraint." *American Criminal Law Review* 28: 233–243.

Hall, J. (1935). *Theft, law, and society.* Boston: Little, Brown.

Hall, T. (1990). "Fatal accidents are down as U.S. becomes vigilant." *New York Times,* October 7, pp. A1, A32.

Halleck, S. (1980). "Vengeance and victimization." *Victimology* 5(2): 99–109.

Hanley, R. (1994a). "Crime victims call for hard labor." September 28, p. B6.

———. (1994b). "Three lives converge in a killing." *New York Times,* January 5, p. B6.

———. (1999). "Killer of New Jersey officer faces at least 4 more years." *New York Times,* November 11, p. B3.

Hansell, S. (1996). "Identity crisis: When a criminal's got your number." *New York Times,* June 15, p. E1.

Hansen, M. (1997). "Repairing the damage: citizen boards tailor sentences to fit the crimes in Vermont." *ABA Journal* 83 (September): 20.

Harland, A. (1979). "Restitution statutes and cases: Some substantive and procedural restraints." In B. Galaway and J. Hudson (Eds.), *Victims, offenders, and restitutive sanctions* (pp. 151–171). Lexington, MA: Lexington Books.

———. (1981a). *Restitution to victims of personal and household crimes.* Washington, DC: U.S. Department of Justice.

———. (1981b). "Victim compensation: Programs and issues." In B. Galaway and J. Hudson (Eds.), *Perspectives on crime victims* (pp. 412–417). St. Louis, MO: C. V. Mosby.

———. (1983). "One hundred years of restitution: An international review and prospectus for research." *Victimology* 8(1): 190–202.

Harlow, C. (1985). *Reporting crimes to the police. BJS special report.* Washington, DC: U.S. Department of Justice.

———. (1987). *Robbery victims. BJS special report.* Washington, DC: U.S. Department of Justice.

———. (1988). *Motor vehicle theft. BJS special report.* Washington, DC: U.S. Department of Justice.

———. (1991). *Female victims of violent crime. BJS special report.* Washington, DC: U.S. Department of Justice.

———. (1999). *Prior abuse reported by inmates and probationers. BJS selected findings.* Washington, DC: U.S. Department of Justice.

Harrington, C. (1985). *Shadow justice: The ideology and institutionalization of alternatives to court.* Westport, CT: Greenwood Press.

Harris, M. (1979). *Sentencing to community service.* Washington, DC: American Bar Association.

Harshbarger, S. (1987). "Prosecution is an appropriate response in child sexual abuse cases." *Journal of Interpersonal Violence* (March): 108–112.

Hart, T., and Reaves, B. (1999). *BJS Bulletin: Felony defendants in large urban counties, 1996.* Washington, DC: U.S. Department of Justice.

Haugrud, L., Gratch, L., and Magruder, B. (1997). "Victimization and perpetration rates of violence in gay and lesbian relationships: Gender issues explored." *Violence and Victims* 12(2) (Summer): 173–185.

"Hawaii return-witness program turns tide against crime." (1982). *Criminal Justice Newsletter,* June 7, p. 1.

Hays, C. (1992). "Family to get $1.5 million in slaying by mental patient." *New York Times,* July 29, p. B6.

Healy, K. (1995). *NIJ Research in Action. Victim and witness intimidation: New developments and emerging responses.* Washington, DC: U.S. Department of Justice.

Healy, K., and Smith, C. (1998). *NIJ Research in Action. Batterer programs: What criminal justice agencies need to know.* Washington, DC: U.S. Department of Justice.

Heinz, A., and Kerstetter, W. (1979). "Pretrial settlement conference: Evaluation of a reform in plea bargaining." *Law and Society Review* 13(2): 349–366.

Heinz, J. (1982). "On justice to victims." *New York Times,* July 7, p. A19.

Hellerstein, D. (1989). "The victim impact statement: Reform or reprisal?" *American Criminal Law Review* 27: 390–434.

Hellman, P. (1993). "Crying rape: The politics of date rape on campus." *New York Magazine,* March 8, pp. 32–37.

"Help for the terrified elderly." *New York Times,* April 2, p. A18.

Henderson, G. (1924). *Keys to crookdom.* New York: Appleton.

Henderson, L. (1985). "Victim's rights and wrongs." *Stanford Law Review* 37: 937–1021.

Hendricks, J. (1992). "Domestic violence legislation in the United States: A survey of the states." In E. Viano (Ed.), *Intimate violence: Interdisciplinary perspectives* (pp. 213–228). New York: Hemisphere.

Henican, E. (1998). "Pretty names don't make these laws effective." *Long Island Newsday,* July 29, p. A40.

Herman, J. (1981). *Father-daughter incest.* Cambridge, MA: Harvard University Press.

———. (1992). *Trauma and recovery.* New York: Basic Books.

Herman, S. (1998). *Viewing restorative justice through victims' eyes.* Arlington, VA: National Center for Victims of Crime.

———. (1999). "Interview: the director of the National Center for Victims of Crime." *Law Enforcement News,* November 30, pp. 8–11.

Herrington, L. (1982). "Statement of the chairman." In the *President's Task Force on Victims of Crime, Final report* (pp. vi–vii). Washington, DC: U.S. Government Printing Office.

———. (1986). "Dollars and sense: The value of victim restitution." *Corrections Today* (August): 156–160.

Herszenhorn, D. (1999). "Alarm Helps to Fight Domestic Violence." *New York Times,* July 27, p. B6.

Hester, T. (1987). *BJS bulletin: Probation and parole, 1986.* Washington, DC: U.S. Department of Justice.

Hewitt, S. (1998). *Assessing allegations of sexual abuse in preschool children.* Thousand Oaks, CA: Sage.

Hickey, E. (1991). *Serial murderers and their victims.* Pacific Grove, CA: Brooks/Cole.

Hillenbrand, S. (1990). "Restitution and victim rights in the 1980s." In A. Lurigio, W. Skogan, and R. Davis (Eds.), *Victims of crime: Problems, politics, and programs* (pp. 188–204). Thousand Oaks, CA: Sage.

Hills, S. (1981). *Demystifying deviance.* Englewood Cliffs, NJ: Prentice-Hall.

Hilton, N. (1993). *Legal responses to wife assault: Current trends and evaluation.* Newbury Park, CA: Sage.

Hilts, P. (1994). "6% of women admit beatings while pregnant." *New York Times,* March 3, pp. A1, A23.

Hindelang, M., Gottfredson, M., and Garofalo, J. (1978). *Victims of personal crime: An empirical foundation for a theory of personal victimization.* Cambridge, MA: Ballinger.

Hinds, M. (1988). "The new fashioned way to steal money: Fake credit." *New York Times,* December 31, p. A28.

Hochstedler, E. (1981). *Crime against the elderly in twenty-six cities.* Washington, DC: U.S. Department of Justice.

Hoffman, J. (1994). "May it please the public: Lawyers exploit media attention as a defense tactic." *New York Times,* April 22, pp. B1, B7.

Hofstadter, R., and Wallace, M. (1970). *American violence: A documentary history.* New York: Knopf.

Holloway, L. (1994). "Impersonators bearing badges of dishonor." *New York Times,* November 12, pp. B1, B28.

———. (1995). "Despite the bitter cold, many homeless resist the shelters." *New York Times,* February 8, p. B3.

Holmes, R. (1994). *Murder in America.* Newbury Park, CA: Sage.

Holmes, R., and DeBurger, J. (1988). *Serial murder.* Newbury Park, CA: Sage.

Hook, S. (1972). "The rights of the victims: Thoughts on crime and compassion." *Encounter* (April): 29–35.

Hoover, J. (1994). *Technical background on the redesigned National Crime Victimization Survey.* Washington, DC: U.S. Department of Justice, BJS.

Hoover, J. E. (1966). "The car theft problem: How you can help beat it." *Congressional Record: Senate,* September 22, p. 23621.

Horn, M. (1993). "Memories lost and found." *U.S. News & World Report,* November 29, pp. 52–63.

Hotaling, G., Finkelhor, D., Kirkpatrick, J., and Straus, M. (1988). *Coping with family violence: Research on policy perspectives.* Newbury Park, CA: Sage.

House Subcommittee on Health and Long-Term Care, Select Committee on Aging. (1992). *Hearings on elder abuse.* Washington, DC: U.S. Department of Justice.

Howell, J. (1989). *Selected state legislation: A guide for effective state laws to protect children* (2nd ed.). Washington, DC: National Center for Missing and Exploited Children.

Hudson, J., and Chesney, S. (1978). "Research on restitution: A review and assessment." In B. Galaway and J. Hudson (Eds.), *Offender restitution in theory and action* (pp. 131–148). Lexington, MA: Lexington Books.

Hudson, J., and Galaway, B. (1975). *Considering the victim: Readings in restitution and victim compensation.* Springfield, IL: Charles C Thomas.

Hughes, R. (1993). *Culture of complaint: The fraying of America.* New York: Oxford University Press.

Hunzeker, D. (1992). "Stalking laws." *National Conference of State Legislatures' State Legislative Report* 17(19): 1–6.

Inciardi, J. (1976). "The pickpocket and his victim." *Victimology* 1(3): 446–453.

Infolink. (1999). *HIV AIDS legislation.* Arlington, VA.: National Center for Victims of Crime.

Ingrassia, M., and Beck, M. (1994). "Patterns of abuse." *Newsweek,* July 4, pp. 26–33.

International Criminal Police Organization (Interpol). (1998). *1998 Annual Report.* Paris: Interpol.

Irwin, T. (1980). *To combat and prevent child abuse and neglect.* New York: Public Affairs Committee.

Island, D., and Letellier, P. (1991). *Men who beat the men who love them.* New York: Harrington Park Press.

Jackson, N. (1998). "Lesbian battering: The other closet." In N. Jackson and G. Oates (Eds.), *Violence in intimate relationships: Examining sociological and psychological issues* (pp. 181–194). Woburn, MA: Butterworth-Heinemann.

Jacob, B. (1977). "The concept of restitution: An historical overview." In J. Hudson and B. Galaway (Eds.), *Restitution in criminal justice* (pp. 45–62). Lexington, MA: Lexington Books.

———. (1989). "Movie fan is killed in theater argument over a popcorn line." *New York Times,* July 4, p. 33.

———. (1990). "Bronx jurors fail to indict in slaying." *New York Times,* November 28, pp. B1, B3.

Jacobs, S., and Moore, D. (1994). "Successful restitution as a predictor of juvenile recidivism." *Juvenile and Family Court Journal* 45(1): 3–14.

James, G. (1990). "Bronx jurors fail to indict in slaying." *New York Times,* November 28, pp. B1, B3.

Jankowski, L. (1991). *Probation and parole, 1990. Bureau of Justice Statistics Bulletin.* Washington, DC: U.S. Department of Justice.

Janofsky, M. (1994). "The 'why' of youth's fatal beating in Philadelphia is elusive." *New York Times,* December 5, p. A16.

Jasinski, J., and Williams, L. (1998). *Partner violence.* Thousand Oaks, CA: Sage.

Jeffrey, C. (1971). *Crime prevention through environmental design.* Beverly Hills, CA: Sage.

Jennings, K. (1986). "Dispute on abuse survey." *New York Newsday,* August 12, p. D3.

Jensen, G., and Brownfield, D. (1986). "Gender, lifestyles, and victimization: Beyond routine activity." *Violence and Victims* 1(2): 85–99.

Jensen, G., and Karpos, M. (1993). "Managing rape: Exploratory research on the behavior of rape statistics." *Criminology* 31: 363–385.

Johann, S., and Osanka, F. (1989). *Representing battered women who kill.* Springfield, IL: Charles C Thomas.

Johnson, G. (1941). "The Negro and crime." *Annals of the American Academy of Political and Social Science* 217: 93–104.

Johnson, J. (1989). "Horror stories and the construction of child abuse." In J. Best (Ed.), *Images of issues: Typifying contemporary social problems* (pp. 5–19). New York: Aldine de Gruyter.

Jones, A. (1980). *Women who kill.* New York: Fawcett Columbine Books.

"Justice by the numbers." (1993). *Law Enforcement News,* December 31, p. 27.

Kalish, C. (1988). *BJS special report: International crime rates.* Washington, DC: U.S. Department of Justice.

Kalven, H., and Zeisel, H. (1966). *The American Jury.* Boston: Little, Brown.

Kanin, E. (1984). "Date rape: Unofficial criminals and victims." *Victimology* 9(1): 95–108.

———. (1994). "False rape allegations." *Archives of Sexual Behavior,* 23(1): 81–90.

Kantrowitz, B., Starr, M., and Friday, C. (1991). "Naming names." *Newsweek,* April 29, pp. 27–32.

Kappeler, V., Blumberg, M., and Potter, G. (1993). *The mythology of crime and criminal justice.* Prospect Heights, IL: Waveland.

Karlen, N., Greenberg, N., Gonzalez, D., and Williams, E. (1985). "How many missing kids?" *Newsweek,* October 7, pp. 32–33.

Karmen, A. (1979). "Victim facilitation: The case of auto theft." *Victimology* 4(4): 361–370.

———. (1980). "Auto theft: Beyond victim blaming." *Victimology* 5(2): 161–174.

———. (1981a). "Auto theft and corporate irresponsibility." *Contemporary Crises* 5: 63–81.

———. (1981b). *Crime victims and Congress.* Paper presented at the meeting of the Academy of Criminal Justice Sciences, Philadelphia, February 15.

———. (1989). "Crime victims and the news media: Questions of fairness and ethics." In J. Sullivan and J. Victor (Eds.), *Annual editions: Criminal justice 1988–1989* (pp. 51–57). Guilford, CT: Dushkin Publishing Group.

———. (1990). "The implementation of victims' rights: A challenge for criminal justice professionals." In R. Muraskin (Ed.), *Issues in justice: Exploring policy issues in the criminal justice system* (pp. 46–57). Bristol, IN: Wyndham Hall.

———. (1992). "Who's against victims' rights? The nature of the opposition to pro-victim initiatives in criminal justice." *St. John's Journal of Legal Commentary* 8(1) (Fall): 157–176.

———. (1995). "Towards the institutionalization of a new kind of justice professional: The victim advocate." *The Justice Professional* 9(1): 1–16.

———. (2000). *New York murder mystery: The true story behind the crime crash of the 1990s.* New York: New York University Press.

Kates, D. (1986). *Firearms and violence: Issues of public policy.* New York: Ballinger.

Katz, L. (1980). *The justice imperative: An introduction to criminal justice.* Cincinnati, OH: Anderson.

Keilitz, S., Davis, C., Efkeman, H., Flango, C., and Hannaford, P. (1997) "Civil protection orders: Victim's views on effectiveness." *NIJ Journal* 233 (September): 23–24.

Kelly, R. (1983). "Addicts and alcoholics as victims." In D. MacNamara and A. Karmen (Eds.), *Deviants: Victims or victimizers?* (pp. 49–76). Newbury Park, CA: Sage.

Kendall-Tackett, K., Williams, L., and Finkelhor, D. (1993). "Impact of sexual abuse on children: A review and synthesis of recent empirical studies." *Psychological Bulletin* 113(1) (January): 164–181.

Kerr, P. (1992). "Blatant fraud pushing up the cost of car insurance." *New York Times,* February 6, pp. A1, D6.

Kesler, J. (1992). *How to keep your car from being stolen.* Houston, TX: Shell Oil Company.

Keve, P. (1978). "Therapeutic uses of restitution." In B. Galaway and J. Hudson (Eds.), *Offender restitution in theory and action* (pp. 59–64). Lexington, MA: Lexington Books.

"Kidnapping summons city to action." (1993). *New York Times,* October 15, p. A24.

Kilpatrick, D. (1985). "Survey analyzes responses of female sex assault victims." *Crime Victims Digest* (February): 9.

———. (1992). *Rape in America.* Fort Worth, TX: National Victim Center.

Kincaid, J. (1993). "Purity, pedastry and a fallen heroine." *New York Times,* June 1, p. A17.

Kinderman, C., and Lynch, J. (1997). *Effects of the redesign on victimization estimates. BJS, NCVS.* Washington, DC: U.S. Department of Justice.

King, P. (1993). "Not so different, after all." *Newsweek,* October 4, p. 75.

King, W. (1989). "Violent racism attracts new breed: Skinheads." *New York Times,* January 1, p. A35.

Kirkwood, C. (1993). *Leaving abusive partners.* Newbury Park, CA: Sage.

Klaus, P. (1994). *Costs of crime to victims. BJS crime data briefs.* Washington, DC: U.S. Department of Justice.

———. (1999a). *Carjackings in the United States, 1992–1996. BJS special report.* Washington, DC: U.S. Department of Justice.

———. (1999b). *BJS Report: Crimes against persons age 65 and older.* Washington, DC: U.S. Department of Justice.

Klaus, P., DeBerry, M., and Timrots, A. (1985). *BJS bulletin: The crime of rape.* Washington, DC: U.S. Department of Justice.

Kleck, G. (1991). *Point blank: Guns and violence in America.* New York: Aldine de Gruyter.

———. (1997). *Targeting guns: Firearms and their control.* Hawthorne, NY: Aldine de Gruyter.

Kleck, G., and DeLone, M. (1993). "Victim resistance and offender weapon effects in robbery." *Journal of Quantitative Criminology* 9(1): 55–81.

Kleck, G., and Gertz, M. (1995). "Armed resistance to crime: The prevalence and nature of self-defense with a gun." *Journal of Criminal Law and Criminology* 86(1) (Fall): 150–187.

Klein, A. (1988). *Alternative sentencing.* Cincinnati, OH: Anderson.

———. (1997). *Alternative sentencing, intermediate sanctions and probation. Second edition.* Cincinnati, OH: Anderson.

Klein, E., and Campbell, J., Soler, E., and Ghez, M. (1997). *Ending domestic violence.* Thousand Oaks, CA.: Sage.

Kleinfield, N. (1995)."Prosecutors paying millions to protect cowed witnesses." *New York Times,* May 30, pp. A1, B5.

Knudten, M., Knudten, R., and Meade, A. (1978). "Will anyone be left to testify?" In E. Flynn and J. Conrad (Eds.), *The new and the old criminology* (pp. 207–222). New York: Praeger.

Kolarik, G. (1992). "Stalking laws proliferate." *ABA Journal* (November): 35–36.

Koppel, H. (1987). *Lifetime likelihood of victimization: Bureau of Justice Statistics technical report.* Washington, DC: U.S. Department of Justice.

Kornbluth, J. (1987). "The woman who beat the Klan." *New York Times Magazine,* November 1, pp. 26–39.

Koss, M. (1992). "The underdetection of rape: Methodological choices influence incidence estimates." *Journal of Social Issues* 48(1): 61–75.

Koss, M., and Cook, S. (1998). "Facing the facts: Date and acquaintance rape are significant problems for women." In R. Bergen (Ed.), *Issues in intimate violence* (pp. 147–156). Thousand Oaks, CA: Sage.

Koss, M., Gidyez, C., and Wisniewski, N. (1987). "The scope of rape: Incidence and prevalence of sexual aggression and victimization in a national sample of higher education students." *Journal of Consulting and Clinical Psychology* 55: 162–170.

Koss, M., and Harvey, M. (1991). *The rape victim: Clinical and community interventions.* Newbury Park, CA: Sage.

Kotecha, K., and Walker, J. (1976). "Vigilantism and the American police." In J. Rosenbaum and P. Sederberg (Eds.), *Vigilante politics* (pp. 158–174). Philadelphia: University of Pennsylvania Press.

Kramgrow, E., Lentzner, H., Rooks, P., Weeks, J., and Saydah, S. (1999). *Health, United States, 1997, with health and aging chartbook.* Hyattsville, MD: U.S. CDC's National Center for Health Statistics.

Krauss, C. (1994). "New York car theft draws police priority." *New York Times,* January 23, pp. 21, 26.

Kristal, A. (1991). "You've come a long way baby: The battered woman's syndrome revisited." *New York Law School Journal of Human Rights* 9: 111–116.

Krueger, F. (1985). "Violated." *Boston* (May): 138–141.

Kuhl, A. (1986). "Implications of justifiable homicide verdicts for battered women." *Response* 9(2): 6–10.

La Fave, W. (1965). *Arrest: The decision to take a suspect into custody.* Boston: Little, Brown.

LaFontaine, D. (1997). *Speak of the devil: Allegations of satanic abuse in Britain.* New York: Cambridge University Press.

LaFree, G. (1989). *Rape and criminal justice.* Santa Fe, NM: University of New Mexico Press.

Lamborn, L. (1968). "Toward a victim orientation in criminal theory." *Rutgers Law Review* 22: 733–768.

———. (1985). "The impact of victimology on the criminal law in the United States." *Canadian Community Law Journal* 8: 23–43.

Land, K., McCall, P., and Cohen, L. (1990). "Structural covariates of homicidal rates: Are there any invariances across time and social space?" *American Journal of Sociology* 95(4) (January): 922–963.

Lander, E. (1988). "Rough sex defense assailed." *New York Newsday,* May 11, p. 26.

Laner, M., and Thompson, J. (1982). "Abuse and aggression in courting couples." *Deviant Behavior* 3: 229–244.

Langan, P. (1985). *BJS special report: The risk of violent crime.* Washington, DC: U.S. Department of Justice.

Langan, P., and Graziadei, H. (1995). *BJS Bulletin: Felony sentences in state courts, 1992.* Washington, DC: U.S. Department of Justice.

Langan, P., and Harlow, C. (1994). *BJS crime data brief: Child rape victims, 1992.* Washington, DC: U.S. Department of Justice.

Langan, P., and Innes, C. (1986). *BJS special report: Preventing domestic violence against women.* Washington, DC: U.S. Department of Justice.

Langan, P., Perkins, C., and Chaiken, J. (1994). *Felony sentences in the United States, 1990. Bureau of Justice Statistics Bulletin.* Washington, DC: U.S. Department of Justice.

Lanning, K. (1992). *Child sex rings: A behavioral analysis.* Arlington, VA: National Center for Missing and Exploited Children.

Largen, M. (1981). "Grassroots centers and national task forces: A herstory of the anti-rape movement." *Aegis* 32 (Autumn): 46–52.

———. (1987). "A decade of change in the rape reform movement." *Response* 10(2): 4–9.

Lasch, C. (1982). "Why the 'survival mentality' is rife in America." *U.S. News & World Report,* May 17, pp. 59–60.

Laster, R. (1970). "Criminal restitution: A survey of its past history and analysis of its present usefulness." *University of Richmond Law Review* 5: 71–98.

Lawry, M. (1997). "Court appointed special advocates: A voice for abused and neglected children in court." *OJJDP Juvenile Justice Bulletin* (March): 1.

Leary, W. (1993). "Guns in home? Study finds it a deadly mix." *New York Times,* October 7, p. A18.

Lederer, L. (1980). *Take back the night.* New York: Morrow.

Lederman, D. (1994). "Crime on the campuses." *Chronicle of Higher Education,* February 2, A31–A42.

Leepson, M. (1982). "Helping victims of crime." *Editorial Research Reports* 1(17): 331–344.

LeGrande, C. (1973). "Rape and rape laws: Sexism in society and law." *California Law Review* 61: 919–941.

Lehnen, R., and Skogan, W. (1981). *The national crime survey: Working papers: Vol. 1. Current and historical perspectives.* Washington, DC: U.S. Department of Justice.

Leo, J. (1994). "Watching 'As the jury turns.' " *U.S. News & World Report,* February 14, p. 17.

Leone, B., and de Koster, K. (1995). *At issue: Rape on campus.* San Diego, CA: Greenhaven Press.

Lerner, M. (1965). "Evaluation of performance as a function of performer's reward and attractiveness." *Journal of Personality and Social Psychology* 1: 355–360.

Letkemann, P. (1973). *Crime as work.* Englewood Cliffs, NJ: Prentice-Hall.

Letters Column Caption. 1996. "What women want is a lot less victimology." *New York Times,* December 22, p. E8.

Levin, J., and McDevitt, J. (1993). *Hate crimes: The rising tide of bigotry and bloodshed.* New York: Plenum.

Levine, J. (1976). "The potential for crime overreporting in criminal victimization surveys." *Criminology* 14(2): 307–331.

Lewin, T. (1992). "Battered men sounding equal-rights battle cry." *New York Times,* April 20, p. A12.

———. (1993). "New laws address old problem: The terror of a stalker's threats." *New York Times,* February 8, pp. A1, B10.

Libai, D. (1969). "The protection of the child victim of a sexual offense in the criminal justice system." *Wayne Law Review* 15: 977–1032.

Libbey, P., and Bybee, R. (1979). "The physical abuse of adolescents." *Journal of Social Issues* 35(2): 101–126.

Lindner, C., and Koehler, R. (1992). "Probation officer victimization: An emerging concern." *Journal of Criminal Justice* 20(1): 53–62.

Lipman, I. (1982). "Ways to protect yourself from burglars, muggers." *U.S. News & World Report,* December 13, pp. 77–78.

Lisefski, E., and Manson, D. (1988). *BJS bulletin: Tracking offenders, 1984.* Washington, DC: U.S. Department of Justice.

Lockwood, D. (1980). *Prison sexual violence.* New York: Elsevier.

Loftin, C. (1986). "The validity of robbery-murder classifications in Baltimore." *Violence and Victims* 1(3): 191–202.

Loftus, E., and Ketcham, K. (1994). *The myth of repressed memory: False memories and allegations of sexual abuse.* New York: St. Martin's Press.

Lorch, D. (1990). "Robbery suspect dies and a neighborhood is silent." *New York Times,* August 24, p. A1, B3.

Loseke, D. (1989). "Violence is 'violence' . . . or is it? The social construction of 'wife abuse' and public policy." In J. Best (Ed.), *Images of issues: Typifying contemporary social problems* (pp. 191–206). New York: Aldine de Gruyter.

Lott, J. (1998). *More guns, less crime: Understanding crime and gun control laws.* Chicago: University of Chicago Press.

Louden, R. (1998). "The development of hostage negotiation by the NYPD." In A. Karmen (ed.), *Crime and Justice in New York City* (pp. 148–158). New York: McGraw Hill Custom Publishing.

Lourie, I. (1977). "The phenomenon of the abused adolescent: A clinical study." *Victimology* 2(2): 268–276.

Lubenow, G. (1983). "When kids kill their parents." *Newsweek,* June 27, pp. 35–36.

Luckenbill, D. (1977). "Criminal homicide as a situated transaction." *Social Problems* 25: 176–186.

Lundman, R. (1980). *Police and policing: An introduction.* New York: Holt, Rinehart & Winston.

Lundsgaarde, H. (1977). *Murder in space city: A cultural analysis of Houston homicide patterns.* New York: Oxford University Press.

Lurigio, A. (1990). *Victims of crime: Problems, policies and programs.* Newbury Park, CA: Sage.

Lyall, S. (1989). "Rape charge is dropped in case at L. I. School." *New York Times,* May 11, p. B1.

Lynch, R. (1976). "Improving the treatment of victims: Some guides for action." In W. MacDonald (Ed.), *Criminal justice and the victim* (pp. 165–176). Beverly Hills, CA: Sage.

Lynn, W. (1981). "What scientists really mean by 'acceptable risk.' " *U.S. News & World Report,* March 30, p. 60.

MacDonald, J. (1971). *Rape: Offenders and victims.* Springfield, IL: Charles C Thomas.

MacDonald, J., and Michaud, D. (1995). *Rape: Controversial issues—Criminal profiles, date rape, false reports and false memories.* Chicago: Charles C Thomas.

MacNamara, D., and Sullivan, J. (1974). "Making the victim whole: Composition, restitution, and compensation." In T. Thornberry and E. Sagarin (Eds.), *Images of crime: Offenders and victims* (pp. 79–90). New York: Praeger.

Madison, A. (1973). *Vigilantism in America.* New York: Seabury Press.

Maghan, J., and Sagarin, E. (1983). "Homosexuals as victimizers and victims." In D. MacNamara and A. Karmen (Eds.), *Deviants: Victims or victimizers?* (pp. 147–162). Newbury Park, CA: Sage.

Maguire, K., and Pastore, A. (1994). *BJS sourcebook of criminal justice statistics—1993.* Washington, DC: U.S. Government Printing Office.

Maguire, K., Pastore, A., and Flanagan, T. (1993). *BJS Sourcebook of criminal justice statistics—1992.* Washington, DC: U.S. Department of Justice.

Makepeace, J. (1981). "Courtship violence among college students." *Family Relations* 30: 97–102.

Malefyt, M., Littel, K., Walker, A., Tucker, D., and Buel, S. (1998). *Promising practices: Improving the criminal justice system's response to violence against women. Office of Justice Programs report.* Washington, DC: U.S. Department of Justice.

Maltz, W., and Holman, B. (1986). *Incest and sexuality: A guide to understanding and healing.* New York: Free Press.

Mannheim, H. (1965). *Comparative criminology.* Boston: Houghton Mifflin.

Manshel, L. (1990). *Nap time.* New York: Kensington.

Mansnerus, L. (1989). "The rape laws change faster than perceptions." *New York Times,* February 19, Sec. 5, p. 20.

———. (1999). "Victim's parents reconcile with killer's." *New York Times,* September 28, p. B8.

Maple, J. (1999). *The crime fighter: Putting the bad guys out of business.* New York: Doubleday.

Marciniak, L. (1999). "Adolescent attitudes toward victim precipitation of rape." *Violence and Victims* 13(3) (Fall): 287–300.

Margolick, D. (1994). "Does Mrs. Bobbitt count as another battered wife?" *New York Times,* January 16, p. E5.

Marriott, M. (1989). "With a 'Remember me?' man shoots 3 in subway." *New York Times,* June 12, p. B2.

———. (1991). ". . . And thefts bedevil car renters." *New York Times,* November 16, p. 48.

Martin, D. (1976). *Battered wives.* San Francisco: Glide.

Martin, D. E. (1989). "The line of duty: Special officers help their own." *New York Times,* June 7, p. Bl.

Martin, P., and Hummer, R. (1998). Fraternities and rape on campus. In R. Bergen (ed.), *Issues in intimate violence* (157–167). Thousand Oaks, CA: Sage.

Martinson, R. (1974). "What works—questions and answers about prison reform." *Public Interest* 35 (Spring): 22–54.

Martz, L., Miller, M., Hutchinson, S., Emerson, T., and Washington, F. (1989). "A tide of drug killing." *Newsweek,* January 16, pp. 44–45.

Martz, L., Starr, M., and Barrett, T. (1990). "A murderous hoax." *Newsweek,* January 22, pp. 16–21.

Marx, G., and Archer, D. (1976). "Community police patrols and vigilantism." In J. Rosenbaum and P. Sederberg (Eds.), *Vigilante politics* (pp. 129–157). Philadelphia: University of Pennsylvania Press.

Mash, E., and Wolfe, D. (1991). "Methodological issues in research on physical child abuse." *Criminal Justice and Behavior* 18(1) (March): 8–29.

Mathews, A. (1993). "The campus crime wave." *New York Times Magazine,* March 7, pp. 38–47.

Mauer, M. (1999). *Race to incarcerate.* New York: New Press.

Mawby, R., and Walklate, S. (1993). *Critical victimology: International perspectives.* Newbury Park, CA: Sage.

Maxfield, M. (1987). "Household composition, routine activity, and victimization: A comparative analysis." *Journal of Quantitative Criminology* 3: 301–320.

Mayhew, P., and Hough, M. (1988). "The British crime survey: Origins and impact." In M. Maguire and J. Pointing (Eds.), *Victims of crime: A new deal?* (pp.156–163). Philadelphia: Open University Press.

McCaghy, C. (1980). *Crime in American society.* New York: Macmillan.

McCaghy, C., Giordano, P., and Henson, T. (1977). "Auto theft: Offenders and offense characteristics." *Criminology* 15 (November): 367–385.

McCahill, T., Williams, L., and Fischman, A. (1979). *The aftermath of rape.* Lexington, MA: Lexington Books.

McCormack, R. (1991). "Compensating victims of violent crime." *Justice Quarterly* 8(3): 329–346.

McCurdy, K., and Daro, D. (1994). "Child maltreatment: A national study of reports and fatalities." *Journal of Interpersonal Violence* 9: 75–94.

McDermott, J. (1979). *Rape victimization in 26 American cities.* Washington, DC: U.S. Government Printing Office.

McDonald, D. (1988). *NIJ crime file study guide: Restitution and community service.* Washington, DC: U.S. Department of Justice.

McDonald, W. (1976). "Criminal justice and the victim." In W. McDonald (Ed.), *Criminal justice and the victim* (pp. 17–56). Beverly Hills, CA: Sage.

———. (1977). "The role of the victim in America." In R. Barnett and J. Hagel III (Eds.), *Assessing the criminal: Restitution, retribution, and the legal process* (pp. 295–307). Cambridge, MA: Ballinger.

———. (1978). "Expanding the victim's role in the disposition decision: Reform in search of rationale." In B. Galaway and J. Hudson (Eds.), *Offender restitution in theory and action* (pp. 101–110). Lexington, MA: Lexington Books.

———. (1979). "The prosecutor's domain." In W. McDonald (Ed.), *The prosecutor* (pp. 15–52). Beverly Hills, CA: Sage.

McFadden, R. (1993a). "Armored car suspect confirmed inside job." *New York Times,* February 5, pp. B1, B4.

———. (1993b). "A stranger is stabbed saving a life." *New York Times,* May 14, p. B3.

McGillis, D. (1982). "Minor dispute processing: A review of recent developments." In R. Tomasic and M. Feeley (Eds.), *Neighborhood justice: Assessment of an emerging idea* (pp. 60–76). New York: Longman.

———. (1986). *NIJ issues and practices: Crime victim restitution: An analysis of approaches.* Washington, DC: U.S. Department of Justice.

McGillis, D., and Smith, P. (1983). *Compensating victims of crime: An analysis of American programs.* Washington, DC: U.S. Department of Justice.

McGrath, K., and Osborne, M. (1989). "Redressing violence against elders." *NOVA Newsletter* 13(2): 1, 4, 5.

McIntyre, D. (1968). "A study of judicial dominance of the charging decision." *Journal of Criminal Law, Criminology, and Police Science* 59 (December): 463–490.

McKinley, J. (1991). "Merchant and burglar die in police shootout." *New York Times,* May 3, p. B3.

McKnight, D. (1981). "The victim-offender reconciliation project." In B. Galaway and J. Hudson (Eds.), *Perspectives on crime victims* (pp. 292–298). St. Louis, MO: C. V. Mosby.

McPhee, M. (1999). "Agonizing wait for mom." *New York Daily News,* December 20, p. 4.

Meiners, R. (1978). *Victim compensation: Economic, political and legal aspects.* Lexington, MA: D. C. Heath.

Meloy, J. (1998). *The psychology of stalking: Clinical and forensic perspectives.* San Diego, CA: Academic Press.

Mendelsohn, B. (1940). "Rape in criminology." Translated and cited in S. Schafer (1968), *The victim and his criminal.* New York: Random House.

———. (1956). "The victimology." *Etudes Internationales de PsychoSociologie Criminelle* (July): 23–26.

Menninger, K. (1968). *The crime of punishment.* New York: Viking Press.

Merrill, L. (1994). "A defense that won't go away." *New York Daily News,* April 7, p. 6.

Messner, S., and Golden, R. (1992). "Racial inequality and racially disaggregated homicide rates: An assessment of alternative theoretical explanations." *Criminology* 30(3) (August): 421–447.

Messner, S., and Tardiff, K. (1985). "The social ecology of urban homicide: An application of the 'routine activities' approach." *Criminology* 23: 241–267.

Miers, D. (1989). "Positivist victimology: A critique." *International Review of Victimology* 1: 3–22.

Miethe, T., Stafford, M., and Sloane, D. (1990). "Lifestyle changes and risks of criminal victimization." *Journal of Quantitative Criminology* 6(4): 357–375.

Mignon, S. (1998). "Husband battering: A review of the debate over a controversial social phenomenon." In N. Jackson and G. Oates (Eds.), *Violence in intimate relationships: Examining sociological and psychological issues* (pp. 137–160). Woburn, MA: Butterworth-Heinemann.

Miller, F. (1970). *Prosecution: The decision to charge a suspect with a crime.* Boston: Little, Brown.

Miller, S. (1992). "Arrest policies for domestic violence and their implications for battered women." In R. Muraskin and T. Alleman, (Eds.), *It's a crime: Women and justice* (pp. 334–359). Englewood Cliffs, NJ: Regents/Prentice Hall.

Miller, T., Cohen, M., and Wiersema, B. (1996). *Victim costs and consequences: A new look.* Washington, D.C.: U.S. Department of Justice.

Milner, J. (1991). "Introduction: Current perspectives on physical child abuse." *Criminal Justice and Behavior* 18(1) (March): 4–7.

Mitchell, A. (1992). "Strange school ties: A near fatal student-teacher pact." *New York Times,* October 23, p. B3.

Mithers, C. (1990). "Incest and the law." *New York Times Magazine,* October 21, pp. 44–63.

"Mixed verdict for six youths in fatal beating." (1996). *New York Times,* February 6, p. A9.

Mones, P. (1991). *When a child kills: Abused children who kill their parents.* New York: Simon & Schuster.

Moore, E., and Mills, M. (1990). "The neglected victims and unexamined costs of white collar crime." *Crime and Delinquency* 36(3): 408–418.

Moore, L. (1985). "Your home: Make it safe." *Security Management* (March): 115–116.

Morganthau, T., and Shenitz, B. (1994). "Too many guns? Or too few?" *Newsweek,* August 15, pp. 44–45.

Mothers Against Drunk Driving (MADD). (1988). "Victim rights: How far have we come?" *Maddvocate,* (Spring): 13.

Muehlenhard, C., Powch, I., Phelps, J., and Giusti, L. (1992). "Definitions of rape: Scientific and political implications." *Journal of Social Issues* 48(1): 23–44.

Mueller, G., and Cooper, H. (1973). *The criminal, society, and the victim.* Washington, DC: National Criminal Justice Reference Service.

Munson, D. (1989). *The child victim as a witness: OJJDP update on research.* Washington, DC: U.S. Department of Justice.

Murphy, W. (1999). "Massachusetts initiates victim 'Miranda' law." *The Crime Victims Report* 3 (4) (September): 49, 50, 55.

Mustaine, E., and Tewksbury, R. (1998a). "Predicting risks of larceny theft victimization: A routine activity analysis using refined lifestyle measures." *Criminology* 36(4) (November): 829–857.

Mustaine, E., and Tewksbury, R. (1998b). "Victimization risks at leisure: A gender-specific analysis." *Violence and Victims* 13(3) (Fall): 232–249.

Mydans, S. (1994). "The other Menendez trial, too, ends with the jury deadlocked." *New York Times,* January 29, pp. A1, A8.

Myers, J. (1998). *Legal issues in child abuse and neglect.* Thousand Oaks, CA: Sage.

Myers, M. (1977). *The effects of victim characteristics on the prosecution, conviction, and sentencing of criminal defendants.* Unpublished doctoral dissertation. Ann Arbor, MI: University Microfilms.

Myers, M., and Hagan, J. (1979). "Private and public trouble: Prosecutors and the allocation of court resources." *Social Problems* 26(4): 439–451.

Myrdal, G. (1944). *An American dilemma: The Negro problem and modern democracy.* New York: Harper & Row.

Nathan, D., and Snedeker, M. (1995). *Satan's silence: Ritual abuse and the making of a modern American witchhunt.* New York: Basic Books.

National Advisory Commission on Criminal Justice Standards and Goals. (1973). *The courts.* Washington, DC: U.S. Government Printing Office.

National Center for Child Abuse and Neglect (NCCAN). (1978). *Child sexual abuse: Incest, assault and sexual exploitation.* Washington, DC: U.S. Department of Health, Education, and Welfare.

National Center for Educational Statistics (NCES). (1998). *Indicators of school crime and safety, 1998.* Washington, DC: U.S. Department of Justice.

National Center for Missing and Exploited Children (NCMEC). (1986). *State legislation to protect children: An update on the nation's progress to implement effective laws preventing child victimization.* Washington, DC: Author.

———. (1987). *Accomplishing great things.* Washington, DC: Author.

National Center for Victims of Crime (NCVC). (1996). *The 1996 victim rights sourcebook.* Arlington, VA: NCVC.

———. (1999). *The NCVC does not support the current language of the proposed crime victims' rights constitutional amendment.* Arlington, VA: NCVC.

National Clearinghouse on Child Abuse and Neglect Information. (1997). *What is child maltreatment?* Washington, DC: National Clearinghouse on Child Abuse and Neglect Information.

National Commission on the Causes and Prevention of Violence (NCCPV). (1969a). *Crimes of violence.* Washington, DC: U.S. Government Printing Office.

———. (1969b). *The offender and his victim.* (Staff report by D. Mulvihill, L. Curtis, and M. Tumin). Washington, DC: U.S. Government Printing Office.

National Committee for Prevention of Child Abuse (NCPCA). (1993). *Current trends in child abuse reporting and fatalities.* Chicago: National Committee.

National Crime Prevention Institute. (1978). *Understanding crime prevention.* Louisville, KY: Author.

National Institute of Justice (NIJ). (1984). *Vehicle theft prevention strategies.* Washington, DC: U.S. Government Printing Office.

———. (1998). *New directions from the field: Victims' rights and services for the 21st century.* Washington, DC: U.S. Department of Justice.

National Insurance Crime Bureau. (1993). "The public speaks out on fraud and theft." *Spotlight on Insurance Crime* 2(3) (Winter): 1–2.

———. (1995). "Eye on insurance crime." *Spotlight on Insurance Crime* 3(3) (Winter): 8–9.

National Organization for Victim Assistance (NOVA). (1988). *Victim rights and services: A legislative directory—1987*. Washington, DC: Author.

———. (1989). "Bipartisan victim rights bill introduced in U.S. Congress." *NOVA Newsletter* 13(3): 1, 5.

———. (1991). "U.N. convention on the rights of the child." *NOVA Newsletter* 15(1): 1–9.

National Sheriffs' Association (1999). *First response to victims of crime*. Washington, DC: Office for Victims of Crime, U.S. Department of Justice.

National Victim Center (NVC). (1990). *Crime victims and corrections*. Fort Worth, TX: NVC.

———. (1991a). *America speaks out: Citizens' attitudes about victims' rights and violence*. Fort Worth, TX: NVC.

———. (1991b). *National victim services survey of adult and juvenile corrections and parole agencies. Final report*. Fort Worth, TX: NVC.

———. (1992a). *Infoline: Constitutional rights for crime victims*. Fort Worth, TX: NVC.

———. (1992b). "Restitution statutes." *Infoline* 1(58): 1–4.

———. (1993). *Civil justice for crime victims*. Fort Worth, TX: NVC.

Neidig, P. (1984). "Women's shelters, men's collectives and other issues in the field of spouse abuse." *Victimology* 9(3–4): 464–476.

Nelson, S. (1998). "Bill aims to aid search for missing." *Long Island Newsday*, February 4, p. A26.

Neubauer, D. (1974). *Criminal justice in middle America*. Morristown, NJ: General Learning Press.

Newberger, E. (1987). "Prosecution: A problematic approach to child abuse." *Journal of Interpersonal Violence* (March): 112–117.

Newman, D. (1966). *Conviction: The determination of guilt or innocence without trial*. Boston: Little, Brown.

Newman, M. (1992). "Gang fatally beats a mistaken target, Bronx witness says." *New York Times*, August 20, pp. A1, B3.

Newman, O. (1972). *Defensible space: People and design in the violent city*. London: Architectural Press.

New York Police Department (NYPD). (1992). *Auto theft: A growing business*. New York Police Department Auto Crime Division.

New York State Crime Victims Board. (1988). *Annual report, 1987–88*. Albany, NY: Author.

New York State Law Enforcement Council. (1994). *Legislative proposals, 1994*. New York: Author.

"NICB study shows vehicle theft trends." (1993). *Corporate Security Digest* August 3, pp. 1–2.

News Wire Services. (2000). "GOP senator advocates push for victims rights." *Bergen* (New Jersey) *Record*, February 6, p. A21.

Nicholson, E. (Ed.). (1988). *Sexual abuse allegations in custody and visitation cases*. Washington, DC: American Bar Association.

Niemeyer, M., and Shichor, D. (1996). "A preliminary study of a large victim/offender reconciliation program." *Federal Probation* 60(3) (September): 30–34.

Nieves, E. (1994). "Prosecutors drop charges in abuse case from mid-80s." *New York Times*, December 3, pp. A25, A29.

Normandeau, A. (1968). "Patterns in robbery." *Criminologica* (November): 2–15.

Nossiter, A. (1994b). "Judge awards damages in Japanese youth's death." *New York Times*, September 16, p. A12.

———. (1996). "Putative damages: The non-cash value of $43 million." *New York Times*, April 28, Section 4, p. 5.

O'Brien, R. (1985). *Crime and victimization data*. Beverly Hills, CA: Sage.

———. (2000). "Crime facts: Victim and offender data." In J. Sheley (Ed.), *Criminology, third edition* (pp. 59–83). Belmont, CA: Wadsworth.

O'Brien, T. (2000). "Officials worried over a sharp rise in identity theft." *New York Times,* April 3, pp. A1, A19.

Ochberg, F. (1978). "The victim of terrorism: Psychiatric considerations." *Terrorism, An International Journal* 1(2): 147–167.

O'Connell, P., and Straub, F. (1999). "Why the jails didn't explode." *City Journal* 9 (2) (Spring): 28–37.

"Offenders get wrists slapped: Car thefts total a million a year." (1975). *Salem* (Massachusetts) *News,* October 2, p. 2.

Office of Justice Programs, BJS. (1997). *Implementing the national incident-based reporting system: A project status report.* Washington, DC: U.S. Department of Justice.

Office of Justice Programs (OJP). (1997). *National Victim Assistance Academy (NVAA) handbook.* Washington, DC: U.S. Department of Justice.

———. (1998). *Stalking and domestic violence: The third annual report to Congress under the Violence Against Women Act.* Washington, DC: U.S. Department of Justice.

Office of Juvenile Justice and Delinquency Prevention (OJJDP). (1998a). *When your child is missing: A family survival guide.* Washington, D.C.: U.S. Department of Justice.

———. (1998b). *Guide for implementing the balanced and restorative justice model.* Washington, DC: U.S. Department of Justice.

———. (1998c). *National directory of restitution and community service programs.* Washington, DC: U.S. Department of Justice.

Office of Victims of Crime (OVC), National Institute of Justice. (1997). *Restorative justice fact sheet.* Washington, DC: U.S. Department of Justice.

Ofshe, R., and Watters, E. (1993). *Making monsters: False memories, psychotherapy, and sexual hysteria.* New York: Scribners.

Ohlin, L., and Tonry, M. (1989). "Family violence in perspective." In L. Ohlin and M. Tonry (Eds.), *Crime and justice: A review of research, Volume 11: Family violence* (pp. 1–18). Chicago: University of Chicago Press.

O'Neill, T. (1984). "The good, the bad, and the Burger court: Victims' rights and a new model of criminal review." *Journal of Criminal Law and Criminology* 75(2): 363–387.

Onishi, N. (1994). "Stray gunfire kills man in Bronx." *New York Times,* May 26, p. B3.

Orcutt, J., and Faison, R. (1988). "Sex-role attitude change and reporting of rape victimization, 1973–1985." *Sociological Quarterly* 29: 589–604.

Outlaw, M., and Ruback, B. (1999). "Predictors and outcomes of victim restitution orders." *Justice Quarterly* 16(4): 847–869.

Pagelow, M. (1984a). *Family violence.* New York: Praeger.

———. (1984b). *Women battering: Victims and their experiences.* Beverly Hills, CA: Sage.

———. (1989). "The incidence and prevalence of criminal abuse of other family members." In L. Ohlin and M. Tonry (Eds.), *Crime and justice: A review of research, Volume 11: Family violence* (pp. 263–313). Chicago: University of Chicago Press.

Paglia, C. (1993). Interview on CBS's *Sixty Minutes.* August 1.

———. (1994). *Vamps and tramps.* New York: Vintage.

Parent, D., Auerbach, B., and Carlson, K. (1992). *Compensating crime victims: A summary of policies and practices.* Washington, DC: U.S. Department of Justice.

Parker, K. (1999). "Moral pendulum swings back." *The Denver Post,* November 22, p. BIO.

Parker, R. (1995). "Bringing 'booze' back in: The relationship between alcohol and homicide." *Journal of Research in Crime and Delinquency* 32(1): 3–38.

Parker, R., and Rebhun, L. (1995). *Alcohol and homicide: A deadly combination of two American traditions*. Albany: SUNY Press.

Parsonage, W. (Ed.) (1979). *Perspectives on victimology*. Beverly Hills, CA: Sage.

Parsonage, W., Bernat, F., and Helfgott, J. (1994). "Victim impact testimony and Pennsylvania's parole decision-making process: A pilot study." *Criminal Justice Policy Review* 6: 187–206.

Paternoster, R. (1984). "Prosecutorial discretion in requesting the death penalty: A case of victim based racial discrimination." *Law and Society Review* 18: 437–478.

Payne, L. (1989). "Her boyfriend says: Tawana made it up." *New York Newsday,* April 27, pp. 1, 3.

Peacock, P. (1998). "Marital rape." In R. Bergen (ed.), *Issues in intimate violence* (pp. 223–235). Thousand Oaks, CA.: Sage.

Peak, K. (1986). "Crime victim reparation: Legislative revival of the offended ones." *Federal Probation* (September): 36–41.

Pendergrast, M. (1994). *Victims of memory: Incest accusations and shattered lives*. San Francisco: Upper Access.

Pepinsky, H. (1991). "Peacemaking in criminology and criminal justice." In H. Pepinsky and R. Quinney (Eds.), *Criminology as peacemaking* (pp. 299–327). Bloomington, IN: Indiana University Press.

Peters, D., Wyatt, G., and Finkelhor, D. (1986). "Prevalence." In D. Finkelhor (Ed.), *A sourcebook on child sexual abuse* (pp. 50–60). Beverly Hills, CA: Sage.

Pfohl, S. (1984). "The discovery of child abuse." In D. Kelly (Ed.), *Deviant behavior* (pp. 45–65). New York: St. Martin's Press.

Pilon, R. (1998). "Victims would be better served by looking to the states, where most laws are enforced." *Insight on the News,* August 31, p. 25.

Plate, T. (1975). *Crime pays*. New York: Simon & Schuster.

Platt, A. (1968). *The child savers*. Chicago: University of Chicago Press.

Pleck, E. (1989). "Criminal approaches to family violence, 1640–1980." In L. Ohlin and M. Tonry (Eds.), *Crime and justice: An annual review of research, vol. 11: Family violence*. (pp. 19–57). Chicago: University of Chicago Press.

Pleck, E., Pleck, J., Grossman, M., and Bart, P. (1978). "The battered data syndrome: A comment on Steinmetz' article." *Victimology* 2(4): 680–684.

Podhoretz, N. (1991). "Rape in feminist eyes." *Commentary* (October): 30–36.

"Police chief and others do not fit victim stereotypes." (1993). *Crime Victims Digest* (September): 6–7.

Pollitt, K. (1989). "Violence in a man's world." *New York Times Magazine,* June 18, pp. 16, 20.

———. (1991). "Naming and blaming: The media goes wild in Palm Beach." *The Nation,* June 24, pp. 833, 847–852.

Porter, E. (1986). *Treating the young male victim of sexual assault: Issues and intervention strategies*. Syracuse, NY: Safer Society Press.

Pranis, K. (1999). "Victims in the peacemaking circle process." *The Crime Victims Report* 3(4) (September): 51.

President's Task Force on Victims of Crime. (1982). *Final report*. Washington, DC: U.S. Government Printing Office.

Press, A., Copeland, J., Contreras, J., Camper, D., Agrest, S., Newhall, E., Monroe, S., Young, J., and Mattland, T. (1981). "The plague of violent crime." *Newsweek,* March 23, pp. 46–54.

Press, A., McCormick, J., and Wingert P. (1994). "Overview: A crime as American as a Colt .45." *Newsweek,* August 15, pp. 22–43.

Prestia, K. (1993). *Chocolates for the pillows—Nightmares for the guests*. Silver Spring, MD: Bartleby Press.

Prison Research and Action Project. (1976). *Instead of prisons*. Genesee, NY: Author.

"Prosecutorial discretion in the initiation of criminal complaints." (1969). *Southern California Law Review* 42 (Spring): 519–545.

Purdum, T. (1986). "Link is sought in 5 City U. robberies." *New York Times,* February 19, p. B3.

———. (1988). "The reality of crime on campus." *New York Times Education Supplement,* Sec. 12, April 10, pp. 47–51.

Purdy, M. (1994). "Workplace murders provoke lawsuits and better security." *New York Times,* February 14, pp. A1, B5.

Purnick, J. (1986). "Manes retracts story and says he cut himself." *New York Times,* January 22, p. 1.

Quinn, M., and Tomita, S. (1986). *Elder abuse and neglect: Causes, diagnosis, and intervention strategies.* New York: Springer.

Rand, M. (1993). *Crime and the nation's households, 1992. BJS Bulletin.* Washington, DC: U.S. Department of Justice.

———. (1994a). *Carjacking: Bureau of Justice Statistics crime data brief.* Washington, DC: U.S. Department of Justice.

———. (1994b). *Guns and crime: BJS crime data brief.* Washington, DC: U.S. Department of Justice.

Ranish, D., and Shichor, D. (1985). "The victim's role in the penal process: Recent developments in California." *Federal Probation* (March): 50–56.

Raskin, L. (1968). "A heist a minute." *Nation,* April 7, pp. 434–436.

Ratnesar, R. (1998). "Should you carry a gun?" *Time,* July 6, p. 48.

Rauber, M. (1991). "Rape victims get a legal break." *New York Post,* May 21, p. 22.

Ray, L. (1984). "Dispute resolution: 'A muffled explosion.'" *NIJ Reports* 185 (May): 9.

Reaves, B. (1993). *National incident-based reporting system: Using NIBRS data to analyze violent crime. Bureau of Justice Statistics Technical Report.* Washington, DC: U.S. Department of Justice.

———. (1998). *Felony defendants in large urban counties, 1994.* BJS State Court Processing Statistics. Washington, DC: U.S. Department of Justice.

Reckless, W. (1967). *The crime problem.* New York: Appleton-Century-Crofts.

Reiff, R. (1979). *The invisible victim.* New York: Basic Books.

Reilly, J. (1981). "Victim/witness services in prosecutor's offices." *The Prosecutor* (October): 8–11.

Reiman, J. (1990). *The rich get richer and the poor get prison: Ideology, class, and criminal justice* (3rd ed.). New York: Wiley.

Reiss, A. (1971). *The police and the public.* New Haven, CT: Yale University Press.

———. (1981). "Toward a revitalization of theory and research on victimization by crime." *Journal of Criminal Law and Criminology* 72(2): 704–713.

———. (1986). "Official and survey statistics." In E. Fattah (Ed.), *From crime policy to victim policy* (pp. 53–79). New York: St. Martin's Press.

Rennison, C. (1999). *Criminal victimization 1998: Changes 1997–1998 with trends 1993–1998. BJS NCVS.* Washington, D.C.: U.S. Department of Justice.

Renzetti, C. (1992). *Violent betrayal: Partner abuse in lesbian relationships.* Newbury Park, CA: Sage.

"Report finds 'Crisis of children killing children.' " (1994). *Crime Victims Digest* (January): 3.

Resick, P., and Nishith, P. (1997). "Sexual assault." In R. Davis, A. Lurigio, and W. Skogan (eds.), *Victims of crime, second edition* (pp. 27–52). Thousand Oaks, CA: Sage.

Reuters News Service. (1996). "Loss of evidence impeded inquiry into boy's death." *New York Times,* February 18, p. 30.

Rhode, D. (1989). *Justice and gender: Sex discrimination and the law.* Cambridge, MA: Harvard University Press.

Rhodes, N. (1992). "The assessment of spousal abuse: An alternative to the conflict tactics scale." In E. Viano (Ed.), *Intimate violence: Interdisciplinary perspectives* (pp. 27–36). Washington, DC: Hemisphere Publishing.

Rhodes, W. (1978). *Plea bargaining: Who gains? Who loses?* (PROMIS Research Project No. 14). Washington, DC: Institute for Law and Social Research.

Richardson, J., Best, J., and Bromley, D. (Eds.). (1991). *The satanism scare.* New York: Aldine de Gruyter.

Riedel, M. (1987). "Stranger violence: Perspectives, issues, and problems." *Journal of Criminal Law* 78(2): 223–259.

Riedel, M., and Mock, L. (1985). *NIJ report: The nature and patterns of American homicide.* Washington, DC: U.S. Government Printing Office.

Rittenmeyer, S. (1981). "Of battered wives, self-defense and double standards of justice." *Journal of Criminal Justice* 9(5): 389–396.

Roberts, A. (1990). *Helping crime victims.* Newbury Park, CA: Sage.

———. (Ed.) (1998). *Juvenile justice: Policies, programs, and services. Second edition.* Thousand Oaks, CA: Sage.

Roberts, S. (1987). "Criminals, authors, and criminal authors." *New York Times Book Review,* March 22, pp. 1, 34–35.

———. (1989). "When crimes become symbols." *New York Times,* March 7, Sec. 4, pp. 1, 28.

Robin, G. (1977). "Forcible rape: Institutionalized sexism in the criminal justice system," *Crime and Delinquency* (April): 136–152.

Robin, M. (1991). "The social construction of child abuse and 'false allegations.' " *Child and Youth Services* (15): 1–34.

Roche, J. (1967). "Statement to Senate." *Congressional Record: Senate,* March 22, p. 7594.

Roehl, J., and Ray, L. (1986). "Toward the multi-door courthouse: Dispute resolution intake and referral." *NIJ Reports* 198 (July): 2–7.

Rohter, L. (1993a). "Fearful of tourism decline, Florida offers assurances on safety." *New York Times,* September 16, p. A14.

———. (1993b). "Tourist is killed in Florida despite taking precautions." *New York Times,* September 9, p. A16.

Roiphe, K. (1993). *The morning after: Sex, fear, and feminism on campus.* Boston: Little, Brown.

Rootsaert, D. (1987). A *prosecutor's guide to victim/witness assistance.* Alexandria, VA: National District Attorneys Association.

Rose, V. (1977). "Rape as a social problem: A by-product of the feminist movement." *Social Problems* 25 (October): 75–89.

Rosenthal, E. (1990). "U.S. is by far the homicide capital of the industrialized nations." *New York Times,* June 27, p. A10.

Ross, R., and Staines, G. (1972). "The politics of analyzing social problems." *Social Problems* 20 (Summer): 18–40.

Roth, J. (1994). *Firearms and violence.* National Institute of Justice Research in Brief. Washington, DC: U.S. Department of Justice.

Rottenberg, D. (1980). "Crime victims fight back." *Parade,* March 16, pp. 21–23.

Roy, S. (1990). "Offender-oriented restitution bills: Bringing total justice to victims?" *Federal Probation* (September): 30–35.

Russell, D. (1975). *The politics of rape: The victim's perspective.* New York: Stein & Day.

———. (1982). *Rape in marriage.* New York: Macmillan.

———. (1984). *Sexual exploitation: Rape, child molestation, and workplace harassment.* Newbury Park, CA: Sage.

———. (1986). *The secret trauma: Incest in the lives of girls and women.* New York: Basic Books.

———. (1990). *Sexual exploitation.* Beverly Hills, CA: Sage.

Ryan, W. (1971). *Blaming the victim.* New York: Vintage.

Sabo, D. (1992). "Understanding men in prison: The relevance of gender studies." *Men's Studies Review* 9(1): 4–9.

Sachs, A. (1994). "Now for the movie." *Time,* January 31, p. 99.

Sagarin, E. (1975). "Forcible rape and the problem of the rights of the accused." *Intellect* (May–June): 515–520.

Sakheim, D., and Devine, S. (Eds.), (1992). *Out of darkness: Exploring satanism and ritual abuse.* New York: MacMillan.

Salzinger, S., Feldman, R., and Hammer, M. (1991). "Risk for physical child abuse and the personal consequences for its victims." *Criminal Justice and Behavior* 18(1) (March): 64–81.

Sanchez, R. (1994). "Fake cops' crime wave." *Long Island Newsday,* January 28, p. 31.

Sanderson, B. (1994). "Victim fund slashes its payouts." *Bergen* (New Jersey) *Record,* November 30, pp. A1, A12.

Sargeant, G. (1991). "Battered woman syndrome gaining legal recognition." *Trial* 27(4) (April): 17–20.

Sarnoff, S. (1996). *Paying for crime: The policies and possibilities of crime victim reimbursement.* Westport, CT: Praeger.

Saunders, D. (1986). "When battered women use violence: Husband-abuse or self-defense?" *Victims and Violence* 1(1): 47–59.

Savitz, L. (1982). "Official statistics." In L. Savitz and N. Johnston (Eds.), *Contemporary criminology* (pp. 3–15). New York: Wiley.

———. (1986). "Obscene phone calls." In T. Hartnagel and R. Silverman (Eds.), *Critique and explanation: Essays in honor of Gwynne Nettles* (pp. 149–158). New Brunswick, NJ: Transaction Books.

Sawyer, S. (1987). "Law enforcement officers and their families face special difficulties when victimized." *NOVA Newsletter* 11(11) (November): 1–2.

Schafer, S. (1968). *The victim and his criminal.* New York: Random House.

———. (1970). *Compensation and restitution to victims of crime* (2nd ed.). Montclair, NJ: Patterson Smith.

———. (1977). *Victimology: The victim and his criminal.* Reston, VA: Reston Publishers.

Schanberg, S. (1984). "The rape trial." *New York Times,* March 27, p. A31.

———. (1989) "We should be outraged at all rapes." *New York Newsday,* April 28, pp. 94–95.

Schaye, K. (1998). "Judgment called the end of the Tawana Brawley story." *New York Daily News,* July 27, p.8.

Schechter, S. (1982). *Women and male violence.* Boston: South End Press.

Scherer, J. (1982). "An overview of victimology." In J. Scherer and G. Shepherd (Eds.), *Victimization of the weak: Contemporary social reactions* (pp. 8–30). Springfield, IL: Charles C Thomas.

Schmitt, E. (1994). "Military struggling to stem an increase in family violence." *New York Times,* May 23, pp. A1, A12.

Schneider, A. (1981). "Methodological problems in victim surveys and their implications for research in victimology." *Journal of Criminal Law and Criminology* 72(2): 818–830.

Schneider, A., and Schneider, P. (1978). *Private and public-minded citizen responses to a neighborhood crime prevention strategy.* Eugene, OR: Institute of Policy Analysis.

———. (1981). "Victim assistance programs." In B. Galaway and J. Hudson (Eds.), *Perspectives on crime victims* (pp. 364–373). St. Louis, MO: C. V. Mosby.

Schneider, E. (1980). "Equal rights to trial for women: Sex bias in the law on self-defense." *Harvard Civil Rights and Civil Liberties Review* 15: 623–647.

———. (1991). "The violence of privacy." *The Connecticut Law Review* 23: 973–999.

Schneider, H. (Ed.). (1982). *The victim in international perspective.* New York: Walter DeGruyter.

Schneider, P. (1987). "Lost innocents: The myth of missing children." *Harper's Magazine,* February, pp. 47–53.

Schreiber, L. (1990). "Campus rape." *Glamour* (September): 23–26.

Schultz, L. (1965). "The violated: A proposal to compensate victims of violent crime." *St. Louis University Law Journal* 10: 238–250.

———. (1968). "The victim-offender relationship." *Crime and Delinquency* 14: 135–141.

Schur, E. (1984). *Labeling women deviant: Gender, stigma, and social control.* New York: Random House.

Schwartz, M., and DeKeseredy, W. (1997). *Sexual assault on the college campus: The role of male peer support.* Thousand Oaks, CA: Sage.

Schwendinger, H., and Schwendinger, J. (1967). "Delinquent stereotypes of probable victims." In M. Klein (Ed.), *Juvenile gangs in context* (pp. 92–105). Englewood Cliffs, NJ: Prentice-Hall.

———. (1974). "Rape myths in legal, theoretical, and everyday practice." *Crime and Social Justice* 1: 18–26.

Seebach, L. (1999). "How to give the campus left a taste of its own medicine." *Denver Rocky Mountain News,* March 28, p. 2B.

Seelye, K. (1995). "A life saved, a life lost: Gun issue gets personal." *New York Times,* April 1, p. A26.

Seligmann, J., and Maor, Y. (1980). "Punishments that fit the crime." *Newsweek,* August 4, p. 60.

Senate Committee on the Judiciary. (1993). *Report: The violence against women act of 1993.* Washington, DC: U.S. Senate.

Senate Judiciary Committee (Majority Staff). (1993). *The response to rape: Detours on the road to equal justice.* Washington, DC: U.S. Senate.

Sexton, J. (1994). "Brooklyn drivers fear reckless young guns." *New York Times,* December 3, pp. A1, A26.

Shapiro, L., Rosenberg, D., Lauerman, J., and Sparkman, R. (1993). "Rush to judgment." *Newsweek,* April 19, 54–60.

Shelden, R. (1982). *Criminal justice in America: A sociological approach.* Boston: Little, Brown.

Sheley, J. (1979). *Understanding crime: Concepts, issues, decisions.* Belmont, CA: Wadsworth.

Sheridan, R. (1994). "The false child molestation outbreak of the 1980s: An explanation of the cases arising in the divorce context." In K. de Koster and K. Swisher (Eds.), *Child abuse: Opposing viewpoints* (pp. 48–55). San Diego, CA: Greenhaven Press.

Sherman, L. (1986). *NIJ crime file: Domestic violence.* Washington, DC: U.S. Department of Justice.

Sherman, L., and Berk, R. (1984). "The specific deterrent effects of arrest for domestic assault." *American Sociological Review* 49 (April): 261–272.

Sherman, L., Berk, R., and Smith, D. (1992). "Crime, punishment, and stake in conformity: Legal and informal control of domestic violence." *American Sociological Review* 57 (October): 680–690. Washington, DC: Police Foundation.

Sherman, L., Gartin, P., and Buerger, M. (1989). "Hot spots of predatory crime: Routine activities and the criminology of place." *Criminology* 27(1) (February): 27–40.

Sherman, L., Steele, L., Laufersweiler, D., Hoffer, N., and Julian, S. (1989). "Stray bullets and 'mushrooms': Random shootings of bystanders in four cities, 1977–1988." *Journal of Quantitative Criminology* 5: 297–316.

Shipp, E. (1987). "Defense lawyers' tactics: Unfair or just aggressive?" *New York Times,* April 21, pp. BI, B4.

Shotland, L. (1976). "Spontaneous vigilantism: A bystander response to criminal behavior." In J. Rosenbaum and P. Sederberg (Eds.), *Vigilante politics* (pp. 30–44). Philadelphia: University of Pennsylvania Press.

Siegel, J., Sorenson, S., Golding, J., Burnham, M., and Stein, J. (1987). "The prevalence of childhood sexual assault." *American Journal of Epidemiology* 126: 1141–1153.

Siegel, L. (1997). *Criminology, sixth edition.* Belmont, CA: West/Wadsworth.

Silberman, C. (1978). *Criminal violence, criminal justice.* New York: Random House.

Silberman, M. (1995). *A world of violence: Corrections in America.* Belmont, CA: Wadsworth.

Silverman, R. (1974). "Victim precipitation: An examination of the concept." In I. Drapkin and E. Viano (Eds.), *Victimology: A new focus* (pp. 99–110). Lexington, MA: D. C. Heath.

Silving, H. (1959). "Compensation for victims of criminal violence—a roundtable." *Journal of Public Law* 8: 236–253.

Simon, D. (1991). *Homicide: A year on the killing streets.* New York: Fawcett Columbine.

Simonson, L. (1994). "The victims' rights movement: A critical view from a practicing sociologist." *Sociological Imagination* 31: 181–196.

Sinason, V. (1994). *Treating survivors of satanist abuse*. New York: Routledge.

Singer, S. (1981). "Homogeneous victim-offender populations: A review and some research implications." *Journal of Criminal Law and Criminology* 72(2): 779–788.

———. (1986). "Victims of serious violence and their criminal behavior: Subcultural theory and beyond." *Violence and Victims* 1(1): 61–70.

Skogan, W. (1978). *Victimization surveys and criminal justice planning*. Washington, DC: U.S. Government Printing Office.

———. (1981a). "Assessing the behavioral context of victimization." *Journal of Criminal Law and Criminology* 72(2): 727–742.

———. (1981b). *Issues in the measurement of victimization*. Washington, DC: U.S. Department of Justice.

———. (1986). "Methodological issues in the study of victimization." In E. Fattah (Ed.), *From crime policy to victim policy* (pp. 80–116). New York: St. Martin's Press.

Skogan, W., and Maxfield, M. (1981). *Coping with crime: Individual and neighborhood reactions*. Beverly Hills, CA: Sage.

Sloane, L. (1991). "Rising fraud worrying car insurers . . ." *New York Times,* November 16, p. 48.

Smith, B. (1985). "Trends in the victims' rights movement and implications for future research." *Victimology* 10(1–4): 34–43.

Smith, B., Sloan, J., and Ward, R. (1990). "Public support for the victim's rights movement: Results of a statewide survey." *Crime and Delinquency* 36(4): 488–502.

Smith, K. (1994). "Outrage over new attack by freed N.J. kid molester." *New York Post,* September 19, p. 6.

Smith, M. (1988). *Coping with crime on campus*. New York: American Council on Education (ACE).

Smith, S. (1994). "Have screwdriver, will steal." *Car and Driver* (July): 157–167.

Smith, S., and Freinkel, S. (1988). *Adjusting the balance: Federal policy and victim services*. New York: Greenwood Press.

Smith, S., Steadman, G., Todd, M., and Townsend, M. (1999). *BJS Report: Criminal victimization and perceptions of community safety in 12 cities, 1998*. Washington, DC: U.S. Department of Justice.

Snell, J., Rosenwald, R., and Robey, A. (1964). "The wifebeater's wife: A study of family interaction." *Archives of General Psychiatry* 11 (August): 107–112.

Snyder, J. (1993). "A nation of cowards." *The Public Interest* 113 (Fall): 40–56.

Snyder, H., and Sickmund, M. (1995). *Juvenile offenders and victims: A focus on violence. OJJDP Statistical Summary*. Washington, DC: U.S. Department of Justice.

Sorenson, S., and White, J. (1992). "Adult sexual assault: Overview of research." *Journal of Social Issues* 48(1): 1–8.

Southern Regional Council. (1969). *Race makes the difference: An analysis of sentence disparity among black and white offenders in southern prisons*. Atlanta, GA: Author.

Sparks, R. (1981). "Multiple victimization: Evidence, theory and future research." *Journal of Criminal Law and Criminology* 72(2): 762–778.

Spears, J., and Spohn, C. (1997). "The effects of evidence factors and victim characteristics on prosecutors' charging decisions in sexual assault cases." *American Journal of Criminal Justice* 20: 183–205.

Spector, M., and Kitsuse, J. (1987). *Constructing social problems*. New York: Aldine de Gruyter.

Spelman, W., and Brown, D. (1984). *NIJ report: Calling the police: Citizen reporting of serious crime*. Washington, DC: U.S. Department of Justice.

Spitzer, N. (1986). "The children's crusade." *Atlantic* (June): 18–22.

Spohn, C., and Horney, J. (1992). *Rape law reform: A grassroots revolution and its impact*. New York: Plenum.

Spunt, B., Tarshish, C., Fendich, M., Goldstein, P., and Brownstein, H. (1993). "Research note: The utility of correctional data for understanding the drugs-homicide connection." *Criminal Justice Review* 18(1) (Spring): 46–60.

Spunt, B., Goldstein, P., Brownstein, H., Fendrich, M., and Langley, S. (1994). "Alcohol and homicide: Interviews with prison inmates." *Journal of Drug Issues,* 24(1): 143–163.

Stark, J., and Goldstein, H. (1985). *The rights of crime victims: An American Civil Liberties Union handbook.* New York: Bantam Books.

Steinman, M. (1991). "The public policy process and woman battering: Problems and pitfalls." In M. Steinman (Ed.), *Woman battering: Policy responses* (pp. 1–18). Cincinnati, OH: Anderson.

Steinmetz, S. (1978a). "The battered husband syndrome." *Victimology* 2(4): 499–509.

———. (1978b). "Battered parents." *Society* 15(5): 54–55.

———. (1988). *Duty bound: Elder abuse and family care.* Newbury Park, CA: Sage.

Stephens, M. (1988). *A history of the news.* New York: Penguin.

Stets, J., and Pirog-Good, M. (1987). "Violence in dating relationships." *Social Psychology Quarterly* 50: 237–246.

Stillman, F. (1987). *NIJ Research in brief. Line-of-duty deaths: Survivor and departmental responses.* Washington, DC: U.S. Department of Justice.

Stone, L. (1984). "Shelters for battered women: A temporary escape from danger or the first step toward divorce?" *Victimology* 9(1): 284–289.

Straus, M. (1978). "Wife beating: How common and why?" *Victimology* 2(4): 443–458.

———. (1991). "Conceptualization and measurement of battering: Implications for public policy." In M. Steinman (Ed.), *Woman battering: Policy responses* (pp. 19–42). Cincinnati: Anderson.

———. (1999). "The controversy over domestic violence by women." In X. Arriaga and S. Oskamp (Eds.), *Violence in intimate relationships* (pp. 109–119). Thousand Oaks, CA: Sage.

Straus, M., and Gelles, R. (1986). Societal change and change in family violence from 1975 to 1985." *Journal of Marriage and the Family* 48: 20–30.

———. (1990). *Physical violence in American families.* New Brunswick, NJ: Transaction.

Straus, M., Gelles, R., and Steinmetz, S. (1980). *Behind closed doors: Violence in the American family.* New York: Doubleday.

"Street sentence: Vigilante justice in Buffalo." (1983). *Time,* August 15, p. 15.

"Study puts facts behind some child-kidnapping assumptions." (1997). *Law Enforcement News,* August, p. 9.

"Study shows intimidation of witnesses affects verdicts." (1990). *New York Amsterdam News,* October 3, p. 18.

Sugarman, D., and McCoy, S. (1997). "Impact of expert testimony on the believability of repressed memories." *Violence and Victims* 12(2) (Summer): 115–126.

Sullivan, A. (1993). "Gay values, truly conservative." *New York Times,* February 9, p. A21.

Sykes, C. (1992). *A nation of victims: The decay of the American character.* New York: St. Martin's Press.

Sykes, G., and Matza, D. (1957). "Techniques of neutralization: A theory of delinquency." *American Sociological Review* 22: 664–670.

Symonds, M. (1975). "Victims of violence: Psychological effects and after-effects." *American Journal of Psychoanalysis* 35(1): 19–26.

———. (1980a). "Acute responses of victims to terror." *Evaluation and Change* (special issue): 39–42.

———. (1980b). "The 'second injury' to victims." *Evaluation and Change* 7(1): 36–38.

Taibbi, M., and Sims-Phillips, A. (1989). *Unholy alliances.* San Diego, CA: Harcourt Brace.

Tardiff, K., Gross, E., and Messner, S. (1986). "A study of homicides in Manhattan, 1981." *American Journal of Public Health* 76(2): 139–145.

Task Force on Assessment. (1967). "The victims of crime." In The President's Commission on Law Enforcement and Administration of Justice, *Task force report: Crime and its impact—an assessment* (pp. 80–84). Washington, DC: U.S. Government Printing Office.

Tatara, T. (1993). "Understanding the nature and scope of elder abuse with the use of state aggregate data." *Journal of Elder Abuse and Neglect* 5(4): 35–57.

Tavris, C. (1993). "Beware the incest survivor machine." *New York Times Book Review,* January 3, pp. 1, 16–17.

Taylor, B. (1989). *Redesign of the national crime survey.* Washington, DC: U.S. Department of Justice.

"Teaching children how to escape from abduction." (1999). *New York Times,* February 14, p. 32.

Teevan, J. (1979). "Crime victimization as a neglected social problem." *Sociological Symposium* 25: 6–22.

Terr, L. (1994). *Unchained memories: True stories of traumatic memories, lost and found.* New York: Basic.

Thomason, T., and Babbilli, A. (1987). *Crime victims and the news media.* Fort Worth, TX: Texas Christian University Department of Journalism.

Thompson, M. (1984). "MADD curbs drunk drivers." *Victimology* 9(1): 191–192.

Thyfault, R. (1984). "Self-defense: Battered woman syndrome on trial." *California Western Law Review* 20: 485–510.

Timrots, A., and Rand, M. (1987). *BJS special report: Violent crime by strangers and non-strangers.* Washington, DC: U.S. Department of Justice.

Timrots, A., and Snyder, E. (1994). *Drugs and crime facts, 1993. BJS drugs and crime data center and clearinghouse.* Washington, DC: U.S. Department of Justice.

Tittle, C. (1978). "Restitution and deterrence: An evaluation of compatibility." In B. Galaway and J. Hudson (Eds.), *Offender restitution in theory and action* (pp. 33–158). Lexington, MA: Lexington Books.

Tjaden, P., and Thoennes, N. (1998). *Stalking in America: Findings from the national violence against women survey.* Washington, DC: National Institute of Justice.

Toby, J. (1983). "Violence in school." In M. Tonry and N. Morris (Eds.), *Crime and justice: An annual review of research (Volume 4)* (pp. 1–47). Chicago: University of Chicago Press.

Tomasson, R. (1991). "Man acquitted in shooting at courthouse." *New York Times,* July 26, pp. B1, B16.

Tomz, J., and McGillis, D. (1997). *Serving crime victims and witnesses, second edition.* Washington, DC: U.S. Department of Justice.

Travelers Insurance Company. (1977). "Your car's a steal in more ways than one." Hartford, CT: Author.

Treanor, W. (1986). "The missing children's act has been misused, abused." *Juvenile Justice Digest,* August 25, pp. 7–10.

Trescott, P. (1987). *Diplomatic crimes.* Washington, DC: Acropolis Books.

Triebwasser, J. (1986). "Court says you can't run from restitution." *Law Enforcement News,* June 28, pp. 6, 8.

———. (1987a). "Court leaves death penalty alive and well." *Law Enforcement News,* June 9, p. 5.

———. (1987b). "Victims' non-impact on sentence." *Law Enforcement News,* September 29, p. 5.

Turman, K. (1999). *Breaking the cycle of violence: Recommendations to improve the criminal justice response to child victims and witnesses.* Washington, DC: Office for Victims of Crime, U.S. Department of Justice.

Turner, J. (1990). "Preparing individuals at risk for victimization as hostages." In E. Viano (Ed.), *The victimology handbook: Research findings, treatment, and public policy* (pp. 217–226). New York: Garland.

Umbreit, M. (1987). "Mediation may not be as bad as you think; some victims do benefit." *NOVA Newsletter* (March): 1–2, 6.

———. (1989). "Violent offenders and their victims." In M. Wright and B. Galaway (Eds.), *Mediation and criminal justice: Victims, offenders and community* (pp. 99–112). Newbury Park, CA: Sage.

———. (1990). "Victim-offender mediation with violent offenders: Implications for modifications of the VORP model." In E. Viano (Ed.), *The victimology handbook: Research findings, treatment, and public policy* (pp. 337–352). New York: Garland.

———. (1994). "Victim empowerment through mediation: The impact of victim offender mediation in four cities." *Perspectives* (American Probation and Parole Association) (Special Issue) (Summer): 25–28.

———. (1995). "Restorative justice: Implications for organizational change." *Federal Probation* 59 (1) (March): 47–54.

Umbreit, M., and Coates, P. (1993). "Cross-site analysis of victim-offender mediation in four states." *Crime and Delinquency* 39: 565–585.

Umbreit, M., and Greenwood, D. (1998). *National survey of victim-offender mediation programs in the United States.* Washington, DC: Office of Victims of Crime, U.S. Department of Justice.

Uniform Crime Reporting Section, FBI. (1993). *Law enforcement officers killed and assaulted, 1992.* Washington, DC: U.S. Department of Justice.

United Nations, Department for Economic and Social Information. (1998). *Demographic yearbook, 1996.* New York: United Nations.

U.S. Attorney General's Advisory Board on Missing Children. (1986). *America's missing and exploited children: Their safety and their future.* Washington, DC: U.S. Department of Justice.

U.S. Center for Disease Control (CDC), National Center For Health Statistics. (1999). *National Vital Statistics Report* 47(25) (October): 27–28.

U.S. Congress Senate Committee on the Judiciary. Subcommittee to Investigate Juvenile Delinquency. (1954). *Hearings.* 83rd Cong., 2nd sess., January 15. Washington, DC: U.S. Government Printing Office.

U.S. Department of Health and Human Services (U.S. HHS). (1999). *Child fatalities fact sheet.* Washington, DC: National Clearinghouse on Child Abuse and Neglect Information.

U.S. House Committee on the Judiciary. (1980). *Victims of Crime Act of 1979: Report together with dissenting and separate views.* 96th Cong., 2nd sess., February 13. Washington, DC: U.S. Government Printing Office.

"U.S. Supreme Court holds: No constitutional duty to protect." (1989). *NOVA Newsletter* 13(2): p. 6.

Vachss, A. (1993). *Sex crimes.* New York: Random House.

Van Ness, D. (1990). "Restorative justice." In B. Galaway and J. Hudson, (Eds.), *Criminal justice, restitution and reconciliation* (pp. 7–14). Monsey, NY: Willow Tree Press.

Van Ness, D., and Strong, K. (1997). *Restoring justice.* Cincinnati: Anderson.

Verhovek, S. (1994). "Gang intimidation takes rising toll of court cases." *New York Times,* October 7, p. A1, B8.

———. (1995). "States seek to let citizens carry concealed weapons." *New York Times,* March 6, pp. A1, B8.

Viano, E. (1976). *Victims and society.* Washington, DC: Visage.

———. (1983). "Victimology: The development of a new perspective." *Victimology* 8 (1–2): 17–30.

———. (1987). "Victim's rights and the constitution: Reflections on a bicentennial." *Crime and Delinquency* 33: 438–451.

———. (1989). "Victimology today: Major issues in research and public policy." In E. Viano (Ed.), *Crime and its victims: International research and public policy issues* (pp. 3–16). New York: Hemisphere Publishing.

———. (1990a). Introduction, "Victimology: A new focus of research and practice." In E. Viano (Ed.), *The victimology handbook: Research findings, treatment, and public policy* (pp. xi–xii). New York: Garland.

———. (1990b). "The recognition and implementation of victim's rights in the United States: Developments and achievements." In E. Viano (Ed.), *The victimology handbook: Research findings, treatment, and public policy* (pp. 319–336). New York: Garland.

———. (1992). "Violence among intimates: Major issues and approaches." In E. Viano (Ed.), *Intimate violence: Interdisciplinary perspectives* (pp. 3–12). New York: Hemisphere.

"Victim's counseling records may be reviewed for exculpatory evidence." (1999). *The Crime Victims Report,* 3(4) (September), pp. 55–56.

Villmoare, E., and Neto, V. (1987). *NIJ research in brief: Victim appearances at sentencing under California's victims' bill of rights.* Washington, DC: U.S. Department of Justice.

Vollmer, A., and Parker, A. (1936). *The police and modern society.* San Francisco: University of California Press.

Volpe, M. (1989). "The police role." In M. Wright and B. Galaway (Eds.), *Mediation and criminal justice: Victims, offenders and community* (pp. 229–240). Newbury Park, CA: Sage.

Von Hentig, H. (1941). "Remarks on the interaction of perpetrator and victim." *Journal of Criminal Law, Criminology, and Police Science* 31 (March–April): 303–309.

———. (1948). *The criminal and his victim: Studies in the sociobiology of crime.* New Haven, CT: Yale University Press.

Von Hirsch, A. (1988). "Punishment to fit the criminal." *The Nation,* June 25, pp. 901–902.

Voss, H., and Hepburn, J. (1968). "Patterns in criminal homicide in Chicago." *Journal of Criminal Law, Criminology, and Police Science* 59: 499–508.

Walker, L. (1984). *The battered woman syndrome.* New York: Springer.

Walker, S. (1982). "What have civil liberties ever done for crime victims? Plenty!" *ACJS (Academy of Criminal Justice Sciences) Today* (October): 4–5.

———. (1994). *Sense and nonsense about crime and drugs: A policy guide* (3rd ed.). Belmont, CA: Wadsworth.

Walklate, S. (1991). "Researching victims of crime: Critical victimology." *Social Justice* 17(3): 25–42.

Waller, I., and Okihiro, N. (1978). *Burglary: The victim and the public.* Toronto: University of Toronto Press.

Walsh, A. (1992). "Placebo justice: Victim recommendations and offender sentences in sexual assault cases." In E. Fattah (Ed.), *Toward a critical victimology* (pp. 295–311). New York: St. Martin's Press.

Walsh, M., and Schram, D. (1980). "The victim of white collar crime: Accuser or accused." In G. Geis and E. Stotland (Eds.), *White collar crime* (pp. 32–51). Beverly Hills, CA: Sage.

Warchol, G. (1998). *BJS Special Report: Workplace violence, 1992–1996.* Washington, DC: U.S. Department of Justice.

"Warned not to testify, theft victim is shot." (1991). *New York Times,* June 25, p. B5.

Warner, J., and Burke, V. (1987). *National directory of juvenile restitution programs.* Washington, DC: U.S. Department of Justice.

Warrior, B. (1977). "Transition house shelters battered women." *Sister Courage* (Boston) (February): 12.

Warshaw, R. (1988). *I never called it rape.* New York: Harper & Row.

Webster, B. (1988). *Victim assistance programs report increased workloads. National Institute of Justice, Research in Action.* Washington, DC: U.S. Department of Justice.

Weed, F. (1995). Certainty of justice: Reform in the crime victim movement. Hawthorne, NY: Aldine de Gruyter.

Weigend, T. (1983). "Problems of victim/witness assistance programs." *Victimology* 8(3): 91–101.

Weinberg, S. (1955). *Incest behavior.* New York: Citadel Press.

Weinraub, B. (1994). "Michael Jackson settles suit for sum said to be in millions." *New York Times,* January 26, pp. A1, A18.

Weis, K., and Borges, S. (1973). "Victimology and rape: The case of the legitimate victim." *Issues in Criminology* 8(2): 71–115.

Wells, R. (1990). "Considering victim impact: The role of probation." *Federal Probation* (September): 26–29.

Wertham, F. (1949). *The show of violence.* New York: Doubleday.

Wexler, R. (1990). *Wounded innocents: The real victims of the war against child abuse.* Buffalo, NY: Prometheus Books.

"When judges make the punishment fit the crime." (1978). *U.S. News & World Report,* December 11, pp. 44–46.

"Where's the car?" (1992). *U.S. News & World Report,* March 30, p. 51.

Whitaker, C. (1989). *BJS special report: The redesigned National Crime Survey: Selected new data.* Washington, DC: U.S. Department of Justice.

Whitcomb, D. (1986). *NIJ research in action: Prosecuting child sexual abuse: New approaches.* Washington, DC: U.S. Department of Justice.

———. (1988). *Evaluation of programs for the effective prosecution of child physical and sexual abuse.* Washington, DC: Institute for Social Analysis.

———. (1992). *When the victim is a child* (2nd ed.). Washington, DC: Office of Justice Programs.

White, J., and Wesley, J. (1987). "Male rape survivors: Guidelines for crisis counselors." *Crime Victims Digest* (April): 3–6.

Whitman, H. (1951). *Terror in the streets.* New York: Dial Press.

Widom, C. (1989). "Child abuse, neglect, and violent criminal behavior." *Criminology* 27(2): 251–270.

———. (1992). "The cycle of violence." *NIJ Research in Brief* (October). Washington, DC: U.S. Department of Justice.

———. (1995). *Victims of childhood sexual abuse—later criminal consequences. NIJ Research in Brief.* Washington, DC: U.S. Department of Justice.

Wiehe, V. (1997). *Sibling abuse: Hidden physical, emotional, and sexual trauma.* Thousand Oaks, CA: Sage.

Wiehe, V., and Richards, A. (1995). *Intimate betrayal: Understanding and responding to the trauma of acquaintance rape.* Thousand Oaks, CA: Sage.

Wilbanks, W. (1987). *The myth of a racist criminal justice system.* Pacific Grove, CA: Brooks/Cole.

Will, G. (1993). "Are we a nation of cowards?" *Newsweek,* November 15, pp. 93–94.

———. (1998). "President feeds the culture of victimology." *Houston Chronicle,* July 31, p. A42.

Williams, K. (1976). "The effects of victim characteristics on the disposition of violent crimes." In W. McDonald (Ed.), *Criminal justice and the victim* (pp. 172–214). Beverly Hills, CA: Sage.

———. (1978). *The effects of victim characteristics on judicial decisions: PROMIS research project report.* Washington, DC: Institute for Law and Social Research.

Williams, L. (1984). "The classic rape: When do victims report." *Social Problems* 31: 459–467.

Williams, T. (1987). "Post traumatic stress disorder: Recognizing it, treating it." *NOVA Newsletter* (February) 1–2, 7.

Willis, C., and Wells, R. (1988). "The police and child abuse: An analysis of police decisions to report illegal behavior." *Criminology* 26(4): 695–714.

Winerip, M. (1983). "Rape case: Vengeance and furor." *New York Times,* August 1, p. B1.

Witkin, G. (1994). "The great debate: Should you own a gun?" *U.S. News & World Report,* August 15, pp. 24–31.

Wolf, R., and Pillemer, K. (1989). *Helping elderly victims: The reality of elder abuse.* New York: Columbia University Press.

Wolff, C. (1993a). "Former police officer stabbed while intervening in an attack." *New York Times,* May 19, p. B3.

———. (1993b). "Hostages mean hard lessons for police." *New York Times,* February 7, p. A37.

———. (1993c). "Massive cabdriver protest of 35 killings snarls traffic." *New York Times,* October 27, pp. B1, B4.

Wolfgang, M. (1958). *Patterns in criminal homicide*. Philadelphia: University of Pennsylvania Press.

———. (1959). "Suicide by means of victim precipitated homicide." *Journal of Clinical and Experimental Psychopathology and Quarterly Review of Psychiatry and Neurology* 20: 335–349.

———. (1965). "Victim compensation in crimes of personal violence." *Minnesota Law Review* 50: 229–241.

Wolfgang, M., and Ferracuti, F. (1967). *The subculture of violence: Towards an integrated theory in criminology*. London: Tavistock.

Wolfgang, M., and Riedel, M. (1973). "Race, judicial discretion, and the death penalty." *Annals of the Academy of Political and Social Science* 407 (May): 119–133.

Wood, N. (1990). "Black homicide—a public health crisis: Introduction and overview." *Journal of Interpersonal Violence* 5: 147–150.

Wooden, K. (1984). *Child lures: A guide to prevent abduction*. St. Louis, MO: Ralston Purina.

Woodward, K., Friday, C., Quade, V., and Sparkman, R. (1993). "The sins of the fathers . . ." *Newsweek,* July 12, p. 57.

Wright, E. (1973). *The politics of punishment*. New York: Harper & Row.

Wright, J. (1995). "Guns, crime, and violence." In J. Sheley (Ed.), *Criminology: A contemporary handbook* (2nd ed.) (pp. 495–514). Belmont, CA: Wadsworth.

Wright, J., Burgess, A., Burgess, B., and Laszio, A. (1996). "A typology of interpersonal stalking." *Journal of Interpersonal Violence,* 11(4): 487–502.

Wright, J., Rossi, P., and Daly, K. (1983). *Under the gun: Weapons, crime, and violence in America*. New York: Aldine.

Wright, L. (1994). *Remembering Satan*. New York: Knopf.

Wright, M. (1985). "The impact of victim-offender mediation on the victim." *Victimology* 10(1): 630–646.

———. (1989). "Introduction." In M. Wright and B. Galaway (Eds.), *Mediation and criminal justice: Victims, offenders and community* (pp. 1–13). Newbury Park, CA: Sage.

———. (1991). *Justice for victims and offenders*. Philadelphia: Open University Press.

Wyatt, G. (1985). "The sexual abuse of Afro-American and white American women in childhood." *Child Abuse and Neglect* 9: 507–519.

Wyatt, G., and Powell, G. (1988). *Lasting effects of child sexual abuse*. Newbury Park, CA: Sage.

Yapko, M. (1994). *Suggestions of abuse: True and false memories of childhood sexual trauma*. New York: Simon & Schuster.

Yapko, M., and Powell, G. (1988). *Lasting effects of child sexual abuse*. Newbury Park, CA: Sage.

Yllo, K., and Bograd, M. (1988). *Feminist perspectives on wife abuse*. Newbury Park, CA: Sage.

Young, C. (1999). "Feminists play the victim game." *New York Times,* November 26, p. A43.

Young, M. (1991). "NOVA protests NBC's 'Naming Names.' " *NOVA Newsletter* 15(4): 1.

Younger, E. (1977). Introduction to the American Bar Association, *Victims of crime or victims of justice?* (pp. 1–5). Washington, DC: Author.

Zawitz, M. (1994). *Domestic violence: Violence between intimates. Bureau of Justice Statistics selected findings*. Washington, DC: U.S. Department of Justice.

Zehr, H. (1998). "Justice as restoration, justice as respect." *The Justice Professional* 11(1): 71–87.

Ziegenhagen, E. (1977). *Victims, crime, and social control*. New York: Praeger.

Ziegenhagen, E., and Brosnan, D. (1985). "Victim responses to robbery and crime control policy." *Criminology* 23(4): 675–695.

Zimring, F. (1986). *NIJ crime file study guide: Gun control*. Washington, DC: U.S. Department of Justice.

———. (1987). "Why the Goetz verdict was not a landmark precedent." *New York Times,* June 21, p. E20.

Zimring, F., and Hawkins, G. (1997). *Crime is not the problem: Lethal violence in America.* New York: Oxford University Press.

Zimring, F., and Zuehl, J. (1986). "Victim injury and death in urban robbery: A Chicago study." *Journal of Legal Studies* 15(1) (January): 1–40.

Appendix

INTERNET WEB SITES TO MONITOR IN ORDER TO OBTAIN CURRENT INFORMATION ABOUT VICTIM ISSUES

WEB ADDRESS	ORGANIZATION AND CONTENT
	GENERAL INFORMATION ABOUT ALL KINDS OF CRIME VICTIMS
www.victimology.nl/	*World Society of Victimology* Offers a newsletter of an international organization of academics and practitioners, and conference notices
www.ojp.usdoj.gov/ovc	*Office for Victims of Crime (OVC) of the Office for Justice Programs (OJP)* Lists links to resources, state compensation programs, training opportunities,events
www.ncjrs.org	*National Criminal Justice Reference Service Justice Information Center* provides full text government documents about all categories of victims
www.ncvc.org	*National Crime Victim's Center (NCVC)* Provides overviews about the plight of many groups, a digest of recent news articles, plus notices about meetings and conferences
www.wadsworth.com	*Wadsworth Publishing Company* Provides links to a wide range of criminal justice Web sites

Statistics About Crime Victims

Website	Organization / Description
www.ojp.usdoj.gov/bjs/	*Bureau of Justice Statistics* Posts the latest data from the annual *National Crime Victimization Survey,* plus many reports, graphs, data sets
www.fbi.gov	*Federal Bureau of Investigation* Posts the annual *Uniform Crime Report*
www.albany.edu/sourcebook/	*Sourcebook of Criminal Justice Statistics* Presents annual data from many agencies and reports, including past editions of the UCR and the NCVS

Victims of Murder

Website	Organization / Description
www.cdc.gov/	*Center for Disease Control and Prevention* Presents annual national data about fatalities, including homicides
www.icpsr.umich.edu/NACJD/HRWG/	*Homicide Research Working Group* Provides annual analyses and research reports

Victims of Kidnappings and Child Snatchings

Website	Organization / Description
www.missingkids.org	*National Center for Missing and Exploited Children* Provides support, advice, technical assistance, and photographs of missing children

Victims of Child Abuse

Website	Organization / Description
www.calib.com/nccanch	*National Clearinghouse on Child Abuse and Neglect* Issues factsheets and information on prevention, identification, and treatment
child.cornell.edu	*Child Abuse Prevention Network* Serves as a center for resources and links
childhelpusa.org	*Child Help USA* Offers research findings, training, and prevention activities

Victims of Elder Abuse

Website	Organization / Description
www.gwjapan.com/ncea	*National Center on Elder Abuse* Offers a newsletter, legislative updates, and a connection to a clearinghouse on abuse and neglect of the elderly.

Victims of Spouse Abuse

Website	Organization / Description
www.ojp.usdoj.gov/vawo/welcome.html	*Violence Against Women Office of the OJP* Provides links to groups assisting victims of stalking, battering, and sexual assault

Victims of Sexual Assaults

Website	Organization / Description
www.ncasa.org	*National Coalition Against Sexual Assault* Works to end sexual violence through education, advocacy, and reform of public policy
www.rainn.org/	*Rape, Abuse, and Incest National Network* Offers a newsletter for staffs of rape crisis centers which provides a digest of news, commentary, and statistics
www.wellesley.edu/WCW/projects/mrape.html	*Wife Rape Information Page* Collects articles and resources about marital rape

Victims of Stalking	
www.soshelp.org/	*Survivors of Stalking* Offers advice, support, advocacy, and readings
www.stalkingvictims.com	*The Stalking Victims' Sanctuary* Provides readings, support, and legal resources

Victims of Drunk Driving Collisions	
www.madd.org	*Mothers Against Drunk Driving* Offers data and prevention strategies

Victim-Offender Reconciliation and Restorative Justice	
www.voma.org	*Victim-Offender Mediation Association* Offers a newsletter for program staffs, advocacy, and training opportunities
www.vorp.com	*Victim-Offender Reconciliation Programs* Serves as a resource center for advocacy, training, and technical assistance
ssw.che.umn.edu/rjp/	*Center for Restorative Justice and Peacemaking* Advocates establishing community programs, offers training
www.humboldt.edu/~isadr/	*Institute for the Study of Alternative Dispute Resolution* Provides professional training in mediation skills, conducts research
www.fresno.edu/dept/pacs	*Center for Peacemaking and Conflict Studies* Offers graduate education in conflict management
www.crenet.org/	*Conflict Resource Education Network* Serves as a clearinghouse for developing school- and university-based conflict resolution programs and curricula

Victims' Rights	
www.nvcan.org	*National Victims' Constitutional Amendment Network* Advocates legal reform in Congress and state legislatures

Victim Assistance	
www.musc.edu/cvc/	*National Crime Victims Research and Treatment Center* Supports medical and psychological research into the impact of victimization and the effectiveness of treatment
www.selfhelpweb.org	*National Self-help Clearinghouse* Advocates mutual aid, and provides technical assistance and referrals
www.try-nova.org/	*National Organization for Victim Assistance* Offers information packets and training programs, and runs conferences

Victims Seeking Redress in Civil Court	
www.victimbar.org/	*National Crime Victim Bar Association* Offers database of civil litigation and referrals to lawyers specializing in civil suits

Name Index

T

U

V

W

Y

Z

Subject Index